CALLING the GAME

BASEBALL BROADCASTING FROM 1920 TO THE PRESENT

STUART SHEA

GARY GILLETTE, EXECUTIVE EDITOR

SOCIETY FOR AMERICAN BASEBALL RESEARCH, INC.
PHOENIX, AZ

Calling the Game: Baseball Broadcasting From 1920 to the Present
by Stuart Shea
Executive Editor: Gary Gillette

ISBN 978-1-933599-40-3
(Ebook ISBN 978-1-933599-41-0)

Cover and book design: Gilly Rosenthol

Cover photos:
Mel Allen, Ernie Harwell, Vin Scully: National Baseball Hall of Fame Library, Cooperstown, NY
Bob Uecker, Nations Association of Broadcasters
Harry Caray, publicity photo, uncredited

The Society for American Baseball Research, Inc.
4455 E. Camelback Road, Ste. D-140
Phoenix, AZ 85018
Phone: (800) 969-7227 or (612) 343-6455
Web: www.sabr.org
Facebook: Society for American Baseball Research
Twitter: @SABR

TABLE OF CONTENTS

III. National Broadcasting

ACKNOWLEDGEMENTS

WHILE A BOOK MAY BE CREDITED TO ONE OR TWO AUTHORS, IN reality dozens of people are needed to make any such undertaking possible.

The following friends, baseball researchers, and writers, most of them Society for American Baseball Research (SABR) members, read various parts of this manuscript and/or added information, feedback, and stories to make it better than it would have been otherwise:

Dick Beverage, Gord Fitzgerald, Mary Groebner, Chris Hand, Kevin Hennessy, Tom Hufford, Dic Humphrey, Bill Nowlin, Frank Schetski, Met — er, Matt Silverman, and Doug White — a multi-skilled lineup of friends and colleagues — went above and beyond the call to ensure that what I wrote was accurate. Any mistakes left are my own damn fault.

In addition, Jeff Bower, Mark Campbell, Barbara Davis, Barbara Devine, Michael Duca, Dave Eskenazi, Tom Gaines, Thom Henninger, Howard Luloff, Welford McCaffrey, Art Mugalian, Rod Nelson, Jim Planamento, Stew Thornley, John Shea II, Stephen J. Walker, Katherine Wayne, and Peter Yee served as reviewers and sources. Muchicimas gracias a todos!

That you all would share with me your corrections, connections, insights, and memories is a big part of why I treasure my baseball relationships and, in particular, those in the SABR community.

Gary Gillette edited this manuscript, but he did much more. Some years ago we decided to create what we hoped would be the world's best baseball broadcasting database. After that, a book was the next logical step. His belief that I could write it was essential, and his work — much of it on the national broadcasting essay — elevated the finished product to a new level.

As a researcher, writer, project director, and generator of ideas, Gary's name is already etched in baseball's book of life, and I'm proud to call him, Vicki, Kamil, and Karolina friends. More than friends — family.

Pete Palmer is a generous man who has done incalculable work to advance the facilitation of baseball knowledge. He assisted with the creation of the data tables you see in this book and also read over the Red Sox chapter, offering memories and insights with his characteristic selflessness. Thanks, Pete, for all your help over the years.

During the later stages of this book I had the good fortune to come into contact with Jacques Doucet, who I believe is the only man to cover the Montreal Expos (on radio and in the newspapers) over their entire major-league tenure. He graciously agreed to pen some of his memories for our benefit, for which I am most grateful. Merci. I am overjoyed that as of 2012 he is back on the air covering big-league baseball and I eagerly anticipate his upcoming two-volume history of *Nos Amours*.

Pat Hughes, the voice of the Chicago Cubs, is not only a superb broadcaster but also a keen historian of the art form; just go to BaseballVoices.com for the proof. Thanks, Pat, for your interest and contribution.

Jim Walker and Rob Bellamy, authors of *Center Field Shot*, THE history of baseball on television, contributed an essay that made this book more complete. (If you liked this book, get CFS if you don't already have it and line up to read their history of baseball on radio.)

Tom Shea, baseball fan and writer and collector of stylin' vintage jerseys, assisted in the research for this book.

The always helpful Mike Selleck of the Oakland Athletics made some important information available to me, for which I am grateful.

For their research assistance, I bow to the mighty Mid-Continent Public Library, the Chicago Public Library, Paper of Record, the New York Public Library, and the St. Paul Public Library. John Horne at the National Baseball Hall of Fame and Museum supplied photographs with speed and good cheer.

Others have written about baseball broadcasting and deserve credit for, among other things, lighting the path. The work of Curt Smith, Ted Patterson, Jim Walker & Rob Bellamy, and Eldon Ham, in particular, is invaluable to anyone interested in this field. I also appreciate that many of the great pioneers of sports broadcasting penned their stories, keeping alive legends and lore otherwise bound for obscurity.

Friends and colleagues with whom I've shared baseball have shaped my thought. Some of these folks are Dave Aretha, Mark Campbell, Mark Caro, George Castle, Kevin Cuddihy, Toby Dye & Kitty Knecht, Dan Epstein, the Garibay family, James Finn Garner, Andie Giafaglione & Carlos Orellana, Chris Hein, Kevin Hennessy, Thom Henninger, Christina Kahrl, Frank Kras, Steve Leventhal, Jack O'Regan, Claudia Perry, Bob Purse, Gary Skoog, Rory Spears, Sheila Spica, Joe Stillwell, and John Thorn.

From generous souls Bart Johnson, Grover "Deacon" Jones, the late Curt Motton, the late Wilbur "Moose" Johnson, the late Larry Gross, and especially the late Lenny Yochim, I learned much of what I know about baseball. Their lifelong experiences in the game remind me that what there is to know is infinite.

Marc Appleman, Eileen Canepari, Nick Frankovich, Peter Garver, Bill Nowlin, Susan Petrone, and John Zajc, SABR stalwarts of the past and present, are each, in their own way, responsible for a chunk of this book's existence. Thank you all. Among this crew, Cecilia Tan in particular was especially active and helpful in managing the progress of the book.

Nothing would be complete without thanking three very special lights in my life: Marco, Carolina, and Ava Garibay.

Thanks also to my mom, Marion Clare Smith Light, and dad, John S. Shea II, for introducing me to baseball and sharing memories of their favorite voices for this book. And salutes to brothers John and Tom, who watched so many ballgames with me.

My only regret about this book is that three very special people did not live to see its completion.

First is Larry Epke, lifelong Cleveland Indians supporter and fellow SABR member, who shared many great baseball moments with me. I miss him, his friendship, and his love of the game nearly every time I think about baseball.

My uncle, Larry Smith, was among the world's biggest boosters of Harry Heilmann. I was lucky enough to be able to show Larry an early draft of this book's Tigers essay, and he enjoyed reliving memories of Heilmann's broadcasts as well as those of Ty Tyson and Ernie Harwell. To him, and my other relatives growing up listening to the Tigers on the radio, I dedicate the Detroit chapter.

Finally, there is Greg Spira, Queens resident, Mets devotee, skeptic, dreamer, friend, and finder and fixer of errors big and small. He was a great resource for this book, and it was no small honor to co-write the Mets chapter with him. I am still sad that we'll never see a game together at Citi Field.

After salaams to so many good friends, relatives, and colleagues, I reserve my biggest and most joyful thanks for Cecilia Garibay. Not only does she help me see things more clearly, she also helps me remember, by her shining presence, what I'm looking for.

FOREWORD

by Pat Hughes, Voice of the Chicago Cubs, WGN Radio
www.baseballvoices.com

I FEEL FORTUNATE TO HAVE GROWN UP DURING A GREAT AGE FOR sports broadcasters.

During the 1960s, national baseball broadcasts featured immortals such as Mel Allen, Curt Gowdy, and Dizzy Dean, men linked to the past but describing the greats of the time.

My hometown team was the San Francisco Giants, who were blessed to have Russ Hodges and Lon Simmons at the mikes.

Another Bay Area legend, Bill King — voice of the NFL's Raiders, NBA's Warriors, and later the Oakland Athletics — is in my opinion the best radio sports play-by-play broadcaster who has ever lived.

Growing up in an area and at a time in which few games were televised, radio was my prime conveyor of baseball. I developed a healthy respect for the great announcers' ability to paint pictures using words and sound to help the listener feel that he or she is simply across the room rather than hundreds, or even thousands, of miles away.

When I chose to enter the broadcasting field, my goal was to reach the major leagues. After five years of calling minor league games in San Jose and Columbus, I was fortunate enough to land a job as a cable television announcer for the Minnesota Twins, and the next year joined Bob Uecker on the Milwaukee Brewers radio crew.

Teaming with a legendary announcer like Bob Uecker was wonderful; I learned a great deal about the game of baseball. We had a lot of fun and I was lucky enough to be in the booth to watch Robin Yount's 3,000th hit, Juan Nieves' no-no, and Paul Molitor's hitting streak.

When I was offered an opportunity in 1996 to become the voice of the Chicago Cubs, calling games from legendary Midwestern radio powerhouse WGN, how could I resist? This is one of the great jobs in sports.

The team's radio network reaches close to 50 stations in 12 states, affording first Ron Santo, then Keith Moreland, then Ron Coomer and I the chance to bring Cubs baseball to fans all over the country. And thanks to Internet broadcasting and satellite radio, you can listen to the Cubs, or any other big-league club, everywhere from Belfast to Bombay.

It's a big responsibility to share the exploits of such a legendary team with so many fans. But as a fan and student of baseball broadcasting, I know that my path has been paved by Red Barber, Russ Hodges, Ernie Harwell, Vin Scully, Harry Caray, and so many others. In my career I have met many of the voices who have inspired me. It's an honor to be part of this great tapestry, and I hope to continue calling baseball for many years.

Calling the Game tells the story of major league baseball broadcasting on a team-by-team basis. I met Stuart Shea while we were working on different assignments at Wrigley Field, and he shares my interest in the game's radio and television history. I'm looking forward to reading the book and hope that you enjoy it, too.

THE ORIGINAL 16 FRANCHISES

TBS: TOTAL BRAVES ON SATELLITE

BOSTON/MILWAUKEE/ATLANTA BRAVES BROADCASTING HISTORY

"If we'd thought a bit 'bout the end of it
When we started painting the town
We'd have been aware that our love affair
Was too hot not to cool down."
— Cole Porter, "Just One of Those Things"

THE BOSTON BRAVES AND RED SOX WERE, FOR MANY YEARS, THE only major-league teams in the Northeastern U.S. to broadcast their games on radio. While the Yankees, Giants, and Dodgers largely eschewed the airwaves until 1939, the Sox and Bees (an old nickname for the Braves) were on the air beginning in 1926. They spread the word not only on their longtime flagship, WNAC, but also on a linked group of stations called, at various times, the Yankee Network and the Colonial Network.

Massachusetts was quite a hotbed of radio and television invention. The first Massachusetts radio station took to the air in 1923, and the State of Massachusetts even had an experimental television — or, as it was called then, "radio vision" — station in 1928.

For more than two decades, the Red Sox and Braves shared a radio carrier, as WNAC beamed home games of both clubs throughout the East. Much of the broadcast history of the Braves is also that of the Bosox.

Fans as far as New York, Philadelphia, and even the District of Columbia became familiar with the tones of Fred Hoey, a former sportswriter who called the games from 1927 through 1938 and was one of the area's most popular radio voices. The Boston Garden, home of the

NHL Bruins, even named Hoey — a huge hockey booster in the town — as its assistant general manager in 1929.

During this time, WNAC and the Yankee Network — one of the first such linkups in sports radio — involved 16 stations in markets as large as Providence, Rhode Island; Portland, Maine; and Manchester, New Hampshire. They competed directly with the broadcasts of those cities' own minor-league teams.

These broadcasts had millions of listeners in the Northeast, but minor-league clubs in several cities felt that the big-league teams' Sunday broadcasts hurt their gate receipts on the most important day of the week for attendance. In 1932, the Eastern League officially called on the Red Sox and Braves to halt airing games on those days and, by 1934, the clubs acceded.

After a humiliating episode at the 1933 World Series in which Hoey was rumored to be "under the weather" (coded language of the day for being inebriated), he rebounded to call the 1936 All-Star game for Mutual and continued his highly-rated Boston game broadcasts and nightly sports show.

Following the 1938 campaign, the Yankee Network's sponsors tried to fire him, desiring more "pep" in their broadcasts. An unexpected firestorm of protest from local fans, however, forced the network to swallow hard and rehire Hoey for two more years in January 1937.

Prior to 1939, however, the Bees and Red Sox got a new sponsor, Atlantic Refining, which successfully ousted Hoey in favor of former big-league star Frankie Frisch, whose big name trumped the fact that he had never broadcast before. Atlantic Refining felt that Hoey was too closely aligned to the network's previous sponsors, and probably also believed that the times had changed — along with them, the need for an announcer to be more "colorful" and less dry. Hoey ended up doing a daily sports report on WBZ.

The move to hire Frisch despite a total lack of experience was part of a new trend of using ex-ballplayers in the broadcast booth; professional radio men of the time detested this movement with all their hearts. Behind the mike Frisch was taciturn and sometimes unintentionally funny ("[N]ow the Braves will send up a pin shitter"), with a high-pitched, reedy and scratchy voice. Many fans in Boston and, later, New York probably agreed that it was appropriate that "the Fordham Flash" left the booth in 1940 to manage again.

WAAB snagged rights to Boston baseball in 1937, carrying games through 1941 over the Colonial Network. WNAC resumed airing the Boston home games in mid-1942, with General Tire co-sponsoring with Atlantic Refining. Nineteen network stations carried the Sox and "Bees," as the Braves were often called in those days, with locals Jim Britt and Tom Hussey manning the mikes following Frisch's departure.

Atlantic Refining remained Boston's radio sponsor for most of the decade, with Ballantine Brewery and Narragansett Brewing also taking turns buying ad time. Only the Cardinals, among contemporary NL teams, could boast a network nearly as big as that of the Boston Braves.

Britt began his career in Buffalo doing all sports and made a name for his versatility and facility behind the mike. The extent to which he became a national presence is best reflected by the fact that he described the All-Star Game for Mutual Radio in 1942 and, later, from 1947 through 1951. He also telecast the 1949–51 World Series on NBC, and called the 1946 Fall Classic on radio.

Perhaps most germane to Hub fans, he and Mel Allen also collaborated on the 1948 World Series radio broadcast, the only time the Boston Braves reached the World Series in the electronic media age. (During the series, Allen became very sick and was laid up at home for a few weeks afterward.) Allen and Britt also televised Notre Dame football in the late 1940s and early 1950s.

In 1946, WMEX secured the rights to broadcast the Braves' night home games, putting Frank Fallon — who later spent years as the PA announcer for the NBA Celtics and NHL Bruins — behind the mike. Decades later WMEX would land the Red Sox' radio package.

WHDH purchased the baseball radio rights for 1947, with Atlantic and Narragansett serving as sponsors. Britt did spring games of both clubs from the Grapefruit League, as well all home regular-season contests. The power of television, however, was beginning to wreak substantial changes on the media landscape in the Northeast.

General Tire and WNAC radio co-owned WNAC-TV, which split coverage of the Sox' and Braves' home games with WBZ from 1947 through 1952. Chevrolet bought a piece of the TV broadcasts for several seasons starting in 1949, and Ballantine beer did the same in 1950. On WHDH radio, Atlantic Refining and Narragansett continued as sponsors.

Television cameras cost about $20,000 each in 1949, and two were used on Boston's baseball telecasts, one from above home plate and the other some 200 feet down each ballpark's right-field line. Some advertisements were shown on film from the TV studio as early as 1949, with others done live from the park. The Zoomar (later "zoom") lens was first used on a Boston baseball broadcast in 1950.

Britt, by this time, had erased most of the memories of Hoey's broadcasts. One of the truly beloved sports broadcasters in the city's history, he was — like most of his felt-hatted radio contemporaries — a witty, sometimes boisterous raconteur, a man-about-town who liked a drink. As one of the most popular men in Boston, Britt sparked the annual "Jimmy Fund" drive, did public service announcements pushing treasury bonds, and vocally advocated ending racial prejudice.

In addition to doing 154 ballgames per summer, he was busy in the offseason, hosting a daily sports show — which sometimes lasted up to two hours — and even worked weekends.

But in 1951, he lost half his gig. The Red Sox chose to break off from the Braves and air all their games, both home and road, on WHDH radio. The Braves were forced to follow, going exclusively to WNAC. The NL club, just three years from its last pennant, had 31 radio affiliates. Britt chose to broadcast the Braves, while the Sox hired a couple of new guys, including a youngster named Curt Gowdy.

So for the final two years of the Braves' long history in Boston, Britt and Les Smith described the action to a shrinking fan base on WNAC. They also narrated the pictures to 59 home games each year, including 14 night contests, on WBZ and WNAC. Boston only had two TV stations in early 1950s, so baseball broadcasts filled a lot of the available real estate.

Prior to the 1949 season, Britt got new broadcasting digs at Braves Field, with a better view than previously. Unfortunately, the team wasn't that exciting after 1948, and attendance fell sharply. Baseball in 1950 had five cities with two or more teams; a decade later it had just one as the "weaker" clubs in St. Louis, Boston, Philadelphia, and New York moved to new markets.

Louis Perini became the first MLB owner to shift a franchise in 50 years when he uprooted the Braves and moved them to Milwaukee. This relocation was a long time in the making: Perini had bought the Milwaukee Brewers' minor-league franchise in 1946 and had been building relationships in the Midwest. Eventually he induced Milwaukee County to build a new ballpark for his minor-league team, with the idea that it could be quickly expanded for big-league baseball. On March 13, 1953, Perini petitioned the NL to allow the Braves to move, and five days later the shift was ratified. The Triple-A Brewers never occupied the venue that was ostensibly constructed for them.

Britt went to New York immediately after the Braves flew the coop, taking a nightly sports gig on the city's NBC television affiliate. He then signed on to handle play-by-play for Cleveland Indians telecasts from 1954–57, but never again reached the prominence of his heyday.

The Braves' move became a Cinderella story. Despite moving to Milwaukee during spring training, the club was an instant hit in a city which after the 1901 season had never been regarded as worthy of the major leagues. The club broke attendance records and soon built a radio network of 39 stations, third-most in the NL, by 1956.

One important thing that the Braves did right was follow in the Jim Britt tradition by getting a good broadcaster who knew the area. Earl Gillespie, born in Chicago, was just 31 when the Braves came to Milwaukee. In 1951, he'd called Marquette football and, then, as sports director of station WEMP, had described NFL Packers games the next year. He also called 1952 NFL championship game for Mutual Radio and, getting his baseball bona fides in order, did Brewers' games on WEMP from ancient Borchert Field in 1951 and 1952.

Gillespie himself had played four years of professional baseball in the 1940s without ever advancing above Class D. He knew the game like the back of his hand and, like many great Midwestern voices, had no problem showing his enthusiasm. He pulled for the Brewers and, later, the Braves, and in this way endeared himself to the team's fanatical rooters.

The Schlitz Brewery had long been interested in establishing a beachhead for baseball in Milwaukee, offering Lou Perini $750,000 for the major-league territorial rights to the city back in the early 1950s — the sponsor was interested in buying the rights without a ballclub in the picture. Perini, however, declined, since he already had established a relationship with Miller Brewing.

In 1954, Miller paid the Braves a million dollars for a five-year advertising package, gaining complete sponsorship rights. Oddly enough, both WTMJ and WEMP radio carried the same feed of the games; no other big-league club simulcast its broadcasts like this at the time. Gillespie paired with WTMJ announcers, working with Bob Kelley in 1953 and Blaine Walsh from 1954 on.

Gillespie hit the ground running, covering the new Milwaukee Braves' exhibition games from Florida, starting in late March. By Opening Day, 15 stations had joined the team's radio network. By midseason, the Braves were leading the National League in attendance. To increase understanding of the game among the town's fairer sex, the Braves held two baseball clinics for women fans during the season, with Gillespie as one of the panelists.

Gillespie's word was bond in the area. In 1954, Jackie Robinson accidentally threw a bat into the stands at County Stadium, and Gillespie reacted negatively, leading to widespread booing. Reports that Gillespie had called Robinson an "agitator," however, proved to be false.

The hard-working, hard-rooting Gillespie collapsed during the middle of the Braves' 20-game spring broadcast schedule in 1955 with what was originally called a stomach ailment, but was actually a mild heart attack. He recovered, however, to call the All-Star Game on radio with Cleveland's Bob Neal that summer.

The next year, Clark Oil paid Miller handsomely to become co-sponsor on the Braves' radio games. By this time, enough money was in the budget for a 30-minute pregame show as well as a postgame program.

The amazing Braves won the club's first NL pennant in Milwaukee in 1957, and then upset the mighty Yankees in the World Series, with Gillespie and Neal calling the action on radio for Gillette. (Milwaukee fans taunted the Yankees with the phrase "Bushville Wins!" after the seventh game.) With the club's original radio rights contract expiring, several companies and stations bid for the privilege of backing the team's broadcast. Miller and Clark came through with increased sponsorship dollars, and WTMJ and WEMP continued to air the games. Kent cigarettes also sub-leased time on the broadcasts; the three companies were the team's exclusive sponsors through 1962.

Gillespie, ever the busy man, not only called the Braves at this time but also did national college football and basketball, plus even minor-league hockey. He and Walsh used big fishing nets in the Milwaukee booth to catch foul balls, and the pair estimated in 1960 that they caught 75 or so balls a year, or roughly one per game. On April 15, 1958, Opening Day at County Stadium, a fan in the upper deck dropped a 10-pound fish into the net the first time Gillespie tried to snag a ball.

While future national football, basketball, and bowling announcer Chris Schenkel did work some Braves games in the 1950s before heading to New York, Blaine Walsh was Gillespie's best-remembered sidekick, good at injecting sidebars and capable of handling play-by-play when needed. In fact, Walsh called the ninth inning of the Braves' 1958 pennant-clincher at Cincinnati while Gillespie headed for the clubhouse to do interviews.

Gillespie reprised his World Series assignment in autumn 1958 for Gillette, this time paired with Bob Wolff. The Braves, however, lost their rematch with the Yankees after taking a three-games-to-one lead.

Voted 1959 Wisconsin Sportscaster of the Year, Gillespie by now was legend in the Upper Midwest. He had his key phrases, like saying that an outfielder "picked that ball off the wall out there" when he described a good catch. A bases-loaded situation was translated into "F-O-B" (for "Full of Braves"). Though he never claimed to be the first to say it, Gillespie would often yell "Holy Cow!" when surprised. *Go Get 'em Braves*, a record album stuffed with 1950s Braves highlights as called by Gillespie and Walsh, sold a lot of vinyl in the upper Midwest.

In those fondly remembered years, Earl and "The Blainer" provided Wisconsin's summer soundtrack as they brought the world of big-league baseball to the living rooms, porches, and cars of teens, brewery and factory workers, and seniors around the state — all bursting with pride at finally being considered "major league" after years of being patronized.

In a hugely disappointing 1959 season, the preseason favorite Braves spent most of the summer in third place before rallying in late September to finish in a tie for first. Milwaukee then lost a best-of three playoff series to Los Angeles in two games, both decided by one run, the second game featuring a three-run comeback by the Dodgers in the bottom of the ninth that tied the contest. The Dodgers — picked to win by almost no one before the season — won the pennant in the 12th, as the bloom fell from the Wisconsin rose.

Despite their huge statewide popularity, the Braves earned only $200,000 in broadcast revenue that season, ranking seventh in the NL, just ahead of the Giants. Not allowing local telecasts was the primary factor, although the club did make some compensating money from national games — which, in a cruel twist, the local fans couldn't watch either, since Perini refused to give permission.

Therein lay a major problem. While the Braves' radio strategy was strong, the franchise took an ostrich-like approach to the exploding popularity of television.

Having televised all of their home games in the late 1940s and most of them in 1951–52 to a hungry Boston audience, the club completely renounced TV coverage upon moving to Milwaukee. Perini, believing that television — rather than his team's inconsistency and deteriorating ballpark — had caused the Braves' massive post-1948 attendance drop in Boston, was opposed to showing home games, and he unwisely chose not to underwrite the substantial costs of televising road contests, even from Chicago.

While the decision to abandon television may have upped Perini's gate receipts in the short run, it was terrible long-term strategy. Fans all over the country got to see the Braves, who were featured regularly on network "Game of the Week" telecasts, yet the club's loyal Wisconsin fans found themselves frozen out. The team's no-TV strategy must have been particularly galling to old-school Milwaukee baseball fans who remembered that WEMP had televised American Association Brewers games in the 1940s.

By the late 1950s, it was substantially cheaper to produce road game telecasts and, by then, Milwaukee had four television stations for the Braves to work with. A television package could have restored some of the lost excitement as well as wooed back estranged fans. Lou Perini could have poured some of his enormous profits into telecasting road games. Moreover, Perini could have aired a few carefully selected home games — for example, sellouts or midweek day games against poor teams — during the club's boom years. But the parsimonious owner hewed fast to his short-sighted policy.

Facing rising ticket prices at County Stadium, some Braves fans in the early 1960s found other pastimes to engage their passion — most prominently, the Green Bay Packers. Under uber-coach Vince Lombardi, the NFL club rode the rapidly rising popularity of pro football as it inherited the mantle of the state's champions from the Braves. Milwaukee attendance declined and, by the time the Braves finally chose to telecast some ballgames to promote the club, it was too late.

Attendance, outsized for the team's first few years, began to dip. Fans were prohibited in 1961 from bringing their own beer into County Stadium, causing a furor in a town where beer was a staple and thousands of brewery workers could get it for free.

Faced with a sharp decline in attendance, the Braves finally contracted in 1962 to televise 15 road games over WTMJ-TV. Miller, Kent, and local Rambler dealers were the sponsors. With the new TV rights fees, the club's media revenue in 1962 reached a new high of $375,000. Retired pitcher Ernie Johnson did the pregame and postgame on telecasts, starting an on-air career with the franchise that would last nearly three decades. The Braves' initial TV game originated from brand-new Dodger Stadium on April 14.

Perini decided it was time to cash out, selling the team after the 1962 season to a group led by Chicago insurance executive Bill Bartholomay. The new ownership moved quickly to explore relocation of the franchise, which would turn out to be a bloody process for Milwaukee fans.

The following season, Gillespie and other insiders began to sense that something was very wrong. First, Miller dropped its sponsorship of the team's radio games, meaning that WTMJ, in turn, stopped carrying them. Blaine Walsh was suddenly gone from the broadcasts, with Tom Collins, a WEMP staffer, replacing him.

With Miller's departure, Schlitz entered into the picture, increasing the club's radio rights. The Braves now earned $475,000 for their radio package and a 25-game television schedule over WTMJ and three network stations. This figure, though, still ranked eighth among the NL's 10 clubs.

Walsh and Mike Walden, who soon departed for the West Coast, televised games in 1963 for Blatz Brewery. For the first time, the club showed a few home games on the tube, allowing five broadcasts from an increasingly empty County Stadium. Walsh was also hired by

WEMP on to do road games on the radio, as the station hoped to recapture some of its old magic.

In December 1963, a despondent Gillespie resigned his post as the Braves' announcer, though he remained as WEMP's sports director. He also took a job as a sportscaster on WITI-TV, which he held for more than a decade. While Gillespie said at the time that he wanted to spend time with his family, he would later admit that he knew that the team was going to move soon.

On January 17, 1964, the Braves announced that Merle Harmon, formerly of the Kansas City A's, had been hired as the team's voice. Harmon held court over a 56-station network, the team's largest ever. In early March, the club added a new television voice from far afield: Bill Mazer, a New York sportscaster who jetted to Milwaukee to work with Walsh on weekend games on WTMJ-TV and four network channels. This was to be Mazer's only stint broadcasting big-league baseball.

When the Braves rebounded somewhat in 1964, finishing only five games out, attendance rose significantly. Milwaukee management announced in late 1964, however, that the team would relocate to Atlanta. The city of Milwaukee was absolutely crushed. Local politicians forced the team and the National League into court, where the Braves were prohibited from leaving until 1966. Therefore, the club played the entire 1965 season as a lame duck, creating a terrible situation for everyone concerned, including the broadcasters.

No Milwaukee TV station would touch the team's 1965 games and, although Harmon and Walsh had a deal to call the games on the radio, the sponsors who had previously signed up wanted nothing to do with the team. So the 1965 Braves' radio programming carried no advertising. Without any advertising or sponsorship revenue, four parties — WTMJ, WEMP, a group called Teams Inc. that was trying to obtain a replacement team for Milwaukee, and the club's ad agency — were forced to underwrite the costs of the broadcasts.

Much happier were the Atlanta residents who, during this lame-duck year, got to know their new club via one of baseball's best-known voices. Mel Allen, dumped the previous fall by the Yankees, was hired in early March 1965 to broadcast Braves games to Atlanta 53 times on WSB radio and 17 times on WSB-TV.

Earl Gillespie was the first major league baseball voice of the upper Midwest, helming Milwaukee Braves broadcasts from 1953 through 1963. With his net for catching foul balls and his "Holy Cow" shouts, Gillespie was thoroughly invested in his team's success. (National Baseball Hall of Fame and Museum)

Once in Atlanta, the Braves got their broadcasting strategy right, assembling a reasonable 20-game road television package. The Southeast's first major-league club saw its games carried on large radio and TV networks that ranged from North Carolina to the east, Florida to the south, and Mississippi to the west. WSB signed on as the team's radio flagship and continued as such through 1983.

Atlanta employed a director of broadcasting, a rarity for the time, who lined up 36 radio stations and 19 television outlets — the most in the majors — to carry the team's inaugural season. Coca-Cola, Falstaff, Lorillard Tobacco, and Pure Oil composed an impressive advertising lineup.

Unfortunately the team stumbled in choosing the men to actually call the games after sifting through more than 500 applications for the two jobs. Cheerful Ernie Johnson, a loyal soldier, got the gig along with Larry Munson, who came from the University of Tennessee and would become a broadcasting legend at the University of Georgia. The big surprise of the trio was announced on November 4, 1965: Milo Hamilton, who had been Bob Elson's sidekick on White Sox games. There were conflicting stories about why Alabama native Mel Allen, then just 53 and a huge name, wasn't retained.

Hamilton was professional if not exciting, Johnson added the ex-player view, and Munson was loved for his presence. Bringing in Dizzy Dean for a few guest appearances in 1967 and 1968, and Bob Uecker for the same reason in 1969, underscores how dull those late 1960s Braves' broadcasts might have seemed to some listeners.

In 1967, the team broadcast over an impressive 43 radio stations in addition to WSB. The Braves counted 22 out-of-town TV stations that carried 14 weeknight and six Sunday road games. Hamilton became a pillar of the community, attending special dinners and engaging in myriad charitable causes, as he has in every city in which he has worked. In 1968 he was named director of the local chapter of the Epilepsy Foundation of America.

Despite winning the initial NL West Division title in 1969, the Braves quickly declined on the field, and attendance and ratings plunged in the early 1970s. Bartholomay sold his controlling interest to local television magnate Ted Turner in January 1976, although the former owner remained in the picture as chairman of the club.

Turner owned WTCG, Channel 17 in Atlanta. When the Braves wanted to expand their TV package for 1973, they shifted to independent WTCG (WSB was a network affiliate) and increased their telecasts from 20 to 52.

Ahead of his time, Turner saw the future of television and divined that its regional potential for sports represented an enormous, untapped market. Upon purchasing the Braves, Turner opined, "The television station has been financially successful and we decided to use its profits to move into the professional sports field." As a down payment for the team, Turner effectively used the money that he had already committed to spend when he had secured the club's television rights.

Even though the Braves were terrible in the late 1970s, they were the South's only major-league baseball team, and consequently sold out their sponsorship slots as companies on the outside banged on the doors. In 1973, his first year televising the club, Turner built a 26-station network, the biggest in the majors except for the Montreal Expos, who enjoyed a national network.

Egotistic, driven, and brilliant, Turner had a clear vision of a linked-up future, and he was one of those who made it happen. By airing large numbers of Braves games, he made the daily vicissitudes of his team into compelling TV for Southern fans, benefitting from a previously untapped market, much like the Braves had in Wisconsin two decades earlier. Braves fans began to follow their team via television in a similar manner as fans throughout the majors had used radio: as a conveyance that provided them with daily news, soap operas, crime dramas, and sporting events.

Under Turner's watch, the Braves started over with a new broadcasting team, as Milo Hamilton departed for Pittsburgh. This time, the team in the booth would last a quarter-century. Pete Van Wieren, who had nearly landed a job in Chicago as Harry Caray's sidekick, gladly came to Atlanta. After beginning his media career a sportscaster, Van Wieren had worked in several smaller markets before landing a job calling Triple-A Tidewater Tides games in 1974. Starting in 1976, he spent 33 years behind the mike in Atlanta, becoming famous for his preparation and for his easygoing manner.

Meanwhile, Skip Caray, who had called NBA Atlanta Hawks basketball on WTCG for three years, joined the crew for the 64 television games that aired in 1976. The White Sox made an offer to Skip to team with his father in 1976 on Chicago's WSNS-TV, but the son declined the opportunity.

Employing some of his father's trademark bluster, Caray made his mark with a sense of humor, a deep knowledge of baseball, and an ability to instantly shift from laid-back conversation to excited descriptions of big moments. He quickly became one of the most recognizable voices throughout the South.

Van Wieren and Caray provided the Braves with the needed personality quotient on-air to liven up Johnson's reliable but uninspiring work. Johnson also directed the team's broadcast operations, assembling a 60-station radio network.

Sensing an infusion of excitement about the franchise once Turner had taken over, WSB inked a long-term radio pact in 1978. Turner had shown 98 games on Channel 17 in 1977, including 24 at home, but by 1981, the ambitious owner was scheduling an amazing (for the Braves) 147 contests on free television. By then, the TV pioneer was thinking globally, not just regionally.

In December 1976, Turner uplinked WTCG's signal to the Satcom 1 communications satellite, changing both baseball and television forever. Most over-the-air stations of that time were worried about being seen in non-local markets, deterred by the cost of satellite rebroadcast, by the difficulty of charging for ads, and by the uncertainty of not knowing who would be watching. But Turner was thinking in terms of millions of viewers and billions of dollars.

Soon, viewers across the U.S. were tuning to the Atlanta station via their cable system, following WTCG's programming of reruns and old movies — and Braves games. While the Braves' media revenue amounted to only one million dollars in 1979, the figure was deceptive, comprised almost fully of radio fees. After all, Turner, as owner of both WTCG and the Braves, didn't need to pay himself a rights fee.

In 1980, WTCG changed its call letters to WTBS (Turner Broadcasting System) and continued its growth into would soon be known as a "superstation." Nearly all cable operators in the U.S. and Canada, as well as some overseas, added Turner's programming, allowing Turner to increase his advertising rates. By 1981, WTBS was viewed on nearly 2,700 regional and local cable systems, for a potential audience of nearly 11 million households. The club's return to excellence on the field in the early 1980s couldn't have come at a better time, and the Braves soon became known as "America's Team."

To be sure, Ted Turner had his quirks, which manifested themselves in odd ways. He wanted pitcher Andy Messersmith to wear "Channel 17" on the back of his jersey, and he installed himself as the team's manager for one game in 1977. MLB commissioner Bowie Kuhn suspended Turner for this and banned him from entering the dugout again. But the "Mouth of the South" generally kept his hands off the merchandise and, when he worked on promoting the team's story, he showed himself to be a genius.

Taking what looked like a bad situation — a flat team in what some thought of as a bad baseball market — Turner made himself rich and made the Braves a winner by simply letting baseball fans watch. He didn't hold out for pay-TV like Walter O'Malley, Horace Stoneham, or others; instead, he put his team on free TV and basic cable and let the fans come to him — like the Mets in New York and the Cubs in Chicago would later do.

Aggravated that Braves games were being broadcast into their markets, many MLB clubs pressed Commissioner Peter Ueberroth for financial relief. In 1985, Turner agreed to pay $30 million to MLB's Central Fund (where national broadcast revenue was collected before being disbursed equally to all teams) over five years to indemnify the other owners against "losses" caused by his superstation. Turner didn't admit to doing anything wrong; he paid up to get the other owners off his back.

With more TV games being shown in the early 1980s, more on-air talent was needed. So Atlanta sifted through Darrel Chaney, John Sterling, and Billy Sample before landing former Dodgers pitcher Don Sutton in 1989. Sutton, with the confidence of a former star, a shock of fuzzy hair, and a distinct ability to dissect the game, was truly at home on the Braves' broadcasts and became one of the game's foremost analysts. Joe Simpson, who joined the Atlanta team in 1992, was nearly as good, with an easy but incisive manner. The "four musketeers" described the action on radio and TBS through 2006, when Sutton departed.

Between 1991 and 2005, the Braves won the NL East title every season (except 1994, the strike year, when no title was officially awarded). The team was red-hot on the field, at the gate, and on the air. TBS's Glenn Diamond, one of the top TV producers in sports by the

1990s, managed a large on-air broadcast team and production crew that created a well-paced, exciting seasonal narrative.

Continuing to expand his empire, Turner created an extensive array of cable channels the early 1990s. Some of these carried Braves games as WTBS decided to schedule more entertainment programming.

When Turner merged his global operations with media giant Time Warner in 1996, however, the Braves became just another corporate subsidiary. And once Atlanta moved many of its games to other regional networks, the club's carefully cultivated brand began to deteriorate. The quality of the announcers on these cable games was not up to the TBS standard, with Tim Brando, Ernie Johnson Jr., and Bob Rathbun — all far better known for their basketball and football work — calling the action.

The Braves' ascent to their status "America's Team" in the 1980s came from having their games shown in one place. In recent years, Atlanta broadcasts have been all over the map: Peachtree TV, FSN, TBS, Turner South, and SportSouth, among others. In 2010, the Bravos were featured on three separate channels, making it hard for fans find the games. Spreading games among multiple channels may have been good for short-term profits, but it also diluted the brand. Fandom is a covenant between the club and its customers; why make it hard to spread the team's gospel?

Along with the shifting terrain, the Braves broadcasts became less compelling. Caray passed away suddenly in 2006, and Van Wieren announced his retirement shortly thereafter. Simpson has been paired with a succession of announcers on TV, including Jon Sciambi, who might have become a long-term favorite but who decided to head off to ESPN prior to 2010. While Simpson had shown himself capable of play-by-play, Atlanta hired Chip Caray and eventually made the third-generation legacy the lead voice on all the team's telecasts.

When Time-Warner sold the Braves to Liberty Media in 2007, Turner Broadcasting — at that time part of Time-Warner — structured an ironclad 20-year television deal rumored to pay the club somewhere between $10 and $20 million a year, far below what every other major league club now makes for its local television rights. All the entities that have shown Braves games since that point (SportSouth, Fox Sports,

Following a career as a relief pitcher for the Braves, Ernie Johnson moved into broadcasting and remained a calming presence on the air for 35 years. (National Baseball Hall of Fame and Museum)

When the Braves moved south to Atlanta in 1966, Milo Hamilton won their #1 announcer's job and acclimated southern fans to the ways of the big leagues for a decade. (National Baseball Hall of Fame and Museum)

and Peachtree) are owned by Turner. Obviously this was a terrible deal for the club, but just fine for Turner as it exited the scene.

The Braves' newest radio voice is Jim Powell, a Georgia native hired in 2009 after spending 13 years as Bob Uecker's second in the Brewers' booth. Powell, who is quite pleasant, speaks no more than necessary, and learns from his work, is capable of becoming a star of the magnitude of predecessors like Britt, Gillespie, Caray, and Van Wieren. Powell teams well on the radio with Sutton.

Unfortunately, the Braves' current radio situation is a mess. For 2010, the team awarded rights to WCNN, an AM sports-talker, and WNNX, an FM rocker. Neither station clears 12,500 watts in the evening, which makes it tough for listeners in some parts of the sprawling Atlanta metro to hear the games. A few smaller stations have signed on to carry the games to address this problem, but the overall plan remains far from ideal.

Following the 2012 season, the Braves discontinued their agreement with Peachtree TV (formerly WTBS) and for the first time since moving to Atlanta in 1966 are no longer showing any games on over-the-air television. The entire package is now split between SportSouth and Fox Sports in a deal that most analysts believe has seriously crippled the team's ability to acquire free-agent talent. Chip Caray and Joe Simpson call the games, leaving Ernie Johnson, Jr. free to focus on other sports.

Covering three different cities in very different sections of the country, the Braves' franchise has enjoyed more than eight decades on the radio, plus nearly six decades on TV. In many ways the club has been a broadcast pioneer, despite the regressive period in Milwaukee (in terms of broadcast strategy).

The lessons from the Braves' successful history on the air are: Plan for the long term, deal quickly and decisively with the ups and downs, and tailor the team's broadcast to the characteristics of its market. The Braves' best announcers — Hoey, Britt, Gillespie, Skip Caray, Van Wieren, Simpson, Sutton, Powell — came from the area they represented, sounded like they belonged, knew baseball, and obviously enjoyed what they were doing.

Pretty darn simple. Also very profound.

PITCHING BEER AND BAD BALLCLUBS

ST. LOUIS BROWNS & BALTIMORE ORIOLES
BROADCASTING HISTORY

"Ain't the beer cold!"
— Chuck Thompson

BEFORE THE MOVE TO BALTIMORE, THE ST. LOUIS BROWNS AND Cardinals shared Sportsman's Park and, until the end of the Second World War, announcers, sponsors, and radio stations. Therefore, much of the two franchises' early broadcast histories are either shared or overlapping.

In the pioneering days of baseball broadcasting, stations only covered home games. This meant that in two-team cities like Boston, Chicago, and St. Louis, the same broadcasters described the action for both clubs. No notion of broadcaster "loyalty" to one team really existed until economic conditions allowed for one-team, one-station relationships to develop in two-team markets.

St. Louis, home of the *Sporting News*, has always been baseball crazy and, as a result, took to broadcasting its favorite sport early. KMOX, the city's first radio station, presented its first games in 1926 — a fateful year for both Mound City teams. It was in 1926 that the Cardinals won their first National League pennant and their first World Series, setting the club on the path to becoming one of the NL's premier teams. In contrast, 1926 was the year that the Browns fell apart: after a period of respectability that saw them finish in the first division of the American League for five of the six previous seasons, the Browns slumped to seventh. In 13 of the next 15 years, the Browns inhabited the league's nether regions.

Thomas Patrick Convey sat in the press box at Sportsman's Park doing play-by-play on KMOX for a month early in the 1926 season. Garnett Marks succeeded him — until the clubs apparently decided that the radio guys were using too much electricity and pulled the plug!

The following year, however, three local stations were itching to broadcast baseball. In fact, competition for the St. Louis radio dollar meant that neither the Browns nor the Cardinals were ever on just one station from 1927–1946. In 1937, for instance, KMOX's games were sponsored by General Mills and KWK's by Socony Vacuum Oil. These companies, along with Atlantic Refining, were then the game's biggest financial guarantors nationally.

France Laux, St. Louis' first star baseball announcer, joined KMOX in 1929 and soon dominated the ether. Laux, an Oklahoma insurance man, gained attention while re-creating the 1927 World Series for KVOO in Tulsa. Two years later, at age 32, he vaulted all the way to St. Louis, doing games solo: Laux didn't get a color man until 1937. The popular Laux had an authoritative voice that described action as it happened without adding much opinion, color, or inflection.

In 1937, the prestigious *Sporting News* voted Laux its Announcer of the Year; during the 1930s and 1940s, Laux broadcast nine World Series and nine All-Star Games for CBS Radio. In 1939, the Yankees and Giants came calling, hoping that he would announce their home games, but Laux had found his home in the Gateway City and declined the offer.

Little audible evidence exists of Laux's work today, and even less survives of Convey, Ray Schmidt, Eddie Benson, Cy Casper, Jack Neblett, and other early voices of Browns and Cardinals baseball. The Browns were the river town's poor relations, finishing higher than sixth in the American League just three times from 1926–1941 while the rival Cardinals captured five National League pennants and three World Series in the same span, only thrice finishing in the second division.

The frustration engendered by the perplexing Brownies on the field extended to the booth as well: in 1939, the club fired manager Jim Bottomley, immediately moving him to their broadcasts.

World War II gave the Browns a chance to shine, as from 1942–1945 they became surprisingly competitive. KMOX, previously the St. Louis outlet for General Mills' baseball network, was no longer in the game, however. Following the 1940 season, KMOX — along with other CBS Network stations — deserted baseball due to pressure from sponsors who were annoyed that the games stole precious airtime from their favored soap operas.

Laux moved to three-year-old KXOK and an eight-station network in 1941, sponsored by Hyde Park Breweries (which had bought out of his contract with KMOX). Big changes were coming in St. Louis baseball broadcasting in the twin shapes of a nutty, cowboy-hatted Texan and a crude populist.

Former Cardinals hurler Dizzy Dean began his broadcasting career in 1941 with Johnny O'Hara on KWK, sponsored by Falstaff. The new duo immediately ate into Laux's audience — especially with their veteran competition on a smaller, less important station. On the air, "Ol' Diz" was the same wacky, crazy-like-a-fox presence that he had been as a player, and fans ate it up. Dean was paid $12,000 for his work in 1941, but quickly got a raise as, suddenly, Laux seemed a tad old-fashioned. By the time the Browns were enjoying their solitary pennant-winning year in 1944, Dean and O'Hara were a popular alternative on WEW during the day and WTMV at night.

The second threat to Laux's stature came in the presence of Harry Caray, a confident youngster from the Hill section of St. Louis. Hired as KXOK's sports director in early 1944, Caray immediately set out to convince Hyde Park Brewery management that he was more exciting than his own colleague, France Laux.

Hyde Park was persuaded by the brash Caray and shelved Laux. After calling the home games of the Browns and Cards during the magical year of 1944, Caray set his sights on Griesedieck Brewery, brewers of Falstaff beer. Ditching KXOX for WIL — a station that hadn't done baseball since 1931 — in 1945, Caray called the plays alongside Gabby Street, former manager of both the Cards and the Browns, under Griesedieck sponsorship.

Had the tremendously popular Dean been doing baseball in 1945, Caray probably couldn't have gained such a foothold. But Falstaff eschewed sponsoring games that year; instead, the brand used Dean — with whom it had a long-term contract — on various entertainment programs on KWK and as a representative of the brewery, sending him around the country to speak to servicemen. WEW and WTMV hired Laux in 1945 to narrate games with Johnny O'Hara but, with Diz returning to baseball in 1946, Laux was again pushed aside.

The first postwar season in 1946 was the final year that the Cardinals and Browns shared announcers and stations. Dean and O'Hara called all home and some road contests on WIL, while Caray and Street worked on WEW and WTMV. Re-created road games were rarely transmitted, since there was almost always a home game at Sportsman's Park.

The big split came in 1947, a cataclysmic year all around the game. Cardinals owner Sam Breadon went in a new direction, choosing to sever his broadcasts from the Browns'. The Cardinals, with Griesedieck, aired all 154 games on one radio network with Caray and Street. Redbirds road games were transmitted live from Cincinnati and Chicago, but otherwise re-created from wire feeds.

Dean, left in the cold by his beloved Cardinals, was crushed, but he signed to cover the Browns for Falstaff on WIL for 1947, sharing the mike with O'Hara. The duo again described all home games live, also doing some road games live, and others from wire reports. Dean, who had signed a five-year deal with Falstaff for a total of $100,000 prior to 1946, used whatever opportunity he found to rip Breadon.

On the air, Dean was country cornpone, but his folksy style didn't mask the former star's deep understanding and appreciation for the game. Like most great baseball announcers, Dean seemed one step ahead of the action, and he knew exactly what he was doing with his malapropisms and ungrammatical speech.

The Browns were desperate enough in 1947 that they signed the 37-year-old Dean — who repeatedly opined that he could pitch better than the humpties the Browns were running out to the mound — to a player contract as a publicity stunt. On the season's final day, Dean took the hill for the first time in six years and, amazingly, tossed four scoreless innings against the White Sox, allowing just three hits and also poking a single to left field.

Another big event in St. Louis in 1947 was the debut of KSD, the city's first television station. J. Roy Stockton, St. Louis Post-Dispatch sports editor, called the plays for 34 Brownies home games on the new channel, assisted by the station's Frank Eschen. For these telecasts, KSD set up its two cameras, its announcers, and a statistician in a new booth below the upper deck on the first-base side of Sportsman's Park.

Despite rumors that he was headed to Boston to manage the Red Sox, Dean returned to do Browns radio in 1948, pairing with Laux on WIL. Dean's return had been in doubt because Falstaff strongly considered not underwriting the 1948 season, eventually agreeing to advertise on only 77 broadcasts — meaning that half the club's games had no commercials between innings. Falstaff did, however, advertise on the Browns' TV contests in 1948 and again in 1950.

During 1948, KSD telecast the All-Star Game from Sportsman's Park; this was the first Midsummer Classic to be televised. Several other stations around the country paid to pick up the video feed.

With broadcasting Browns games increasingly looking like a dead end, Dean was happy to explore other options, so in 1948 he began his national broadcasting career with a 15-minute NBC Network radio show originating from KSD. The following year, Falstaff deemed Dean to be too valuable for something as low-end as Browns games. Instead, Dean hosted a half-hour daily show on KSD-TV. The Yankees wanted to bring Dean to New York, but Falstaff wouldn't release him from his contract until 1950.

Without Dean, the Browns instead turned to Johnny O'Hara and Tom Dailey on WEW during the day and KWK at night. Only the evening games were able to attract a sponsor in the form of Old Judge Coffee.

Because WEW and KWK began 1950 with no sponsors, they couldn't afford experienced broadcasters. Former infielder Buddy Blattner, a St. Louis native who had retired specifically to go into broadcasting, sat at the mike until Falstaff finally ponied up a small fee that allowed for live home broadcasts and road re-creations with unknowns Bill Snyder and Les Carmichael calling the action. Carmichael didn't even last till the end of the season, being replaced in September by longtime hurler Bobo Newsom. On television, KSD, also sponsored by Falstaff, paired Blattner with longtime airman Bob Ingham.

For 1951, 25 Midwest stations affiliated with Gordon McLendon's Liberty Radio Network carried the Browns' day games. Howie Williams, formerly Arch McDonald's second in the Senators' booth, relocated west to team with Blattner on KWK radio as well as on KSD's five telecasts.

Bill Veeck bought the bereft Browns in midseason 1951, immediately trying to bring Dizzy Dean back to the club's broadcast team on KXOX. Ol' Diz did about 60 Browns' contests in 1952, working around his commitments on the Mutual Network's national Game of the

Day. For the first time, the Browns originated all their broadcasts live from the ballpark, although with Howie Williams having returned East, Blattner worked alone for much of the season.

Falstaff once again sponsored not only the Browns, but also the Chicago Cubs and a large slate of Mutual's national radio package. Only seven Browns games were televised, one of them the franchise's first-ever road telecast on July 4 from Chicago.

In his autobiography Veeck — as in Wreck, the Browns' new owner confessed to cooking up a plan to have Blattner use a remote mike to broadcast a game while playing second base. The Phillies, who owned Blattner's playing contract, demanded $10,000 of Veeck, knowing he'd never pay up, thus ending the innovative (or harebrained?) scheme.

After the 1952 season, St. Louis baseball went through a lot of change in a short time. Both Veeck and Cardinals owner Fred Saigh asserted that they would not allow other clubs to televise their 1953 games against the Browns and Cardinals unless the St. Louis teams received some of the revenue from those telecasts. This was, essentially, an early large market vs. small market faceoff, one doomed to fail.

Veeck's hard-line stance brought instant retaliation as the Yankees and Indians in turn banned any broadcasts from their parks back to St. Louis. As further penalty, the Yankees, Indians, and Red Sox all promised to move their 1953 home games against the Browns to the afternoon, thereby reducing the share of gate receipts for the visiting Browns.

Faced with this opposition, Saigh chose to sell the Cardinals. After considering moving the Redbirds to Houston, amazingly, he found a local angel: Anheuser-Busch. The Browns had seen significant market growth in 1952, but brewing magnate Gussie Busch, always a sportsman, promised to invest a huge amount of money into the NL team and grow the Cardinals as never before.

Veeck immediately knew that he was beaten since he could never compete with Busch's financial might in the small St. Louis market. Therefore, Veeck began exploring a move to either Milwaukee or Baltimore for 1953, but a group of AL clubs led by the Yankees thwarted him.

With Griesedieck out as a Cardinals sponsor, its Falstaff brand threw the brewery's weight behind the Browns on KXOK and its fifteen-station radio network. Blattner again occupied the lead chair, this time assisted by Bill Durney, also employed as the Browns' traveling secretary.

Knowing he was overmatched, Veeck backed down from his no-telecast-without-remuneration stance. Falstaff expanded its television presence as Blattner and Dean traveled to Washington, D.C. to cover the Yankees-Senators AL season opener on April 13 — the first time the league's traditional inaugural game was shown on TV. The fledgling ABC network picked up the telecast and beamed it to fifteen stations stretching west to San Francisco, but none in the Northeast.

This was Falstaff's opening shot in a fusillade of new baseball broadcasts on ABC. Three AL clubs — the Athletics, White Sox, and Indians — sold ABC the rights to telecast their

Saturday games into non-major-league markets, with Blattner and Dean behind the mikes for the first national network broadcast schedule of regular-season games. When Blattner was on network duty, France Laux returned to the Browns' booth, working with Durney.

The local television picture wasn't as bright. KSD was scheduled to show a few Browns games in 1953, but Veeck wanted more TV exposure. In April he signed a deal with WTVI, St. Louis' second television station that was slated to begin broadcasting in May on channel 54, to air 33– 50 games, which would net the cash-strapped Browns approximately $1,000 per broadcast. Along the way, Milo Hamilton began his nearly sixty-year big-league career when, as WTVI's sports director, he helped out on its 20 Browns telecasts.

Bad weather, however, caused delays in installing the station's antennas, so no games were shown until an August 10 exhibition benefit game against the Reds. On September 27, the Browns ended the 1953 season with a 2-1, 11-inning loss to the White Sox at Sportsman's Park as Bill Veeck was hung in effigy in the stands. Two days later, the beleaguered owner sold the club to Baltimore interests.

The new Orioles understandably chose to make a clean break from the Browns, including their choice of broadcasters. The Birds and National Brewery, the team's new sponsor, chose not to pursue Blattner and instead hired Ernie Harwell in January 1954, pairing him with Bailey Goss, a local long associated with National. Howie Williams quit his Senators' PR job to be third man on the broadcasts.

This was Harwell's first lead broadcast role in the majors after serving in Brooklyn in 1948–1949 and with the Giants from 1950–1953. Harwell described the action over 10,000-watt WCBM and a network that started at 10 stations but quickly grew. By January 1954 the Orioles and National had also finalized a 59-game television plan. The new club on the western shore of the Chesapeake Bay was an immediate hit.

For 1955, Chuck Thompson joined the local network team, with Williams moving behind the scenes. Baltimore's three television stations split a slate of 59 games. Harwell, Thompson, and Goss also broadcast the NFL's Baltimore Colts during this period, with National sponsoring.

Many people now remember National Beer and Orioles baseball enjoying a constant relationship. After a three-year run with National, however, the Orioles — displeased that the brewer had begun sponsoring Senators games as well — sold their sponsorship to rival the Gunther brewery for 1957 as the games shifted to 50,000-watt monster WBAL (50,000 watts is the maximum power for AM radio). Goss and Thompson, considered too closely affiliated with National, decamped to Washington, and Gunther hired Herb Carneal and Larry Ray. Interestingly, WTTG in Washington still elected to telecast 26 Orioles games that season.

Gunther Brewing (acquired by Hamm's in late 1959) sponsored the Birds from 1957–1961. It also inaugurated the major league career of Carneal, who would eventually serve as a Twins airman for more than 40 years. Ray returned to Kansas City in 1958, a year in which the Birds secured new radio and TV deals. WJZ obtained exclusive television rights, which they would hold through 1961 and again from 1964–1978. WBAL took over on the radio, remaining as the team's flagship for two decades. In 1958, it broadcast 13 exhibitions from Florida as well as the full regular-season schedule. The next year, WJZ, airing 54 games, took on Phillies Cigars as a co-sponsor with Gunther as Baltimore's broadcast revenue of $425,000 ranked fifth among the eight AL clubs.

Following the 1959 season Harwell departed for Detroit, where he would enjoy a four-decade career. To replace him, Baltimore reached into Boston's stockpile of broadcasters and selected rich-voiced Bob Murphy, who became top dog, with Carneal as an able second. Local sportscaster Joe Croghan, best known for his gridiron work, joined as the third voice when the other two were on television.

The 1960 Orioles' TV plan sliced home games from 21 to only 11 (all Sundays) but added extra road contests, including seven from Cleveland and six each from New York and Chicago. Hamm's added local co-sponsors to both radio and TV to bring in extra income. Once again, with about half a million bucks in broadcast rights fees, Baltimore was in the middle of the pack — light years better that than its 1954 figure in St. Louis of less than $9,000. In 1962, WBAL-TV began televising some Orioles games in prime time. Lorillard, manufacturer of Old Gold Cigarettes, signed on as co-sponsor.

National regained the Orioles' account and, in early September 1961, announced a two-year deal to sponsor 1962–1963 games. The sponsorship change meant a whole new broadcast crew for 1962, consisting of loyal soldiers Thompson and Goss plus the team's former public relations man, Jack Dunn III, whose grandfather had owned the International League Orioles franchise in the 1910s and 1920s.

Murphy and Carneal, therefore, worked as lame ducks for the 1961 season's last month. Both landed on their feet, as Hamm's transferred Carneal to Minnesota, while Murphy hooked on with the expansion Mets in the Big Apple.

Chuck Thompson was back in the Orioles booth, where he belonged all along. Thompson began his radio career in 1939 in Reading, Pennsylvania as an 18-year-old dance-band singer. He transferred to Philadelphia's WIBG in 1941. After the war, Thompson returned to the station; in 1946 he was pressed into emergency duty at an A's game when regular announcer Byrum Saam couldn't get to the booth in time after a pregame ceremony.

After learning the ropes on the Athletics' and Phillies' broadcast crews in 1947–1948, Thompson took a job in Baltimore broadcasting the International League Orioles. As his regional popularity grew, he also took on network TV football assignments. His signature phrase was "Go to war, Miss Agnes!" which he used for any exciting happening on the field; this saying came from a golfing buddy who wouldn't swear. He rooted openly for the Colts and Orioles; when things were going well for the home team, he'd exclaim, "Ain't the beer cold!"

Thompson did his share of national baseball and football as well as calling the Colts from 1955–1960, consuming plenty of rubber chicken on the off-season banquet circuit while personifying the "pleasant living" credo of National Beer. Thompson meant as much to Baltimore as Jack Brickhouse did to Chicago or Mel Allen to New York.

For 1962, Natty Boh and the Orioles chose to televise just a few home games but more than half their road schedule — nearly all the away weekend games — which cost more but was deemed a better strategy.

Goss, the "voice of National Beer" on their ads, was slated to cover only home games in 1962 due to his other duties. Unfortunately, he was killed in a drunk driving accident that April 30 when he lost control of his car after attending a company function. He was 49. A grief-stricken Thompson, Goss' close friend and golf partner, didn't hit the links again for more than 10 years.

Following the 1962 season, Dunn returned to the Orioles' front office with Croghan, by now a WBAL sportscaster, replacing him. Croghan lost that gig, however, when WJZ retook the Birds' television rights for 1964.

The new second to Thompson was Frank Messer, who from 1956–1963 had earned plaudits for his broadcasts of the International League's Richmond Virginians. In addition to serving as Thompson's caddy, Messer also called the action for the Colts from 1964–1966. The new WJZ deal puffed up the Orioles' broadcast rights revenue to some $700,000 a year, fourth best in the American League.

The Orioles in 1965 had a 40-station radio network. National, hoping to maximize its investment in the club, no longer wanted exclusivity, instead selling spots to local concerns Esskay Meats and Central Savings as well as national companies such as Lorillard, General Cigar, and Pepsi-Cola. This didn't mean National was losing interest; just the opposite, in fact. In May 1965, National — with Jerry Hoffberger in control — actually purchased the Orioles in a complex deal.

For 1966, the Orioles hired a third man for the booth, Bill O'Donnell, who had broadcast University of Syracuse football for 13 years. O'Donnell remained on the broadcast team until 1982.

By this time, National occupied the roles of the Orioles' chief sponsor, their broadcast rights holder, and the club's owner. Birds announcers could understandably have felt they were in a rather sticky position. In 1973, however, O'Donnell told Jack Craig, the *Sporting News'* TV-radio columnist, that he never felt pressure from the top to be a "house man" or to minimize bad news. Obviously O'Donnell had impressed with his impartiality, because by the early 1970s, he was also handling NBC baseball and football assignments.

After the Orioles won the World Series in 1966, they had an advantage in their negotiations with WJZ. Their new TV deal for 1967–1968 netted them a cool million dollars per year, roughly a fourth of the team's income. (Major league clubs often misreported their broadcast revenues to the trade magazines which tracked these things, either to hide the true figures or because they were accounting things differently on yearly bases. Most of these revenue numbers are probably on the low side.)

Not only did the club grow its radio network to 60 stations by the mid-1960s, but it also could boast a television network ranging as far south as Louisiana, with all TV games presented in color starting in 1967. The TV plan didn't change much, however, no matter who had the contract or how many people watched. From 1958–1981, the club allowed 46–54 games per season to be telecast per season, nearly all from the road.

Messer departed after 1967 for a role on the Yankees' broadcasts. Jim Karvellas, better known for broadcasting the NBA's Baltimore Bullets and, later, the New York Knicks, joined the crew for two years. The Orioles had always manned their booth without employing ex-athletes, but a three-man team with no ex-jocks was rare by this time.

Karvellas, voted Maryland's top sportscaster in March 1969 by the National Sportscasters and Sportswriters Association, left before the 1970 season. His replacement was John Gordon, who had been named South Carolina's top sportscaster by the same group in 1969.

The late 1960s and early 1970s were halcyon days for manager Earl Weaver's powerful club — built around three future Hall of Famers in Frank Robinson, Brooks Robinson, and Jim Palmer and featuring other popular stars like Boog Powell and Dave McNally. Baltimore won another world championship in 1970, plus AL pennants in 1969 and 1971, and AL East Division titles in 1973–1974.

Despite this success, there was trouble at the mill. Like most older industrial cities, Baltimore had lost a large share of its upper class and middle class to the suburbs after the war. Attendance peaked in 1966. The Orioles' radio network dropped to 55 stations by 1973 and plunged to just 25 two years later. The $775,000 Baltimore made from its radio-TV rights in 1973 ranked ninth among 12 AL clubs as broadcasting revenues had doubled in cities like New York and Boston.

National Beer, struggling to cope with much larger brewers, merged with Carling in 1975; the new company took over sponsorship and rights for Orioles television and radio. Uncomfortable with the advent of free agency, Jerry Hoffberger decided to sell the club. Ironically, Bill Veeck almost grabbed the brass ring, but everyone was concerned that Veeck would relocate the team. With the expansion Washington Senators having recently left for Texas, the idea of having no team in either Baltimore or D.C. was inconceivable. As a result, the club wasn't sold until 1979, when wealthy Washington attorney and powerbroker Edward Bennett Williams acquired it. Williams was also president of the NFL Washington Redskins.

In addition to new ownership, the Birds got new radio and TV homes for 1979. When the Orioles and WBAL, at the end of a one-year contract, disagreed about travel expenses, WFBR pounced on the situation, gaining the rights to air radio accounts on a 48-station network. Tom Marr of WFBR, at that time a sports anchor but later a political commentator, joined the radio team. The TV contract went to WMAR, which hired Brooks Robinson (who had retired the previous season) to join Thompson and O'Donnell.

The down-to-earth Robinson, who would suck his teeth on the air after a particularly tasty plate of ribs, certainly was dear to Baltimore's blue-collar heart. He worked on over-the-air telecasts until 1993, but never on radio.

WFBR's broadcasts caught fire in the summer of 1979, when the Orioles won the AL flag. The station repeatedly played back game highlights, increasing interest and grew the radio network substantially. By 1982, 70 stations were airing Orioles games.

Early in 1982, Bill O'Donnell, a model of stability in the booth, was diagnosed with cancer. Marr took a bigger role in the broadcasts, which did not sit well with Thompson. On October 29, O'Donnell died at 56, thus effectively bringing an end to an era of Orioles baseball. The 62-year-old Thompson, sad to lose another partner and not interested in working with Marr, cut back his schedule and worked exclusively on telecasts, calling 40–50 games each season with Robinson before retiring in late 1988.

The club's 1983 TV and radio agreements poured $2 million per year into the club's coffers as Baltimore hired Jon Miller to be its new radio voice. Fresh off a stint with the Red Sox and already a veteran of three major league teams, Miller quickly forged a strong identity with a new generation of Orioles fans with his humor, rich voice, and feel for the game. Miller and Marr paired through 1986, when the team's contract with WFBR expired.

With owner Williams' encouragement, cable television became part of the Orioles' broadcast package in the early 1980s. Ted Patterson, a broadcasting junkie and a fixture on area radio since the early 1970s, helped wangle a deal for Super TV — a UHF channel which scrambled its signals for pay broadcasts — to relay 16 Orioles games in 1982. Rex Barney, the club's popular public address announcer, teamed with Patterson.

The pay presentation proved popular, so Super TV aired another 16 home contests in 1983, though Barney missed some after suffering a stroke. For 1984, recognizing the value of this new field, the Orioles granted rights to HTS (Home Team Sports), one of the first regional sports cable networks, for 80 games. The Birds initially received $30,000–$50,000 per game from HTS, buttressing the team's low over-the-air broadcast revenue, which was stuck at late 1960s levels.

The cable TV revolution completely changed the way baseball was shown on television and altered the game's financial structure. With cable networks providing aggressive competition to both local and network broadcasting, major league teams could and did demand more money and control. No longer were sponsors the biggest players in the picture. With more options, teams began to bringing their broadcasting functions in-house, hiring their own managers, advertising sales people, and talent.

While having teams hire their announcers seemed like a major change, it was not as if announcers were independent in the "good old days" of the postwar era when major tobacco and liquor brands, carmakers, oil companies, and the like guaranteed the broadcasts. Chuck Thompson was most certainly beholden to National Beer for his job in Crabtown, and Bob Elson described every home run in the Windy City as a "White Owl wallop." On the banks of the Mississippi, listeners wouldn't go an inning without hearing announcers describe the great taste of Busch Bavarian. East coast fans constantly heard about the cool refreshment of an Old Gold cigarette and the great work done by Atlantic Refining. Despite being hired by the teams themselves, or with the teams having veto power, most men and women at the baseball mikes these days are professional and fair.

Taking on a significant schedule of mostly home games for 1984, HTS needed high-impact professional announcers. The big role went to Bullets broadcaster Mel Proctor who, like

Miller, had previously worked for the Texas Rangers. Barney and media gadfly Larry King did color commentary as Orioles fans now could watch an unprecedented 132 games on the box.

As TV greatly expanded its role, Jon Miller used his popularity to increase his stature. The Cardinals made Miller a $150,000 offer to join KMOX as Jack Buck's partner for 1984, but Miller decided to stay put when WFBR raised his pay to $100,000. The next fall, the Cubs offered Miller a huge raise to work alongside Harry Caray in 1986, but Miller again chose to remain in Baltimore — this time negotiating a new pact that gave him editorial control of all facets of the radio broadcasts.

When WFBR's radio deal expired after 1986, WCBM, a 5,000-watt station, made a $5 million, three-year bid and captured the rights. Jack Weirs became Miller's No. 2 on

What are the odds that a lawyer from Maine would end up one of sports' most recognizable voices? Gary Thorne called baseball in Chicago and New York before landing in Baltimore, where he has starred on television since 2007. (Keith Allison)

WCBM in 1987, relocating from Hawaii for the job. After just one season, however, the radio station ran out of money and defaulted on the contract. After some behind-the-scenes machinations, WBAL ended up with the rights for 1988.

Weirs returned to Honolulu as Joe Angel became Miller's new second banana on WBAL. On cable, HTS shelved Rex Barney in favor of a parade of ex-Orioles, including Jim Palmer, John Lowenstein, and, later, Rick Dempsey and Mike Flanagan.

From 1991–2000, Chuck Thompson appeared again on Orioles broadcasts in a part-time role until eye problems forced him to retire for good. It was a lovely, sentimental coda for a man who evoked for older fans the simple pleasures of local beer and local baseball.

With sponsors no longer controlling baseball broadcasting as they had in the 1950s and 1960s, clubs were now free to engage in long-term relationships with their on-air talent. The Orioles are one of the clubs famous for this. Palmer has been an Orioles TV fixture since 1988. Miller was the Orioles' distinctive voice until 1996, when he left after a salary dispute. Fred Manfra has been on the crew since 1993, Jim Hunter since 1997, and Buck Martinez called games from 2003–2009. Angel has spent much of the last two decades at the mike at Camden Yards. None of these more recent voices has achieved anywhere near the level of affection engendered by Miller or Thompson. Many fans love Palmer, but others can't stand him. Angel is much more a professional voice than a local hero.

In 1994, longtime TV carrier WJZ recaptured the over-the-air contract, airing 55–70 contests per season through 2006 before the age of free TV ended in favor of the megamillions that regional sports networks (RSNs) could generate.

Comcast, a dominant Philadelphia-based cable operator, purchased HTS before the 2001 campaign and carried the team on cable through 2006 when the Orioles went in a new direction as a direct result of … the Montreal Expos?

Peter Angelos, a very successful personal-injury lawyer from Baltimore, had purchased the Birds in 1993 after former owner Eli Jacobs went bankrupt. Building upon the incredible popularity of trend-making Oriole Park at Camden Yards, the Orioles became immensely profitable. As the owner of that gold mine, Angelos was not used to being dictated to, and was tremendously vexed when Major League Baseball chose to move the Expos to Washington, D.C. prior to the 2005 season.

Despite Angelos' strenuous opposition, baseball owners decided on D.C. because no viable alternative existed for relocating the struggling, MLB-owned club. The Orioles' claim over the D.C. territory was resolved when Angelos agreed on the condition that he could televise the Nationals' games on his brand-new RSN, the Mid-Atlantic Sports Network (MASN). In negotiations to allow the Expos to share the Orioles' territory, MLB paid to acquire a 10% stake in MASN for the Washington club. As part of the arrangement, the Nationals ownership share of the RSN will gradually increase to 33%.

While Chuck Thompson began his big-league career in Philadelphia and also worked in Washington, it is for his years in Baltimore that he is best remembered. At once homespun and attentive to details, his joyful "Ain't the Beer Cold!" summed up baseball in Crabtown for nearly 40 seasons. (National Baseball Hall of Fame and Museum)

The Orioles themselves did not appear on MASN until 2007, when their contract with Comcast expired, but the new RSN carried the Nationals immediately. MASN paid the Nationals $20 million for the right to show 70 games in 2005. With the Orioles moving to MASN, only 48 games appeared on WJZ in 2007–2008 before a cutdown to just 20 games a season.

Comcast did not go down fighting, suing twice to force the Orioles to remain on its network. When both cases were thrown out of court, Comcast — which owned many of the local cable systems in the Orioles' viewing territory — responded by refusing to carry MASN in some areas.

Mike Flanagan, the former Orioles pitcher and general manager, died a suicide on August 24, 2011. The following season, onetime Orioles shortstop Mike Bordick moved into a television analyst role, working approximately half of the club's games on MASN and WJZ with Palmer continuing as analyst for the other contests.

The year 2014 marked the eleventh year together in the booth for radio men Joe Angel and Fred Manfra with no changes in sight.

The complex infighting over the team's TV rights would have been more dramatic had the Orioles been a good team. Covered by Gary Thorne, Palmer, and Angel, a team that finished last or next-to-last in its division for all but one of 14 seasons was far from must-see TV or gotta-hear radio, but matters improved once Buck Showalter took over as manager.

The broadcast histories of the Browns and the Orioles share some common threads: long stretches of bad teams, intimate ties to breweries, and a plethora of short-time talent behind the mike. Yet the teams' broadcast histories are dissimilar in two profound ways. The Browns were always patching things together, without an effective long-term strategy.

The Orioles, in contrast, have managed their broadcast rights very well overall. More importantly, in Baltimore the club was, at least in the older days, able to create an intense bond between the community and key announcers — the kind of relationship necessary for long-term loyalty to a baseball team.

HUBCASTING

BOSTON RED SOX BROADCASTING HISTORY

"When sorrows come, they come not as single spies but in battalions."
— *William Shakespeare, Hamlet*

IS TRAGEDY INBORN FOR RED SOX FANS? PERHAPS IT USED TO BE.

Ned Martin, the dean of Boston broadcasters for his 32 years of service, occasionally used the above quote from the Bard when things went wrong for the Olde Towne Team. In watching over 5,000 Red Sox games beginning in 1961, Martin had plenty of time to ruminate on sadness.

It is truly a shame that Martin, Curt Gowdy, Ken Coleman, and many other great Red Sox broadcasters did not live to see the team win a World Series. Fans born in the 1980s and 1990s have always known the Red Sox to be competitive and often dominant.

Showing devotion sometimes matched, but not bettered, by partisans of other clubs, Red Sox Nation — from Dorchester to Orono and all points east and west — can now follow the team by radio, television, satellite, and the Internet. Like all of the other "original 16" teams of the early and mid-twentieth century, though, Red Sox fans began their romance with broadcasting back on the low-tech AM dial.

Perish the thought, but the Red Sox began their broadcast history on a string of stations called the Yankee Network — the name, of course, referring to New Englanders' collective persona as "Yankees" rather than to their long-hated foes. Beginning in 1925, the Yankee Network broadcast home games of both the Red Sox and the National League Braves, who shared Beantown before leaving for Milwaukee in 1953. Road games were sometimes re-created in the studio from ticker tape during the early days of Boston baseball broadcasts, and often not covered at all.

Gus Rooney is credited with doing the first Red Sox and Braves broadcasts in 1925 over WNAC (now WRKO). Fred Hoey, however, is remembered as the club's first full-time voice. Hoey had worked as a sportswriter since 1909 at the now defunct *Journal*, *Post*, and *American*, later becoming the Braves' official scorer. He was deemed a natural for the radio waves.

Back in those days, Hoey was baseball in Boston. Starting in 1933, WNAC broadcast all Red Sox home games. Each broadcast in this era began 15 minutes before game time, when pregame host Jerry O'Leary greeted listeners with his signature, "It's a beauuuuuuuuutiful day for the ball game!" O'Leary, a popular local advertising man, held his position on the broadcasts from 1930 through the early 1960s. Baseball historian Pete Palmer recalls that O'Leary also did a pregame segment from the Fenway Park stands in the 1950s in which he asked young fans baseball questions. Those who answered four questions earned four silver dollars.

By 1936 the Yankee Network's broadcasts of Red Sox games reached 10 stations, with more than 20 stations eventually becoming part of the network. General Mills was the main sponsor, as indeed they were for most big-league teams' radio packages of that era. Socony Vacuum Oil Company also bought ad time on the Yankee Network, as well as on other teams' broadcasts.

The New York Yankees — who broadcast no games out of fear that putting a product on the air "for free!" would cut into ticket sales — were angry at both Boston clubs for airing their games down the Eastern seaboard. As punishment, the Yankees would not allow the Red Sox to broadcast their games against New York. (Broadcast agreements always require the consent of both teams.)

Selected for the prestige job of calling the national broadcast of the 1933 World Series, Hoey had to be removed from the microphone during Game 1 on October 3. The scuttlebutt was that Hoey showed up at the park intoxicated. The veteran announcer steadfastly denied this, attributing his performance to laryngitis and nervous tension, and CBS Radio claimed that Hoey was replaced because of a "tired voice."

Not everyone agreed that Hoey was out of it that day. The Portsmouth (New Hampshire) *Herald* published an editorial supporting the Red Sox' announcer on October 4: "No one noticed any crack in his voice on account of the cold. His broadcast came clear and distinct and his story was well and intimately told. . . . Roger Baker of Buffalo who succeeded him . . . may be all right as a football announcer, but he is certainly not in the class with Fred Hoey in handling a baseball broadcast."

Hoey was beloved in Boston and the environs for his no-nonsense descriptions, but the times were changing. Sponsors canned Hoey in 1936 because he was not "chatty" enough, but public outcry — including words of support from President Franklin D. Roosevelt — forced his rehiring. Hoey proudly returned to the airwaves, but was permanently dismissed two years later.

By that time WAAB had taken over the Sox' radio broadcasts, with the games returning to WNAC in 1942 and continuing there until 1946. The 64-year-old Hoey died in the kitchen of his suburban home on November 17, 1949, by accidental asphyxiation from a gas stove.

When Hoey left the airwaves, inexperienced Bronx-born Frankie Frisch took over. Frisch, however, left his first broadcasting job in midseason 1940 to manage the Pittsburgh Pirates, which is probably just as well for the nation's grammar teachers and speech tutors.

Jim Britt jumped into the void, having cut his teeth on football at Notre Dame and on baseball in Buffalo.

Britt was an immediate hit with his erudite and accurate reporting. Fans for many years later fondly recalled his signature sign-off, "Remember, if you can't play a sport, be one, will you?"

In 1943–45, Britt served in the military, and sidekick Tom Hussey replaced him on both Sox and Braves broadcasts. George Hartrick briefly became the new no. 2. Longtime Hub radio and TV personality Leo Egan also helped out on the broadcasts in both the late 1930s and late 1940s.

By the time Britt returned from the military, television had moved in. WHDH had bought the exclusive rights to Red Sox radio in 1946, and the Red Sox and Braves began telecasting on WBZ and WNAC in 1947. Britt, Hussey, and former pitcher Bump Hadley manned both the radio and TV mikes.

Despite his obvious talent as an announcer, Britt had his critics. Some fans thought he was pompous. Occasionally he had a drink too many, and he was pulled over more than once by the police. He was intensely popular, however, performing yeoman service for the Jimmy Fund, which remains to this day the select charity of the Red Sox.

Britt made what in retrospect was a poor career decision, too. Hoey, Britt, and company had been re-creating road games off ticker-tape since the 1930s, but only in 1951 (after most clubs had already done so) did the Red Sox decide to cover road games live. Fatefully, Britt decided to stay in Boston and eschew traveling to cover Braves games exclusively.

The Braves' move to Milwaukee in 1953 cost Britt his chance to continue doing big-league play-by-play in Boston, and his mistake

Before he was the voice of NFL football or host of the "American Sportsman," Curt Gowdy was the voice of the Boston Red Sox. He held that job from 1951 through 1965, at which point he left for NBC Sports and greater national fame. (National Baseball Hall of Fame and Museum)

opened the door for Curt Gowdy's ascension. Britt died, nearly forgotten, in California in 1981 at age 70, three decades after his days of glory.

Gowdy earned his audition in Boston by virtue of his work in 1949 and 1950 describing Yankees games as Mel Allen's second. When he arrived in Boston in 1951, Gowdy quickly ingratiated himself to Red Sox fans over WHDH and a 50-plus-strong member station network, sponsored by Atlantic Refining and Narragansett Brewing.

Gowdy was called a "man's man" in the vernacular of the day. Hailing from Wyoming, he was an outdoorsman whose hearty and enthusiastic manner carried him through situations that demanded detailed knowledge. Never a true baseball expert, Gowdy instead conveyed the excitement of a particularly well-spoken guy hanging out at the hunting lodge.

Although he earned his stripes in baseball, Gowdy became more famous for his basketball and football work. When Gowdy first came to Boston, he also called Celtics games for three seasons on radio and later became a successful football announcer. Because of this, many people today do not realize that Gowdy was a baseball voice for nearly three decades, describing Ted Williams, the "Splendid Splinter," in his twilight years while greeting Sox fans with a convivial, "Hi, neighbor! Have a 'gansett!"

Gowdy's first sidekick in Boston was Bob Delaney — a self-described salesman who apparently didn't even like baseball. Delaney flopped and left following the 1953 campaign. Tom Hussey was the third man in the booth through 1954, at which time Bob Murphy joined Gowdy.

The late Murphy, best remembered for broadcasting the Mets for their first 42 seasons, cut his teeth at Fenway. While the teams the two announced from 1954 through 1959 were not especially good, Gowdy's rough-hewn and excitable country style mixed memorably with the more precise, scholarly-but-friendly demeanor of the Oklahoma-raised Murphy.

Beginning in 1955, the Bosox went with a two-man booth for a few years. After Gowdy missed much of 1957 with a back problem, though, the team brought in Bill Crowley. Crowley held the third chair through 1960, when he took a job as the team's public relations director.

Art Gleeson joined the team in the booth in 1960, replacing Murphy, who began a gig with the Orioles. More significant was when 37-year-old Ned Martin came aboard a year later to fill Crowley's post. Philadelphia-raised and most recently the voice of Detroit's Class AAA club in Charleston, West Virginia, Martin was relaxed and knowledgeable, perfect for Boston's fanatical and well-informed fan base.

By this time the Red Sox were carried on WHDH's AM, FM, and television stations. After showing all 77 home games between 1949 and 1953, the club settled into a pattern of telecasting a mix of 51–56 home and road contests per year through 1971.

Atlantic Refining and Narragansett Brewing continued buying commercial time on Red Sox broadcasts well into the late 1960s. Several other companies — including Boston-area Ford dealers, American Tobacco, General Cigar, and the local Hood Dairy — subscribed to one-third sponsorship shares on the broadcasts in the late 1950s and early 1960s.

With the Braves gone, the Sox consolidated their status as Boston's team and began to cash in, earning $300,000 in 1957 from their radio and television rights. The following year, the club signed new deals and increased its take to $450,000, fourth among American League clubs.

Most of the club's telecasts in the 1950s and 1960s were weekend games. Nearly all home and road Saturday and Sunday games were televised, along with the occasional weeknight. This was a solid strategy, balancing home and road, although the Sox probably would have increased their gate had they not aired all their weekend games.

This was obviously a calculated decision that the extra advertising dollars would outweigh any reduction in gate receipts. Other big-market clubs like the Cubs and Yankees made similar choices.

Boston broadcast revenues continued to increase in the 1960s, as the club earned $600,000 for its rights by 1963. Yet the Yankees made $1,200,000 for their media rights at the same time, and even the Twins were earning as much as the Red Sox. The problem was that the product wasn't very good: "What's the matter with the Red Sox?" was the oft-repeated cry. It was only after the team improved in the latter part of the 1960s that Boston's broadcasting rights came into line with the size and income of the club's territory.

Art Gleeson died of a heart attack at age 58 on November 27, 1964, in a small town in Oregon where he had just arrived for a family reunion. In the wake of Gleeson's passing, the Red Sox shifted Martin to the second chair and brought in popular former pitcher Mel Parnell, who served on the broadcasting team for four years.

Gowdy left Boston in 1966 for NBC to call the network's TV Game of the Week and the World Series, to host the American Sportsman, and to continue his gridiron work, which had begun with ABC and the infant American Football League. No one in the history of TV sports announced so many big events, and given the current highly segmented nature of sports media, it's unlikely that anyone ever will.

Martin became the lead voice on Red Sox radio, where he would remain through 1978; he was also the second announcer on televised games through 1971. After nearly two decades on the job on a daily basis, he accepted a lesser role, manning on over-the-air broadcasts from 1979–87.

Ken Coleman came aboard to replace Gowdy, beginning a career in Boston nearly as long and memorable as that of Ned Martin. The enthusiastically gruff Coleman, born in suburban Quincy in 1925, was a Red Sox fan from birth. After a decade of telecasting the Indians, Coleman came home and almost immediately was tested in the cauldron of 1967. In the summer of *Sgt. Pepper*, the Detroit riots, Monterey Pop, and the Six-Day War, older Bostonians recall nothing more fondly than the "Impossible Dream" — the Red Sox' first pennant of the TV age and the franchise's first World Series appearance since 1946. Coleman seconded Martin in the radio booth and was the lead announcer for televised contests.

Prior to the season, the long-standing Yankee Network was disbanded, with WHDH assembling a group of 44 Northeastern stations before the Hughes Sports Network began managing the Sox' radio relationships in 1970.

Martin, Coleman, and Parnell became, for the summer of '67, the soundtrack of New England. Doing so, they helped revitalize the game in Boston, raising fans' expectations that their hometown heroes would always be in the hunt. Fortunately, from 1967 onward, the Red Sox have contended most of the time. Unfortunately, Boston has also suffered from enough pathos to make for a memorable Greek tragedy.

WHDH and the Red Sox finalized a three-year TV and radio rights deal prior to the 1967 season, locking Boston's rights up at about $700,000 per. So as ratings rose that year and afterward, the club was still earning early-1960s rates for its programming: their rights payments were lowest in the AL except for Washington and Minnesota.

Subsequent contracts in 1969 and 1970 with WHDH-TV and WHDH radio did not appreciably increase the Red Sox' rights fees, indicating that the club might have been getting a share of the advertising revenue as well.

For many years, the team had three sponsors on radio and television: Narragansett, Arco, and General Cigar. By the early 1970s, Narragansett had taken a powder, replaced by Schaefer beer, with other companies, many of them local, buying smaller slices of commercial time.

During the late 1960s and early 1970s, Coleman and Martin were the voices of summer in Boston, aided by former infielder and fan favorite Johnny Pesky, hired in 1969 at the behest of a friend who just happened to be WHDH's station manager.

When WHDH-TV ran into license renewal problems in 1972, WBZ took over the broadcasts and brought in a new group of sponsors. The following year, the team's announced broadcast revenue was up to one million dollars. WBZ telecast Red Sox games from 1972 through 1974.

In 1975, the Sox' TV rights were acquired by WSBK (Channel 38), which held them until 1995. TV-38 won an intense and costly bidding war for the rights, pouring an extra half-million dollars per year into the club's coffers.

When acquiring a prime new sports property, stations often establish their own brand by picking their own broadcasters. WSBK retained neither Coleman as its play-by-play man nor Pesky as analyst, choosing Dick Stockton and former Red Sox slugger Ken Harrelson. Stockton, a generalist who has covered many sporting events, was almost the opposite of the baseball-minded Martin. He had only 19 games of baseball experience (from a handful of Yankees telecasts on the Home Box Office pay cable network in 1974) when WSBK chose him for the job, though he had also called one year of Celtics games and had served as WBZ's sports director for three seasons.

The outspoken, attention-grabbing Harrelson's broadcasting career got off to a rocky start. Nonetheless, the opinionated cowboy held forth on television until 1981 before heading west to broadcast the White Sox. Even though the Red Sox did not have the right to approve

WSBK's on-air talent, Harrelson's departure may have been hastened by a 1980 incident in which he referred to the club's front office as a "laughing stock."

From 1975 on, the Sox became more aggressive in their broadcasting policies, airing an increasing number of games on the tube, reaching 100 for the first time in 1982. TV-38 also provided audio and video feeds to stations throughout New England a few times per week, with Red Sox games sometimes appearing on two stations in the same market on Sunday afternoons.

Cable television's debut came fairly late to Boston compared to other big-league cities. It was only in 1984, after eight other AL teams had already begun to experiment with the promising medium, that cable made its first appearance at Fenway. Despite their late start, the Red Sox cleverly exploited the enormous potential of cable.

NESN (New England Sports Network) began its association with the club in '84 with 87 games described by Kent Derdivanis and former Boston second-sacker Mike Andrews. The Red Sox co-founded the network with the Boston Bruins, showing foresight in their plan to control content and advertising revenue. The Sox typically provided NESN — a 24/7/365 operation — with at least half their non-network games and eventually moved them all to cable.

Between 1985 and 1986, NESN's subscriber base leapt from 30,000 to 90,000 as the channel was well on its way to long-term success, even if it took a while to get the announcers right. WSBK joined the cable game as well, following in the footsteps of independent stations in Chicago, New York, and Atlanta by getting on the Satcom 1 satellite and using its sports coverage to become a superstation in the 1980s. TV-38 enabled Red Sox broadcasts to penetrate the New York market — shades of the Yankee Network! — but the venture did not last.

WHDH held the club's radio rights through 1975, and this time the money would work out right for the Red Sox. The club won another AL pennant that year, giving it great negotiating leverage for a new deal. WHDH said it could not pay increased fees that the club needed and, with some regret, it let go. WMEX emerged with five years' worth of radio rights, and the deal brought the club's overall broadcast revenue to $2 million, its highest ever at that time.

The new station was happy to bring Ned Martin on board, and hired veteran Jim Woods to join him. George Grande, future play-by-play man for the Yankees, Cardinals, and Reds, was a studio host for Sox games at WMEX at this time. (The station was sold in early 1978; new management changed the call letters to WITS and the format to talk radio.)

The station retained the radio rights, meaning they sold the ads and kept all the profits. Trying to milk the maximum amount of money from the broadcasts, WMEX began to stuff games with more and more advertising, even during at-bats. This chafed at both Martin and Woods, not to mention irritated Sox fans.

Martin had long been admired in New England for his balanced, intelligent broadcast style, but the radio executives wanted someone more company-oriented. Furthermore, Boston owner Tom Yawkey was said to be annoyed by Martin's lack of overt homerism.

During 1978, tensions between the broadcasters and the businessmen continued to grow; by the end of the season, Red Sox broadcast director Gene Kirby had persuaded WITS president Joe Scallan to cashier Martin. Scallion told William Leggett of *Sports Illustrated* that he fired Martin for failing to spend enough time mingling with the team's sponsors in Fenway Park's VIP lounge, thus depriving the station of "constant marketing exposure." Martin and Woods were also accused of not showing adequate enthusiasm for the constant commercials they were forced to read during games.

Woods, disgusted by Martin's sacking, rebuffed Scallion's overtures to return and resigned in protest. Martin and Woods were replaced by a returning Ken Coleman and by former Sox star Rico Petrocelli, who had no previous on-air experience. Woods never worked again as a regular announcer in the major leagues, instead serving from 1981 through 1983 as a play-by-play man for MLB games on the fledgling USA cable network before retiring.

Ned Martin was an institution in New England for his measured, literary calls of Red Sox games as well as for his work on Ivy League football. In all, he spent 32 years describing Red Sox games on radio, TV, and cable, more than any other announcer in the team's history. When WITS fired Martin, it was a given that he would remain somewhere on the team's broadcasts, and so he moved to television. The small screen was not his medium, however, and the magic was gone.

The fallout from Scallion's ill-considered decision melted WITS' ratings and, by 1983, the team's stock on the field had fallen as well. The best radio deal available was on WPLM-FM, flagship for the Campbell Sports Network. With the advent of Roger Clemens and improvement in the mid-1980s (including going to the World Series in 1986), interest was high enough by 1989 that a much larger station, WRKO, acquired the rights via a lucrative new package. In 1995 the radio rights were sold to WEEI — by this time an all-sports station — and the two stations split the team's games.

Coleman assumed the radio call on WITS in 1980–82, assisted by young Jon Miller, who would later earn fame in Baltimore and with ESPN. Former Red Sox backup catcher Bob Montgomery joined Boston's TV team in 1982 after Harrelson left for Chicago. Montgomery started with Martin then teamed with Sean McDonough, developing genuine on-air rapport.

When Miller moved on after 1982, Joe Castiglione replaced him on radio. In the last three decades, Castiglione — like Coleman, having done Indians games despite being born and bred in New England — has worked his way into local fans' hearts, as much a part of the team as David Ortiz. Castiglione has also taught broadcasting at Northeastern University since the mid-1980s. In 2004 he had the distinction of being the first radio announcer in franchise history to proclaim that the Red Sox had just won a world championship.

Coleman retired in 1989, with Castiglione remaining number two under journeyman Bob Starr with the move to WRKO. From 1993 on, Castiglione has been the top dog. For 14 years he teamed with former Astros and Expos radio veteran Jerry Trupiano. Trupiano was dismissed following the 2006 campaign in favor of Dave O'Brien and Glenn Geffner.

Geffner was found wanting and departed after one season, but O'Brien — a thoroughly professional voice who had hung his shingle in several cities — became a stable and complement for Castiglione. The Sox also worked local radio personalities Dale Arnold and Jon Rish into the broadcasts.

Engaging and enthusiastic, Castiglione's effect wasn't limited to the radio. Don Orsillo, a Red Sox television broadcaster since 2001, took classes from Castiglione at Northeastern. Orsillo replaced the popular Sean McDonough, who did over-the-air telecasts from 1988 through 2004 on WSBK, WABU, and WFXT. McDonough, son of the late, powerful Boston newspaper columnist Will McDonough, found himself on the outside with the franchise's increasing focus on cable broadcasts, and a couple of unfortunate roistering incidents did not help. He left after the 2004 season, a year before Boston TV games began carriage exclusively on cable, to pursue other opportunities, including a weekly ESPN baseball telecast.

NESN was granted more and more of the club's telecasting rights over time and, in 2003, the cable net showed 120 games. From that point, over-the-air TV coverage quickly petered out. By 2006 the only way to watch the team outside of the ballpark was on cable (and nationally televised games). Of course, the huge size of Red Sox Nation and the club's current popularity means that the Red Sox are shown far more often on Fox and ESPN than nearly any other team.

NESN expanded its operations after Fenway Sports Group, headed by John Henry, bought the club after the 2002 season. The Red Sox purchase price was $700 million, then an MLB record. A large portion of that price was attributed to the team's 80 percent stake in NESN, so maximizing revenue from the channel with additional games and a surfeit of round-the-clock Red Sox programming made perfect sense. Chairman Tom Werner, a TV executive and former Padres owner, received credit for properly assessing the value of NESN and its strategic place in the growing empire, New England Sports Ventures, he directed with Henry. (NESN was renamed Fenway Sports Group in 2011.)

The tenures of McDonough and Orsillo told a tale about contemporary baseball broadcasting: the two were nearly interchangeable in tone and style, sporting the standard television "announcer voices" — well-trained, authoritative, and generally dispassionate — currently in vogue.

The TV team's color man is different. While NESN sifted through several different play-by-play voices in the last 20 years prior to choosing Orsillo, since 1988 the network has used just one analyst: Jerry Remy. The former Boston second baseman's style is down to earth, contrasting with Orsillo's "competent" tone.

Immensely popular in New England, Remy is an ex-jock who can break down the game without tooting his own horn. He sounds like an ordinary person, not a professional voice.

His impact has been seismic, and his status grew to cult level. Remy owns a pair of restaurants, one a block from Fenway Park.

NESN has grown from "just" a cable TV network into a major player. The Red Sox own nearly all the network (the NBA Bruins own the rest) and have complete editorial control. Yet Remy — like other ex-players who have nothing to fear because of their huge popularity — can be critical of Red Sox misplays when warranted without fear of reprimand.

NESN telecasts in 2009 went on without Remy, who missed most of the season when he was diagnosed with lung cancer. Dennis Eckersley, for most home games, and Dave Roberts, for most road games, filled in until Remy came back in August. With another off-season to recuperate, Remy made a full-time, healthy return to the booth in 2010.

Eckersley and Roberts have spent most of their time at NESN as in-studio analysts, joining a long parade of former Sox stars — and lesser lights — who opine before and after games. Rico Petrocelli, Jim Rice, Dave McCarty, Lou Merloni, and Sam Horn have all been featured.

For the last 20 years the Red Sox have made it possible for Spanish-speaking fans to hear the team's games on the radio. Bobby Serrano and Hector Martinez did the honors through the 1998 campaign, joined in 1993 by former Boston pitcher Mike Fornieles. The games initially aired on WRCA, then on WROL and WLYN through 2002.

J.P. Villaman, known as "Papa Oso," took over the color duties from Martinez in 1999. When Serrano left following the 2001 campaign, Luis Tiant Jr. and Juan Baez entered the booth. Baez departed after the one year in favor of Uri Berenguer — nephew of former pitcher Juan — who has become a respected play-by-play man. Tiant departed after 2004. But the big change came as a result of tragedy.

THE JIMMY FUND

Jim Britt is only one of the many Red Sox broadcasters to have raised money for the Jimmy Fund, which since 1953 has been the team's official charity. The Jimmy Fund supports children with cancer and their families.

Ken Coleman, longtime Red Sox voice on radio and television, was appointed executive director of the Fund in 1983. After serving as Coleman's deputy, Mike Andrews, NESN's first analyst, took over the Jimmy Fund and has run it for more than 30 years.

Uri Berenguer, the Boston's Spanish-language voice, came to Massachusetts as a sickly youngster. After getting treatment at the Jimmy Fund Clinic, he hasn't forgotten how the clinic helped save his life, and is present at myriad Jimmy Fund events. WEEI and NESN are deeply involved in fundraising, and current radio voice Joe Castiglione is also active with the Fund.

On May 29, 2005, Villaman, returning from a Red Sox series at Yankee Stadium, was killed in a highway accident. Bill Kulik, who had built the Spanish Beisbol Network into a growing concern, joined Berenguer in the booth until Juan Oscar Baez was hired. The games have aired on WROL since 2003. Kulik now has several teams' Spanish broadcasts under his wing.

With Fenway Park sold out for the past decade, and with away games featuring thousands of fans in all manner of Red Sox regalia, the club has profited from the insatiable appetite of Red Sox Nation. As of 2014 the Boston radio network now incorporated 62 stations, and there are parts of New England where Sox games can be found on three or more places on the dial, plus in Spanish on the five stations that carry the club.

Needless to say, despite baseball fans' fondness for nostalgia and the sport's exploitation of its own history, there's no chance of Boston's radio network being renamed the "Yankee Network" in the near future.

Despite the club's high profits and excellent on-field performance, however, the 2013 season was traumatic in Boston due to the terrorist bombings at the Boston Marathon and the murder charges raised against Patriots tight end Aaron Hernandez.

All was not well in the Red Sox' broadcast booths, either. Jon Rish, the club's pregame and postgame radio host and #3 announcer, resigned in April 2013 after being asked to take a 30% pay cut by WEEI's parent company, Entercom.

Rish, 40, felt that his future would be stronger were he a software developer, so he quit the radio game and began taking classes. That an announcer for a profitable team on a profitable station would be asked to take such a humiliating punishment beggars description.

Sean Grande, a WEEI host and basketball announcer, took over some of Rish's assignments spelling Dave O'Brien, who spends most Mondays doing an ESPN national telecast. Former Bosox infielder Lou Merloni was also tabbed to assist Joe Castiglione on occasion.

The biggest issue affecting Red Sox broadcasts in 2013, however, was the exit of Jerry Remy. First, he missed a month from late May to late June recovering from a bout of pneumonia, with Dennis Eckersley and WEEI radio's Rob Bradford sitting in.

Then on August 16, Remy's son Jared was arrested for the fatal stabbing of his girlfriend, Jennifer Martel. Jerry Remy left the NESN booth and did not return for the rest of the season, even though — surprisingly — the network gave him the option of coming back in late August.

Dennis Eckersley took on most of the analyst assignments for the remainder of the 2013 campaign. Jon Rish came back for a few games, and Peter Gammons joined Orsillo in the booth for one contest.

Jared Remy worked for the Red Sox security force but was fired in 2008 after allegations that he sold steroids to another employee. After this, Jerry Remy had clearly run out of favors for his son with the team's front office.

Toting a rap sheet of violence against lovers and strangers long prior to the 2013 murder, it is amazing that Jared Remy, an admitted abuser of steroids, was even a free man. Many in the area wondered whether the father's fame made the police and local media go easy on the clearly disturbed and dangerous son.

This is the kind of scandal that can, in addition to destroying families, ruin a career, and Jerry Remy's tenure with the Red Sox came under some scrutiny, although he returned in 2014.

THE CHICAGO CUBS ARE ON THE AIR!

CHICAGO CUBS BROADCASTING HISTORY

"And they had this big fat clown of an announcer sayin', 'Ah, the Cubs are gonna have
a great year, the Cubs are gonna have a great year…'"
— *Sox fan, author, and humorist Jean Shepherd*

"I don't care who wins, as long as it's the Cubs!"
— *Bert Wilson*

THE FIRST MAJOR-LEAGUE BASEBALL GAME BROADCAST ON RADIO
was the Friday, August 5, 1921 contest between the Pittsburgh Pirates and Philadelphia
Phillies at Forbes Field. The host Pirates won 8–5 as Harold Arlin laid down the action on
Pittsburgh's pioneering station KDKA for the few people in the world that owned the
equipment needed to listen.

That fall, radio fans heard the Yankees-Giants World Series on KDKA, Newark's WJZ,
and Boston's WBZ (all stations owned by Westinghouse). The following year's series, again
featuring the Yankees and Giants, was also broadcast.

Catering to the universal love for baseball, radio stations all over the land soon began
reading ticker-tape results from their local nines' games; these broadcasts were almost
immediately seen as enticements. A July 10, 1925, Washington Post article noted that the
Saks clothing store at Seventh Street and Pennsylvania Avenue had set up a loudspeaker
in front of the main entrance tuned to station WRC, which broadcast "returns," as they
were then called, of road games played by the Senators.

Baseball fans might be surprised to find that the most significant broadcasting city in the history of the national game is Chicago, rather than New York City, Washington, Los Angeles, Pittsburgh, Boston, or Philadelphia. The history of Chicago Cubs radio and television mirrors, in many ways, the history of baseball broadcasting itself.

The Cubs, encouraged by owner William Wrigley, made it known in the early 1920s that they welcomed stations that wished to broadcast their games on the radio. Wrigley felt that the publicity would be good for his team, though other clubs recoiled in horror from this belief.

Sen Kaney was among the earliest stars of the new medium, operating in Chicago, which took to the medium like nobody's business. Originally employed by KYW, Kaney transferred to WDAP on April 19, 1924 as program director and on-air personality. (WDAP was soon renamed as WGN, then as now owned and operated by the *Chicago Tribune*.)

In the city's first-ever local radio transmission of major league baseball, WGN carried the entire Cubs–White Sox 1924 postseason City Series, with Kaney sitting on the Wrigley Field rooftop next to the press area to describe the action. While Kaney was no baseball expert, he was reportedly witty and engaging on the air. (He anchored, on the NBC radio network, national coverage of the first professional night baseball game, which took place in Des Moines, Iowa on May 2, 1930.)

Opening Day, April 14, 1925, marked the first regular-season broadcast on WGN, with Quin Ryan replacing Kaney on the Wrigley Field grandstand roof during an 8-2 win over visiting Pittsburgh. The few existing sound bites of Ryan, a local writer and boxing expert, reveal a genial presence with a friendly, ethnic tone which would seem completely out of place in today's homogenized broadcasts.

That fall, Ryan and Graham McNamee, in a first, aired coast-to-coast national broadcasts of the Pittsburgh-Washington World Series on WGN, which carried the World Series for many years. In 1931, Commissioner Landis granted just two radio networks — NBC and CBS — permission to broadcast baseball's Fall Classic, and WGN picked up NBC's feed, featuring the popular McNamee.

WGN and Ryan contracted to air every 1926 Saturday afternoon Cubs home game as well as their Opening-Day tilt. More games were added during the season, however, as the Cubs' games proved to be popular programming.

In another indication of just how different baseball broadcasting philosophies were at the time, Ryan was joined in the booth by two comic actors responsible for WGN's locally popular *Sam 'n' Henry* program.

Of course, when baseball on the radio was young, no template existed for "standard practice," or for what constituted "appropriate" commentary for the game. The idea of broadcasting baseball games was only implemented because enough advertisers showed interest in paying for the program. And in those days before sophisticated Arbitron and Nielsen surveys, it was anyone's guess as to what the family gathered around the wireless set in their living room would enjoy.

Starkly illustrating this lack of orthodoxy was station WMAQ, which also began broadcasting Cubs and White Sox games. Their announcer, sportswriter Hal Totten, first broadcast from Wrigley Field on June 1, 1925. Totten had a sense of humor drier than the Sahara, with a voice that varied little from its signature monotone. These days, a man with Totten's spare delivery might not rise past broadcasts on public-access TV.

WGN began regular broadcasts of Cubs and White Sox home games in 1927, with Ryan describing the entire home schedule for both clubs. By this point, Ryan had been moved into the work area that the writers called the "press coop."

As was true for most early radio performers, Ryan was not just a sports guy. As "Uncle Quin," he handled youth programming, reading the *Tribune* Sunday funnies to kids in the studio and hosting a *Punch & Judy* children's show. In addition, Ryan anchored political conventions and covered other news events.

Totten and WMAQ were also on hand for the entire 1927 schedule. Other stations eventually joined in the fun including, at different times, WIND, WBBM, WJJD, and WCFL. At one point in the 1930s, five stations aired both Cubs and White Sox home games. Only later, in the 1940s, did teams begin to arrange for a single radio station to air all of their games, using exclusivity as a mechanism to increase rights fees for the club.

That kind of thinking was years away, however. Radio was still so novel that neither the thought of exclusivity nor of radio stations paying teams to air their ballgames existed. Since Phil Wrigley wanted local stations to flood the airwaves with Cubs baseball and, thus provide free advertising for the Cubs, the struggling White Sox — having fallen in the public's esteem in the wake of the Black Sox scandal — were forced to allow broadcasts as well.

At this point, broadcasts usually began only a few minutes before the first pitch. Call-in shows or a long pregame buildups were years away. Immediately before the first pitch in 1927, for example, WGN's *Lyon & Healy Artist Recital* brought popular and classical music to listeners tuning in to hear their hometown team.

WGN also broadcast other events from Wrigley Field, including Bears NFL games, prizefights, road races, and the Kentucky Derby. Baseball, though, was then and for several decades to come the blue-chip radio sport.

Rough-voiced but friendly, Vince Lloyd — with Hall of Fame shortstop Lou Boudreau — called Cubs games together on radio for two decades. (National Baseball Hall of Fame and Museum)

To cater to fans from both sides of town, WGN announcers (and, most likely, those of other stations) read ticker-tape reports of the results of Sox road games between innings at Wrigley Field. They would do the same for the Cubs when Ryan was broadcasting from Comiskey Park. Announcers also updated the fans by reading the scores of out-of-town games for all the other clubs.

What was in all likelihood the first Cubs' radio re-creation took place on September 18, 1928, when WGN "broadcast" the Cubs–Braves game from Braves Field in Boston.

On this day, the White Sox were not playing, but the station wanted to slake the public's thirst for baseball. Therefore, Irving Vaughan, the *Tribune's* beat writer covering the Cubs, sat in the press box in Boston and, on an open telephone line, relayed every play to the WGN studios, where Ryan would then describe the action to listeners as if he himself were there.

It wasn't too long before WGN and other stations began re-creating afternoon road games as primetime evening programming, using ticker-tape transmissions of each pitch as grist for their re-creation mill. Sound effects, such as crowd noise and the crack of hickory on horsehide, became a staple of the program, spicing things up and making fans feel as though they were actually listening to a live contest.

While Ryan was busy in the studio re-creating Cubs games, the legendary Bob Elson began his big-league career covering White Sox games at Comiskey Park for WGN.

Elson, of Peoria, Illinois, won a contest to become an announcer on KWK in St. Louis in 1928, but WGN jumped in and offered him a job as soon as they heard about the contest. Soon to be known as "The Commander," Elson headed north and began to fill in at the park for Ryan, who was already overworked. The newcomer quickly became popular with Chicago-area fans for his no-nonsense, businesslike delivery.

Sponsors quickly lined up to advertise on these popular broadcasts. By 1929, when the Cubs won the National League pennant, the John R. Thompson quick-lunch restaurants and the Baskin/Hart, Schaffner, & Marx stores served as primary sponsors of both the Cubs and White Sox on WGN. John R. Thompson himself even joined Ryan in the WGN booth during Cubs games in 1930. In 1934, the Walgreen's drug store chain began nearly 80 years of on-off sponsorship of the Cubs.

In February 1931, Quin Ryan re-assumed his old duties as WGN's station manager. Baseball was never his favorite sport, and he had suffered hay fever serious enough to keep him from working some games. With Ryan back in the office, Elson was the natural choice to take over full-time diamond duties. At this point, Elson had a 15-minute pregame show, normally beginning at 2:45. (Games at this time typically started at 3:00, with doubleheaders opening at 12:30 or 1:30.) Thompson's was again a major sponsor.

WGN had stiff competition on the radio dial for baseball during these halcyon days. WBBM's popular Pat Flanagan brought his signature brogue and clipped delivery to the games; WIBO had Jimmy Corcoran and Bob Hawk on board. Totten, sponsored for many years by Texaco, reigned first at WMAQ and later at WCFL, the famous station owned by the Chicago Federation of Labor (hence its call letters). Even noted radio raconteur Norman Ross took a turn with baseball in 1932.

Announcers often moved between stations because their voices and personalities became identified not with a particular station, but rather whatever sponsor was associated with the broadcast. Thus, many of the Chicago broadcasters worked for more than one local station.

Because the Cubs won NL flags in 1929, 1932, 1935, and 1938, working the popular Chicago broadcasts could serve as a steppingstone to national success for many young radio men. Jack Brickhouse began his big-league career in 1942 as Elson's protégé at WGN, while other soon-to-be-famous broadcasters — including Russ Hodges, Jack Drees, Gene Elston, Jimmy Dudley, Milo Hamilton, and Bill Brundige — spent early-career summers covering games in Chicago.

Chicago announcers often became famous across the nation because of their stations' wide listening areas. Elson and Flanagan were picked to do the 1932 World Series, for instance, and Elson would call many more.

One fellow who re-created Cubs games on WHO in Des Moines, Iowa, during the 1930s ended up as a Hollywood actor. Later, after leaving the Democratic Party for the Republican Party, the broadcaster-turned-thespian would be elected governor of California and, ultimately, president of the United States. Ronald Reagan — who back in the 1930s and 1940s, pronounced his name "Ree-gan" — was always a big baseball fan.

Gimmicks were common. Prior to the 1936 season, the Cubs bought time at 7:00 p.m. on WIND to present a one-hour capsule re-creation of that day's home game. Hal Berger, imported from KNX in Los Angeles, did the honors. During road dates or after rainouts, WIND presented re-creations of famous games from the past.

In 1937, WBBM frequently featured guest commentators during games. Joe E. Brown, Three Finger Brown, Joe Tinker, Johnny Evers, Lew Fonseca (who two seasons later would get a regular commentating gig on WJJD), Tris Speaker, and Walter Johnson were among the featured voices.

One of the first Cubs' road games to be broadcast came in 1935 on the occasion of the team's first night game at Cincinnati. Russ Hodges, formerly at Cincinnati station WCKY, relayed the action back to Chicago on WIND.

When Elson went into the navy during World War II, Bert Wilson took his place on the Cubs' airwaves. Wilson was among the more charismatic announcers the North Siders had ever heard. A genial bear of a man, he was an eternal optimist, a fan both on and off the air, and often the butt of jokes. Excitable and highly partisan, Wilson was so popular that when Elson returned from his military duty, he was reassigned exclusively to the then-moribund South Side White Sox.

Some future big-league broadcasters in the Midwest, such as Gene Elston and Milo Hamilton, were clearly influenced by Wilson's style, though they never quite seemed to capture the excitement that the big fellow generated in the booth.

By 1944, the days of multiple stations broadcasting games were mostly over. Radio was now such a high-profit business that stations wanted exclusivity. Like other teams, the Cubs were happy to hand over their broadcast rights to a single bidder with deep pockets — although club owner Phil Wrigley probably did not negotiate for as much money as he could have. WJJD surprised those in the business in 1944 by coming in with the high bid, but WIND captured the rights the following season. WGN regained the Cubs radio broadcasts in 1958.

For several years, Old Gold cigarettes and Walgreens had sponsored competing broadcasts. Starting in 1944, though, the two companies combined to provide the ads on Cubs games for many years.

Taking on a heavy schedule, Bert Wilson worked alone at the microphone, doing all nine innings of all 154 games, home and road. Even after the war and its resulting travel restrictions ended, the Cubs' radio team was still re-creating some road games, not ending that practice until the early 1950s.

In 1950, Bud Campbell came aboard as Wilson's sidekick. Meanwhile, following World War II, the Cubs sank into a two-decade stretch of misery. From 1946 through 1966, the Bruins finished above .500 only twice: as a result, Wilson called far more losses than victories during his years behind the mike at Wrigley Field.

Not surprisingly, the constant travel took a toll on Wilson. He missed two weeks of action in 1952 due to high blood pressure then announced in September 1955 that he would resign from WIND at the end of the season. The veteran mikeman had planned to take on a lighter schedule in 1956, telecasting Cincinnati Reds games. He had suffered from heart trouble for quite a while, however, and passed away on November 5, 1955, in Mesa, Arizona.

The new voice of the Cubs was Jack Quinlan, who had come on board in 1953 as a third man. Quinlan had a friendly and talkative style and worked well with other soon-to-be-famous voices like Elston (with the Cubs from 1954–1957) and Hamilton (1956–1957).

Generally believed to be one of the rising stars in sports broadcasting during the early 1960s, Quinlan reigned as top dog on Cubs radio during some of the franchise's worst seasons. During the late 1950s and early 1960s, optimism and Ernie Banks were the only things long-suffering Cubs fans could hold on to.

Though they experienced more than their share of futility on the field after World War II, the Chicago Cubs, in addition to being among baseball's radio pioneers, were also leaders in television. Early in 1946, WBKB-TV announced plans to televise Opening Day at Wrigley Field. Unfortunately, transmission problems involving their downtown antenna and an inconveniently placed office building forced them to delay telecasting the Bruins' home games until July 18.

Jack Gibney handled the commentary on the first TV game, but he was not destined to become one of Chicago's great sports announcers. In 1947, "Whispering" Joe Wilson, joined by Jack Brickhouse, took over in the WBKB booth for all 77 Cubs home contests.

Brickhouse, like his mentor Bob Elson, had come up to the big city via Peoria. But Brick would cultivate an on-air style completely unlike "The Commander." Thin and bespectacled in his younger years, the "gee-whiz" broadcaster soon bulked up and lost most of his hair. Elson had helped Brickhouse get a job on WGN in the early 1940s; in 1945, with Elson in the military, "Brick" assumed the No. 1 role on the White Sox' broadcasts.

The next year, however, Elson returned from the service, leaving Brickhouse without a job in Chitown. Brickhouse, therefore, migrated to New York City in 1946 to announce New York Giants games at the Polo Grounds with neophyte Steve Ellis. Brickhouse did not hit it off with the flinty Ellis, though, and he returned to Chicago the following season to join Joe Wilson at WBKB.

Early on, Brickhouse presciently cottoned onto television as the next big thing. "I wanted to get into this television thing and find out what it was all about," he wrote years later. At first, it certainly wasn't about getting rich, as WBKB paid Wilson and Brickhouse the princely sum of $35 each per game in 1947.

Around this time, Brickhouse developed his signature call for home runs, the hearty "Hey, Hey!" that would sometimes leave his voice cracking. He also used plenty of other interjections — like "Whee!" when the Cubs did something well, and "Oh, brother!" when they didn't. Elson, who viewed himself much more seriously, would never have used such informal expressions. Unfortunately for Cubs fans, Brickhouse read more "unhappy totals" at the end of ballgames than "happy totals" over his many years of covering the Cubs.

WGN, Channel 9 on the dial, decided to enter the television business in 1948, hiring Brickhouse away from WBKB as its lead announcer. He was joined in the Channel 9 booth by Marty Hogan for one year, then by Harry Creighton through 1956. Brickhouse's remarkable 34-year tenure in the broadcast booth helped shape the understanding as well as the baseball vocabulary of millions of Cubs fans of different generations.

As in the early days of radio, the baby-step years of TV were not about exclusivity. In 1948, three stations each televised all 77 Cubs home contests. Besides WBKB and WGN, WENR also was in on things on the North Side, employing Bill Brundidge and legendary former Cubs second baseman Rogers Hornsby to call the action.

WENR dropped out after that one year, leaving WBKB and WGN competing for the hearts and eyeballs of loyal Cubs fans until 1951. Following that season, Joe Wilson and WBKB faded into memory.

In those days, television broadcasts of baseball games typically featured only two or three cameras, one in the upper deck behind home plate and one down each foul line, either stationed at field level or in the upper deck. The key innovation of positioning a camera in the center field stands to capture pitch location, which most historians of the medium credit to WGN, came in the late 1950s.

Back then, teams saw TV mostly as a promotional tool, much as they had done in the early days of radio. Chicago put its home games on the air in order to bring Wrigley Field into the fans' homes and into the taverns where they gathered, mostly as a means of enticing those people to come out to the park and buy tickets. The idea of taking a television crew on the road with the club would have been ridiculous; hauling a crew and a truck of huge cameras around the country, and paying the high costs of phone-line transmission, served as prohibitive factors. While teams had for several seasons worked with independent radio engineers on their road broadcasts, independent TV production companies were still a few years in the future.

Therefore, Brickhouse spent his summers almost entirely in Chicago, attaching words to the pictures of WGN's Cubs and White Sox home games. The first Cubs' road telecast did not occur until 1960. By then, the throaty, friendly, enthusiastic Vince Lloyd had slid comfortably into the TV booth, backing up Brickhouse after Harry Creighton's departure.

Lloyd did occasional play-by-play and between-inning commercials, not to mention the popular "Lead-Off Man" pregame interviews on both the Cubs' and the White Sox' telecasts. One of Lloyd's greatest moments was an irreverent 1961 Opening-Day interview at Griffith Stadium in Washington, D.C. with President John F. Kennedy. That moment, as well as many of the most memorable Chicago baseball moments of the 1950s and early 1960s, came with Brickhouse and Lloyd calling the action for the White Sox.

May 15, 1960, however, marked a great moment in Cubs history. In the first game of a doubleheader against the Cardinals at Wrigley Field, Don Cardwell, just acquired from Philadelphia, fired a no-hitter. Film of the eighth and ninth innings plus the postgame of this contest still exists; WGN's feed, with Brickhouse and Lloyd at the mike, is the earliest extant video of a regular-season no-hitter.

When the Cubs and Sox (occasionally) telecast road games, the WGN-TV crew split, with staff announcers such as Lloyd Pettit or Len Johnson handling the extra work. Only after the Pale Hose departed WGN for the monetarily greener pastures of the UHF dial did the Cubs ramp up their schedule, increasing road games from but five in 1967 to a hearty 63 in 1968.

Following the end of his successful playing career, Lou Boudreau had gone on to not-so-successful stints as manager of the Boston Red Sox and the Kansas City Athletics. After the lowly A's canned him, Boudreau was signed on December 12, 1957 by WGN radio. There the popular ex-player joined Jack Quinlan in the booth, replacing Milo Hamilton and Gene Elston.

In many ways, this was a new beginning for the Cubs. WGN had regained the team's radio rights after the 1957 campaign by signing a five-year deal, and it was glad to bring the then-30-year-old Quinlan over from WIND. Boudreau's selection as color man was a surprise, as he became the first former player in the team's radio booth since megaphone-voiced Lou Fonseca in the 1940s. Nevertheless, the future Hall of Famer would go on to forge a long career with WGN and to become as beloved by fans in Chicago as he had been in Cleveland.

Boudreau was not a natural announcer, so he rarely handled play-by-play. Instead, he used his experience and his huge storehouse of baseball knowledge to add colorful analysis to Quinlan's (and later, Lloyd's) mellifluous broadcasts.

This being the Cubs, however, anything was possible. When aging Charley Grimm proved unsuitable as the skipper of the team only 17 games into the 1960 campaign, the club's management arranged to trade announcer for manager, moving Grimm into the booth to team with Quinlan, sending Boudreau back to the dugout as the Cubs' manager!

So Boudreau served out the remainder of the 1960 season as manager, faring no better in that role than he had with the A's or Red Sox. In 1961, as the Cubs initiated their controversial five-year experiment with their "College of Coaches," Boudreau retook his place at the microphone as the banjo-playing Grimm toddled off into retirement.

In the late 1950s and early 1960s, Walgreens cut back to sponsoring just the Cubs' postgame show. The suburban Oak Park Federal Savings stepped in as a key sponsor of the team's games, along with Goebel Brewing, Phillips 66 gasoline, and Phillies Cigars. On TV, the OK Oklahoma service station chain and Hamm's Beer did the honors.

Quinlan and Boudreau were paired together through 1964. During this time, Quinlan assumed the mantle as WGN radio's top sports voice, covering Big Ten football as well as doing closed-circuit telecasts for the gridiron's Chicago Bears, winners of the 1963 NFL championship. He also handled, with Chuck Thompson, the national radio coverage of the 1960 World Series. Boudreau, a three-sport star in high school, would also later cover NBA basketball and NHL hockey for WGN — a station that kept its employees mighty busy back then.

Tragedy ultimately broke up the Quinlan-Boudreau "dream team," still felt by some to be the best ever to cover games in the Second City. On March 19, 1965, returning from a spring-training golf date, Quinlan's car skidded off a highway outside of Phoenix. Ramming a parked truck, the 37-year-old Quinlan was killed instantly, leaving a widow and four children.

Less than a week later, WGN promoted Vince Lloyd to the lead radio job. Lloyd would partner with Boudreau on radio broadcasts through 1981, entertaining and educating millions of fans. Lloyd Pettit became Brickhouse's full-time television partner, a post he held through 1970.

Vince Lloyd Skaff, born in 1917, dropped his last name when he began his broadcasting career in 1940. He served an apprenticeship in Peoria — like Elson, Brickhouse, and Quinlan — before joining WGN's television and radio sports staff in 1949. Lloyd worked his way up slowly, thus being well-prepared for the opportunity when he became a lead sports voice.

The excitable Lloyd's signature call for a great Cubs play was "Holy Mackerel!" In his first regular-season Cubs game as the No. 1 radio announcer, Lloyd called an unusual 10-10 tie between the Cubs and Cardinals at Wrigley Field halted after 11 innings by darkness.

Old Style beer began a long-term relationship with the team in the late 1960s and has sponsored the North Siders ever since, most of the time on the radio.

After a poor 1965 and a last-place finish in 1966, Lloyd, Boudreau, Brickhouse, and Pettit got a jolt from the surprising 1967 Cubs, who vaulted into third place under the management of acid-tongued Leo Durocher.

With a core of Ernie Banks, Billy Williams, and Ron Santo bolstered by recent acquisitions Randy Hundley, Fergie Jenkins, and Bill Hands and supplemented by farm products Ken Holtzman, Glenn Beckert, and Don Kessinger, the Cubs remained competitive through the early 1970s — though the star-crossed team never won a pennant.

Through those exciting years, Lloyd, Boudreau, Brickhouse, and Pettit (replaced by Jim West in 1971) ascended to new heights as Chicago's voices of summer, especially after the White Sox slid downhill in 1968. Transplant announcer Harry Caray helped to pull the Sox from the mire when the Pale Hose became competitive again in the 1970s, yet the Cubs retained their place at the top of the city's sporting scene on WGN radio and TV.

Starting in 1968, the Cubs televised nearly all their games, home and road, treating a whole generation of fans to nearly twice the television action. Director Arne Harris, one of the most creative forces ever involved in local TV broadcasting, became famous around town for the broadcast innovations he directed. Cubs games at Wrigley Field in the 1970s involved a plethora of interesting replay angles, shots of fans' goofy hats, and superb camera work acknowledged as among the best in the industry.

Nothing lasts forever, of course. Brickhouse, who had been in the business for nearly 50 years, announced late in the strike-riven 1981 season that he would retire at the season's end.

Milo Hamilton, a well-traveled veteran hired by WGN in 1980, was slated to take over as the team's TV voice in 1982. But the Tribune Company, which had purchased the Cubs in 1981 from the Wrigley estate, had other ideas.

Harry Caray, for a decade the biggest star the White Sox had, left the Sox in the winter of 1981–82 over a disagreement about new owner Jerry Reinsdorf's decision to put a majority of the team's games on his new cable television setup, SportsVision. Caray didn't want to lose the much wider exposure that free TV provided, feeling that he was established enough not to have to "start over" in an unproven medium. He also wasn't happy with the dollars in the contract.

Widely known as the "Mayor of Rush Street" for his frequent appearances in drinking establishments around Chicago's best-known nightlife neighborhood, Caray took the initiative. He called the *Tribune*, met with company officials to begin a whirlwind courtship, and ended up signing a contract with the Cubs in early 1982.

Hamilton was stunned. The top job had been promised to him, yet he had been deposed by someone he personally and professionally disliked. Despite this turn of events, Hamilton stayed on in Chicago. After one year, the team made an accommodation for him; in 1983, Hamilton dislodged Lloyd from the radio play-by-play role for six innings then went to television booth for the middle three frames while Caray moved to the radio mike.

The new arrangement meant that the venerable Lloyd, a full-time play-by-play announcer since 1965, was now uncomfortably relegated to color work. Moreover, Boudreau's ongoing presence resulted in a confusing three-man radio free-for-all.

Caray, a calculating, intelligent professional, wooed the North Side and never looked back. The veteran broadcaster with the big ego knew that he was in position to call the shots, and he took over the North Side as he had the South Side a decade earlier. Caray bellowed his "Holy Cow!" calls as his enthusiastic "Voice of the Fan" persona and his unquestioned knowledge of baseball quickly made him, by some estimates, the most popular Cubs' broadcaster ever.

In 1983, Caray teamed for the first time with Steve Stone, a former Cy Young Award winner with the Orioles who had also pitched for both the White Sox and Cubs in the 1970s. Witty, smart, and blessed with a fine voice, Stone — despite a relative lack of experience behind the mike — immediately proved an enormously popular foil for both Caray and Hamilton on WGN-TV.

When WGN was added to most basic cable systems during the 1980s, Caray and the Cubs became America's sweethearts, quite an unexpected turn of events given Caray's initial lack of regard for cable and pay television.

This package attracted advertisers, especially breweries. Miller had advertised on Cubs telecasts during the 1970s and early 1980s, but Budweiser — building a new relationship with Harry Caray, who'd served as a pitchman for the company back in St. Louis — bought the sponsorship for 1983. While Miller had paid around $500,000 per year for the rights to advertise on Cubs games, Bud was willing to fork over more than three times that annually.

The St. Louis megabrewery got its money's worth. The beery "Cub Fan — Bud Man" campaign built around Caray and his outsized personality ran on local television for many years, and spread across the land on cable systems.

The Cubs' 1984 NL East Division title further cemented the franchise as a national sports heavyweight. Following that season, Hamilton fled the Windy City for Houston's warmer clime, while the Astros' No. 2 man Dewayne Staats made his way north to Chicago.

The Cubs were first broadcast in Spanish in 1981 on WOJO radio. Play-by-play man Leon Martinez held that role through 1994 (except for 1993) on various stations with differing numbers of games being broadcast. From the end of the 1995 season through 2008, however, the Cubs did not broadcast a single game in Spanish, though the White Sox continued to carry games *en Español* for their Latino fans.

With 18 of 30 major league clubs featuring some form of Spanish-language broadcasting by the latter part of the decade, the Cubs' lack of a similar initiative — considering that Chicago has one of the largest Spanish-language populations in the country — was puzzling and embarrassing.

Change finally came in 2009, when the team announced that WRTO would broadcast 20 home night games in Spanish — not that many, but a start.

For six decades, from the 1930s through the 1980s, Cubs viewers and listeners had been served well by a series of unpolished but thrilling broadcasters like Lloyd, Boudreau, Pat Flanagan, Wilson, Brickhouse, Pettit, and Caray.

Since then, the accession of "professional types" that began with Hamilton in 1980 has continued, dramatically changing the tone and tenor of Chicagoland baseball broadcasts. Some of these imported pros lent a high quality note to the two clubs' broadcasts, but some have not worked out.

Truly, Caray, Brickhouse, and Lloyd were from a different age when they could be not only stewards of their own special language, but also occasionally extreme in their homerism. The key was that Chicago fans always loved them that way. Stone proved a perfect foil to Caray's careening-on-the-edge style without falling into the subservient pattern sometimes adopted by "professional voices."

Lloyd, one of the best play-by-play men Chicago has ever known, faded from the picture, assuming in 1985 stewardship of the Cubs' extensive radio network. Boudreau hung around through 1987. The two old warhorses weren't easy to replace, as experiments with inexperienced color men — former Cubs manager and GM Jim Frey in 1987 and Davey Nelson in 1988 and 1989 — ended poorly. Nelson was the team's first-ever African-American broadcaster.

In 1990, to augment the aging Caray (who had missed several weeks in 1986 due to a stroke), the Cubs hired Thom Brennaman as the team's lead radio voice. The Tribune Company believed that Brennaman, scion of longtime Cincinnati broadcaster Marty Brennaman, was on his way to a great career. Its faith was so great that it brought the young broadcaster in even though he had just two years of part-time TV coverage under his belt.

Lacking experience or any local connection, Brennaman the Younger did not quite work out in Chicago, though he scaled greater heights in Arizona and Cincinnati and on FOX Sports national telecasts. Former players Bob Brenly and Ron Santo — both without broadcasting experience — also joined in 1990 as color men. Brenly lasted just one year before returning to the dugout as a coach, but Santo carved himself a new career as one of city's most beloved radio personalities.

More than any other player of his generation of Wrigley Field baseball heroes, Santo bled Cubby blue. In the 1960s and 1970s, Ernie Banks was "Mr. Cub," but after Banks' exile from the organization in the early 1980s, Santo acceded to the throne in the 1990s as the nostalgic "new face" of the Cubs' past. A hero for his work benefiting the Juvenile Diabetes Foundation — he himself eventually lost both legs to the disease — Santo was unsophisticated, frank, emotional, and entertaining. The former third baseman was arguably loved by Cubs fans even more as a broadcaster than he had been as a player.

Santo's unpolished style didn't really come alive on the air, however, until former Minnesota Twins and Milwaukee Brewers second-banana Pat Hughes entered the scene as the Cubs' lead radio voice in 1996.

Hughes, previously Bob Uecker's straight man in the County Stadium booth, immediately took to the primary job in Chicago. Showing an excellent sense of humor of his own along with a smooth delivery and a terrific knowledge of the game, Hughes' booming voice and calm demeanor created synergy with Santo.

Santo was not really capable of handling play-by-play duty, as demonstrated during some terrifying trial runs in the mid-1990s. Therefore, Hughes manned the mike for all nine innings of every game for years. WGN brought a third voice, Andy Masur, into the radio booth starting in 2003, to handle a half-inning of action.

Masur showed enough promise in limited action to land a full-time job with the Padres in 2007. WGN also became a stepping-stone for Masur's successor, Cory Provus, who did two years in the No. 3 role in the Cubs' booth before graduating to the No. 2 chair of the Milwaukee Brewers' radio team, then to the top spot in Minneapolis-St. Paul.

In 1993, the Cubs finally joined the cable TV revolution, in a measured, conservative, *Tribune*sque way. Because of local TV blackouts necessitated by MLB's new ESPN national contract, the Cubs needed an outlet for their Wednesday night games. The Tribune Company transferred those contests to CLTV, its 24-hour local news channel. CLTV continued to show Cubs games through 1998, when FOX Sports set up an RSN in Chicagoland.

By then, the Cubs had lost Harry.

Talented young Josh Lewin, formerly with Baltimore, had spent the 1997 season helping out with the play-by-play in the Cubs' booth before reportedly being pushed out by Harry Caray to make room for his grandson Chip, who was at that time announcing for the Seattle Mariners.

Despite Chip's hiring by the Cubs for 1998, the family affair never came to pass. After broadcasting Cubs games for 15 seasons, Harry Caray passed away on February 18, 1998. His age was given as 84.

Caray's death, which received in Chicago the attention that one would expect for a head of state, marked another major transition in the television booth. Chip Caray, excitable but not particularly distinctive, never really won over Chicago fans. To be fair, that was almost inevitable for anyone succeeding a bigger-than-life legend like grandfather Harry.

Fill-in play-by-play man Wayne Larrivee, a football and basketball announcer who worked Cubs games on weekends when Chip Caray called regional games for Fox, struggled to hold his own on baseball broadcasts.

As an ongoing tribute to Caray, his signature singing of "Take Me Out to the Ballgame" continued between the top and bottom of the seventh at Wrigley Field. Instead of using a tape of Harry, or simply letting the fans sing the song, Cubs marketing director John McDonough turned the memorial serenade into an opportunity. The stagy "celebrity seventh-inning stretch" has continued since early 1998, featuring many actors and actresses from WGN television programs and WGN radio. Other seventh-inning guest lead singers have included players and ex-players from other sports.

Stone came down with a nearly fatal case of a rare heart disease called valley fever in 2000, missing most of the season. Former Cubs players Randy Hundley, Bob Dernier, and Dave Otto filled in. None had much experience behind the mike; only Otto lasted past the end of the season.

In 2001, with Stone retiring to regain his health, Otto took over on cable telecasts while Joe Carter began a bumpy two-year stretch on games telecast on WGN and local UHF station WCIU. WGN had become a member of the fledgling WB television network in the late 1990s; taking on that network's schedule of primetime programming meant that Cubs games had to be shifted elsewhere. Most of the games went to cable, with a handful handed off to low-rated WCIU.

The team and the telecasts both improved in 2003 as Stone returned to the analyst chair alongside Chip Caray. The Cubs came within five outs of going to the World Series that season before being devastated by losing the NLCS to the surprising Florida Marlins.

Under new manager Dusty Baker, the Cubs were supposed to make 2003 a new beginning, yet it turned out to be merely a glimmer in the darkness. As the club fell apart in the last week of the 2004 season, players began sniping at Caray and Stone in the television booth, as odd and illogical as that seemed.

The brouhaha started when a few Cubs players began criticizing the club's announcers for being too quick to credit players on other teams with good performances. It was a remarkable exercise in buck-passing by the underachieving Cubs, not to mention that objectivity is generally regarded as a good thing in broadcasting. Following the season, both announcers were let go as the organization caved in to pressure from its too-sensitive players and manager.

Comcast, the giant Philadelphia-based cable operator and sports network, outbid FOX for the rights to carry the Cubs on cable in 2005. The new Comcast Sports Net Chicago — owned by the Cubs, Sox, NBA Bulls, and NHL Blackhawks — hired another former Brewers mikeman, Len Kasper, to take over on TV for 2005. Bob Brenly, the Cubs radio color man in 1990 who later skippered the Arizona Diamondbacks to a world championship in 2001, joined Kasper in the booth on all telecasts.

After an up-and-down first year, in which Brenly received criticism for treating a struggling team with kid gloves, the duo stabilized its game in 2006 as the team fell into the cellar for the first time since 2000.

The future on the air for the Cubs is unclear. WGN has been synonymous with Cubs baseball, both on TV and the radio. Yet the TV station will likely lose the Cubs' rights beyond the end of its current deal in 2014, especially with the club having been sold by the Tribune Company (WGN's owners) to the Ricketts' family, which has no intrinsic ties to the team's longtime flagship station.

In recent years, several radio rightsholders like KDKA with the Pirates, KMOX with the Cardinals, and WCCO with the Twins, lost their longstanding relationships (although the Cardinals returned to KMOX in 2011). A big factor in this transition has been the availability of all the clubs' broadcasts on the Internet, which has made rights fees prohibitively expensive for some stations.

WGN and the Cubs have been bound together since the 1920s, growing up together during the radio era and then prospering during TV age. The growth of cable and the Internet have put strains on that partnership, yet it is almost impossible to think of the Cubs without also thinking of WGN.

Pat Hughes continues to anchor the Cubs' radio broadcasts with style and humor. His partner Ron Santo, an icon in Chicago for decades, passed away December 3, 2010 at age 70.

Many Cubs fans simply loved Ron Santo for his infectious enthusiasm, his on- and off-field heroism related to his diabetes, and his singular on-air presence. Others disdained his blatant homerism and the admitted lack of priority that he placed on straightforward analysis. Few, however, denied that in recent years, he — rather than the far less visible Ernie Banks — had donned the royal robes of "Mr. Cub."

Following a decent interval, the grieving Cubs interviewed a batch of candidates to fill the sudden vacancy. That the new color man would be an ex-Cubs player was presumed; the candidate corps grew to include Mark Grace, Gary Matthews, Dave Otto, and Rick Sutcliffe. On February 16, 2011, however, the Cubs announced that Keith Moreland, a popular infielder and outfielder who'd been on the celebrated 1984 squad, would get the coveted job.

The 56-year-old Moreland had spent several years on the University of Texas football and baseball broadcasts — he'd played both sports at UT before entering pro baseball — and had previously filled in on a few Cubs broadcasts.

Moreland proved no match for Santo in the charisma department — who could be? — but knew baseball and lessened Hughes' workload in the booth.

Following the Cubs' awful 2012 season, TV color man Bob Brenly fled the booth for the warmth of Arizona, spurning a two-year deal for a spot in the Southwest. The Cubs' up-in-the-air media rights situation meant that nobody associated with the television broadcast would be guaranteed beyond 2014.

In Brenly's place came Jim Deshaies, who since 1996 had served in the Astros' television booth. Deshaies is a friendly presence who can break down pitching. He and play-by-play man Len Kasper mesh well, and most writers and fans were satisfied with the change.

The near future holds massive change for the Cubs' television presentation. Comcast SportsNet already airs more than half the team's contests, and since the Cubs have a piece of CSN, that number could well increase; Comcast and the club has a deal through 2019. The team is also said to be weighing the idea of building its own RSN in the style of the Mets and Yankees.

Radio commentator Keith Moreland was popular enough that WGN radio's November 6, 2013 announcement that the announcer had resigned to spend more time with his family in Texas came as no little surprise. (Ron Coomer, a onetime Cub, was named his replacement five weeks later.)

Bigger news came the same day, when the Cubs confirmed that they would exercise their right to opt out of their contract with WGN-TV following the 2014 season. The station, which at this point purchased about 70 games a year either to show or farm out to WCIU, paid the Cubs $20 million a season in a deal structured to run through 2022. WGN-TV, under the opt-out clause, had 30 days to agree to a much higher rights figure or lose the ability to purchase games for 2015 and beyond. With the station continuing to rebuild itself with a youth-focused prime-time lineup, and the Cubs scheduling fewer day contests, the fit between the two no longer exists. The team wants to explore all of its options — including the possibility of building its own RSN, which in reality probably won't happen until at least 2019.

Another bombshell dropped later that afternoon, as the team named Rick Renteria as its new manager. He is the Cubs' first Latino manager since 1980 and the first ever Mexican to helm the team. As a result, the club's Spanish broadcasting presence may — and certainly should — change significantly. The Cubs currently have more games available on the radio in Spanish than they have since 1994. In 2014, WRTO aired 60 Cubs games, 4 of them on the road.

Whether the Cubs manage to retain their almost mythical popularity in coming years, changes are in store, both on the radio and television fronts as traditional mass media undergo an Internet- and web-driven transformation. Regardless of what happens, the Cubs' seminal role in the history of baseball broadcasting will remain secure.

Telecasting the Cubs from 1948 through 1981 (and the Sox from 1948 through 1967) on WGN, Jack Brickhouse left an indelible mark on the consciousness of Chicago fans. His influence was far greater, for example, than that of Harry Caray. (National Baseball Hall of Fame and Museum)

SPORTS AND, SOMETIMES, VISION

CHICAGO WHITE SOX BROADCASTING HISTORY

"And it's a White Owl wallop, and a box of cigars, for Orestes Minoso."
— Bob Elson's home-run call

THE AMERICAN LEAGUE FIRST PERMITTED HOME RADIO BROADCASTS in 1927. WGN, beginning a tradition that continues today as a major player in Chicago radio sports, carried all the White Sox' games from Comiskey Park with Quin Ryan and Frank Dahm at the mike.

Other stations soon followed suit. At times during the 1930s, five radio stations broadcast both White Sox and Cubs games. Since teams did not broadcast many road games back then, the idea of a station carrying just one team in a two-team town was unheard of.

Through the early days of Chicago radio, therefore, stations carrying baseball used the same announcers for both teams. Hal Totten, John Harrington, and Pat Flanagan spent years in Chicago describing the action on both the North Side and the South Side. National figures such as Russ Hodges, Jimmy Dudley, Jack Drees, and Johnny O'Hara passed through the booth at Comiskey over WGN, WCFL, WBBM, WIND, WIBO, WJJD, and WENR.

A 1931 *Washington Post* article claimed that Chicago-area sponsors paid the following amounts per year to stations for games: WMAQ received $25,000; WENR, $35,000; WBBM, $40,000; WJJD, $8,000; and WIBO, $12,000. WGN earned $150 per game. WCFL's broadcasts were underwritten by a local finance company, which may have been General Finance, for many years a sponsor of Sox games.

Bob Elson soon emerged as the biggest name in baseball broadcasting in the Second City. In 1931, when Ryan decided he didn't want to do any more baseball, the station hired Elson as a staff announcer with a focus on baseball. He called all White Sox and Cubs home games.

WGN's policy at this point was to do only home games, but if a team was contending for the pennant, the station would follow them exclusively and forsake coverage of the other team. Elson traveled to important away games to announce the Cubs, but never the White Sox, as the Sox rarely contended after 1920, finishing as high as third only three times between 1921–51.

A disciple of early broadcasting legend Ted Husing, Elson was a legendary gin rummy player as well as the city's top baseball voice. He quickly appeared on World Series and All-Star broadcasts and soon became a national presence. In addition to baseball, Elson covered society functions and political meetings. By the 1950s, he was chairing a famous two-to-four-hour daily talk show from Chicago's Pump Room restaurant. Elson's wife, Jeanne, led the local Children's Crusade of Mercy.

Back in these days, top broadcasters worked hard. Since working only in baseball was nearly unheard of, famous announcers wore many hats. Elson gave sports reports in the evening, covered football games in the fall, and attended society gatherings, concerts, dances, and political events in the winter. Imagine Ed Farmer covering a political convention or Hawk Harrelson describing a hockey game!

Most of the radio announcers covering sports in those days had a dry newsreader's cadence and tried to sound as authoritative as they could. This may have been a legacy of pre-radio days, when announcers had to be "big" to be heard on stages and in clubs.

In 1934, Hal Totten did double duty, calling games for WMAQ from the ballpark every afternoon then handling a re-creation every night of another game over WENR (like WMAQ, also an NBC network station). NBC radio eventually forced WMAQ to stop carrying baseball in favor of more profitable soap operas, so the Chicago station outsourced its baseball programming to local rival WCFL.

While stations covering the White Sox were not charged exorbitant sums for the privilege of carrying the games, they had to be consistent; team president Charlie Comiskey informed radio stations in April 1935 that they had to carry all the team's home games or none of them. "We will not permit a station to return here once they discontinue our games," he told the *Chicago Tribune*.

General Mills, makers of Wheaties, allocated major advertising dollars into Chicago in 1937, paying $125,000 to broadcast games over WJJD. Part of this money went to comic Joe E. Brown, who was called in to provide commentary along with Harrington for a reported $3,000 per week. Local pharmacy chain Walgreens spent $100,000 with WGN to sponsor Cubs and Sox broadcasts that season.

In 1944, the White Sox and the Cubs decided to award their radio rights for home games to only one channel: WIND. With Elson in the Navy, the Sox asked the now-forgotten

Walt Lochman to call the action. Jack Brickhouse, a protégé of Elson's, did the honors the following year.

Elson returned in 1946 and began a 25-year run of calling Sox games exclusively. WIND carried all the team's night dates, while WJJD — run by the Marshall Field family, owners of a popular Chicago-area chain of department stores — took care of the daytime contests. Two years later, WEFM became the first FM station to carry Chicago baseball when it signed up for the Sox' evening broadcasts.

The Cubs were first telecast in 1947, but the Sox had to wait till 1948 when WGN took out an option for all 77 of the Pale Hose's home games, with Brickhouse and Harry Creighton in the booth. Brickhouse took a chance by forsaking radio in favor of television, but he made the right choice and remained a WGN telecaster for more than three decades.

Elson's second banana in the late 1940s was Ed Short, who eventually became the White Sox' general manager and deserves some credit for building the successful 1950s Sox. Following Short's ascendancy to the front office, Elson worked in 1952 with Dick Bingham before beginning an eight-year association with Don Wells in 1953.

By this time, the Sox were carried exclusively on WCFL, which had begun airing Sox night games in 1950. The Sox sold their radio rights that year for $70,000, with Muntz TV stores and Fox de Luxe Beer the key sponsors. Though the team negotiated with several different TV channels, Sox games remained on WGN (which reportedly paid $100,000 in 1950 for TV rights for all 77 home games) until 1967.

As the Sox became competitive in the early 1950s, the fans returned to Comiskey Park; attendance nearly doubled when Paul Richards assumed the managerial reins. By 1952, the Sox were sending Elson and Short on the road, ending their re-creations.

Beginning that year, the Sox stopped televising night home games, partially to increase attendance and partially because WGN couldn't give all its time to baseball. The Sox did not televise road games since 1) the cost of sending video over phone lines was prohibitive, and 2) WGN was airing all the Cubs' home games.

By 1957 Marty Hogan — a born salesman and an ex-Cubs broadcaster — was running the show at WCFL, supervising the popular Sox broadcasts featuring Elson and Wells, who called Sox games on a huge network of nearly 60 stations that stretched from Illinois and Indiana to Tennessee and the deep South. Radio was still the biggest game in town, though both the Cubs and Sox lost radio network affiliates in the Upper Midwest when the Braves moved from Boston to Milwaukee in 1953.

The Go-Go Sox captured the 1959 AL flag after finishing second to the dynastic Yankees the previous two seasons. Unfortunately, Elson didn't get to call the only World Series the White Sox would appear in while he was at the mike, as Brickhouse teamed with Vin Scully on NBC-TV while Mel Allen and Byrum Saam did the radio accounts for Gillette. At this time, local radio rights holders were not allowed to put on their own World Series broadcasts; this policy did not change until the early 1980s. Elson was long bitter about this, justifiably.

During these years, the Sox' steadiest broadcast sponsor — and their exclusive spring training advertiser — was General Finance, a local loan company. Elson, in his casual, ingratiating way, referred to the company's fictional head, "Friendly Bob Adams," so often and so effectively that some listeners thought Adams was a real person. Other longtime sponsors of Sox broadcasts in the 1950s and 1960s included Budweiser, General Cigar, and Butternut Bread.

On television, the Sox' contests (as well as the Cubs') were funded by ads for Hamm's Beer and Oklahoma Oil, which ran a chain of Midwestern service stations.

While the Sox were often thrilling in these years, Elson was no homer, and to some, his stentorian, reporter-like tones dimmed the excitement surrounding the club.

The Sox still did not televise many road telecasts, but with the team bearing down on the 1959 AL crown, Brickhouse and Lou Boudreau journeyed to Cleveland to call the September 22 pennant-clincher. Existing audio of the contest shows that Brickhouse, often painted as a Cubs partisan, was absolutely thrilled by the South Siders' triumph.

Even with a large radio network and 54 home games on television, the White Sox made just $400,000 for their media rights in 1959, sixth among the eight AL teams, barely ahead of Kansas City. This seems low, but Chicago was the only two-team city in the major leagues in 1959, and the Cubs were earning the same amount for their broadcasts as the Sox. In New York, for example, the Yankees were paid $875,000 for their rights, just a bit more than the total of the two Chicago clubs.

For 1960, WGN began showing a few Sox road night games, devoting even more time to baseball. Brickhouse was now assisted by Vince Lloyd, who like Elson and Brickhouse before him had come up through Peoria. On Opening Day 1961 in Washington, with the Sox about to take on the expansion Senators at Griffith Stadium in the new franchise's first game, Lloyd conducted a short but memorable interview for the "Lead-Off Man" pregame show with President John F. Kennedy, who had been in office for less than three months.

Things were changing in radio. Don Wells had been with WCFL for nearly a decade, calling Sox games as well as NFL Chicago Cardinals football. He was respected and liked. But Bill Veeck, who purchased the White Sox in 1959, saw Wells as a perhaps too-public supporter of Charlie Comiskey, scion of the family patriarch. (Comiskey lost control of the White Sox when Veeck outmaneuvered him.)

Following the 1960 campaign, in which the Sox did not defend their title, Veeck — never afraid to move quickly and decisively — had Wells bounced from the broadcasts. The highly regarded announcer mulled an immediate offer from the freshly relocated Minnesota Twins, but opted for the sunnier climes of Southern California and the expansion Angels.

After firing Wells, the White Sox and WCFL received more than 200 applications for his job. Veeck pushed wacky Sox outfielder Jim Rivera for the job, but "Jungle Jim" did not want to retire. Instead, Ralph Kiner, a retired slugger who had been vice president of the PCL's San Diego Padres, started his broadcasting career in 1961 on WCFL, spurning a competing offer from a Pittsburgh TV station.

Bob Elson famously disdained what he called "ex-jock announcers," and rookie Kiner was a bubbling fount of bloopers and garbled syntax. Pairing the crusty Elson with the overly self-confident Kiner — who'd had the stones to ask broadcasters to pay him for doing radio interviews back in the 1950s — truly created an "odd couple."

An 11-state network of more than 60 stations carried the Sox in 1961. WCFL was the city's true baseball radio station; as a Mutual Network affiliate, it also broadcast Mutual's Game of the Day if the national game didn't conflict with the White Sox.

Elson missed time with a virus during the 1961 season, so Bob Finnegan, WCFL's monotone-voiced sports director and Comiskey Park PA announcer, filled in. A bigger change was coming at the conclusion of the 1961 season, however, after it had become clear that Elson would not continue with Kiner. With the former slugger publicly searching for another job, WCFL snapped up Milo Hamilton.

When Kiner inked with the expansion Mets as a broadcaster in February 1962, WCFL promoted Hamilton to the second chair in the WCFL booth. Bob Feller had campaigned for the job, but Elson's well known distaste for ex-players made it a foregone conclusion that Feller wouldn't be picked.

Hamilton, an acolyte of the Elson style, had called Cubs games on WIND in 1956–57 but, when WGN bought out the club's radio rights, became a full-time disc jockey, spinning top 40 tunes and hosting record hops while pining for another chance at baseball. In August 1961, Hamilton, perhaps anticipating the WCFL job opening, had quit WIND over what was called a "policy matter."

On the television side, Brickhouse continued his role and also hosted a daily WGN radio sports highlights and discussion program. Like other big-name local media personalities of the day, he also interviewed celebrities and did political conventions as well as covering sports. "Brick" even went to the West Coast to cover the 1964 Republican convention, leaving Vince Lloyd and Lloyd Pettit to narrate Cubs and Sox TV games in his absence.

Even as a veteran of three decades behind the mike, Elson still called prizefights and football and sat at his famous Pump Room interview roundtable. In the early 1960s, both Hamilton and Jack Quinlan of the Cubs moonlighted as offseason disc jockeys — although the thought of Milo Hamilton spinning the newest Beach Boys 45 is mind-boggling.

Among WGN's many advances in broadcasting was the use of color TV for baseball. In 1960, the station beamed all 43 Sox home games (and all 77 Cubs home games) in color; the only other locally broadcast regular-season games in color that year were 23 Cincinnati Reds home contests.

The Sox contended through the early 1960s and almost won in 1964, but storm clouds were appearing. WCFL, the White Sox' home since 1953, was moving more toward a teen-oriented music format, making the somewhat old-fashioned Elson a bad fit. In June 1965, the Sox were rumored to be considering an offer from WBBM radio.

Just after the 1965 season, WCFL dumped Elson's daily interview show. The station set up a new nightly program for Elson called *Contact* that was supposed to deal with topical issues, but it was canceled before it even hit the air. In October 1965, WCFL re-upped for only one more season, leading the White Sox to the conclusion that it was time to find a new radio home.

A month later, Hamilton jumped WCFL to take his first of several No. 1 jobs: calling games on radio and television for the recently relocated Atlanta Braves. In January 1966, Finnegan, WCFL's sports director, named himself as Hamilton's replacement. Using someone already on the payroll with limited big-league experience (and none after 1966) showed that the station wanted to spend nothing extra in its last year covering the Sox.

On August 4, 1966, the Sox officially ended their 15-year affiliation with WCFL in favor of WMAQ, Chicago's NBC radio affiliate. The four-year contract was signed without Elson being included, but about 10 days later, the announcer agreed to terms. After considering former Yankees star Yogi Berra as the color man, WMAQ drafted Red Rush — the station's voice of Loyola University basketball and Northwestern University football — to assist Elson. Rush had the necessary personality to work with the domineering Elson. The new sidekick called the middle three innings, did the intros and wrap-ups, laughed at Elson's jokes, and played the pigeon at gin rummy.

WMAQ gave Elson an interview show in November 1966 to keep their new man busy in the offseason. For 1967 and, in fact, each year of the four-year deal, WMAQ did the entire White Sox spring training schedule. General Finance and Old Style Beer signed on as sponsors in 1967, with Walgreen's supporting the pregame show. The contract, though promising for both sides, was almost immediately fraught with tension. WMAQ was trying to improve its local presence, but the network executives in New York were angry that the channel had tied up so much airtime with the White Sox.

The 1967 season was a pivotal one in White Sox history, ending an era of perennial contention that had begun in 1951. The 1967 Sox should have won the AL pennant, but blew their last five games against the A's and Senators and finished fourth, three games out. This bitter disappointment led the front office to make some ill-advised trades that destroyed the club.

The ashes of 1967 also gave birth to a new era, as the Sox chose at season's end to depart WGN-TV, where they had always felt second-best to the Cubs, and take their games to WFLD, a UHF channel owned by Field Enterprises, publishers of the *Chicago Sun-Times*.

With WFLD desperate for programming, Sox fans could now see their club an amazing 144 times in 1968 — all games except those played in Oakland and Anaheim. It was by far their highest number of telecasts to date.

Unfortunately, WFLD's announcers were not exciting. Fifty-one-year-old Jack Drees, who had called White Sox games on radio some thirty years before, was no thrill, and his second, Dave Martin — a WFLD staffer — was found wanting after just one season. In fact, in his five years on WFLD, Drees worked with four different color men: Martin, Mel Parnell, Billy Pierce, and Bud Kelly (the only one to last two seasons). Former big-league infielder Al Rosen was offered the job for 1969 but did not want to leave job as a stockbroker.

Each of the four analysts served as well as their short tenures would indicate, and WFLD's often grainy, snowy picture made a dull second-division team even less appealing.

WMAQ radio added some new sponsors for 1968, including local Oldsmobile dealers, Zenith, and B.F. Goodrich. Ratings plunged as the Sox lost their first 10 games of the season and stumbled to a ninth-place finish.

It was a bad year all around on the South Side, with racial tensions rising across the U.S. and MLB attendance dipping as the improved Cubs garnered what attention local media gave to baseball. The White Sox seemed suddenly old-fashioned, even vacating Comiskey to play 20 "home games" in 1968–69 in Milwaukee, helping Bud Selig and his group in their efforts to land a new team. The White Sox networked those games via Milwaukee station WVTV.

The White Sox malaise was exemplified by a preseason 1968 Cubs-Sox exhibition game at County Stadium televised by both WGN and WFLD. The Cubs' broadcast draw five times the Sox' audience.

WMAQ preempted the Sox seven times during the summer of 1968 to broadcast reports from the Democratic Party's Chicago convention, and the team sued the station for non-fulfillment of its contract as well as for underreporting profits from its broadcasts. WMAQ, in turn, claimed that their contract with the Sox guaranteed a profit for the station, which the club did not deliver. The litigation led to bad blood between station and club and, by July 1969, Elson and Rush had been banned from team flights!

With the Cubs contending, it was a bad time for the second-division Sox to be looking for a new radio deal. During 1970, its final season with the Sox, WMAQ featured General Finance, Old Style, and Zenith as Sox sponsors. Walgreen's took on the pregame, with the postgame sponsored by AAMCO Transmissions and a local Chrysler dealer. It became crystal clear by midseason, however, that the last-place White Sox could not find a major station to carry it for 1971.

So on October 13, 1970, Bob Elson and Red Rush signed a one-year deal to do play-by-play for Charlie Finley's Oakland Athletics. Rush apparently initiated the deal, and Elson went along because he didn't want the horrible 1970 Sox team to be his swan song. The Elson era, which spanned more than 35 years, was over in Chicago, and the Old Commander would be replaced by someone whose style was completely the opposite.

With the White Sox out in the cold for 1971, former Cardinals radio mainstay Harry Caray — himself pushed out of Oakland after just one year of battling his on-air partner Monte Moore, as well as A's owner Finley — said he would drop his usual rate and come to Chicago for just $50,000.

The Sox, desperate for attention, named the voluble Caray their new voice in January 1971. The big question: Who would hear the voice? The Sox used three tiny suburban outlets — WJOL-FM of Joliet, WEAW-FM from Evanston, and WTAQ-AM in LaGrange — as its flagship channels. While the club planned to air on a network of other high-fidelity FM stations, only two were carrying the club by Opening Day.

The financial details reveal how little leverage the Sox had: each station paid the team $25 per game, sold its own ads, and kept all the revenue. This meant that five stations airing all 162 games earned the White Sox a little over $25,000 in radio rights fees!

Caray and Ralph Faucher, heretofore a staff announcer on WTAQ, broadcast weekend spring training games from Sarasota, Florida, as well as all 162 regular-season contests. Meanwhile Drees and Bud Kelly — a soporific DJ on light-rock station WBBM-FM — lulled fans to sleep 129 times on WFLD-TV.

At least the new radio broadcasts injected some energy and panache into Sox games. The Sox had some talented young players in 1971, and Caray, with his outsized presence, was just the man to bring the new message to a bored and disinterested fan base. While Elson is justly famous for his longevity and his accomplishments, he was past his prime by the early 1960s. Most Chicago fans don't have distinct memories of Elson even if they heard him, because over his last decade with the White Sox, he would simply go on about this or that old-time celebrity he'd interviewed, or some restaurateur who had given him a free dinner on the last road trip.

Older Chicago baseball fans remember Vince Lloyd and Jack Brickhouse. Younger ones can talk about Hawk Harrelson, Pat Hughes, and Ed Farmer. Some diehards even have memories of Red Rush. All of them of a certain age, plus those who know the club's history, remember how Harry Caray, along with front-office executives Roland Hemond and Stu Holcomb and enigmatic slugger Dick Allen, saved the White Sox.

Caray was profane, sloppy, often annoying, and completely in tune with the game. His common-man act was at least part salesmanship, but his language and bearing was refreshing to long-suffering fans numbed by stony-faced spokesmen narrating a black-and-white picture of a dull gray team that contrasted with a world that had long since embraced color.

And, boy, were the Sox colorful, with their red pinstripes adorning power hitters like Allen, Carlos May, and Bill Melton, knuckleball pitcher Wilbur Wood, and hard throwers Terry Forster and Rich Gossage. Those Sox didn't win, but — boosted by Caray's beery baritone — they drew 68 percent more fans in 1971, and their 1973 attendance was more than two-and-a half times as big as in 1970.

The "radio broadcaster as newsman" role was never better filled than by Bob Elson, "The Commander," who spent 35 years calling the Chicago White Sox on radio. His fans called him accurate and easygoing; his detractors found him uninteresting. (National Baseball Hall of Fame and Museum)

In 1972, the final season of the two-year pact with WTAQ and friends, the Sox broadcast 12 exhibition games and the regular-season slate on a five-state, 22-station network. WTAQ's 5,000 watts dropped to just 500 watts at night, but the station still got comparatively huge ratings with Caray behind the mike.

During the season, the White Sox wrapped up a new radio contract with WMAQ for 1973. Hamm's, General Finance, Chevrolet, Gonnella Bakery, and Zenith formed a heavy-weight set of sponsors, and a local men's clothier paid for the pregame. The deal ended Faucher's career in the big-league booth and began a long-running series that could have been titled "Who's Harry's Partner?"

The truth is that very few people could work with Harry Caray in Chicago because he rarely let them. If Harry perceived a new partner as a shill or an interloper — sometimes both — he refused to collaborate. Caray's first sidekick on WMAQ was Gene Osborn, an itinerant who'd toiled for the Pirates and Tigers.

The team also signed a new television outlet for 1973: WSNS, Channel 44, with a better signal than WFLD. Caray — with the help of young Bob Waller, who'd done games in Cincinnati in 1971 — improved the telecasts significantly, extending his reach beyond simply radio. Falstaff, familiar with Caray from St. Louis, elected to become the main TV sponsor, joined by Chicagoland Chevrolet Dealers, Motorola, Com Ed, and Chicago area McDonald's operators.

Caray earned extra money for doing television as well as radio, and his presence had an invigorating effect for WSNS and the Sox: At the end of the 1973 season, the club announced that TV ratings had risen 70 percent from the previous year.

Caray didn't much care for Osborn, who was replaced in 1974 by Bill Mercer, a longtime Texas broadcaster who'd done two years of Rangers games. Osborn took a job with KBMA-TV in Kansas City but passed away in November 1975 at age 53.

Although the Sox doubled Mercer's salary to $50,000, it was a tough time for the new No. 2. Harry, fueled by his popularity and really feeling his oats, lashed out at anything he saw as a representation of authority. He battled with players and management and saw Mercer — who was nothing if not professional — as a house man.

Everyone wanted in on Sox broadcasts for 1974: the club had 11 sponsors for the games and a different sponsor underwriting the pregame. Even with this success, however, trouble was brewing as Caray feuded with everyone, including manager Chuck Tanner and WMAQ management. The station decided to simply dump the whole package, but the decision was changed after WMAQ was sold. The new management elected to bring the Sox back for 1975 and to raise Caray's salary to $100,000.

On TV, Bob Waller had followed Caray's lead in criticizing Tanner, et al. But he was sacrificed, likely as a concession to the manager and to the front office. Waller had already blabbed his way out of a job in Cincinnati by being too overtly critical; he told it like he saw it, but didn't have the power to do so. While Caray made a couple of public statements in support of his fired colleague, he didn't go to bat to save Waller.

Years later, Caray told Curt Smith, "One year [sic], I had an assistant named Bob Waller — no great shakes there." Caray had used Waller as a cat's paw to get at management, and the younger man, perhaps thinking that he had Caray's support, sawed himself off a limb.

Baseball makes strange bedfellows; Waller ended up as Monte Moore's second chair in Oakland in 1975, after having said publicly in October 1974, "I don't think I'd particularly enjoy working all year with Monte Moore." Moreover, Waller later ended up calling games for another team managed by Chuck Tanner, after Finley hired him to manage the Athletics in 1976.

Perhaps the bitterest pill for Waller, and Caray, was that the new man in the booth was J.C. Martin, a former White Sox catcher with no broadcasting experience. Martin was handpicked by the front office to say nice things about the team, and Caray treated him with barely disguised contempt in their year together.

With Martin and Bill Mercer departing the scene after 1975, Caray was — again — alone. But he had a new boss: Bill Veeck, who stepped in and purchased the Sox when it appeared the club might move.

With other, more pressing, matters to be dealt with, Chicago didn't sign a replacement second broadcaster until spring training, when the team hired Lorn Brown, a Chicagoan who'd called games for the Sox' Triple-A team in Iowa City in 1973 and 1974 as well as the Chicago Bulls on TV in 1975–76 with Andy Musser (later a Phillies broadcaster).

To get the Sox' gig, Brown beat out Lanny Frattare and Pete Van Wieren, who went on to enjoy long careers in Pittsburgh and Atlanta, respectively. Brown, not an employee of the club, was no hatchet man, but he didn't try to shine Shinola, either.

After Veeck had a year to evaluate everything, he decided — not surprisingly — to shake things up even more prior to the 1977 season. So he brought Jimmy Piersall, who had impressed during a brief appearance with Caray in 1976, into the booth.

A great defensive outfielder who had fought his way through a nervous breakdown in the 1950s, Piersall — a loose cannon — claimed to "Tell it like it is." One problem was that Piersall rarely seemed to consider the consequences of his actions. He and Caray were often simultaneously hilarious, tasteless, and incisive, and Chicago's never heard anything like them since. Piersall got into a lot of trouble for things he said on the air, and at his very best was a lightning rod for controversy — all of which meant that people tuned in to hear him.

Only Piersall's high-voltage act could have made the signing of Mary Shane seem like an afterthought. Caray had noticed the 31-year-old Shane working as a radio reporter in the County Stadium press box in 1976 and, on a lark, asked her into the booth to do a bit of play-by-play. (That season, Caray had no regular partner.) Shane was an instant sensation as well as a novelty, and WMAQ hired her to do 20 games in 1977. The pioneering female announcer was introduced to the media the day that Chicago's mayor, Richard M. Daley, died, which held down the coverage a bit.

Although she wasn't the first woman on a local baseball broadcast — Betty Caywood had done a couple of weeks' worth of games for the Athletics in 1964 — Shane knew sports, knew journalism, and was well-spoken and intelligent.

Unfortunately, according to Piersall, Veeck didn't like her and, after a few gaffes, Shane was yanked from the air late in the season. She passed away in 1987 after a successful run as a sportswriter in Massachusetts.

One day in 1976, when Caray was singing his usual "Take Me Out to the Ballgame" to himself in the booth, an engineer decided to open the microphone and air Harry's private homage to the game through the public address system, reportedly at Veeck's urging. This caused a sensation. Soon, Caray's boozy rendition of baseball's anthem was a necessary part of the Comiskey experience. In fact, late in 1976, the Sox commissioned a flexi-disc — a thin, soft plastic phonograph record — which included several renditions of the song. The Sox gave away the disc at a game against Toronto in April 1977.

Caray's legend grew: he even cut a disco version of "Take Me Out to the Ballgame." He was the biggest man in town, and when he hung out at a particular nightclub, the crowds would follow.

The Sox transferred to WBBM radio for 1980, meaning that Lorn Brown was out and Joe McConnell, the station's football announcer, was in. Piersall and Caray were mostly doing TV by this time, and were essentially out of control — especially Piersall, who repeatedly got into hot water with his big mouth. In mid-1980, he insulted Veeck's wife Mary Frances on the air. A month later he skipped out on a telecast, and shortly after that tried to strangle a local sportswriter. The next season he went so far to smear the Sox players' wives as "horny broads," and was finally suspended.

Veeck wouldn't own the White Sox for long; the economic realities of the free-agency era made running a team on a shoestring impossible over the long haul. So the ingenious maverick owner sold out in January 1981 to a limited partnership headed by Jerry Reinsdorf and Eddie Einhorn, and the White Sox embarked upon one of the most interesting chapters in baseball broadcasting history.

Einhorn, the club's new president, had a long string of successful sports television ventures on his curriculum vitae, including founding the TVS syndication network while still in his 20s and later becoming head of CBS Sports, where he won Emmys and garnered high ratings in the mid-to-late 1970s. The White Sox became a lab for his experiments. While several other clubs had tried pay television with middling or poor results, the White Sox went into it more aggressively than anyone.

On October 11, 1981, the White Sox announced the formation of SportsVision, a cooperative project including three other Chicago professional sports franchises: the NBA Bulls, the NHL Black Hawks, and the Sting of the North American Soccer League.

SportsVision operated via a scrambled signal over WBBS, Channel 60, an affiliate of ON-TV, operators of similar pay channels around the country. ON-TV already featured a few Angels, Dodgers, and Tigers games on its Los Angeles and Detroit pay channels.

Blazing a trail others would follow, the Sox planned SportsVision as a year-round operation that would drive the club's entire media package. Other clubs had only dipped their toes into the cable pool, while Einhorn and Reinsdorf were bringing a revolution to a populace already pretty satisfied with the way things were.

The Sox intended for SportsVision to debut on April 1, 1982. If viewers in Chicago already had the ON-TV service, SportsVision cost $14.95 a month. If not, the tab was $21.95. The service also required a $52.95 installation fee. Perhaps most surprising — and galling to many subscribers — was that counter to the philosophy of early pay television, SportsVision would feature commercials.

Not surprisingly, SportsVision was a tough sell, and not only because of the high cost. Chicagoans had become, over the years, used to seeing more baseball on "free TV" than any other market in the country except New York City. In 1980, for instance, the White Sox had aired 125 of 162 games in their last year on WSNS, and Cubs fans saw their team 148 times on WGN.

Sox ownership expected the viewing public to quickly embrace SportsVision, and perhaps too confidently tried a hard sell, initially claiming that no games would be on free TV in 1982. This caused friction with many fans already angry at the previous year's landmark player strike. Even though SportsVision started off with some ham-handed public relations, the Sox really did need to address their television situation in a proactive way.

By 1981, the team's contract with WSNS had run out, and the White Sox could find no other outlet except WGN, again making them second-best to the Cubs. WGN scheduled just 64 Sox games and 148 Cubs games, although the midseason strike wiped out many of both teams' telecasts. WGN's Rich King and Lou Brock helped out Caray and Piersall on the 1981 broadcasts, but the future Hall of Fame outfielder was uncomfortable on the air and did not return.

It wasn't as if the Sox hadn't considered already cable and pay television; before selling the team, Veeck had even signed a development pact with Cablevision's SportsChannel. Einhorn had no problem, though, with disregarding previous contracts. He unilaterally opted out of both the Cablevision agreement and WGN's 60-game deal for 1982, leading to lawsuits. Einhorn eventually agreed, as compensation to WGN, to use the station's crews and equipment for all SportsVision home games in 1981, 1982, and 1983.

Waking up to the reality that SportsVision wouldn't succeed overnight, the Sox in December 1981 signed a three-year deal to air 30 games per season on WFLD. Even with that concession to the market, most of the club's telecasts were headed for pay cable. As the driving force behind SportsVision, the Sox had a lot to lose — and, almost immediately, they lost Harry Caray.

Always conscious of his visibility, Caray — making $225,000 with the Sox — wanted no part of a problematic, uncertain new venture which might limit his exposure. He wasn't crazy about the Sox' new owners, either, who he felt were low-balling him on a new contract offer.

Several weeks after the 1981 season, Caray began meeting in secret with WGN executives, who had been pleased with his work on the previous season's Sox telecasts and thought he might be a good replacement for the just-retired Jack Brickhouse on Cubs games.

The Sox offered Caray a one-year deal, but heard nothing. Not having Caray under contract affected not only their television package, but also the Sox' new radio deal. Four stations were interested, but WMAQ came away with the rights for the third time in a 15-year period. The station inked a five-year deal in mid-December, hiring away McConnell from WBBM and pledging to cover all spring training games. Ten other stations were on the team's network in 1982.

Rumors began leaking out late in 1981 that the Sox had hired Don Drysdale and Ken "Hawk" Harrelson as their lead broadcasters for television, indicating that the club had moved on from the Caray era.

Drysdale, who had broadcast for several other teams as well as on ABC's short-lived *Monday Night Baseball*, agreed to a five year, $200,000 deal early in 1982. The tough ex-pitcher was not a rooter, but rather a slick, professional voice with a distinct West Coast persona. (He didn't understand, for instance, that while Angelenos referred to their metropolitan area as "greater Los Angeles," nobody in Chicago referred to its metropolitan area that way.)

Paired with Drysdale was the outrageous Harrelson, a former star slugger and pro golfer who had done some broadcasting with the Red Sox. He was funny and casual, and, like Drysdale, could break down a game. Harrelson still had a lot to prove in 1982, however, and hadn't yet developed the set of signature phrases that pleased many listeners while annoying others.

On January 12, 1982, the Sox unveiled hard-bitten ex-pitcher Early Wynn (who had pitched for the Sox for five years late in his long career) as Joe McConnell's sidekick, making Caray's departure a foregone conclusion. Four days later, the Cubs — now owned by the *Chicago Tribune* — announced that Caray had joined WGN for a $275,000 salary. So the White Sox, trying to sell a brand-new pay-TV network in a city accustomed to free TV, had lost their biggest attraction.

While Jack Brickhouse had been rumored to be joining SportsVision, he could not come to terms with the new network. Veteran Merle Harmon was tabbed to anchor the telecasts, with Piersall offered a chance to do pregame and postgame commentary. McConnell also was part of the SportsVision team.

The question then became: Would anyone get to see these new broadcasters? By January 1982 it had become clear that SportsVision wouldn't be ready to show Sox games until May. While installation problems were blamed for the endless delays — among other things, the converter boxes were apparently difficult to produce — few households were signing up anyway.

So Einhorn and Reinsdorf bit their lips and decided to add 15 more early-season White Sox games to WFLD's slate, although Opening Day was not one of them. WFLD only received a few advertising spots of their own to sell, as the team held onto most of the ad inventory.

In February, SportsVision tried to address its lack of subscriptions by giving away tickets to Sox, Sting, Bulls, and Hawks games to induce sign-ups. Chicago papers began carrying ads for trial offers to ON-TV and SportsVision.

As of April 15, 1982, SportsVision had landed a big sponsor — Budweiser — but could count just 5,000 subscribers, well below the initial goal, as the Sox had hoped for 30,000 new paying customers by May 13. SportsVision was supposed to go live that day, but had only 8,000 subscribers by May 4. When the *Tribune* printed this, Einhorn accused the newspaper of protecting the interests of its subsidiaries, WGN and the Cubs, by wishing ill on SportsVision.

As another inducement to sales, the channel put its early May White Sox games and its Black Hawks playoff contests on for free. The hockey games brought in a lot of new subscribers, as the Hawks played unexpectedly well, going all the way to the conference finals.

SportsVision finally went live, for pay, on May 25, 1982, transmitting its signal to approximately 10,000 Chicago-area homes. The channel invested in its future by building a new infrastructure featuring new switching technology, a clear picture, new broadcast facilities at Comiskey Park, and a full schedule, as the service also telecast 32 non-White Sox MLB games in 1982. It also featured occasional technical problems, with transmitters blowing out and such.

By late July, the network had just 17,000 subscribers, well below the goal, so SportsVision brought in a new sales staff and began seeking affiliations with local cable systems. Even so, at the end of the season, the service was only in 22,000 homes.

During 1983, Einhorn teamed with Group W Communications to build an ad hoc network of regional teams to increase the amount of baseball programming that each station could offer, beaming games from other markets on nights or afternoons when the home team wasn't playing. The Detroit Tigers and Minnesota Twins were involved in their own cable ventures, and Milwaukee, Kansas City, and St. Louis were also considering deals. Cable TV was causing the ground under baseball to shake.

The bigger local earthquake, however, emanated from Piersall's mouth. He feuded constantly with Sox manager Tony La Russa, and was occasionally warned by the Sox and SportsVision, but he was popular enough to keep his job even after Caray, his biggest champion, had departed. When he blasted the White Sox' front office on Opening Day 1983, however, it was the final straw. SportsVision canned him the next morning. He managed to keep his job on WMAQ, though, as the Sox were in no position to demand that the radio station simply dismiss a popular commentator.

That year, the White Sox won the AL West, and Reinsdorf and Einhorn happily garnered the resulting good publicity. Lorn Brown came back to fill in on the air and remained on the broadcast team through 1988, working on radio with incisive ex-catcher and manager Del Crandall and Frank Messer, a veteran of more than two decades in the baseball booth who by then had seen his best days. The White Sox received no rights fees from WFLD for their 1983 telecasts, but kept all of Anheuser-Busch's ad dollars as well as 50 percent of any other ads the station vended. In April, WFLD had 20 percent open spots but, by the end of the season, all its ad space had been sold.

SportsVision, meanwhile, lost $300,000, but got a big break late in the season, when the ON-TV network — in far more homes than SportsVision — signed an $8 million deal for 1984–85 to show some 200 SportsVision games, including most of the White Sox' contests. ON-TV moved to Channel 44 and assumed SportsVision's operating costs. This merger put SportsVision in the black.

ON-TV, the country's largest pay-cable system, was betting that the City of Chicago would continue to lag behind in wiring homes for basic cable. Late in 1984, though, Cablevision of New York closed a deal with SportsVision, assuming rights to show the Sox, Bulls, and Hawks through 1990, showing that Cablevision executives were confident that the area would soon be fully wired and that they could muscle their way on to local basic cable systems rather than keep SportsVision as a pay service.

This deal pumped more money into SportsVision and indeed, the channel was soon added to basic service on nearly all Chicago-area cable systems. This move fatally wounded ON-TV, which had spent a huge sum of money on a product that nearly every local viewer would now get for free if they were a cable subscriber.

During the 1985 season, ON-TV, which had already gone dark in most of its other markets, shut its doors in Chicago, despite having already paid the White Sox to show their games. Games that had been earmarked only for ON-TV and not for SportsVision were, therefore, not aired at all.

White Sox fans still saw 67, 67, and 66 games on free TV from 1987 through 1989, indicating that SportsVision's stated mission — to move the Sox' TV package mainly to cable — was not entirely successful. SportsVision was tremendously successful, however, in earning the Sox, Bulls, and Hawks a pile of money.

The announcers changed chairs during these years. Drysdale and Harrelson went full-time to TV in 1984, and McConnell was dumped from the broadcasts because Harrelson didn't like him. Former player and manager Joe Torre, rumored to be coming to Chicago in 1985, instead took a job calling Angels games. Harrelson soon consolidated his power by taking an ill-advised promotion to the position of general manager of the club for one chaotic year, then decamped to New York for a job in the Yankees' booth before returning to Chicago, somewhat chastened, in 1990. In 1986 and 1987, Drysdale did television work with Messer before leaving for his native California to work Dodgers games.

By this time the White Sox had begun a regular schedule of games on Spanish-language radio, becoming one of the first teams in the American League to do so. The club had always drawn upon a Latino fan base on the western side of the city and in the west and southwest suburbs. The Sox had initially broadcast games in Spanish in 1978, but did not do so not again until 1986, when Frank Diaz and Jose Flores called 33 home contests on WTAQ (the same low-power suburban station that broadcast the Sox *en Ingles* back in 1971–72). By 1989, the package included all home and some road contests, but after that high-water mark, the station lost its advertising.

WTAQ cut back to 39 home games in 1990 as popular former Sox shortstop Chico Carrasquel joined Diaz as a color man. Carrasquel, a Venezuelan who had played in Chicago just before fellow countryman Luis Aparicio, became a valued member of the Sox family, acting as an ambassador to Chicago's Spanish-speaking community until his retirement in 2002. He formed a popular on-air team with Hector Molina on WIND — which had carried the Cubs and Sox in the 1945os and 1950s in English — from 1992 through 1996.

WIND let Carrasquel go during the 1996 campaign, claiming budget problems; this led some angry listeners to tune out. Molina continued on WIND alone through 1999; after his departure from the Sox' booth, the club's Spanish-language games simply dried up. In 2005, Molina returned to call a handful of games with Ozzie Guillen Jr., son of the White Sox manager, during Chicago's world championship season.

Oscar Ramos Jr. took over for Molina in 2009 when the latter became more involved with Milwaukee Brewers telecasts. The club put 46 home games on the radio on WRTO in 2010, the most Sox broadcasts in Spanish for more than a decade.

When Chicago abandoned Comiskey Park in 1990 to move to what is now called U.S. Cellular Field, the club's broadcasting situation benefitted from plenty of upgrades, with larger and better press and broadcast accommodations, some new voices, and the return of WGN as the Sox' over-the-air carrier after a decade's absence.

With the Sox in a new home, and interest high in a team expected to contend, WGN made room for 42 South Side games in 1990. Jim Durham, the NBA Bulls' telecaster who had also called games for the Houston Astros, worked with former Sox first baseman–outfielder Tom Paciorek, who also teamed with Harrelson on the local outlet of the national SportsChannel network, which had bought into SportsVision in 1984.

Harrelson and Paciorek formed a memorable pair, with the approachable Paciorek giving the consciously rustic "Hawk" some necessary ballast. The two paired on all White Sox telecasts from 1991–99, and their often funny, occasionally combustible presence hasn't been approached since.

On the radio side, Wayne Hagin — who had previously described Giants and Athletics action — ventured east in 1989 to work in the Comiskey booth with John Rooney, formerly of Minnesota. Rooney, with just one year of Twins games and some experience on CBS radio, had come to Chicago in 1988, calling the Sox on WFLD's telecasts. His style truly was more suited for radio, however, and he immediately made himself comfortable with his witty banter, his spot-on impersonations of Vin Scully and Milo Hamilton, and an affinity for the Midwestern lifestyle borne from years doing Triple-A ball in Louisville.

WMAQ paid markedly more to Rooney and Hagin than they had to their old radio team of Brown and Crandall. "I guarantee it'll be more exciting than Del and Lorn," promised station manager Jeff Pearlman.

And it was. Due to Rooney's popularity, however, Hagin was essentially eclipsed. Following the 1991 season, the Sox and Hagin amicably parted ways, with the broadcaster in the running for the job succeeding Ernie Harwell in Detroit. (Unfortunately for Hagin, the job went to Rick Rizzs.) Joining Rooney in 1992 was Ed Farmer, a former hard-throwing Sox pitcher and Chicago native who has, over the last two decades, carved a particular niche in the local consciousness.

The two paired on WMAQ and, later, WMVP for 14 years, becoming one of the most popular radio teams in Chicago baseball history, breaking up only when Rooney got the plum lead job in St. Louis for 2006. Farmer took over on play-by-play, teaming with another ex-Sox player, Chris Singleton, who wasn't really suited for the role and lasted only two seasons. In 2008, Steve Stone, who remains one of the best analysts in the business, joined Farmer for a year before switching to TV to work with Harrelson, with Darrin Jackson becoming Farmer's co-pilot.

Farmer, at first a gravelly-voiced color man with an unusual tone and bizarre inflections, has become a gravelly-voiced play-by-play announcer with an unusual tone and bizarre inflections. With no professional training, Farmer often puts the emphasis on the wrong word in a sentence. Listening to "Farmeo" for a while, however, and one can understand his odd charm: he knows the game so well that he often sums the situation up in a few words, leaving time for listeners to paint their own pictures. Sometimes his thoughts come out in strange ways, and Farmer is not to everyone's taste, but most Sox fans love him.

With Rooney doing weekend games for CBS radio during the 1990s, the Sox needed a third man to do play-by-play. Ken Korach and Dave Wills filled those part-time jobs during the decade, and both received enough exposure to earn MLB play-by-play jobs elsewhere.

WMAQ had bought the rights to the Sox and Bulls (a package deal, as Jerry Reinsdorf owns both clubs) in 1981 and held them through 1995, when interest in baseball had dropped substantially in the wake of the cataclysmic work stoppage of 1994–95.

In November 1995, the Sox and Bulls inked with WMVP radio. The station had, for several years, prided itself on its tough commentary on Chicago sports teams, but its talk show hosts predictably began soft-pedaling criticism of its two new clients. WMVP never became a rubber stamp for the White Sox, however, and was able to maintain credibility throughout its 10-year run carrying the club.

Following the 1998 campaign, Fox Sports, a majority partner in SportsChannel, decided to take over the brand. For the next six years, the Sox were seen on Fox Sports Chicago. In 2000, Darrin Jackson replaced Paciorek, who had resigned to spend time with his family (but reportedly was also tired of working with Harrelson).

"DJ," a former Sox player with no previous broadcast experience, was everything Harrelson could have wanted in a sidekick: malleable and easygoing to the point of deference. Jackson breaks down hitters well and is a likeable, folksy commentator, but playing second fiddle to a dominant force like Harrelson made it tough to stand out.

During 2004, Fox's last season covering the White Sox, the station experimented with an alternate audio feed intended for younger, more casual fans. Eric Collins — who got a job describing Dodgers' road TV games beginning in 2009 — teamed with Pat Reidy for 10 games starting in July.

While the experiment was not continued, it was interesting. Fans already have the option of hearing Spanish Audio Programming on many broadcasts, and digital TV, with an seemingly infinite number of audio channels, could make alternate audio — a stathead broadcast, an old-fashioned game-call, a female-oriented broadcast — a reality in the coming years.

Comcast SportsNet entered the picture in 2005. The Philadelphia-based company opened a franchise in Chicago and came in aggressively, guns blazing, to kill off Fox. Comcast retained a 20 percent stake in its new channel, offering to split the remaining 80 percent evenly between the White Sox, Cubs, Bulls, and Hawks, thus giving each team a major stake in the network's success. Much of the success of the White Sox' cable endeavors has been credited to the late Jim Corno, among the most respected executives in sports television until his passing in 2013.

One reason that the teams found this venture attractive was increased control over their own broadcasts. Fox Sports Net was not owned by the teams and, therefore, not easily influenced by them, either in editorial control or presentation. In addition, owning the network also allowed the teams to sell advertising and keep a higher percentage of the take. FSN Chicago, immediately deprived of its most important content, collapsed within a year.

WGN, while retaining a contractual option for more than 50 White Sox games per year, does not present all of those games. In 2000, the station began optioning some Sox contests — usually midweek contests against less interesting rivals — to independent UHF station WCIU, which now telecasts some 25 games each season.

Chicago retains a large number of games on broadcast television. This makes perfect sense, given the city's nearly 55-year heritage of free telecasts. Those traditional telecasts, along with those on Comcast, improved in 2009 when Steve Stone moved to the Comcast booth. Stone, who had run the gauntlet working with Harry Caray in the 1980s and 1990s, has the requisite ego and gravity to stand up to Harrelson's hurricane-force winds, though the two at first did not jell.

Darrin Jackson's 2009 move to WSCR radio (which took over the Sox' audio in 2006) to partner with Farmer made the radio games a bit less incisive and, surely, one of the stranger MLB radio experiences. Neither is a traditional play-caller, and each might be better as a strongly opinionated TV color man.

The White Sox currently enjoy a very popular set of broadcasters, though the need to replace one or more of the veteran trio of Harrelson, Farmer, and Stone is probably not that far away. During the 2014 season, in fact, the 72-year-old Harrelson announced an intention to cut back on traveling.

During the 2013, Sox fans noticed a thawing of relations between Harrelson and Stone. Whatever the reason for the improved on-air chemistry, it was one tolerable feature of the team's a 63–99 finish.

Beginning in 2012, the Pale Hose began airing all games in Spanish on a digital radio station with Hector Molina and Billy Russo at the mikes. They are the first team to use digital radio as part of its on-air plan.

In the Reinsdorf era, the White Sox have always had a clear vision of how they wanted to position the club on the air. Einhorn and Reinsdorf have moved decisively into new sports broadcasting technologies and media arrangements. Some of their pioneering steps did not work out perfectly, but the overall result has been very successful as the twenty-first century White Sox, with profitable video and radio operations, are in better position to compete on air in Chicago than they have been for most of the last half-century although their attendance continues to lag.

The immediate future holds distinct possibility of change in the broadcast situation. The Cubs' contract with WGN is up following the 2014 season; should the Cubs ditch WGN, the station might pick up more Sox games.

Harry Caray: Two men saved the Chicago White Sox: Dick Allen (the 1972 AL MVP) and Harry Caray. The latter joined the South Siders in 1971 after a long stint in St. Louis and one year in Oakland and revitalized the Sox. His profane, party-hearty persona at times disguised his deep knowledge of baseball, but his impact at 35th and Shields was seismic—far greater than what he achieved for the Cubs beginning in 1982. (National Baseball Hall of Fame and Museum)

WAVES OVER QUEEN CITY

CINCINNATI REDS BROADCASTING HISTORY

"This is the old left-hander, rounding third and heading for home…"
— Joe Nuxhall

THE QUEEN CITY'S FIRST RADIO STATION WAS WMH, WHICH FIRST signed on in 1921. As part of its coverage of all things Cincinnati, the station aired a Reds game in 1924 with Gene Mittendorf — later WKRC's program director and football announcer — at the mike.

Powel Crosley, a local auto parts manufacturer, had founded station WLW in 1922 largely as a vehicle to sell the radios his company made. WLW, with frequent boosts in power, boasted by 1930 the strongest radio signal in America.

The first regular Reds' broadcasts came in 1929, when WSAI's Bob Burdette aired 40 games from Redland Field. But in those early radio days, the best-known baseball station in Cincinnati was WFBE, and the man — hulk, really — at the mike was a 5-foot-6, 300-pound ball of energy named Harry Hartman.

Born in 1903, Hartman started broadcasting games in 1928. Owner of a local clothing store, his career behind the mike began when an announcer scheduled to narrate a fight on the radio didn't show up. Hartman stepped in, did the job with enthusiasm despite a limited vocabulary, and suddenly had a new career.

What was Hartman like? Unlike many stalwarts of early radio, he was no Ted Husing wannabe, being completely uninterested in erudition or propriety. He would take off his shirt if the weather got hot. He yelled "Socko!" and "Blammo!" and "Belto!" when batters hit the ball hard. Some historians credit him with inventing the phrase "Going, going, gone!" MediaHeritage.com even notes that he collaborated with a local bandleader on the song "Bam! It's Going, Going, Gone." He took infield practice with the players and accompanied the club to spring training long before it became fashionable for announcers to do so. In short, he was a ton of fun.

Hartman's nightly sports review was one of the city's top radio programs, and his national profile rose quickly. When *The Sporting News* went off on one of its anti-radio screeds, it was Hartman who wrote in to defend the new medium in the November 1932. That winter, Hartman came in second in the weekly newspaper's national fan poll of favorite broadcasters.

It was only fitting that the first real competition to WFBE's radio reign in Cincy came from a polar opposite to the rotund, Jewish, street-educated Hartman: an abstemious Mississippi-born Christian named Walter Lanier Barber.

Barber had made something of a name for himself in Florida, quitting school in order to focus on broadcasting, a trade he had not been much interested until he realized that he was good at it. When Crosley bought the Reds in February 1934 and renamed the ballpark Crosley Field, he decided to place game broadcasts on WLW's sister station, WSAI, which had gone on the air in 1923.

Crosley charged Larry MacPhail, his new majordomo, with locating a good young broadcaster. Barber got the gig, earning $25 per week from WSAI in 1934 which, during the Depression, was a handsome wage for an inexperienced young man. Barber announced a few games, filled in as needed in his position as "staff announcer," and, most importantly, watched and learned from big-league players, writers, and radio men.

Barber was not a disciple of the Hartman school — not that there could have been anyone much like Hartman — instead tilting toward the big, authoritarian, learned voices of early mikemen like Ted Husing and Graham McNamee.

When "Red" Barber (so-called for his shock of flaming hair) called games on WSAI, some fans preferred his prepared, dispassionate style to that of Hartman, and the station raised the youngster's pay to $50 per week for 1935. That season, through Crosley's connections, General Mills began to sponsor Reds games on WSAI, and the giant company's marketing muscle began to pull that station's games even with those on WFBE.

That fall, Barber called Ohio State football on WLW, further burnishing his regional reputation. In 1936, WSAI began broadcasting every Reds home game and re-creating all road contests, except those originating from Brooklyn and New York. WSAI did not broadcast games on the Sabbath, but WCPO (formerly WFBE) did all home games and some road re-creations and proudly aired games on Sundays.

In 1936, Hartman won *TSN*'s listener poll for best baseball radio announcer, with Barber coming in sixth. That fall Barber benefitted from a series of swapped favors. The Mutual Network which, at that time, had just three stations, wanted permission to broadcast the upcoming World Series. Commissioner Landis said that a three-station network wasn't much, and Mutual volunteered to add WLW in Cincinnati to the list if that would help.

Landis approved, and the decision was made to use Barber, who had not called games over the big station, but was a Crosley employee.

So Barber got what at the time was referred to as a "hurry-up call" to sit in on the Fall Classic broadcasts and add the occasional comment. This happenstance catapulted "the Redhead" into the national spotlight.

WSAI gave Barber an assistant for 1937: Dick Bray, who for several years had chaired the team's pregame show and had done "fan in the stands" interviews. Starting in 1937, neither WSAI nor WCPO were allowed to broadcast from Crosley Field on Sundays.

Following the 1938 campaign, Barber followed Larry MacPhail to Brooklyn, where he would gain nationwide fame announcing the Dodgers. This is where most storytellers, cognizant of Barber's rise to fame and Hartman's resulting obscurity, repeat the oft-quoted trope that Red "ran Harry Hartman out of town." The truth, however, is more complex. Hartman never left Cincinnati: it was Barber who departed, lured by bigger money, a much larger potential audience, and more control over the broadcasts.

While Barber built his empire in Brooklyn, Hartman married a local girl and remained on WCPO, broadcasting games through 1941. Four years later, he was feted by local writers and players who remembered how important he had been to developing the game and its radio presence, both locally and far beyond the Ohio Valley.

Hartman was not destined for a long life, passing away in 1956 at age 53 of a heart condition. His granddaughter, playwright Karen Hartman, wrote a play about him in the early 2000s called *Going Gone*. Unfortunately, few alive remember how Hartman sounded, and the next tape someone unearths of this nearly forgotten pioneer will apparently be the first.

With Barber gone, WSAI hired Roger Baker, who had cut his teeth in Buffalo, to announce the Reds in 1939. Hedging their bets, General Mills and Socony Vacuum Oil co-sponsored games on both WSAI and Hartman's WCPO; placing ads simultaneously on competing stations was unusual for the time.

In addition to covering home games live, WSAI also featured dramatic re-creations of each day's game at 9:00 p.m. There was plenty of drama, as the Reds won the NL pennant in 1939, their first in two decades, and then repeated the feat *and* won the World Series the following season.

With Hartman's departure from Reds broadcasts in 1942, Sam Balter, former Olympic basketball player, took over on WCPO. He lasted just one year, though, and the station then gave up baseball until 1945. The most important new baseball man in town was Waite Hoyt, who WKRC hired to initiate its baseball broadcasts in 1942.

Hoyt's hiring turned out to be a genius move, but things could have easily turned out very differently. WKRC had initially pursued Dizzy Dean, but the ex-Yankees' pitcher got the nod instead. Barber may have recommended Hoyt, as he had given Hoyt his first opportunity in radio on the Dodgers' postgame show in 1941. Hired by WKRC, Hoyt teamed with Dick Nesbitt.

Cincinnati Gas & Electric sponsored Baker & Bray's calls on WSAI, while Burger Beer soon began a relationship with Hoyt that lasted more than two decades.

Hoyt's hiring bothered a lot of radio men. The number of ex-players in the booth was increasing and Hoyt, with no play-by-play experience, was initially more than a little raw. Yet the ex-jock's way with words won over a lot of fans.

Following the 1944 season, the Reds sold exclusive rights to WCPO, meaning that Baker and Bray were through on WSAI. Baker went into radio administration, while Bray hooked on with WCKY. (Interestingly, while many sources say that the Reds allowed no home contests to be broadcast on the Sabbath, Cincinnati newspapers of the time clearly show Sunday games on their radio schedules.)

Lee Allen, who would become one of baseball's preeminent historians before his untimely death in 1969, served in 1945 as Hoyt's assistant, but was bounced after the season when he tried to get his salary increased.

It was all Waite Hoyt from that moment on, working alone for Burger from 1946 through 1951 in Crosley Field's roofless press box, which let in rain, burning-hot sun, the songs of the boo-birds, and even the occasional feathered bird.

When it rained, Hoyt would tell stories. Stories about his days with the Yankees, with Ruth and Gehrig and Dugan and Shawkey and Huggins. His stories, in fact, were such hits that a local company issued two record albums full of them: *The Best of Waite Hoyt in the Rain*, volumes 1 and 2.

As a matter of accuracy, the taciturn but oddly emotive Hoyt always called his games in the past tense ("Pinson swung and hit the ball to shortstop. Davenport threw it to first and the batter was out"). Some broadcast historians feel that he is the best ex-player to ever call play-by-play. Many former players have enjoyed fine careers as analysts, but only a few have carried the play-by-play load with distinction; this short list is topped by Jack Graney, Bob Uecker, Ken Singleton, Buddy Blattner, and Duane Kuiper. Some might add Ken Harrelson to that list, over the strenuous objections of others.

Hoyt lived hard early in life. He drank to excess on many occasions; on June 19, 1945, he disappeared after a game and went missing for two days. No contemporary explanation was given for why he disappeared, but it easily could have been related to his alcoholism. After this, Hoyt checked himself into AA, cleaned up, and became healthy enough to live to a ripe old age.

There were occasional blips along the way. On Opening Day 1946, Hoyt's microphone wire was accidentally cut and he talked into a dead mike for 45 minutes — the type of embarrassment that would soon become impossible given the many people involved in producing each broadcast.

Like many other clubs, the Reds began building an extensive radio network following World War II. Thirteen stations were on the line by 1947; 27 by 1950. Hoyt got an assistant in 1952, Bob Gilmore, who was hired to take some of the load off the veteran broadcaster, who had added television to his resumé.

Red Thornburgh, who back in the 1930s had worked on WCPO with Hartmann, hosted the first Reds' television games, which aired in 1947 on Crosley's experimental television station WX8CT. Newspapers noted that only 100 sets were owned by Cincinnatians at the time, but that crowds flocked to local watering holes to view the games on tiny little screens.

Thornburgh remained a local media fixture for years. The next season, however, Hoyt's WCPO radio calls were simulcast for the 32 home games carried by WLWT, the city's first television station. (WLWT was yet another Powel Crosley venture.) The Reds even beamed two exhibition games from Crosley Field. Before the season began, WLWT upped its power enough to send images within a 40-mile radius of Cincinnati.

WLWT was the only TV station in town until spring 1949, when WKRC and WCPO took to the air. Crosley decided to show all 77 of the team's home games, almost immediately assigning them to WCPO. Burger Beer was the team's first television sponsor, bringing along its already strong brand identification with the team's radio broadcasts.

Hoyt once again was working alone, this time in two media! Only the more wealthy fans could afford the luxury of a TV set in 1948, however, as these primitive receivers cost $200–$300, and maintenance and installation could run the bill up another hundred bucks.

Crosley's importance to the history of radio and television — especially his role in spreading the technology to Middle America — cannot be overstated. Using baseball to bring listeners and viewers to his stations, he literally helped build a new sports-media culture.

Following 1949, the Reds adopted a more reasonable TV strategy, airing only on WCPO. WLWT had become an NBC affiliate after Crosley had sold his company in 1945 to what later became Avco Corporation. The club showed many home day games but did not televise Sunday and night games so as to not adversely affect their gate.

Hoyt and Gilmore did all the radio and television through 1954. Early that August, Gilmore — who did statistics and read commercials as well as handing some play-by-play — criticized the sixth-place Reds and their General Manager, Gabe Paul. On August 7, he was forced to resign under pressure from Burger Beer, though he returned to his daily radio sports show on WCPO four days later.

Gilmore noted at the time that the Reds "wanted a cheerleader instead of a reporter." Hoyt, in turn, averred that Gilmore was very good at his job, and that the Reds had never told him what to say, "But then I never criticize or editorialize, and I'm very optimistic." (Truly words of wisdom for someone wanted to keep a sports broadcast job for a decade or more.)

Perhaps not coincidentally, Burger took the Reds to WSAI radio for 1955, and Jack Moran became Hoyt's new sidekick. An all-purpose broadcaster — disc jockey, kids' show host, and sportscaster — Moran was given to loud sports jackets and was an enthusiastic booster of "Smoooooooooth Burger" beer. He lasted just one year on TV, but remained with Hoyt on radio until 1962.

In 1955, the Reds decided to begin producing some live road telecasts over WCPO. Despite this innovation, their television situation soon became almost haunted — one might call it Gilmore's Curse.

WLWT outbid WCPO for the Reds' TV rights in 1956, retaining those rights for nearly 40 years. With the change in stations came a new sponsor, Hudepohl — another of the many regional beer brands popular before giant national breweries such as Budweiser and Miller crushed or bought out their smaller rivals.

WLWT and "Hudie" wanted a bold new television presence so, in September 1955, they signed Bert Wilson, who had been the Cubs' radio voice since the early 1940s, as their voice for 1956. Always overweight and beset by nerves, Wilson had three days earlier retired from the Cubs' booth, literally exhausted from the work and the travel.

Doing just 53 games — 30 of them on the road — on television for the Reds would be a great chance for Wilson to gear back somewhat and stay in the business while relaxing his jumpy demeanor. Wilson had little more than a month to anticipate his new opportunity, though. He passed away on November 5, 1955 at age 44 in Mesa, Arizona. In the hospital for two weeks to deal with nervous exhaustion, he died of a massive, sudden heart attack.

WLWT called on veterans George Bryson and Mark Scott to cover the telecasts in the wake of Wilson's death. Scott, voice of the Pacific Coast League Hollywood Stars earlier in the 1950s, served as second chair on Reds telecasts in 1956 and 1957. Following that, he did some television in Los Angeles, then created and hosted the popular Home Run Derby show in 1959. He also died of a heart attack on July 13, 1960, at age 45.

Bryson, born in 1914, had called basketball for the NBA Cincinnati Royals and the University of Cincinnati and had previously been, for more than a decade, the play-by-play man for Fresno's California League team. He continued as top dog on Reds broadcasts until 1960. Bryson worked with former Reds first baseman Frank McCormick from 1958 through 1960, then returned to California for a big-league job with the expansion Angels in 1962. Weirdly, Bryson also died well before his time, passing away from heart trouble in late 1964 while working Kansas City Athletics games.

Ed "Gus" Kennedy — who had narrated television accounts of NBA Royals games — took over TV play-by-play in the club's pennant-winning 1961 season and kept the job through 1970.

Despite evolving far from the media centers on either coast, the Reds' television broadcasts in these years were groundbreaking, thanks in part to adventurous policies established years before by the forward-thinking Crosley. In 1960, the team was one of only three (the others being the Cubs and the White Sox) to show games in color, bringing 23 home contests' worth of bright hues into living rooms and bars via WLWT and three network affiliates. WLWT became, in the mid-1960s, the first station in the U.S. to broadcast entirely in color.

Among the many innovations or pioneering aspects of Cincinnati's telecasts on WLWT were using a four-camera set up while other teams made do with only two. The Reds also adopted Zoomar (Zoom) lenses before many other clubs, and WLWT carried exhibition games, which few other teams televised, as well as extensive preseason programming.

Hudepohl Brewing, as the Reds' primary sponsor on WLWT, sponsored an advertorial column "written" by Gus Kennedy called "That's My Opinion …What's Yours?" which ran in area newspapers. Other late 1950s advertisers on Cincy TV games included Standard Oil of Ohio (Sohio) and local Ford dealers.

The team's broadcast revenues at this point were $350,000, about what the Cardinals, Cubs, and Pirates were earning. (Of course, the Cubs were one of two teams in the huge Chicago market.)

By the early 1960s, Hudie had a half-sponsorship on the telecasts, with other companies (Sun Oil, General Cigar, R.J. Reynolds, and Brown & Williamson tobacco) buying smaller shares. The team's surprise NL flag in 1961 helped it negotiate higher rights fees. Unfortunately, the Reds then locked themselves into a long-term deal that guaranteed $500,000 in annual broadcast fees. While that was very good money in 1962, it was well below-market by 1969 — only half of what most other NL clubs were earning for their rights.

Waite Hoyt, back to radio exclusively, kept sailing along. By 1957, WKRC had nabbed the air rights and had 45 stations on its network. In 1962, Jack Moran quit the station to take another job, and Gene Kelly — a 6-foot-8 former pro baseball player who'd spent 10 years on the Phillies' broadcast team — signed to team with Hoyt.

After just two years, though, Kelly departed to become a staff broadcaster for KMOX in St. Louis, never to do baseball play-by-play again. On January 27, 1964, Burger announced that Claude Sullivan would be Hoyt's new No. 2 on radio.

Sullivan, who had called radio sports since 1945, was beloved in the area for his award-winning broadcasts of University of Kentucky basketball and football. Eight-time Kentucky Sportscaster of the Year, Sullivan had even described Olympic basketball from the 1960 games in Rome.

The Reds almost won in 1964, coming up achingly short, and manager Fred Hutchinson died of cancer after the season. In summer 1965, Sullivan also began experiencing throat and chest maladies.

After the 1965 season, the Reds parted ways — after more than two decades — with Burger Beer. Another regional brewery, Wiedemann of Northern Kentucky, signed on as the team's new sponsor, a move that might have had something to do with Claude Sullivan.

Wiedemann did not desire Hoyt's presence on the air because of his long-standing identification with Burger. Therefore, the legendary mikeman was allowed to "retire" from the broadcasts and remain with his longtime employers as a PR representative.

Amid rumors that the brewery and WCKY would select Mel Allen, Ken Coleman, or Reds PA announcer Paul Sommerkamp to head the radio broadcast, Sullivan himself got the lead job in October 1965, with Jim McIntyre picked as his sidekick. McIntyre had earned his local bona fides by calling minor-league games in Louisville.

Sullivan soon began a rapid, unexpected descent from his broadcasting peak. In July 1966, he was hospitalized with a malignant tumor in his chest and missed a month, returning in mid-August. Eric Bose of WCKY did the pregame in his absence, and McIntyre pulled extra duty at the mike.

Early in 1967, with Sullivan's health still an issue, the Reds persuaded popular pitcher Joe Nuxhall to retire as a player and join the radio team. Sullivan gamely soldiered on, finishing the season and continuing his treatments at the Mayo Clinic, where he passed away at age 43 on December 6, 1967.

Sullivan, lauded to this day at the University of Kentucky, was a rare breed of sports broadcaster: a generalist who knew all of his sports and could adjust his cadence and his technique to each. With his passing, Nuxhall became the No. 2 on radio, with McIntyre ascending to the top. Nuxhall was never smooth on play-by-play, but the left-hander was a favorite in the Queen City, hailing from nearby Hamilton and carrying the legend of his boyhood big-league debut.

In August 1968, the Reds and a new sponsor, Stroh's Beer, inked a two-year deal with radio powerhouse WLW. What started as a short-term engagement turned into a 45-year partnership with no end in sight. WLW was clearly going heavily into sports, also nabbing the rights to Royals basketball in June 1969.

Frank McCormick departed the telecasting team after 1968; a few years later, he joined the front office of the Yankees. Needing a color man to work with Kennedy, the Reds were delighted to snap up Pee Wee Reese in March 1969, days after NBC had cut the Dodgers' legend from their Game of the Week telecasts. Reese had to read about his termination in the newspapers.

Kennedy and Reese announced 40 telecasts in both 1969 and 1970, 35 of them on the road. The Reds vacated outdated Crosley Field in mid-1970, beginning their era of dominance as baseball's "Big Red Machine" at new Riverfront Stadium.

The 1970 Reds mashed their way to an NL West title and won the second National League Championship Series. NBC used McIntyre on its radio and TV coverage of the World Series, which Cincinnati lost in five games to Baltimore.

McIntyre suddenly retired due to a serious health issue shortly after the World Series, necessitating a search for a new radio voice. The Reds considered Harry Caray, but perhaps his long association with Budweiser and Busch beers was not a plus from Stroh's point of view. Instead, the Reds reached into the minors and emerged with 26-year-old Al Michaels.

Michaels had spent the previous three seasons as sports director for a pair of Honolulu TV stations and, more importantly, doing play-by-play for the PCL Hawaii Islanders games. (Harry Kalas and, later, Ken Wilson also leapt from Hawaii to the majors.) Marathon Oil joined Stroh's as a co-sponsor in 1971, when the Reds also broadcast 15 exhibition games.

WLWT's new sponsor for 1971, Pabst Beer, deemed Pee Wee Reese and Ed Kennedy too old-fashioned. In a prime example of how one should never ditch Plan A without having a Plan B, the Reds then spent six years with short-lived and little-remembered TV broadcast teams, using three play-by-play men and five different color men during that span. Bob

Waller, the No. 2 in 1971 to colorless Tom Hedrick, was fired for his overt criticism, a pattern that Waller would repeat when with the White Sox.

The Reds' reliance on non-local, workmanlike TV play-by-play broadcasters like Hedrick, Charlie Jones, and Ken Coleman didn't work. It was completely out of step, moreover, with the club's time-tested and successful process of selecting their radio broadcasters: a sound strategy of finding talented young voices and giving them the reins.

As the Reds continued to play great baseball, Michaels impressed with his feel for the game and with his golden voice. He and Nuxhall worked closely for three years, after which Michaels headed to San Francisco to become the Giants' top voice.

The loss of Michaels hurt, but it allowed the Reds to recruit the man who to this day remains the club's voice. On January 21, 1974, the Reds announced the hiring of a new radio play-by-play man: 31-year-old Marty Brennaman. Coming off his third consecutive award as Virginia Sportscaster of the Year, Brennaman had called International League Tidewater Tides games for three years, also announcing ABA Virginia Squires basketball for four seasons.

The young talent's first-ever Reds game was a trial by fire as, on Opening Day 1974, Hank Aaron tied Babe Ruth's career record of 714 home runs. Brennaman's call was excited but assured, and he was on his way.

Over the years, Brennaman has become as much a part of Cincinnati baseball as any player or ballpark. He never appears to relax, and his intensity is his foremost trait and probably his greatest asset. Like Harry Caray, Bob Prince, and others, Brennaman has always had an edge to his voice that intimated something great — or awful — was about to happen to the boys. His persona and his delivery make for riveting listening.

From 1974 through 2007, Brennaman and Nuxhall on 700 WLW were one of the most-loved and most enduring broadcast pairs in baseball history. Brennaman's edginess left plenty of room for Nuxhall to hang back, and each benefitted by learning from the other. The duo became best friends and chaired a remarkably popular radiocast, as the dynastic club's network grew to more than 125 stations by 1978, with Stroh's remaining as the key sponsor. A local company even produced and sold "Marty and Joe's" potato chips.

Because of his enormous popularity among Reds fans, which translates to ironclad job security, Brennaman has been one of the few successful broadcasters in baseball history who could be characterized as a "ripper." Part of that dynamic is that Brennaman has used his sharp tongue mostly on opponents, their fans, and the umpires.

Unlike many successful, driven men in the public eye, Brennaman can make fun of himself — once referring to himself as "Morty Birmingham" after an angry listener wrote that, if the announcer was going to call Houston's team "The Astronomicals," then he should refer to himself by a new name, too. Brennaman brought a bust of Elvis Presley into the radio booth for luck, where it remained for a season.

In 1988, Commissioner Bart Giamatti summoned Brennaman and Nuxhall to his office in New York City over their role in the Dave Pallone–Pete Rose incident, when the Reds' player-manager allegedly poked the umpire during an argument. Giamatti called the

For more than 40 years, Marty Brennaman has made sure that Queen City fans know that "This One Belongs to the Reds!" (Wikimedia Commons)

broadcasters on the carpet for their understandably pointed commentary, which was alleged to have incited the fans against the umpire. Nuxhall, in particular, got in trouble for accurately referring to Pallone as a "scab."

Perhaps saltier and even less worried about reprimand, Brennaman came under fire in 2007 for calling a particularly rough road trip the baseball equivalent of "the Bataan Death March." The following year, he insulted Cubs fans on the air.

Marty and Nuxie built their legend on radio while the Cincinnati television picture was fuzzy for many years. While the club's TV announcers weren't consistent, at least the club's plan was. From 1963–80, the Reds' telecast 34–45 games per season, most of them from the road, to avoid overexposure. By 1978, Pabst beer was the team's largest sponsor on the tube.

Bill Brown, a WLWT sportscaster, joined the Reds' TV team in 1976. Brown has been announcing in the majors ever since, although some find his play-by-play perhaps a bit dry. Brown worked in the Queen City until 1983, when he left to do cable work in Pittsburgh before finding a permanent home with the Astros.

Ray Lane and Ken Wilson continued the lackluster parade on television until 1984, when future Hall of Famer Joe Morgan became the first (and, so far, only) African American Reds broadcaster in 1985.

In 1986, the Reds began using Brennaman and Nuxhall on both TV and radio, filling out their booth for a few years with another series of undistinguished broadcasters. They included Steve Physioc, Andy MacWilliams, Jay Randolph, and much-admired ex-catcher Johnny Bench — who lamentably was asked to do a job he wasn't capable of.

Cincinnati made some short-lived forays into cable in the early 1980s. The SportsTime regional network aired 52 home games in 1984 before going belly-up. Cable games did not return to Southern Ohio until 1990, when the anodyne Steve Lamar ("That's a striiiiiiiiiiiiike!") and former Reds first baseman Gordy Coleman called the action on SportsChannel Ohio. Brennaman's signature presence was deemed necessary enough that he, too, was worked into the cablecast team.

In 1993, the Reds finally found a solution on television. George Grande lasted two decades in Cincy after calling games for the Yankees and Cardinals for two years each. While Grande was not distinctive, he was a true professional who never embarrassed the club and brought out the best in his color man, former pitcher Chris Welsh. The two did 90 games on cable and WLWT in 1993.

The 1994–95 labor war took a lot of the heart out of baseball in the smaller markets, so WLWT, under pressure from NBC to free up more prime time hours for network shows, chose to get out of baseball at the end of its contract in 1995. This essentially killed baseball on "free TV" in Cincinnati, though WSTR aired 50 games in 1996 and split 45 more with WKRC the next two years. From then on, the Reds chose to put their whole television package on cable.

SportsChannel was rebranded as Fox Sports Ohio in 1999. It has been the club's telecast outlet ever since, showing 100 games for the first time in 2003 and increasing to 145 games in 2007. Marty Brennaman, preferring his first home in radio, has eschewed television work since 1998.

Grande was signed to work 100 games per season, and chose not to call the extra 45 games that the club planned to air in 2007. Therefore, Fox Sports and the Reds added Marty's son Thom — who had broadcast the Cubs and Diamondbacks as well as serving as a baseball and football voice for Fox — to the broadcast crew. Neither he nor ex-Reds pitcher Jeff Brantley, hired in 2006, could fill the extra-large shoes of Marty and Joe. The club's decision to let Brantley — whose voice is as thick as molasses and is often behind the play — handle radio play-by-play is perplexing.

WLW cut back its commitment to Nuxhall, whose advancing age had made him noticeably slower on the air, around the same time. The move caused a predictable firestorm. The "old left-hander's" passing in December 2007 was the end of an era for Reds fans, and the team has not yet been able to replace him on the radio. Brennaman hoped that his hand-picked choice, Steve Stewart, would catch on. Reds fans never really bonded with Stewart, though, and he decamped for Kansas City after four years.

Waite Hoyt: Former Yankees pitching star Waite Hoyt entertained Queen City fans on radio and television from 1942 through 1965. His rain delay stories, in which he recalled his times with Ruth, Gehrig, et al., were just as popular as his game broadcasts. (National Baseball Hall of Fame and Museum)

Grande's decision to take nearly the entire 2010 season off from Reds TV broadcasts did not cause the same level of fan heartbreak as Nuxie's passing, but it did shine a spotlight on the club's uncertain plans. With Marty cutting back on his games, and with Thom doing Fox network duty on weekends, Cincinnati has at times in the recent past employed as many as eight broadcasters. Fans for a time rarely had any idea of who would work a particular broadcast.

How much does that lack of stability matter? Sometimes, the intense loyalty fans feel for "their" announcers can overcome the letdown from a mediocre team. In a market with a long, revered tradition like the Queen City, the importance of much-loved broadcasters ranging from Harry Hartman and Marty Brennaman — behind the mike on Reds games for almost 40 years — certainly matters a great deal.

TRIBAL GATHERING

CLEVELAND INDIANS BROADCASTING HISTORY

*"I consider it a kick in the teeth and a lousy thing to happen
after all the years I have been with the Indians."*
— Jimmy Dudley, after being fired in 1968

WHAT DOES IT MEAN TO HAVE A SUCCESSFUL CAREER IN BASEBALL broadcasting, and what kind of shelf life does a broadcaster have? How much of a team's identity is tied up in its voices?

The Cleveland Indians have been broadcasting for more than 80 years, but few of their voices have penetrated the national consciousness. As a result, the Tribe's list of memorable broadcasters is nowhere near as long as the team's history.

In part, this is because Cleveland is surrounded on all sides. With Pittsburgh to the east, Detroit to the north, Cincinnati to the south, and Chicago to the west, the Indians' media network is circumscribed geographically.

Cleveland's top baseball broadcasters overlapped in an 80-year chain, from Tom Manning to Jack Graney to Jimmy Dudley to Ken Coleman to Herb Score to Tom Hamilton. While these mikemen all had/have their adherents in Northeast Ohio, they are not well known nationally.

One reason is that the Indians have historically not been proactive in their broadcasting, rarely investing in developing quality young voices. When the club did this — as with Dudley, Hamilton, and Matt Underwood — the results have been good. Yet from the 1950s through the 1980s, the team took a reactive and, often, ham-handed approach to its broadcasting.

Even though he wasn't the first to call baseball on the radio in Cleveland — a former local semi-pro player and radio host named Floyd Bradley called some early-season contests on WHK in 1927 — Tom Manning was the most popular for several years.

Manning was first the club's public address announcer, using a megaphone at League Park to inform the fans of pitching changes and lineups. The Tribe brought him aboard to do radio in 1928, figuring he had a big voice, and they were right; Manning was so loud that he blew out a microphone in his first broadcast.

Unlike Red Barber or Ted Husing, Manning had a quintessential "regular guy" voice: his tone was earthy and his manner enthusiastic. Manning was hired to cover the 1929 World Series on radio and, even though he was not a regular broadcaster in 1932, also called the Fall Classic for NBC.

The *Sandusky Register* noted in 1932 that "Manning's style of announcing is particularly suited to world series broadcasts as it is more colorful than some of the more technical or professional baseball announcers."

By 1932 Manning's employer, WTAM, was part of the NBC network and therefore forced to carry more programming from New York. That meant that the station had to give up Indians baseball; WHK secured the rights instead.

Ellis VanderPyl began the season as the Indians announcer, but was soon fired by the club's sponsor. Tribe GM Bill Evans thought that Jack Graney would fit the job better, and the former outfielder called home games and re-created road games for the remainder of the campaign.

Graney, the first ex-ballplayer to make any kind of a mark as a broadcaster, had a high-pitched voice and liked to spice up his broadcasts with humor — a habit that some serious-minded fans and reporters did not necessarily appreciate. His knowledge of each American League ballpark as a former player allowed Graney to inject these sometimes dry recaps with real baseball insight and color.

On July 20, 1933, Graney was seriously injured in an auto crash, later suing the driver of the car he was riding in for $75,000. After recuperating, Graney returned in 1934 to a new broadcasting box built expressly for him and WHK, where he covered all but Sunday contests at League Park. Sponsored by General Mills, Graney entertained Northeast Ohio and buffed up his national profile by serving as an announcer for the 1935 World Series.

Interestingly enough, Tom Manning was named Cleveland's Broadcaster of Year in 1935 by fan vote, despite not serving as a regular broadcaster! Though Manning called nine World Series, he has been nearly forgotten despite his one-time national profile.

General Mills and co-sponsor Socony Vacuum Oil came up with all sorts of sponsorship tie-ins during the 1930s and 1940s. In June 1940, for instance, Graney and sidekick Pinky Hunter re-created some Indians-at-Boston games while at a Cedar Point grocery as part of the store's "Wheaties Days."

During World War II, baseball took its role as the national game quite seriously, raising money for the war effort and cementing its place in the community. On July 7, 1942, the

National League All-Star team, having captured the annual Midsummer Classic two days before, took the field against a team of Army and Navy stars in Cleveland, collecting $700,000 for military relief funds. Graney was behind the mike for that special exhibition, along with Bob Elson and Waite Hoyt.

On May 12, 1943, Graney's son John was killed in a plane crash at Fort Bragg, North Carolina, and the father learned the terrible news while calling a game at League Park. Pinky Hunter finished the game and handled the broadcasts on his own for several days after.

Cleveland had no regularly scheduled broadcasts in 1945, with WHK — now a Mutual Network station — forced to carry soap operas and other daytime programming. But when Bob Feller returned from the service to take the mound on August 24, WGAR carried the contest with Graney and Bob Neal calling the action.

With the Indians reportedly up for sale in 1946, no Cleveland radio station would commit to broadcasting the Indians' games. Though no aircasts were scheduled, the club retained the popular Graney as its publicity director.

When Bill Veeck bought the team from Alva Bradley's majority stockholders in June 1946, he immediately threw open the airwaves, allowing any station to broadcast home games and re-create road contests. Four stations took advantage of Veeck's offer, starting on June 28.

WGAR was the sole survivor for 1947, inking a three-year deal with Veeck and tabbing Graney and Van Patrick to cover the action. General Mills remained the sponsor. On July 22, "Wheaties Days" festivities featured Graney and Van Patrick re-creating a road game from Meyers Lake Amusement Park.

Standard Brewing signed up as the Tribe's sponsor in 1948, and WJW arranged to take over the contract and air the games. Jimmy Dudley, who years earlier had served as Russ Hodges' wingman in Chicago, joined the Tribe's radio team as its no. 1 voice. Old pro Graney assisted Dudley. The Indians' games were carried by a regional network that began the season at 12 stations and grew to 26 by September.

Even though 1948 would be a great year for the Indians — the club won the World Series and its broadcasters covered road games in person for the first time — WJW struggled to clear airtime for its baseball games. The station had network commitments until 3:00 p.m. each day and couldn't carry any action that started before then.

The Indians added television in 1948, with Patrick and Paul Hodges calling the action over WEWS, with the club's first telecast on May 15. WEWS used four cameras (a high number for the time) and a staff of 15 for the games. Only about 3,400 sets were estimated to be in use in Northeast Ohio at the time, but the club's clinching of the pennant led to hundreds of fans buying TV sets to watch the World Series.

Patrick departed for Detroit for 1949, as Bob Neal took over calling the action on television as well as emceeing a weekly WEWS roundtable program starring Veeck. Leisy Brewing sponsored the Indians' TV package in 1950 and 1951. Neal, who also worked NFL Browns games, remained connected with the Indians for a quarter-century.

Standard Brewing, maker of Erin Brew, sponsored games both on new rights holder WERE-AM and FM and on WXEL-TV, paying $250,000 for the combined package in 1950. WERE carried the Tribe on radio through 1972, retaining the Indians' radio rights as various television stations gained and lost the privileges.

Because of the team's success on the field in the late 1940s and early 1950s, other radio stations wanted to stay connected to the Indians. As an example, WJW hired stars Al Rosen and Bob Lemon to play DJ and host a program called "Pitching Platters."

Neal and Red Jones, a former AL umpire, called the Tribe's games on TV in 1952 and 1953 before the club took control of broadcast personnel in 1954 and made some changes. Former Boston play-by-play man Jim Britt became the new No. 1, while Ken Coleman, already the Cleveland Browns' announcer, served as his second.

Change was also necessary on the radio because, in August 1953, Jack Graney announced that he would retire. On September 4, the Indians held a tribute night for Graney at Cleveland Stadium, with Tris Speaker as Master of Ceremonies. Fans kicked in $8,000 as a parting gift for the beloved broadcaster.

The Indians won an AL record 111 games en route to the pennant in 1954. Dudley, by now flying his own airplane on road trips, called the All-Star Game and the World Series on radio for the Mutual Broadcast System. His new partner on WERE was 30-year-old Ed Edwards, who had been with the station for only a few months after calling minor-league games in Rochester and Hartford. For this season, Standard Brewing sublicensed half the ads to local Chevrolet dealers.

With a hugely popular team powered by a stellar pitching staff, the Indians attempted to boost attendance at home by becoming the only AL team (along with the NL Cardinals) to televise all their road games, despite the expense of renting phone lines and hiring crews in other cities. After 1954, however, WXEL cut back dramatically on the number of telecasts and, following 1955, became a CBS affiliate as WEWS regained the Cleveland TV rights.

The Indians canned Edwards on February 1, 1956. The club gave the press no reason for the move, but Edwards had previously lost one minor-league job for making intemperate remarks at a banquet and was later bounced from a job with the Athletics.

Gil Gilhooley of Toledo was mooted as a potential replacement for Edwards. A former major-league player, Gil was father of the late Frank Gilhooley, who broadcast Toledo Mud Hens baseball and many other sports from 1953 to 2009 and was much beloved in northwest Ohio.

But the new guy who came on-board to assist Dudley in 1956 was actually an old guy: Tom Manning. The 57-year-old veteran lasted just one year, though; he could barely see the ball and quit on the advice of his doctor.

Britt departed after doing four years of Indians TV games. Ken Coleman became the lead voice, assisted from 1958 through 1960 by Bill McColgan, yet another Browns announcer brought over to do baseball.

Nobody knew that the Indians would not win another pennant for more than four decades. Cleveland, still a marquee club, received $350,000 for their media rights in 1957, and their $500,000 rights fees in 1958 ranked second in the AL, tied with Detroit. The Carling Brewery was the key sponsor on both television and radio, with Standard of Ohio taking a share on the tube and Central National Bank doing the same on the wireless.

Bob Neal, out of the picture since losing his TV job in 1953, was now back, working on radio with Dudley on a 45-staton network. Neal was well known for his work on CBS college football and for covering the Browns for six years; he had also called the Game of the Day and the World Series for Mutual Broadcasting in 1955 and 1956.

Unfortunately, Neal and Dudley did not get along at all. Dudley was the top dog and Neal wanted that job in the worst way. The two could not stand each other's presence, and they did not talk to each other either on the air or off. In 1960, Dudley endured another headache when the IRS hauled the broadcaster into court, saying that he had claimed too many business deductions.

Certainly their styles differed: Dudley was pleasant, breezy, and uncontroversial, while Neal loved to needle, second-guess, and display his rapier-like wit. Longtime Tribe beat writer Terry Pluto wrote in *The Curse of Rocky Colavito* that Neal's tone was "bitter and sarcastic," while Dudley's biggest sin as a broadcaster might have been his "lack of variety."

For most of the period from 1957 through 1967, tethered together but hardly a team, Dudley and Neal narrated the fortunes of a decaying franchise. The frigidity in the booth provided a distinct contrast to Cleveland's increasingly chummy and incompetent front office clique.

WJW gained the club's television rights for 1961 and held them for nearly two decades. Bill McColgan was pushed aside, a casualty of conflicts with Browns football. His replacement was 39-year-old Harry Jones, a sportswriter for the *Plain Dealer* and the chair of the local BBWAA. Carling and Sohio sponsored the broadcasts as media rights shot up to $700,000.

The next year Sugardale Provisions, a meats company, took a one-third sponsorship. Neal was moved to TV to separate him from Dudley, while Jones shifted to radio. This arrangement lasted through 1964 and allowed Neal to announce the Japanese baseball All-Star game, live from Tokyo, on ABC with Jim McKay in July 1962.

The Indians at this time were utilizing seven cameras for the games on their TV network, with five for local contests. The production crew needed an extra-powerful Zoom lens for the mandatory center field camera location because the fence at canyon-like Cleveland Stadium was so far from home plate.

In late 1963, with Ken Coleman busy calling Browns football, former Tribe pitcher Herb Score auditioned as a television commentator during two late-season contests. Fan and press reaction was good enough that the Indians replaced Coleman with Score on the broadcast crew for 1964, making him the first ex-player in the team's booth since Graney.

That December, Coleman took part in an interesting venture, describing the play-by-play of the Chicago Bears-New York Giants NFL championship game for a pay-per-view company called The Theater Network, which showed the gridiron title game on giant screens in several movie theaters in blacked-out Chicago.

Dudley suffered a heart attack between the 1963 and 1964 seasons, but recovered in time to resume his duties. In 1964, neophyte Score and veteran Neal worked together; in later years Score acknowledged the help Neal gave him when the ex-pitcher was getting acclimated.

Carling was still chief sponsor on both radio and television; however, more companies were buying smaller spots on the broadcasts as the trend away from major sponsors accelerated. Six companies were now advertising on Indians radio broadcasts, with three more on TV.

Pregame and postgame shows had their own sponsors as well — usually smaller, local companies like 1966 local postgame TV show underwriters BPS Paints and Harry Weintraub Clothes.

The rivalry in the radio booth was ratcheted up when WERE and the Indians named Neal and Dudley co-lead announcers in January 1965 with Score remaining on television. With Dudley and Neal nominally co-equal, the situation became even worse.

WJW signed a new three-year TV deal for 1967 and, for the first time, beamed all 46 games (mostly on weekends) in color. Carling, Sugardale, Pure Oil, and Allstate bought ad time. A 28-station network, sponsored by Duquesne Brewing, General Cigar, Sun Oil, Society National Bank, and Kahn's Meats, carried the club's action on radio, where Dudley and Neal continued as teammates and enemies.

After more than a decade of tension, Neal finally won the battle. On January 19, 1968 WERE — with the approval and input of the Indians — announced that Dudley, their radio voice for two decades, would not be rehired. Over the years, Dudley had spent his off-seasons in Tucson where the Indians had their spring training base, while Neal had solidified his relationships with the front office in Cleveland. An indication of Neal's increasing level of security was his good-natured lampooning of GM Gabe Paul at more than one off-season dinner hosted by the Cleveland BBWAA chapter.

Dudley's era was doubtlessly past by 1968. Moreover, with the Indians positing a winning record only once from 1960 through 1967, management needed to do something to convince their fans that they were worth listening to — and it was far easier to change broadcasters than clean out Cleveland's country-club front office.

It is no disrespect to Jimmy Dudley to acknowledge that times change. Styles had changed in broadcasting, in the same way that all men wore hats in the 1940s, but by the 1960s young men wouldn't be caught dead in a fedora. By the 1960s, baseball fans wanted something more from their hometown broadcasters: clinging to Red Barber's old-fashioned style of staying distant from the action and describing it with understatement did not excite the audience any longer.

Sports often serves to reinforce memories of the halcyon days of the fans' and players' youth, yet asking fans to listen daily to a voice from yesteryear is a tough sell unless the man at the mike has become a legend who can transcend changing times. Jimmy Dudley called All-Star Games and World Series; years later, he would be honored with a Frick award. He had a 20-year run as a big-league announcer — a pretty fine career for a man who was a good broadcaster but not a legend.

Gabe Paul made Bob Neal's dreams come true, trading experience for youth at the same time by installing Herb Score in the radio booth. (Score had worked as Harry Jones' analyst on television for the previous three seasons.) Happy to have someone he could mentor after undermining Dudley, Neal crowed, "Never before in the history of Cleveland Indians broadcasts has there been any rapport between the two men who did the job. This is going to be a combined effort."

Even though Dudley was a holdover from another era, so was Neal, and public reaction was sharply negative: fans didn't understand the move, which had little to do with baseball and a lot to do with office politics. Though he won the battle, Neal never matched his rival's popularity, partly because he was perceived by many contemporaries as one the game's "rippers." Fellow broadcaster Shelby Whitfield wrote in 1973, "Harry Caray and Bob Neal are a couple of veterans who have been known to second-guess managers and players from the booth. They often have been accused by players of not being fair in their reporting and slanting their reporting to the advantage of club management."

The Indians wanted another ex-player to replace Score as their radio analyst, but couldn't find anyone that to suit them. A month after Dudley was canned — too late for him to get another job for 1968 — Cleveland hired New York legend Mel Allen, bounced from the Yankees' air team in late 1964, to replace Score.

Allen's tenure on the shores of Lake Erie was not successful, including the famous occasion in which he recited a portion of "Song of Hiawatha," Henry Wadsworth Longfellow's nineteenth-century epic poem, on the air! Allen underwent surgery in December 1968, and did not broadcast baseball again until the 1980s.

Emblematic of their lack of a plan, the Indians had therefore rejected both the Red Barber and the Mel Allen broadcast philosophies, yet they still had no idea what they wanted their broadcasts to sound like.

WJW inked a new contract for TV rights in 1969, giving the club a slight raise to $800,000 in total media rights. That meant that in more than a decade, the team's rights increased less than 15%.

Neal had a minor heart attack in 1969 and missed a month. The next season, he sparked an ugly feud with star Indians pitcher Sam McDowell, calling it a "national disgrace" when McDowell failed to win his 19th game of the season for a club that finished 76-86. The newspapers, fans, and the Indians' players lined up to take their shots at Neal.

Continuing somehow to survive controversy, Neal hung on to his job when the Indians and WERE signed a new three-year deal in early 1971, beating out WGAR and WJW radio. The club got no bump in its radio rights fees, though, because WERE claimed it could not sell all of its commercial spots. By 1972, Cleveland's rights fees were eighth among AL teams.

During these fallow years, the Tribe's radio network shrank and advertising sales went down to the wire because the team was so bad. Early in 1972, WERE nearly reneged on its commitment to air exhibition games. Both club and station were operating in a country-club milieu where it seemed that nobody had to work particularly hard.

WJW sports director Dave Martin, who had replaced Score three years earlier, replaced himself on the telecasts in 1972 with Rocky Colavito. The popular former Indians' slugger had tried to insinuate himself into the picture as Cleveland's manager, but instead had to settle for a part-time coaching position and telecaster.

Finally, change came to the radio booth after 1972 when low-power, ineffectual WERE declined its option and WWWE — owned by the Indians' new owner Nick Mileti — assumed the radio rights.

The Texas Rangers had approached Herb Score about their top radio job, but Score chose to stay with the Indians, who promoted him to No. 1. Joe Tait, already the broadcaster for Mileti's NBA Cavaliers, joined Score in the radio booth. Bob Neal — having lost his patrons at the radio station and in the front office — was now out after nearly 25 years.

Mileti pushed other changes in the team's broadcast culture. In 1973, the Indians hooked up with Home Box Office cable channel (HBO), airing some Indians' games on cable systems in Northeastern Pennsylvania where HBO began. This was the first "pay cable" MLB game shown anywhere since 1964.

Unfortunately for the Indians, Bowie Kuhn asked the club not to continue the telecasts as the season went on. (Northeastern Pennsylvania was solid Yankees territory, with some Mets and a few Phillies fans.) Even before Kuhn's "request", Bob Brown, Cleveland's public relations director, said, "I doubt if it lasts." The next year, the Yankees made their own deal with HBO to broadcast 19 games.

Home Box Office, which in 1973 also showed the Cleveland's NBA Cavaliers and WHA Crusaders, was founded in New York City by Charles Dolan with the backing of media giant Time-Life. Dolan's brother Larry would purchase the Indians three decades later.

WJW retained the Tribe's over-the-air TV package in 1973 for one year, with the club retaining the rights to sell ads. Harry Jones was paired with another new partner: former Indians pitcher Mudcat Grant. The duo lasted four years but, even with Cleveland hiring Frank Robinson to be the majors' first black manager, these were hardly highlight-reel times for the Indians.

For 1976, WJW signed a new deal, paying the team $100,000 more — bringing its media income to $900,000 — in exchange for getting back the rights to sell ads. (In April 1977, WJW was forced by the FCC to change its name to WJWK-TV.)

Jones, shown the door after 1977, rejoined the Indians in 1978 to do PR work. With the club's fortunes at a low point, it would have been a great time to look for a young voice to team with Score and Joe Tait and help establish a new image for the franchise.

Instead, in 1978 WJKW selected Eddie Doucette, a basketball play-by-play man with little baseball experience, to work with the station's sports director, Jim Mueller, yet another ex-Browns and Cavaliers announcer. The pair lasted only one season. Local sportscasters Fred McLeod and Joe Castiglione called the games on TV during the final season of the station's contract in 1979 — the fourth different TV crew in four years.

WUAB signed up as the Indians' new television home in 1980, and the new deal raised the televised games from 40 to 70 and the rights fees to $1.1 million. Busch Beer was the big sponsor. Joe Tait shifted to the tube as WWWE sports director Nev Chandler teamed with Score on the radio. Chandler served with Score for five years and later announced Browns games, like almost all Indians broadcasters who weren't ex-ballplayers. The popular mikeman died at age 48 of cancer, 10 years after leaving the Tribe's broadcast team.

Despite the lack of stability in the Indians' broadcast policy, the club received a windfall in 1982 from the Cavaliers' new owner, Ted Stepien (who had fired Joe Tait in spring 1981). Stepien, intending to build an empire in the burgeoning cable industry, paid $500,000 for the rights to show 20 regular-season Indians games and six spring training contests on a new cable venture called TenTV. Bob Feller was the big attraction on the broadcasts, providing color while Castiglione handled play-by-play.

The subscription-based TV channel had a novel business plan: their $8 monthly fee was split between TenTV and the local cable operator. Some local operators in Cleveland also experimented that year with "cable radio": high-quality audio pumped through cable TV connections.

WUAB renewed its commitment to carry the Tribe's games on television in 1983; this, along with another year of cable revenue, elevated the team's rights fees to $3.4 million as TenTV changed its name to SeasonTicket and signed a new three-year contract. Feller was joined by Professional Bowling Association voice Denny Schreiner and young Jack Corrigan, who had been hired by Stepien to replace Tait on Cavs games.

Unfortunately, the city of Cleveland was not yet wired for cable, and the 487,000 subscribers on 18 suburban and exurban cable systems did not provide enough of an audience to make the channel profitable. Stepien and the Cavs therefore stopped showing Indians games in 1984 and 1985, although the existing deal promising SeasonTicket cable exclusivity required them to continue making payments to the Indians.

When that deal expired before 1986, the Tribe was left with no cable TV deal. New WWWE and WUAB contracts brought the team's broadcast income to $3 million, which ranked higher than only Seattle in the American League.

Now showing flashes of on-field competitiveness, the Indians on August 10, 1989 signed a deal with SportsChannel to telecast 11 late-season games, followed by 45 each in 1990 and 1991. Rick Manning, a former Indians outfielder and fan favorite, was the big beneficiary of SportsChannel's entry into the market. After initially teaming with Steve Lamar in 1989, Manning has since remained part of the Tribe's on-air team.

After being saddled with a series of cookie-cutter second bananas, Score — and the fans — lucked out when Tom Hamilton, former voice of Triple-A Columbus, was hired in 1990 to assist on the radio. Possessor of a hearty delivery and parsimonious with annoying

Tom Hamilton, a member of the Indians radio team since 1990, is one of baseball's best radio announcers—informative, genial, and excitable. (Erik Drost)

jargon and cute catchphrases, Hamilton is a baseball announcer. He and Score made an excellent team.

Cleveland's fan base was saddened by Score's retirement after 1997; he had been a local celebrity for more than four decades as a player and broadcaster. While never overly analytical or smooth, Score's work — including his penchant for misstatements — was loved by the fans.

Hamilton has served capably as the team's voice since 1998. The Indians made another strong long-term hire in 2000, adding Matt Underwood, a 32-year-old local television reporter and producer, as the third man on radio broadcasts. Underwood had worked on the pregame and postgame shows for several years before being brought on board. When Underwood took over TV play-by-play on television in 2007, the club's broadcasts improved substantially. He joined Mike Hegan, a former big-league first baseman who began broadcasting for the Tribe in 1988. Hegan was competent and dry, the epitome of a noncontroversial jock-analyst.

As the 1990s progressed, local media rights fees skyrocketed in baseball, driven by competition between cable and over-the-air TV. Some clubs allowed their radio and television rightsholders to sell ads in order to realize larger rights fees, while other clubs brought all aspects of their broadcasts in-house.

Larry Dolan (along with what was called a "family trust" in the local media) purchased the Indians from Dick Jacobs for what was then a record $323 million in 2000. From 2002 through 2005, the Indians put all their TV eggs in the cable basket, appearing exclusively on Fox Sports Ohio. FSO's majority owner was Cablevision, the pioneering New York–area MSO (for multi-system operator, or one company that runs several different cable systems) founded and controlled by Charles Dolan, Larry's brother, who had earlier acquired Cleveland-area RSN SportsChannel Ohio.

The FSO arrangement was disrupted in 2003 when Dish Network protested FSO's carriage fees by picking up just 75 of the club's 150 TV games. In 2005, Larry Dolan formed and financed a new sports cable network which, unlike earlier Cleveland-based ventures, was successful immediately. A major factor in STO's success was that its owner also owned the Indians — it is very difficult to launch a regional sports network without having an MLB team, which supplies an enormous amount of programming necessary to anchor the RSN.

Dolan's SportsTime Ohio (STO) has cablecast between 130 and 140 of the club's contests each season since 2006. It is not clear, however, whether STO is paying the Indians a fair price for the broadcast rights; deals between clubs and their RSNs do not usually reflect actual market rates.

Recognizing the need to build the Indians' brand on over-the-air television as well as cable, Dolan partnered with WKYC, the local NBC affiliate, to show 20 games per year on "free TV." WKYC also provides production facilities to STO for its Indians' telecasts and for Browns preseason games, as well as for college football and basketball.

WKYC's sports anchor, Jim Donovan, served for a few seasons as a play-by-play voice on the station's Indians broadcasts. He'd done a year of Class-A Vermont Reds games in the 1980s, so Donovan wasn't a total novice, but his lack of high-level experience meant that many fans were happy when he stepped aside in favor of Underwood in 2009. Donovan was the latest Browns announcer to be given the reins with the Indians as well.

In 2007, STO hired Bruce Drennan, an Indians telecaster from 1980 to 1982, as a daily talk show host and sometime Indians pregame and postgame presence. Drennan had been convicted of income tax evasion in 2004 for failing to report gambling winnings from betting on baseball. In a cheeky move, STO titled Drennan's show *All Bets Are Off*.

Cleveland waved a fond good-bye to longtime analyst Mike Hegan, who retired after 2011 following 23 years of service. He passed away late in 2013. Jim Rosenhaus, who had worked his way up through the minors before nabbing a gig as no. 3 in the radio booth, stepped capably into Hegan's shoes — making for what appears to be another solid long-term hire.

Following the 2012 season, Fox Sports purchased STO for a reported $230 million and brought it into the fold, rebranding as Fox Sports Time Ohio.

As a practical matter, it would be impossible for a Major League Baseball franchise to avoid any broadcast cross-pollination with the other three major professional leagues. Nevertheless, baseball clubs are generally better off in the long run when they resist sharing veteran voices. Piggybacking off the identities of other local teams makes it much more difficult for a ballclub to establish a unique identity on the air, which is essential when asking the fans to buy into seven months of nearly daily broadcasts from March through September.

In Cleveland, the tendency to go with the flow and stick with familiar voices created

Ken Coleman: One of sports' most identifiable voices of the 1960s and 1970s, Coleman did ten years of baseball (and 14 years of football) in Cleveland before moving to Boston. (National Baseball Hall of Fame and Museum)

thousands of mediocre baseball broadcasts. Reversing decades of reactive behavior and poor decisions, the Indians since the 1980s have a much better track record of investing in broadcasters not associated with the city's other teams.

The Tribe's current lead voices are fairly young, have traction with the team and its fan base, and are easy to listen to. That's worlds better than what's existed for most of Indians history, and more than many contemporary teams can claim.

LONG GONE, BUT NOT FORGOTTEN

DETROIT TIGERS BROADCASTING HISTORY

"Harry Heilmann, the old Tiger outfielder who broadcasts the Detroit games, is, we think, the best play-by-play man in the business."
— *Shirley Povich*, Washington Post, 1946

DETROIT'S WWJ WAS THE FIRST COMMERCIAL RADIO STATION IN the United States; the *Detroit News*-affiliated channel took to the air in 1920. By the mid-1920s, several big-league clubs had begun to dabble in radio, but Tigers owner Frank Navin initially wasn't interested in the new communications technology.

Michigan broadcast pioneer Ty Tyson, however, changed the team's history. Tyson had called some University of Michigan home football games in 1924 and attendance almost immediately shot up. Navin took notice and finally, in 1927, let the radio men into his ballpark.

Beginning April 19, 1927, WWJ aired all of Detroit's weekday and Saturday home games and, contrary to the expectations of many around the game, the broadcasts — in reality, very valuable free publicity — didn't hurt one bit. The Tigers, while not the first team on the air, were the first to regularly broadcast their games.

Most major league teams at the time refused to broadcast their Sunday games for fear of hurting attendance. The Tigers held to this strategy longer than most clubs, refusing to air home games on the Sabbath until after World War II.

Tyson's style was laconic and austere, but not unfriendly. He used slang, didn't talk down to his listeners, and didn't clog up the airwaves trying to prove how smart he was. Some, like Red Barber, found Tyson's economy almost unprofessional, but Detroit fans loved him perfectly fine for a couple of decades.

WWJ was one of the NBC network stations that carried the 1934 Tigers-Cardinals World Series. Ford Motor Company, which had paid $100,000 to sponsor the Fall Classic, used its muscle to force Commissioner Kenesaw Mountain Landis to reverse himself and allow the popular Tyson as one of the broadcasters. Afterward, radio broadcasts of the World Series almost always included at least one local announcer who had the advantage of following the club all season. Tyson was also on the crew for the 1936 NBC broadcast of the October Classic.

WXYZ, another local station, came up with an interesting idea to spread the Tigers' gospel prior to the 1934 campaign, paying $25,000 to set up a six-station Michigan Radio Network, which carried Tigers games over the rest of the state while leaving WWJ's local broadcast undisturbed.

So while Ty Tyson became the voice of the Tigers in the Motor City, few outstate Michigan baseball fans knew him at all. WXYZ's announcer, former Tigers outfielder Harry Heilmann, was the voice of baseball for Detroit fans outside of Southeast Michigan.

It's hard to overstate what baseball announcers meant to sports fans back then, as the men at the mike spent two hours or more virtually every day for six months beaming baseball into fans' living rooms and cars. Tyson's word was bond in the city, while the hold that Heilmann had on western and upper Michigan was almost incalculable.

Starting in 1935 on WXYZ at $40 a week, Heilmann was a classic storyteller, perfect for the small-town public that tuned in. Over the years he made appearances all over Michigan, doing play-by-play or public address duties at youth games as far west as St. Joseph and as far north as Ironwood.

Both WWJ and WXYZ were sponsored by General Mills and Socony Vacuum Oil, the biggest national guarantors of baseball at the time. WWJ was able to find advertisers for a 15-minute pregame show as well. A third local radio powerhouse, WJR, employed Jimmy Stevenson to re-create games at night to capture the industrial city's blue-collar audience, but these recaps did not impinge on the popularity of either Tyson or Heilmann.

By 1940, WXYZ was also airing evening re-creations of Tigers road games and Heilmann's recaps were broadcast in the Motor City proper as well as in the hinterland.

General Mills and Socony still sponsored both WXYZ and WWJ's broadcasts until 1943 when General Mills pulled out, leaving WWJ without the underwriting to continue baseball. WWJ may also have had NBC network commitments that forced the Tigers out. Either way, Heilmann now was the Tigers' sole voice.

The Tigers' road re-creations were produced in the 1940s at a studio-cum-theater on Woodward Avenue near Hudson's giant department store in downtown Detroit. This studio featured, among other attractions, continuous Movietone newsreels running all day.

In 1945, with Goebel Brewing now the sponsor, the Michigan Network had grown to 15 stations. Detroit won the first postwar world championship, besting the Chicago Cubs in a seven-game series, but the club soon fell into the doldrums. The 1950s were the beginning of Detroit's fall as one of the country's major cities, but few saw the decline at the time.

WJLB took over as the club's flagship station both on AM and FM in 1945. Two years later, the Michigan Network sported 22 stations, the biggest radio hookup in baseball. After the war, Tyson and Heilmann often appeared together on the former's daily interview show on WWJ, aired from the Michigan Central Depot near Briggs Stadium. Kids who showed up for the show received packages of Chuckles® candy.

While the Tigers were slow to grasp the strategic advantage of radio, they were quick to see the possibilities of television. WWDT, the city's first TV channel, presented the team's initial telecast on the afternoon of June 3, 1947, as the Yankees shut out the Tigers 3–0. Tyson, by now WWJ's sports director, and Paul Williams (who later held the same position) called the action.

To provide a home for Tyson and his 12-man TV crew, a new perch was built just above home plate, attached to the façade of the upper deck. This crow's nest-like broadcast booth was famous for its intimacy as well as for easily being the closest to the action in the majors. Just one week before the first telecast, the city of Detroit had honored Tyson for his 25 years at WWJ radio.

While the Tigers were happy to show games on TV, the team never made rash decisions with the new medium as some other clubs did. Detroit refused to over-commit or over-saturate the region with games, keeping a sensible and consistent approach to its broadcasting. From 1949–1974, the hometown nine was seen on the tube between 35 and 44 times each season. Through 1953, the Tigers allowed only weekday home telecasts, viewing the club's TV slate as a means to promote weekend and night games rather than reduce attendance at them.

Heilmann triumphed over alcoholism later in his life and his popularity only grew. On September 11, 1948, fans presented him with a red convertible between games of a doubleheader at Briggs Stadium. After discovering he had lung cancer in July 1950, Heilmann gamely continued to work, aided by that fact that the Tigers' radio crew still did not travel to road games.

Some of the former star slugger's friends, knowing how sick he was, began a campaign to push for his Hall of Fame induction. In January 1951, Heilmann fell just 17 votes short of earning his bronze plaque. In March, while doing exhibition games for WUBK and a 46-station radio network, Heilmann collapsed in Florida. Goebel announced Ty Tyson as the temporary replacement on April 2.

Harry Heilmann died in Detroit on July 9, one day before the 1951 All-Star Game was played at Briggs Stadium. The crowd stood for a pregame tribute to its fallen hero, who was posthumously elected to Cooperstown in January 1952.

Tyson finished out the 1951 season, the first in which Detroit road games were covered on-site, and then stepped back from the broadcasts for the final time. Goebel's new man in Detroit was Van Patrick, "The Old Announcer," an indefatigable and incorrigible Texan.

Prior to assuming Tigers radio and TV duties, Van Patrick had made his name calling NFL Detroit Lions games on WJR, which he would continue to do through 1973. He worked incredibly hard, also chairing newscasts and calling Notre Dame gridiron action along with his baseball and pro football duties. Patrick was a self-referential professional voice who loved the attention and the glory of his job.

Bob Reynolds, WWJ's new sports director, served as Patrick's second in 1952, but Goebel wanted an ex-player involved. After receiving an offer to join Goebel's team, popular veteran Bengals pitcher Dizzy Trout — who had been traded to the Red Sox during the season — retired in January 1953 to become Patrick's new co-pilot.

Trout was even folksier than Heilmann in the booth. The rookie analyst lasted only three years, largely because Patrick couldn't stand him. Trout didn't even pretend to be sophisticated, and his cornpone delivery was thick even for Detroit, which had a large population of transplanted Southerners working in the car factories.

Mel Ott, former Giants slugger and manager, had spent 1955 calling the diamond action on Mutual's Game of the Day. The Tigers and Goebel announced his hiring in January 1956, sending Trout back to the family farm.

Telephone line charges and employee travel costs had made airing road games too expensive in the early years of sports telecasts. By 1954, however, with independent companies now providing camera crews and television production trucks in each major league city, the Tigers opted to show some road contests. From seven in 1954 the total steadily increased, reaching 30 in 1960. Patrick and Trout, then Ott, did double duty on radio and TV.

Beginning in 1956, Dearborn's WKMH produced Detroit's radio games, feeding WJR night games and WWJ afternoon games. Patrick and Ott provided play-by-play to 36 stations on the radio network and a six-station television net originating with WJBK. Goebel & Speedway gasoline sponsored both radio and TV.

That year the Briggs family sold the Tigers to a group led by John Fetzer of Kalamazoo, who owned a profitable chain of radio and television stations. Fetzer assumed majority control of the team by 1958, becoming one of the most influential owners in the American League. The broadcast pioneer also spent a lot of time in the next two decades helping craft baseball's national television plans.

On November 21, 1958, the 49-year-old Ott died in New Orleans a week after a serious automobile crash in Mississippi. He had made strides in his new vocation and was seen as a rising star behind the mike. After a brief period of mourning, the Tigers snapped up another Southerner as his replacement: Arkansas native George Kell, who had broadcast one season of CBS's Game of the Week.

Throughout its history on the air, the Tigers have never been short of former players in the booth, most of them with local connections. Heilmann, Trout, Kell, Al Kaline, Jim Price, Norm Cash, and Jim Northrup are but some of the former hometown heroes who have served as Motown mikemen.

Immediately popular in Detroit, Kell was genial, easygoing, and didn't make as many howling mistakes as many other inexperienced ex-players. His first year, on WKMH in 1959, was the last with Goebel as the club's chief sponsor. That was bad news for Van Patrick, who had become very closely identified with the brewer, a competitor of the sponsor-to-be, Detroit's Stroh Brewery. Stroh's searched for a new announcer and found 41-year-old Ernie Harwell calling games in Baltimore.

Harwell, who began his career broadcasting the Atlanta Crackers, got his first big-league action in Red Barber's booth at Ebbets Field. He then moved on to cover the New York Giants before becoming part of the Baltimore Orioles' first announcing crew in 1954. Kell, who'd finished his playing career with the Orioles in 1958, recalled years later that the Tigers had solicited his input and that he enthusiastically recommended Harwell. The hiring was announced on October 12, 1959.

Beginning in 1960, Harwell and Kell worked together on the radio; when the game was also televised, they'd trade places in the fifth inning. While a disciple of Barber's, Harwell was more personally involved with the broadcasts than his mentor. Harwell wasn't exactly an overt fan, but he clearly showed emotion when the Tigers did well.

It didn't take long for Harwell to become the city's most beloved voice, mixing the older style of Barber with a parochial connection to his adopted hometown. "A fan from Romulus (or Bay City, Ortonville, or Capac) caught that ball," Harwell whimsically intoned when a foul ball was hit into the seats at Tiger Stadium.

Serendipitously, the Tigers became a contender almost as soon as Harwell arrived, winning 103 games in 1961, being eliminated on the final day in 1967, then capturing the World Series in 1968. The extremely popular club was credited with helping to soothe a racially divided city after the devastating riots in 1967, but the reality is that racial discrimination in Detroit was so deep and pervasive that nothing could save the troubled town. Kaline & Co. took a "last hurrah" AL East title in 1972.

Harwell's narration made Tigers games required listening, which was reflected by a third advertiser joining for 1959: Phillies cigars.

Hall of Fame outfielder Harry Heilmann brought his descriptions of Tigers games to stations all over Michigan from 1934 through 1950, serving as the eyes and ears of those for whom Tiger Stadium was only a distant dream. His death in 1951 elicited widespread mourning all over the Midwest. (National Baseball Hall of Fame and Museum)

Stroh's and Speedway Petroleum, as the main sponsors, each took one third of the ad space in 1959. Lucky Strike took the third spot in 1961 and 1962.

More sponsors, and more ads, soon crowded not only Detroit broadcasts, but also most baseball games across the land. The move to multiple sponsors was part of a new media strategy, which made more sense for the rights holders; the stations could sell a greater volume of ads to many more clients at ever-increasing rates. Teams were not upset about abandoning the exclusive sponsorship model either, because those sponsors often wielded an uncomfortable amount of control over a club's broadcast product and image.

The $600,000 the Tigers made for their radio-TV rights in 1960 ranked ahead of only downtrodden Kansas City among AL clubs. Fetzer would soon work his magic, however, and dramatically pump up the value of the club's media rights.

During the late 1950s and 1960s, Detroit usually telecast about a dozen home games — often on Saturday — plus 30 or so from the road. WJBK was the home of TV games from 1953–1974, with an outstate network of 10 stations at its peak.

Kell, tired of the travel, departed in 1964 to spend more time in Arkansas with his family. Bob Scheffing, fired the previous year as the Tigers' manager, uncomfortably occupied the No. 2 role for a year before becoming a scout.

The team's radio network in the early 1960s reached 50 stations, but in 1964 a new deal removed WKMH from the picture and the size of the network dropped. WWJ took the day games and WJR the night, but in 1965, WJR paid $300,000 for exclusive radio rights and installed Gene Osborn as Harwell's second. Originally from Albuquerque, Osborn was familiar to local fans since 1960 for his broadcasts of the NBA's Pistons.

The Tigers split their TV and radio teams for first time in 1965. Harwell and Osborn worked radio exclusively, and WJR had plenty of new sponsors lined up for them to plug, including Pure Oil and General Cigar. That January, the Tigers and WJBK announced that George Kell would return to the broadcast team, solely on television. Kell also had ABC's *Game of the Week* on his plate as Ray Lane, a local sportscaster, joined Kell in the Detroit TV booth. Lane moved to radio in 1967, with Larry Osterman coming aboard on TV the same year.

The franchise began to innovate in television, retaining the right to sell ads; the Tigers front office by 1966 had a director of TV network sales. Detroit actually had two separate TV networks, one for Michigan and one for stations in northern Indiana and northwestern Ohio which sold its own ad time. These changes enabled the Tigers to clear $900,000 from their TV broadcasts in 1965, pushing their total media income to $1.2 million, tied with the Yankees for highest in the AL. Unlike most other clubs, though, the Tigers broadcast just a game or two each week from spring training.

By 1966, General Cigar, Pure Oil, Stroh's, National Bank of Detroit, and B.F. Goodrich paid the tab on radio, while on television Pabst, Sun Oil, and Hygrade provided the support. Household Finance, which for decades underwrote the White Sox on the radio, also sponsored pregame shows for several years in Detroit. Tigers' games had plenty of auto industry sponsors, of course, including AC Delco, AAA Auto Club, and various oil companies, along with local consumer products like Faygo soda pop.

The Tigers named Larry Osterman their new TV voice in December 1966. The 31-year-old had previously headed the Fetzer Broadcasting's sports division for eight years and remained sports director of WKZO of Kalamazoo. In 1967, WJBK telecast more than half of its schedule in color, including all 11 home games.

The 1968 season, during which WJBK showed all its games in color, was glorious on the field as the Tigers corralled the World Series. Strangely, though, the team's media revenues fell to one million dollars in 1969. Estimates had the Tigers netting $700,000 in TV revenue. WJR renewed its radio rights for 1970, kicking about $400,000 into the kitty. Part of the operation was simply moving money from one pocket to another in the same pair of pants, as the Tigers' television network included several stations owned by John Fetzer. As baseball in general, and a mediocre Tigers club in particular, began to lose popularity, the club's media revenue shrank. Their 1974 rights were still estimated at a million a year, a total which at this point ranked in the middle of the AL pack.

When WJBK bailed on the Tigers' TV games, WWJ, the local NBC affiliate, took over in 1975. The new deal increased TV revenue to $1.2 million but mandated that WWJ handle ad sales. For the first time, the team showed some Sunday home games on local television, but not on its network.

Harwell, who had become a Christian in the late 1960s and developed a lasting reputation as one of the best people in the game, signed a new contract for 1973. He would have a new partner, as Ray Lane's work with WJBK-TV caused him to leave. Paul Carey, WJR's assistant sports director and voice of the Pistons, joined Harwell in the radio booth, calling the fourth through sixth innings and also engineering the broadcasts. Carey beat out 150 applicants for Lane's job. Harwell's new sidekick was blessed with a deep, rich voice of a type rarely heard on broadcasts today. By 1979, "Ernie and Paul" were providing drama and companionship to listeners on a radio network approaching 60 stations.

Detroit legend Al Kaline essayed a few games on TV with Osterman and Kell in 1975, and the following January, the Tigers announced that Kaline would permanently join the broadcast team. Kaline teamed with one of WWJ's various sports anchors for home games and with Osterman on the road. None of the WWJ staff play-by-play men — Joe Pellegrino, Don Kremer, or Mike Barry — lasted more than two seasons.

WWJ changed its name to WDIV in 1979. The following season, the station wisely chose to let Kell and Kaline pair in the booth. The very popular team held court on Channel 4 until 1995. With Kell's induction into Cooperstown in 1983, they became the first 100% Hall of Fame broadcast team, and as beloved eminences, were immune from criticism.

Osterman was off the Tigers' broadcasts from 1979–1983, but returned once the club was fully invested in the realm of cable television. In 1980, the local ON-TV outlet, WXON, began showing Tigers home games. The plan expanded in 1981, and through 1983 subscribers could use a box connected to their TV set to decode the station's scrambled signal and enjoy

20 weeknight home tilts each summer. Local TV host Larry Adderley headed the coverage, assisted by former Tigers Norm Cash and Hank Aguirre.

The team's media rights rose to $2 million by 1983, still lowest in the AL East. With ON-TV ready to go under, Fetzer pulled the trigger and the Tigers created their own cable network: the Pro-Am Sports System (PASS).

PASS, which cost $10 per month for subscribers, was — unlike many early cable homes for baseball — a 24-hour operation. Detroit's estimated 1984 media dollars ranked tenth in the league, odd because 1983 Tigers broadcasts on WDIV pulled huge 20 ratings and 40 shares, the best in the majors. The discrepancy had to be due to the related-party transactions.

Detroit burst out of the gate in 1984 with a 35–5 start and cruised to an easy AL East crown before blowing away the Royals in the ALCS and crushing the San Diego Padres in the World Series. This happened with a new owner, as Fetzer had sold the Tigers and PASS to Domino's Pizza magnate Tom Monaghan after the 1983 season. Interestingly, while Domino's sponsored the Tigers on TV in 1984, competitor Little Caesar's was the club's chief radio guarantor.

WJR had inked a new five-year contract after 1983; two years later, it had 30 different advertisers. With the club on top of the baseball world, estimated media rights in 1985 grew to $4 million, in the middle of the AL. The Tigers continued to register the game's highest over-the-air television ratings from 1984–1986. As a result, WDIV could sell out an entire 30-minute pregame show.

In 1986–1987, PASS subscriptions leapt 60%, elevating the team's media rights to $5 million. By 1990, PASS had a very healthy 625,000 subscribers, and in 1992 the Tigers netted an estimated $14 million in broadcasting revenue.

Osterman was now the team's play-by-play voice on cable, teaming with Bill Freehan for two years and Jim Northrup for several more. Harwell, who'd won the Ford Frick Award in 1981, continued on radio with Carey, while Kell and Kaline cruising along on broadcast TV. The WJR/WDIV/PASS situation appeared as if it would continue forever, with money enough for everyone. But the next several years saw the entire broadcasting setup wiped out in a stunning series of developments.

In 1990, the news leaked that WJR was going to replace Harwell, ostensibly because the mike legend wanted to retire. The club's new GM, Bo Schembechler, former University of Michigan football coach and college football legend, formally announced in December that the 79-year-old legend's contract would be allowed to lapse after the 1991 season. Harwell was as gracious as ever, thanking the club for how well he had been treated over the decades and acknowledging their right to go in a different direction. But he wouldn't say that he wanted to leave, despite reported pressure to do so.

The press was inflamed, and the fans were outraged. The club and the station defended their plan as generous and compassionate, as Harwell would be allowed to take a victory lap around the league throughout the 1991 season. It didn't help one bit, and in 1992, new announcers Rick Rizzs (from Seattle) and Bob Rathbun (from the East Coast) were brought in on three-year contracts only to face a hostile reception. Meanwhile, Harwell agreed to announce a handful of games for the California Angels.

Competing Michigan pizza baron Michael Ilitch of Little Caesar's bought the Tigers in midseason 1992 from an increasingly cash-strapped and erratic Monaghan. Smartly, Ilitch made it a high priority to repair the festering wound. The new owner brought Harwell back to the Detroit radio crew for 1993, having him do three innings of each game — which obviously made for an uncomfortable situation with Rizzs and Rathbun. In 1994, Harwell moved over to cable TV, calling the action on PASS in place of the retired Osterman and continuing to work as a TV announcer until 1998.

Rizzs and Rathbun were not asked to return for 1995. Instead, big-dog local sportscaster, former voice of the NFL Lions, and longtime University of Michigan football announcer Frank Beckmann assumed the play-by-play role on WJR. Detroit native and onetime Tigers pitcher Lary Sorensen was hired as his color man. Beckmann — engaging and a bit authoritarian — aided the franchise in regaining local respect.

Following the end of that strike-marred season, WDIV decided that it could live without baseball. For the first time, a UHF station began presenting Tigers games as WKBD gained the rights to 56 games in 1996 — George Kell's last summer in Detroit. By then Jim Price had assumed a role on the TV team; the former Tigers reserve backstop has been a constant presence since 1994 on Tigers broadcasts.

The Post-Newsweek Group bought PASS in 1992 after Ilitch had purchased the club, converting PASS from a pay channel to the local basic cable tier. A year after Fox Sports moved into the Detroit market in 1996, obtaining the rights to Pistons games, the Post-Newsweek Group folded PASS and ceded the territory to Fox, with the media giant agreeing to buy out PASS's remaining sports rights. Fox Sports Net (now Fox Sports Detroit) has cablecast the Tigers ever since.

Fox Sports Net hired Josh Lewin, fresh off a season with the Chicago Cubs, as its Tigers play-by-play voice for 1998, with 1984 World Series hero Kirk Gibson in the color role. Fox carried 85 games, the most by a cable channel in club history to that point. The 1998 season also brought change to WJR when Sorensen quit the broadcast team in May for what were termed "personal reasons."

Handsome and articulate, with a full-time job in radio and prior experience on the Baseball Network and ESPN in 1994–1995, Sorensen soon lost nearly everything. Previously suspended for cocaine use as a player in 1986, Sorensen sank into full-blown alcoholism after leaving the broadcast. In 2005, he was jailed for repeated DUI convictions. Though Sorensen never returned to the broadcast booth, he eventually did manage to straighten out his life.

Replacing Sorensen, Price moved from TV to the radio side, first assisting Beckmann. For 1989, Beckmann shifted to over-the-air television, teaming with Kaline, while Harwell resumed his treasured role as the club's radio voice. Assuming a bigger role, Price provided the analysis while supporting a true legend, as Tigers fans reveled in Harwell's return to radio.

Ernie Harwell (L) came to Detroit a veteran of the Dodgers, Giants, and Orioles as well as the Atlanta Crackers. He spent 40 years at the mike for the Tigers. (National Baseball Hall of Fame and Museum)

Harwell retired after the 2002 season, and Dan Dickerson, who had apprenticed as No. 3 to Harwell and Price for three years, settled comfortably into the lead chair. He and Price have an easy rapport. Dickerson's voice isn't distinctive, but he always knows what's going on and communicates the situation quickly, capably, and seamlessly. He survived the absolutely horrid summer of 2003 with attitude and humor healthy and intact — no mean feat when calling every play of a 119-loss season.

Following the major league trend, the broadcast television picture in Michigan began to dim. WKBD showed 40 games per season from 1997–2003, then just 26 in 2004. Various stations picked up about a dozen games each year for a couple of more summers, but the Tigers had essentially shifted all their games to cable giant Fox by 2005.

Lewin left for Texas in 2003, with former Angels radio announcer Mario Impemba — a student of baseball broadcasting who worked his way up through the minors — replacing him. When Gibson returned to coaching in 2004, Rod Allen, yet another former Tigers player, joined the television crew.

The club's unexpected but exciting return to the postseason in 2006 boosted radio and TV ratings and cemented the current quartet's status. The 2014 season was the twelfth consecutive year that all or almost all of Detroit's games will be covered by the same four voices. Both teams are tightly interwoven on-air, and Allen has become a local hero for his unpretentious, folksy sayings and analysis.

Radio color man Jim Price missed ten games in 2012 for health reasons, with former Detroit hurler Dan Petry stepping into the breach. Price returned strong, however, and continues to assist Dan Dickerson in the booth.

The Detroit Tigers' television and radio history has been one of remarkable stability, beginning with Ty Tyson and Harry Heilmann and continuing through George Kell, Al Kaline, and the immortal Ernie Harwell. Though all of these titans are now "loooong gone" (in Harwell's memorable home-run call phrasing) from the booth, they are definitely not forgotten.

Three of the Bengals' four current voices are young and, following the Detroit fashion, none of the current broadcasters is overly critical. The club's broadcasts remain in good hands as Messrs. Dickerson and Impemba seek to continue the Tigers' tradition of long-lived announcers and intense fan loyalty.

A TALE OF THREE REDHEADS

BROOKLYN/LOS ANGELES DODGERS BROADCASTING HISTORY

"They're tearing up the pea patch out there!"
— Red Barber

"¡Se va, se va, y se fue ... despidala con un beso!"
—Jaime Jarrin

THE DODGERS HAVE BEEN AMONG BASEBALL'S PREEMINENT
franchises for more than six decades, both on the field and on the air. Who is most responsible
for making the Dodgers a broadcast behemoth? Not Red Barber. Nor Vin Scully. Not even
Walter O'Malley. It was one the most mercurial and most innovative men ever to run a
big-league ballclub: Larry "The Roaring Redhead" MacPhail.

Let's go back a bit. Contrary to its reputation as media center of the universe, New York's
entertainment scene did not embrace radio in the 1920s and 1930s, for understandable
reasons. A city dependent on live theater, concerts, and newspapers had much to lose from
the growth of radio, and New York's baseball teams felt little enthusiasm for the new medium.

As a result, in 1934, the three New York teams signed a five-year pact to not air their
games on the wireless. From 1934 through 1938, while baseball on radio grew in leaps and
bounds in nearly every other major-league market, Gotham fell well behind the curve.

The Dodgers, for most of the early part of the twentieth century in the dumps due to
poor ownership, were at the forefront of the ban. Not only did the Dodgers not broadcast

their own games in the mid-1930s, they also refused to let visiting teams even air play-by-play re-creations of games played at Ebbets Field!

Then the "Roaring Redhead" rode into town. Following a successful stint running the Cincinnati Reds, in which he pushed radio hard and established night baseball in the majors, the hard-partying, hard-working MacPhail was named Dodgers executive vice president in early 1938. Two months later, when owner Steve McKeever died, MacPhail ascended to the team presidency.

MacPhail changed the Dodgers' uniforms, painted the ballpark, and instituted night games in Brooklyn in 1938; in the first night game at Ebbets Field, Johnny Vander Meer threw his second straight no-hitter. For 1939 the Dodgers reconstructed the press box and set their sights on upping the club's stature via broadcasting. MacPhail had already picked his man: Walter Lanier (Red) Barber.

Barber began his radio days as a 20-year-old at WRUF, the University of Florida's station, in 1929. He was initially a reluctant announcer, but proved good at it — and careers could accelerate quite fast in those days for talented young men in radio. By 1934 MacPhail had brought Barber to Cincinnati to broadcast Reds games on WSAI. The erudite Barber was popular enough to conquer local radio. Some even thought that he eclipsed Reds voice Harry Hartman.

As a staff announcer for the station, Barber did everything that was needed, calling football in the fall and baseball in the summer. This versatility served him well later. He called the World Series from 1935 through 1938 on national radio, plus several early All-Star Games, becoming a national presence by age 30.

By January 1939, MacPhail had negotiated a deal with General Mills, baseball's biggest radio sponsor of the time, to bring Barber to Brooklyn. WOR in Newark, the 50,000-watt Dodgers' flagship and the lead channel of the Mutual Broadcasting Network, broadcast the club's exhibition games and all games from Ebbets Field that season, re-creating road games. WHN in New York City also picked up most games.

Risking being left in MacPhail's wake, the Giants and Yankees scrambled to get their games covered, sharing a station, sponsor, and announcers for their home games even though their

Following a successful stint in Cincinnati, "Red" Barber brought his endearing, stentorian tones and colorful language to Brooklyn in 1939. He described the Dodgers to local fans through 1953, when he left amid a dispute with Walter O'Malley. (National Baseball Hall of Fame and Museum)

hearts weren't in it. In 1939, Dodgers were aired home and away on WOR/WHN, while the Giants and Yankees only aired home games on weekdays and Saturdays. (The Giants' and Yankees' road games were re-created during the evening on WINS.) Because the Polo Grounds didn't get lights for another year, and Yankee Stadium not till 1946, all their live broadcasts were in the afternoon.

General Mills paid Barber $8,000 his first year and paid $70,000 to the Dodgers for exclusive broadcast rights. Years later, Barber wrote of this disparity with some bitterness, as even the best broadcasters were poorly paid in the early days of radio (and later in television).

Nonetheless, Barber, from his lofty perch in Brooklyn, became "the most influential sportscaster in American history," according to Chicago Cubs play-by-play man and broadcast historian Pat Hughes.

Brooklyn's 1939 radio program was bound to succeed, just as those of the Yankees and Giants were bound to fail. The Dodgers put all their games on the radio live, while the Yankees and Giants, sharing one station, could not. Brooklyn hired Barber, while the Yankees and Giants shared their own Southern broadcaster, Arch McDonald, who in comparison to Barber could not help but be second-best. Barber became ubiquitous, while McDonald — through no fault of his own — was hamstrung by his employers' reticence and lack of buy-in.

This was a big break for the Dodgers, as well as for Barber. Had the Yankees and Giants put all their games live on the radio, Barber's effect would have been blunted. In 1939, however, he had nights and Sundays, when he could command the attention of working-class fans, entirely to himself (aside from the limited competition from re-created games where the outcome was already known).

Barber was an immediate smash: New Yorkers had never heard the daily rhythms of a baseball season described live by anyone, and certainly not by someone of Barber's capability.

The Old Redhead was by far the most detail-oriented play-by-play voice of his day. He prepared endlessly and obsessed over accuracy. He had his own syntax and cadence. He believed it inappropriate for him to root for the Dodgers, because he saw himself as a reporter, not as a fan or as some kind of hanger-on. Barber could weave a narrative with the best storytellers, but his voice was always authoritative, a constant reminder that you were listening to him. It was not a dialogue.

Barber had a seismic impact in the field. He and Bob Elson of Chicago, who had a similar "newsman" approach, influenced scores of broadcasters around the land, among them Ernie Harwell and Vin Scully (who both worked with Barber), Milo Hamilton, Gene Elston, Merle Harmon, and Dick Enberg. These well-known voices made it their business, as had Barber, to deliver baseball crisply and professionally.

Should an announcer root for his team? There are at least two schools of thought on the issue. The disciples of Barber, many of whom are Easterners, say never. An announcer, from this viewpoint, is a journalist reporting on an event. Others, however — including most Midwesterners — came to expect their team's broadcasters to root along with them.

To be sure, Barber's approach wasn't the only way, even in New York. When Mel Allen assumed the Yankees play-by-play job in 1940, he was far less pedantic, more enthusiastic, and obviously invested in the outcome. Adherents of the Allen style included contemporaries McDonald, Russ Hodges, Dizzy Dean, Rosey Rowswell, and Harry Caray, as well as later announcers Bob Prince, Lindsey Nelson, Vince Lloyd, Jon Miller, and Bob Uecker. These legends in the field raised their voices in excitement and won over listeners with their hearts-on-sleeve enthusiasm.

Is a baseball game a news event? Or entertainment, meant to be enjoyed? While one could enjoy both Barber's broadcasts and those of Russ Hodges in the 1950s, most fans felt drawn toward one approach or the other. The loud and excitable Dave Niehaus probably wouldn't have played well in New York and, just as likely, St. Louis fans of the 1950s wouldn't have enjoyed the sometimes dispassionate Vin Scully.

In 1978, Allen and Barber became the first broadcasters honored with the prestigious Ford Frick Award (which is frequently though inaccurately equated to being a Hall of Famer). The two giants of baseball announcing represented two distinct approaches to calling the game, but still worked together from 1954 through 1964 on Yankees broadcasts.

While many of the Barber style of announcers (Scully, Harwell, Ned Martin), are and were excellent, some of today's "professionals," with their Newhouse-trained voices, studied home-run calls, and utter lack of individuality, could have been stamped out at a plant.

Listening to Red Barber for an inning, one could tell that the man behind the mike came from somewhere. He used Southern colloquialisms that were familiar to him. A hitter with a 3–1 count was "sitting in the catbird seat." A hot team was "tearing up the pea patch out there" or "walking in the tall cotton." A happy player was "grinning as big as a watermelon." A team in trouble was "in the pickle fat." Barber's richly textured and unique speech reached all levels of society: James Thurber's classic 1942 *New Yorker* short story "In the Catbird Seat" used Barber's phrases as a distinguishing feature of its goofy lead female character.

In later years, Barber self-consciously burnished his own myth of impartiality and honesty. The construct that he created — where he simply described the action on the field as it happened — is not to be taken literally. The Old Redhead injected as much of his personality into his description of the game as did Caray or Prince or anyone else. It was merely a different personality, one that Brooklyn fans dearly loved.

In that wild year of 1939, Barber called a 23-inning road re-creation, did the World Series for Mutual radio with Stan Lomax, and even narrated a game on August 26 for experimental NBC TV station W2XBS. In this first televised big-league game, the crew used two cameras, one at field level and one in the third-base stands. Following the season, *The Sporting News* named Barber its announcer of the year, as it would again two years later.

By the early 1940s, Barber was firmly in control of the huge New York market. The Yankees and Giants did not even bother broadcasting in 1941 and 1943 because they couldn't find a sponsor who would underwrite their games when they would be competing with Barber and the Dodgers.

With MacPhail and Barber eager to push the envelope, the Dodgers were at the forefront of other video innovations, scheduling the first Opening Day telecast in 1940 as well as the first night TV game in 1941. While television technology was still primitive, the fascination of seeing moving pictures outside of movie theaters — often in bars, restaurants, or store windows — excited enough people for baseball to take notice.

From 1939 through 1941, "Big Al" Helfer teamed with Barber. At this time, the No. 2 announcer read commercials, provided between-innings banter, and called an inning or two of play-by-play to allow the lead voice to rest a bit. With Helfer in the Navy in 1942, Alan Hale, who had called Cubs and White Sox games on WJJD in 1941, assisted Barber.

Barber was also the voice of the NFL Brooklyn Dodgers football team in 1940, then called the NFL Giants from 1941–45, usually for the same companies that sponsored his baseball broadcasts. W2XBS also televised Barber's early football assignments.

The more popular the Old Redhead became, the more he worked. In addition to baseball and football, Barber worked on various entertainment and sports commentary shows. He was probably the most famous radio voice in the country within three years of his ascendency to the Brooklyn mike.

The popularity of Barber's broadcasts — both his descriptions from Ebbets and his dramatic re-creations of road games — led WOR to institute a postgame program in 1940. Waite Hoyt, the former Yankees hurler, was the host. Barber had a major role in Hoyt getting the job, and for 1942, next year, the Reds hired Hoyt as their play-by-play man.

The Dodgers wanted more revenue than the $85,000 they had earned from General Mills in 1941, and thus teamed with Old Gold cigarettes in 1942. The broadcasts moved fully to WHN, an independent rather than a network station, with famous racing announcer Clem McCarthy's race results pushed off WHN as a result.

Of course, the extra money from Old Gold came with a quid pro quo. In 1942, Old Gold was promoting that it had won a cigarette taste-test, and Barber and Hale were obligated to pump the results. This was one of the downsides of "old-time" radio, where the sponsors controlled the broadcasts. It's also why an announcer could claim to be neutral, because he wasn't actually working for the team.

That summer, the first season of World War II, Barber and Hale did extra work for Brooklyn's Red Cross blood drives. The additional appearances strained Barber enough that he developed a serious throat problem and, by the end of the season, was exhausted and forced to completely rest his bleeding vocal cords for several weeks.

Hale headed to California in 1943, and Connie Desmond, an Ohio native who had assisted Mel Allen on Yankees and Giants games in 1942, joined the Dodgers' broadcast team. Desmond called the fifth inning and read the usual advertisements and score updates.

Desmond was quite good and highly regarded and could have been a lead announcer for many teams. It wasn't to be, though, due to the debilitating alcoholism that cost him his career, his family, and, ultimately his life. How big was this loss? Red Barber said of Desmond, "Before his illness, he was the best man I ever shared a microphone with."

By this time the Dodgers featured both pregame and postgame shows with Marty Glickman and Bert Lee. Barber also helmed a Wednesday night entertainment program for Old Gold in 1943, which meant that Connie Desmond covered Wednesday night games himself. Old Gold paid the Dodgers $130,000 for exclusive broadcast rights in 1943 and remained the club's sole sponsor through 1947.

Despite the big money represented by these radio rights, on-air talent was not valued nearly as highly as today. Broadcasters did not earn much and were expected to work very hard: in 1943, Barber again worked long hours chairing the Red Cross Brooklyn blood drive, emceeing events and frequently donating blood himself. They performed their jobs in cramped, low-tech facilities. At Ebbets Field, Barber, Desmond, and Howie Williams (later an announcer and advertising salesman on Senators and Orioles broadcasts) were crammed into a 20-foot wide by 4-foot deep booth with a broadcast engineer and all the bulky equipment needed for the broadcast.

It certainly helped Barber's stature that the Dodgers became so successful under MacPhail and Branch Rickey. From 1939–56, Brooklyn won seven NL flags and finished lower than third only once. Barber broadcast five NL pennant-winners at Ebbets Field and was credited with helping the club's attendance skyrocket in the 1940s.

Though both Barber and Desmond were classified 1-A, they weren't conscripted, so they kept announcing during the war. In 1944 they did 10 exhibition games along with the regular slate. In 1945, Barber tried to team with singer Burl Ives to host a radio program about folk ballads, but the pair couldn't find a sponsor.

By 1945, the hard-working Barber had begun negotiating tougher with his sponsors and had earned better terms. But the star announcer had never heard an offer anything like the one Larry MacPhail made him just after the war.

MacPhail had left the Dodgers for the Yankees, charged with making the staid old Bronx Bombers more dynamic. Prior to the 1946 season, MacPhail offered Barber the Yankees' radio job, along with full control of the booth, at $100,000 for three years. Feeling a sense of loyalty to the Dodgers, Barber told Branch Rickey of the offer, and Rickey matched what MacPhail had proposed. So Barber remained in Flatbush, but far better compensated; both he and Desmond received new three-year deals.

In July 1946, Barber was named director of CBS sports, succeeding Ted Husing. He hosted a regular CBS radio program in addition to his Dodgers duties, which soon expanded to television contests.

The rapid postwar proliferation of households and businesses like bars owning TV sets led to a new broadcasting paradigm. Americans were agog over the tube, and big-league clubs began airing games on the new device in 1946. The Cubs and Yankees put a few games on TV, but the Dodgers were out in front, with WCBS showing 18 contests. Bob Edge, CBS Director of Sports Televising, narrated the telecasts.

During that year's major-league winter meetings, television was the main topic. Each club was forthwith awarded the right to televise its games within a 50-mile radius of its home park; televising outside of that area could not occur without consent of the other team.

It cost TV stations an estimated $1,000–$2,000 to televise a home game in 1947 — at that time, quite an expensive proposition. Thirteen of the 16 major-league clubs presented games on television, nearly all of them home contests due to the extraordinary expense of using AT&T's telephone and television coaxial cables to transmit images from remote locations.

The Dodgers showed all 77 home games in 1947, with General Foods and Ford becoming baseball's first television sponsors. Brooklyn's sponsors wanted voices on their telecasts that were distinct from what the fans were hearing on radio, so Edge, who had quit CBS to become a freelance announcer, provided the narration.

The 1947 Yankees-Dodgers World Series was one of the high watermarks of baseball, featuring Bill Bevens' near no-hitter, Al Gionfriddo's legendary catch of Joe DiMaggio's long drive, and a seven-game New York victory. It was a thrilling series but, amazingly, not shown on network television. With TV networking still in its infancy, and line charges prohibitive, only viewers in the New York, Philadelphia, Washington, D.C., and Schenectady, New York areas were serviced.

For 1948, the Dodgers decided to cover their road games live on the radio, rather than re-creating them in a studio. Starting July 15, all Brooklyn games were produced live from whatever ballpark the Dodgers were playing in. This extra travel didn't help Red Barber's health. He'd covered the 1948 Winter Olympics from St. Moritz before joining the Dodgers for the season, calling the fifth and sixth innings on television and the rest on radio.

Barber then returned to Europe to report on the Summer Olympics in London while Desmond worked radio solo and Edge did TV by himself. Shortly after Barber returned, exhausted, from Europe, he was hospitalized with a bleeding ulcer in Pittsburgh and missed nearly a month.

One man's misfortune provided another man's big break. In early August, Ernie Harwell, voice of the Southern Association Atlanta Crackers, got the call to come to Brooklyn, beginning his nearly 50-year big-league career as a substitute. Harwell was so good, though, that the Dodgers used a three-man radio team through 1957.

Much has been made of the story in which Harwell was released from his contract with Atlanta when Brooklyn GM Branch Rickey agreed to send minor-league catcher Cliff Dapper to the Double-A Crackers in exchange. This is a great story, but it was a *fait accompli* that Harwell was headed to Brooklyn. Like Barber, Harwell was under contract to Old Gold — which sponsored both the Dodgers and the Crackers — and not employed by the club itself. So the young announcer was obligated to go where the sponsor told him to.

Harwell worked at Ebbets Field for two years before heading across town to the Polo Grounds, where he called Giants games through 1953. When Barber returned from the hospital, his first game back at the mike was Rex Barney's September 9 no-hitter. Barber broadcast that year's World Series as well. Barber later would mistakenly claim in his memoirs that the 1948 Fall Classic was the first televised World Series, which is not accurate: Bob Stanton described the 1947 Series for those viewers who had a chance to watch it on NBC-TV.

Old Gold sponsored two-thirds of the club's 1948 television package for $135,000, with Ford as the club's other television sponsor. On radio, Old Gold and Post Cereals did the honors.

Despite the popularity of Dodgers broadcasts, chief sponsor Lorillard, makers of Old Gold cigarettes, changed direction for 1949, deciding to direct their advertising dollars toward women rather than men. This meant that Old Gold was out of the baseball business and that the Dodgers needed new sponsors.

Companies lined up to pay for an association with Barber and the Dodgers. General Foods and Schaefer Beer won the bidding for the radio package, while Schaefer alone underwrote all 77 TV games. The club's radio home changed its name from WOR to WMGM and added an eponymous FM station; Brooklyn's beloved Bums remained there until they left for the West Coast. The 1949 season would be the Dodgers' last on WCBS-TV, which began showing more network programming and had little time left for baseball.

WMGM really pumped its baseball programming, airing, in addition to the Dodgers, a daily 30-minute re-creation of two other top major-league games with Glickman and Lee at the mikes. In 1951, Dodgers PR man Harold Parrott called the station every morning during the season to give a live update on the team. WMGM also teamed with the Brooklyn Red Cross to issue a health manual entitled *The Care and Protection of Dodger Fans*.

With a three-man radio team, traveling expenses were much higher, so the Dodgers and WMGM devised a plan by which only two of the three broadcasters traveled, but all three worked games at Ebbets Field.

All seemed peaceful in the pea patch, but when Branch Rickey — who had enjoyed a fruitful relationship with Barber — departed the Dodgers in 1950, tensions between the star announcer (who was closely identified with Rickey) and owner Walter O'Malley worsened, although the situation would not come to a head for another year or so.

Prior to the 1950 season, the Dodgers hired a new third man to replace Ernie Harwell, who moved across town to work with Russ Hodges on Giants broadcasts. Barber's choice for the role was young Vincent Scully, who survived a one-month spring training trial and is now the last direct descendant of Barber's broadcasting lineage. Scully is well into his sixth decade with the club, having learned from the best in a humbling fashion. "Nobody was going to get a big head working for Red Barber," he recalled decades later.

Unlike most other clubs, the Dodgers did not farm out their broadcasts to smaller stations on a radio network; a one-year trial in 1949 did not succeed. The club claimed that it did not want to kill the minor leagues by spreading major-league radio. Beginning in 1950, though, a large group of nationwide CBS radio network stations carried Dodgers Saturday home games.

The following season, O'Malley devised an innovative way to expand the Dodgers' radio presence outside of the region, increasing both the club's income and visibility. Since many stations could not afford to pick up games sent over the wires from Brooklyn, the Dodgers built a network in Virginia which would, for a much lower cost to small stations, re-create the games from ticker-tape and broadcast this feed.

This cheaper way of doing broadcasts allowed stations with smaller budgets in the South and Southeast to carry Dodgers games; by 1952, more than 100 stations from Ohio to Florida had signed on. Nat Allbright and Bill Best announced these games. Current Reds voice Marty Brennaman, who grew up listening to the broadcasts in Virginia, has made a point of crediting Allbright as one of his inspirations. Allbright said later that one of the great highlights of his life was receiving a 1955 Dodgers world championship ring.

Brooklyn around this time also bolstered its television package. Beginning in 1950, the club presented a pregame and postgame show on weekdays and Saturdays. The host for the postgame *Talk to the Stars* interview show and the pregame *Knothole Gang*, sponsored by Curtiss Candy Co., was Happy Felton, a 6-foot-2, 290-pound, bespectacled former vaudeville actor.

In March 1951, Schaefer and the Dodgers signed an eyebrow-raising, open-ended deal that gave Schaefer Beer the option to sponsor the club's radio and television broadcasts for up to 10 years for a total price nearing $5 million. That year, WOR, the Dodgers' new telecaster, aired three games in color (the initial one on August 11), another sports broadcasting first.

While electronic broadcasting had finally earned some grudging respect from the newspapers, the ink-stained wretches still took any chance they could to castigate their electronic cousins. During the 1951 season, Brooklyn manager Charlie Dressen was quoted (by a print reporter) ripping his own pitcher, Erv Palica. Connie Desmond stated on the air that Dressen denied the report. *The Sporting News* went crazy, wagging its finger for Desmond to "know his place" and not try to be a reporter. Red Barber, in response, wrote a six-page letter to *TSN*, of which the Bible of Baseball deigned to print only a small quote.

Desmond and Barber were true partners, working the Dodgers as well as non-baseball

Being Vin Scully's second couldn't have been an easy job, but after years working in the Texas League, Jerry Doggett was overjoyed to make the majors. He did solid work for the Dodgers from 1956 until his retirement in 1987. (National Baseball Hall of Fame and Museum)

events such as the 1951 Orange Bowl for CBS radio. Desmond's excessive drinking, however, was starting to take its toll.

Starting in 1952, Lucky Strike cigarettes joined Brooklyn-based F. & M. Schaefer Brewing as radio sponsors for Dodgers games on WMGM. Simmering tensions between O'Malley and Barber — and between Barber and BBD&O, the ad agency handling the Schaefer account — were about to boil over. Rumors had Barber leaving for the Yankee Stadium booth prior to the 1953 season, but the Brooklyn icon stuck around for another season and another Dodgers pennant.

Interestingly, a strike by WOR-TV's technical staff forced the Dodgers off the air in mid-August, knocking out seven telecasts before WABD took over the chores on August 28.

The big break between Barber and the team came in late September. Tired of working the World Series for the $200-per-game pittance offered by Gillette, Barber turned down the gig. No other announcer had ever stood up to the Gillette Company, which had been a heavyweight in sponsoring major sporting events since the 1939 World Series. The company's popular Cavalcade of Sports radio and TV programs were sports cultural touchstones in 1940s and 1950s America, and Gillette was the nation's top sports advertiser for thirty years.

An annoyed Walter O'Malley nominated Scully to take Barber's place, and the Dodgers' very first announcer, angered but not surprised by what he viewed as a lack of support, decided it was time to leave.

BBD&O and the sponsors reaped some financial benefit from the departure of the high-salaried, entrenched Barber, and were able to exercise more editorial control over the broadcasts as well. O'Malley, meanwhile, perhaps jealous of Barber's long-term relationship with Rickey, was happy begin a new era. Scully slid comfortably into the lead chair for 1954, with Desmond retaining, for the moment, his status as second chair.

The new third man was, in baseball parlance, a curveball. Andre Baruch, a Paris-educated disc jockey, bandleader, newsreel narrator, and announcer on radio's syndicated *Your Hit Parade*, joined the broadcast team. It didn't hurt that for many years he was associated with Lucky Strike cigarettes, or that he had broadcast some Yankees games back in 1931.

Baruch, while recommended by Barber to O'Malley in 1953 for future work, was not highly regarded for his baseball skills. He served with Scully and Desmond on WMGM for two seasons before hanging 'em up to return to music.

Another of the many Dodgers' broadcasting firsts was their Spanish-language game coverage. The legendary Buck Canel had broadcast for many years from New York to South and Central America over the Caribbean Radio Network. For 1955, he actually was in a booth at Ebbets Field on a regular basis, describing a select slate of home games over WHOM through 1957. Once in Los Angeles, the Dodgers increased their Spanish-language radio presence.

Glam was also part of the Dodgers' package. For 1955, the pregame and postgame shows had a new commentator along with Glickman, Jim Gordon, and Ward Wilson: former professional tennis player Gussie Moran. Moran, who had caused a ruckus at Wimbledon in 1949 by wearing a short skirt that showed off her legs as well as a particularly frilly pair of knickers, didn't know much about baseball at the start, but she worked at her craft and became popular among fans of all stripes. She appeared as part of WMGM's Dodgers programming through 1957, perhaps as a counterpoint to the Giants' use of Leo Durocher's wife, actress Laraine Day, also a pregame host.

The 1955 campaign began inauspiciously, at least on the radio, as the Dodgers aired just four spring exhibitions. As the club took over first place in the initial week of the season and established its dominance of the NL, Connie Desmond reeled out of control. He was sent home (officially on a "leave of absence") while Scully assumed a heavier load.

After losing their five previous October battles since 1941 with the lordly Yankees, the beloved "Boys of Summer" Dodgers finally won the World Series in 1955. Vin Scully was on NBC's national television broadcast, sharing the mike with Al Helfer, and called the final inning.

Baruch resigned prior to the 1956 season, and Desmond was assumed to be out of the picture as well. Bob Pasotti, formerly of Armed Forces Radio, was a candidate for the Dodgers' job — he had kept statistics in the radio booth for Red Barber years before — but Helfer was hired instead. Desmond also received one last chance to keep his spot on the broadcast team.

In 1956, the switched-on Dodgers telecast 25 road games on WOR, visiting every park but Forbes Field in Pittsburgh (which prohibited it) and the Polo Grounds, since the Giants beamed all their home games to New York City anyway. The stakes were high enough for the sponsors and BBD&O that the ad agency actually sent a man on the road with the Dodgers to ensure that the broadcasts went smoothly.

The Dodgers attempted for the second time to build a regional radio network, signing up 18 stations for all regular-season and 35 exhibition games in 1956.

Unfortunately, Desmond could not keep it together and resigned, this time for good, in August. What could have been a great career ended with unanswered questions. How good could Connie Desmond have been if not for his fatal weakness? Could he have been Barber's successor had he stayed sober? If so, what would that have meant for Vin Scully?

Jerry Doggett replaced Desmond, joining the radio-TV crew on Labor Day. In radio since the late 1930s, he had done Liberty Network baseball for two seasons and had been broadcaster and PR director for the Double-A Texas League Dallas Eagles since 1951.

The Dodgers' final season in Brooklyn began in 1957 with WMGM airing 36 exhibitions, again sponsored by Schaefer and Lucky Strike. The Dodgers finished third that summer amid reports of rowdyism at Ebbets Field and rumors about the club leaving town.

Amidst a blizzard of charges and countercharges came an outcome that no one seemed to want: The Dodgers abandoned Brooklyn and the Giants fled Manhattan for sunnier climes after the 1957 season. Helfer, who had done the 1957 All-Star Game and World Series on TV, was left behind and Happy Felton emceed his last *Knothole Gang*.

Once the Dodgers settled in Los Angeles, O'Malley did a complete turnaround on television. Brooklyn had shown, over WCBS then WOR, nearly every home game between 1947 and 1957. Out West, however, the franchise televised only two regular-season home games over-the-air in its first 20 years in California. In fact, from 1958–68, O'Malley permitted only a handful of *road* contests — only those played at San Francisco — to be telecast.

Some commentators believed that O'Malley soured on TV, believing that he was angry at having given away his product back in Brooklyn, which had negatively affected his bottom line. But O'Malley had only soured on so-called free TV; the Dodgers' mogul had grand plans for the big box, though these plans were not fully realized for two decades.

In June 1953, O'Malley publicly stated that pay television, a new innovation, would save Major League Baseball. The next year, the Dodgers started working with a California corporation called Skiatron to develop a system whereby fans would pay to watch individual games in their own homes. Skiatron and O'Malley were in agreement that pay TV could help offset Brooklyn's attendance decline, as demand was apparent for more sports on television than the few commercial channels of the time could offer.

Matty Fox, Skiatron's president, noted that a pay channel that would also show movies and concerts might cost viewers about three bucks per month, with an extra buck or so to watch each Dodgers game. Behind the scenes, Fox was trying to convince O'Malley to move to California, where Fox — as a former film producer — had a lot of political, media, and business contacts, and where he believed a wealthy audience was starving for big-league baseball.

As early as May 1955, all three of Gotham's major-league teams, according to the New York Times, had shown interest in Skiatron — or another vendor — putting games on pay TV for 1956. It would be much harder to build the necessary infrastructure, however, than anyone thought.

The potential for pay TV raised hackles among ordinary citizens as well as from movie theater owners, Broadway owners, and — especially — the established broadcast networks, which were terrified of the prospect of competition.

Had the Dodgers and Giants seen a more positive response from New York politicians about pay television and new ballparks, they might not have relocated. But during Congressional hearings in 1957 intended to determine whether the four major pro sports should be placed under antitrust laws, powerful Brooklyn Democrat and House Judiciary Committee chair Emmanuel Celler proved distinctly hostile to O'Malley's plans.

From its inception, many powerful players had lined up against pay television. News stories and editorials referred to Skiatron in an inflammatory way as "the closed-circuit medium that may end free televised baseball games." Pay TV would do nothing of the sort, of course; this was just fear-mongering. Matty Fox claimed, correctly, that so-called "free TV" was not free because of the hidden cost of the advertising built into the products that paid for the broadcasts. The public antipathy was more than a bit odd, as championship prizefights and some football games were being sold on a pay-per-view basis in movie theaters by the mid-1950s.

Fans then as well as now seem to hold baseball to a different standard than other sports, as there has always been a strong sentiment that the national game should to be free for everyone to watch on TV. Writers in the 1950s spilled buckets of ink raising the terrifying notion of viewers having to pay to see the World Series. Similar concerns were raised in the 1990s when the trend of clubs moving games from broadcast TV to cable TV greatly accelerated, and again when MLB started placing postseason games on cable in the 2000s.

The Dodgers wanted to put their TV games on a pay-per-view system in 1955 for 50 cents per contest. The entire debate was heating up, and investigative journalistic icon Edward R. Murrow presented a program about pay television on CBS as part of his *See It Now* series. O'Malley, that July 14, was one of his interviewees.

With the Dodgers' interest in Skiatron an open secret, a second company entered the picture in 1957. ITV offered to pay $2.5 million in a long-term deal to produce Dodgers and Giants games on pay TV if the two clubs would remain in New York City. "There's no reason why the Giants and Dodgers must go to California for closed circuit television when they could get more money here," said ITV's president, Max Kantor.

It was too late. Skiatron had already handed $2 million to the Dodgers in 1957 for exclusive pay TV rights, according to mayor George Christopher of San Francisco. Well before the Dodgers actually left Brooklyn, everyone already knew that the team was on its way out and that the earth-shaking move was largely because of the promised riches that pay TV was expected to provide.

O'Malley at first denied that pay television was a reason the club wanted to leave Brooklyn, but he admitted the relationship with Skiatron — and the payment — in in June 1957, a week or so after *Variety* reported that both the Giants and Dodgers had granted Skiatron exclusive rights.

Television entrepreneurs of the time were faced with either battling the Federal Communications Commission for the right to use the public airwaves or building their own incredibly expensive cable networks, which had the major advantage of being outside the FCC's purview. The FCC — beholden to the broadcast networks by the 1950s — couldn't legally outlaw pay television, but it could hold lengthy hearings and attempt to sway public opinion against the concept. Which it did.

At an impasse in negotiations for a new ballpark with the city and with extremely powerful bureaucrat Robert Moses, and realizing the extent of local anger at the specter of pay television, O'Malley and Stoneham chose to relocate to the Golden State and try their luck with new politicians and new media strategies. Stoneham's concurrence was critical to the Dodgers' gambit, and the Giants owner apparently only agreed to head west with O'Malley if the Giants had a stake in the pay TV game as well.

Vested interests in Los Angeles were lining up to help O'Malley. In a vote that appears to have been decided well in advance, the Los Angeles City Council approved giving Skiatron and a competitor, Telemeter, pay TV licenses on October 18, 1957. While most of the bad publicity from the vote was spread by the movie theater industry, much of the public was apparently annoyed by the closed-door process of awarding the franchises.

Telemeter pulled out early in 1958 because it felt that Angelenos were not willing to embrace pay TV, and thus would be wasting money by developing the expensive networks. Skiatron soon asked the City of Los Angeles to withdraw its 1957 license for the same reason.

As a result, no games aired on pay TV in 1958. Since O'Malley also kept the networks from showing any *Game of the Week* broadcast in Los Angeles — even when the Dodgers were on the road or playing at night — Los Angeles residents now could watch no Major League Baseball on television. Until, that is, the Dodgers owner agreed as a "public service" (his words) to allow Westinghouse to present the team's 11 games in San Francisco over KTTV, an independent station.

Warren Giles, NL president, was in favor of the Dodgers' and Giants' television strategy, and said so. Early in 1959, plans were in motion to put both teams on the pay box by July. But once again, Skiatron couldn't make it happen due to intransigence from local forces and the high cost of laying coaxial cable. Matty Fox was alleged to have signed a deal in 1958 with AT&T to lay the cable, but the work was never done. Early the next year, Twentieth Century–Fox explored buying Skiatron, but Matty Fox refused to sell.

Pabst and American Tobacco were the Dodgers' 1959 sponsors, paying a combined $300,000 for the club's rights, sixth among eight NL clubs but above the Giants. KTTV telecast the club's 11 games at San Francisco, but the Dodgers asserted that they would again reap no money from these programs, largely because of the agreement with Skiatron that prevented other broadcasting arrangements. Chuck Bennett did pregame and postgame work on these KTTV telecasts for many years.

O'Malley turned down short-term revenue from broadcast TV with his eyes open. He decided that, with big-league baseball a novelty in Los Angeles and with his club playing in the 90,000-seat LA Coliseum, it would be silly to televise games for free as he had done in Brooklyn.

In April 1959, Skiatron claimed it would be able to hit the air on April 1, 1960, and the company's stock instantly shot up. After scrutiny from the Securities and Exchange Commission, however, Skiatron was criticized by the agency for misrepresenting its readiness to telecast games and misrepresenting its financial stability in order to increase stock activity and price.

Both the Giants and Dodgers, as shareholders in Skiatron, share some blame for this manipulation. In 1959, Horace Stoneham had even claimed to have a contract with Skiatron, perhaps to up the company's prestige — although it turned out not to be true. The under-funded company, reeling from the spate of bad publicity, soon bit the dust, although Matty Fox immediately set about raising money for another, more advanced, pay venture.

The Dodgers left KMPC for a new radio flagship in 1960, signing a long-term deal with more powerful KFI. Union Oil, the club's new sponsor, shared spots with American Tobacco Company, which also sponsored the Giants. The new Union Oil arrangement — which also included having the company float a large, low-interest loan to O'Malley to help him finance the construction of Dodger Stadium — earned the Dodgers a million dollars each year from 1960 through 1963 for its radio rights. This was the top media revenue stream in the National League, and second in baseball only to the Yankees.

That such a huge sum came entirely from radio is attributable largely to Vin Scully, who became the voice of the game in Southern California. He and Jerry Doggett worked together through 1976, growing in stature as the region discovered their abilities.

Vincent Scully, who grew up in New York City's Washington Heights, was an aggressive young professional willing to work hard to get ahead. He learned from Red Barber how to talk baseball, and would later call Barber the biggest influence in his life.

What Scully took from Barber was his preparation, his sense of impartiality — even today one can't tell from his call which team is winning — and his lack of interest in ripping anyone. He withstood pressure from Walter O'Malley more than once about becoming more pro-Dodgers on the air, defending his philosophy to "go down the middle" in his descriptions.

An East Coast native but a California resident for more than a half-century, Scully favors old-fashioned terms like "She is gone!" and "Forget it" for home runs, or describing a regular guy as a "butter-and-egg man." An adherent of an old-time style, Scully doesn't crowd the broadcast with statistics. He has, however, loosened up a bit in recent years and is somewhat more colloquial than during the 1950s and 1960s.

Robert Creamer wrote of Scully's omnipresence on the West Coast for *Sports Illustrated* in 1964: "When a game is on the air the physical presence of his voice is overwhelming. His pleasantly nasal baritone comes out of radios on the back counters of orange juice stands, from transistors held by people sitting under trees, in barber shops and bars, and from cars everywhere — parked cars, cars waiting for red lights to turn green, cars passing you at 65 on the freeways, cars edging along next to you in rush-hour traffic jams."

By 1964, Scully — an employee of the team rather than the radio station or the sponsor — was earning $50,000 per year, more than most players. The trend for clubs to hire their radio voices began partially as a reaction to Barber's exit from Brooklyn, as club owners realized they were giving far too much control of their product to sponsors that had no long-term stake in the franchise's fortunes.

Doggett, for his part, was excitable and loyal and bled more blue than Scully. He was a good co-pilot and could have been the primary announcer in some cities, but being Vin Scully's right-hand man was a quality job, if not a simple one.

The Dodgers, without pay television plans for 1962, telecast their home opener — the first game played in Chavez Ravine and the first-ever Dodgers home game seen on TV — in addition to the usual slate of games from San Francisco.

Showing their usual indifference to building a large radio network, the Dodgers had just 10 radio stations on the line by 1963, the fewest of any NL club. Even though the Dodgers showed just nine games on television and had no TV network, they still made a million dollars in media rights. Only the Mets in the NL equaled that, and only the Yankees (at $1.2 million) exceeded it.

After Skiatron folded, Matty Fox founded Tolvision, which became the biggest shareholder in another new venture, Subscription Television (STV). Onetime NBC radio and TV president Pat Weaver, who had created the landmark *Today* and *Tonight* shows, ran STV.

STV began operating in Los Angeles and San Francisco, in proximity to O'Malley and Stoneham. But STV also had plans to expand into other major metropolitan areas with three channels that would telecast sports, movies, live theater, and even kids' programs.

Major corporate backers of STV were the R.H. Donnelly group, based in Chicago, which handled sales, and Lear-Sigler, a California electronics manufacturer responsible for STV's home installation and technology.

In late 1963, the SEC received notice that a $22 million initial stock offering would be made by STV. The Dodgers invested $142,000 and the Giants $108,000; with that and other initial cash investments, Weaver hired Tom Gallery, formerly NBC sports director, to assemble the new channel's programming.

Already, closed-circuit television, showing sports and entertainment, was succeeding in Toronto and New Haven, Connecticut. STV, with more and better backers than Skiatron, clearly threatened the status quo. The Giants and Dodgers both stood to profit enormously if STV's forecast of 700,000 subscribers by 1968 was realized; by that time, the company would have been obligated to pay each club $10,000,000 per year.

This was no simple task, though. Building a private cable network — one free from FCC regulation — was extraordinarily expensive, and the costs of constructing and installing cables was the biggest factor.

Ironically, Matty Fox never saw a game on the legacy of his brainchild, having died of a heart attack on June 2, 1964 in Chicago at age 52. After months of hand-wringing from worried Hollywood moguls and network TV executives as well as populist fist-shaking from various congressmen, STV finally debuted in Los Angeles on July 17, 1964.

That night, live from Dodger Stadium, the home team edged the Cubs 3–2 in the first color baseball telecast ever seen in Southern California. About 2,500 subscribers had paid STV a $5 installation fee for a small box which sat atop their TV sets and could be activated when a program was to begin; an article in the *Christian Science Monitor* claimed that 1,600 sets were tuned into the game.

STV, which used five cameras for the telecasts — more than usual for the time — also collected a $1 monthly service charge, with Dodgers games costing an extra $1.50 each.

Frank Sims, at one time a Phillies telecaster, called the play-by-play with Dodgers executive Fresco Thompson handling the color. Sims was given the job after Scully declined the opportunity to be part of the new venture. From July 17 onward, the pair described the remainder of the club's 1964 home contests.

On opening night, STV threw a party for 1,000 at its Hollywood studio. But trouble was brewing, as a consortium of movie theater owners and television network executives, both with deep pockets and powerful friends, managed to get an anti–pay TV initiative, Proposition 15, on the November 1964 state ballot.

The opposition used fear-mongering via misleading advertisements and PR campaigns to paint STV as a threat to the rights of free people everywhere. By a 2–1 margin, California voters banned pay television in the state.

Though that ban was later declared unconstitutional by the state Supreme Court, the vote was fatal to STV, which capsized from debt and relentless bad publicity. The company refunded the $5 installation fee to its 6,000 subscribers and dismissed its employees — and that was the end of pay television in Southern California for several years.

The FCC decided, in 1966, to assert control over all cable (CATV) systems in the United States. When the California ballot initiative banned pay TV, it was clear that the Dodgers had, as in the early days of radio, gone up against a company town. This time, however, they lost. Since O'Malley couldn't execute his television plan, the Dodgers — the rich, successful Dodgers, who won world championships in 1959, 1963, and 1965 — went on televising only a handful of games per season.

This very conservative — some might say spiteful — strategy showed in the Dodgers' bottom line. No longer were the Dodgers earning more money than most other clubs for their broadcasts; in fact, by 1966, the Yankees, Tigers, Phillies, Braves, Mets, Astros, and even the Angels earned equal or higher rights fees than the big-market, big-name Dodgers.

Strangely, however, the Dodgers claimed in 1970 that the rights figures they had been providing to broadcasting industry trade magazines in the last 1960s were wrong, and that the team was actually earning nearly two million dollars a year.

In 1967, TV and radio manufacturer Packard Bell Electronics became a Dodgers sponsor. It's probably no coincidence that this was the first year the club showed its TV games in color. Union Oil remained the Dodgers' top guarantor, taking one-quarter to one-half of the ads on Dodgers' games, and would do so well into the 1980s. Interestingly, in the late 1960s, Los Angeles was the only MLB club not sponsored by a brewery or winery.

With no pay TV to build around, Los Angeles finally invested heavily in building a regional radio network in the late 1960s, going for quality rather than quantity by moving into profitable markets and competing with broadcasts of minor-league clubs. In 1967–68, the club linked to 17 network stations, but lost some affiliates to the expansion San Diego Padres the next year.

By the 1970s, though, the Dodgers' network was up to 20 stations, connecting with major radio outlets in Phoenix, Honolulu, and Las Vegas to become the area's signature team.

In 1969, the Dodgers telecast all their road games from San Francisco and San Diego, earning an extra $200,000 from KTTV. In 1970, the club altered its plans, airing 21 away games, only one against the Padres. This was a favor from O'Malley to the expansion team's president, longtime former Dodgers executive Buzzie Bavasi, intended to help the new club's weak attendance.

It was around this time that the Dodgers' relationship with their star broadcaster got a little bumpy. While Scully's 60-plus years with the Dodgers seem from a distance to have been smooth, the two parties almost came apart in the early 1970s.

Scully had commented as early as 1968 that he wanted to spend more time with his family, and complained about having to call games during the summer in sweltering cities like Cincinnati and Philadelphia, where the broadcast booths in the old ballparks were not air-conditioned.

There was also the question of how much time he had in a day. Scully was one of the most recognizable voices in the West, with his own syndicated TV game show, *It Takes Two*, carried in several markets. Some said his ego had gotten too big, or that the veteran radio man had developed a case of "television-itis," predicting that Scully would leave the Dodgers in favor of bigger assignments.

During 1970, Scully turned down an offer to do an NFL *Game of the Week* telecast, but he did, however, negotiate 26 vacation days from baseball broadcasts, much of that coming during spring training. Mike Walden, voice of USC Trojans college football, took over for Scully for some Grapefruit League and regular-season road games in 1970. Walden did not receive good reviews for his baseball work, though, and departed after that year.

Prior to the 1971 campaign, Scully signed a new long-term contract. His TV game show eventually stopped production, but the Dodgers' voice would still spend much of the offseason in the 1970s narrating golf on television. Eventually, Scully's baseball and non-baseball pursuits came into balance.

Los Angeles by now was pretty savvy at negotiating media deals, being among the first clubs to hire a high-level broadcast executive. James Bealle was the club's vice president of radio and TV in the early 1970s. Dave Van De Walker, who had coordinated Dodger broadcasts for a couple of local ad agencies, joined the club in 1970 as the director of its radio network.

As befits a team in a showbiz town, the Dodgers went into recordings, too. Danny Goodman, the team's promotions director, did big business in souvenirs. The club put out several records in the early 1960s featuring songs like "Charge" and "D-O-D-G-E-R-S," using Vin Scully to narrate spoken passages and to read "Casey at the Bat." Goodman also marketed seven-inch records of Scully narrating the ninth innings of Sandy Koufax's 1965 perfect game and Bill Singer's 1970 no-hitter.

Another important component of the Dodgers' media strategy was increasing their Spanish-language broadcasting as soon as they got to LA. (Aside from being smart business, this certainly helped counter the bad publicity O'Malley received when the final residents of Chavez Ravine, nearly all Latinos, were forcibly removed so the city could hand over the land to the club for construction of Dodger Stadium.) Creating a Spanish-language component was a proactive move to build a new audience via radio. KWKW was the club's first Spanish-language flagship; it carried the team through 1973, mostly with the same sponsors as on KFI — likely another first for the Dodgers' broadcasting history.

Rene Cardenas of Nicaragua was the Dodgers' first Spanish-language voice, calling the games from 1958 through 1961 before departing to call the expansion Houston Colt .45s. Cardenas, known all over Latin America, spent four years in LA paired with a variety of voices. Cardenas' protégé Jaime Jarrin, who had joined the Dodgers' broadcast team in 1959, took over from his mentor.

Jarrin, an Ecuadorian who knew nothing of baseball before coming to America as a teenager, was an immediate hit, teaming with Jose "Fats" Garcia from 1962 onward on all home games. They re-created nearly all the team's road contests by listening to Scully's and Doggett's English narration. The club did send Jarrin and Garcia to cover games live in San Francisco and, later, San Diego.

In 1970, Jarrin, who also called football on KWKW, became the first Latino to win a Golden Mike award from the Radio and Television News Association of Southern California. He also took the trophy the next year as well. An unusual measure of Jarrin's importance to the area's Latino consciousness was demonstrated by the August 1972 hijacking of a Frontier Airlines plane in New Mexico. The hijacker specifically asked that Jarrin be brought to LA International Airport to interview him about the plight of Mexican-Americans in Los Angeles.

In fall 1972, "Fats" Garcia passed away. Rudy Hoyos, previously a KWKW newscaster for 20 years, replaced him on the broadcast team.

By 1972–73, the Dodgers were earning $1.8 million each season on television and radio revenue — the most of any team in baseball. This impressive total was achieved despite having only 10 network radio stations, having no supplemental TV network, and authorizing very few telecasts. How did the club accomplish it? Aside from the Dodgers' tremendous popularity, a key element was that, in the 1960s, the club began to manage its own broadcast operations, buying time on radio stations, selling ads itself, and pocketing the profits.

The Dodgers switched radio stations in both languages in 1974. Southern California's most powerful radio station, 50,000-watt clear-channel KFI, wanted to change its programming direction. As a result, shortly before spring training, the team hammered out a deal with KABC. The club's new radio home had far less power than KFI and could not reach some areas of the San Gabriel Valley, necessitating that the Dodgers add network stations in San Bernardino and Ventura.

The club's new Spanish-language outlet, XEGM, improved reception for fans south of LA because it was transmitting from Tijuana, Mexico. Reaching a whole new group of Latino fans in the fast-growing area from Orange County to San Diego, it also competed directly with the Padres' Spanish broadcasts. (The Angels did not begin broadcasting *en Español* until 1982.)

Despite the early reception problems, KABC remained the Dodgers' radio home for more than 20 years. Scully and Doggett solidified their stature in the public consciousness on radio and continued to call some 20 television games per season.

Scully had signed a deal with CBS in 1975 to call various sports on television, and in 1977, the club added Ross Porter to the broadcast crew to help carry the load. Porter wasn't an immediate hit, but then few could measure up to Scully's rep.

Porter began broadcasting at age 14 in 1953, in Oklahoma. He had a folksy voice and was somewhere between a rooter and a neutral party. CBS radio had him call the 1977 World Series, and he also did some NBC Game of the Week telecasts. He remained with the Dodgers for 28 years, taking over as the No. 2 when Doggett retired in 1987.

One of the most fascinating games the Dodgers ever broadcast was a June 3, 1989, tilt at the Astrodome that went 22 innings. Scully called the affair with Don Drysdale on television, while Porter worked the whole seven-hour and 14 minute epic alone on the radio, possibly setting some kind of record.

The Dodgers were still earning $1.8 million per season for their broadcasting rights in 1977, but that was no longer the most in majors. By that time, the staggeringly popular Red Sox were netting $2 million per year. So Los Angeles searched around for new revenue streams and came up with a new/old idea: pay television.

In 1977, with opposition to the pay concept having subsided, a local concern, National Subscription Television, began broadcasting over a scrambled UHF channel using a decoder box. Better known as ON-TV, the new network had plans to expand all over the country.

Initially, ON-TV paid for the rights to show six Dodgers home games, sans commercials, with Geoff Witcher — who had covered LA's Triple-A farm club in Albuquerque — at the mike. The games selected were against quality opponents that would draw fans to the park anyway.

By 1979, the Dodgers had upped the amount of home games on ON-TV to 12 and were being paid $75,000 for each. Witcher was not the most gifted at play-by-play, but he was a loyalist who bled Dodger blue. He worked for years as a talk show host and helmed the Dodgers' radio pregame.

To a limited extent, Walter O'Malley's vision of two decades earlier was coming true, but the disruptive effect of changing technologies bedeviled the franchise. Following the 1984 season, ON-TV went out of business in California; the channel's success led entrepreneurs to wire the area for coaxial cable, which in a cruel twist made scrambler-box television obsolete. DodgerVision, a collaborative new venture between the club and Metromedia Cable, hired Eddie Doucette — a roving announcer better known for his basketball work — to team with ex-Dodgers Al Downing and Rick Monday.

Los Angeles for many years kept its pay TV broadcast crew separate from its regular radio and television announcers. Scully did no cable games in the 1970s, 1980s, or early 1990s, nor did Ross Porter or Don Drysdale, who had journeyed home to the Dodgers' booth in 1988 after his contract with the White Sox ran out.

Soon, the Dodgers shifted their pay telecasts to Z Channel, a local operation best known for its high-quality film selection. In 1988, local sports anchor Tony Hernandez did the play-by-play, but Doucette was back in the saddle in 1989, again working with Downing.

SportsChannel, a Cablevision network, opened a Los Angeles affiliate in 1990, and the Dodgers and Angels immediately moved their cable packages to this new channel for three years. Fans had to pay a premium to get SportsChannel LA (SCLA); as a result, the channel and the baseball teams it carried never got the same saturation of the NBA Clippers and Lakers and NHL, who were on the basic-cable Prime Ticket. A series of mediocre announcers and color men didn't help the SCLA broadcasts.

Following this experiment, the Dodgers forsook cable and pay television until 1997, instead showing 46–50 games on their new television affiliate, KTLA, which snagged the rights that KTTV had held since 1958. The relatively small number of TV games was definitely unusual for a major-market franchise.

Drysdale passed away in a Montreal hotel during the 1993 campaign, and Rick Monday joined the Dodgers' crew on a full-time basis to replace him. Monday is a certified hero in Los Angeles for his division playoff series–winning homer in 1981 and for his saving of an American flag while with the Cubs in 1976, but he has struggled with play-by-play.

Scully, Porter, and Monday moved to a new radio home, KXTA, for five years starting in 1998. Beginning in 2002 KCOP took the over-the-air TV package, signing up for a three-year slate of 50 games per season.

The club returned to cable in 1997. From then through 2005, Fox West 2 carried Dodgers' games, peaking in its last year with a staggering (for the team) 125 cablecasts, leaving just 25 for KCOP to show over-the-air in a one-year deal. Following that season, Fox West 2 was folded into Prime Ticket, which would carry approximately 100 Dodgers games per year.

In early 1998, the O'Malley family sold the club to Rupert Murdoch's News Corporation subsidiary, Fox Television, for some $311 million. Most local observers believed that the 1997 deal with Fox West 2 was done with knowledge that the sale to News Corp. was going to happen.

Six years later, Fox sold the Dodgers to Boston real-estate developer Frank McCourt. Fox continued to show games, though, on its Prime Ticket channel, maintaining the best things about its relationship with the club without the hassles of actually having to run it.

Following the 2004 season, Ross Porter was not renewed, as the Dodgers instead hired the polarizing former ESPN studio host and boxing announcer Charley Steiner, who had spent three years in the Yankees' radio booth. It was a sea change in style that many locals found jarring.

In 2005–06, Steiner, Scully, Monday, Jerry Reuss, and Al Downing rotated in and out of the booth, a confusing arrangement, especially for fans used to stability while watching and listening to their Dodgers games.

KCAL became the club's over-the-air carrier in 2006, telecasting mostly away games. Scully reduced his schedule in 2005, calling only home games and those played in San Diego, San Francisco, Phoenix, and Denver.

Steiner moved to radio on a full-time basis in 2006, working with Monday to form one of baseball's least substantial pairings, although Scully continued to simulcast the first three innings on radio. During the 2007 season, negotiations with KFWB for a new contact collapsed, so the team once again pulled up stakes and signed with KABC radio.

Scully has worked exclusively on television since 2007, doing the games solo as befits his huge talent and his temperament. As one of the all-time greats, he is fully capable of being his own virtual color man, drawing on his decades of expertise and experience. Almost impossibly, the living legend sounds nearly as sharp now as ever — perhaps working alone shows how truly great he is.

In 2009, Eric Collins assumed the play-by-play mike for Dodgers road games that Scully didn't work, paired with hyperkinetic ex-player Steve Lyons on what is regarded as a more youthful-oriented (sometimes smart-alecky) broadcast. Collins, one of very few African Americans in a baseball booth, proved good at smooth, entertaining play-by-play, but did not seem to capture the fans' imagination.

Through all of these changes, Jamie Jarrin continues to roll on as the team's Spanish voice. A reunion with Jarrin's former mentor Rene Cardenas from 1990 through 1998 ultimately proved unworkable as the booth eventually wasn't big enough for the two patriarchs of Spanish-language broadcasting. Fernando Valenzuela joined the radio team in 2003, giving some star power to the broadcasts. Interestingly, the club's Spanish-language home since 2008 has been KHJ, in previous years the club's *English* home base.

In their constant effort to extend their reach, the Dodgers began a tentative set of Korean-language broadcasts in the early 1990s. This occurred mostly through the good offices of constant booster Richard Choi, who has described the action in Korean over a variety of stations over these past 20 years. Interest is highest when Korean natives such as Chan-Ho Park, Hee-Seop Choi, and Hyun-Jin Ryu play for LA. The Dodgers also briefly tried broadcasting in Chinese in 1993.

In addition, the Dodgers produced a female-centered Webcast in 2009 with Jeanne Zelasko — at that time *Fox Saturday Baseball*'s studio host — doing play-by-play with former pinch-hitter supreme Mark Sweeney on color. This broadcast streamed exclusively over the Dodgers' website for all Wednesday home contests. Zelasko had been a finalist for the 2009 road TV job, and the Webcast was seen a way to keep her in the family and perhaps test her for a bigger role. The project only lasted one season, however, and Zelasko eventually landed at ESPN.

Over their nearly 60 years on the west coast, the Dodgers have expanded their audience to the Pacific Rim and Latin America while sometimes alienating fans at home with their broadcasting policies.

Prior to 2012, the Boys in Blue moved to a new radio home: KLAC. The station's first order of business was to dump Joe Block and Josh Suchon, co-hosts of *Dodger Talk*, the club's popular postgame show. Block landed on his feet, joining Bob Uecker in Milwaukee's radio booth, but Suchon — a onetime beat writer in the Bay Area — found no immediate replacement work.

Kevin Kennedy, controversial former Rangers and Red Sox skipper as well as a longtime minor-league manager in the Dodgers' system, took over the postgame chair. Kennedy worked on Fox's national broadcasts as well as on TV in Tampa Bay in 2009–10; he is better suited to the studio role than to live action.

KLAC signed the Dodgers to a three-year deal for 2013–15. Scully continues to simulcast the first three innings on radio and TV for home games and most for NL West road games, while Steiner and Monday do the final six innings of those contests on radio and all nine innings for other games. How long Scully will want to continue calling a large slate of games is unknown.

The television side of the equation was as chaotic as the radio picture was stable. Dodgers owner Frank McCourt — nearly broke and locked in a bitter divorce with estranged wife and former club CEO Jaime — attempted to save his ownership by negotiating a record new TV rights deal with Fox Sports West.

After drawing $30 million in unsecured loans from Fox to meet the team's payroll, McCourt cut an audacious new 17-year deal in spring 2011 to extend the RSN's TV rights. Commissioner Bud Selig, who had already appointed former Rangers president Tom Schieffer to oversee Los Angeles' finances, vetoed the $3 billion deal with its crucial $385 million upfront payment, which caused McCourt to put the franchise into bankruptcy.

The ugly mess continued to play out over the summer and fall with McCourt and Fox threatening to sue and Selig trying to assert MLB's control while remaining above the fray. Eventually on November 1, 2011, all sides agreed to a court-supervised sale of the club and related assets like Dodger Stadium.

Driven by the lucrative potential auction of the Dodgers' television rights, the sale price for the club hit an astounding $2.3 billion. Guggenheim Partners, a financial services conglomerate, led the group that purchased the club.

The deal hinged on whether the value of the team's TV rights could be raised. And after a bidding war with Fox, Time Warner Cable emerged late in 2012 as the winner, guaranteeing the Dodgers some $8.3 billion over 25 years to run a new RSN called SportsNet LA.

Debuting in 2014, the channel is built around and owned by the Dodgers and features a round-the-clock on-air schedule.

Baseball broadcast pioneers for most of their history, the Dodgers' new owners sail into an uncertain but promising future. MLB approval of the new TV pact came slowly and with some concessions, as the revolutionary deal was structured so as to keep most of the Dodgers' revenue away from MLB's revenue-sharing fund.

Unfortunately for the Time Warner, their $210 million annual payout to the club led to the need to charge very high fees to other local cable systems that wanted to pick up SportsNet LA. Time Warner has some 32% of coverage of the area, but another large operator (DirecTV, with a 27% carriage share) balked at paying the $4-$5 cost, per subscriber, per month, to carry the Dodgers' channel. Additional carriers Cox, Dish, and Verizon also refused to carry SportsNet LA.

RED BARBER'S 14 RULES FOR MEN AT THE MIKE

1. Always be yourself. Be natural. You have to ad lib so much that artificiality will kill you off if you want to adopt a strained style.

2. Do not affect any cliques. Do not develop any hates, any strong likes or dislikes, and foist them on the public. Make up your mind to like all the writers, players, managers, and owners, and never say an unkind word.

3. Remember, you are no umpire, referee, judge, or manager. Call them as you see them, and do not second-guess.

4. Maintain a close, friendly, intimate if possible, contact with players and managers. Keep asking questions.

5. Never stop studying the players and the game. Get to the ball park with the first player, hang around the dugout, follow all leads, regard no detail as too small.

6. Accept fan mail with thanks and a level head. Read all your pan mail closer than your fan mail. The panners help you more than the pat-on-the-backs.

7. Read *The Sporting News* through every week. Read your sports pages. Carefully, religiously.

8. Read your thesaurus and dictionary every day. You are a merchant of words and you can never have enough words with which to express yourself. Pick up expressions, divers (sic) ways of saying the same thing.

9. Keep your own baseball scores. Keep your own statistics. Post them every morning.

10. Never for a moment forget that announcing is your life work. Forget the glamour, the kids chasing for autographs. You cannot pay your rent in laurels.

11. Never forget that peculiar quality of radio—what is said remains said. You cannot erase it. One boner may kill your career.

12. Build up confidence everywhere—among your listeners, the writers, players, managers, owners. Be honest always.

13. Get the background of your city, of your ball club, of your players. Learn all you can about your listening public, about the city and its suburbs and humanize your announcing.

14. Keep physically fit. Broadcasting is a strain. I lose ten pounds a season. One big night sets you back a whole week. Never drink at all, and if you must take a drink, don't do it until your day's work is done. That means even beer.

—from the December 14, 1939 *Sporting News*

The impasse — being fought over the largest fee in the country charged for a local sports network — continued through the 2014 season, with no end in sight. And the increased scrutiny over rights and carriage fees is not good news for the secretive MLB and cable industries.

After helming the first season on SportsNet LA, Vincent Scully signed on to continue his broadcast schedule in 2015, though he vowed to further cut his road schedule. When the inevitable day arrives that Scully retires from the booth, it should be fascinating to see if Los Angeles can come up with another broadcaster who can even begin to fill his shoes.

The Dodgers took some steps to address this point in December 2013. After declining to retain TV voices Eric Collins and Steve Lyons, Los Angeles hired Orel Hershiser, who pitched for the club for 13 seasons, as its

For baseball fans who love and remember the "old ways," Vin Scully's continuing presence in the Dodgers booth in a career spanning more than 60 years is one of the game's great blessings. (National Baseball Hall of Fame and Museum)

new television color man for road games. Hershiser, late of ESPN radio and television, is expected to work on home games as well when/if Scully decides to hang 'em up.

Also coming aboard were Nomar Garciparra and Jerry Hairston Jr., who work mostly as in-studio commentators, and Alanna Rizzo as the by-now necessary on-field reporter. Larger studio crews, sideline reporters, and microphone-wielding talking heads roaming the stands are now part of most major league baseball broadcasts; it's a long way from one announcer doing 23 innings.

THREE MEN AND A MIKE

WASHINGTON SENATORS/MINNESOTA TWINS BROADCASTING HISTORY

"I quickly learned that the pictures on the tube were the new stars. My job was to enhance that picture for the viewer by adding information or insight or emotion to make the viewer's enjoyment even more complete."
— *Bob Wolff on calling television games (2011)*

THE HISTORY OF SENATORS AND TWINS BROADCASTING BOILS down to three men: Herb Carneal, Bob Wolff, and Arch McDonald. Ford Frick Award winners all, the three form a nearly uninterrupted chain of 75 years of excellence in Washington and Minnesota.

When Clark Griffith chose to air Senators games for the first time in 1934, he handpicked the garrulous 33-year-old McDonald, who in 1932 had won a *Sporting News* poll as most popular minor league radio announcer while with Chattanooga's WDOD.

Before taking to the mike, McDonald had been, among other things, a soda jerk, a patent-medicine salesman, a roustabout, and a second for boxer Jack Dempsey. One day, hanging around the Chattanooga ballpark, he was asked to test out a PA system. McDonald was a natural: he sounded so good that he eventually got the radio job.

Like other major league teams in the 1930s, Washington aired road contests only as re-creations from tickertape accounts. McDonald proved to be expert at these half-theater/half-sports events. His homespun manner and hillbilly phrasing won over the nation's capital — still very much a Southern city before the explosive growth brought by the Second World War.

Essentially a populist, McDonald opened his nightly sports radio shows with a recording of the sorrowful country/bluegrass number "They Cut Down the Old Pine Tree." He called runners "ducks on the pond." His home run call was, "There she goes, Mrs. Murphy!" McDonald was "dizzy" before Dizzy Dean took the mike, and as authentically "rosy" as his contemporary Rosey Rowswell. Arriving on the scene even before Red Barber, McDonald was the first unapologetically Southern voice to succeed as a big-league broadcaster.

Hired by WJSV, a 10,000-watt CBS station, in 1934, McDonald preached to a huge audience, including listeners to his 15-minute 6:30 p.m. sports show sponsored by People's Drug Stores. The Senators, defending AL champions for the last time, permitted McDonald to air their 1934 Opening Day game live from Griffith Stadium. As unlikely as it seems, though, the new announcer really made his mark with his popular re-creations.

Broadcasting from a glassed-in storefront at the People's Drug Store on G Street near the White House, McDonald was a show to watch as well as to hear. A big man who got bigger the more he enjoyed life, McDonald would gesticulate wildly during his re-creations, banging gongs and quoting song lyrics.

Eventually these "faked games" would originate from a theater that seated more than 300 fans, with McDonald often working before a full house. In the November 2001 edition of the Old Time Radio Club's *Illustrated Press*, Jerry Collins wrote that McDonald stayed a half-inning behind the action in case the incoming wire feed went dead.

As the years went by, McDonald became more successful in Washington despite a patina of sadness in his persona. "The Old Pine Tree" was an odd choice for a signature tune, dealing as it did with the Southern practice of cutting down a pine tree to make a casket, in the song for the dead love of the protagonist. Perhaps Arch McDonald, a drifter in the classic sense, had seen enough sorrow that he was determined to live his life to its fullest.

From 1935–1937, the Senators decided not to broadcast any home games, but McDonald's re-creations and nightly summaries bewitched the region. In 1936, the voice of the national capital finished second to Cincinnati's Harry Hartman in a *TSN* fan vote for favorite major league broadcasters. Also in 1936, McDonald did his live program from the Nationals' camp in Orlando during spring training — the longest-distance live radio hookup in the country at the time. That year, General Mills, a huge sponsor during baseball's early radio days, took over as sponsor of WJSV's recaps and re-creations.

McDonald's legend grew almost as fast as his girth. In November 1936, he won a famous "eat-off" against Washington coach Nick Altrock at a birthday banquet for Calvin Griffith.

Prior to the 1938 campaign — the first in which the Senators aired their home games — McDonald attended and addressed a baseball broadcasting conference at the Edgewater Beach Hotel in Chicago. Ford Frick and Donald Davis of General Mills were the keynote speakers, and the company's voices from across the land were expected to attend.

During these early days, General Mills had a behavior code for its announcers. Accuracy and nonpartisanship were major planks in the company's platform, though McDonald openly rooted for the Senators. Even more important, however, was General Mills' dictum that broadcasters should not "rip" players or umpires for poor performance, instead letting the listeners sort things out for themselves.

The first baseball broadcaster known for "ripping" (i.e., consciously going negative on players) was probably Harry Caray, disliked and feared by St. Louis players for many years. An announcer needs plenty of traction with the fans in order to carry that off, and few broadcasters have lasted long enough to be able to fire when ready. Cincinnati's Marty Brennaman may be the only current voice who might be considered a "ripper," although his criticisms are usually pointed at umpires, other teams' fans, or Reds opponents.

Once the Senators started airing home games, the three New York teams became the only clubs to ban on-site radio, as the Gotham powers had agreed in 1934 not to sell radio rights for five years.

These were heady times in radio, with innovations producing many of the things now taken for granted. On June 9, 1938, WJSV experimented with a separate microphone pointed at the field to pick up the crack of bat, the banter of players, the calls of the home plate umpire, and the sounds of the crowd.

Later that month, McDonald broke his ankle and was hospitalized, so he had a tickertape machine installed in his room and did his updates from the infirmary! That kind of dedication and love for his work made the toast of the District a prime candidate for even bigger jobs, and soon, the New York Yankees and Giants came calling. After getting Griffith's blessing to leave D.C., McDonald — selected above 612 other applicants — migrated north to air Yankees and Giants home games in 1939.

Replacing McDonald in Washington was legendary pitcher and Hall of Famer Walter Johnson, assisted starting at mid-season by Harry McTigue. Johnson, a county commissioner in Maryland as well as a farmer, was in the vanguard of a wave of former athletes migrating to the air waves: ten old-time players were major-league announcers in 1939. General Mills remained the club's sponsor.

In June, when Johnson took some time off to attend the inaugural induction ceremony at the grand opening of the Hall of Fame in Cooperstown, McDonald was master of ceremonies at the event.

Northern culture and McDonald did not mesh well. Oddly — given Red Barber's success in Brooklyn — some baseball rooters in New York cared little for what they saw as a cornpone delivery, despite McDonald's popularizing the phrase "right down Broadway" and nicknaming Joe DiMaggio "The Yankee Clipper." Following his first year in New York, McDonald asked to be let out of the remainder of his contract.

Johnson was happy to return to his Maryland farm and leave the broadcasting to McDonald who, as WJSV sports director, earned a $25,000 salary. The Big Train ran a losing campaign for Congress in 1940 as "The Old Pine Tree" resumed his familiar place behind the mike in the District of Columbia. However, in reaction to a 35 percent drop in attendance in 1939, the club permitted no Sunday or holiday home broadcasts.

Things were changing, though. After the 1940 season, CBS radio — pressured by its non-baseball sponsors — forced WJSV and its other affiliates to drop the National Pastime in favor of soap operas. As a result, the Congressionals found themselves without a station. After a battle with WOL, WMAL emerged as the club's new radio home. At Griffith's insistence, WJSV loaned McDonald to WMAL expressly for the Senators' games. While the Senators had asked for $30,000 for broadcast rights from WMAL, they got just $20,000. (For many years, the perception that Washington had a weak local fan base because it was a city populated primarily by people from somewhere else deflated the value of the club's broadcast rights.) General Mills was again the key sponsor.

During World War II, McDonald, one of the most popular men in the capital, worked hard on the home front. He led blood drives at his own radio station and sold $250,000 of war bonds, increasing the National Game's profile during the conflict. Because of this and his astronomical popularity, he was named as the *Sporting News'* 1942 major league announcer of the year.

What was McDonald's secret? He broadcast with unfeigned enthusiasm, speaking for and to the folks sitting in the bleachers and the grandstands. "Use penny words," McDonald philosophized in 1942, "and let the dollar words take care of themselves."

One day he remarked excitedly that, if the Senators didn't win a game he was re-creating, "Then I'm Scarlett O'Hara." The Senators didn't win, and the next day, he came to the studio wearing a long dress and a wig. McDonald kept tons of pets at his Maryland home, ran unsuccessfully for Congress, wore ten-gallon cowboy hats, and ate like a herd of elephants — he was not just another regular guy.

Shirley Povich recalled years later that McDonald was a mixture of a ballgame and "a hillbilly act without the music." The legendary Washington sportswriter distilled McDonald's essence as "as natural as your next breath, as unstilted as a hearty laugh."

In tandem with his hearty laugh, McDonald employed a wicked sense of humor. During a 1952 exhibition broadcast, McDonald put on his listeners, the *Washington Star*, WWDC, and the club by claiming that 400 tickets for the club's sold out Opening Day game were in the hands of *Star* sportswriter Burton Hawkins. The resulting calls tied up switchboards at the club, the paper, and the radio station.

In 1943, Old Gold Cigarettes, a Lorillard brand, began a four-year run as sponsor of the Nats' broadcasts on WOL. General Mills was withdrawing its local baseball sponsorships, and nearly every team at that time counted cigarette makers or breweries as chief radio sponsors.

Old Gold sponsored the Cubs, White Sox, Dodgers, and Senators, requiring each of "their" announcers to promote the product during the game with a special phrase. To Arch, a nice day for a game was "as pleasant as a pack of OGs." His new sidekick, Russ Hodges, was required to greet each Senators safety with, "It's a hit — same as Old Golds!"

The beefy, popular Hodges had come aboard in 1942 after several years of baseball in Chicago. He was named the Mutual Network's top football announcer in 1943. Like McDonald, he did yeoman work in the war effort; Hodges received a special award from the Army for spending time with rehabbing patients at Walter Reed Hospital.

Hodges continued his quick rise to the top of the broadcasting world by snaring the Yankees No. 2 job, working with Mel Allen, on March 1, 1946. McDonald partnered with Stan Stoller and Ray Morgan from 1946–1948, but it was the arrival of 27-year-old Bob Wolff in 1947 that began the second era of Senators broadcasting.

The indefatigable Wolff, who in 2014 celebrated his 68th year in broadcasting, became legendary for his tolerance for — indeed, his appetite for — a schedule that would have defeated most others. Wolff did not miss a single Nats game from 1947 through 1959. Curt Smith wrote of his style, "He has a sense of humor — with the old Senators, he had to — and he was always honest. There is no phony baloney with Bob Wolff."

Wolff started his career at the mike in 1939 while studying at Duke University, where he played baseball for Jack Coombs, who had gone 31-9 for Connie Mack's 1910 Athletics! He then moved to the Navy, producing films and books, which kept him in the nation's capital, rather than overseas, during World War II. Wolff landed his first radio job in 1945.

A friendly, get-along guy in a world where such skills were highly valued, Wolff was also somewhat of a hipster. Along with using vernacular such as "like" and "man," in the early 1950s Wolff even played ukulele for the Senators' vocal group, the Four Base Hits. (Most teams of the time had vocal groups, a tradition dating back to the 1880s.)

Washington brought Wolff along to narrate their first season on television when WTTG, a DuMont Network station, put all 77 Senators home games on the telly in 1947. The season opener on April 19 featured the first-ever televised image of a president (Harry Truman) flinging the season's first ball. This telecast was special enough that it was also broadcast in New York via coaxial cable.

On the radio side, McDonald regaled the fans on behalf of sponsors Sinclair Refining and Diamond Cab, but the Senators did not have a network of stations to broadcast his voice. WWDC-AM and WWDC-FM aired night games, while WPIK covered the rest of the Washington schedule.

The Senators televised all home games through the 1950 season as Wolff became staggeringly popular in Washington for his voice, professionalism, and ubiquity. Ford Motors sponsored the club in 1948, but the following season, Chesterfield cigarettes paid $200,000 to become the club's sole radio-TV sponsor — and, save for one billboard, in Griffith Stadium.

Though it seems hard to imagine, many people didn't quite understand the potential of radio and TV advertising at that time. An example was that, in 1950, WWDC received just $110,000 from Chesterfield for its radio rights (not including the park signage).

For 1951, Clark Griffith actually sold a sponsorship to local brewer Heurich — brewers of Old Georgetown — even though he had never actually sold beer at Griffith Stadium! Huerich paid Griffith $125,000 for park signage, radio, and 21 TV games' worth of advertisements. The Senators would finally allow beer to be sold at their home games in August 1956, but by then, both Huerich and Clark Griffith were gone from the picture.

Because back then baseball teams tended to view television primarily as a marketing tool and not as a major revenue generator, most of the Nats' 1951 telecasts were night games in the first half of the season — an unbalanced schedule designed to promote games later in the season when the kids were out of school.

By this point, Wolff had become even busier. Working with McDonald on radio starting in 1950, he also provided a daily sports report and taped player interviews. He also found time to write a newspaper column as well as re-create an afternoon AL game if the Senators were scheduled to play at night. In 1952, McDonald missed time with a kidney problem that required surgery, putting even more pressure on Wolff.

That season, the Senators were still re-creating road games, although they did live broadcasts of 12 exhibitions from Florida and added a 12-station radio network. Washington, on orders from Griffith — whose spendthrift ways were noticed by adopted son Calvin — was the last team in the majors to re-create road games, paying for their broadcast team to travel to all road games only beginning in 1955. Prior to that year, the budget-conscious Senators only did live road radio when they also televised.

The 1953 Opening Day Yankees at Senators game was not shown in Washington but, strangely, was telecast by St. Louis' KSD and a 14-station network, composed of stations scattered around the US, using the Browns' announcing team. (Local TV stations in the 1950s would sometimes link up in ad hoc "networks" to cover important events ignored by major television networks NBC, CBS, and DuMont. KSD was a big station in the Midwest.)

Bailey Goss, a local announcer long affiliated with Baltimore-based National Brewing, joined McDonald and Wolff in the booth for 1953. The budding relationship with the brewer eventually would have serious repercussions for the Nats. That season, the Senators expanded their TV plan from 26 to 54 games, and, in a local first, WTTG televised at least one game from each American League city.

The following season, National paid $750,000 for an exclusive three-year pact to sponsor the Senators on radio, TV, and in the park. With Goss shifting to Orioles games, National Brewing hired longtime PR guy and sometime mikeman Howie Williams to coordinate all aspects of the broadcasts both for the Orioles and Senators.

During 1954, with a 31-station radio network down the line from WWDC, Washington broadcast 15 spring games and the full regular-season schedule. Although the network had grown to 39 stations two years later, two years after that it had fallen to just 13. The lackluster Senators were mired in the second division and, by 1957, Arch McDonald was gone.

National Brewing's relationship with the Senators pumped money into the club's coffers in return for a huge amount of editorial control, an arrangement which was typical at the time. In some cases, in fact, the sponsors had more of an editorial role than the teams themselves. National and Arch McDonald simply did not get along, and after 1956, McDonald decided to step down.

This was a mutual decision. The popular 55-year-old was not overly fond of the extra travel involved in doing live road games, and his health had declined. Despite the shocking announcement, McDonald retained his daily sports show, his position as WTOP sports director, and his role as the voice of both Redskins and University of Maryland football.

McDonald continued to entertain Washington and its environs until November 16, 1960, when he died of a heart attack on a train back from New York after broadcasting a Redskins-Giants game. After being hospitalized in 1958 and 1960, the veteran mikeman chose to enjoy what time he had left. So McDonald died doing what he loved most: talking sports and playing cards. The pine tree they cut down for him must have been a strong one.

Wolff became the team's lead voice in 1957, by which time he had already begun burnishing his national reputation. During the winter of 1954–1955, he had covered events — hockey, basketball, and the like — at New York's Madison Square Garden. He also was busy on the gridiron; Wolff's call of December 31, 1954's Gator Bowl was, amazingly, his 250th sports broadcast of the year. He did national broadcasts of the 1956 All-Star game and World Series, sitting behind the mike for a memorable call of Don Larsen's perfect game.

During the late 1950s and early 1960s, Wolff worked baseball broadcasts with eager young producer and statistician Maury Povich — Shirley's son, who years later became a well-known media personality. On at least one occasion, Maury Povich did play-by-play when Wolff had to leave the booth and catch a plane to New York.

On January 8, 1956, WTTG presented what may have been the first-ever baseball nostalgia television program. The *Washington Nationals Show* aired from 11:00–11:15 p.m. on Sundays, showing historical Senators footage and featuring an in-studio guest. Soon, WTTG was airing four different baseball programs besides the games themselves: a pregame show, a postgame show titled *Dugout Chatter*, the aforementioned Nats show, and a fifth 15-minute program called *TV's Baseball Hall of Fame*.

National and the Senators signed a three-year, $1.5 million sponsorship deal before the 1957 season. For their $500,000 annual fee, National received exclusive ballpark signage and 4½ innings each game of exclusive radio/TV sponsorship. The National deal also put 30 Senators games on television in Baltimore each season through 1961. The cross-market broadcasts went both ways: in 1957 WTTG aired 27 Orioles games in D.C. in addition to its slate of 48 Senators tilts.

At the behest of National Brewing, Chuck Thompson — much more pliable to the sponsor's will than the sometimes cantankerous McDonald — came north to assist Wolff at the mike in 1957–1958. That arrangement ended in 1959 when, unexpectedly, National and the Senators broke up.

What happened? Prior to the 1959 season, WTOP, a radio-TV conglomerate owned by the Washington Post, outbid everyone to purchase the club's radio and TV rights. Calvin Griffith — who had become the owner when his father died in 1955 — wanted to sharply limit TV games, showing just 13 in 1959. Although Griffith said that this was "advantageous" for the club, the team netted but $125,000 for its media rights — just one-third of what the Boston Red Sox, for example, netted.

For several years, Griffith — complaining about low attendance and low broadcast rights fees — had threatened to flee west. The threats intimidated the District into committing funds to build a new, modern stadium. However, progress on the facility was slow and Griffith kept looking for an opportunity to escape. Ultimately, District of Columbia Stadium, the first superstadium, would open in 1962, a year after Griffith and his promising team had relocated.

It's not surprising that a bad team in a crumbling venue, owned by a bottom-line business-man with a wandering eye, would struggle to draw crowds, listeners, and viewers. For 1960, the club's last season in D.C., the Senators received just $250,000 for their radio and TV broadcasts, the smallest amount in the majors. Appropriately, their 24 telecasts were also the fewest in the AL.

By the 1960s, American League clubs were televising far more of their games than National League clubs. In 1960, the Yankees telecast 124 games, then the most-ever and the most in the majors by a large margin. All junior league teams put at least some games on the tube, and six AL clubs aired more than 40 games. In the senior circuit, however, neither the Braves nor the Giants telecast anything, and only the Cubs aired more than half their games. As a result, network broadcasts tended to tilt more toward the National League.

Local broadcasters went on strike briefly in 1960. With Wolff and Thompson (back for a year between other jobs) unavailable, Arch McDonald Jr., a broadcast executive, took to the WTOP booth to cover a couple of games, apparently handling matters capably.

On October 26, 1960, the Senators wangled permission from other AL owners to move to Minneapolis, which embraced the club once the plans for the rival Continental League went bust. The sports landscape in the Twin Cities was changing dramatically, as Bob Short had moved the NBA Minneapolis Lakers to Los Angeles earlier that year and the NFL Vikings had taken the field a month before the announcement of the Senators' move.

Calvin Griffith said that one reason to move was the potential for increased broadcasting revenue; he hoped to realize a half-million annually. That target was unrealistic in the short term but, rebranded as the Minnesota Twins, the franchise's financial position did improve materially. Griffith was about to benefit from a felicitous combination of an eager fan base, increased media revenue, and the development of his young, talented team.

Wolff anchored the initial broadcasts over WCCO radio, which remained the club's flagship through 2006, one of the longest continuous relationships for a radio flagship in big-league history. The second play-by-play voice was Ray Scott, already popular in the region for his calls of Green Bay Packers football on CBS.

The Twins got one heck of a third broadcaster in Halsey Hall, beloved for decades as a newspaperman and sportscaster in the Twin Cities. Hall was quite a character: he did play-by-play for baseball, football, and basketball; officiated high school basketball games; wrote millions of words; and was married to the same woman for 55 years despite the stresses of his lifestyle. Hall is said to be the first to use the exclamation "Holy Cow!" while calling a baseball game.

Hall had tastes for history, puns, green onions, cigars, alcohol, and baseball, not necessarily in that order. During a 1968 broadcast from Chicago, his cigar ash set afire a pile of ticker tape, burning his jacket. Twins catcher Jerry Zimmerman cleverly noted, "Halsey's the only man I know who can turn a sports jacket into a blazer." (The Twin Cities' Society for American Baseball Research chapter is named in honor of Hall.)

WTCN-TV, the area's second TV channel, beamed five Friday night home games and 45 road tilts in 1961. WTCN had just lost its ABC network affiliation, so it had plenty of primetime air available for baseball. Eventually Twins games were beamed to fans in five states. Hamm's Beer, a Twin Cities–based brewer that had expanded nationally during Prohibition by making soft drinks, was the big early sponsor of the Twins on radio and TV, but over the years the team enlisted a large cast of occasional advertisers.

Twins games were an immediate hit with the fans, both in the park and over the air. Wolff, however, turned out to be a bad fit for Minnesota — not because he was unpopular, but because he was too far from his family and his East Coast bases in Washington and New York. Very big out east, Wolff was largely unknown in the Upper Midwest.

Though Wolff was in the running for the lead job with the expansion Mets, he didn't get it. Instead, he forsook the Twins in favor of NBC-TV's national baseball telecasts in 1962, pairing with Joe Garagiola for 50 Saturday and Sunday games. Following the 1965 season, his last calling baseball, Wolff took a job with Madison Square Garden. To this day, Wolff reports on sports for a Long Island television station.

Minnesota welcomed Herb Carneal as the Twins' primary voice for their second season, broadcast on WCCO and a 32-station network. As a 21-year-old in 1954, Carneal had assisted By Saam and Claude Haring in Philadelphia then three years later hopped aboard the Orioles' train on WMAR, which he rode for five seasons.

Hamm's had sponsored Orioles games in the late 1950s, and this connection had much to do with Carneal's ascendance to the No. 1 job in Minnesota. He was a known quantity to the brewery, which remained affiliated with the team into the 1970s.

The unprepossessing Carneal was known as a gentleman who eschewed carousing and read incessantly; unlike many others in the press box, he was keenly interested in non-sports subjects. His rich, friendly tone came to embody the Upper Midwest: chatty without being catty, informative without being patronizing.

From 1962 through 1966, Carneal, Scott, and Hall described the exploits of an exciting, talented Twins team. By 1966, the club's 55-station radio network spanned the Upper Midwest, with 15 more stations in the Rocky Mountain Northwest carrying the games on weekends. On television, the Twins took to color before many clubs, so beaming nearly two-thirds of them in 1966.

The Twins' advertisers in the mid-1960s included Western Oil and Fuel, Pure Oil, and Northern States Power. But Hamm's remained the biggest guarantor, inking a new three-year pact with the Twins in late 1966 for $600,000 per.

For personal reasons, Scott resigned his Twins position after the 1966 season. From that point, most of his work involved football and golf. Former Athletics and network baseball announcer Merle Harmon joined the Twins' broadcast team in 1967.

Despite having geographically the largest television and radio networks in the American League, the Twins in 1969 netted only $650,000 total from their radio and television rights. That was not much more than they had realized eight years previously, and higher than only the expansion Royals, the Senators, and the badly-run Red Sox in the AL.

From 1965 through 1970, Minnesota fans experienced a lot of exciting baseball. The Twins' made their first World Series appearance in 1965; came up one game short in a disheartening, *closeasthis* second-place finish in 1967; and won the first two division titles in the new AL West in 1969 and 1970. The franchise then went into a 15-year decline, however, as aging stars, poor scouting, and Griffith's penurious ways made a bad match with the advent of free agency.

The down cycle on the field was complemented by a lack of consistency in the team's broadcasts. Prior to 1970, Hamm's — purchased two years earlier by Connecticut-based brewer Hueblein — dropped its commitment to the Twins as Midwest Federal Savings inked a seven-year deal to become top sponsor, retaining all rights (and profits) from sub-selling both TV and radio ads.

With the Seattle Pilots rumored to be headed for Milwaukee in spring 1970, Merle Harmon made it known that he wanted the relocated club's top radio job. The Twins reduced Harmon's projected role for 1970 to TV games in case he stayed, and when the Pilots were legally cleared to move just before Opening Day, Harmon fled.

Harmon's departure and Hamm's withdrawal were followed by a period of virtual chaos; amazingly, the Twins' radio/TV team changed each year from 1970 through 1980, with a baffling array of second-tier play-by-play men and not-so-articulate former players rotating through the booth. The club's on-air presence reflected Minnesota's on-field fortunes, which foundered during the 1970s.

The Robert Wold agency of Los Angeles took over managing the club's radio affairs in 1972. North Star Productions, a Wold subsidiary, built a new — but far smaller — network, selling half the ad time itself and letting the affiliates sell the remaining spots.

Flagship WCCO rolled out its own new advertising paradigm the next year. In the past, ads for games were sold by innings, but the station's new plan stipulated that all ad placements would rotate between game, pregame, and postgame, with each advertiser getting 75% of its spots during the games. Furthermore, all spots would now be sold in 30-second increments, and buying more spots got the sponsors increased promotional time during the station's non-baseball programming.

This innovative plan was successful, with the Twins pulling in many new local and national advertisers, but the on-field product had deteriorated. Ray Scott returned for the TV play-by-play in 1973, but he didn't even call the Opening Day telecast because he was already committed to the Masters Golf Tournament. Veteran Jack Drees filled in, calling his final big-league game.

Halsey Hall's retirement in 1973 at age 75 didn't help; the Twins never enjoyed another like him. Hall passed in 1977. Weathering the storm of changes, Carneal stood tall in the North Country, describing with dignity the lesser players who strolled the diamonds previously trod by demigods like Tony Oliva, Jim Kaat, Harmon Killebrew, and Rod Carew.

Perhaps the most interesting new Twins' broadcaster of the 1970s was Carol Kerner, a 37-year-old radio reporter who did color on a pair of games on WCCO in April 1977 after hosting the pregame for the Vikings the previous fall. While the station apparently wanted her to succeed in baseball, she did not return to the Twins' broadcasts.

The Twins moved from the suburbs to downtown in 1982, from cozy but obsolete Metropolitan Stadium to the modern, antiseptic Herbert H. Humphrey Metrodome. Carneal and Frank Quilici began the final season of a three-year term on WCCO, while Bob Kurtz and Larry Osterman did their fourth of five years televising 50 games on KMSP.

The team's radio network continued to decline dangerously, as other Midwestern clubs like the Royals and Cardinals put together far more attractive teams and network packages for radio stations in small cities across the Upper Midwest and Great Plains.

In 1983, local media consortium and WCCO owner Midwest Radio-TV acquired the team's full media rights from Midwest Federal and subleased the television rights to KMSP, prior to selling them outright to the station for 1985. The following season, Carneal paired with short-termers Tim Moreland and Ron Weber.

A controversy arose when cable-TV venture Spectrum Sports was sold the rights to air 50 home contests in 1983, with Dick Bremer and Pat Hughes in the booth. Midwest Radio-TV thought it had locked in complete television rights, but the Twins disagreed. After an early 1984 ruling that Midwest Radio-TV indeed had legal rights to the cablecasts, a settlement was reached that allowed Spectrum to remain on the air. Hughes departed for Milwaukee, but Minnesota native Bremer teamed with Harmon Killebrew for two more seasons before Spectrum Sports went belly-up. That left the club with no cable package for 1986. On KMSP, Kurtz — radio voice of the NHL's Minnesota Wild since the franchise's inception — ended his eight-year tenure with the Twins, working with Killebrew.

The following season brought big surprises, as the 1987 Twins stormed their way to their first world championship, upsetting the Cardinals in a dramatic Fall Classic. Above the field, the team's broadcasting situation simultaneously reached new heights. First, John Rooney came aboard after several successful years apprenticing in Louisville on Triple-A broadcasts, assuming the play-by-play chair on KMSP and also helping on radio. Displaying both talent and potential, Rooney would leave for Chicago after one year and establish a national reputation.

Second, John Gordon joined WCCO as Carneal's co-pilot, replacing anodyne Joe Angel. After years of experience on Orioles and Yankees broadcasts, Gordon was ready for a new home. Deeply involved with the Fellowship of Christian Athletes, "Gordo" remained at the mike in Minnesota for a quarter-century. Although his radio descriptions were less rich in detail in his later years, the enthusiastic broadcaster remained popular.

Finally, Twins Vision, the area's second sports cable network, made its debut with Bremer, who had worked three years with Spectrum, as its lead voice. Bremer featured a classic baritone reminiscent of By Saam or Ray Scott. In 1993, he assumed all Twins television play-by-play chores. Since 1995, Bremer has paired successfully with former Twins hurler Bert Blyleven, whose use of a Telestrator to "circle" Metrodome fans on the TV screen led to a local rock band recording a song called "Circle Me Bert."

From 1988 through 1992, Ted Robinson handled the play-by-play on over-the-air broadcasts on KMSP, WCCO, and KITN. Prior to Blyleven's hire, Bremer and Robinson teamed with a variety of former players, sharing airtime with the Jim Kaat (insightful), George Frazier (creditable), and Al Newman and Tommy John (neither of whom lasted long).

Carneal and Gordon worked without interruption through 1999, an old-fashioned, veteran baseball radio team in the tradition of Prince & Woods or Allen & Hodges. The demands of baseball on the radio cause most teams to employ second, or even third, chairs that can also handle some play-by-play, and the Twins have rarely expected their No. 2 announcer to strictly provide color. Because television's play-by-play role is much less demanding than radio's, many more ex-players have become prominent on TV, making former players who do a good job with radio play-by-play (like Richie Ashburn and Waite Hoyt) rare and valuable.

Midwest Sports Channel, a cable venture of WCCO that originally showed mostly collegiate sports, broadcast Twins games for 12 years starting in 1989. Many of those contests, including most at home, were aired on a pay-per-basis. Few clubs, however, were successful with pay-per-view, though the Twins tried for several years. Eventually, they moved more than 100 of their games annually to MSC.

Following the 1994–1995 strike, the Twins' TV fortunes plummeted and their over-the-air schedules were reduced to fewer than 30 games per season. More games were switched to cable when Liberty Media bought the struggling MSC and merged it with Wisconsin Sports Network in 1995. Fox Sports purchased MSC in 1999, with the channel taking the FSN (Fox Sports North) branding two years later.

The Twins made a major strategic mistake in 2003 when owner Carl Pohlad attempted to emulate other MLB franchises with his own RSN by launching Victory Sports Network. The old FSN contract, which ended in 2002, had paid the Twins about $6 million per season for television which, by the time the deal expired, was well below the going rate.

After rejecting a new, $12 million annual offer from FSN, Twins management made big plans for their own startup cable channel, which was to feature a lineup comprised of Twins baseball, University of Minnesota basketball, local high school sports, and outdoor sports programming. Most cable providers in the region, however, would not pay $2.20 per subscriber

Back in the days when sponsors dictated announcers, Herb Carneal — with five years experience on Orioles broadcasts — was shifted to Minnesota for 1962. He remained the Twins' voice until passing away in April 2007, a model of stability, civility, and good humor. (National Baseball Hall of Fame and Museum)

for an essentially baseball-only channel, especially when FSN cost only $1.70 per subscriber, and so Victory folded on May 7, 2003 after just 19 Twins broadcasts.

After this disaster, the club was forced back to FSN, signing a 10-year contract through 2012 for $12 million annually — given the inflation in sports TV rights fees during that period, it was a steal for Fox. Bremer and Blyleven remained comfortably ensconced in the TV booth.

The Twins inked a five-year deal with a radio affiliate KSTP after 2006, ending their 46-year relationship with WCCO. KSTP would never feature the voice of revered Herb Carneal, who passed away April 1, 2007 at age 83. Carneal had called only home games for the previous seven seasons, with Dan Gladden initially serving as the road analyst but later working most games and assuming some play-by-play duty as well. The Twins played in 2007 with commemorative uniform patches honoring Carneal.

Gordon announced early in 2011 that the season would be his final one in the booth. With Gordon covering only 89 games, team management auditioned Kris Atteberry, Twins pregame host and the voice of the independent minor league St. Paul Saints. Atteberry called 52 games, with Kurtz and Robinson returning for 25 games each in a bow toward nostalgia.

But rather than bring Atteberry on full-time, Minnesota hired 33-year-old Cory Provus, who had spent the previous three seasons as Bob Uecker's reliable second in Milwaukee, as the club's lead voice. Before making the decision, the club interviewed Atteberry, Royals TV play-by-play man Ryan Lefebvre, and Josh Whetzel, a broadcaster with Triple-A Rochester. Local observers were surprised that Lefebvre did not get the job.

Provus' first big-league experience came as the third man on the Cubs' radio network, and his businesslike personality was quite a contrast to Gordon's genial on-air style. Gladden's ongoing presence maintains some continuity, with Twins fans now getting a slightly more analytical broadcast than in previous decades.

Thus the remarkable 74-year chain of overlapping broadcast stars — Arch McDonald, Bob Wolff, and Herb Carneal — ended quietly in 2008, with veteran Gordon exiting the stage three years later. While Bremer and Blyleven are beloved up north, Twins fans won't hear the likes of the old big three for some time.

BRONX BANDWITH

NEW YORK YANKEES BROADCASTING HISTORY

"[Mel Allen] gave the Yankees his life…and they broke his heart."
— Red Barber

THE COGNOSCENTI OF NEW YORK DID NOT TAKE TO RADIO IN THE
1920s and 1930s. A town whose reputation as a cultural center was built on newspapers,
live music, and theater had much to fear from an electronic device that could inform and
entertain the populace in the comfort and safety of their own living rooms. "The press" — as
newspapermen of the day liked to call themselves, usually with self-important over-
tones — found itself in a bitter battle for power and influence with the rapidly growing
new medium.

Even the metropolis' baseball clubs found it disadvantageous to discuss the new gadget,
although the Yankees did allow some broadcasts, including home openers, in the early 1930s.
During the mid-1950s, after being hired by the Dodgers, announcer Andre Baruch noted
that he had called some 35 Yankees games in 1931. This would most likely have come on
WABC, the station employing him at the time.

Perhaps with some prodding from theater owners, the Yankees, Dodgers, and Giants
formally agreed to embargo broadcasts of their games for a five-year period beginning in 1934.

During that time, New York fans could only hear their heroes during the World Series.
But in sharp contrast to today, where TV networks soil themselves rushing to put East
Coast teams on the air at all costs, Ford Motor Company — sponsors of the 1934 through
1936 World Series on the CBS, NBC, and Mutual radio networks — dropped its ads from

the 1937 Giants-Yankees World Series. According to *The Sporting News*, Ford "felt that an all–New York World Series was *something of an anti-climax.*" (Emphasis added.)

Baseball could still be found on the airwaves in Gotham, however. Even in 1938, with no regular broadcasts of local games, fans could listen to contests from out-of-town stations like WJZ of Boston, WCAU of Philadelphia, or any of the various New England stations broadcasting Boston Red Sox and Braves games via the (unrelated) Yankee Network.

The Yankees detested the Red Sox for airing Boston's games throughout the Northeast. While most clubs visiting Yankee Stadium in the 1930s were free to relay accounts of their games back home for re-creation, the Red Sox were banned from doing so because New York management worried that the Boston broadcasts might impact the Yankees' home attendance.

Things changed when Larry MacPhail roared into Brooklyn in 1938 and made it clear that he would broadcast the Dodgers' games the following year, forcing the Giants and Yankees to act. On January 25, 1939, the two New York clubs announced that they would share one radio station, one set of sponsors, and one announcer for both of their Monday through Saturday home games.

General Mills, Socony Vacuum Oil, and Proctor & Gamble secured WABC — at that time a CBS station — for the games, then asked Frankie Frisch to serve as broadcaster. Frisch, however, who had never called a game before, spurned New York as well as Cincinnati to take the microphone in Boston.

Arch McDonald, heretofore the baseball voice of Washington, D.C., was hired in early March, 1939. Beating out 612 other applicants for the job, McDonald became the highest-paid sports broadcaster in the country.

Unfortunately for all concerned, McDonald and New York did not mix. The comfortable, corny banter that worked for McDonald down South did not play well in the more urbane, cynical and self-conscious Big Apple. McDonald managed to coin some memorable phrases — like calling Joe DiMaggio the "Yankee Clipper" and saying pitches came "Right down Broadway" — but, when he asked in December 1939 to be released from his contract, nobody stood in his way.

The following season the Yankees and Giants moved to phase two of their radio program, which earned them far less in sponsorship guarantees than in 1939. This time, the sole sponsor was Reynolds Tobacco, makers of Camel cigarettes.

McDonald's departure made a first-time regular of 26-year-old Melvin Allen Israel. The native of Birmingham, Alabama, described 154 games from Yankee Stadium and the Polo Grounds in 1940, including the Giants' first home night game. Coincidentally, Allen had originally been tabbed to replace McDonald in Washington in 1939, but the Senators wanted their former mound legend Walter Johnson instead. (That choice didn't work out.)

Prior to arriving in New York in 1937, Allen had earned a law degree from the University of Alabama, where he became known for calling the school's football games. Once at CBS, he understudied for legendary newsman Bob Trout and worked under Ted Husing on various sports assignments, including the 1938 World Series.

Allen found himself thrust into the local baseball scene in 1939 because of another announcer's misfortune. Garnett Marks, McDonald's first assistant in New York, twice referred on the air to Proctor & Gamble's Ivory Soap as "Ovary Soap." Exit Marks, enter Allen.

Unlike local rival Red Barber, Allen was deeply invested in the outcome of a ballgame. While not an open rooter, he was emotionally involved in his broadcasts. Allen and the old Redhead, however, did not feud; in fact, the two professionals respected each other's work, liked each other personally, and later would work together. Said Barber, many years later: "There was no fault to be found with Mel's mike ability or his voice or his reliability."

Both Allen and Barber had very strong opinions and kept tight control of their booths. Working as Mel Allen's assistant wasn't easy, but it could provide a springboard. Russ Hodges and Curt Gowdy landed No. 1 jobs after understudying in the Yankees' booth, and Art Gleeson and Bill Crowley joined Gowdy in Boston following their rookie stints in New York. Connie Desmond and Jim Woods also furthered their broadcasting careers working under Allen.

Mutual Radio tabbed Allen to host the 1940 World Series pregame and postgame. But Allen's glory at the top was short-lived. In 1941, New York was the only big-league city where no games were placed on the radio. The Yankees and Giants, running into stiff competition from Brooklyn by the name of Red Barber, found no sponsor willing to cough up enough cash to make going head-to-head with the Dodgers worth the trouble.

For 1942, however, WOR snagged the rights, with $75,000 going to both the Yankees and the Giants. General Mills (makers of Wheaties) and Macy's Department Stores served as principal sponsors. With the U.S. now at war, a whole new series of government regulations forced a preseason gathering of all baseball broadcasters sponsored by Wheaties so that the new rules could be reviewed. For example, announcers were now prohibited from discussing weather conditions, which made announcing rain delays tricky.

Allen and Barber teamed up that fall to call the World Series on Mutual. While the two often worked together, New York was split

While Dodgers and Giants fans might disagree, Mel Allen is the greatest broadcaster of baseball's "golden age." Passionate, hard-working, dedicated to the Yankees, and incredibly talented, Allen lost his job in 1964 but decades later returned to New York via cable telecasts and to the nation via "This Week in Baseball." (National Baseball Hall of Fame and Museum)

in three by its baseball passion, and few fans were neutral about their radio voices; NL partisans and Yankee-haters (and there were a lot of them) took their antipathy out on Allen. A great many other New Yorkers, though, viewed Mel Allen as engaging, enthusiastic, and exciting.

Being emotionally involved in the broadcasts was a failing to some, but this deep passion and investment in the result made Allen's star shine even more brightly to others. It's all a matter of style: What do you like? Lager or dark beer? Bebop or big band jazz? Allen or Barber?

Gillette wanted to assume sponsorship for the Yankees and Giants games for 1944. Allen was called into the service, and Gillette doggedly recruited Red Barber to cross town for the gig. But Barber, playing the situation effectively, got a raise from Brooklyn and stayed put. Therefore, Gillette sponsored Yankees and Giants home games featuring Don Dunphy and baseball clown Al Schacht in 1944 then Bill Slater and Al Helfer on WINS in 1945. WINS remained the Yankees' radio home until 1957.

Once World War II ended, the big news in New York baseball was that, for the first time, the Yankees would broadcast all their games, airing Yankee Stadium games live and road games via re-creations. Larry MacPhail, who had crossed town to run the Yankees in 1945, wanted a dedicated radio station for his club. The inevitable scheduling conflicts made it impossible for WINS to carry two teams, and Horace Stoneham's Giants decamped to WMCA. MacPhail once more attempted to get Barber to change loyalties, but the Old Redhead chose to remain with the Dodgers.

When Allen returned from the service, it was not guaranteed that he would retain his job. Sponsors had no particular loyalty to him, nor did the Yankees, who conducted a series of interviews and listened to a lot of audition tapes while considering who to hire.

Dan Topping, co-owner of the Yanks with Del Webb, was in Allen's corner, however, and his opinion apparently carried the day. Allen teamed with Russ Hodges — heretofore announcing for the Washington Senators and the NFL Detroit Lions — on Yankees broadcasts.

The Yankees remained on WINS, but with a new sponsor: Ballantine Ale, the most popular malt beverage in the region. In the days before refrigeration technology allowed for national distribution of perishable foods, each area of the country had its own distinctive beers, potato chips, bread, etc. Most teams, therefore, had a local brewery as a sponsor.

Ballantine's influence on Yankees broadcasts was as least as significant as that of Burger in Cincinnati, Budweiser in St. Louis, or National Brewing in Baltimore and Washington. The sponsor chose, or at least approved, the announcers, and also set budgets for travel, equipment, and personnel.

Under MacPhail's lead, the now radio-friendly Yankees also aggressively embraced television. DuMont Network bought the club's 1946 television rights for $75,000, using Allen and Hodges in the TV booth.

For 1948, with Ballantine and White Owl again the sponsors, Allen signed his name on a new four-year contract that paid him a total of $175,000. As one of the country's best-known voices, Allen was in demand for voice-over work, football play-by-play, and even as a disc jockey.

That April 23, a technical problem caused WINS and the Yankees some grief. Somehow an angry telephone caller had his line switched onto the broadcast line during a game. When the caller uttered an obscenity, WINS engineers cut the line immediately.

Allen worked with Hodges on both WINS and WABD-TV in 1948, simulcasting home games, a new idea in broadcasting.

Russ Hodges had signed a four-year deal in 1947 for $22,000 a year to call the action of the Yankees' baseball and football clubs. Yankees president and co-owner Dan Topping also owned the football club. (The All America Football Conference had a four-year run in the late 1940s competing with the NFL. Two of the AAFC's charter franchises were located in Gotham: the New York Yankees and the Brooklyn Dodgers.) After two years, however, with Hodges' fame rising, the Giants made him an offer to be their lead broadcaster, and he spent the rest of his career working for Horace Stoneham.

By 1950, the Yankees and their sponsors had decided that their broadcasts needed more "personality." New Yorkers, therefore, got a dose of former pitcher Dizzy Dean, who had called games in St. Louis with singular grammatical construction and surprising insight. For $25,000 per year in 1950 and 1951, he handled home pregame and postgame duty on TV. For half of those contests, he also joined Allen and new sidekick Curt Gowdy in the booth.

When Gowdy departed for Boston in 1951, the Yankees' sponsors added Art Gleeson to the broadcasting team. Before calling *Game of the Day* with Al Helfer in 1950, Gleeson had served as the voice of the Pacific Coast League Los Angeles Angels.

In 1951, WPIX and the Yankees began a relationship that lasted nearly a half century. WPIX, owned by the *New York Daily News* (then and now a Tribune company), began as an independent television station famous for its sports programming, local personalities, and popular movies.

Dean returned to St. Louis for 1952, and the Yankees inked newly retired superstar Joe DiMaggio to replace him at double the cost. The Yankee Clipper, however, never got comfortable in his on-air role and lasted just one season.

After DiMaggio failed in his only attempt at broadcasting, the Yankees tried comic actor Joe E. Brown on pregame and postgame. Brown's hiring was the latest in a series of "entertainers" in the New York booth; in addition to Dean, broadcasts had previously featured character actor J.C. Flippen in 1940 and Al Schacht in 1944. Unfortunately, despite some experience working baseball broadcasts in other cities, Brown did not make a hit in New York.

The other 1953 newcomer was Jim Woods, who had earned the Yankees' gig with his play-by-play work for the Southern Association Atlanta Crackers. According to Curt Smith, Woods was the first minor-league broadcaster to do an entire season of television work when he called Double-A Crackers games in 1949.

Woods' nickname was the "The Possum." Understudying for Allen was his first big-league job; the Southern import would be behind the mike in the majors for the next 25 years.

The ink had barely dried on the spate of 1953 postseason newspaper stories about the Yankees' 15th World Series win in 27 seasons when the shocking news broke that Red Barber had been forced out of Brooklyn.

Landing like the proverbial cat, Barber simply moved his mike to another borough, taking up residence at Yankee Stadium as the club's new television host and relief broadcaster for Allen. Tired of traveling, Barber was used almost exclusively on home games.

For 1954, Barber called 2½ innings of radio play-by-play and 2½ frames of TV play-by-play as well as handling TV pregame and postgame shows. Despite his high profile, though, Barber was clearly the second banana in Mel Allen's booth.

As Barber wrote some years later, "I did not go to the Stadium to challenge Mel Allen, as was written in several quarters when it was announced that I had the job. In no sense was there ever a contest between us . . . when I went over to Yankee Stadium I knew that I was not going to be the principal broadcaster."

In what many call the Golden Era of baseball, the dynastic Yankees were huge, drawing big crowds on the road as well as at home. In 1954, the team transmitted 49 of its home games from flagship WPIX to stations in other cities including Baltimore, Cleveland, and Washington. By now, the Yankees were broadcasting all their away games live on the radio and airing some television contests from the road, too.

Following the close of the 1956 season, during which the Yankees had won another world championship after a two-year drought, Ballantine used its heavy hand to force Woods off the broadcasts. Recently retired Yankees shortstop Phil Rizzuto regularly played golf with a bigwig at Ballantine, who thought that the Scooter would be an ideal "presence" on TV. Rizzuto had reportedly been negotiating to work on Orioles TV games, but he leapt quickly at the Yankees' opportunity.

Former Yankees shortstop Phil Rizzuto (L) got his job in the broadcast booth thanks to a friend at Ballantine Beer, the team's sponsor. While he was never erudite, Rizzuto was charming on the air and, of course, knew the game inside out. (National Baseball Hall of Fame and Museum)

The bushwhacked Woods was allowed to claim that he had resigned. Interestingly, Baltimore did not add an ex-player to its broadcast team for another 26 years.

A year later, Ballantine forced another change, this time adding Jerry Coleman, Rizzuto's ex-double-play partner, to the air team for 1958. Both Coleman's and Rizzuto's hirings came over Allen's and Barber's distinct objections. Ballantine even tried to reduce Barber's salary in order to make room in the budget, but Barber stood his ground and the brewer found some other way to pay Coleman.

George Weiss, the Yankees' GM, left not long after, and the club awarded Ballantine the rights to sell ad time on the games as well as on the pregame and postgame shows for a fixed rights fee. Soon, as many had predicted, New York Yankees' games carried a dizzying array of sponsors, and what had been interesting and unique pregame and postgame shows were increasingly transformed by a blizzard of ads.

The 1955 season had been the last in which the Yankees telecast no road games. The club's new and aggressive television strategy demanded a large broadcast team, and the desire to put glamorous ex-Yankees on the air was understandable. The gaffes and goofiness emanating from the inexperienced Rizzuto and Coleman in those years, however, were said to be something to hear. Coleman's well-known malapropisms and Rizzuto's lack of polish turned some people off, but others enjoyed their good-natured by-play.

Both former infielders eventually improved in the booth, but it must have been very difficult for perfectionists like Allen and Barber to work alongside ex-athletes who struggled to transfer their thoughts from their brains to their voice boxes.

The Yankees sailed along, winning eight pennants in the 1950s. After 1957, the Bronx Bombers were the only team in town when the Dodgers and Giants departed for California. The next spring the Yankees added Gussie Moran, former pro tennis player and onetime Dodgers pregame personality, to their own radio pregame show.

But New York was about to taste bitterness in the upcoming seasons. From 1955 through 1960, the Yankees lost three tight World Series. After the last one, Casey Stengel was fired. With Ralph Houk taking the managerial reins for 1961, WCBS snatched away the radio rights after a bitter fight with WMGM. After more than a decade, WINS was out.

WCBS aired all the team's games in 1961 on its FM station, with all but 20 weekday afternoon games also broadcast on the AM dial. New York, as always, made more money from its media package than any other American League team, especially with the Dodgers and Giants now gone.

The Yankees took full advantage of the four seasons when they had the world's biggest media market to themselves. In 1961 WPIX televised 125 Yankees games, by far the most in the majors, with several regional affiliates taking a smaller slate. Ballantine again sponsored on both TV and radio, jointed on the former by R.J. Reynolds and on the latter by Atlantic Refining. The wealthy club realized about a million dollars per year in rights fees.

The following year, Atlantic dropped out, with Ballantine and Reynolds covering all the advertising as the team's media revenue leapt to $1.2 million — highest in the game — even though the expansion Mets had set up shop at the Polo Grounds in Manhattan, directly across the Harlem River.

New York captured two more World Series in 1961 and 1962. During Game 4 of the 1963 Fall Classic, however, in the midst of a sweep of the Yankees at the hands of the Los Angeles Dodgers, Mel Allen lost his voice during the national television broadcast. Vin Scully, the second broadcaster in the booth, had to rush in to fill the void, leaving Allen a target for all sorts of damaging personal and professional speculation.

At the time, the Yankees were the U.S. Steel of baseball; it was hard to root for them due to their seeming sense of entitlement as well as their enormous wealth. CBS, sharing the network *Game of the Week* franchise with NBC, allocated most of its telecasts to covering the exploits of Mantle & Co. Because the national TV contract revenues were not split evenly amongst the teams as they have been since the mid-1960s, second division teams like the Athletics and Senators received very little TV money because their games were not often telecast nationally.

In 1964, for instance, CBS turned over more than half of the $895,000 the network spent on baseball to its most frequently featured team, the Yankees. When it became clear that Messrs. Topping and Webb wanted to sell the prize franchise, CBS decided to just buy the club outright that August.

What could be better for the "Tiffany network" than to own the perennial American League champion in the biggest media center of the country? As it turned out, the presumed sports/entertainment/media synergy never materialized as the club almost immediately fell from its near-perennial perch atop the American League.

CBS paid just over $11 million for 80 percent of the Yankees who, along with the Phillies, would be the only big-league clubs not featured during 1965's national broadcasts. (The Phils simply felt they could make more money televising locally.)

(In 1965 CBS changed its offering to the *Yankees Game of the Week*. ABC joined the national party for one year then turned over the national package to NBC. From 1965 on, the *Game of the Week* was broadcast in all local television markets; prior to 1965, big-league cities were blacked out in order to protect each club's local TV ratings from the effects of *GOTW* broadcasts. The lure of national advertising money, which logically needed to reach the biggest markets in the country, was too great for the lords of baseball to resist.)

The CBS acquisition of the Yankees received microscopic scrutiny from New York state and national lawmakers during 1964. All this occurred amidst a strange year for the Yankees who, under new skipper Yogi Berra, struggled to hold off the White Sox and Orioles to win another AL pennant in a somewhat unconvincing way.

In September, a couple of weeks after the CBS sale had closed, Dan Topping, still titular head of the Yankees, called Mel Allen into his office and informed him that his contract would not be renewed. A flabbergasted Allen was nevertheless expected to finish the season despite being blindsided; the Yankees did not make this news public. In the interim, the ever-professional but heartbroken Allen soldiered on, hoping to find a sympathetic ear somewhere in the front office.

The first external sign that Allen was in trouble was the Yankees' effort to keep him off the 1964 World Series telecast. Phil Rizzuto was selected for the games instead, shutting Allen out of the Fall Classic for the first time since 1954. No one from the club would explain publicly why Allen had been replaced, which led to rumors of a sex scandal, drug use, or greed. None was true; the team was simply greasing the skids for his exit.

In December 1964, a few weeks after the Yankees' seven-game World Series loss to St. Louis, Allen was publicly axed. How could, and why did, the Yankees fire Mel Allen?

Barber felt that the Yankees were simply tired of Allen's attitude. The Yankees averred that they and Ballantine had decided it was time for a change. Allen himself said later that struggling brewer Ballantine needed to cut costs, but that he would have taken a pay cut to stay on. The team's voice was then earning all of $60,000.

To fill their new on-air vacancy, the Yankees first recruited Tigers TV voice George Kell, who declined. Their next choice was Joe Garagiola, another ex-athlete celebrated for his lighthearted attitude about the game and himself. Some other broadcasters, including Harry Caray and Barber, had found or would find Garagiola difficult to work with.

It was sad and regrettable, that the Yankees — as with the Indians and Jimmy Dudley, or the Pirates and Bob Prince, or the Phillies and Gene Kelly — would treat a fan favorite and long-term broadcaster as shabbily as the Yankees did Allen, and with such obvious disregard for what fans may have felt. Because the amount of dollars at stake have always been huge, and the egos of the advertising and broadcasting industries' executive ranks have been concomitantly inflated, legends can sometimes be unceremoniously discarded.

Allen pondered but declined an offer from Athletics owner Charlie Finley to relocate to Kansas City. It was more important to Allen at that time to remain in the area that he loved and where he had been on top than to take another big-league job in a much smaller market. Finley never let his dream die, though, as he also wanted Allen when the club relocated to Oakland. Allen did take gigs calling games for the Braves and Indians in 1965 and 1968.

Barber, now working with Garagiola, Coleman, and Rizzuto, was hemmed in by the new jockocracy. He began to loosen his tongue a bit on the broadcasts, perhaps feeling that he had little to lose. The Yankees' dynasty immediately crumbled after Allen's departure, with the team becoming truly bad for the first time since World War I.

On September 22, 1966 — three days after Dan Topping sold his last 10 percent of the Yankees to CBS — Barber met his Waterloo. Calling a rainy weekday makeup game at the Stadium against the White Sox in late September, the veteran broadcaster made a point of noting on WPIX that only 413 people were in attendance, and that this, the smallest crowd ever at Yankee Stadium, was the big story.

With the club headed for its first last-place finish since 1912, in the Yankees' fifth straight season of declining attendance, few of the club's brass appreciated Barber's nose for news. Immediately after Barber's on-air comments, the front office, by phone, instructed the broadcast's director not to show any shots of the empty stands, and to use nothing but tight views of the playing field. Barber as well as others assumed that the directive came from new team chairman Michael Burke.

Four days later, Burke fired Barber. Burke said that the decision to can the Old Redhead had been made before he took control, but that he supported it. If the Yankees hadn't already lost the sympathy of the press for their poor play, they certainly lost it for the way they let go of Barber.

At the time, Barber said that he wanted another baseball broadcasting job, but he instead moved on to a new career as an author and to a more relaxed life with his devoted wife Lylah.

Although CBS owned the Yankees, WCBS radio showed little interest in renewing its radio rights for 1967. WHN, previously the Mets' rightsholders, took over the Yankees' package. As one could expect, moving to the Mets' old station — the Mets! — was another drop in status. Marv Albert did add some needed zing to the Yankees' games with his pregame and postgame reports.

More major changes were in the offing. The day after Barber was fired, Ballantine — losing market share to bigger national breweries — pulled its Yankees sponsorship, which amounted to a million dollars per year.

With Ballantine now no longer able to do any damage to the Yankees' broadcasts, most of the links to the club's great past were gone. Stengel was retired. Dan Topping and Del Webb were out of the picture. Mel Allen and Red Barber were history. Whitey Ford was only months from hanging up his pinstripes, and the great Mickey Mantle would stumble through the 1968 season. CBS had no idea of how to right the ship; the only thing the network could do was throw open the gates to new advertisers.

While other sponsors waited in the wings, the Yankees were in no position to demand big money, and New York was the only team in the majors whose radio-TV revenue declined in 1967. The team now chose to control its own radio rights, selling ad time and allowing radio and the Yankees' TV affiliates to sell a few spots of their own. More sponsors joined the broadcasts, increasing the potential for income-building relationships when the team improved.

WPIX telecast 65 home games and many road games in color. While the productions did not feature center field camera views, a new editorial policy was in place: cameras could now focus on anything going on in the park, whether fights in the stands, umpire-player arguments, or, presumably, small crowds.

Three ex-players in the booth made the flow of the play-by-play messy. Garagiola, Coleman, and Rizzuto had trouble describing the action, but the bonhomie seemed to flow freely. Joe Garagiola had also gotten a job hosting the NBC-TV game show *Sale of the Century*.

Even with all the turmoil, the New York club ownership was taking its broadcast policy seriously, as expected for a team that was part of a network. By 1967 the team had hired a vice president of sales and broadcast affairs and, within a few years, had added an executive producer of broadcasting as well as a broadcast coordinator, making it among the first MLB teams with an in-house broadcast department.

General Cigar, Pabst, and American Airlines underwrote the big TV sponsorships in 1968, with Krueger Brewing buying half of the ads on WHN.

That season, Frank Messer — who had been Chuck Thompson's co-pilot in Baltimore since 1964, and before that had called games for the Yankees' Triple-A club in Richmond — replaced Garagiola, who had increased his role on NBC by announcing the *Game of the Week*. Messer, at least, was a proper play-by-play man, and provided some ballast to the ex-jock levity on Yankees broadcasts for nearly two decades.

The Yankees hadn't returned to their customary winning ways in the late 1960s and perhaps as a result looked to revisit their glory days. In 1969, Whitey Ford joined the on-air team for 50 or so games, most of them at Yankee Stadium.

Jerry Coleman moved west, joining the San Diego Padres' broadcast crew for 1970, creating a vacancy in the Yankees' booth filled by unknown Bob Gamere. The 31-year-old Gamere had no major-league experience. His resume was thin: three years of Red Sox pregame shows on WNAC in Massachusetts and Holy Cross football. Gamere had met a WPIX agent on vacation in Aruba in fall 1969 and apparently made some sort of impression.

Gamere flopped, but the fault was not all his. He asserted later that he had been instructed during broadcasts, through earphones, not to mention that certain players were in slumps — Mike Burke apparently had heard enough candidness from Red Barber. This is just one example, but Gamere proved immediately unpopular and was not rehired for 1971.

Gamere afterward bounced around various on-air and administrative radio jobs in the Northeast, including doing Harvard football. He was stabbed near Fenway Park in 1988 under mysterious circumstances, and the next year lost his TV sportscasting job after being accused of male-on-male sexual harassment charges that were eventually dropped. In 2008 Gamere was arrested in Boston on child pornography charges; two years later, he was sentenced to a five-year prison term.

The Yankees shifted to WMCA radio for 1971, and former big-league first baseman Bill White beat out some 200 other applicants for the vacancy in the club's broadcast booth. White became the first full-time black announcer in Major League Baseball, a full half-century after the first big-league game was broadcast. Jackie Robinson had done some network television analysis in the 1960s, but nothing long-term, so the Yankees deserve credit.

White, who had some broadcasting experience on the Phillies' pregame and postgame shows , became a favorite in New York. White covered the Yankees on the air for 18 years before becoming president of the National League in 1989. He wasn't afraid to express sharp opinions and cultivated a fiercely independent persona: White's 2011 autobiography was entitled *Uppity*.

As the Bombers fought their way back to the top of the AL East, the club enjoyed continuity on the air: Messer, Rizzuto, and White worked for Yankees games as a team from 1971 through 1985.

CBS, having run the Yankees during the franchise's worst period since the Deadball Era, sold the club in 1974 to George Steinbrenner, an owner committed to winning at all costs.

New York signed a one-year radio extension for that year with WMCA but the station, oddly, could not sell enough ads to produce pregame or postgame shows even though they paid enough in rights fees to help make the club's $1.3 million in radio-TV revenue highest in the AL.

That season, the Yankees became the second team to show games on the nascent Home Box Office service, following an experiment by the Indians the previous season. New York reduced the number of games on WPIX to 72 — the club's fewest to date on "free" television — in order to allow HBO to feature 19 Tuesday, Wednesday, and Friday broadcasts.

HBO was a venture of pioneering RSN Madison Square Garden (MSG); at this time, the channel was carried on 22 cable systems in New York, Pennsylvania, and New Jersey. The first Yankees cablecast came April 18 at Baltimore.

The fledging network hired young Dick Stockton, veteran New York sports presence Marty Glickman, and onetime Yankees infielder Gil McDougald as announcers. The first two had already worked for HBO, Stockton covering the Professional Bowlers Association and Glickman a fixture on Knicks and Rangers games since the late 1960s.

While the Yankees and HBO seemed interested in continuing the arrangement in 1975, there was no extension of the deal, possibly because of pressure from the Commissioner Bowie Kuhn, who was wary of this new technology. Stockton went on to a long career in a variety of sports, starting with Red Sox baseball, and the Yankees had to wait a few more years for another cable outlet.

For 1975, the Yankees and WMCA signed another three-year deal, with a regional packager, Manchester Broadcasting, selling advertising time and setting up a new 40-station radio network. Dom Valentino, a vice president at Manchester, joined the radio broadcast team, but lasted only one season. Well-liked by White and Rizzuto, he unfortunately suffered two heart attacks and was in an auto collision during his ill-fated time in the Bronx.

The team returned to Yankee Stadium in 1976 after sharing Shea Stadium for two years while Yankee Stadium was completely rebuilt. A major facet of the park's reconstruction was the creation of state-of-the-art press box and broadcast booths.

Like most other teams, the Yankees' broadcasts by this time featured myriad local and national sponsors. In 1976, national brands like Miller beer, Gabriel shock absorbers, Getty Oil, Toyota, AAMCO, and Jack-in-the-Box shared airtime with local brands like Yoo-Hoo, Yankee Franks, and Morsan Sporting Goods stores. A decade of failing to win, however, had left Yankees ratings far from the reliable dollar machine of old, and several other AL teams were now netting higher media rights fees than New York.

During 1977, the Yankees brought the first woman into regular rotation on a baseball broadcast when Pam Boucher (her maiden name; she was actually Pam Jones at the time) joined the radio team for a year. Boucher was rarely, if ever, given a chance to be an analyst or to call play-by-play, instead doing between-inning score rundowns and postgame shows, but she was a pioneer. She also did administrative work and held the job of the team's director of broadcasting through 1979.

The 1977 Yankees won the franchise's first World Series in a decade and a half, increasing the team's marketability on TV and radio. New York transferred its radio package to WINS, its home from 1939 through 1957. By 1980, the Yankees were earning an estimated $3 million in radio-TV revenue and now had joint control of their television ad sales.

WPIX, still the Yankees' TV partner, went up on the satellite in 1978, becoming one of the first television superstations. The increased national exposure for the Yankees increased the team's profile, but never had the effect on the nation's baseball consciousness of WGN or WTBS, each showing at least 120 Cubs and Braves games a year.

In 1979, George Steinbrenner made his first move to beef up his on-air team, adding recently released catcher Fran Healy to the broadcasts. Healy is an archetype of the amiable ex-jock, an insider who despite his front-line access never strayed into tough topics and was never controversial — survival skills that kept him employed on both Yankees and Mets telecasts for nearly two decades. Healy, along with White and Messer, were the first Yankees' voices heard on a new cable outlet called SportsChannel.

SportsChannel began operation in 1976 as Cablevision Sports 3 and first covered the Yankees in 1979, the same year it was renamed. SCNY's success led to SportsChannel RSNs in other cities; the network went national after it became a joint venture between Cablevision and NBC in 1988. As the first regional sports network in the U.S., SportsChannel changed the way Americans watched sports.

SportsChannel was a subsidiary of Cablevision, founded in 1973 by Charles Dolan and one of the nation's biggest cable system operators. Dolan would become a huge player in the New York sports and entertainment industries and would try to buy the Yankees in the late 1990s. Dolan would also try to acquire the Red Sox in the early 2000s.

Even with SportsChannel in the mix, WPIX happily inked a new $25 million contract for 1980–84. During that span, WPIX showed 100 games per season, while SportsChannel aired 40–50. Amazingly enough, in 1981, SportsChannel aired some of its Yankees' games on tape delay, rather than live.

The next year, in a smart move, SportsChannel hired Mel Allen. The legendary voice spent several years on the network's Yankees telecasts, enjoying a profitable second life in his long career that also featured his narration of the syndicated show *This Week in Baseball*. Allen's greatest latter-day call may have been Dave Righetti's July 4, 1983, no-hitter. SportsChannel was a great opportunity for Allen to come full circle and to go out on top.

By 1987, the market had changed. SportsChannel was now the biggest player in town, broadcasting 100 Yankees games, leaving only 40 for WPIX. When the Yankees' deal with SportsChannel ran out, Steinbrenner negotiated a groundbreaking 13-year contract with the competing MSG Network (including three option years). The deal shocked the sports world because it brought in an average of $42 million per season for the Yankees, starting in 1989.

The 1989 deal also gave MSG the rights to over-the-air Yankees games, which the cable provider then sold to WPIX. In both 1989 and 1990, Channel 11 showed around 75 games, since the MSG Network couldn't clear a whole season's worth of airtime while also broadcasting both the NBA Knickerbockers and the NHL Rangers.

After being spurned by Steinbrenner, Cablevision eventually gained control of Madison Square Garden itself as well as the MSG Network, the Knicks, and the Rangers — but despite reports that Cablevision was about to purchase the club in 1998, never the Yankees.

During the 1980s and 1990s, the Yankees broadcasts seemed to lose direction, as if the team and MSG felt that more voices guaranteed a better broadcast. Whatever the reasons, the Yankees' broadcasting booths seemed to have had turnstiles installed. In addition to ubiquitous locals like Dave Cohen and Spencer Ross, various roving professionals like Joe Angel, John Gordon, Dewayne Staats, George Grande, Tommy Hutton, Greg Gumbel, and Paul Olden drifted into and out of New York after a year or two or four.

In 1996, for example, the Yankees, between their various radio and TV deals, employed 13 different broadcasters, not counting pregame and postgame anchors or radio beat reporters.

Many Hall of Famers have called Yankees games. A *son* of a Hall of Famer has called Yankees games. Even a former umpire called 'em as he saw 'em from the Yankee Stadium booth. Having worn the native pinstripes wasn't a requirement, but it certainly helped, as more than 15 ex-Yankees have toiled in the New York booth since 1980.

Among the many personnel changes in the last three decades in the Bronx, the passion for ex-jocks in the booth got out of hand. In the last 30 years, the Yankees and their broadcast outlets have employed at least 22 different ex-players with microphones. Some of them, such as Tom Seaver, Jim Kaat, and Ken Singleton, were already good. Some became pretty good, like Bill White and, eventually, Rizzuto. Some never got past the typical early-career struggles that most ex-players experience.

In 1989, John Sterling earned a shot at the team's No. 1 radio slot, and has held the job ever since. Formerly one of the Atlanta Braves' broadcast crew, the gregarious and oft-lampooned Sterling also had local experience calling NBA New Jersey Nets games in the late 1970s and early 1980s. He first worked on WABC, which acquired the Yankees' radio rights in 1981.

When Joe Angel left the booth in 1992, Michael Kay, a New York sportswriter who had covered the team as a beat reporter for five years, joined Sterling as color man. Kay eventually took over some play-by-play duties, showing a facility for the microphone.

The Yankees have claimed that Kay — who had made his name at New York City's two tabloids, the *Post* and *Daily News* — was the first full-time beat reporter to jump into any sport's broadcasting booth. That is not accurate, however; longtime Cleveland sportswriter Harry Jones called Indians games in the 1960s and 1970s, as did ex-scriveners Jacques Doucet and Richard Griffin in Montreal. As far back as the 1930s, moreover, Chicago newspaperman Hal Totten had moved into radio to become the Cubs' and White Sox' voice.

Amid all the moving of various broadcasters, some of the talent developed strong followings. Former pitcher Jim Kaat and late Yankees outfielder Bobby Murcer were much appreciated, the former for his superb ability to break down a game and the latter for his warm, genial presence. Ken Singleton, one of the best ex-players ever to work a baseball broadcast booth, remains excellent. Phil Rizzuto had achieved legendary status by the 1980s, and Spanish-language mikemen Armando Talavera and Beto Villa (later the No. 1 voice) began a 10-year stretch working Yankees games in 1997.

The 1994–95 player strike, however, damaged the Yankees' radio and TV partners. Fewer games in 1994 and 1995 resulted in a smaller ad inventory to sell, so when the Yankees rolled out their plans for replacement baseball, nobody was buying. The Yankees dismissed WABC's request for relief on its rights fees; the station, believing (as did most others) that games with replacement players would be a disaster, sued in March 1995 for breach of contract. Had the 1995 regular season begun with the replacement teams the owners planned on fielding, MSG — also denied a reduction in rights fees by the team — would have sued the Yankees, too.

Rizzuto called his last game on WPIX in 1996 after nearly six decades of service to the Yankees' organization as a player, broadcaster, and ambassador. The spring after his retirement, writer and poet Hart Seely collated some of "Scooter's" best on-air calls and musings into a delightful book of "found poetry." *O Holy Cow!* is perhaps the best possible memorial to Rizzuto's broadcast legacy.

The nearly 50-year relationship between WPIX and the Yankees ended in 1998. Four years earlier, MSG — then owned by media conglomerate Paramount Communications, formerly Gulf & Western and home to Paramount Pictures — had tried to keep all games to itself and not make any available to Channel 11. But public outcry against the potential loss of games on "free TV" led the cable provider to back off. Later in 1994, Madison Square Garden was purchased by a partnership of ITT and Cablevision.

Cablevision acquired complete control in 1997 of MSG, which owned the Knicks and Rangers as well as the MSG Network. That meant Cablevision controlled the local TV rights to all seven available New York–area clubs: the MLB Yankees and Mets, the NBA Knicks and Nets, and the NHL Rangers, Islanders, and Devils. (The NFL centralizes all clubs' TV rights and sells them as part of its national package, so the only televised games controlled by NFL clubs are their preseason exhibitions.)

After 1998, with Cablevision owning MSG, WPIX decided it had had enough and, surprisingly, signed a deal to televise 50 Mets games each year. WNYW gained the Yankees over-the-air rights, and carried the team for three years.

In 1999, Steinbrenner formed a surprising partnership with the NBA New Jersey Nets and created a holding company called YankeeNets that owned both clubs. Since the Nets were worth nowhere near as much as the Yankees, Steinbrenner received a reported $225 million payment to equalize the equity. The two franchises hoped to substantially increase their leverage and, thus, their media revenue by jointly negotiating their future broadcast rights with the de facto monopoly Cablevision had created.

If YankeeNets failed in ratcheting up each club's TV rights, its ace in the hole was the threat of creating its own regional sports network that would compete with Cablevision's

RSNs (MSG and SportsChannel New York) — which is exactly how things played out. After YankeeNets generated little interest from Cablevision, Time Warner, or other media companies in forming a new RSN with YankeeNets, the clubs created an RSN of their own, dubbed YES for the "Yankees Entertainment and Sports" Network. As a prelude, after being sued by MSG during the machinations over the Yankees' TV rights, the Yankees paid MSG $30 million in 2001 just to buy back MSG's cable rights to Yankees games.

Beginning in 2002, this new RSN made the Yankees the centerpiece of its schedule, offering around 120 games each year, plus expanded pregame and postgame programming. YES also featured lots of sepia-toned programming from the plethora of great moments, games, and seasons in Yankees history. Initially, YES was majority owned by a separate corporation, Yankee Global Enterprises LLC, created in 2003 when YankeeNets was dissolved. Yankee Global Enterprises also owns the Yankees.

YES immediately built a strong relationship with Viacom, which owned the local CBS television and radio affiliates. In 2002, WCBS-TV in New York arranged to carry 20 games annually for three years.

When YES and WCBS began showing the Bombers, Michael Kay took over the play-by-play on TV, teaming with Ken Singleton and Jim Kaat in one of the best-ever three-man broadcast teams. Combining the insights of a former hitter and a former hurler, the broadcasts benefitted from each member's unique insights.

That same year, all-news WCBS-AM, the Yankees' radio flagship for six years in the 1960s, snagged the Yankees' radio package with a five-year deal that paid the club nearly $10 million per season beginning in 2002. The team's new radio flagship came with a new No. 2 announcer, former ESPN anchor and boxing commentator Charley Steiner. For three years, Steiner and Sterling comprised what some listeners felt to be a particularly brassy and opinionated duo before Steiner departed to Los Angeles.

When Steiner departed, the Yankees broke a barrier by making Suzyn Waldman the first full-time female broadcaster in the majors. A longtime stage actress as well as sports reporter, she is the only big-league color announcer ever to co-star on Broadway with Richard Kiley in *Man of La Mancha*. Waldman had joined the WPIX team as a reporter and color commentator in 1996; beginning in 2005, she teamed full-time with Sterling in the WCBS booth.

The pair has been criticized as mere shills, but Sterling certainly has a presence big enough for The Big Apple, and Waldman works very hard — probably harder than a man in a comparable position would have to — and takes full advantage of her experience as a reporter. Waldman has received some criticism for occasionally crying on the air during dramatic moments, which seems like the typical double standard for female broadcasters. Is it any different than when Russ Hodges shouted, when Marty Brennaman exults, or when Ted Leitner affectionately refers to "my Padres"? Even Harry Caray cried on the last broadcast of one of his Cubs seasons. Waldman both knows her stuff and is emotionally involved in the game, which makes her equal to most and better than some other baseball broadcasters.

The first full-time black major league baseball announcer, Bill White may not have had the best voice for radio, but his knowledge of the game was unbeaten and his willingness to share his opinions much missed in today's well-scrubbed radio atmosphere. (National Baseball Hall of Fame and Museum)

Since 2005, WWOR, a New Jersey station that for many years was the Mets' television flagship, has aired the Yankees' small package of over-the-air contests. The unusual merry-go-round of stations, seen again following the 2013 season when the Yankees supplanted the Mets on WFAN radio, has a parallel in both teams' use, at various times, of announcers Tim McCarver, Tom Seaver, and Fran Healy.

Following 2011, the Yankees re-upped with radio home WCBS, but after the 2013 campaign, shifted to WFAN. Despite rumors of their impending demise, Sterling and Waldman remain in place at the radio mikes.

In 2012, Rupert Murdoch's News Corporation acquired a 49% stake in YES, with the option to increase that to 80% within three years. By acquiring a controlling interest in YES, News Corp. added it to Fox Sports' stable of 19 RSNs as Fox planned for the 2013 debut of the national Fox Sports 1 cable channel that would compete head-to-head with ESPN.

YES paid the Yankees a reported $85 million for the club's TV rights in 2013 on a long-term contract that provided for 4–7% increases annually through 2022. After 2022, the annual fees paid by YES (under Fox control) will reportedly escalate to $350 million in the final option year of the agreement in 2042. YES would happily show every New York game, but exclusive national telecasts on Fox and ESPN annually siphon off about 20 Yankees contests, and another 20 or so are on local WCBS. (Of course, those telecasts also funnel money into the club's coffers via the Yankees' share of MLB's national broadcast agreements.)

After decades of what seemed like constant change that at times bordered on turmoil, the Yankees now have a strong on-air team. Most of the time the broadcast crew successfully strikes a reasonable mixture of homerism and honesty — a difficult balancing act that not all broadcast teams can manage. In New York, both are expected, which is a pretty tough mandate. On television, veterans Kay and Singleton are usually joined by John Flaherty or Al Leiter, while Waldman, Sterling, and Beto Villa (in Spanish) hold court on radio.

The New York Yankees are one of the two or three most valuable sports properties in the world, and savvy media management is a huge part of that. In 2010, Forbes estimated the franchise's value at $1.6 billion, partly based on YES paying the club $84 million in broadcast fees.

With higher ratings and visibility than ever, plus a luxurious new Yankee Stadium, the Yankees are seemed to be well-situated to both make money and continue to outspend everyone in MLB for the foreseeable future. The huge rights fees promised to the Rangers, Angels, and Dodgers in the past two years, however, have changed the landscape, and the effects of that major shift have yet to play out in Gotham.

WHITE ELEPHANTS ON PARADE

PHILADELPHIA/KANSAS CITY/OAKLAND ATHLETICS BROADCASTING HISTORY

"He's handled radio the same way he's handled his ballplayers.
He's going to do it his way or there's no way."
— Bill Dwyer, KNBR radio general manager, of Charles O. Finley in 1977

BY THE TIME THAT FAST-DEVELOPING CONSUMER TECHNOLOGY
made it possible for teams to reach a wide range of potential customers via radio, the Golden
Age of the Philadelphia Athletics had already ended. The franchise's 1931 AL pennant was
its last until 1972 — though nobody would have expected that at the time — and the first
regular broadcasts of games in the Quaker City wouldn't come for several years.

By the early 1930s, several teams had experimented with radio broadcasts, but neither
Philadelphia franchise embraced the new medium. No sponsors had yet stepped forward
to award major-league clubs money for their broadcast rights and, aside from the Red Sox,
no East Coast team was entrepreneurial enough to understand radio's great potential as a
promotional tool.

For the 1933 season, only half of major-league clubs — the Braves, Red Sox, Cubs, White
Sox, Reds, Tigers, Cardinals, and Browns — allowed regular game broadcasting.

After failing to find a sponsor willing to indemnify them at least $25,000 for possible lost
gate revenue, the Athletics again said "no" to radio in 1934. Following their lead, the Phillies
banned broadcasting from Shibe Park. As a substitute, depending on which team was at

home, Athletics star first baseman Jimmie Foxx or Phils coach Hans Lobert alternated 10-minute programs on WCAU radio six nights per week during the baseball season.

Things began to change in 1935, after the Athletics had fallen into the AL cellar, a distant 34 games behind Detroit. Mack's bunch, still the dominant team in Philadelphia, finally bit the bullet and allowed radio broadcasts for 1936. The moribund Phillies followed.

The Sporting News reported in October 1935 that General Mills, baseball's top national guarantor, was prepared to spend half a million dollars broadcasting the National Pastime in 1936, and hoped to add WCAU to the rolls of stations carrying big-league games.

With too much money at stake for a deal not to happen, three local outfits broadcast Phillies and Athletics home games in 1936. WCAU, the most popular station locally, boasted Bill Dyer behind the mike for both the Phils and A's. WIP, one of the city's earliest radio outlets (it began operating in 1922), hired NL umpire Albert "Dolly" Stark, a salary holdout, to do the accounts. WFIL hired *Philadelphia Inquirer* sportswriter Joe Tumulty to describe some games. Unfortunately, no known recordings of these pioneer broadcasters — or of any local Philadelphia Athletics broadcasts — have escaped into the streams from which baseball audio collectors fish.

From 1935 through 1954, the White Elephants finished sixth, seventh, or eighth 15 times. Despite the wretched on-field material, Dyer and WCAU were a huge and immediate success on the airwaves in 1936. Following the season, General Mills awarded trophies to WCAU and to Dyer, naming them their top nationwide baseball promoters and broadcasters.

In fall 1936, CBS hired the elfin Dyer to pair with France Laux of St. Louis on its World Series broadcasts. (CBS, Mutual, and NBC all featured the Fall Classic that year.) In 1937, Dyer was again feted as one of the game's up-and-coming radio stars, with General Mills and Mobil providing sponsorship for Philadelphia baseball broadcasts. Dyer snared the prestigious 1937 World Series gig, too.

Little was said about "Dolly" Stark's work for WIP; amid rumors he would not be rehired, Stark returned behind the mask after his year behind the mike. WIP was out of luck for 1937, having paid $15,000 to broadcast games yet being unable to use Atlantic Refining as its sponsor because WCAU's earlier and larger contract with the Phillies and A's stipulated that no energy company besides Mobil could advertise on a Philadelphia game.

In 1938, Byrum Saam took his seat in the big chair at WIP and immediately became the Athletics' primary voice as WCAU and Dyer went exclusively with the Phillies. WIP put together an eight-station network for Athletics games, thus boosting Saam's audience in the Middle Atlantic.

Late in the 1939 season, the A's held a day for slugger "Indian Bob" Johnson, also giving suitcases to both Saam and Dyer. Saam, who had just married a young woman who worked in the WIP offices, ostensibly used the valise on his honeymoon. Dyer, however, ended up packing his bag and leaving Philadelphia.

As a member of the CBS Radio Network, WCAU was bound by CBS's new policy that prevented its stations from broadcasting much local sports. Dyer took a job broadcasting the International League Baltimore Orioles in 1941 and would later serve simultaneously as GM of the Basketball Association of America and (later) NBA Baltimore Bullets for four years. While a major figure in that Maryland metropolis, he never regained national fame.

For 1941, WCAU leased its broadcast rights to smaller WPEN, which had big plans; *The Sporting News* reported that the station was working to recruit Red Barber! This fascinating possibility never came to pass, and Barber said nothing about it in his autobiography. WPEN's plans were doomed from the get-go, though they did cover a few A's and Phils night games that season with Ira Walsh at the mike.

WIBG had planned to enter the local broadcast picture in 1941, but troubles with increasing the station's broadcast power delayed it for a year. General Mills arranged for Saam to take the mike for all Phillies and Athletics games on WIBG starting in April 1942, with Atlantic Refining the main sponsor by 1944.

During the Phillies' and Athletics' dark years of the 1940s and early 1950s, By Saam brought the Pennsylvania metropolis its baseball. Saam [discussed in depth in the Phillies' chapter] had a deep register and an affable yet somewhat formal manner. Beginning in 1944, his booming voice was paired with Claude Haring, who had begun his baseball career in 1936 as Dyer's assistant. The bespectacled Haring had aired Pirates games for WWSW in the interim, but was at heart a Quaker, remaining a Philadelphia broadcaster through 1962.

While small towns over America feasted on national broadcasts, baseball in major U.S. cities was very local. At this time, newspapers and radio stations covered "city series" in two-league markets like Chicago, Philadelphia, and St. Louis with an intensity reflecting their readers' rooting interest. When their local heroes weren't in contention, highly partisan fans often viewed these intra-city series as more important than regular-season games, and WIBG made a point of airing these preseason or postseason exhibitions.

As was true for all two-team cities during these years, there was no imbalance in airtime, with both the sad A's and the awful Phillies having all home games broadcast. Saam earned his legendary status with an incredible body of work during the baseball season; starting in 1943, he not only did he call all A's and Phillies home games, but he also manned occasional road recreations while doing a 15-minute sports summary on WIBG six nights each week.

Haring left to televise Phillies and A's games on WPTZ in 1947, leaving radio duty to Saam and young Chuck Thompson, who proved so good as a second banana that he soon moved to bigger and better things.

Baseball on TV was an immediate hit in Philadelphia. For 1950, WIBG decided to cover all games live for the first time, meaning that its broadcasters would now travel. Saam and Haring went exclusively with the A's, and so missed the Fightin' Phillies' pennant, its first since 1915.

This arrangement was confusing to listeners, however, because WIBG chose to air all home games for each club, with the station doing live cut-ins to road games if the Phillies and A's were playing simultaneously.

The Athletics network included more than a dozen regional stations during the war years, but their popularity sagged dramatically in the early 1950s amid constantly swirling rumors that the team was to be sold and moved. Superannuated Connie Mack retired following the 1950 season and, with the exciting "Whiz Kid" Phillies surprising everyone by taking the NL flag, the White Elephants' tenuous hold on Philly fans deteriorated even further. From having all 77 home games telecast in 1950, by 1954 only 25 A's home games were shown on the tube, with those spread among three stations.

The Phillies' success and the desire of Connie's sons to cash out made the Athletics' exit a foregone conclusion and the family sold the franchise, which relocated to Kansas City for 1955. This was the third franchise shift in three years, with all three franchises fleeing a two-team town (St. Louis, Boston, Philadelphia) in favor of virgin territory — or so the Athletics thought.

It is said that Byrum Saam, who broadcast the Philadelphia Athletics from 1938 through 1954 and the Phillies from 1938 to 1949 and again from 1955 through 1975, saw more losing baseball than any announcer ever. That's a shame, as his big, booming, friendly voice carried the authority of a higher power. (National Baseball Hall of Fame and Museum)

Arriving in the theoretically wide-open spaces of western Missouri and eastern Kansas, the Athletics unpacked to find that area had already been seeded and harvested by the St. Louis Cardinals. For decades the only good baseball team within shouting distance of the western portion of the huge Mississippi-Missouri River basin, the Redbirds had by 1956 developed an intensely loyal fan base covering the western prairie and the Great Plains from North Dakota to Oklahoma and from western Illinois to Wyoming.

When the Athletics opened their inaugural campaign in Kansas City in 1955, a respectable 33 stations in eight states signed on to air their games. The Cardinals' radio network, however, featured popular, larger-than-life Harry Caray and boasted 89 stations, the most by a wide margin of any major-league club. An indication of the relative market position of the two teams was that St. Louis had an affiliate in Topeka, the state capital of Kansas that was west of and far closer to KC than to the Gateway City.

During their 13 years in Missouri's second city, the Athletics posted losing records every season, finishing last or next-to-last 10 times, understandably never capturing the affection of many fans. That the club's two owners — Arnold Johnson and Charley Finley — in Missouri were irascible made the downtrodden A's even more difficult to love. Unfortunately their on-air product wasn't much better than the mess on the field.

The KC Athletics' first voice on flagship station KMBC was Merle Harmon, familiar from his collegiate work on University of Kansas football and basketball. Harmon was too vanilla to become beloved, but he later enjoyed some national success. The Athletics, trying to escape the reputation of decay that had pervaded their later years in Philadelphia, were lucky to have an ambassador with a pleasant timbre and demeanor.

Harmon's first on-air colleague was Larry Ray, who had broadcast Kansas City Blues Triple-A games from 1949 to 1954. The two had teamed on Blues games in 1954 in what might have been an extended audition. The franchise remained focused on local voices and professional broadcasters rather than on former players throughout its time in Missouri and even after its move to California — surprisingly, the Athletics did not hire a ex-jock as a full-time radio analyst until 1986.

Even with the club's lack of popularity, most of KC's exhibition games were carried on the team's radio network. By the 1970s, far fewer MLB exhibition games were broadcast than 20 years before. Only in the 1990s did the amount of spring training contests on radio return to 1950s levels.

Schlitz was the lead sponsor on KMBC, paying the Athletics $220,000 for that privilege in 1955. Sam Molen (author of a 1959 book of sports anecdotes called *Take Two* and *Hit to Right*) hosted *Sam Molen's Lead-Off* before the broadcasts. While their radio production was in fine shape, the A's were immediately hamstrung by an inability to get a television deal, even though Molen was also sports director of KMBC-TV. The relocated franchise was the only one in the AL in 1955 without a TV contract.

KMBC's promotion folks had some wacky ideas. During that first season, the team held a series of beauty pageants, with one local beauty selected for each station in the Athletics' radio network. The overall winner, named "Queen of the Athletics Network," ruled over two late August games and a dinner dance. The following season, the Kansas City Chamber of Commerce tried to generate some excitement by hosting a closed-circuit telecast of an A's exhibition game against the Pirates from New Orleans.

Ray resigned in December 1956 to take the no. 2 radio job in Baltimore, as Harmon then worked with Ed Edwards (Jimmy Dudley's former sidekick on Indians broadcasts) for a year and a half. Edwards ran into trouble in July 1958 for his desire to quit the A's broadcasts and buy a radio station in 1959. After *The Sporting News* revealed the plan, the Athletics immediately replaced him with sportscaster Bill Grigsby. Grigsby's tenure with the A's, which lasted through 1961, was ordinary; he later gained much greater fame broadcasting the NFL's Kansas City Chiefs through 2009.

The A's installed a new press box at Municipal Stadium in time for the 1959 season. WDAF assumed the role as broadcast partner, inking a three-year deal to air radio games and televise 60 games over the life of the contract. In 1959, Harmon and Grigsby telecast 10 games, four from Detroit and three each from Cleveland and Chicago. In 1961–62, the pair described 20 and 30 TV road games, respectively, as the club continued to founder.

The star-crossed team went from the frying pan to the fire when Arnold Johnson —
despised in Kansas City for crooked deals that had sent many of the team's best players to
the Yankees — died in March 1960. Afterward, the team passed into the hands of Charles
O. Finley. The Indiana insurance magnate had tried to buy the A's in 1954, but the Mack
family wouldn't sell to him. Now, with few suitors for the basement-dwelling franchise,
Finley took the reins while his fellow owners held their noses. Finley was erratic, idiosyncratic,
and iconoclastic, constantly offending with his blustering, empty threats and foolish
displays of power.

The new owner canned Harmon following the 1961 season, ostensibly because the announcer wouldn't take part in a "Poison Pen" ceremony making fun of a local sportswriter.
Finley repeatedly hired and fired people, perhaps (as Bill James has written) trying to erase
his failures and inadequacies, or possibly to flaunt his authority by acting as if everyone else
was replaceable.

Television and radio stations were loath to develop relationships with the A's in the 1960s,
because Finley began threatening to move the team almost immediately after acquiring it.
Therefore, every season's rights negotiations became an unfriendly poker game between
Finley and various broadcasters. When the team signed a new deal for 1962, Finley retained
the right to hire and fire broadcasters at his whim. Since allowing the club to retain this
kind of control was a major concession, Finley probably forewent significant dollars to get
this clause. As it was, the 1960s KC Athletics netted less for their broadcasting rights than
any other big-league club except, occasionally, the Washington Senators.

The one guy Finley didn't fire was Monte Moore, who became the team's lead broadcaster
in 1962. Moore stayed with the A's until 1980, departing only when Finley sold out, and even
returned for some cablecasts in the 1990s. Bland and inoffensive, Moore was very loyal to
Finley — a loyalty that Bill James has written included Moore's passing along sensitive
information about players to the front office.

Moore, another University of Kansas voice, and his 1962 sidekick Bruce Rice, mostly
remembered today for his work with the NFL Chiefs, got their first chances to call major-
league games not because of their great baseball knowledge but rather because they had
already worked in the sports department of KCMO, the team's new radio-TV rightsholder.

The late Rice lasted but one season, going on to a long career as a popular local sports
anchor while also working on the Chiefs' radio crew. (The Royals' Pitcher of the Year award
is named for him.) The innocuous Moore paired with four different sidekicks — Rice,
George Bryson, Red Rush, and Lynn Faris — in a six-year span, but it didn't matter. The
A's were terrible, and few fans listened or came to the park. By 1962, the club's radio network
had dropped to only 10 stations.

The team's annual scramble for a television deal during the Finley years was almost comical,
with the number of TV games decreasing from 41 in 1963 to just 20 by 1967. Finley's television revenue fell from $325,000 to $250,000 to $167,000 over the team's final three seasons
in Kansas City while TV dollars were growing in most other markets.

After the 1962 season, Moore worked directly for Finley and, thus, was grandfathered into whatever radio and TV deal Finley negotiated. Moore announced for WDAF's radio and TV operations in 1963 and again for KCMO from 1964 through 1967.

Even the club's attempts to increase their local profile weren't effective. Starting in 1961, the team's general manager chaired a 15-minute weekly baseball discussion show on WDAF-TV, but the GM, who hosted *Ask Frank Lane*, could hardly have been less engaging.

Convinced going into 1963 that he needed a bigger name in the broadcast booth, Finley hired George Bryson, a onetime used car dealer who had been a Reds voice in the late 1950s and had served in the Angels' front office in 1961–62. Some viewed Bryson as a rising star, and NBC picked him for the network's radio broadcast of 1963 All-Star Game. In spring 1964, Bryson took ill, but was back on the job by Opening Day.

In another typical Finley flight of fancy, Betty Caywood joined the A's broadcast team on September 18, 1964, inking a contract through the end of the season. Ms. Caywood, a 32-year-old then doing TV weather in Chicago, knew little about baseball. Caywood was not the first female broadcaster on a major-league game — golfer Helen Dettwiler did some work on General Mills network games in the 1940s — but she was clearly not qualified for the role.

When asked in 2008 in a radio interview (later excerpted in a *Chicago* magazine blog) about the job, Caywood replied, "My first response to him was, 'Charlie, I don't know the first thing about baseball.' He said, 'I know, but you've got the gift of gab, and all you have to do is color.' And I didn't even know what color was…I was paid so much, to do something I knew nothing about, that it was quite extraordinary…and kind of silly."

Strangely, Finley insisted that Caywood's promotion couldn't wait until 1965. While these machinations were going on, Bryson was losing his fight for life. He reentered a Kansas City hospital on September 25, a week after Caywood's debut, and died on October 14 at 51 from a longstanding heart condition. In the wake of Bryson's death, Caywood's option was allowed to lapse. Four decades later, Betty Caywood Bushman returned to the booth for a Kansas City T-Bones game in the independent Northern League.

Having outlasted everyone Finley brought in to work with him, Moore assumed the reins as the Athletics' lead voice, working with Rush — Loyola University of Chicago's basketball voice — in 1965, then with Faris (who'd done minor league games in New Orleans) in the franchise's final two seasons in KC.

Once he'd finally airlifted the franchise to Oakland, Finley paired the reserved, devout Moore with huge, profane "Big Al" Helfer in what would be the latter's final regular MLB announcing job. Helfer, once the big man on the Mutual Network's *"Game of the Day"* broadcasts and a news reporter from 1964 through 1967, lasted two seasons in Oakland.

The A's were first heard in Northern California on KNBR radio, which inked a five-year deal in 1968 as the lead for an 11-station network. On the tube, the A's were seen on KBHK-TV via a 25-game, road-only package on the brand-new UHF outlet and three network channels in 1968–69.

Even though the Athletics had become good by 1969, they found for the second time that moving into already occupied territory — this time preceded by the Giants — greatly restricted their financial gain. Finley made the situation even worse. He consistently asked for impossible sums in negotiations, which caused the talks to drag on perilously close to Opening Day, hamstringing any decent marketing campaign the team or their broadcasting partner might mount.

One thing the Athletics did right was to immediately arrange Spanish-language broadcasts on KBRG-FM. Victor Manuel Torres, who had tried for some time to interest the Giants in such an enterprise, signed on with Finley and called A's games in Spanish until 1971 when, tragically, he was paralyzed in an auto crash. Torres died in 1997.

Having first whetted his appetite for the broadcasting style of his youth by hiring Al Helfer, Finley next hauled in Harry Caray — the Cardinals' voice and the A's primary broadcast competition in KC — for 1970 after KMOX and Anheuser-Busch had fired him. That experiment, played out on KNBR and six affiliates, lasted but a year.

The next old pro to occupy the chair next to Monte Moore in the booth was Bob Elson, whom the White Sox had put out to pasture. Red Rush, no stranger to the Athletics, accompanied Elson from Chicago to the East Bay. The odd ménage-a-trois broadcast the green-and-gold over tiny KEST — a 1,000-watt AM station that was the best Finley could do once 50,000-watt KNBR decided to drop all its sports programming. It was quite a comedown for the pioneering Elson, who had begun his career calling baseball four decades earlier. Following a 1971 campaign that produced an AL West Division title, the Athletics' first championship of any kind since 1930, Elson signed off as a baseball broadcaster for the last time.

In 1972, Oakland won its first of three consecutive World Series. Athletics fans made do for the first two of those championship seasons with Moore and yet another veteran second banana, Jim Woods, on San Jose's KEEN. Famous loose cannon Jim Piersall added some flavor (and some tension) to the radio booth during 1972 home games, while veteran manager Bill Rigney took over the no. 3 position in 1973 until Finley fired him in September.

To replace Rigney in the playoffs, Finley hired Bob Waller, a 30-year-old announcer who had spent the regular season with the White Sox. Waller worked Oakland's 1973 postseason games, but then said publicly that he didn't much like working with Moore and returned to Chicago. The White Sox let Waller go a year later, and he returned to Northern California, presumably with tail tucked between legs, as Moore's co-pilot from 1975 through 1977.

Future Giants and ESPN voice Jon Miller got his first major-league job with the Athletics in 1974, paying his dues for a year in the Finley circus before moving on to Texas, Boston, and Baltimore. Miller was given the job in Oakland just two years out of college, as Finley showed an ear for talent along with his eye for saving money.

Miller and Moore broadcast over KEEN (which inked a new three-year pact with Finley) and KPIX-TV, which began an eight-year run as the club's television partner. Unfortunately, KPIX, as a network station, made no extra time for pregame or postgame programming.

Finley continued his habit of opening negotiations by asking for ridiculous figures and not becoming reasonable until the season was about to begin. The trade press view was that constantly going down to the wire led to Finley getting much less money than he would have had he negotiated in good faith from the start. Not only did the Athletics have to struggle to find broadcast partners, but they also struggled to land sponsors. Few advertisers wanted to be associated with such a flaky character, and the A's major sponsors tended to change each year.

In 1976, Finley was forced to pay KNBR $300,000 to put on A's games on the air, deciding to sell advertising time himself to maximize radio income. This deal was done at the last minute, as usual, and KNBR aired road games on tape delay.

For 1977, Moore's last on radio, the A's and KNBR once again battled before coming to terms on a radio deal just a week before the season started. KNBR would have broadcast the club's games for free, but Finley — in no position to demand anything — wouldn't agree until it was too late to do any meaningful promotion. Oakland finished last in the West that season, lagging even expansion Seattle. The biggest young star debuting with the A's that year was 15-year-old Stanley Burrell — Finley's ballpark gofer and informant — who called an inning of play-by-play from the Coliseum on May 11. Years later, Burrell found extraordinary success in pop music as M.C. Hammer.

Finley's fecund brain hatched plenty of harebrained schemes, including a stillborn plan to put Athletics games on CB radio. When his 1977 attempt to move the club to Denver fell apart, no local radio station would touch the A's.

Therefore, the previously proud Athletics' franchise — owner of eight world championship banners — began 1978 season broadcasting from the University of California–Berkeley. KALX was a student-run, ten-watt FM station whose signal barely carried as far as the Oakland–Alameda County Coliseum. Two students called the games: Larry Baer, who went on to a successful career as a Giants' executive, and Bob Kozberg, later a CBS news producer.

The KALX deal lasted just 16 games, by which time most area fans had given up trying to tune in. The club then made a deal with KNEW, which brought in locals Jim Peterson, Bud Foster (who had aired PCL Oakland Oaks games in the 1940s and 1950s), and former big-league outfielder Curt Flood to complete the 1978 schedule.

After a single season on KXRX, another San Jose station, in 1979, the Athletics' broadcast purgatory came to a merciful end following the 1980 campaign when Finley, tied up by divorce proceedings and a long-term stadium lease, was forced to sell. That season's radio broadcasts on microscopic KDIA featured the inscrutable Red Rush ("Rudi is playing 143 feet off the left-field line") and Dom Valentino ("Right you are, Red") calling the plays.

Long-suffering A's fans were finally rewarded when Walter Haas Jr., patriarch of the family that controlled the Levi's blue jean empire, purchased the club. For 1981, the Athletics again had a respectable radio deal and a respected announcer: Bill King, already the voice of the NBA's Golden State Warriors and the NFL's Oakland Raiders. King, hired by the club as Director of Broadcast Operations, would hold that job for the rest of his life. Born in Illinois, the cosmopolitan and urbane King brought his travel, culture, and military experience to the broadcasts, balancing out the highs and lows on the diamond with his descriptions while earning accolades as a masterful sports voice.

From 1981 through 1992, Oakland baseball fans heard their team on KSFO. The vigorous, ribald, and passionate King teamed with former Giants broadcaster Lon Simmons from 1981–94 on radio and from 1981–87 on television. Young Wayne Hagin was also along for the ride until 1984, and the trio of mikemen enjoyed a good relationship. In 1982, team public relations director Jay Alves added a new angle to the package, making the A's the first MLB club to use computer-generated stats on their radio broadcasts.

In addition to getting their English-language radio affairs in order, the Athletics also began to cultivate a relationship with the local Latino community. In 1981, Amaury Pi-Gonzalez began a 13-year run broadcasting the team's home games in Spanish. He had worked with the A's previously, but not with this level of commitment from the club. In 1991, in fact, Pi-Gonzalez aired every one of the club's games, and nearly all of them the following two years.

Even as the A's refurbished their tattered reputation in the 1980s, they were still a distant second in the market to the Giants, to say nothing of other local pro sports teams like the NFL's 49ers and Raiders and the NBA Warriors. Oakland fans had never even seen 50 games on TV in a season until 1988, and for many years the team's over-the-air television and cable broadcasts featured strictly middle-of-the road main dishes like Greg Papa, Wayne Walker, Dick Stockton, Ken Wilson, and Tim Roye. Reggie Jackson and Harmon Killebrew served brief stints doing color, without distinction.

A's fans have, fortunately, been able to enjoy the sometimes witty and always insightful Ray Fosse since 1986 both on radio and television. Fosse is one of those ex-jocks who clearly gets it, communicating the nuances of the game to both casual and informed listeners.

When Simmons retired in 1996, Ken Korach, formerly a fill-in with the White Sox, replaced him as King's second. Over the last two decades the A's have been on six different radio stations — most often with an FM oldies rock channel. Korach has been a steady presence throughout, combining a slightly sandpaper voice with strong preparation, taking over as the lead voice when King passed away following the 2005 season.

The Athletics have embraced the information age in many ways, from Billy Beane's celebrated use of sabermetrics to the club's use of the Internet, and their willingness to try out new technology age has benefitted the team's fans. For example, the A's became one of the first teams to put some spring training broadcasts exclusively online, with Robert Buan (the club's longtime pregame and postgame host) at the mike. These games were added as a promotional tool to augment those games already aired over terrestrial radio.

As with other broadcast changes in the club's history, the changeover from over-the-air to cable telecasts came late to the Athletics. In 2009, for the first time, the team telecast exclusively on cable, with Comcast signing a long-term deal and airing an all-time high 145 games.

Pi-Gonzalez, after several years with other clubs, returned to do Spanish broadcasts for an audience that had been without *los Atleticos* since 2003. Oakland signed a five-year pact before the 2009 season with KDIA and KDYA to cover all 162 games in Spanish, marking the first time that Oakland broadcast every game in two languages. Bill Kulik's Spanish Broadcasting Network became the club's partner; Kulik's company now controls Spanish-language broadcasts in Oakland, Philadelphia, Boston, and Washington.

On the whole, things are just fine on the air in Oakland. The current English-language television voice is Glen Kuiper, who has served capably for a decade in his role. He is the brother of Giants broadcaster and former big-league infielder Duane. A third brother, Jeff, produces Giants telecasts for Comcast.

Early in the 2012 season, radio voice Ken Korach missed 21 games after undergoing knee replacement surgery. Johnny Doskow, lead announcer for the Athletics' Triple-A club in Sacramento, took over on KGMZ.

The same year, Comcast began working former A's infielder Scott Hatteberg into the television broadcasts as an analyst. Ray Fosse, shunted over to radio for those games, was not happy about the move and said so, though he had no unkind words for Hatteberg himself.

With a legacy full of long periods of despair and inadequate marketing, and with continuing rumors that they will relocate — possibly to the South Bay, possibly out of the state — the Athletics face a huge challenge creating a large fan base. The loyalty engendered by several first-rate broadcasters can only go so far when the future is perpetually cloudy.

FROM BY TO WHITEY TO HARRY THE K

PHILADELPHIA PHILLIES BROADCASTING HISTORY

"I think you're going to find in the future that a person will own not only a team and a stadium, but also a means to electronically transmit his team's games."
—*Jim Barniak, PRISM broadcaster, 1981*

WITH TWO MAJOR-LEAGUE TEAMS, PHILADELPHIA WAS BLESSED with a home game nearly every day of the baseball season from 1901 through 1954. But in the first two decades of the radio age, most of these games meant little in the standings.

It says a lot about Philadelphia's love for baseball that the city supported, even at a minimal level, both the Phillies and the Athletics in the 1930s and 1940s. The city's sports fans have always been passionate, and they have cared not only about their athletes, but also about who called their games. Most local fans know about Byrum Saam, Harry Kalas, Gene Hart, Bill Campbell, Whitey Ashburn, Merrill Reese, and Tom Brookshier, but few know about the role that Atlantic Refining played in the city's baseball broadcast history.

Atlantic Refining Company, headquartered in Philadelphia, spent 40 years as lead sponsor for Philly's radio baseball games and wielded a tremendous amount of power in how those contests were presented. Once part of John D. Rockefeller's Standard Oil Trust, Atlantic Richfield was spun off in 1911.

In 1936, the Phillies and Athletics approved two stations to broadcast their home games. WCAU, with Bill Dyer and Claude Haring, sang the praises of General Mills' Wheaties. Meanwhile on WIP, former National League umpire Dolly Stark stumped for Atlantic. Each sponsor paid approximately $25,000 for the privilege.

Stark didn't last, but Atlantic did. By 1939, WIP's games, featuring Byrum Saam and Stoney McLinn, aired on Atlantic's own network, while Dyer and General Mills remained on WCAU.

As a CBS station, however, WCAU was forced in 1941 by network policy to stop broadcasting baseball, and WIP took over exclusive rights to both teams' games. Putting the games on one station was a big deal at a time when exclusive arrangements were not the norm, and the Phillies and the sponsors worked hard to recruit Red Barber from Brooklyn. But when Barber decided to remain in Flatbush, Byrum Saam, three years into the job, cemented his position as the top man at the sports mike in the City of Brotherly Love.

Born in Texas, Saam had a deep timbre to his voice, admittedly similar to that of Ted Husing, the CBS broadcaster who by the mid-1930s was among the most recognizable voices in America. Coming to Philadelphia via Minneapolis, Saam did college sports until 1937 when, at age 22, he developed a lasting relationship with Atlantic Richfield.

From that point, broadcaster and sponsor were inseparable. Saam, a loyal soldier, tailored his style to his Eastern audience. "We're rolling along," he would say during his broadcasts, with a deep, rich, tremulous voice that conveyed excitement as well as warmth.

Baseball broadcasts don't feature many deep-toned, "big-voiced" announcers anymore. Until the 1980s, booming voices were everywhere: Saam, Gordon McLendon, Al Helfer, Bob Wolff, Bob Murphy, Gene Kelly, Bob Kelley, Ray Scott, Russ Taylor, Dave Niehaus, Paul Carey, Bob Starr, and many more. Some of these men were physically large, but not all of them. Their impressive voices resonated richly and deeply.

Only a few baseball mikemen continue that tradition now, notably John Sterling, Pat Hughes, and Jon Miller. We have far more adenoidal announcers these days, men who speak from upstairs rather than from their diaphragms. Maybe that has been influenced by modern microphone technology, or maybe it is simply the way people prefer to talk today. Even in the lower levels of the minors, the more nasal voices — which minimize or eliminate regional accents — get the jobs. Many of today's top announcers have voices that could come from anywhere rather than from one part of the country, which is perhaps the point.

Byrum Saam broadcast a lot of terrible baseball as the lead voice for both the Phillies and Athletics through 1949. From 1940 through 1949, 11 of the 16 Philadelphia teams Saam covered finished last. Bespectacled Claude Haring shared the pain with Saam much of that time. During the war years, WPEN and WIBG divided the Phillies broadcasts, with around a dozen outlying stations on the network. Atlantic remained the sponsor.

Haring transferred to television exclusively in 1947, with Chuck Thompson assuming the second chair on radio. Atlantic Refining and General Mills continued as co-sponsors over a 10-station network.

In 1948, the Phillies made $500,000 for their TV-radio rights. That was a substantial sum of money for the time, but over the next decade, the club's rights fees remained almost completely stagnant.

Three stations shared the local baseball TV broadcasts in the late 1940s and early 1950s, eventually showing more Phillies than Athletics games. While in 1947 and 1948 the telecasts featured just two cameras, crews were using four by 1955.

In 1950, Ayer (the ad agency representing Atlantic Refining on WCAU's baseball broadcasts) decided that all the games for both teams should be covered live on the radio. This meant travel, and that each club would have one discrete broadcast team.

This forced Saam to choose who he would cover: the Phillies or the Athletics? Saam chose the A's and continued to call their games with Haring through the 1954 season.

Given that the A's went in the tank in 1950, observers believe that Saam must have made the decision based on his relationship with Connie Mack. What seems difficult to understand in hindsight, however, wasn't so clear then. Both the Phillies and Athletics had posted 81–73 records in 1949, and it was not conclusive that the Phils would become the better club. The Mackmen had gone 84–70 in 1948, while the Phillies had finished 66–88.

Unfortunately for Saam, the Athletics collapsed while the "Whiz Kids" Phillies captured the 1950 NL pennant as several regulars had their best seasons and young Robin Roberts and Curt Simmons combined for 37 victories. The Fightin' Phils galvanized the city before a quick four-game loss to the Yankees in the World Series. During the series, the national television broadcast of Game 1 went out for two innings.

Harry Kalas – "Harry the K" – came to the Phillies in 1971 following six years with the Houston Astros and by 1977 was the club's top broadcaster. He had both the pipes and the knowledge of the game to command an audience, and his death in 2009 ended an era in Philadelphia. (National Baseball Hall of Fame and Museum)

Ayer and Atlantic selected 6-foot-8 Gene Kelly to call Phillies games on WPEN radio and WPTZ-TV. The Brooklyn-born Kelly, a former minor-league pitcher, also called the NBA Philadelphia Warriors. He worked with Bill Brundige for two years, with Haring in 1952, and with George Walsh in 1953–54. Herb Carneal joined them on weekends starting in July 1954.

After the 1950 pennant, the Phillies fell back to the middle of the pack while the Athletics, changing managers and strategies seemingly every year, remained in the doldrums. Organized Baseball soon concluded that Philadelphia, like Boston and St. Louis, wasn't big enough to support two teams, and the A's pulled up stakes.

Once the Athletics transferred to Kansas City for 1955, the Phillies placed more games on television to fill the programming gap, showing most home and road weekend contests. Saam, benefitting from his long association with sponsor Atlantic Refining, was able to switch back to the Phillies.

Sponsored by Atlantic, Chesterfield cigarettes, and Valley Forge Beer, Saam partnered in 1955 with Haring and Kelly, who had been deposed from his lead role. Walsh, who had been the lead television voice for home games with both the Phils and A's, moved back to Louisville, where he had broadcast for a decade.

Kelly was no slouch; he had done the national broadcast of the 1953 World Series, and it must have been difficult for him to adjust to a secondary role with the Phillies when Saam reassumed the No. 1 spot.

No longer competing with the A's, the Phillies expanded their radio network. By 1956 the net had grown to 17 stations, with Atlantic Refining, Ballantine, Phillies cigars, and Tasty Baking providing the advertising support.

Atlantic Refinery's 1956 Junior Sportscaster Contest (a competition the company revived several times) produced one of life's lovely little coincidences. The Phillies solicited entries from aspiring voices 18 and under, with the youngster judged to be the most promising given the big prize: calling part of a game on WIP with Gene Kelly.

The winner was a callow youth named Andy Musser, who showed up on a full-time basis in the Phillies' booth a couple of decades later.

In 1959, WFIL took over as the club's exclusive TV outlet for first time. Affiliated with the *Philadelphia Inquirer*, WFIL was an ABC affiliate with a history of picking and choosing which New York–based network programming it would air. This tendency allowed the channel to put on as many games as it wished.

With the club's radio games now on WIP's AM and FM frequencies, the Phillies earned $600,000, highest in the NL, for their broadcast rights in 1959. After the season — perhaps to placate Saam, who had just called the 1959 World Series on national radio — Atlantic Refining canned Kelly. To Kelly's resentment, the Phillies apparently did not try very hard to stop the firing. The popular broadcaster was allowed to "resign."

While Kelly hoped to snare the vacant Orioles' radio job, he failed and broadcast no baseball in either 1960 or 1961 before landing on the Reds' broadcast team for 1962. Later he shifted to St. Louis and KMOX, where he called the Indy 500 and college football. He passed away in 1979 at 60.

Kelly's replacement was Frank Sims, sports director of WKMH radio in Detroit, which for a time had been the Tigers flagship. Sims spent three years on the crew with Saam and Haring, but eventually made his biggest mark as a top executive for The Sports Network, the era's biggest supplier of crews and equipment for remotely televised sporting events.

WFIL won exclusive rights to the Phillies in 1960, airing the club's games on both radio and TV through 1967. Atlantic Refining remained the primary sponsor, but by this time used only a quarter-share of the commercial time on the games, selling the rest at a tidy profit.

In 1961, a miserable year for the Philadelphia, WFIL radio aired 20 exhibitions plus all 154 regular-season games on its 20-station network. The Phils lost 23 straight at one point and finished 47–107, but that disastrous campaign was also a turning point, as the team's young players made it through hell and came out stronger.

When Richie "Whitey" Ashburn hung up his spikes after spending 1962 with the woeful expansion Mets, it was a natural that the Phillies would add the immensely popular outfielder to their broadcast team. Ashburn became the first former big-league player to ever broadcast for the Phils, and after relocating from his native Nebraska to Pennsylvania, he cemented his place as a key face and voice of the organization.

The Phillies also brought Bill Campbell, sports director at local WCAU and a longtime voice of the NFL Eagles and NBA Warriors, into the booth. To make room, Haring — who had been doing Phillies games for 20 years — was deposed along with Sims, who then called games for the Dodgers' Double-A Texas League club in Albuquerque.

By 1963, the team's broadcast revenue was just fourth in the NL and eighth in the majors. The Phils leapt out to a big lead in 1964 and seemed to be a lock to win the pennant, but folded disastrously down the stretch. Despite the heartbreak, however, the club's rise was great for business as the Phillies commanded a new three-year deal from Atlantic Refining and WFIL.

This contract doubled the team's estimated broadcast revenue to $1.3 million per season, second-highest in baseball behind, surprisingly, Houston. WFIL radio expanded its network to 25 stations, while WFIL-TV saw enough advertising interest to present a 30-minute pregame show before each of its 51 Phillies telecasts in 1965.

Key to this deal was the assurance that WFIL would have complete exclusivity in the area. As a result, the Phillies were one of only two teams not shown on ABC-TV's 1965 Game of the Week package. (The other was the Yankees, owned by CBS.)

WFIL radio changed to a top 40/rock-and-roll format in 1966, making for a very bad fit with adult-oriented sponsors like Atlantic Refining, R.J. Reynolds, and Ballantine. Following the 1967 season, WFIL's radio contract expired and was not renewed.

Noting Ashburn's popularity, the Phillies increased their jock presence on the air. Bill White, the club's first baseman, began hosting a radio pregame show in 1967. (White joined the Yankees' broadcast crew in 1971, and that year Phillies pitcher Jim Bunning, in his last year before retiring, hosted a 10-minute radio postgame.)

Following a near-Hall of Fame career as a center fielder for the Phillies, the beloved Richie Ashburn joined the team's broadcast lineup in 1963 and kept on calling games until his death during the 1997 season. (National Baseball Hall of Fame and Museum)

By this time the Phillies had begun showing a lot of weekend games on television, long before many other teams did so. With weak attendance at deteriorating Connie Mack Stadium, club management obviously concluded that the increased advertising dollars outweighed the risk of decreased gate receipts.

Both the radio and TV packages came up for bids in 1968. CBS affiliate WCAU secured the team's radio rights, bringing in some new sponsors, and would continue to broadcast the Phillies through 1975. WCAU headed a 25-station network that aired the full regular-season schedule as well as 20 spring games.

Meanwhile, WFIL retained the Phillies' television rights, presenting the games in color for the first time. Atlantic Richfield did not pay for television exclusivity during this contract, allowing the Phillies to be seen on the *Game of the Week*.

Unfortunately by this time not too many people wanted to watch the Phillies, on television or at the park. By 1969, the team's TV broadcasts featured only five-minute pregame shows.

Following the 1970 season, WFIL finished its 21-year run as Philadelphia's TV outlet. The team landed a new, five-year, $13.5 million television contract with WPHL, a UHF station. With the team moving into new Veterans Stadium, Schmidt Beer took over for Ballantine (which had just been sold and was hemorrhaging money) as a secondary sponsor.

Schmidt apparently mandated that a younger voice join the broadcasts. Who would the new man be, and who would go to make room for him? Atlantic Refining insisted that Saam remain as the team's primary voice, and the Phillies would not permit the firing of Richie Ashburn. That left 47-year-old Bill Campbell in the crosshairs.

Harry Kalas, 34 years old yet with six seasons of broadcasting the Houston Astros already under his belt, came aboard to provide "youth" in the Phillies broadcast booth. Bill Giles, at the time Phillies vice president of business affairs, said that he recommended Kalas — a colleague from their days in Houston — only after the decision was made to fire Campbell. Local sportswriting legend Bill Conlin would later report, however, that Giles campaigned actively to have Kalas replace Campbell.

Like most of the great baseball broadcasters, Kalas developed his own home run call. During his days with Triple-A Hawaii, he had said, "That ball's aloha." In Houston, Kalas observed, "That ball's in Astro-orbit." In Philly it became, "That ball's outta here" or, later, simply, "It's outta here." Simple, but when Kalas wrapped his delightful, full voice around it, it became a rising cadence of joy.

Philadelphia fans, never enamored of the reserved, precise Red Barber style, fell in love with Kalas almost immediately. He openly pulled for the boys, but he had credibility — Kalas was no ripper, but he called 'em like he saw 'em.

In addition to its new personnel, WPHL buffed up the staid Phillies' telecasts in 1971 with the use of slow-motion, instant replay, and a fourth camera. The station aired a then–team record 67 games, plus three spring contests.

The new TV deal earned the Phillies $1.5 million annually in 1971–73 and $1.55 million in 1974–75. Management also signed a new three-year radio contract with WCAU, which immediately hired Campbell as a morning sports anchor.

The sponsors insisted that veteran radio-TV producer Gene Kirby run the Phillies' broadcast operations in 1971. Kirby was known for his twin abilities to keep costs under control and to cosset advertisers. With new money in the budget, the Phillies' 1972 telecasts featured two seven-and-a-half minute pregame segments, one targeted specifically at kids and one toward women. That interesting experiment only lasted a year, during which the club won just 59 games despite Steve Carlton's 27–10 record.

The baseball world was changing rapidly in the 1970s. The game was faster when played on artificial turf. Giant new superstadia decreased home runs and scoring. World Series games were being played at night. Everybody had sideburns, and many had mustaches. And after 1973, Atlantic (now Atlantic Richfield) pulled out of sponsoring Phillies games; no longer would one company dictate so much of the club's broadcast strategy. The decline of the single-sponsor broadcast meant better business for the teams and, arguably, better service to the viewers and listeners as smaller local sponsors became part of the Phillies' broadcasts in 1974.

Byrum Saam, nearing 60, was beginning to struggle to see the ball while announcing. Everyone knew that the team would have to make a change soon. This was a bitter irony for Saam, who called Phillies games for so many mediocre or bad teams, because in 1975, Philadelphia fielded its best team in a decade.

New ideas were about to spice up the Phillies' television situation. After a year of showing games in New York, the still new Home Box Office cable channel wanted to air Phillies games on cable in their market. WPHL's sponsors, however, were guaranteed exclusivity by their contracts, forcing HBO to back off.

This doesn't mean, however, that the Phillies eschewed cable television; they just took the new technology closer to home, working with Ed Snider, owner of the NHL Flyers and the Spectrum arena in South Philadelphia. Snider was a former vice president and minority owner of the NFL Eagles and was the prime mover in getting the expansion Flyers franchise in 1967. In the mid-1970s, Snider began his own sports-and-movies cable network, calling it PRISM (Philadelphia Regional In-Home Sports and Movies). PRISM took the air in 1976, showing 30 Phillies home games, Flyers and NBA 76ers contests, and college sports to Philly fans whose homes were wired for cable. PRISM also showed movies and specials and quickly made money, apparently enough to compensate WPHL and the station's sponsors for the lack of exclusivity.

A venture of Snider's conglomerate Spectacor, PRISM was the first local cable television network to show major-league games since the abortive 1964 STV project on the West Coast. More importantly, it was the first such venture to demonstrate that broadcasters and teams could successfully charge fans for watching sports content. PRISM was a game-changer; the Phillies under owner Bill Giles played a little-known but key role as television pioneers in MLB in the 1980s and 1990s.

On the field, things were looking way up. The Phillies surged to second place in 1975 after finishing last or next-to-last in the NL East for the first five years of its existence in 1969–74. This set up the team's new 1976 radio and television contracts quite nicely.

WIBG outbid several other stations to become the new radio broadcaster. For the first time, the Phillies retained the radio rights, selling ad time themselves but also paying broadcaster salaries and expenses. WIBG retained the rights to sell ads on pregame and postgame programming. WPHL signed a new television deal as well.

The biggest change was that after nearly four decades at the microphone, Byrum Saam retired. Kalas became the "Voice of the Phillies" to two generations of fans. Andy Musser, 20 years after winning the Junior Broadcaster contest, joined as the third man. Musser had worked in Philly for a few years before breaking through as voice of the NFL San Diego Chargers and the NBA Chicago Bulls. He had no professional baseball experience, but did his job effectively.

In a tremendous gesture, when the Phillies played a five-game series in Montreal in late September 1976, the club flew Saam to Quebec to call the play-by-play for the NL East–clinching game — the only clinching game the broadcast legend would call in a career that began in 1938.

KYW assumed the Phillies' radio rights for 1977. As one of the first all-news stations in the country, KYW made a much better fit for the Phillies than did WIBG's easy-listening format. Once again, the Phils retained ad sales rights.

With more television broadcasts scheduled, the club hired Chris Wheeler, a local who had been with the team's public relations department for several years. Not a traditional sports voice, "Wheels" was among the rare analysts not to be an ex-player. He became known for breaking down the finer points of a game.

In the 1970s and early 1980s, Kalas, Ashburn, Wheeler, and Musser made for a close-knit broadcasting group, calling the action for one of baseball's most exciting teams. Wheeler never achieved the fame of Kalas or Ashburn — not everyone can become a legend, after all — but he forged a very long career.

In 1979, the Phillies made a huge splash by signing the biggest free-agent in the game, Pete Rose, to a huge deal. WPHL-TV helped ensure that Rose came to Philly by sweetening their rights deal in an innovative way: if ad revenues exceeded a certain threshold, WPHL promised to award the team $600,000. (It was a fairly common practice at the time for 50 percent bonuses upon reaching agreed-upon targets.) This virtually guaranteed extra cash undergirded the Phillies' winning offer to Rose.

Following the 1978 season, the Phillies — pushed by WPHL — nearly replaced Musser. The team called for resumes and tapes from prospective candidates; however, despite a huge response, nobody impressed management enough to win the job. Musser remained on the club's broadcasts for another 23 years, and is said to have missed only two games in his 26-year tenure.

Philadelphia's estimated $2.95 million in 1979 media revenue from television rights, radio ad sales, and PRISM fees, was by far the largest in the game. KYW had 33 stations on its network.

In 1980, the Phillies took on a new broadcaster, Tim McCarver. The former Cardinals and Phillies catcher proved such a quick study behind the mike that he was considered for network positions as early as 1981. After 1982, McCarver headed to New York, where he worked on Mets games for 16 seasons.

The Phils won the world championship in 1980, the franchise's first in almost a century of existence. But local fans were outraged that Kalas & Company were nowhere to be found during the Fall Classic. Major League Baseball's outdated and protectionist rules still prohibited clubs from broadcasting on their own radio network during the World Series, forcing them to listen to the CBS radio network accounts. The angry response from legions of Phillies fans helped push MLB into amending this rule.

The surprising World Series win helped the club up its broadcasting earnings to $4 million in 1981. That spring, Musser was injured in an auto accident. Adding insult to injury, departing Phillies manager Dallas Green as much as called Musser a shill, saying that, perhaps in his new job in Chicago, he should "hire Musser to bully the fans" for four years until he could build the Cubs into a contender. It seemed strange then and seems strange now that Green, himself often accused of bullying, would call out the reserved Musser in such a fashion.

Cable TV was a huge part of the Phillies' windfall. In 1981, PRISM paid an impressive one million dollars to air 30 home games. PRISM counted more than 200,000 subscribers that year and proceeded to sign a five-year contract with the team. Meanwhile, WPHL carried an all-time high of 81 games, including nearly all the Phils' road schedule.

For 1982, the Phillies earned an astonishing $6.5 million in broadcast revenue, tied for second-best in the game with the brewery-supported Expos, who were at their high-water mark, and behind only the mighty Yankees. Two things boosted the Phillies' revenue: WCAU inked a new 11-year radio deal, in which the team ceded ad sales rights in exchange for a hefty fee, and both PRISM and WPHL-TV increased their rights payments.

The next year, in which the Phillies again won the NL pennant, WTAF-TV took over as the club's over-the-air partner, inking a 10-year deal that paid the club a flat fee plus a percentage of advertising sales. WTAF was then an independent UHF channel, but in 1986 became part of the new Fox TV Network, and in 1988 changed its call letters to WTXF to officially reflect that. In a highly unusual twist, however, WTXF continued to brand itself on-air as WTAF-TV 29 until the mid-1990s!

Several MLB teams signed long-term media deals in the early 1980s, but few of them ultimately proved good for either party. The clubs that signed them received upfront money and what seemed at the time like great terms, but which turned out to be far less attractive as rights payments escalated elsewhere in the industry. Stations and advertisers, for their part, found their programming and advertising flexibility limited by such deals. The Phillies renegotiated some of these deals or terminated some of them early.

By 1983 PRISM boasted more than 300,000 subscribers in the Delaware Valley, each paying between $10 and $11 a month. That year, Rainbow Media acquired PRISM and its sister channel PRISM New England, but retained the original PRISM channel in Philly as a separate brand. Rainbow launched SportsChannel Philadelphia in 1990 as a basic-cable sports net that carried the lower-profile Phillies games that neither PRISM nor WTXF wanted.

The Phillies' stalwart four-man crew rolled along undisturbed from 1977 through 1996, with a succession of other announcers helping out on cable telecasts. Kalas burnished his resume by calling the 1984 NLCS on national radio and, more importantly, becoming the voice of NFL Films that same year.

The $8.5 million the Phillies earned in 1985 from their broadcast rights ranked behind only the mega-market Mets and Yankees. Nonetheless, despite the barrels of money coming in, the Schmidt-Carlton-Maddox team's glory era on the field had passed. From 1984 through 1992, Philadelphia finished above fourth just once.

PRISM began showing road games for the first time in 1986, the first year of a new eight-year contract. In 1990, the two parties renegotiated the contract when SportsChannel debuted.

In 1988, 123 Phillies contests were televised. The team retained advertising sales on PRISM telecasts, but both WCAU radio and WTAF-TV sold all of their own ads.

Like other clubs, the Phillies had a balance of local and national sponsors. The 100-year-old local Tasty Baking Company, makers of Tastykakes, has advertised on broadcasts for decades. Tasty has issued Phillies trading cards, and a card in their 1984 set featured a photo of Kalas, Ashburn, Wheeler, and Musser.

The Phils aired 149 games in 1990 on WTAF, PRISM, and SportsChannel Philadelphia, which in its first season got mostly midweek road contests played against mediocre teams. Musser, getting his first lead assignment, called the SportsChannel games. In 1992, he began working with ex-Pirates and Phillies reliever Kent Tekulve.

WOGL took over the club's radio rights in 1991 via a four-year deal, with WPHL becoming the club's new over-the-air partner for eight seasons. From 1991 through 1994, the club telecast 80 or so games on WPHL, approximately 25 on SportsChannel, and about 40 on PRISM.

Jim Barniak, PRISM's longtime sports director, passed away suddenly on December 30, 1991, at age 50 from a gastrointestinal hemorrhage. Before coming to PRISM when it was launched in the 1970s, Barniak — the 76ers' play-by-play voice — had been a columnist for the evening *Bulletin*.

In 1990–91, Barniak had resumed his 1970s role behind the mike on PRISM's Phillies games, working with Mike Schmidt and Garry Maddox. Following Barniak's passing, Chris Wheeler was assigned his first play-by-play job, doing PRISM games in 1992.

Philadelphia earned $13.5 million in media rights fees in 1993, a year in which the hard-scrabble veteran Phillies rose from the doldrums to surprise everyone and win the NL flag. In 1994, WGMP snared the radio rights for a three-year span. Since 1996, the Phils have aired on WGMP, WPEN, WPHT, WPEN again, and WPHT again. This station-hopping has become common in recent years, with short-term deals leading to frequent turnover.

Radio and television stations often find airing sports an irresistible pull because the sports fan demographic is large, mostly male, and affluent. The problem with airing sports is that rights fees are high and viewership rises and falls with a team's on-field success. This unpredictability is just one reason that broadcasting relationships can change very quickly. It takes flexibility on both sides for such a partnership to last.

WPSG, for instance, began an 11-year run as the team's over-the-air television channel in 1998. Following the 2000 season, the club made a major change in its television strategy, cutting over-the-air games from 70 to around 40 per season, still quite a few for most teams but an unexpectedly low number in major markets with a long history of games on "free" television.

Another area in which the Phillies have been ahead of the curve is in Spanish-language broadcasting. After abortive efforts in 1994 and 2001, the Phils teamed with entrepreneur Bill Kulik in 2005 to put games on WPWA. After one season of doing home games at the park and road games from TV feeds, Kulik and Denny Martinez began traveling to all games. Kulik's Spanish Broadcasting Network is an influential power in the rapidly growing Spanish-language baseball market.

The 1994–95 labor war hurt all MLB clubs' broadcast revenue but, by 1997, the Phillies had weathered the storm. *Broadcasting & Cable* estimated that the club's television package earned it some $25 million that year. But those numbers couldn't numb the loss that team employees, fans, and fellow media members felt when Richie Ashburn died at 70.

"Whitey," who was telling friends that he would retire following the close of that campaign, passed away on September 9, 1997, at his hotel in New York City a day after calling a Phillies-Mets game. Kalas was grief-stricken at the loss of the man who had become one of his best friends.

Larry Andersen, a former relief pitcher known for his wit, joined the Phillies in 1998 as Ashburn's replacement. The quick-witted former relief pitcher became the seventh of nine former Phillies players to serve as a broadcaster since 1976. Unlike some of the ex-jocks who passed quickly without making a mark, Andersen stuck around, becoming a popular and worthy successor to Ashburn.

The other big change for 1998 was that Comcast took over the Phillies' cable television rights, replacing PRISM and SportsChannel. Comcast, a local cable provider, was founded in 1963; it had become a big player in the cable TV market and would soon become a huge player in broadcast sports, helping to drive the shift of live sports to RSNs. Ed Snider sold his controlling interest in Spectacor — which owned the Flyers and managed sports arenas all over the country — to Comcast in 1996, then used that money to purchase a controlling interest in the 76ers. The deal allowed Comcast to control video rights for the Phillies, 76ers, and Flyers. Thus on October 1, 1997, both PRISM and SportsChannel went dark.

Comcast launched its first RSN in Philadelphia and, since then, has expanded into Baltimore-Washington, Chicago, the Bay Area, and Houston.

After two years of splitting TV games with WPSG, Comcast carried 113 Phillies' telecasts in 2001. Kalas, Wheeler, and Andersen formed the three-man crew on all telecasts, with Musser closing out his career on radio and new hire Scott Graham learning the ropes. John Kruk helped out for a year on TV in 2003, and the next season Tom McCarthy came aboard.

Graham and McCarthy had their fans, but they — like Musser and Campbell before them — represent professional broadcasters brought into baseball after having established themselves announcing other pro and college sports. These kinds of professional voices represent low-risk tradeoffs and can be reassuring when compared to non-artful jocks like, say, Gary Matthews, who joined the Phillies' air team in 2007. Popular ex-players can achieve heights of popularity that few professional announcers ever do, but sometimes flame out after brief trials.

Following the 2006 season, Graham was let go. No official explanation for the dismissal was given, leading to all sorts of rumors. Scott Franzke, who had spent time filling in for Josh Lewin on Rangers telecasts, took Graham's place, doing pregame and postgame work and calling the middle three innings on radio. By 2008, Franzke had assumed the No. 1 job.

Kalas was still doing three innings of radio on each game, but the iconic voice was spending most of his time on television, teaming with Matthews, with Wheeler chipping in. In July 2008, Kalas missed some time after undergoing surgery to fix a detached retina. During this season, the Phillies captured their second World Series, beating the Tampa Bay Rays.

The joy of the 2008 championship faded quickly the following spring. On April 8, 2009, the Phillies received their World Series rings, and Kalas was asked to throw out the first ball. Five days later, Kalas collapsed and died in the press box before a game at Nationals Park in Washington.

Virtually everyone in Philadelphia grieved at the loss of the beloved 73-year-old announcer, who lived his life to the fullest, whether it was calling ballgames, singing at piano bars, or hanging around with the players he came to know so well. Tom McCarthy, who had spent 2006 and 2007 on Mets broadcasts before returning to Philadelphia for 2009, assumed the top roles on WPHL and Comcast.

With many years ahead of them, Franzke and McCarthy put the Phillies in a good position for the future. In 2012, the club began simulcasting its radio games on WIP-FM, bringing the games to homes and car radios in glorious stereo.

Because of their large market and astute strategic thinking from the 1970s onward, the Phillies have made a lot of money in broadcasting. The club enjoys in a gigantic and wealthy market, with Comcast and Citizens Bank Park now providing the muscle.

Just how much muscle the network could flex became clear following the 2013 season. Comcast and the team hammered out a groundbreaking 25-year deal reportedly worth $5 billion. The contract pumped immediate money into the team's coffers — the rights fees alone will pay some $100 million a year — but also gave the network more editorial control over the broadcasts.

That new editorial control blared loudly on January 8, 2014 when Comcast dismissed Chris Wheeler and Gary Matthews — both Phillies employees — from Philadelphia's television team. "Wheels" had been in the broadcast booth for 37 years, Matthews seven.

 Brought in to replace the veteran pair were former Phillies Jamie Moyer and Matt Stairs, both hired directly by Comcast. Mike Schmidt also began appearing on Sunday telecasts. Another former Fightin', pitcher Ricky Bottalico, hoped for a booth job but was instead hired as a studio analyst.

Another facet of the huge Comcast/Phillies deal is that the team assumes a 25% ownership stake in the network. This is the wave of the future that Jim Barniak talked about way back when, one that only a few teams so far have reached successfully.

Beamed around the region on radio, TV, and cable, memorable voices like Byrum Saam, Richie Ashburn, Harry Kalas, Gene Kelly, Larry Andersen, Chris Wheeler, and Bill Campbell thrilled baseball fans for decades. None of these men chose the detached "Red Barber" style, nor did any reduce themselves to Harry Caray–like bluster. The Phillies' best announcers have molded themselves after their passionate and knowledgeable — if often impolite — audience, skillfully walking the fine line between loyalty to the team and honesty to the fans.

GOOD NIGHT, SWEET PRINCE

PITTSBURGH PIRATES BROADCASTING HISTORY

"If [Bob Prince] hadn't shown such hubris in his fight against Westinghouse, if he'd shown a hint of humility, he'd have broadcast the Pirates till he died. But he hadn't, and it cost him the thing he loved the most."
— *Milo Hamilton, in Curt Smith's* Voices of the Game

NO MATTER HOW HISTORICALLY BAD THE PIRATES HAVE BEEN FOR most of the past two decades, nobody can take away one key achievement from the franchise: Pittsburgh was the first big-league team to broadcast a baseball game over the radio.

Radio essentially grew up with the twentieth century. Guglielmo Marconi introduced his wireless sound transmitter to President Teddy Roosevelt in 1904 and, within 10 years, both sides in World War I were using the new device.

Commercial applications beckoned; by the early 1920s, most large cities had radio stations. Pittsburgh's KDKA, owned and operated by local industrial giant Westinghouse, was among the first. In 1921, according to research by Ted Patterson in *The Golden Voices of Baseball*, KDKA did the first radio sportscast: a boxing match, with sportswriter Florent Gibson describing the action.

Two months later, the description of Jack Dempsey's title fight was relayed over a primitive "network" of wires hung from railroad cars; this hookup produced a broadcast audible from several hundred miles away on the day's crystal radio sets.

Harold Arlin was one of radio's Horatio Alger stories. The farm boy from Illinois, working at Westinghouse, heard of an announcer's position at KDKA, auditioned for the job, and got it. He stepped, largely unprepared, into a new field where he covered dances, news, and sports. Due to the nascent station's reach, Arlin accidentally became one of radio's first stars.

He also became baseball's first announcer. On August 5, 1921, Arlin was at Forbes Field to describe the action between the Phillies and Pirates. He also called radio's first football game, a Pittsburgh–West Virginia tilt, that fall.

The 1921 World Series was the first broadcast over radio. Legendary sportswriter Grantland Rice sat at the microphone on a network headed by WJZ in Newark, New Jersey (which, decades later, was the New York Mets' first flagship). Arlin also announced the Series action on KDKA.

These local stations were, at the time, worldwide. With few stations competing for space on the dial, people could tune into KDKA, WJZ, or Chicago's WGN from almost anywhere: Australia, the high seas, or Paris. Harold Arlin was, in his time, as big a star as Rush Limbaugh, Wendy Williams, or Piolín are today.

Listeners all over the globe paid good money to hear programs in their living rooms. $59 was a common price in the 1920s for a quality radio set; that is equivalent to more than $700 today. Stations in the U.S., Canada, and Europe brought news, music, and chat into the homes of people around the world, changing the lives of millions who might never have been able to hear what someone from Pittsburgh, Dallas, or Paris actually sounded like.

Baseball broadcasts proved popular with fans as well as shut-ins who didn't even know the game, but many of the game's executives loathed "giving" listeners something "for nothing."

Some minor leagues prohibited radio broadcasts outright. The Southern League, for example, didn't allow broadcasts of their games in the late 1920s, and other leagues followed suit into the 1930s. Prohibiting broadcasting games in smaller towns was far more defensible than doing so in major-league markets; the decision to keep all radio personnel out of ballparks in New York, for instance, seems shortsighted to the point of being silly.

For most of the 1920s, the baseball press considered the emerging radio fad to be a threat. *The Sporting News*, the "Bible of Baseball," had previously excoriated anything mounting the slightest challenge to what it saw as the established order — or, at least, challenging the vested interest of *TSN* and its friends. (Those threats included the Federal League, baseball scores on ticker-tape machines in bars, and players' unions.)

This excerpt from *TSN*'s April 27, 1922, issue — before even a single club had instituted a regular broadcast schedule — indicates how the smug baseball press viewed itself as the only conduit through which anyone should experience the game. It also revealed a paranoid, but largely accurate, prediction about television.

> Mr. Radio is going to butt into the business of telling the world all about the ball game without having the world have to go to the ball game to find out … this new radio craze is already crimping attendance at anything where the feast is for the ear rather than for the eye … next we will have the whole works shot to pieces because instead of mere sounds the radio will be repro-ducing in every home that has a ten-dollar equipment the picture of the play

... when Ruth hits a homer or Sisler slides into the plate, a film will catch him in the act, wireless will carry it a thousand miles broadcast, and the family sitting in the darkened living room at home will see the scene reproduced simultaneously on the wall ... then what will become of baseball?

It is difficult to understand, in retrospect, why *Sporting News* editors were so worried: all radio did was increase interest in baseball and create new fans among those who couldn't go to the park. Had the Bible of Baseball, along with the more intractable club owners, had their way, those folks would never have been able to truly experience the game, and baseball might have regressed to the level of a quaint late nineteenth-century spectator sport, perhaps as popular in America today as cricket or mumblety-peg.

Radio, and Babe Ruth, saved baseball, introducing it to millions of fans during the 1920s and 1930s, a time when people had limited entertainment dollars but increased entertainment options. The image of a family sitting around listening to a baseball game on the radio could hardly have been more pleasant, regardless of *TSN*'s whining — indeed, as time marched on and progress could not be halted, millions of families enjoyed baseball together on radio, on television, and, yes, even at the ballpark.

Of course, the ink-stained wretches of the press corps were jealous of the radio men and uncomfortable with the idea of competition. But radio announcers in big-league cities — some of them ex-newspapermen — soon became trusted personalities to the public, many with voices as familiar as those of close relatives.

Most major-league clubs and their mouthpieces grasped the promotional benefits of radio fairly quickly. Following the 1925 World Series, broadcast nationally on the wireless, even *TSN* saw fit to opine, "[T]he National League allows certain of its games to be broadcast during the regular season; it is a good investment in good will and a bit of missionary work ... the bottom has fallen out of the argument that to broadcast a sporting event keeps the customers away."

Regardless of this sensibility, *TSN*'s opinion on radio broadcasting of games continued to waddle between pro and con until the late 1930s, by which time nearly every team had a majority of its games on the wireless — and even the old newspaper men had accepted that they had company.

By this time, the pioneering Pirates had stopped broadcasting regular-season contests. Arlin took his final turn at the mike in 1924 and then, for nearly a decade, the Bucs were off the air because of owner Barney Dreyfuss' intractability about the medium.

In 1933, however, with the aged Dreyfuss having lost some influence, WWSW 1490's sports director, Walt Sickless, contracted with the club to re-create all 77 Pittsburgh road games. Al Helfer, who later worked with the New York Giants and other teams, was for a time Sickless' assistant. The following season, KQV joined the re-creation parade and over the next few years presented a passel of different voices, none of which endured in the public mind.

The first great sports broadcaster of Pittsburgh was a stick-thin writer, public speaker, and all-around gadfly named Rosey Rowswell (pronounced 'ROSE-well'). Emerging from a crowd of three stations doing games in 1936, Rowswell — calling re-creations over WJAS — built a big local following with his homespun delivery and goofy slogans.

WWSW announcer Jack Craddock ditched radio and returned to his career as an evangelist prior to the 1937 campaign, and suddenly Rowswell was the top dog in the Steel City. (Oddly enough, Craddock returned to Pittsburgh years later to serve as Rowswell's sidekick.) Other broadcasters who couldn't beat him included Jimmy Dudley and Claude Haring, who went on to enjoy long radio careers with other clubs.

In these days, no clear advancement path existed in radio, much less the niche of sports

The diminutive and excitable Rosey Rowswell commanded the Pirates' radio ship from 1936 until 1954, a period in which he was one of the most popular men in town. (National Baseball Hall of Fame and Museum)

radio. The field was too new. Only in the mid-1930s did broadcasting schools gain traction, and, as many famous baseball announcers of the time remarked years later, any old bozo could walk into a station and get a job if he had the right amount of moxie. It wasn't unusual for preachers, actors, comedians, or singers — anyone with a big voice, really — to double as a baseball announcer.

It also wasn't unusual for bureaucrats, advertising salesmen, or engineers to be behind the mike. Without a way to gain experience other than by doing, broadcasters then were as green as summer lawns, and on-air talent was rarely viewed as an end in itself. As is the case today, when many second and third men in radio booths are expected to have engineering or computer sound-processing skills, many mikemen in the 1930s had to do something else to keep a job, whether it involved running the equipment, selling ads, sweeping the floors, or lobbying government for increased wattage.

Radio, already a huge business, had to do its share of lobbying. Following the 1936 season, baseball commissioner Kenesaw Mountain Landis — citing "evidence" that attendance was hurt by radio — forced stations broadcasting the games to pay fees to the major-league clubs.

Clubs certainly deserved indemnification against possible box-office losses, and there was enough money in the business for radio stations, sponsors, and the teams themselves. Soon, the clubs — seeing the example of the Chicago Cubs, whose success in using radio was unparalleled — had assumed increased control of the broadcasts to maximize revenue.

As is true today, the big money behind early broadcasts came from industry. General Mills was a huge early sponsor of baseball, as were various automobile, oil, liquor, cigarette, and consumer goods companies. Hundreds of thousands of dollars were at stake for an announcer, who had to hold his listeners' interest in order for those between-innings commercials to have their full effect.

There was no formula for who would be an effective announcer. Some clubs used folksy storytellers, others stentorian lecturers. Still others employed ex-players with on-field experience or sportswriters who claimed to have the "inside dope."

Then there was Rowswell, who by 1938 was the only man in town doing "the Buccos," as he called them. Rowswell was already 54 years old in 1938, and had the homey style of a fan lucky enough to find himself behind a microphone. During re-creations, when a Pirates player homered, Rowswell would scream, "Open the window, Aunt Minnie!" Craddock, or an engineer, would then drop a tray full of utensils, glass, nuts, and bolts, signaling that poor Aunt Minnie couldn't get to the window in time to avoid it being smashed by the flying baseball.

Obviously, out-of-town baseball recreations — often aired in primetime, several hours after the actual game's conclusion — were pure entertainment, and the re-creation aspect gave announcers plenty of poetic license. Rowswell may have had more fun doing these than being at the ballpark, although surviving evidence shows that he more than enjoyed himself at Forbes Field.

The Bucs for 1940 rethought their stance on home games, airing all but holidays and Sundays with WWSW (now at 970 on the dial) and KDKA (at 1020) sharing the signal. Rowswell missed some action when he caught pneumonia during spring training. KDKA stopped carrying the Bucs in 1941 but, with longtime partner ARCO Refineries (a division of Atlantic Refining) as its biggest sponsor, WWSW aired the contests on both AM and its brand-new FM technology.

The following year, with more and more stations popping up all over the country, the Pirates created a five-station regional network to bring games to those fans throughout Western Pennsylvania who might not be able to pick up the WWSW signal. The Pirates' radio network grew to 13 stations by 1947, and nearly 50 by the 1960s.

Popular singer and movie star Bing Crosby bought into the Pirates in 1946. When in town, "Der Bingle" would join Rowswell and Bob Prince (who had replaced Craddock when he went back to religion for good in 1948) in the Forbes Field booth, reading commercials, doing occasional play-by-play, and sharing his knowledge of current baseball.

While the club's broadcasts were popular for their regional flavor, they were becoming old-fashioned. Rowswell's facility at re-creations, his increasingly poor health, and especially the high costs of transmitting broadcasts via telephone lines made the Bucs the last team in baseball to cover road games from the ballpark. By the time Pittsburgh's radio broadcasters had started traveling on a full-time basis in 1955, television had become a force in the Grand Old Game.

Following the war, television really took off, finding fertile ground in a new postwar society that was moving to the suburbs. Craving entertainment and flush with discretionary income, burgeoning suburban families were a perfect market for TV. Those fans still living in the cities often hung out at watering holes that had purchased a set or two to lure more customers. Fans in Chicago and New York became used to seeing most, if not all, of the team's home games televised.

By 1948, in fact, all major-league teams had begun televising at least a few games — except the Pirates. This was due, in part, to the city of Pittsburgh not even having a TV station until that year. WDTV, the city's first channel, was a DuMont Network station, and management found it much cheaper to pick up network programming. Therefore the Bucs didn't telecast until most clubs had already sorted out their initial broadcasting strategies and had built long-term advertising relationships.

The Bucs weren't much to watch anyway; in each season from 1950 through 1957 they had finished either seventh or eighth in the eight-team NL. Finally, on Saturday, August 29, 1953, the Pirates became the last of the 16 franchises to telecast a game, beaming their 5–4 loss to visiting St. Louis to local fans on WENS, channel 16.

Tom Johnson, co-owner of the Pirates, fronted the money to build WENS, the city's second station, and the August 29 game was actually the channel's debut. Several past and current Pirates — including Bob Prince and slugger Ralph Kiner — held stock in WENS, which earned some money back by feeding the game by phone lines to KSD in St. Louis.

WENS televised 24 more games in 1954. It had big plans but even bigger financial problems, and the Bucs found themselves without a television home for the next two years. The station went off the air for good three years later.

Perhaps a bigger loss came on February 6, 1955, when Rosey Rowswell died suddenly at home in the suburb of Fox Valley. At 71, he'd lived a happy life, with an audience of thousands of devoted fans. Bob "The Gunner" Prince assumed the chair as the Pirates' No. 1 man, teaming with Dick Bingham to cover all the team's games on radio. The pair would be the first Pittsburgh broadcasters to travel.

Prince, who began his radio career in 1940, worked his way up from 15-minute daily sports shows to doing play-by-play for the

Nicknamed "The Gunner," the hard-living, hard-working Bob Prince began as Rosey Rowswell's assistant in 1948 and took over the top job seven years later. Beloved in Western Pennsylvania, Prince epitomized the era when baseball broadcasters were stars and their word was bond with fans. (National Baseball Hall of Fame and Museum)

Pirates, Penn State football, the Pittsburgh Steelers, boxing matches, hockey, and dozens of other assignments. Following in the footsteps of the popular Rowswell, Prince found it necessary to drop impartiality and root for the home team.

He knew baseball inside out and did his homework, but Prince also knew that Pirates fans had come to regard the broadcasts as a show. It had been a while since the team was any good, so he would talk about his golf game, his buddies in show biz, and the restaurants in the city the team was playing — all at a rapid-fire pace that, in part, contributed to his nickname of "The Gunner." His nickname also described his out-of-control personality. As a young man, Prince rode the rails, rode wild horses, and sold insurance until his broadcasting career took off.

Despite the Pirates' low profile, Prince attracted attention for his outlandish on-air antics and his crazy sports jackets. He worked hard and played harder, and things improved for him and the fans once the Pirates returned to TV, got some good players, and moved their radio broadcasts to the biggest station in town.

KDKA took over the Bucs' radio games and also committed to a 24-game TV package in 1957. Prince, the lead broadcaster on radio, also did the television play-by-play. On those days, Paul Long, also a licensed pilot who flew his own plane to games, assisted Bingham on radio.

From 1957 through 2006, the Pirates were KDKA and KDKA was the Pirates. The two had a 50-year relationship, the third-longest tenure for a ballclub and a radio station in history: the Cubs and WGN were partners from 1958 through 2014; the Cardinals and KMOX's 51-year relationship ended in 2005, though it resumed a few years later.

In 1958, Jim "The Possum" Woods took over from Bingham — a KDKA disc jockey — as Prince's second. Gunner and the Possum became one of baseball's best-loved on-air teams, serving as foils on the air and drinking buddies off it. Woods had a deeper, more homespun voice than the excitable Prince, and the two were perfectly set to describe the Bucs, who captured the 1960 World Series and contended almost every year for the rest of that wild decade.

Following the team's world championship, a local company hastily assembled *The Impossible Pirates*, a commemorative 12-inch record album full of Pirates history and highlights of the previous season's exciting moments. It sold for $3.95 by mail.

In 1965, Pittsburgh began piping its spring training broadcasts to a station at its Grapefruit League home, Fort Myers. The club had a network of approximately 30 stations for most of the 1960s, spreading the word to parts of Pennsylvania, Ohio, and West Virginia.

Pittsburgh did get a new deal with KDKA for 1966, one that allowed the station to use one-third of the advertising time to promote its own shows. The contract bumped the team's rights fees up $100,000 to $450,000. All televised Pirates games were shown in color beginning in 1968.

The size of the Pittsburgh market meant that the club's broadcasting revenue was long the smallest of National League teams. Over the years, local concerns such as Foodland

Supermarkets, Iron City Beer, Sipes Paint, Allegheny Airlines, Mellon Bank, and Giant Eagle have chosen the Bucs' broadcasts to tell their stories.

Some things, however, only could have played in Pittsburgh. During the 1966 season when the Pirates finished just short of the pennant-winning Dodgers, Prince picked up on Pirates trainer Dan Whelan's weird hex — waving a green rubber hot dog at opponents — and spread an area-wide mania for what he dubbed "The Green Weenie." Pirates fans began showing up at Forbes Field with big green rubber hot dogs. Not content with starting one goofy craze, Prince, noting that Willie Stargell owned a fried chicken outlet in Pittsburgh's Hill neighborhood, began greeting homers by Pops with a shout of "Chicken on the Hill!"

Long's departure after 1962 began a slightly eerie string of "third broadcasters" behind Prince and Woods. First, Claude Haring, who had worked on games in Philadelphia for two decades, returned to Pittsburgh, seeing duty in 1963–64 with Prince and Woods. Haring then retired, passing away of a heart attack in October 1967. He was replaced by the fiery Don Hoak, former Pirates third baseman, who lasted two seasons in the booth (1965–66) before he died of a heart attack three years later.

Following the 1966 campaign, the third job went to former Bucs hurler Nellie King, who had prevailed over nearly 50 other applicants — including former Pittsburgh moundsmen Bob Purkey and Bob Friend. The Pirates have, since that time, felt that featuring an ex-Bucs pitcher in the booth was important. Since 1966, the club has employed a prominent ex-Pirates hurler on its broadcast team for all but two years (in the late 1970s).

King served as the third man in the booth from 1967 through 1969, after which he assumed the second spot when Jim Woods replaced the fired Harry Caray in St. Louis. With Jack Buck a clear first in the Mound City, however, Woods departed after two years. He later put in five years in Boston and also worked in Oakland.

Prince and King — who had prepped for his job by serving as sports director at a West Virginia radio station — paired for nine years on KDKA, doing both radio and television. The early 1970s were salad days for the historic franchise, as Pittsburgh won NL East Division titles in 1970–72 and 1974–75 and copped the 1971 World Series.

Amazingly, though, the Pirates didn't see an increase in rights fees from KDKA until 1973. Until 1972, the club was still earning just $450,000 from its television and radio package, the lowest in the majors. The big increase to $1,000,000 in 1973 helped, but even then the Bucs were ahead of just three other NL clubs in broadcast revenue.

Even as the Pirates continued to win in the 1970s, trouble was brewing. Prince's salary was always one of the highest in the business, and KDKA (owned and operated by giant Westinghouse) and the Pirates began to worry that perhaps their golden boy had let his status go to his head.

In the early 1970s Prince began bristling at Westinghouse's sales staff's penchant of bringing customers and sponsors into "his" radio booth, where they would yell drunkenly, sometimes loudly enough to be heard on the broadcast. More than once, Prince decried this behavior on the air, which causing some consternation with the men in the suits.

Prince's relationship with KDKA slowly deteriorated. After the 1975 season — during which the famed announcer told his bosses that heretofore, nobody from the parent company was welcome to enter "his" booth — the station did the unthinkable, cashiering Prince with the Pirates' tacit approval.

Despite huge public outcry — a protest parade drew some 150,000 fans, a drop in ticket sales, boycotts of the station and of Iron City beer (a Pirates radio sponsor), the firing stuck. Wanting a new voice who would never say a cross word to his bosses, Westinghouse selected Milo Hamilton to take Prince's spot. King, caught in the crossfire, escaped the baseball radio game, but returned in 2000 as a guest on the radio during the last broadcast from Three Rivers Stadium.

Prince, meanwhile, didn't know what to do with himself. Now bereft of the true love of his life — the Pirates — he hopped to Houston's booth and to ABC's *Monday Night Baseball* in 1976, but both assignments lasted only for that season. The Gunner really only played in Pittsburgh so, in 1977, he began announcing for the NHL Penguins' hockey team and continued to host all sorts of roasts, celebrity dinners, and benefit events.

KDKA's decision to hire Milo Hamilton for the top spot was the bomb of the century in Pittsburgh. Hamilton, a professional voice who only retired in 2011, was no favorite in the Steel City; of course, Prince's friends in high places would have made it hard on anyone. Hamilton's new partner, Lanny Frattare, was viewed as a "good hire," however. Frattare had the advantage of loyalty and "local" experience, having worked his way up the team's minor-league chain.

It has been argued that, in retrospect, KDKA's decision to drop Prince was the first important stage of the collapse of the Pirates, arguably the NL's strongest franchise during the 1970s. Whether that connection is true or not, it is very clear that the bottom fell out after the club's 1979 World Series win.

MLB's mushrooming drug scandal in the late 1970s and early 1980s proved disastrous to the Pirates' team image, and the fans' seething anger over the 1981 strike hurt badly in what was always a working-class town. Meanwhile, the rise of the four-time Super Bowl champion NFL Steelers in the 1970s made pro football far and away the top sport in blue-collar Western Pennsylvania. Even the popular and successful Barry Bonds–led Bucs of the early 1990s couldn't stave off the collapse of the Pirates in the city's sports consciousness.

Following four tough years, Hamilton beat an understandable retreat to the relative calm of Chicago. KDKA, hoping to land Bob Starr, turned down Prince's offer to return ("I'd crawl back on my hands and knees if they asked me"). Rebuffed by Starr while rebuffing Prince, Westinghouse instead settled on the familiar Frattare as the club's lead voice for 1980.

A good game-caller dedicated to the club, Frattare worked, over his nearly 30 years in the big chair, with a variety of assistants and color men. They included the vanilla Dave Martin in 1980 (fresh from *Good Morning America*), "We are Family" 1979 World Series hero Jim Rooker (1981–93), and another former Pirates pitcher, Steve Blass (1994–2008).

Most of Frattare's analysts have been colorful. Rooker, always entertaining, gained unwanted prominence in 1989 for saying during a game at Philadelphia — in which the Bucs led 10–0 — that he would walk home if the team lost. Unfortunately, the Phillies roared back to win the game, and Rooker smartly turned the gaffe into an opportunity to walk across the state for charity after the season.

Rooker was suffering, however, from alcohol problems, and took leave from the club in 1991 to enter treatment. He retired from broadcasting in 1993, ran unsuccessfully for Congress, and then settled down to a new career of writing children's baseball books.

Like Rooker, Blass is revered in Pittsburgh for his key role on a World Series–winning club; in this case, 1971. As the club's living legend in the booth and a well-loved presence like Mike Shannon in St. Louis or Jerry Remy in Boston, Blass made his on-air debut as part of the team's cable telecast crew in 1982.

Cable TV should have been the best thing in the world for the financially undernourished Bucs when they began planning for the new medium in the late 1970s, especially when "Pops" Stargell's very likeable team won its second world championship of the decade in 1979. By the early 1980s, the Pirates' fan base had eroded, and a severe economic depression in the steel industry hit the city very hard.

The team's first cable carrier, Action TV, aired in 1981, pairing Prince — who, despite falling out of favor with KDKA, still had allies within the club itself — with veteran Ray Scott, calling what was supposed to be a 20-game schedule. This was the first time that the Pirates had permitted a local home telecast since July 16, 1970, when the first game was played at new Three Rivers Stadium. The 1981 cable plan was gutted by the strike. The following season, Prince and Blass called a few games on a cable channel called TPC.

In 1983, Home Sports Entertainment, a national cable entity owned by Warner-Amex, took out a contract (with an unusual, annually renewable five-year option) on Pirates cable rights and paired Prince and Blass with Bill Brown, who had previously done some Reds TV, along with recently retired slugger Willie Stargell. The foursome covered 60 home games in 1983 and 76 games, mostly at home, the following year. Not coincidentally, Warner-Amex had purchased nearly half of the Pirates' stock in late 1982.

Doom loomed on the horizon, however. The Pirates were not an immediate success on pay television. HSE was doing well in the South, but had few subscribers in Pittsburgh or Cincinnati. Warner-Amex unloaded the entire operation in July, selling HSE to a consortium that included the Houston Astros and Texas Rangers, who already had games airing on the network.

After the 1984 season, when the Pirates finished last for the first time since 1955, HSE signed off permanently in the Steel City, and the club had no cable coverage the next year. During this time, the Bucs had continued showing their usual 35–50 road contests each season on KDKA. John Sanders, the station's sports director, provided prosaic play-by-play from 1981–89, after which he took a similar job with the Cleveland Indians. Alan Cutler and Kent Derdivanis, also of KDKA, also took turns at the mike without distinction.

The Pirates and KDKA — perhaps from sentimentality, more likely in an attempt to find some way to get people to pay attention — asked Prince to return from exile to the Buccos' radio team in 1985. Frattare diplomatically averred that he was looking forward to working with the 67-year-old prodigal, who dutifully showed humility and expressed his thanks when rehired.

Unfortunately for all concerned, Prince's number was about up. Years of hard living had caught up with the legend who, in a bitter stroke of irony, underwent surgery in April to remove cancerous growths from his mouth. He returned to the booth on May 3, but was unable to handle the stress and called just three games before reentering a local hospital. Prince passed away on June 10, 1985; although his life ended sadly, Prince certainly had a long run at the top, and was still one of the biggest men in town at his demise.

TCI, another regional cable operator, signed on with the Bucs for 1986. Its operation — which for two years featured future NHL Penguins voice Mike Lange at the mike — was initially known as Pirates Cable Network but was soon branded as KBL Entertainment Network.

For a time, KBL showed entertainment programming as well as other local sports, modeling itself after successful cable channels like PRISM in Philadelphia and ON-TV in Southern California and the Midwest. Soon, however, KBL dropped everything except sports. In 1994, Prime Sports bought the channel from TCI, renaming it Prime Sports KBL and showing annually as many as 60 (mostly home) Pirates games.

After 1993, when Derdivanis and Rooker departed, KDKA hired another former pitcher, Bob Walk, as a radio-TV analyst. Walk proved as durable in the booth as on the mound and remains with the club, as does that year's other new hire, Greg Brown.

Brown is a "lifer": he interned with the Pirates in 1979 while in college, then spent 10 years as a club employee in various departments, and was the PA announcer in 1987. He received seasoning at the Pirates' Triple-A club in Buffalo, calling the American Association Bisons as well as NFL Buffalo Bills games for five years.

The disastrous collapse of the 1990–92 club that won three consecutive NL East titles and twice came within a game of the World Series was followed quickly by another disaster when, following the 1994 strike, KDKA-TV bowed out of the picture. For the next few seasons, the once-proud franchise bounced embarrassingly around local TV outlets, never showing more than 15 games in any year on "free TV" until cutting out over-the-air coverage entirely in 2003.

Prime sold KBL in 1996 to Fox; eventually the Pirates ramped up their cable TV games to well over 100 by 2008 on FSN Pittsburgh (previously Fox Sports Net Pittsburgh).

Long a source of stability, the club's radio situation changed completely after the 2006 season, when KDKA bowed out after five decades and made way for WPGH-FM. Everyone that cared about the Pirates felt more than a little sorrow over the parting, and they became the only team in the NL without an AM flagship station.

Greg Brown became the Pirates' No. 1 when Frattare called it a career after 2008. Frattare had taken time off in 2004 to deal with depression, and he never achieved the level of loyalty that earlier Pittsburgh voices had. Brown is pleasant to listen to, and has become the voice of the club perhaps more through longevity than through excitement over his work. The same can be said for minor-league veteran Tim Neverette, who joined the Bucs' TV team for 2009, though his progression through the bush leagues is to be admired.

During the 2008 season, Fox sold its Pittsburgh, Seattle, and Denver cable sports operations to Liberty Media. In 2011, those three channels were rebranded as Root Sports. The announcers for Pirates telecasts remained the same, and to the joy of local fans, Root debuted showing more than 150 Pirates games.

For 2012, the Bucs returned to KDKA radio, this time only on the FM dial. Strong ratings for the first portion of 2011, when the team played very well, led KDKA-FM reps to seek out a new multiyear deal that includes at least 16 spring-training games annually for a radio network that included 38 stations in 2011.

The return to KDKA was a smart move, but the team only gained real traction with its surprising 2013 playoff season. No group of broadcasters — no matter how able and dedicated — could repair the morbidity of a team that set the record for most consecutive losing seasons, as it finished below .500 every year from 1992 through 2012. Brown & Co. certainly had fun describing the return of the Black and Gold to the playoffs in 2013.

DON HOAK

Hoak, who manned the hot corner for 11 years in the majors, was popular and obsessed with baseball. He was the hardest-driving and most aggressive player of his day, and didn't lack confidence or self-esteem.

Before he'd even uttered a word on a Pirates broadcast, Hoak boasted to *The Sporting News*, "I told Prince and Woods that I might be starting a new job, but if they expect me to be No. 3, they're wrong. I'm aiming for No. 1, not necessarily in Pittsburgh, but in some broadcasting booth in the majors."

After just two years in the booth, Hoak jumped back to the field, joining the Phillies as a first-base coach for a year, then spending two seasons managing in the minors. On the fast track, Hoak openly campaigned for the Pirates' job following the 1969 season when Larry Shepard was canned.

On October 9, Hoak — who had earlier said he wouldn't stay in the Bucs' system if he didn't get the job — found out that the assignment went to his old skipper, Danny Murtaugh. Later that day, Hoak's brother-in-law's car was stolen. Hoak, who was at the scene, went chasing after it, collapsed on the street, and died of a massive coronary.

When the Pirates were horrid in the 1950s and 1980s, they still had powerful presences imbued into their broadcasts: men whose voices and personalities formed intense bonds with their audience. Of course, intensity can provoke controversy, which is something most corporations scrupulously try to avoid.

The progression from Bob Prince to Greg Brown symbolizes the removal of strong local flavor from baseball broadcasting. Listening to MLB announcers today, one would never know what part of the country most hail from — their diction, inflection, tone, and phrasing are as homogenized as American fast food.

The spicy local and regional cuisines of the classic age of sports broadcasting have been removed from the menu. The best of the professional class of modern broadcasters call the game well, invoke memory, establish continuity, and induce fans to bond with their team. The worst of the cohort — none of whom currently work in Pittsburgh — are simply palate-cleansers whose descriptions evaporate five minutes after the game is through.

In their nearly 90-year radio history, the Pirates have had only two truly memorable voices: Rosey Rowswell and Bob Prince. Both are long dead, sadly, along with the distinct style of work they embodied.

BIRD ON A RADIO WIRE

ST. LOUIS CARDINALS BROADCASTING HISTORY

"[Harry] told it like he thought it was, and that's different from telling it like it is."
— Jack Buck in That's a Winner!

THE ST. LOUIS CARDINALS' RADIO HISTORY IS BOUND UP WITH THAT
of the long-departed Browns. Like other franchises in two-team cities, the Redbirds and
Brownies shared airwaves and broadcasters during radio's early history.

While the Cardinals eventually developed the biggest radio network in baseball, their
early experiences with the medium were not always progressive. By 1933 the team was on
the radio every day except Sunday at home, but St. Louis management believed it could
veto visiting team broadcasts of their games in St. Louis. The next season, the club tried to
ban visiting teams from re-creating games being played at Sportsman's Park. The Pirates
fought that ruling and won.

Perhaps looking to challenge General Mills' ubiquity as a sponsor in baseball broadcasting,
Kellogg's sent local announcer France Laux to Chicago to call two Cubs-Cardinals games
in September 1937. These games, though, did not result in any long-term broadcasting relationship between the club and the food company.

The "Gas House Gang" Cardinals were clearly the city's most popular team in the 1930s,
but St. Louis' population was decreasing and the fight for baseball dollars always tough. St.
Louis had been capable of supporting two baseball teams at the turn of the century, and
the Browns had competed successfully with the Cardinals for Mound City fans until the

mid-1920s but, from 1926 until the Browns left in the 1950s, the Cardinals completely dominated the market.

As late as 1941, Laux — working with Cy Casper and Gabby Street — was the town's dominant baseball broadcaster, working for Hyde Park Brewery and its network of stations in Missouri and Illinois. During the 1942 campaign, the status quo changed when former Cardinals hurler Dizzy Dean entered the Falstaff-sponsored KWK booth, working with Johnny O'Hara. Dean was a huge hit, and in 1943, *The Sporting News* named O'Hara its baseball announcer of the year.

O'Hara, who had been a radio operator on an ocean liner then called games in Chicago before coming to St. Louis, saw his baseball career come to a close only a few years later, largely because of the efforts of Harold Carabina, better known as Harry Caray.

When the local Griesedieck brewery chose to hire Harry Caray and Gabby Street for its 1944 Cardinals and Browns program schedule, the company took on heavy competition. The ambitious Caray, who had worked at several smaller stations before coming to St. Louis, essentially convinced Griesedieck leadership that he was better than Laux, better than O'Hara, better than Dean — better than anyone. But even as Caray brimmed with confidence, he was counting on the baseball knowledge of Street, a former big-league player and manager.

"No partner I've ever had meant as much to me as he did," Caray wrote in his memoir *Holy Cow!* And while Caray certainly had the gift of gab — the first play-by-play he had ever called was of St. Louis Flyers hockey, a sport he had never previously seen — it took him a while to hone his style and develop his identity.

An orphan from St. Louis' Hill neighborhood, Caray was raised by an aunt and learned the game of survival early. His aggressive style was a perfect fit for the fluid world of radio, which in the late 1930s and early 1940s had not yet developed an orthodoxy.

During the 1945 season, Street hosted a pregame program, sponsored by Old Judge coffee, on WIL prior to Browns and Cardinals games. He was the star of the show; while Caray was well-liked, Street was a local hero.

Amid the team's triumphal 1946 campaign came a note of tragedy when Johnny Neblett, who had assisted O'Hara's broadcasts in 1941–42, was killed in a September 15 airplane crash in Chicago.

The Cardinals, as 1946 world champions, earned $50,000 from Griesedieck in both 1947 and 1948 for their radio rights. Early in 1947, however, fans were given a glimpse into the earliest days of the medium. From April 13 through April 16, a battle between local electricians and local telephone workers meant that broadcasts were broadcast by shortwave radio instead of on AM.

Caray's persona and his legend would eventually grow so huge that it is now difficult to imagine a world in which it were otherwise, but Harry Caray wasn't always Harry Caray, living legend. He had assumed his mantle of national stardom by 1948, when *The Sporting News* selected him as the National League's top broadcaster for the third straight year. He also would take the prestigious award in 1950. Perhaps the fact that TSN was published in

St. Louis allowed the paper to fully appreciate his message and his unique style, but it is undeniable that Caray was seismically important to the American Midwest.

Bob Ingham had manned KSD's Cardinals telecasts in 1948, but he shifted to a studio role in favor of the more popular Caray. Ingham claimed the big honor, however, of calling the 1948 All-Star Game on TV from Sportsman's Park, the first Midsummer Classic to be telecast.

For 1949, the Cardinals split from the Browns to produce their own 162-game broadcast schedule, the full slate of regular-season games plus eight exhibitions. Griesedieck paid $100,000 for the Cardinals' radio rights, and team owner Sam Breadon wanted Caray as his No. 1 broadcaster, partially in gratitude for Caray's actions at a 1947 postseason testimonial banquet. After J. Roy Stockton, *St. Louis Post-Dispatch* sports editor, had drunkenly ripped Breadon from the dais, Caray took an unscheduled turn at the mike to rouse fans in support of the Cardinals and, by extension, their owner.

The Cardinals had aired 48 games on TV in 1948 but cut back to 34 in 1949, fearful of overexposing the team and dissuading outstate fans from making weekend road trips to St. Louis. The team continued to pare down its telecasts over the next several seasons.

As the Cardinals shied away from television, though, they grew their radio package into an on-air powerhouse. In 1949, when Breadon sold the Cardinals to Fred Saigh, the team's broadcasts were carried on 54 stations in Missouri, Iowa, Illinois, Arkansas, Kansas, and points as far west as Wyoming. That number, impressive as it was, would rise.

Gabby Street passed away prior to the 1951 season. From this point the Cardinals were Harry Caray's show on both TV and radio. Caray answered to nobody, and his future second- and third-bananas would not be allowed to threaten him in any way. Stretch Miller is one example: He joined as the third man in the booth that season from Bloomington, Illinois, despite never having done big-league baseball before, and he never would again after his term with St. Louis.

Another passing marked the 1951 season; Ray Schmidt, who had appeared on St. Louis radio in 1937 and 1940, died that May at 44 from liver troubles. Schmidt had also called the 1940 All-Star Game with Tom Manning.

The Cardinals' first-ever road telecast came July 27, 1952, from Brooklyn. KSD (the city's first and, at the time, only TV channel) aired two games that season. With both NBC and CBS network programs to choose from, KSD didn't clear much time for baseball.

Following 1952, the Cardinals and Browns asserted that they would no longer allow opposing teams to televise games in which they were involved unless they received some revenue. This was, essentially, a large market versus small-market argument. The Cardinals' complaint was primarily directed against the Giants, Dodgers, and Cubs, who played in cities with more than one TV station and, therefore, could show as many games as they wanted, while KSD in St. Louis wasn't even on the air every day.

While the Browns continued to fight this battle, Cardinals owner Fred Saigh eventually decided he wanted out and sold the team in early 1953 to Gussie Busch, chairman of the giant Anheuser-Busch brewery. The resulting infusion of cash saved the Redbirds and drove Bill Veeck's struggling AL Browns out of town. Once Busch became owner, the Cardinals stopped televising home games entirely. After the 1952 season, the club did not allow a single home telecast until 1982.

Griesedieck had an option to sponsor the team's 1953 telecasts, but declined as the brewery's executives didn't want to spend money promoting a club owned by a rival brewer. For the few road games KSD aired in 1953, Anheuser-Busch took the sponsorship.

The Cards made some big on-air changes for 1954. Management mixed up the broadcasting team and ditched WIL and KSD for new radio and TV packages. On October 11, 1953, the Cardinals reassigned Caray's color man, Gus Mancuso — who had been rumored on his way out for a year — to a scouting role. Ten days later, Anheuser-Busch named Jack Buck, a Triple-A play-by-play man in Rochester, New York, as Mancuso's replacement.

Buck won a Purple Heart serving in Europe with the U.S. Army during World War II then worked on riverboats up and down the Mississippi. In 1951 he was doing minor-league radio play-by-play when he hooked on with Columbus, Ohio's, WBNS-TV. He made an unexpected leap to the Triple-A Rochester Red Wings in 1953 after their announcer, Ed Edwards, told an off-color story at a team banquet and was canned. Buck re-created Red Wings road games using ticker-tape reports.

Bing Devine, GM at Rochester, the Cardinals' top farm club, soon went to work for Gussie Busch in St. Louis, and Anheuser-Busch bought the Red Wings' sponsor, Old Topper Beer, in 1953. The stars were aligning for Buck, who was sent to New York City to telecast a Cardinals game as an audition for becoming an assistant to Caray in 1954.

Buck got the job, but over Caray's wishes, and he later remarked that Caray wanted Chick Hearn, who later became a great NBA basketball announcer. Since Caray had been, for many years, associated with the Griesedieck brewery, Buck read most of the Busch commercials on the air, and was always far closer to Anheuser-Busch than Caray.

The Cardinals' radio network remained among the biggest in baseball, with St. Louis games even broadcast into the cities of their minor-league affiliates. While radio stations in these smaller markets made good money, the policy understandably put the owners of the minor-league clubs in a terrible bind. Under threat of Congressional action, Gussie Busch early that spring dropped plans to air games in nine cities (ranging from Muskogee, Oklahoma, to Houston, Texas) with struggling minor league franchises. Clubs in smaller towns were seeing dangerous drops in attendance due, at least in part, to television and increased radio network coverage from bigger cities.

With the relocation of the Browns to Baltimore for 1954, the Redbirds had the undivided attention of local sports fans. Why not, club executives thought, consolidate their gains? So the Cardinals chose to air all their road games on WTVI, a new independent station. In making all their games available on television, the team and station were also making a concerted effort to cut into the popularity of evening horse racing in St. Louis.

Once the Cards decided to televise all 77 road games in 1954, a third broadcaster was needed to assist Caray and Buck while Caray did the TV work on the road. Milo Hamilton of KTVI was added to the broadcast team, but he did not get along with Caray professionally or personally.

The team's radio contract elapsed after 1954. It made some sense for KMOX, a clear-channel, 50,000-watt station that was by far the biggest in the region, to go after Cardinals baseball now that the franchise was owned by Anheuser-Busch. The Redbirds and AM 1120 joined forces in what for decades would be a shining example of how a team and radio station could work together.

For 1955, the team boasted Anheuser-Busch, General Finance, and Marine Petroleum as sponsors. Caray, feeling his oats, wanted to be paired with one of his pals on the air so, at his urging, Anheuser-Busch fired Hamilton in favor of fellow Italian-American and St. Louis native Joe Garagiola, a former catcher. The Cardinals also hired Garagiola's wife Audre to be Sportsman's Park's organist.

The new broadcaster supported his friend and patron in July, writing a letter to *The Sporting News* that questioned Milwaukee radio man Earl Gillespie's use of the term "Holy Cow!" Garagiola credited the exclamatory phrase to Caray, although later research would establish that Minnesota's Halsey Hall actually has a strong claim to having first popularized the phrase.

While he only broadcast the Cardinals for a few seasons in the 1940s, Jay Hanna "Dizzy" Dean's lazy drawl and homespun witticisms—the ease of which belied the craft behind his image—led to national fame on radio and television through the 1960s. (National Baseball Hall of Fame and Museum)

Working hard and striving to succeed, Garagiola studied tapes of his broadcasts in order to improve, though he struggled to figure out the limits of a color man and often talked over the words of his on-air partner. Buck was pushed down to third by Garagiola's hiring, but Anheuser-Busch kept its main man busy with other local sports in baseball's offseason.

By 1956, the Cardinals had reduced the television schedule to 65 road games, omitting some weekend contests. In 1958, KTVI (formerly WTVI) sliced that number by more than half. The Cardinals aired their games over 80 radio stations in 12 states in 1959. Busch Bavarian, one of Anheuser-Busch's bigger brands, paid $400,000 for the full sponsorship rights. Anheuser-Busch was also by now a half-sponsor of NBC's *Game of the Week.*

Following the season, Anheuser-Busch wedged Buddy Blattner — taken off TV's *Game of the Week* because of a feud with Dizzy Dean — into the Cardinals' broadcasts, which pushed Jack Buck out of the Sportsman's Park booth.

Understandably aggrieved, Buck considered leaving and considered play-by-play offers in Baltimore and Detroit, but the brewery convinced KMOX to hire Buck just to keep him around. So Buck spent a year making promotional appearances for the station and hosting a talk show, an idea considered revolutionary in the industry. Rarely were radio shows two-way affairs at that time, but Bob Hyland, KMOX's director, asked Buck to host a show called *At Your Service*, which became a surprise smash hit.

The busy Buck called bowling as well as baseball and AFL football for ABC-TV in 1960. Soon, Buck left ABC on bad terms for a role as one of CBS-TV's top NFL voices, covering the Chicago Bears for many years. He was on the first broadcast team of the NHL's St. Louis Blues in 1967.

After the 1960 campaign, Buck rejoined the Cardinals' broadcast team, replacing Blattner, who left to take a job with the expansion Los Angeles Angels in 1961 rather than stay as a side man in what had become a fractious St. Louis booth.

By now, Garagiola's reputation and ego had grown to match Caray's. Once friends, the two now could not stand each other. After 1962, Garagiola departed to work New York Yankees broadcasts. Caray and Buck, while never close friends, served professionally and also ably as the Cardinals' top two broadcasters for the next seven years, which proved among the most successful in franchise history.

Caray, by now an institution, was the local baseball oracle, a national presence on postseason radio, and even the voice of University of Missouri football. Rarely did anyone tangle with him and win.

Hard-drinking, hard-living, lusty, and profane, Caray was also the most passionate and, many felt, the best baseball voice of his time. Self-consciously calling himself the "voice of the fan," Caray was not afraid to rip the home team, and his disdain for slumping Cardinals players, especially Ken Boyer, was well-known. Because Caray did not use much discretion when going after those who disappointed him, many St. Louis players despised the man they called "Old Tomato Face."

Buck was far less critical and less passionate, but he cared deeply for the game and the people of St. Louis. Harry and Jack both became broadcast legends, winning the hearts of sports fans in utterly different ways.

Major League Baseball's first expansion, in 1961, was also the last season for any single-sponsor broadcasts. The final holdouts for this tradition were both Missouri clubs: the Kansas City Athletics, sponsored by Schlitz, and the Cardinals, run by Anheuser-Busch, which had surpassed Schlitz in the 1950s as the biggest domestic brewer. The two brewing giants were fierce competitors for decades. From this point, all broadcasts had multiple sponsors.

More sponsors meant increased financial opportunities for clubs and radio stations. Increased demand for ad space, especially for good teams, meant higher ad rates and more revenue. Removing control of the broadcasts from one or two corporations also gave the team more flexibility in its choices of which on-air talent to hire, which games to show, and the overall editorial tone of the broadcasts. The Redbirds had four radio sponsors in 1962, plus three on television; Anheuser-Busch and American Tobacco were sponsors both on the wireless and the box.

The approach also had risks, however. Using too many sponsors tended to dilute each one's individual message, and a team and station chasing a wide variety of sponsors risked turning some of them off. These are the kinds of issues that broadcast executives have concerned themselves with since the inception of radio and, as in the past, short-term profits had to be balanced with long-term issues of control, image, and desired listenership.

Cardinals attendance dipped with a string of mediocre teams in the late 1950s and early 1960s, and Anheuser-Busch decided to sell a one-third sponsorship to American Tobacco beginning in 1962.

St. Louis was, in 1958, the 10th largest U.S. television market, which seems impressive, but because the major leagues hadn't expanded yet, it ranked higher than just two other NL markets, Cincinnati and Milwaukee — and the Braves did not televise any games.

The Cardinals halved their slate of road telecasts in 1962, switching to from independent KPLR back to KSD (now an NBC affiliate) for bigger dollars and better exposure. The marriage endured for a quarter of a century.

In those days, some clubs were deathly afraid of television overexposure, which they believed gave the public too much baseball "for free" and cut down home attendance — a stance certainly understandable for minor-league clubs as well as big-league franchises in smaller markets.

With Blattner and Garagiola both gone, Jerry Gross, an East Coast native who had previously worked in Ohio, joined KMOX as a sports reporter and third man on Cardinals games. He also served as the voice of the NBA's St. Louis Hawks.

Anheuser-Busch split the 1963 radio sponsorship with American Tobacco, with the Cardinals' baseball network now at almost 100 stations — still the game's largest.

Busch, American Tobacco, Lincoln-Mercury, and General Finance carved up the commercial inventory on KMOX in 1964. Shell & American Tobacco covered the advertising for the 21 road contests televised on KSD.

The team's large geographical reach — prior to the Athletics' move to Kansas City in 1955, St. Louis was the westernmost club in the majors — made it feasible and logical to build a large radio chain. Another reason for the club's domination of the radio dial was the Cardinals' policy of allowing their network stations to sell their own pregame and postgame ads. This trade of dollars up front in exchange for affiliate loyalty differed from how most other clubs ran their radio relations, and it obviously worked well.

In 1964, the Redbirds captured their first NL title in nearly two decades. Harry Caray called the pennant-clinching game from a box seat next to the Cardinals' dugout at Sportsman's Park. The joyous mayhem that erupted after the last out — as Caray, Gussie Busch, and various fans shouted incoherently into an open mike while the announcer clambered onto the field to conduct player interviews — is one of the great moments of on-air anarchy in baseball history.

That October, St. Louis capped its surprise season with a seven-game World Series triumph over the fading Yankees. Coming off a world championship, the team's 1965 TV-radio revenue rose to $500,000, still below any other NL team but Pittsburgh and lame-duck Milwaukee.

This exciting victory didn't do much, however, to lift St. Louis into the realm of top earners on radio and television as the Cardinals continued their broadcast strategy of trading TV revenue for attendance by not broadcasting any home games. The 1964 Cardinals' TV games on KPLR had drawn a very impressive 25 rating, but the metropolitan area just wasn't big enough to guarantee a huge amount of eyes for potential sponsors. Furthermore, because the ballclub was owned by its biggest sponsor, there is no way to know exactly how much the Redbirds' media rights were actually worth on an open market.

At this point, the Cardinals began to sell sponsorship shares in packages as small as eighths, with Busch sponsoring a third of the radio accounts and taking half the inventory on TV games. The Redbirds also instituted a television network to show their Sunday road contests all over the Midwest.

Four Midwestern teams — the Cardinals, Twins, Reds, and White Sox — owned the game's biggest radio networks in 1967. The first three franchises played in areas surrounded by lots of small towns and open space, while the White Sox had long been an aggressive marketer to areas south of Chicago. That year, KMOX beamed 28 preseason games plus the Cardinals' entire regular-season schedule to its chain. On television, all of KSD's games were, for the first time, available in color.

After the team's 1967 World Series victory, Jerry Gross left St. Louis to take a job broadcasting the NBA San Diego Rockets. He would go on to call the first three years of Padres baseball as well. Caray and Buck soldiered on as a duo.

Busch remained the club's top sponsor in 1968, with ads now sold in tenths as the club's television network had grown to 16 stations in five states. All 24 games on KSD were beamed to the network. For the first time, KSD was allowed to sell 20 minutes per game of its own commercial airtime that year, and also in 1969.

On November 3, 1968, the Cardinals' voice was almost permanently silenced when a car plowed into Harry Caray on a rainy night in St. Louis after he stepped into the street from between two parked cars. Hurled some forty feet by the impact, Caray suffered two broken legs, serious internal injuries, a busted nose, and a broken shoulder.

Buck stepped in to take over Caray's University of Missouri football assignments on Saturdays then called his customary NFL game for CBS the next day. While Caray recovered in time to return to the Cardinals' booth in spring 1969, the relationship between the announcer and the team's radio and television sponsors — which was never really warm — became distinctly cooler.

In the past, Caray had been called on the carpet by both KMOX and the advertising men in charge of Anheuser-Busch, but the announcer's warm relationship with Gussie Busch had saved him. But now, he was in deeper trouble.

Caray, often jokingly salacious, was rumored — while married to his second wife, Marian — to be carrying on with at least one female member of the Busch family, although the allegations were never proven. Caray didn't care about the potential for scandal; years later, in a 1984 *Inside Sports* interview, he recalled in a less-than-classy way, "At the time, all I said was I never raped anyone in my life."

Plenty of insiders at Anheuser-Busch wanted Caray out simply because he was too close to Gussie Busch. Others thought that Caray was a ticking time bomb. Some envied the size of his paycheck. But few denied that Harry Caray was a great salesman for Busch Bavarian. Introduced in 1955, Busch Bavarian was for decades the primary beer linked with Cardinals broadcasts.

After winning a world championship in 1967 and following up with another NL pennant before falling in seven games to the Tigers in the 1968 Fall Classic, the Cardinals had become the senior circuit's marquee club. Their media rights payment of $600,000 in 1969, however, again ranked above only two clubs in the league, the Pirates and the newborn Expos.

St. Louis didn't win in 1969, staggering to a disappointing third after the squad's emotional center, slugger and 1967 ML MVP Orlando Cepeda, was dealt to Atlanta during spring training. Bigger changes were in the air, too. On October 7, KMOX suddenly yanked Caray's 10-minute daily sports show from its lineup. Two days later, after denials from all sides that the change had any significance, the Cardinals officially announced that Harry Caray would not be returning. KMOX had, for weeks, been quietly commissioning audition tapes from announcers around the country.

Caray went out guns a-blazing, calling television cameras to his favorite haunt and openly drinking cans of Schlitz — which he later admitted he couldn't stomach — in order to get under the team's skin. Caray laid most of the blame for his sacking on Al Fleishman, whose publicity firm served as Anheuser-Busch's entire PR operation, but if any of the rumors around his departure are true, Holy Cow himself was at least partially responsible.

While Anheuser-Busch and KMOX considered Pittsburgh's Bob Prince a good potential replacement for Caray, the brewery instead promoted Buck — who had known in advance about Caray's upcoming sacking — to the lead slot.

Not many Frick Award-winning play-by-play men (commonly though inaccurately called Hall of Famers) spend 15 years as a second banana like Jack Buck did. Perhaps even more surprising is that Buck didn't even get his first crack at being a No. 1 baseball announcer until he was 46. But from 1970 on, Jack Buck became the Cardinals' ambassador to the club's vast mid-American fan base. He also outlasted the competition to become KMOX radio's sports director.

The team needed a new assistant. Early rumors had Pee Wee Reese and even Pat Summerall becoming Buck's new sidekicks, but Jim Woods, heretofore Prince's partner in the KDKA booth, was picked.

Unfortunately, Woods did not get along with Buck, and he bolted at the close of his two-year contract. Woods thought Buck to be a comedown from Prince in substance and style, and that St. Louis was something of a closed shop to outsiders. For their part, local fans didn't take to the gravelly-voiced mikeman nicknamed "Possum."

Cardinals broadcasts in 1970 featured Budweiser and other Anheuser-Busch products sponsoring half of both the radio and television package. KSD televised 24 games, feeding about half of them to a 20-station network. The next season, the Cardinals and Anheuser-Busch instituted two separate radio sponsorship plans with different time allotments per game, investing in affiliate relations in order to retain as big a network as possible.

Woods' departure after 1971 left a hole in the broadcast team, one that would be filled by a former player for the first time in a decade. Popular third baseman Mike Shannon, whose career had been prematurely ended by nephritis, was chosen — some said by Gussie Busch himself — to join Buck. While the move seemed strange at first, it paid huge dividends.

Shannon has never been smooth and it took him a while to get the feel for his job. His voice is rough, his cadence a bit laid-back and a bit military. But Shannon parlayed his in-depth knowledge of the game and his unique approach into a strong analytical profile and, eventually, into solid play-by-play. Cardinals fans love him the way that Yankees fans loved Phil Rizzuto, Cubs fans adored Ron Santo, and Phillies fans took to Richie Ashburn: as a genuine local hero with intimate ties to the team's glory days. Shannon matured into better play-by-play calling than most former athletes.

Payments from KMOX and KSD garnered $800,000 for the team in 1972, by which time the radio network had grown to more than 120 stations, with Busch continuing to package the broadcasts. The Cardinals sold out a pregame and two postgame radio shows; on KMOX, the 10-minute Mike Shannon Show was also aired before the network pregame.

The 1972 TV network included 19 stations ranging across nine states. KSD's new sports director, Jay Randolph, handled television pregame and postgame programming, and the next season moved into play-by-play. While Randolph had been the voice of the NFL Dallas Cowboys, he had precious little baseball experience.

St. Louis again went through a trial trying to find a permanent third for the broadcasting team. Don Drysdale worked on a few telecasts in 1971, Myron "Mike" Walden assisted in 1972, and Harry Walker — popular former Cardinals outfielder and manager — teamed with Buck on radio in 1973 when Shannon joined Randolph on TV. None of them impressed.

By this time, several local concerns, First National Bank of St. Louis and Famous-Barr Department Stores, took sponsorships along with Anheuser-Busch on radio and television. Ron Jacober replaced Randolph in 1973 as KSD's pregame host.

The 1974 Cardinals' radio net was still the largest in baseball, with its 120 stations ranking just ahead of the Reds'. KMOX and the brewery, however, underwent a particularly contentious rights renewal negotiation that year, and the delay in signing a new contract made promotion and ad sales difficult.

For 1975, the Cardinals and their broadcast partners agreed to deals bringing the team's radio-TV revenue to a million dollars, equaling those of Houston, Atlanta, and Montreal, and surpassing San Diego.

In yet another attempt to find a third man for the broadcast team, KMOX hired Bob Starr — a former minor-league catcher — in 1975. He covered radio games when Jack Buck assisted in calling the 30 road games on KSD, at least one against each NL opponent. Eleven of those televised contests came on Sundays, with the others in weekday prime time.

While Buck might have been happy doing Cardinals baseball and NFL football forever, he found it hard to resist an early 1976 offer to relocate to New York and host NBC's *Grand Stand*, a nationwide sports program. Starr assumed the play-by-play seat that spring next to Mike Shannon. KSD now had nine sponsors, while KMOX featured six, and the team was finally making plenty in ad revenues.

Even in 1976, though, the Cardinals did not see television as its own profit center. Club officials were quoted saying that they did not want to overexpose the team and that they viewed the games on KSD as promotions to increase home attendance.

Buck's tenure in New York was unsuccessful, as was *Grand Stand* itself. Both he and the Cardinals were happy to resume their relationship in 1977. Starr remained in the picture as a second play-by-play man both on television and radio.

The team's media revenues remained in the million-dollar range in 1979, while those of other teams stagnated or declined due to recession. The Cardinals no longer had the biggest radio network in the game, though, as that honor was claimed by the Reds, enjoying the wave of popularity from the Big Red Machine dynasty. The fact that the Redbirds' cross-state rivals, the Royals, were a championship-caliber team with an expanding radio net had an impact, too.

KSD (soon to rename itself KSDK) that season beamed 40 games, the most Cardinals fans had seen on television since 1960.

For 1980, Anheuser-Busch allowed its control of radio and television rights to expire, and KSDK and KMOX bid successfully on five-year contracts to produce the broadcasts themselves. These new deals lifted the team's media revenue to $1.5 million per year. By this time, only one club — Seattle — maintained control of its own radio and television broadcasts.

With Starr decamping for the California Angels' broadcast booth, KMOX's hockey voice, Dan Kelly, began a five-year run as an assistant on the Cardinals' broadcasts. Kelly's brother Hal had called many years of Triple-A baseball in Toronto and Montreal.

Despite not controlling the broadcasts directly, Anheuser-Busch continued as a major sponsor on radio and TV, and remains the club's biggest guarantor to this day. Busch Bavarian, renamed simply as Busch in the 1970s, was no longer the company's top-selling brand, ceding that honor to their premium brew, Budweiser. Other major sponsors like TWA, Texaco, and Southwestern Bell joined the sponsorship rolls in 1982.

In addition to KSDK's 39-game package, some fans could now follow the club on cable TV. Cox aired seven games on a subscription basis as part of its new Preview service on KDNL, Channel 30. Joel Meyers of KMOX, at this point also the Cards' public address announcer, snared his first big-league baseball gig on these telecasts, working with retired St. Louis great Lou Brock, who had appeared as a White Sox TV announcer the previous season.

The Cardinals won the 1982 NL East Division crown, their first title in 15 years, and went on to capture the World Series. As a result, the team's media rights package rose to $1.7 million even without a cable deal: Preview had flamed out, and few cable professionals felt that any local system had enough market penetration to make a venture profitable.

So the one local enterprise that could afford to invest in such a potentially lucrative but risky venture — Anheuser-Busch — chose to undertake it. Busch, taking half ownership, went into business with Telecommunications of Denver and Multimedia of Greenville, South Carolina in a new venture called Sports Time Cable, which debuted on April 3, 1984, in 15 states. STC had an ambitious plan to blanket the Midwest with sports events from all over the region.

The regional operator would bring all sorts of new baseball content to its member cities. Kansas City, for instance, would not only get to see the Royals, but also the Reds and Cardinals, as those three teams comprised the core of STC's major league network. Other local systems, like SportsVision in Chicago and PASS in Detroit, also supplied games, which were shown both live and on a tape-delayed basis. Sports Time also signed with the Cleveland Indians' cable outlet, Season Ticket, but that channel soon ceased operations.

STC drew from a pool of six million potential subscribers that would pay between $9 and $12 monthly, depending on the local cable system, plus an installation fee. Sports Time's corporate headquarters were in St. Louis, with production facilities in Cincinnati.

Sports Time's 1984 deal with the Cardinals lifted the team's media rights to $2.6 million. The 52 games televised on cable featured newcomer Bob Carpenter doing play-by-play assisted by Buck and popular former pitcher Al "The Mad Hungarian" Hrabosky. The rough-and-ready former closer also announced STC's telecast of the Class A Midwest League All-Star Game with Mike Newell.

After the baseball season, Sports Time aired Major Indoor Soccer League (MISL) soccer, NHL hockey, and NCAA basketball, plus 50 college football games. The net planned to show 200 MLB games in 1985, including 60 Cardinals contests (50 at home) and 52 Royals games, paying a million dollars to each club for the privilege.

Sports Time, however, was in deep trouble. Executives had projected signing 200,000 subscribers by September 1984 but had fallen way short, and revenue was disastrously low. In a desperate attempt to increase sales, STC ran free previews and lowered its subscription fee to just $6 per month with free installation.

Having paid millions in rights fees to baseball clubs — not to mention the NHL, MISL, the Big Eight, the Big Ten, the Missouri Valley Conference, and others, Sports Time could not survive such a low level of buy-in. Some sources reported that Sports Time was losing as much as an unsustainable million dollars per month.

The Cincinnati Reds soon dealt STC a death blow by opting out of the network for 1985, and on February 28, 1985, Sports Time announced that it would close. In its sole year of operation, STC had amassed but 37,000 paid subscribers.

Maybe it shouldn't have been surprising that many early baseball cable ventures failed. At the time, most cable systems were in rural areas, where potential subscribers weren't as closely tied to big-league sports as their city and suburban brethren. Worse, rural households didn't necessarily have the money to spend on a premium cable channel, especially with superstations WTBS and WGN airing the Braves and Cubs for free.

Prime soon stepped in to show some 1985 Cardinals games with projected Sports Time broadcasters Carpenter and Hrabosky, but a new solution was needed for 1986.

Prior to 1985, all the team's broadcasting partners had signed new contracts. Rights fees rose to $3,100,000 (including the Sports Time fee), which was more than the media dollars earned by Pittsburgh, Cincinnati, San Diego, and San Francisco. That figure shrunk, though, when STC wriggled out of its million-buck commitment and paid a smaller "kill fee."

Whitey Herzog's Cardinals captured the NL East in 1985, cementing their status as one of the top teams of the decade. This put the franchise in great shape for a new cable deal, and the local Cencom group — owner and operator of local cable systems with some 200,000 subscribers — paid enough to raise the team's overall rights to $4.6 million for 1986.

Ken Wilson, play-by-play man for the NHL's Blues, started a five-year association with the Redbirds, broadcasting 50 home tilts on Cencom with Hrabosky as his color man. On KSDK, Jay Randolph called 44 away games with Buck and Shannon assisting.

By 1987 the Cardinals' rights had risen to $5.1 million, better than that of seven other NL teams. Cencom at that time had about 11,000 subscriber households per game, plus others who purchased individual games through a pay-per-view system.

Probably unhappy with the growth of cable, KSDK scheduled in 1986 and 1987 only 44 of the 50 games it had optioned. The station and team drifted apart, and for 1988, the Cardinals had a new over-the-air carrier: KPLR. The new contract kicked the team's media rights up to $6 million. With the NFL Cardinals departing for Phoenix, interest in St. Louis baseball skyrocketed with the Redbirds coming off World Series trips in 1985 and 1987.

In the first year of a three-year deal, KPLR aired the 1988 home opener plus 55 road games on a 25 station-network, far more stations than KSDK's. The bland Jay Randolph was out, with the equally generic Ken Wilson assuming his role. Temperamental Hall of Famer Bob Gibson essayed a television pregame show, showing little more distinction than he had during a disastrous trial in ABC's *Monday Night Baseball* booth in the 1970s.

Buck and Shannon rolled along on KMOX as their 130-station network was again the biggest in baseball. In 1989, their TV chain grew to 32 stations, with Gibson now featured on the radio both pregame and postgame. While the St. Louis market size was small, the devotion of the team's fans wasn't: the Cardinals' telecasts were third-highest rated in the game behind those of Cincinnati and Minnesota — two other small-market clubs.

That fall, patriarch Gussie Busch died at 90, leading to whispers that the club would be sold. Busch had always run the club more as a hobby than as a business, and the strong-willed owner had never quite adjusted to the era of free agency.

The Cards inked an extension with KPLR for 1990 that included a stipulation that the team would have no cable broadcasts through 1993. For the Cardinals to give that up, they needed a big payout, and got it: the new three-year contract guaranteed them a total approaching $20 million. KPLR committed to airing 76 games each season, meaning that fans saw more games on broadcast TV but fewer overall.

KMOX re-upped on radio for 1992 as overall rights fees rose to $10.5 million. As usual, the team's broadcasting deals stipulated that all television and radio dollars from Budweiser ad sales went to the team: i.e., back to Anheuser-Busch.

Unfortunately, while the Cardinals relied on the golden radio combo of Buck and Shannon, they were unable to find a distinctive television voice. After Wilson ended his tour of duty in the Gateway City, veteran George Grande took over for two years.

The Cardinals were no longer, by 1993, interested in continuing a deal that precluded them exploring the burgeoning field of cable television sports. Prime snagged the St. Louis cable rights for 1994, and KPLR inked a new contract that reduced its slate of over-the-air games to 60.

Jack Buck's son Joe, a promising voice who had grown up around sports, took over doing television play-by-play in 1993 and quickly proved himself a more than capable heir to the family patrimony.

Within a few years, however, the son had perhaps gotten too big for Cardinals baseball, ultimately eschewing the daily grind of the National Pastime for weekend national assignments, postseason games, and weekly NFL football clashes.

National stardom is a double-edged sword. Network baseball broadcasters, entrusted with describing the game's biggest moments coast-to-coast, are far removed from the daily drama — there is nothing quite like the daily panorama of accompanying a baseball team throughout the long season. While Buck's assignments have gotten bigger, he is perhaps less in touch now with the game than when it was his job to travel with a team.

Joe Buck described the Redbirds on TV on KPLR and Prime until 1996, when Fox Sports Midwest assumed the Cardinals' cable package, which it has held ever since. But Jack Buck's decision to reduce traveling and not cover road games changed the picture in 1997 and 1998: the Cards tried six different TV broadcasters in those two years, and most of them failed to make a mark.

In 1996, a group led by Bill DeWitt — whose father had owned the Browns — bought the Cardinals from the Busch family. Unlike the hands-on philosophy of the previous owners, DeWitt hired good people and let them run the show, planning a new ballpark and wisely trading as much as possible off the club's rich history.

Dan McLaughlin joined the ranks of Cardinals broadcasters in 2000, assuming road telecasts when KPLR's Carpenter declined to travel. McLaughlin soon became the team's top television voice.

When the Redbirds were at home, all seemed well; Jack Buck and Mike Shannon continued to call the action on radio, with Joe Buck or Carpenter on TV with Al Hrabosky. On the road, though, everything was different. Who would be on tonight was the recurring question. McLaughlin? Rich Gould? Ozzie Smith? Bob Ramsey?

Change continued to buffet Cardinals fans as Jack Buck, who had slowed down over the years, finally succumbed in June 2002 to several serious maladies, including Parkinson's and lung cancer. The great voice, which had worked for every major TV and radio network in every major sport, was finally silenced.

It took the Cardinals years to find an adequate replacement for Buck; to be fair, any legendary announcer's immediate replacement will almost certainly inherit more than his share of detractors. Joel Meyers, added to the broadcast team before Buck's death, lasted a year, but found the grind too demanding for his already busy schedule.

Wayne Hagin, with experience in several big-league booths, signed a four-year deal in November 2002 to become the team's full-time radio announcer. Despite high hopes on all sides, the solid Hagin did not find it easy to work with St. Louis' other legend, Mike Shannon.

More important, by 2004, it was apparent that Buck's death was the harbinger of change between the Cardinals and with KMOX. In the Internet age, when fans can listen to games from all over the world via their computer or in their cars via satellite radio, a 50,000-watt station like KMOX no longer seemed a necessity. The team wanted more editorial control over the broadcast content and the increasingly important auxiliary programming.

For its part, KMOX no longer wanted to pay large rights fees to broadcast games which could now be heard on the Internet with commercials blocked out. Now one of the nation's top AM talk radio outlets, KMOX also agonized over interrupting popular conservative political commentator Rush Limbaugh's daily show to make room for ballgames. As a result, the strong 52-year bond between KMOX and the Cardinals officially ended on August 4, 2005, when the club announced its purchase of half of local AM station KTRS, which became its new radio flagship.

KTRS 550, broadcasting with just 5,000 watts, had to add several suburban St. Louis affiliates to be heard by everyone in the metropolitan area. The station moved its broadcast headquarters to a building adjacent to new Busch Stadium to more effectively blend itself into the Cardinals' culture.

Fear that the team's radio network would dissolve with the loss of KMOX as its flagship was unfounded. The 2010 Cardinals network topped 100 stations in nine states, ranging as far south as Tupelo, Mississippi, and as far north as exurban Chicago.

With a brand new station came a new voice. Missouri native John Rooney was a natural for the job; he had called games for the White Sox and Twins, for CBS radio, for the University of Missouri, and for St. Louis' Triple-A farm club in Louisville.

Hagin was paid off for the final year of his deal, but the Cardinals' treatment of the veteran broadcaster was less than ideal. Some felt that the whole thing was an "ambush" on Rooney's part, but most close observers believe that the club had already decided to remove Hagin from the mike before deciding to hire anyone else.

A year after jettisoning their longtime radio partner, the Cardinals signed a TV contract with their old TV partner KSDK, which had telecast the team through the 1960s and 1970s. KSDK enthusiastically committed to air 20 Sunday games with Jay Randolph returning to do play-by-play and Rick Horton, a former Cardinals pitcher active in the Baseball Chapel, handling color.

Fox Midwest continued as the team's cable home, showing some 135 games each season with McLaughlin and Hrabosky at the mikes. Hrabosky is a pretty good analyst, though the enthusiastic McLaughlin talks as much as any play-by-play man in the game, rarely leaving any space.

In 2008, during a radio advertising slump, the Cardinals restructured their deal with KTRS, choosing to handle ad sales themselves and retain the resulting revenues. In exchange, KTRS no longer paid a rights fee. This new policy allowed the club to build better relationships with clients and allowed the station to cut its advertising staff.

Relations between KMOX and the Cardinals began to warm up during the late 2000s. By 2010, the two parties were again ready to talk turkey as the KTRS deal expired. What had changed since 2005?

KMOX and the Cardinals had both rationalized their business models for the Internet age, which led them to more clearheaded thinking. More importantly, concerns over KTRS' lack of reach had not abated. While the team felt that co-owning the station created an advantageous synergy, the weak 5,000-watt signal caused problems. The glut of sports talk in the market also raised concerns about KTRS' long-term viability.

A suburban FM station, WXOS, made a strong bid to become the club's sole radio outlet, also proposing an alternate deal where it might simulcast games with KTRS. Redbirds management, however, decided in the end to return home, and on September 1, 2010, the Cardinals and KMOX announced a new five-year deal.

Being carried by KMOX still carries a huge amount of prestige all over the Midwest, probably more than the Cardinals had realized since, according to team management, fan feedback played a huge part in the decision to return to 1120 AM. KTRS remains involved with the team, sponsoring a popular ticket promotion in which fans can purchase last-minute unclaimed tickets for that day's game for just $5.50.

In 2011, the Redbirds moved all their TV games to Fox Sports Midwest, meaning that for the first time since 1947, the club had no local over-the-air affiliate. Only a few Fox national Saturday telecasts were carried on broadcast television. Randolph lost his job, but the

Tall, handsome, and blessed with a golden voice, Jack Buck wore many hats in more than five decades in St. Louis. One of them was as the team's #1 radio announcer from 1970 through 2001, a job he held after being Harry Caray's assistant for some 15 years. How many Frick Award announcers are good enough to be enshrined in the Hall of Fame after being a second banana for that long? (National Baseball Hall of Fame and Museum)

Cardinals expanded Horton's workload, cutting into McLaughlin's and Hrabosky's time.

That worked out in one way, as Hrabosky underwent neck surgery in midseason, but the decision also plunged Horton into play-by-play, which he wasn't ready for.

McLaughlin was arrested in August 2010 for driving while intoxicated then was charged again with DUI on September 30, 2011. The Cardinals and Fox Sports stood behind McLaughlin after his first go-round, but chose to shelve the announcer after the second incident.

As a result, McLaughlin was not behind the mike for the remainder of the regular season, when the Redbirds soared to an un-likely playoff bid, and he saw no further work for Fox Midwest during the club's postseason series and World Series win. McLaughlin was also removed from his college football assignments.

After this layoff, during which McLaughlin admitted he was an alcoholic and apparently got his life back in order, the veteran announcer returned to the Cardinals' TV booth for 2012 in a three-man rotation with Hrabosky and Horton.

Horton has a likeable personality, though he is not an ideal play-by-play announcer. When used as an analyst, he and McLaughlin seem to be trying to fit as many words into a broadcast as possible.

Both Hrabosky and Horton are also occasionally heard as analysts on KMOX radio, as Mike Shannon has started to cut back his schedule. Mike Claiborne called a few games in 2013 in place of lead announcer John Rooney, who had earned a few days off.

History has a huge role in Cardinals baseball. The team's broadcasts have always been produced with one eye on tradition, using familiar ex-players in the analyst's chair while proudly embracing the club's legacy. Some former Redbirds have failed in the role, but Shannon, Garagiola, Street, Horton, and Hrabosky have succeeded.

It will be interesting to see which Cardinals stars of the 1990s and 2000s, if any, ascend to radio and television duty, and to find out whether Rooney and McLaughlin are able to assume the mantle that Harry Caray and Jack Buck wore so proudly for so long.

GIANTICS COAST TO COAST

NEW YORK/SAN FRANCISCO GIANTS BROADCASTING HISTORY

"Charlie Finley said he liked the job Lon [Simmons] and I did but that we could never work for him because we were too objective. To me, that was one of the greatest compliments I ever received."
— Bill Thompson, 1971

DURING THE FIRST TWO DECADES OF THE TWENTIETH CENTURY, the New York Giants were the top team in New York City. Once the American League's New York Yankees began their run of dominance in the 1920s, however, the Giants competed with the Dodgers for second billing on Gotham's giant marquee. New York's dominance of the National League audience in the media capital of the U.S. lasted until Larry MacPhail came to Brooklyn in 1938, ushering in a new era of Dodgers baseball where the Bums from Brooklyn successfully challenged the old regime.

The Giants, like the Yankees and Dodgers, did not regularly broadcast their games in the 1930s but, by late in the decade, the teams began dipping their toes into radio. Three stations covered the Giants' Opening Day game in 1938 from the Polo Grounds: WOR, with Dave Driscoll at the mike; WABC, with Ted Husing on the call; and WMCA, described by Joe Bolton and Dick Fishell.

With the Dodgers blazing the trail for broadcasting in the Big Apple, the other two franchises had to follow. On January 25, 1939, the Giants and Yankees announced that they would share broadcaster Arch McDonald on WABC as the two clubs decided to air all afternoon home games except on Sundays. General Mills, Socony Vacuum Oil, and Proctor and Gamble were the sponsors. WINS also aired re-creations of Giants' 1939 road games with boxing announcer Don Dunphy at the mike.

The following season, R.J. Reynolds' Camels cigarettes became the new sponsor, and Mel Allen began his career as a lead voice, with Joe Bolton by his side. This was strictly a one-year arrangement, though; no advertiser stepped up to cover either the Giants or the Yankees games in 1941.

For 1942, Allen paired with Connie Desmond, airing Giants and Yankees games over two radio stations (one carrying day games, the other carrying night games). Yet again, in 1943, the clubs couldn't find a sponsor and went silent on the radio.

By 1944, Giants owner Horace Stoneham was tired of his team losing and was tired of feeling bettered by the Dodgers. He was also tired of sharing airtime with the Yankees: Stoneham wanted his own announcer and station for 1944 for the Giants, but didn't get them until 1946.

In 1944 and 1945, Giants and Yankees games aired on WINS, sponsored by Gillette. With Allen in the service, Dunphy, Bill Slater, and comic Al Schacht covered the Giants from the Polo Grounds the first season, while Slater and "Big Al" Helfer did the honors in the second.

Finally, in 1946, the Giants broadcast all their games for the first time, although road contests were re-creations. Hoffman, which made soft drinks, and the Pabst brewery lent their names to the broadcasts. The club put together its own broadcasting plan, paying the announcers themselves, and brought in one of the busiest young voices in the business, Jack Brickhouse, who had been sitting in for Bob Elson on Chicago games while Elson was in the service.

Brickhouse interviewed for the Yankees No. 2 job, but lost to Russ Hodges. He then snared the Giants' gig by topping 100 other applicants. Despite being hired as the top man, however, Brickhouse did not enjoy New York. One major problem was that he was paired with radio station WMCA's sports director, Steve Ellis, a boxing and college football voice who had never done baseball. The pair did games in New York and re-created road contests in the studios, but never fully meshed. A second problem was that the Giants were bad.

The games weren't the only Giants-oriented programming on WMCA. The team sponsored a daily 15-minute sports news program with Ellis called *Giant Jottings* as well as a six-hour overnight show on WMCA that aired music for people working the graveyard shift.

Ellis was initially deemed expendable after 1946, with the Giants pushing to get Frankie Frisch to work with Brickhouse. When Brickhouse couldn't get his salary raised to Frisch's level, however, he hightailed it back to Chicago and the Fordham Flash teamed with Ellis, again sponsored by Hoffman and Pabst.

Frisch was no friend to lovers of the English language, with his clipped, old-fashioned diction and his idiosyncratic and erratic sentence structure. But the soon-to-be Hall of Famer (Cooperstown class of 1947) was a genuine hero from the franchise's glorious past — and the Giants needed one.

Ellis transferred to television for 1948, where his lack of baseball knowledge was deemed less critical. He called all 77 Giants home games airing over WNBT, an NBC affiliate and the biggest station in town. Maury Farrell, who began a long and successful career as the University of Alabama's football voice in 1945, teamed with Frisch on radio.

The most important news concerning the radio and television broadcasts in 1948 was the Giants' relationship with Chesterfield cigarettes. Liggett & Myers tobacco purchased complete radio, TV, and Polo Grounds advertising rights for $400,000. The Giants began to schedule more home games at night. WNBT, as an NBC affiliate, couldn't make room in its network schedule to televise them, so independent WPIX stepped into the void.

Following the 1948 campaign, Frisch accepted a coaching job under Giants manager Leo Durocher. Chesterfield, finding both Maury Farrell and Steve Ellis wanting, chose an entirely new broadcast team for 1949. Farrell remained in New York for a few years then returned full-time to Alabama.

With Mel Allen's full blessing, Chesterfield lured Russ Hodges, heretofore Allen's co-pilot in the Yankees' booth, across town to make him their lead announcer. Hodges signed a five-year deal worth $35,000 a season, showing the Giants' commitment to their new voice. Hodges and Allen remained close after working together, hosting a nightly sports show in 1953.

Born in Kentucky in 1911, Hodges — after graduating with a law degree — found his niche in broadcasting, getting his first on-air job in Cincinnati in 1930. After a few years, he traveled to Chicago, calling baseball games on WIND for $45 per week.

Hired as one of General Mills' baseball broadcasters, Hodges was transferred to a minor-league baseball job in North Carolina before hooking on with the Senators, assisting Arch McDonald for seven years until joining with Allen in 1947. In addition to his baseball fame, Hodges was celebrated for his calls of football, basketball, and boxing.

WPIX snagged the team's full TV schedule for 1949 and remained the team's telecaster for the remainder of its time in New York. Stoneham signed new radio-TV deals for 1949 despite being concerned about television's effect on minor- and major-league attendance. "Television can be blamed for the bulk of about 60,000 we lost in attendance (at Jersey City)," he told the press in November 1948, referring to his club's Triple-A affiliate across the Hudson River. Speaking of the crowds at the Polo Grounds, the frustrated owner asserted that "We used to get crowds of about 45,000 under the lights; it's now down to an average of about 35,000."

Following stints in Chicago, Cincinnati, and Washington, voluble Russ Hodges landed a job as the Giants' voice in 1949. He worked for the franchise until he passed away in early 1971. (National Baseball Hall of Fame and Museum)

A week after Hodges signed, Marty Glickman of rival station WMGM was rumored as the new second man, but WMGM re-signed Glickman to a new $30,000 contract and Al Helfer, recently in Cincinnati, took the Giants' job on February 14. WMCA put games on both the AM and FM dials in 1949, continuing to carry Giants games through 1957.

Hodges kept busy in the winter, calling Columbia University football for WINS as well as boxing and basketball. In early 1951 he joined newly retired Yankees outfielder Tommy Henrich to host a TV sports show on WJZ.

Chesterfield expanded its baseball empire, sponsoring Cubs, Giants, and Senators broadcasts in 1950 and buying scoreboard ads in other parks. The tobacco concern formed a "3 to 1 Club" of local cigarette dealers (the name referring to the margin by which the brand was outselling other competing smokes), and in 1951 brought some 6,000 vendors to the Polo Grounds for a game, continuing to cement itself as the cigarette of choice for local fans.

Hodges and new partner Ernie Harwell, who had moved across town from Brooklyn, rotated in the TV and radio booths. Late that season, *The Sporting News* named Hodges its top NL broadcaster.

How good was Russ Hodges? Some detractors feel that he is only honored by the Hall of Fame for his Frick Award because he spent so much time in New York. But is it not arguable that Hodges spent 30 years in a big-league play-by-play booth because he was good?

Friendly and conversational, Hodges carved out his own niche while working in the same town as giants like Red Barber and Mel Allen, and that's no small accomplishment. "Bye Bye Baby," he bade Giants home run balls, and he called a lot of them — including every one that Willie Mays hit through 1970.

The Yankees and Giants linked up again in 1951, sharing WPIX and WABD for their home telecasts. WPIX broadcast all the games, while WABD, a DuMont Network station, cleared space for daytime contests.

The 1951 season was among the most exciting in Giants history, but not until the last seven weeks. Arch-rival Brooklyn had opened up a 13-game lead by August 11 before New York ignited, winning 16 in a row to create a red-hot pennant race. The Giants then went 20–5 in September as the Dodgers crumbled down the stretch, with the two teams ending the regular season in a tie.

After the Giants and Dodgers split the first two games of the three-game playoff series that would determine the pennant, the whole season hung on Game 3 at the Polo Grounds. All three were televised nationally, with the second and third games the first nationally televised sporting events ever to be fully sponsored, with Chesterfield picking up the tab. The broadcasts originated from independent WPIX-TV, but were sent nationwide via NBC. Harwell called the action on national television for Games 1 and 3, switching to radio for Game 2. Hodges did the opposite.

Bobby Thomson's "shot heard 'round the world" won the game and the pennant for the Giants in the last of the ninth. Four different radio broadcasts and one TV broadcast went out over the airwaves that historic day. Red Barber's radio call from the visitor's side has been preserved, as were Hodges' from the home team and national radio broadcaster Gordon McClendon's. Harry Caray's call for KMOX and Harwell's television narration, however, have been lost to history.

While Red Barber simply describes what happened on the field, and McClendon revels in the marvel of the finish, Russ Hodges became fully involved in the drama, screaming to an audience of Giants fans, "THE GIANTS WIN THE PENNANT! THE GIANTS WIN THE PENNANT!" for some 15 seconds.

Some broadcasters would have eschewed such a clear display of excitement and joy at the result, but the Giants' voice cared little for the removed style favored by some of his peers. Hodges simply let it all hang out, and is remembered and loved for that.

This is not to say that he was the only one thrilled. Harwell said of Thomson's homer that "All of us were so excited it was a wonder that our picture and commentary could reach from coast to coast."

Harwell, for his part, was no second banana in Gotham. He had already convinced the industry that he was a comer, and in fact Hodges had advised him before 1951 that the Red Sox' job was opening up. Harwell, perhaps feeling that he wasn't quite ready for a No. 1 assignment, let it sit. He was very happy in New York.

After the 1951 regular season, *The Sporting News* tabbed Hodges and Brickhouse as the majors' best TV broadcasters. TSN transcribed and printed Hodges' description of most of the bottom of the ninth of Game 3 of the playoffs. Chesterfield also issued a commemorative 10-inch record album, *The Giants Win the Pennant*, which featured Hodges' call of the fateful ninth inning. This may have been the first commemorative team record album ever issued. Of course, Hodges was pictured on the record sleeve puffing a Chesterfield. The photo wasn't just for show; in 1965, Hodges admitted to smoking at least a pack per game.

Hodges, per the privilege accorded the lead broadcaster for pennant winners, called the World Series on television for Gillette with Jim Britt as New York lost in six games. He continued his off-season boxing and football commentary and also put his name on a collection of baseball stories, *Baseball Complete*.

Starting in 1952, movie star Laraine Day — married to Leo Durocher from 1947 through 1960 — hosted a pregame radio program, *A Day with the Giants*, on WMCA. Eventually that title also graced the team's pregame TV show, which was sponsored by City Service. Day also used the phrase for a book she wrote. Raised a Mormon (and for a short time married to two men at once), Day seemed an unlikely spouse for a smoker, drinker, gambler, and womanizer like Durocher. Years later, Day admitted that she didn't even like baseball.

Late in 1953, Harwell polished his baseball bona fides by penning an article for *TSN* on Harry Wright. On January 4, 1954, the Georgian took over as top man in the booth for the new Baltimore Orioles. The Giants had let him go some time earlier, risking public rancor but certain that Harwell was ready for lead assignment.

In 1954, a Phoenix radio station contracted to broadcast Hodges' broadcasts of 15 Giants spring exhibitions, which were also carried back to New York. Hodges' new partner, Bob Delaney, had paired with Curt Gowdy for several years on Red Sox games.

Delaney, best known for his football game-calling, apparently viewed baseball work as just a job, and was known to hate Horace Stoneham, perhaps because of being uprooted from his home in Massachusetts in favor of New York. Johnny Mize, former slugging star for both the Giants and Yankees, did pregame and postgame commentary in 1954 on WPIX.

Perhaps the first sign that big change was on the way came after the 1955 season, when Chesterfield bowed out. The company had been paying $500,000 per year to the Giants for exclusive broadcast and advertising rights.

On October 31, 1955, with the Dodgers and Giants already rumored to be leaving New York for California, the Giants signed a new advertising contract with Ruppert Brewing, makers of Ruppert, Ruppiner, and Knickerbocker beers and ales — and a name long associated with the Yankees. The deal promised $5 million over a four-year span. That figure included rights fees, air time on both stations, and announcer costs, with the club guaranteed $600,000 free and clear per season.

The Giants never had a big radio network while in New York; only six stations were part of their chain in 1956. Radio was still profitable for WMCA, however, as they had rights to sell all ads for pregame and postgame programming, plus the time between games of the many doubleheaders on the schedule in the 1950s.

While Frankie Frisch was no longer on the Giants' broadcast team after 1948, he hosted a television postgame show after all home contests during the mid-1950s. His program in 1956 was sponsored by Consolidated Cigar.

As rumors swirled around the city about the Dodgers and Giants, WMCA broadcast regular-season games as well as eight spring exhibitions in 1957. Since Delaney didn't like doing play-by-play, Jim Woods — just released by the Yankees — joined the broadcasting team. He, like Ernie Harwell, had announced the Atlanta Crackers before coming north. Woods also did NBC *Game of the Week* telecasts that season, teaming with Lindsay Nelson and Leo Durocher.

Hodges, Woods, and Delaney narrated the comings and goings of the last New York Giants' team, a franchise leaving for the West Coast just three years after winning the 1954 world championship. Giants attendance had declined dramatically, going from the NL's second-highest in 1954 to sixth in 1955 and lowest in 1956. Attendance in that era, however, was closely tied to winning, and the Giants had finished a distant third in 1955 and finished sixth in 1956. The once-grand Polo Grounds, now a decrepit park in a changing neighborhood, symbolized the state of the franchise. Stoneham had no one to blame but himself for the embarrassing condition of his home field, though, since he owned the Polo Grounds.

Stoneham, prone to hanging back and waiting to see what the Dodgers would do, went along with Walter O'Malley's relocation plan, a key part of which was a rosy prediction about the future of pay TV, whose propagators promised millions if the big-league teams would move to the West Coast.

The simultaneous move of the Dodgers and Giants to California provided each club with a regional opponent. Both clubs vowed to eschew over-the-air television in favor of the potentially lucrative new world of subscription television. Skiatron, brainchild of Matty Fox, sold the concept hard, but everyone concerned knew that building the TV infrastructure would take a long time. Fox, whose main relationship was with O'Malley, also brought the Giants into the pay television concept, but Stoneham's commitment never matched that of the Dodgers.

Skiatron had 40 engineers working on cable network logistics in the Bay Area by mid-1958, but Pacific Bell told San Francisco mayor George Christopher that it would cost between $50 and $70 million to install the network in the city alone. Other estimates had the cost at "just" $30 million.

Stoneham claimed that the Giants had signed a deal with Skiatron for 1958 guaranteeing the team equal dollars to what they had been making from TV rights in New York — even if the company was not ready to telecast a single game. Skiatron apparently paid Stoneham a million dollars in 1957 (for the 1958 rights), which covered the club's moving expenses.

As a result, just as in Los Angeles, Bay Area fans could not see the objects of their new affection unless they went out to the ballpark. "There won't be any free television at any time," Stoneham told the *New York Times* in early 1958, dousing rumors that team would sign a 15-year over-the-air deal for a reported $37.5 million. Stoneham even refused KPIX's offer to show the games at no cost to the club, which made sense if the future was indeed in pay TV, but which also looked terrible to the fans and the press.

With no television in sight, the Giants placed prime importance on obtaining a strong radio carrier. Russ Hodges enthusiastically moved west, and amid heavy competition, KSFO landed the plum property, remaining as the flagship station for more than 20 years.

Lon Simmons, KSFO's sports director and, for the previous two years, an announcer for the NFL 49ers, took the job as Hodges' color man. The two paired on both Giants and 49ers games through 1970, becoming among the most beloved local broadcasters ever.

Simmons, a professional ballplayer before entering the broadcast booth, had worked his way up from the booth in Fresno. He knew the game inside and out, but Hodges taught him how to be truly big-league. The two never condescended to their audience, wisely assuming that the fans — who had been watching top-flight Triple-A teams in the area for years — knew the game too.

While Simmons was originally hired to provide color, he proved a natural at calling play-by-play as well, and Hodges soon volunteered to share the role. That was the kind of uncommonly unselfish act that made people on both coasts love Russ Hodges.

During its time as flagship of the Giants' network (in 1958, consisting of eight stations), KSFO always hired and fired the announcers, lending its broadcasts a certain integrity.

Rarely, if ever, were the Giants known to complain about the comments or the tones of their team's voices or about the content of the broadcasts.

Falstaff Beer, a product of St. Louis' Griesedieck brewery, bought sponsorship rights for the Giants' radio games for three years at about $350,000 per year. It was an indication of the changing nature of the brewing industry, as one of the first — if not the first — instances of an out-of-town brewery sponsoring the hometown team's games. Filling out its sponsorship lineup, Falstaff sub-sold ads to Folgers coffee and Tareyton cigarettes.

Franklin Mieuli, a longtime 49ers radio producer and, eventually owner of the NBA Warriors for 25 years, engineered Giants broadcasts for several seasons in the very small booth at Seals Stadium.

In 1958, 28-year-old Bill King was hired out of Bradley University in Illinois to become the third man in the Giants' booth. King became a local sportscaster then took on play-by-play duties with the Warriors, NFL Oakland Raiders, and in 1981, the Athletics. One of the best and most underrated sportscasters ever, King would again pair with Simmons decades after their 1958 work when the latter went to the A's.

New York did not let its old team go easily. From 1958 through 1960, WINS carried re-creations of Giants games called by the late Les Keiter. The widespread coverage of the formation of the upstart Continental League, followed by the NL returning to New York via the expansion Mets, however, caused Big Apple fans to learn to live without their Giants.

In San Francisco, the Giants were a hit, especially after the opening of Candlestick Park in 1960. Skiatron was not getting any closer to putting a cable system into place, however. Knowing that pay television wasn't going to happen anytime soon, Stoneham signed his club up for ABC's *Game of the Week* package to pick up some extra revenue.

The following season, Stoneham grudgingly agreed to a deal with Oakland's KTVU to telecast all Giants games in Los Angeles. (The Dodgers had aired road games from San Francisco since moving west.) These were the only games that San Francisco televised until 1964; LA's KTTV supplied the cameras and crew while KTVU brought its own director. When the Dodgers showed their games from the San Francisco, KTVU reciprocated and provided the crew and cameras.

As the Giants had done with radio partner KSFO, they engaged in a long-term relationship with KTVU, with Channel 2 telecasting the club until 2007. It was one of the longest such partnerships in baseball history.

In 1962, Standard of California became the club's chief sponsor. Even with its few telecasts, the club's radio-TV revenue in 1962 and 1963 — $900,000 per season — was among the highest in the league. San Francisco, at this time, was the nation's seventh-largest television market, so the games were a big draw, just like the club at the park. In 1962 and 1963, the Dodgers and Giants were first and second, respectively, in attendance in the majors.

KTVU beamed two exhibition games in 1962 plus the nine regular-season contests from new Dodger Stadium. In those games, four cameras were used: one behind the plate, one in the stands behind first base, plus a pair in the press box (one used mostly for graphics). By this time, producers nationwide had implemented Zoom lenses to give fans a closer look.

There was at least one good reason why the Giants didn't televise many road games: the prohibitively high cost of line charges for transmitting images. It didn't make financial sense — at least in the short term — to televise games involving high rates for sending the video coast to coast.

Hamm's Brewery began to sponsor the highly-rated Giants TV games. The nine 1964 Giants-Dodgers games beamed from LA on KTVU averaged a 60 share, and twice pulled in 93 shares in a four-station market.

The big TV news for the Giants in 1964 was that STV (Subscription Television), the descendent of Skiatron, finally took the air. A five-year deal with the Giants provided that the club would receive 28 percent of STV's gross receipts from games, with the club percentage increasing to a full third once revenues reached $1.5 million. The company had also signed the NBA Warriors for broadcasts that coming winter.

By August 1964, between one thousand and two thousand local residents had subscribed to the new plan. The $52 annual fee was waived for customers until 1965, with each games costing $1.50 each. On August 14, in the first Giants' game ever telecast locally from Candlestick Park, the Giants shut out Milwaukee 3–0.

The Giants broadcast all their remaining 1964 home games although STV faced stiff opposition whipped up by the film and broadcast television industries. Even the city of San Francisco, whose Candlestick Park still needed to be paid for, fought the infant cable industry.

In November 1964, a ballot initiative to ban pay television in the state passed by a 2-to-1 margin. Eventually it was found unconstitutional, but the damage was done: after nearly a decade, the Giants and Dodgers were back to square one with television as STV capitulated and went bankrupt before the ban was overturned.

For 1966, the Giants expanded their television schedule to include not only the traditional nine Dodgers games from LA, but also eight other road contests, all aired on Sundays. To help handle the extra load, and to lighten things a bit for Hodges and Simmons, KSFO and KTVU added Bill Thompson to the broadcast team.

Like Simmons, Thompson was a former ballplayer who had ended up in radio and had announced the Fresno Giants before joining KSFO. Thompson's job was to direct the broadcasts, handle technical matters, and help out on the air when needed. At this time, Hodges usually called the first and last three innings on television.

Standard Oil and Phillip Morris served as the most frequent sponsors of Giants TV in the mid-to-late 1960s. Allstate Insurance and Gallo Wines took smaller sponsorships in 1966 and 1967, when a new contract with KTVU increased the team's broadcast revenue to $1 million. In 1966, the channel carried around half of its Giants schedule in color, with all of them broadcast in color the next year.

The Giants added two more TV games in 1969, one each against the new Padres and Expos. That year, Willie Mays hosted an interview show on KUDO, owned by Bud Foster, a longtime Bay Area broadcaster. In August, former Giants manager Bill Rigney was fired by the Angels and joined the Giants' broadcast team for the remainder of the season. San Francisco's sponsors on KTVU included Phillip Morris and Standard Oil of California, plus Allstate Insurance, Italian Swiss Colony Wine, and Volvo. The radio guarantors included Burgemeister Beer and Pacific Telephone.

While the Giants were very competitive on the field in the 1960s, things changed when Willie Mays got old and the attendance-depressing effects of chilly Candlestick took hold. The 60-year-old Russ Hodges decided to retire, announcing the unexpected move on November 10, 1970. Though not yet at retirement age, the travel and hard work had apparently worn Hodges down, and some believed that either the Giants or KSFO wanted him out.

The Giants planned to add Hodges to their public relations staff for home games in 1971 and have him call road games on television. This was the first time that Hodges could truly rest in nearly 40 years, and it was both a relief and unbearable for him.

This maneuvering made Lon Simmons the lead voice on radio, supported by Thompson. As old friends, the pair shared a solid partnership, compatible both on and off the air.

The Giants signed new television and radio deals for 1971, but their $1 million in media rights fees was not a raise. Union Oil and Personna Blades acted as TV sponsors, with Gillette, Standard Oil, and Pacific Telephone on radio. For the first time in several years, KTVU did not air pregame or postgame shows, choosing not to disturb its lineup of syndicated programs until game time.

Another big change involved KSFO's employing Wendie Regalia, a local publicist and writer, for pregame and between-game interviews and commentary during doubleheaders. Regalia never worked the games themselves, and left after one season to become an agent for football players, but she was the first woman on a baseball broadcast in the Bay Area and among the first anywhere.

The new broadcast plan, however, unraveled when Hodges died at 60 of a heart attack on April 19 in Mill Valley. Devoted to the Bay Area, the veteran broadcaster was one of few people in New York happy that the Giants moved. He was loved by most and hated by no one, and there's never been anyone quite like him on the air since.

The Giants, during the 1960s, had won one NL flag and finished second five times, disappointing their fans to no end. The team scrapped its way to the 1971 NL West title, but lost the NLCS in the aging club's last hurrah. The Giants then failed to finish as high as second for a decade and a half as their cross-Bay rivals in Oakland rose to prominence.

Nobody could foresee these problems before the 1972 season, though. KTVU's 19-game package featured Buick, Ford, and Union Oil. Radio sponsors were Standard Oil, Chevrolet, Allstate, Hamm's, and Bank of America. In the early 1970s, half of the NL's teams did not televise any home games, so the Giants' small TV plan was not unusual.

That spring, the Giants televised an exhibition game against the Tokyo Lotte Orions, live via satellite from Hawaii. San Francisco's 1972 telecasts were its first to feature slow-motion replays, a technology already in use by most clubs.

The newly crowned world champion Athletics signed a one-year deal with Channel 2 to air their 1973 games, making for an odd situation in which both teams in the same market were carried on one channel. The Giants' games on KTVU had a new play-by-play man: Gary Park, their 10 p.m. newscaster and, later, sports director. Park didn't stand out — except for his penchant for talking about fine wine and Broadway shows — but he called TV games for 15 years.

Longtime radio partner KSFO had bigger changes in store for their Giants' broadcasts. Someone at the station or team wanted to diminish Simmons' role or force him out, and KSFO went hard after Cincinnati Reds voice Al Michaels, considered by many a rising star for his smooth delivery and assertive manner.

In January 1973, various sources reported that Michaels would join the Giants — not that year, but in 1974. Michaels, young and on the way up, was certainly attractive for a slumping team struggling for market share with the suddenly high-profile Athletics. It was a terrible time for the news to be leaked, because Simmons' wife was dying of cancer. She passed away in February 1973.

Grief-stricken, exhausted by road trips, and probably angry at how he was being treated by the team and Michaels (who had on earlier occasions attempted to get the Giants' job), Simmons wrestled with his future. It was reported that he made a proposal to work home games in 1974, but KSFO wanted a full-time announcer. On September 21, the station announced that Simmons was out and that Michaels was in.

Simmons bade good-bye to the fans over the radio on the last day of 1973. Rumors that he would do part-time work for the Athletics if the team were sold did not come to fruition, because Charley Finley held on to the club. So, while continuing his 49ers play-by-play work, Simmons sat out baseball. In support of his friend and partner, Bill Thompson quit the broadcast and was named KSFO sports director in November 1973.

When Michaels came to San Francisco in 1974, he boarded a listing ship. The club was stuck in mediocrity and its broadcast revenue, as a result of a long-term deal signed several years before, was stuck at $1.1 million, seventh in the league. No matter how good Michaels was, he couldn't make the Giants better, especially when teamed with Art Eckman, a former newscaster and basketball announcer with no baseball bona fides.

Ford and Olympia Beer came aboard the television broadcasts. The Giants, who had never possessed a large radio network, boasted 15 stations by 1974, including some powerful California outlets owned by the influential McClatchy newspaper chain.

In early 1975, a season during which the Giants were rumored to be Toronto-bound, the Houston Rockets made the NBA playoffs, meaning that Art Eckman, who broadcast the roundball franchise, missed a bunch of games, during which Bill Thompson stepped back into his old role. Eckman was briefly booted upstairs to become KSFO's sports director following 1975, making way for the surprise return of Lon Simmons.

The venerable voice of the Giants came back after the team was sold because the new ownership wanted Simmons to lend the struggling franchise some respect. The Giants' owners also knew that Michaels would depart for greener pastures when his three-year deal was up after the 1976 season.

During the bicentennial year, Simmons covered three innings on radio while Michaels, burnishing his resume, handled the rest. Joe Angel, former KCBS sports anchor and KSFO sports director, replaced Eckman in the spring; by the end of the year, Angel was positioned to take over for the departing Michaels. The ambitious Michaels went to ABC-TV for the *Game of the Week* and postseason baseball and, eventually, *Monday Night Football*.

In 1976, fans and writers were in stitches over the witty banter between Michaels and Simmons. In early 1977, however, Simmons' wisecracking got him into trouble when some Giants players briefly boycotted going on the air with him due to alleged critical remarks that the players never heard but were relayed by friends and wives.

The 1977 Giants were the only team in the majors whose broadcast rights fees actually plunged; their new contracts paid a total of just $825,000, ranking ahead of only San Diego among NL clubs. It was time for a change and, in September 1978, the Giants announced that KNBR, longtime flagship of the Athletics, would instead become San Francisco's new radio carrier in 1979. KNBR got the contract because its bid came in nearly a half-million dollars higher than that of KSFO and has been the Giants' radio home ever since.

While Simmons was initially expected to return, KNBR management decided to take a different route, cashiering both him and Angel in favor of veteran Lindsay Nelson, who since 1962 had been the lead voice of the New York Mets.

Simmons had to wait until 1981 to make the logical move to the Oakland booth when the Haas family purchased the A's from Finley. In the meantime, Angel called Athletics TV games for one year in 1980.

Nelson's assistant was Hank Greenwald, KNBR's sports director, who'd done some play-by-play on TV for the Athletics the previous year. He, like Michaels and Harry Kalas, had called games for the Triple-A Hawaii Islanders.

KTVU significantly upped its commitment to the club in 1979, increasing its commitment of games by eight to an all-time high of 31.

While Nelson was a very, very fine baseball broadcaster, he didn't catch on with the Giants' faithful in his three years in the Bay Area. People missed Simmons. Following the end of his contract, Nelson rode off to CBS to do college football, never returning to baseball. Young David Glass, who had come on as the third man in 1981, moved up to the No. 2 job.

At this point, the broadcasts became Hank Greenwald's show. Enthusiastic, hearty, and a fan of the game to his core, Greenwald helmed the Giants' radio package through 1996, minus a two-year stint in the Yankees' booth in the late 1980s.

The Giants finally instituted Spanish-language broadcasts in 1981, 13 years after the Athletics had tried it. No station could find the advertising support to make a full-time Spanish-language schedule a reality, but at least San Francisco was heard in Spanish 60 times by 1985.

Tito Fuentes, who had manned second base for San Francisco in the 1960s, worked with a phalanx of play-by-play men, including Ruben Valentin, Edgard Martinez, and Carlos Rivera on KOFY, KLOK, and KIQI before temporarily stepping down in 1992.

The Giants' media rights revenue doubled to $2 million in 1982. Both KNBR and KTVU, however, retained all ad sales at a time when the NL's more progressive and successful front offices (e.g., the Dodgers, Astros, and Reds) were holding their own rights. San Francisco's policy resulted in bigger upfront payments, but lost the bigger earnings on the back end from advertising revenue.

The Giants' radio and TV contracts expired after 1983. While the club considered a cable venture, it did not make that move until 1986. Instead, KNBR and KTVU re-upped with new five-year deals, raising the Giants' rights fees to $2.5 million, ninth in the league.

KTVU aired a new high of 46 road games in 1984, with Lowenbrau beer and Toyota as the major sponsors. At the team's direction, the telecasts were still used largely as promotions for upcoming home games, with comic actor Ronnie Schell starring in a series of commercials that gently made fun of the cold weather at Candlestick. These spots, which ran during games, decreased KTVU's available ad inventory, and contributed to the relatively low rights fees the club received in return.

While the Giants treaded water on the field and with fungible on-air talents such as Wayne Hagin and Phil Stone, the club found a keeper in 1985 when Duane Kuiper moved into the TV booth. The retired infielder immediately proved himself a natural at the microphone, becoming one of the few ex-players who could call a game with the professionals, not just provide color analysis.

The Giants hired Roger Craig as manager in 1986 and, with some good young players, the team became a contender. Ratings and dollars consequently rose. After a proposed cable television deal with Westinghouse fell through, Giantsvision, a pay-per-game service run by San Jose–based Bay Area Interconnect, appeared on local cable systems in 1986. The full 45-game package cost $154, but fans could also opt for two partial plans or purchase, for $5.95, individual games. Stone, Kuiper, and Joe Morgan provided the commentary.

Following an exciting third-place finish in 1986, the Giants captured NL West titles in 1987 and 1989. Giantsvision rolled on, reaching an increasing number of cable systems statewide, with Kuiper and Morgan doing the honors. Hagin teamed with ex-outfielder Ron Fairly on KNBR in 1987–88 when Greenwald spent two seasons with the Yankees after a spat with station management.

Fairly also assisted Park on the broadcast telecasts in 1987; these were sponsored by Toyota, Jack-in-the-Box, and Pacific Bell, among others. That was Park's last go-round in the booth before retiring, as the excitable Steve Physioc spent 1988 as the Giants' TV voice, with the redoubtable Kuiper as his color commentator.

Greenwald's return to the fold in 1989, after having had enough of George Steinbrenner, sparked several changes when he teamed with Fairly on KNBR, pushing out Hagin (who landed in Chicago). When Greenwald called games on KTVU, teaming with Kuiper, Fairly painfully essayed the radio play-by-play. KTVU, having re-upped with the Giants for another six years, broadcast three home and 47 road contests, another new high.

In 1990, Greenwald, Fairly, and Kuiper were rearranged into a three-man crew covering both radio and television. National franchise SportsChannel purchased Giants Vision, meaning that fans no longer had to subscribe or pay a per-game charge to watch Kuiper's and Morgan's 55 cablecasts. Giants fans could now see 105 games on television, far more than ever before.

Anheuser-Busch and the Giants signed a long-term sponsorship deal outside the purview of KNBR or KTVU, while other sponsors of the era included Sizzler Steak House, Toyota, Mitsubishi, and Safeway.

Mike Krukow replaced Fairly on the TV team in 1991. Eventually the ex-pitcher teamed with Kuiper, and the two have become one of baseball's best on-air duos, combining easy humor with just enough analysis and excitement.

Fairly departed for Seattle after the 1992 season, and Morgan went national with ESPN the year after that. Ted Robinson stepped in to help fill the gap. A professional voice adept at football, basketball, and tennis, Robinson served on KNBR and KTVU from 1993 through 2001. He was critical in keeping things together when Greenwald retired after the 1996 campaign.

Greenwald's departure opened the door for Jon Miller, previously the Orioles' voice and already known nationally for his ESPN work. Canned by Peter Angelos, who wanted an announcer that would shill for him and cry when the Birds lost, Miller happily journeyed west to his native Giants. The changeover included a great development for longtime fans, as the Giants also invited Lon Simmons back to assist on telecasts and to cover Sunday games on radio when Miller covered the MLB landscape for ESPN.

Miller is able to imitate other broadcasters to perfection but is proud possessor of his own style. He has always been fun to listen to, and he induced more out of the idiosyncratic and outspoken Morgan than any other partner. While Miller is the lead voice on over-the-air telecasts, most of his time is spent on the Giants' radio side, where his fluidity with language is a better fit.

In 1998, Amaury Pi-Gonzalez, one of the great voices in Spanish-language sports radio history, took over as the Giants' lead announcer on KIQI, which by this time was covering all games, home and road.

In 1999, Erwin Higueros joined the air team, taking over as top voice when Pi-Gonzalez left in 2007. He teamed with Fuentes, who returned in 2004. The Giants no longer have all their games on radio in Spanish, but when KIQI took over from KLOK in 2010, it continued airing about 120 games per season.

The Giants' Spanish-language broadcasts moved to KTRB, the area's ESPN Deportes outlet, in 2012. Higueros and Fuentes do 70 games each year: all home games, except weekday day games, and also any interleague games played in Oakland.

Fox Sports Bay Area assumed the mantle of Giants cable provider in 1999, holding that position until Comcast entered the market in 2007. With fewer and fewer games shown over the air and more on cable, Kuiper's and Krukow's role — and their comfortable on-air rapport — became more significant.

KTVU aired 52 games in 2003, but just 43 each of the following two seasons. When Comcast assumed control of cable games in 2007, it wanted a bigger package, and the Giants were happy to oblige, granting the cable giant the rights to 136 of games in 2008.

This shrinking of the available games led KTVU to bow out after having been the only over-the-air provider the club had known since moving west. KNTV, the Bay Area's NBC affiliate, signed a three-year contract to cover 20 games per season starting in 2008, and re-upped in 2011. One of KNTV's requests was that Miller do the play-by-play. The station's evening news anchor, Raj Mathai (who in the past was believed to be the first India-born sportscaster in the United States), has served as an on-field reporter for many games.

In 2004, KNBR and the Giants hired 26-year-old Dave Flemming as a radio broadcaster. He'd already spent three years at Triple-A Pawtucket. Flemming works almost exclusively on radio, filling a secondary role but stepping into the lead when Miller works on television. He seems like a natural, with excellent skills and ease at the mike.

When Simmons again left the broadcasts following the 2002 campaign, the Giants filled the gap with Tim McCarver (in 2003), Glen Kuiper (Duane's brother, later hired as the A's play-by-play man), Joe Angel, and Dave Raymond. By 2004, the club had settled on Greg Papa as a weekend announcer on both on radio and TV, subbing for Miller.

ESPN removed Miller from its national broadcasts following the 2010 season, when the Giants won their first World Series since 1954. With Miller no longer out of town on weekends, Papa's presence became superfluous.

The Giants are one of baseball's most storied franchises, yet the club has also spent much of the last 80 years in another team's shadow. After being the second (and sometimes the third) team in New York, the Giants moved west almost as an accessory to the pioneering Dodgers. A decade later, the club had to share its market with the Athletics.

From 1958 through 1967, due to their quixotic and disastrous experiment with pay television, the Giants lost time establishing a solid media strategy. In the ensuing years, they have rarely been proactive in their broadcasting approach. As a result, the club simply did not generate the media revenue it could have, because San Francisco's radio and TV plans were essentially reactive.

Comcast has now taken care of that problem, as the cable network has achieved overwhelming presence in the markets it has conquered. The Giants now enjoy pregame and postgame shows, feature shows, a strong online presence, and excellent announcers. Coming off World Series wins in 2010, 2012, they are at long last the undisputed Kings of the Bay.

II. TEAMS OF THE EXPANSION ERA

SNAKES IN A BOOTH

ARIZONA DIAMONDBACKS BROADCASTING HISTORY

"It's time for me to get on my soapbox again about the dangers of maple bats!"
— Diamondbacks color man Mark Grace on many a telecast

WHEN THE ARIZONA DIAMONDBACKS TOOK THE FIELD AS AN
expansion team in 1998, they were extending a long history of baseball in Arizona. Between
the traditions of spring training and the Phoenix Firebirds, San Francisco's Triple-A club
in the Pacific Coast League from 1966 to 1997, fans in the Valley of the Sun have long enjoyed
a high quality brand of the national game.

Phoenix' rapidly expanding population and its young, wealthy demographic were important
factors in MLB awarding the city an expansion franchise. And like so many residents, the
club's personnel came from somewhere else. The Diamondbacks first manager was the relatively young, but experienced, Buck Showalter. When the franchise put together its broadcasting plan, the mix of voices similarly leaned toward "young, with some big-market
experience."

Thom Brennaman, son of Cincinnati Reds mikeman Marty, called the plays on the new
team's television broadcasts. Brennaman the younger had worked two years in Cincinnati
before spending 1990–95 in the Cubs' radio and TV booths, developing his on-air admixture
of laid-back and intense. Arizona hired Brennaman in 1996 to build the club's broadcasts,
just as the club hired Showalter to construct the foundation of the club's baseball operations
several years before the players took the field.

The Snakes' first radio station was KTAR, which began operating in 1922 as KFAD. It won out over several competitors to become the club's flagship, and the Diamondbacks have never aired on any other station. KTAR, which for many years had a news-first format, went all-sports in 2007, also airing games of the NBA Suns and NFL Cardinals. In 2011, KTAR fed the games to 17 network stations in three states.

On the television side, the Diamondbacks initially split games between KTVK, an independent station, and Fox Sports Arizona. From 1998 until 2007, KTVK aired nearly half of the club's contests, with Fox showing 53 in the first year, increasing to 73 by 2007.

Former big-leaguer Bob Brenly teamed with Brennaman in the TV booth. The two had previously worked together in Chicago on Cubs radio games, and Brenly had developed into a fine analyst. Following the 2000 season, Brenly exchanged his mike for spikes and took the reins as the Diamondbacks' manager, guiding the club to a world championship in 2001.

With Brennaman and Brenly both serving as announcers on Fox's national baseball coverage as well, the D-Backs needed weekend TV announcers. The club decided to dip into the city's collective memory and ask Al McCoy along for the ride. McCoy, who had broadcast the Suns since 1971, came west in the 1960s to do minor-league baseball, serving for many years as the Firebirds' voice. He was offered the chance to become the San Francisco Giants' radio voice more than once, but opted for the Suns and their less grueling travel schedule.

For 1998, McCoy worked play-by-play with Joe Garagiola, who kept busy in his "retirement" with various efforts on behalf of indigent ballplayers. While McCoy only spent one season doing the weekend assignments, Garagiola remained part of the Diamondbacks' broadcast team for 15 years, later standing in for Mark Grace while he worked Fox Saturday telecasts.

KTAR had input in selection of the club's wireless announcers. The primary assignment went to Greg Schulte, a longtime KTAR employee who was desirable more for his local fame than for his baseball experience. Schulte's primetime broadcasting work had been as a host and occasional announcer with the Suns and Cardinals, but he had logged some baseball broadcast time doing Arizona State games.

Schulte became a solid baseball announcer, avoiding one of the downsides of giving non-baseball broadcasters the lead role. Rarely are announcers hired to do NBA or NFL work if their resume is mostly MLB — and then only by Fox. Yet calling baseball — the most complex sport of all to broadcast — has long been assumed to be a trade where experience in other sports is transferable. Over the years, men like Keith Jackson, Tom Hammond, Kenny Albert, Howard Cosell, and Brent Musburger, with thin (at best) baseball qualifications, have been given high-profile national broadcasts at which to try their hands.

Schulte has manned the mike for nearly every game in Diamondbacks history. For the first three years of his tenure, he paired with Rod Allen, a former major-league outfielder and minor-league hitting coach. Allen credits Thom Brennaman for getting him interested in broadcasting when the two met in 1996 and hit it off. Eventually Allen did enough demo work to convince people that he could be a solid analyst. As an African American, Allen also lent some much-needed diversity to the on-air staff in Phoenix and among MLB mikemen in general.

Brenly moved into the dugout in 2001, and Schulte began doing weekend TV duty that same year. Allen departed for the Tigers' TV booth after the 2002 season. The changes resulted in shuttling new talent in and out of the Arizona broadcasts booths in a confusing manner. Jim Traber, Victor Rojas, Steve Lyons, and Ken Phelps came and went in the next five years. Matt Williams, a former Diamondbacks star, also hopped on the wagon as a swingman working both radio and TV.

Brad Cesmat worked for a year as the weekend radio pinch-hitter for Schulte on KTAR; public address announcer Jeff Munn stepped into the role in 2003. After struggling to find the right full-time radio color man, KTAR and the club eventually settled in 2006 on ex-pitcher Tom Candiotti and his friendly, unassuming demeanor.

Mark Grace joined the broadcast crew in 2004 after spending his last three active seasons playing for the Snakes. Grace was extremely popular when he played in Chicago, but left the Cubs with hard feelings on both sides of the departure. Brennaman and Grace meshed well in the booth, despite an embarrassing pregame hiccup on September 8, 2005. While speaking into what they did not know was an open mike, the two of them discussed Dustin Nippert, with Grace uttering an expletive at his partner's possibly tongue-in-cheek reference to the young hurler as a "future Mark Prior."

Following 2006, Brennaman waved good-bye to the Southwest to join his father covering the Reds. Daron Sutton, another broadcasting "legacy" and a veteran of assignments in Atlanta, Los Angeles, and Milwaukee, assumed the lead announcer's role without much of a change in style. Sutton was often smart-alecky and sometimes funny, providing a slightly snarky style geared to play with younger fans.

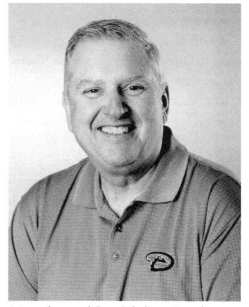

While not to everyone's taste, Sutton and Grace established a solid rapport, frequently sounding more like twentysomethings on Red Bull than middle-aged men. Fox Sports Arizona posted a quite large compendium on its website of various Sutton & Grace sayings, offering reference points to help non-regular fans digest what they heard and understand just what in the world was going on.

Following 2007 the Diamondbacks, as had many other clubs, moved all their telecasts to

Arizona has used Greg Schulte as its radio voice since the franchise's inception. (Arizona Diamondbacks)

cable, with Fox Sports gaining exclusive rights. The RSN aired a franchise-high 151 games in 2008 and another 149 in 2009.

Arizona's Spanish-speaking fans have been well served since the franchise's inception. For the team's first three seasons, KPHX broadcast all home games and some road contests *en Español* with the station's news director, Rene Boeta, handling play-by-play. In 1999, the D-Backs began airing some Spanish-language TV games on various local cable systems, with Miguel Quintana and Oscar Soria beginning their long-standing associations with the club.

Over time, Quintana, Soria, and Arturo Ochoa assumed their places in the radio booth and on SAP telecasts. KSUN now airs all of the team's games in Spanish, both home and road, which is appropriate considering the size of the Diamondbacks' Latino market. A Tucson station also carries these broadcasts, as do six separate stations in Mexico. Most of the club's other telecasts have SAP available in Spanish via the radio audio feed — an affordable solution to the cost of producing a separate Spanish-language TV broadcast.

While everything seemed hunky-dory prior to the 2012 season, the D-Backs' popular television announcing team soon ran into a buzzsaw.

First, lead announcer Daron Sutton was suspended from the broadcasts by the team in late June for offenses still unexplained.

Rumors flew around the game as to why the team would bounce its popular play-by-play man. Some said that he was campaigning a bit too publicly for a role with the Los Angeles Dodgers, while others noted that he had criticized club President Ken Kendrick (who had issued disparaging remarks about injured shortstop Stephen Drew and the intensity of his rehabilitation efforts). Still others focused on Sutton's disagreement with the club's informal on-air dress policy, which he apparently found unprofessional.

Whatever the reason, Sutton — whose contract ran through 2014 — never returned to the Snakes' booth and the team officially cut him loose following the season. By that time, his partner, Mark Grace, was in deep trouble. Grace, who was caught driving while impaired in May 2011, committed a similar offense on August 23, 2012. What's worse, Grace was driving with a suspended license and had disabled the mandatory interlock device on his car.

Under Arizona's mandatory sentencing laws for DUI crimes, Grace was sentenced to four months in prison. The Diamondbacks relieved him of his broadcast duties the day after his arrest.

When the D-Backs suspended Sutton, radio voice Greg Schulte shifted over to Fox Sports Arizona to call the games. Jeff Munn took over from Schulte for the rest of the season on radio play-by-play. Grace's removal from the booth led the club to use weekend analyst Joe Garagiola a bit more often and former Arizona outfielder Luis Gonzalez also took on some games.

The Diamondbacks announced a new television team on October 18, 2012. To replace Sutton, Arizona chose ESPN *Baseball Tonight* and *SportsCenter* host Steve Berthiaume, who came with a national pedigree but little play-by-play experience. His partner is Bob

Brenly, heretofore in the Cubs' TV booth, who lives in Scottsdale and had long been rumored to be going back West; he had not only managed the Diamondbacks but announced for them from 1998–2000.

With the new voices in place, the 87-year-old Garagiola, at the time baseball's most superannuated announcer, retired. His broadcasting career had stretched back to the late 1950s. With neither Berthiaume nor Brenly expected to work network telecasts, a weekend fill-in is no longer necessary.

The jury is out on Berthiaume, but one thing is clear — without Sutton and Grace around, Diamondbacks broadcasts are a lot less…something.

The Phoenix metropolitan area's rapid growth and desirable demographics makes it a solid bet for advertisers. Assuming that the club continues to manage its broadcasts effectively, the Diamondbacks should remain a solid and consistent ratings winner so long as they play competitive baseball.

ROCKY ROAD ON THE AIR

COLORADO ROCKIES BROADCASTING HISTORY

"Todd Helton, a tremendously gifted baseball player, he tried it. I know he tried it because Don Baylor told me. He said to me, 'I told him to get off the juice, that he was a player who didn't need that, get off it. It made him into a robot at first base defensively, and may have altered his swing.'"
— *Wayne Hagin, March 20, 2005*

"I would like to extend a hunting trip to him deep in the woods somewhere."
— *Todd Helton, March 20, 2005*

EXPANSION TEAMS HAVE A TOUGH CHOICE TO MAKE WHEN HIRING broadcasters. For instance, when making the key decision on choosing a play-by-play announcer, does a new club go for...

+ The seasoned baseball broadcaster who knows the game inside and out?
+ An exciting young talent with a fresh style?
+ The dulcet voice that may or not know baseball but has a commanding presence?

When Colorado recruited its first TV voice for the club's 1993 inaugural, it chose "none of the above." Instead, KWGN, Denver's main independent station, featured 71 games called by the 63-year-old Charlie Jones, best known as a football broadcaster. His major-league baseball resume consisted of a few appearances on NBC's *Game of the Week*, 35 games of Cincinnati Reds TV in 1973, and a handful of Angels games in 1990.

The late Jones was homespun and plain. His style — "the kick is up … [long pause] … and it is good" — was dull and somewhat dated. Worse, he was far from a baseball expert. Jones, however, possessed a recognizable voice from his AFL and NFL work in Denver and likely made some non-baseball fans in the area feel a bit more comfortable with their new franchise.

Prior to their debut, the Rockies had inked five-year deals with both KWGN and KOA radio to air the club's games. The approximately $3.5 million earned per year from KOA for the Rockies' radio rights was about average for NL West clubs.

In contrast to the muddled TV picture in the 1990s, the Rockies exhibited foresight and made the right moves on radio. To their credit, Colorado and KOA — owned and operated by Clear Channel Communications, a part of the Rockies' ownership group — realized the importance of a strong local presence in the booth as they built up the team.

Therefore, to back up Wayne Hagin, a "professional voice" who had previously been mikeside with the Giants, Athletics, and White Sox, the club and station hired Jeff Kingery. Kingery had made a name locally calling Denver Bears Triple-A contests for several seasons on KOA as well play-by-play for the NBA Nuggets. While it was unusual to have two announcers without a former player in the booth, the Rockies were able to cross-train both broadcasters. As a bonus, many fewer clichés were flying about due to the absence of ex-jocks.

The excitable Kingery and the slightly smoother Hagin worked well together, as the former had the local chops, the latter the big-league experience. For the franchise's first decade, most fans probably thought of Kingery as the organization's public voice, even though he was nominally the analyst. Hagin stayed with KOA for 10 years and also became a local favorite.

Although the club's initial pick of Jones was quite conservative, the Rockies were responsible for a significant broadcasting first in 1993. On Tuesday, August 3 in Cincinnati, KWGN put Gayle Gardner in the play-by-play chair. A former ESPN anchor and all-purpose sportscaster who had also worked on NBC's *Game of the Week* pregame show, Gardner became the first woman to call the play-by-play of a big-league game in the Rockies' 5-4 loss in Cincinnati.

Despite Gardner's fine performance, no woman has been hired since to do MLB play-by-play, although Suzyn Waldman, part of the Yankees broadcast team since 1996, has done a good job as the team's radio analyst since 2005. In theory, it should be just a matter of time before a woman gets a full-time play-by-play job in the major leagues, but there aren't many women in sports broadcasting to chose from — especially since, in the minor leagues, no women are currently doing play-by-play. Apparently, no woman has ever held a regular job calling baseball play-by-play at any professional level.

Jones held sway on KWGN for three seasons. For his first year, Jones paired with Duane Kuiper, previously an analyst and now a play-by-play man for the Giants. The Rockies and KWGN had hoped to snare Ken Brett from the California Angels, but the former hurler remained in Anaheim.

Kuiper was replaced in the color chair by Dave Campbell, late of ESPN and of Padres broadcasts. Campbell stuck around the Mile High City through 1997, by which time Jones had ridden into the sunset. Succeeding Jones was Dave "Wow!" Armstrong, who called Rockies games through 2001. While most fans liked Armstrong's enthusiastic college basketball work, many found his over-the-top style a poor fit for the national pastime — of which he knew substantially less than about roundball.

The Rockies were late in developing a cable TV presence, getting aboard the Fox Rocky Mountain regional channel only in 1998. This may have been a mistake, as the club led the majors in attendance each year from 1993 through 1999, selling out 203 consecutive games from June 1995 to September 1997. Wider exposure on cable could have helped spread the team's appeal throughout the Mountain West and probably would not have cannibalized attendance. More importantly, it might have better cushioned the large fall-off in the club's gate when the Rockies' on-field fortunes declined.

Kingery ascended to the first chair when Hagin departed after 2002. He teamed with Jack Corrigan, an acclaimed former high-school football coach who had broadcast the Indians for 15 years. The pair had the honor of calling the Rockies' first World Series appearance in 2007.

Hagin's post-Colorado career suffered from a huge controversy. In 2005, while working for the Cardinals, Hagin asserted that Rockies slugger Todd Helton, a star he had covered on Colorado broadcasts for five years, was "juicing" — an allegation swiftly denied by all involved. Although Hagin soon apologized, claiming that his remarks were misinterpreted, he was bounced from St. Louis following that season and had to take a year off before landing his next job with the Mets.

In 2002, following the end of Armstrong's stint in the booth, the Rockies hit upon a fine combination, hiring Drew Goodman as their TV voice and teaming him with former pitcher George Frazier, who'd been doing color work in Denver since 1998. Fox Sports signed a 10-year deal with the team for a 50-game schedule annually, paying $10 million per year and also purchasing airtime on the club's over-the-air broadcasts.

Goodman, whose experience dated back to the old Denver-based Prime Sports Network, had done 10 years of play-by-play for the Nuggets, had been a sideline reporter for hockey and football, and was popular for his work in local sports talk radio.

Though he had been with Fox Rocky Mountain for years, Goodman lacked baseball experience — but he learned fast and knows his way around the game. He has a pleasant timbre and, perhaps most important for a television voice, knows how to get a lot out of his analysts. Both Frazier and Jeff Huson, the team's second TV analyst, are well-grounded behind the mike.

After a decade as the club's over-the-air outlet, KWGN parted company with the Rockies as KTVD became the club's "free TV" partner for 2003. KTVD showed a high of 75 games and a low of 24 through 2008 before Colorado decided to move its games entirely to cable in 2009.

Kingery decided to retire after 2008 to concentrate on his burgeoning screenwriting career. The Colorado brass, however, convinced him to stay for one more year to allow the team ample time to find a successor. This turned out to be a mistake. Following a June 2009 game in Los Angeles, Kingery made an intemperate remark to the team's bus driver. Kingery's outburst — reportedly his second offense of this type — was serious enough to get him permanently barred from the team bus and plane. Supplanted on many occasions in the second half by KOA's Mark Johnson, Kingery's broadcasting career was effectively over.

Neither the club nor KOA participated in the recruiting of a replacement. Media giant Clear Channel — which had already switched some Rockies day games to other local AM stations so as to not preempt Rush Limbaugh's profitable talk show on KOA — handled the national search. Eventually, though, the search ended up in the team's own backyard when the Rockies announced that local voice Jerry Schemmel would pair with Corrigan for 2010.

Schemmel, who in 1992 had replaced Kingery in the Nuggets' booth, had mostly done basketball, working one year in the Class A Pioneer League plus occasional Triple-A Colorado Springs Sky Sox games. Highly regarded and well-known locally, Schemmel had a compelling life story as a survivor of a horrific 1989 plane crash in Sioux City, Iowa that killed 112 people. He wrote a book about it, *Chosen to Live*. Though Schemmel quit his job with the Nuggets to do the Rockies' games, he was not compelled to drop broadcasting Colorado State football and basketball.

Two decades after Major League Baseball belatedly arrived in Denver, the National Pastime — despite its popularity — is still far from the biggest game in town. The Rockies have employed three former NBA broadcasters with local ties and, with Goodman and Schemmel comfortably in place, this likely won't change soon.

Befitting a franchise in a market with a large Latino population, the Rockies scheduled Spanish-language broadcasts from the franchise's inception. Francisco Gamez was the team's initial play-by-play voice *en Español*, with Antonio Guevara later joining him and then taking over as No 1.

Unfortunately, the franchise has not invested heavily in cultivating Latino fans via the Spanish media. While KMXA has been the team's Spanish-language carrier for most of the last decade, the Rockies have rarely broadcast games from the road in Spanish. In some years, Colorado has not done any broadcasts in Spanish.

RAISING THE ROOF ON THE RADIO

HOUSTON COLT .45s/ASTROS BROADCASTING HISTORY

"In Houston, there is grits-and-gravy type who thinks the Astros are made up almost entirely of immortals…whenever an Astros pitcher gets two strikes on any batter, no matter how feeble, he yells, 'Now you're chuckin' in there, boy!' The hop lard [sic] drips from both tonsils."
— Wells Twombly, The Sporting News, 7/28/1973

"Hot ziggity zog and good ol' sassafras tea! Now you're chunkin'!"
— Astros broadcaster Loel Passe

THE NATIONAL LEAGUE'S FIRST MODERN EXPANSION IN 1962 featured two teams that could not have had more different audiences or business plans. The only thing the New York Mets and Houston Colt .45s seemingly had in common was that each played in a substandard facility that would soon be replaced.

The Mets, in New York, needed instant recognition in order to compete for the fans' attention with the mighty Yankees, the perennial American League pennant winners. The Colts, on the other hand, were serving an audience that had no expectations of contending.

This major difference affected the clubs' broadcast plans. While the Mets flooded an already busy media landscape with 133 telecasts in 1962 — including all 81 of their home games — the Colts presented a maximum of 14 games on TV in each of the club's first 11 seasons. While it's hard to imagine now, Houston fans would not be able to watch an Astros home game on television until 1983 — the franchise's 22nd season of existence.

251

Houston had a huge territory from which to draw an audience, and the new team's radio broadcasts were initially carried over a 15-station network. The network soon doubled in size. KPRC, the oldest radio station in Houston, won the initial broadcast rights battle and became the flagship station for the franchise's first 19 years. In the inaugural season, KPRC aired all 31 of the team's spring training games as well as all regular-season games.

The broadcasts' co-sponsors, on both radio and television, were American Tobacco and Pearl Brewing, and the one million dollars they poured into the Colts' coffers ranked ahead of the broadcasting deals that fellow NL clubs in Pittsburgh, St. Louis, and Milwaukee could command.

The Mets needed experienced and recognizable name voices to keep fans interested. In Houston, the club went for a mix of character and reputation, hiring a pair of Mutual Network *Game of the Day* veterans, Gene Elston and Al Helfer, as the team's initial voices.

Robert Eugene Elston came to Houston in 1961 at age 40 at the behest of Colt .45s executive Gabe Paul, who wanted Elston to broadcast the Triple-A Houston Buffaloes games as an extended audition for the upcoming major-league job. Paul lost a power struggle and departed in 1961; even without his patron, though, Elston was offered the big-league job.

Elston had been on the Cubs' radio team from 1954 through 1957, then worked for Mutual for the final three seasons of their *Game of the Day* radio broadcasts. To avoid confusion with White Sox voice Bob Elson, he took the first name "Gene" as his identity upon arriving in Chicago.

In addition to serving as the Colts' radio voice, the measured, almost impartial Elston was a full-time club employee, acting as statistician as well as a tireless promoter on the team's winter caravans. He helped design the Astrodome's press box and also designed and marketed a scorebook used by broadcasters at all levels for many years. Elston was a consummately professional broadcaster: while his style may not have been thrilling, he had the good sense to describe the action and stay out of the way, leaving the personality angle to others.

"Brother Al" Helfer, a tough navy man, broadcast from the 1930s onward for the Reds, Yankees, Dodgers, Giants, and Pirates as well as serving as Mutual's top *Game of the Day* voice from 1950 through 1954. Helfer, already in his 50s, lasted only one season in Houston, as his day had essentially passed and it proved to be his next-to-last major-league posting.

The third member of the radio team was 45-year-old Loel Passe, the only Southerner on the broadcast. His homespun phrases — Houston pitchers who were doing well were greeted with a "Now you're chunkin'!" and a "He breeeeezed him that time!" — were perfect for the team's fan base, although some snooty writers scoffed. An absolute original, Passe didn't miss an Astros game until he left the on-air team in 1976.

According to Robert Reed in *A Six-Gun Salute*, the Astros' broadcasters "were employed solely at the discretion of the ballclub." This was an unusual arrangement for the time; in most cases, sponsors paid for the privilege of approving the announcers. Colt .45s owner

Judge Roy Hofheinz, however, didn't want or need to give up control in exchange for a few extra dollars, so he did it his way.

The club's exhaustive radio schedule was intended to keep the fans fully informed; the 14 Sunday road telecasts were intended largely as promotion. The policy of letting fans watch their team on TV just 14 times per season seems old-fashioned and short-sighted, but in the early 1960s, televised games were not routine, especially in baseball's newer or smaller markets. The fear was that too many games on television — even those originating from the road — would depress attendance. Moreover, renting the dedicated transmission lines to carry the broadcasts back home was expensive enough to make an extensive schedule of road games feasible only for the wealthier clubs.

Hofheinz owned a piece of Houston's ABC affiliate, KTRK, which beamed the team's few televised games. Houston's first telecast on KTRK — scheduled for April 15, 1962 — was rained out, so fans had to wait more than two weeks to see their new team on the tube. On May 2 at Milwaukee, the Colts satisfied their first viewing audience by thrashing the Braves 9–1.

Houston's chief television voice in 1962–63 was Guy Savage, a longtime local broadcaster whose radio career dated back three decades. Savage had televised Houston Buffaloes games as far back as the late 1940s.

The Houston franchise's role as a pioneer in Spanish-language broadcasting is not well-known. With KLVL, the city's first exclusively Spanish-language station, as the flagship,

"Now You're Chunkin'!" Perhaps Loel Passe's southern-fried witticisms could have only worked in Houston, but work they did; he was a popular #2 voice for the club's first 15 years. (National Baseball Hall of Fame and Museum)

the Colt .45s and Astros broadcast a large slate of live home games and road re-creations over a five-station network from 1962 through the mid-1970s.

Hofheinz saw a huge potential market in the Southern United States, Mexico, and in other parts of Latin America for Major League Baseball. To appeal to the Latino market, he lured Nicaraguan-born Dodgers voice Rene Cardenas, who in turn recruited Orlando Sanchez Diago, a Cuban refugee living in Venezuela. The two paired on broadcasts from 1962 through 1976 and again in 1981. Cardenas, the club's Spanish media liaison, announced all sorts of events from the Astrodome and also beamed the 1968 All-Star Game to Latin America.

Cardenas and Diago also conducted Spanish-language tours of Colt Stadium and, later, the Astrodome, and served as the franchise's ambassadors to Houston's Latino community.

For a time, Houston's Spanish-language broadcasts had a far greater reach than their English-language counterparts. In 1966, the U.S. State Department and the team broadcast Astros Sunday games *en Español* over 82 stations in 13 Central American countries. The network continued to operate at a similar size for several more years. When the U.S. government was the sponsor, the games featured no commercials.

Following Houston's first season, in which it finished eighth in the 10-team NL, the Colts initiated a weekday offseason radio program on KPRC. Passe and Elston broadcast live from Colt Stadium's Fast Draw Club, a nineteenth-century, Western-style watering hole and restaurant open all year to season ticketholders who paid an extra membership fee. Most Colts and Astros promotional events took place in the club, a forerunner of today's exclusive ballpark clubs and restaurants.

The Fast Draw Club was at least air-conditioned, unlike the shabby wooden broadcast booths at Colt Stadium that were open to the oppressive heat and to millions of mosquitoes. St. Louis mikeman Harry Caray stripped to his shorts when calling games there, and Colts broadcasters wore short-sleeved shirts in an era of coats-and-ties.

Sportswriter Mickey Herskowitz was added to the broadcast team in 1963, but a July car crash sidelined him, and he returned to the beat instead of the booth in 1964.

On June 2, 1963, the Colts televised a 12:30 game from Milwaukee over their Dallas–Fort Worth affiliate when the Triple-A Dallas–Fort Worth Rangers had scheduled a 2:00 home game. Major League Baseball had an unwritten agreement then not to televise into a minor-league market during a competing minor-league game so, knowing that their decision to televise was on thin legal ice, the club offered $1,000 to the Rangers as indemnity. Out of principle, the Dallas club's management turned down the payment.

The 1964 season was the Colts' last in their original ballpark, and they aired 24 exhibition games over a 26-station radio network that included both English and Spanish affiliates and which stretched west to New Mexico.

The following season the renamed Astros welcomed a new primary sponsor in Schlitz, which inked a $5.3 million, three-year pact. The club also hired a new broadcaster, 29-year-old Harry Kalas, who topped 200 other applicants for the no. 3 job in the booth. Kalas, who had called Hawaii Islanders play-by-play since 1961, did some play-by-play and conducted interviews for the club before and after games.

Former Red Sox voice Curt Gowdy was said to have helped Kalas get hired by the Astros. Kalas had sent an audition tape to Boston when the Red Sox needed a new broadcaster after Art Gleeson's death in 1964, and the tape apparently made a quick, positive impression.

Promoting the fabulous Astrodome was a big part of the announcers' job. For one late 1965 game, the club's three broadcasters were spread around the enormous structure — one in the booth, one the in right field stands, and one in the center field stands — in order to describe to fans the various viewing pleasures of what the club immodestly called "The Eighth Wonder of the World."

Other teams' broadcasters were amazed by the Astrodome's vastness and construction elements, and the Mets actually had Lindsey Nelson describe an April 1965 game from a gondola hanging from a cable high over the infield.

In the early 1960s, the franchise decided to start selling its own radio and television advertising with the help of the Majestic ad agency of Milwaukee. Therefore, the rights fees the team received in those years from their TV and radio partners were small, but their profits were quite grand. Despite this, in 1968 the Astros were the only club in the majors to not to televise their games in color, claiming that the process was far too expensive.

The Astros didn't get much better during the 1960s, but at least they made money. Schlitz recruited other sponsors by 1967, including Coca-Cola, Monsanto (the makers of AstroTurf), and Texaco. By 1970, KTRK was beaming Astros games in color.

Prior to the 1971 season, the Phillies swooped in and picked off Kalas, who gladly accepted Philadelphia's second chair. NBC football voice Bill Enis replaced Kalas on TV, but the Astros went back to a two-man team on radio.

Kalas might not have lasted long in Houston anyway. "It's fun working in a happy booth," he said after decamping for Philadephia. "There was professional jealousy over there, and the only conversation in the booth was strictly business." Though unnamed, the likely target of Kalas' comment was Gene Elston.

An indication of the dominance of football in Texas came on September 11, 1971, when Elston missed his first-ever Astros contest — the 1,601st in club history — to broadcast a Rice–University of Houston football game.

For 1972, the Astros saw a big change in their television picture when KPRC, channel 2, won the club's TV rights to go with KPRC-AM's radio package. In 1973, the team began increasing the number of road telecasts, showing five games in prime time, a first. In both 1972 and 1973, the Astros received one million dollars for their broadcast rights.

Personable Astros hurler Jerry Reuss was hired in 1973 to do a five-minute weekday radio segment on KPRC in the mornings. Reuss went into broadcasting following the end of his long mound career in 1990, eventually manning the radio mike in the majors with the Dodgers.

On December 14, 1973, Bill Enis died in Houston at age 39. The Astros did not replace him, as Elston and Passe held down the fort on both radio and television in 1974–75. KPRC-TV broadcast an all-time high 28 road games in 1975, with their affiliates receiving the 15 weekend contests.

Following the 1975 season, Passe, nearing 60, went solely to television and pregame radio. The veteran mikeman had never missed a game to that point. After one year, Passe left the broadcast team, taking a job with the Houston Sports Association before retiring.

In 1976, the Astros made a surprising hire: Bob "The Gunner" Prince, recently let go by Pittsburgh. Everyone concerned said that the hire was not made out of dissatisfaction with Elston. Astros management also denied a desire to bring in a big name, but both denials rang hollow. Prince still had a high national profile, closing a deal to do 16 weeks of *Monday Night Baseball* play-by-play for ABC.

Unfortunately for the Gunner, his time — like that of Helfer — was already up. A fish out of water outside of Pittsburgh, Prince quickly bombed both with the Astros and on ABC and was relieved of both assignments after just one season.

With their big-name experiment a failure, Houston went instead to the minor leagues and hired 24-year-old DeWayne Staats to team with Elston. Staats had broadcast Triple-A Oklahoma City for two seasons and served as sports director at St. Louis' KPLR-TV. A steady and reliable voice for the general baseball audience, Staats has been broadcasting for more than three decades since, serving in Houston, Chicago, New York, and Tampa Bay as well as on national broadcasts.

Elston and Staats described the biggest-ever Astros TV schedule in 1977, including 28 games in prime time. To carry this load, KPRC split some of the games to its UHF affiliate, KHTV. Though the number of games being broadcast was much greater, the Astros were still getting only a million dollars per season for their broadcast rights, which in 1977 tied for seventh among the 12 NL clubs.

After 1978, KRIV took over the club's television package and brought the Astros into the modern age. Aided by former star Houston pitcher Larry Dierker, Elston and Staats aired 72 road games in 1979.

The next season, KPRC won a hotly contested battle to keep its radio rights, but the one-year deal was the last between the two parties. For 1981, KENR (which changed its name to KRBE in 1983) took over as the team's radio flagship. Finally fielding a good team, the Astros had become a desirable property, and it wasn't long before cable TV came to town.

In 1983, Home Sports Entertainment offered a wide swath of sports programming to cable subscribers across Texas. Eventually the Astros, Texas Rangers, and the NBA Houston Rockets all owned a piece of the channel, which in the mid-1990s went through an ownership transfer and eventually wound up part of Fox Sports' empire.

Fans could now actually watch games played in the Astrodome, as HSE telecast all 81 home contests in 1983. Star reliever Joe Sambito, who missed that season with an arm injury, appeared in the HSE booth with Elston, Staats, and Dierker. Nearly all (158) of the team's games were televised either by HSE or KXTH, which aired the club through 1997.

Early in 1984, Elston was hit by car in Philadelphia while traveling with the club and missed several months of action due to serious injuries. Mike Elliott took over on radio and KXTH, while Jim Durham and Larry Hirsch split the cable duties.

None of the three fill-ins returned for 1985, as the club replaced much of its broadcasting team. Staats and veteran Milo Hamilton essentially traded places, with Staats moving to the Cubs and Hamilton, who lost a power struggle with Harry Caray, finding a new home in Houston. The moves worked out well for both, as Staats stayed in Chicago for five seasons and Hamilton became a fixture in Houston.

HSE decided to put its own imprimatur on its telecasts, hiring Bill Worrell and Jerry Trupiano to handle play-by-play. Elston and Hamilton made the calls on KTXH, with Dierker leaving radio to provide color exclusively on television.

By this time Dierker had already become one of the game's most insightful color commentators. Well-spoken and appropriately critical, he could break down pitchers and hitters and his humor helped keep both his partners and viewers on their toes.

In fact, Dierker became so popular that he was pulled back to radio duty, causing a chain reaction in the Astros' broadcast picture. When Elston retired following Houston's heart-breaking 1986 loss in the NL Championship Series, Bill Brown (who stayed for the long term) and Bill Hoferth and Bruce Geitzen (who didn't) were hired to close the gap.

Brown, who came to Houston after calling games for the Reds and Pirates, is another sound and steady professional voice who describes a lot but doesn't go out on a limb and sometimes doesn't delve too deeply. Those qualities help ensure longevity, and he has worked for the Astros ever since.

In 1987, the Astros resumed Spanish-language broadcasting after a 15-year gap, with a now too-old Sanchez Diago paired with Rolando Becerra on KXYZ through 1992. Diago soon retired and Becerra moved on as Francisco Ernesto Ruiz did play-by-play until 2007, calling home games and re-creating road contests — as many MLB Spanish-language broadcasters have to do because they of strictly limited travel budgets. No big-league club has broadcast English-language re-creations since 1962.

Currently, former Houston catcher Alex Trevino assists Francisco Romero — a veteran of Twins, Diamondbacks, Reds, and Brewers broadcasts — over KLAT, doing all 162 games. The seemingly ageless Cardenas has also appeared on Astros radio occasionally over the last few seasons.

Dierker left the broadcast booth in 1997 to take over as Astros manager, with another former Houston hurler, Jim Deshaies, taking his place. Deshaies and Brown remained a team for 16 years. Both Deshaies and Alan Ashby, an Astros radio voice from 1998–2005, are quality analysts, and Ashby became quite good at play-by-play as well before departing for Toronto.

Hamilton cut back to solely home games in 2006, with minor-league veterans Brett Dolan and Dave Raymond joining the radio team to share the workload.

Fox Southwest showed a record 147 games in 2009, leaving KTXH a truncated eight-game slate, the fewest over-the-air games that Houston has telecast in its history. In 2011, the KTXH aired 24 games in its last hurrah before all Houston games were switched to cable, probably permanently.

The Astros changed everything for 2013. Not only did the club roll out new uniforms, and move to the American League, it also reconstituted its on-air staff.

Radio legend Milo Hamilton retired after 60 years in the booth, and Dave Raymond and Brett Dolan, heretofore describing the action on KLAT, were let go. The Astros signed with new radio carrier KMBE and brought on three brand-new announcers.

Play-by-play announcer Robert Ford is one of just two full-time African American play-by-play men in the majors (the other is Dave Sims in Seattle). A grad of Syracuse's Newhouse School of Broadcasting, Ford truly worked his way up from the bottom, broadcasting in the independent Frontier League in 2003 and 2004 before calling games for three clubs at Classes A and Double-A. He then served three years as a studio host on the Royals' radio network.

Paired with Ford is former big-league pitcher Steve Sparks, who had done pregame and postgame for the Astros in the recent past as well as handling a bit of radio fill-in work. The third man is Crawford Jones, a recent graduate of the University of Houston, winner of a 2012 contest sponsored by the team to become the Astros' "radio apprentice," giving score updates and such.

The Astros also changed their television provider for 2013. After 16 years with Fox Sports as its cable channel, Houston became the sixth MLB organization (Cubs, White Sox, Athletics, Phillies, and Giants) to join the Comcast/NBC stable, taking 46% (a controlling interest) in their new channel. The NBA's Houston Rockets have a 31% share, while Comcast itself owns 23%.

Longtime TV play-by-play man Bill Brown remains with the club, and his new partner for 2013 was actually an old one. Alan Ashby, longtime big-league catcher, left his spot in Toronto's booth to return to Houston, where he served as a radio analyst and announcer from 1998 through 2006. Geoff Blum, former Astros infielder, serves as an analyst on occasion with Ashby shifting to play-by-play, giving Brown a few days off.

Many locals believe that former Astros owner Drayton McLane chased Ashby away from the team the first time because he was too critical of the team's on-field performance. But the Astros' new brain trust selected Ashby over at least one other former broadcaster, Larry Dierker, who — after losing the analyst job — turned down a gig on the pregame and postgame shows, departing the organization in an ugly public tiff with team CEO and President George Postolos, who himself resigned two months later.

While some fans were angry to lose Dierker, Postolos' undoing almost certainly has more to do with an inability to get Comcast Sports Net Houston carried on most local cable and satellite systems. Apparently, the key reason that CSN Houston is not available is that the Astros and Rockets signed a ten-year exclusivity deal with Comcast — a move that is said to have offended other local operators such as AT&T and Time Warner and requires much legal wrangling to amend.

The satellite situation was worse. DirectTV would only negotiate to carry CSN Houston if Comcast was put on a premium payment tier, unlike any other such sports network in the country. This caused the Astros considerable frustration, and they were no happier that other local satellite operators picked up the channel. Clearly everyone wants a deal, but none of the parties are willing to give enough to make it happen.

The lack of cable system coverage (CSN Houston is only on available to 40% of area viewers) and the Astros' on-field ineptitude led to the embarrassing revelation that the club

A thoroughly professional voice, Gene Elston moved from Mutual's *Game of the Day* to the top chair on the Astros radio network. He held that job from 1962 through 1986. (National Baseball Hall of Fame and Museum)

got a 0.0 broadcast rating for a September 2013 Sunday afternoon contest — this means that the amount of Nielsen households viewing the game was statistically measurable at less than one tenth of one percent.

Not getting the club on many Texas cable systems led to low revenues and, therefore, a messy fight between Comcast and the Astros, with the network claiming huge creditor pressure and suing for bankruptcy. The team claims that the only party to which Comcast SportsNet Houston owes money to is the Astros themselves, as Comcast did not pay the club any 2013 monies after early summer.

Astros owner Jim Crane argued that Comcast filed bankruptcy simply to attempt to rearrange their agreement with the club for its own benefit. Crane also stated that he would get his club's games on more systems for 2014 with or without Comcast's help.

Early in November 2013, federal bankruptcy judge Marvin Isgur issued an order allowing the Houston Regional Sports Network to negotiate with other cable systems to build a new business plan by which televising the Astros and Rockets can become profitable. Comcast would remain the clubs' carrier, and still hopes to remain involved in a major way, perhaps by buying the rest of the 78% of the network if nothing else can be worked out.

There's nowhere to go but up.

FOUR DECADES WITH DENNY

KANSAS CITY ROYALS BROADCASTING HISTORY

"Among the pleasures of being a Royals fan, few rank any higher than turning on the radio each evening to receive the 7 o'clock greeting of Mr. Denny Matthews."
— Bill James, in his *1983* Baseball Abstract

FROM THEIR BIRTH IN 1969, THE ROYALS CHOSE TO SEPARATE themselves from their recently departed predecessors, the low-rent Kansas City Athletics, by planning for the long term and by operating with class.

Eschewing the quick-money, counterproductive, year-by-year radio strategy of A's owner Charles O. Finley, the Royals inked a five-year deal with KMBZ radio. Schlitz, through Milwaukee's Majestic advertising agency, signed on as the expansion club's primary sponsor. The brewery sold ad space to Skelly Oil and R.J. Reynolds — the latter soon to be banned from television advertising by government order. Several local concerns, including Guy's Potato Chips, also sponsored the Royals during their first two decades.

Choosing a quality radio voice is correctly viewed as a critical factor in creating a lasting relationship with a baseball team's audience; in the late 1960s and early 1970s, radio was still, for virtually all MLB franchises, the dominant form of media coverage. Television, already dominant force at the national level, was not nearly as important a local presence, especially in smaller markets. (In baseball, this term has reversed since the explosion of cable; baseball on TV is now more important on a local level.)

The Royals made Buddy Blattner, for many years the straight man to both Pee Wee Reese and Dizzy Dean on TV's *Game of the Week*, their first voice. He provided the veteran, nationally known presence in the booth that expansion teams often crave. Blattner was one of few ex-players with the skills for play-by-play.

The Royals selected Denny Matthews, a recent graduate of Illinois Wesleyan (where he played baseball), to be Blattner's sidekick. Matthews would take over as the top man in the booth in 1975 and has built a great career with his pleasant manner, his sharp eye for the details of the game, and his genuine love for sports.

The Royals and KMBZ haggled over a new deal for 1972, but finally came to terms not long before spring training. Schlitz was out as the sponsor since the club, having hired Blattner and Matthews, chose to sell its own advertisements while spreading its games out on a 50-station Midwestern radio network. Kansas City had a lot of open space to its northwest in which to recruit affiliates, but it also bit into traditional St. Louis broadcast territory.

Blattner rode into the sunset following the 1975 campaign, but Matthews remains in the Royals' booth. Blattner's replacement, local college sports broadcaster Fred White, remained on the crew until 1998.

Ryan Lefebvre then served as Matthews' second banana through 2007, at which point former television voice Bob Davis moved to radio. With just a handful of radio broadcasters in more than four decades, the Royals have enjoyed a remarkable record of stability and have given KC fans a high level of comfort.

In addition to continuity in their broadcasters, the Royals avoided for many years the kind of station-hopping that other clubs engaged in while attempting to maximize their rights fees. The club's flagship station was KMBZ through 1974, at which point the team transferred to WIBW in Topeka. To KC-area fans, however, the change was invisible, as KMBZ remained the club's outlet in its home market.

WIBW took over the rights, paying the Royals a flat (but very low) fee and pocketing the ad sales, which picked up in 1976 once the Royals proved themselves competitive. As has often been the case in baseball, smaller local companies sponsored the team's pregame and postgame radio shows, while the bigger companies plumped for in-game ads. In the mid-1970s, the Royals' media revenue was by far the lowest in baseball.

The television side of the picture in KC has often been muddled. Like many teams in the 1960s and 1970s, the Royals rarely televised a home game, instead choosing to air only a handful of weekend and night road contests. Rather than hiring separate telecasters, the club used their radio announcing team, either in a simulcast or by having them go solo for both radio and for TV. Kansas City games were broadcast on six over-the-air TV stations between 1969 and 2007, after which all telecasts went to cable.

Unlike the Kansas City Athletics, though, the Royals were fun to watch. As a result, their TV package — while small — was popular. In 1971, the club's games earned an amazing 60 Nielsen share locally, one of the highest figures in the majors. Even then, though, the small-market club's revenues from radio and television ranked near the bottom of MLB.

In 1974, the Royals (estimated) $650,000 in media rights payments, which ranked 11th among 12 AL clubs. A solid group of sponsors — Hamm's, Dodge, Amoco, and Falstaff — poured money into the team's coffers, though, because Kansas City still managed its own broadcasts and pocketed the advertising revenue

One reason for the team's low revenue was that most of the stations comprising its radio network were smaller, meaning higher line charges and less exposure for potential sponsors. By 1980, the Royals were again trying to package their own radio sales program.

WIBW increased its affiliate loyalty in the early 1980s by offering network stations all its Royals exhibition games at no charge. By 1982, the Royals were claiming a million dollars per year in media rights, as much as some other small-market clubs. Long before the beginning of the 1983 season, the team's radio spots had sold out at $60,000 per minute.

Fred White had been hired in 1974 largely to ease the announcing load during televised games. From that year through 1979, the Royals tried several different TV voices, bringing in Gene Osborn, Dick Carlson, and Steve Shannon, none of whose presence was especially memorable. The club also tried out former Royals infielder Dave Nelson as a color man, with lackluster results.

Moving to WDAF-TV in 1980, the Royals finally found a long-term TV voice. Denny Trease, onetime broadcaster of University of Kentucky football and basketball, held down the fort, working with Al Wisk for three years. Wisk left for the West Coast to do NFL Los Angeles Rams football, but Trease teamed with Matthews and White through 1987.

The 1984 Royals, sponsored by Pabst, Getty Oil, and Datsun, had the largest radio network in the American League, with games distributed for the first time via satellite — cutting costs and improving broadcast sound quality. The following season, WIBW bought its own satellite unit.

Like most small-market clubs, Kansas City initially found it difficult to cash in on the lucrative revenue stream provided by cable-television broadcasts, and the Royals were among the last teams in the majors with a permanent cable TV presence. Despite that, KC was one of the first clubs to try the new medium.

In 1974, KBMA produced five games from Royals Stadium that were sent to a chain of 100 local cable television systems. The experiment went no further but, a decade years later, things had changed with the advent of subscription television, both over scrambled UHF signals and satellites. So the Royals gave cable another try.

For 1984, the SportsTime Cable Network — a joint venture between Anheuser-Busch and cable pioneer TCI — contracted to cablecast games for the St. Louis Cardinals, Cincinnati Reds, and the Royals. Some of these games were also farmed out to fill air time on Chicago's SportsVision and on SportsChannel's schedules in New York and Philadelphia.

SportsTime hired Dwayne Mosley and Phil Stone to describe 50 Royals games (half of them home contests). Veterans of short stints with other big-league clubs, the two mikemen called the club's first West title season.

While SportsTime initially made initial plans to air 52 Royals games in 1985, the entire network fell apart prior to the start of that season. No other operation ventured forward to replace SportsTime, so from 1985 through 1996, the Royals had no cable exposure.

Since Kansas City fans were used to not seeing many of their clubs' games on television — neither the Athletics nor Royals had ever shown more than 47 games a year through the early 1980s — it's not surprising that no entrepreneur felt a need to commit to a cable TV deal. After all, the Royals had a huge radio network; in 1979, their linkup of more than 100 stations was the largest in the American League.

The startup costs of beginning a new venture and the lack of a track record for heavy TV viewing in small cities contributed to the lack of cable presence: small-market clubs like the Pirates, Royals, Brewers, and Mariners hadn't yet demonstrated that a heavy demand existed to watch a majority of their games on TV in any format.

The halcyon days of 1985 were the greatest in Royals history as the team won its only World Series. Despite that success, Kansas City's media revenue was the lowest in baseball again in 1986 due to a lack of sufficient television dollars. That remained the KC story throughout the 1980s and much of the 1990s: a large radio network of small stations, which limited potential advertising dollars, and a dearth of television coverage.

Paul Splittorff, a mainstay of the team's pitching rotation in the 1970s and early 1980s, came aboard as Trease's color commentator in 1988, the initial year of a new five-year deal between the Royals and WDAF. Splittorff remained part of the Royals' broadcast team for two decades.

Unlike some ex-players who simply trade on their celebrity, Splittorff took the craft of broadcasting seriously. He spent a couple of years learning while doing radio pregame and postgame for the Royals — and even covered high-school sports. He also had a successful run as a college basketball commentator.

Miller and Ford were longtime sponsors on Royals telecasts, which were carried by a good-sized network of smaller stations in several surrounding states. The 1988 deal with WDAF boosted the team's media rights payments to $3.1 million, still in the bottom third of AL teams and less than one-fifth of what the Yankees commanded.

WDAF did not renew its deal to televise Royals games after the 1992 season, meaning that Splittorff had to adjust to a new partner. It took the Royals a few years to get it just right. Plain vanilla Dave Armstrong (catchphrase a bland, "Wow!") spent three seasons in the KSMO booth; two other ex-Royals, Steve Busby and John Wathan, joined Splittorff in the booth for one season.

At that point, the team put on the brakes and hired local television veteran Bob Davis, a garrulous, enthusiastic voice who, like many other small-market broadcasters, made his name doing other sports. Davis and Splittorff got comfortable quickly in the booth, and made watching Royals games more pleasurable.

Davis' hiring in 1997 coincided with a long-awaited contract with Fox SportsNet to televise a conservative 30 games per year — most on the road — through 2002. On the radio, Kansas

City remained on WIBW until 1997, but the medium's troubled seas led to increased station-hopping as the club shifted to KMBZ in 1998, WHB in 2004, and KCSP in 2008.

The last move was criticized. First, KCSP — formerly known as WDAF — overbid for the Royals' package in an attempt to solidify its market position. Second, Sunday games had to be transferred to KMBZ, since KCSP already had a commitment to broadcast NASCAR on the Sabbath.

In addition, KCSP's decision to use an untested youngster just out of Syracuse's broadcasting school as its radio host caused some consternation among Royals fans. The hapless host was soon replaced, but the damage was done.

Worse for the spiraling Royals' organization was the club's June 2006 decision to pull the credentials of two radio reporters (one from KCSP) who apparently angered GM Dayton Moore by asking penetrating questions. Both reporters were allowed back into the ballpark the next year, but cutting off access as a way to control the message was a heavy-handed tactic that backfired.

The move from WHB after 2007 was motivated by a short-term cash payout, though KCSP's coverage did improve in 2009 and 2010. The Royals remain on the station, reupping after the 2013 season.

Davis transitioned from TV to radio in 2008, with younger and presumably hipper Lefebvre moving to the screen. Davis and Matthews, working together, presented baseball as it was heard 30–40 years ago, with excitement and geniality but without unneeded flash or silly catchphrases.

Following the end of their 1997–2002 contract with Fox Sports, the Royals started their own cable channel, the Royals Sports Television Network, and moved the bulk of their telecasts to cable. From 2003 to 2007, the Royals showed around 15 games on free TV per season, but have aired none since then. RSTN did not prove profitable, and the Royals returned to the Fox Sports Kansas City RSN for 2008. Fox now shows nearly every game, and out-of-market Royals fans with MLB.tv are able to watch nearly 90 percent of their hometown heroes' contests.

Denny Matthews was named a Frick Award winner in 2007, the highest accolade for a baseball broadcaster. While he cannot last forever in the booth, after more than four decades in the booth — among the longest tenures with one team in baseball radio history — he is a legitimate giant of the industry.

Listening to a team like Matthews and Bob Davis on radio outweighed the rough start that former Royals second baseman Frank White had on television in 2008–09. Showing improvement, the well-liked ex-player remained KC's no. 1 TV analyst for another two years.

Meanwhile, Splittorff — Ryan Lefebvre's longtime second in the TV booth — came down with a serious throat infection in April 2009 that forced him off the mike for most of the rest of that season. His health problems eventually worsened, and the popular lefty's family announced on May 16, 2011, that he was suffering from both mouth and skin cancer. Splittorff succumbed nine days later at 64.

White continued working with Lefebvre through the 2011 season's end, but Royals and Fox chose to go in another direction for 2012, letting him go in the fall. The dismissal of the voluble and proud ex-star precipitated an ugly public scuffle, as White — one of the few public links to the franchise's glory days — fanned the flames in interviews following the club's decision.

Like many other clubs that faced similar predicaments, the Royals should have found a way to keep White involved with the club and the community without asking him to do a job for which he was not truly qualified — but worked hard at anyway.

Before the 2012 season, the Royals hired a voluble and often controversial pair of announcers best known in baseball for their work with the Anaheim Angels. Play-by-play man Steve Physioc and color man Rex "The Wonder Dog" Hudler were brought on board to call action both on radio and television.

Lefebvre and Steve Physioc did play-by-play both on radio and TV, with Hudler handling analysis on television. Steve Stewart continues to fill in on radio for many road games. Matthews, with the club since its inception in 1969, cut down his slate of games; he is now more than five years past conventional "retirement age."

Bob Davis, having voluntarily reduced his role in recent years, retired from the Royals after the 2012 season.

Fred White, a staple on Royals radio and TV during the 1970s and 1980s, passed away

on May 15, 2013. He was 76. That day's television broadcast featured a half-inning of silence to honor White's passing.

The Royals, one of baseball's classic small-market teams, have followed a classic small-market broadcasting pattern throughout their history. Their radio broadcasts have stressed consistency, familiarity, and local color, while their over-the-air and cable telecasts have — often by necessity — featured a wide array of announcers and stations. For many years, the club chose building long-term fan loyalty over maximizing its rights fees, an admirable strategy that served it well in both good times and lean years.

Since the Royals began play in 1969, Denny Matthews has narrated their trials and triumphs. (Courtesy Kansas City Royals)

AIRTIME IN HEAVEN

LOS ANGELES/CALIFORNIA/ANAHEIM ANGELS
BROADCASTING HISTORY

*"When I'm asked who the best sportscasters are today, my answer is anyone good
enough to call baseball on the radio. They are the verbal artists of my profession."*
— *Dick Enberg, in* Oh My!

THE LOS ANGELES ANGELS, OWNED BY GENE AUTRY, WERE ONE OF
baseball's first expansion teams, taking the field in April 1961. Even before lacing up their
spikes, though, the Angels were behind the eight-ball in their own market due to rules
imposed on them that benefited Walter O'Malley, owner of the Dodgers and National
League powerbroker.

Although the National League had no authority to demand concessions from the Angels
or the American League, the mighty Yankees, doing a favor for O'Malley and other moneyed
owners, hog-tied Autry's new club into a restrictive television deal that allowed a miserly
20 games per season. (O'Malley, against free TV and hoping to build a pay-television empire,
wanted to limit the competition.) The power politics of the era allowed the dynastic New
Yorkers to bully, cajole, and bludgeon less powerful clubs to get what they wanted.

Knowing that the Angels would not have a big-league ballpark of their own for some
years, O'Malley forced the Angels to become tenants in Dodger Stadium, the palace that
he was building in Chavez Ravine, which opened in 1962. For four years, Autry's newbies
suffered under their landlord, paying very high rent, with secondary access to facilities, and
with no home television permitted.

The flagship station of Autry's Golden West Radio Network, KMPC, was the Angels' first radio outlet, beginning a relationship that continued for more than three decades. Autry hadn't intended to become a baseball owner; initially his goal was simply to secure the team's radio rights. Nevertheless, once he was convinced by fellow AL owners to head up the ownership group, Hollywood's famous "Singing Cowboy" took to the job with gusto, filling his media properties with team programming.

Regardless of the family connection, KMPC and the Angels still signed only one-year deals into the 1970s. Los Angeles' first sponsors included Falstaff, Brown & Williamson, and Folgers, each of whom took one third of the radio ad spots. All commercial time was sold by February 1961, and the Angels estimated that their rights would earn them $750,000 in their first year, nearly as much as established clubs. KMPC also broadcast 15 pre-season games.

Bob Kelley, the longtime *basso* voice of the Los Angeles Rams, and Steve Bailey, later sports director at KMPC, were tabbed to pair up on the broadcasts. The Angels, however, wanted a bigger name, so GM Fred Haney went east to convince Curt Gowdy to split the No. 1 spot with Kelley. Gowdy refused the offer.

Instead, the Angels hired 37-year-old Don Wells, who had assisted Bob Elson in Chicago for several seasons. Purged the previous fall, Wells said he was happy to be out of Chicago, where he admitted to being "shell-shocked" by Bill Veeck's exploding scoreboard. Wells was referred to as the team's No. 1 announcer when he was hired.

The three announcers also called the action on television. KHJ, channel 9, telecast 10 games from minor league bandbox Wrigley Field in that initial season, plus 10 road games and six preseason contests. Falstaff, B&W, and local Chevrolet dealers purchased commercial time.

Following the season, Kelley quit the broadcast team, claiming that he was simply too busy to do Angels games. Two weeks later, the Angels created a stir by hiring Buddy Blattner, famous for his years with Dizzy Dean on CBS' Game of the Week and fresh off two seasons with the Cardinals.

Blattner signed with the Angels, not with KMPC, thus becoming a club employee. He was regarded as the No. 1 voice, which must have crushed Don Wells. Bailey became the "swing man," doing radio only when games were also televised.

A former major league infielder, Blattner began his broadcasting career in the early 1950s in St. Louis. He saw himself as a hard-working professional, not just an ex-jock, and became known for his clear diction. Defending athletes-turned-broadcasters, Blattner argued that his career on the field gave him insights that announcers who were not former players would not have. While competent, Blattner was not the most interesting listen.

In 1962, oddly, the Angels and Dodgers became the only teams in the majors without a beer sponsor. The club's radio guarantors were Standard Oil, B&W, and Folgers; the TV sponsors were the same as in their inaugural season. The club's 16-station Golden West radio network blanketed California with broadcasts of all regular-season plus 15 preseason games. On the tube, O'Malley's restrictions meant KHJ could air only 20 road games plus six from spring training.

Autry consolidated his empire in 1964, when he granted KTLA — another Golden West station — the Halos' television package, which bumped the team's rights fees to $825,000. KTLA would hold the club's over-the-air TV rights until 1995. As a promotional tool, KTLA aired 10 exhibition games from Palm Springs, all in color. No regular season contests were colorcast, however. While O'Malley's Dodgers put a lot of stock into getting onto pay television via the STV service in 1964, Autry publicly dismissed any interest in the new venture.

Some new sponsors teamed up with the newly renamed California Angels in 1965, as Anheuser-Busch and Lorillard joined the program along with the local Great Western Savings Bank. KTLA showed 20 regular-season road games and 10 from spring training, while KMPC featured its usual full schedule. The club's broadcasting fees were now fourth-highest in the AL and ninth-best in the majors.

Another slate of sponsors (Standard Oil, United California Bank, and Anheuser-Busch) underwrote the Angels in 1966 during their first summer in Anaheim. KTLA presented all 20 regular-season and 10 preseason telecasts in color. KMPC and an 18-station radio network aired a total of 185 games, while local grocery chain Alpha Beta Markets sponsored the pregame and postgame on KMPC.

With their relocation, the Angels also introduced a new voice, albeit in a minor role. Dick Enberg, soon to become one of sports broadcasting's most recognizable names, first appeared with the Halos' broadcast team in 1966 as the TV pregame and postgame host.

While the Angels boasted a shiny new ballpark, their on-field nine in the late 1960s was lackluster, contending only once, and then almost accidentally. In the club's first 18 seasons, the Angels finished above third once, never winning anything till their AL West title in 1979. Yet the lucrative Orange County market guaranteed sponsor dollars and the possibility of high TV and radio ratings.

The Golden West network featured 22 stations in 1968. But the mediocre, weak-hitting Angels were losing the battle of Southern California to the better and more established Dodgers, with California's media rights dropping to 12th in the majors.

After the 1968 season, Blattner, a Midwesterner at heart, left to anchor the expansion Kansas City Royals' broadcasts.

Dick Enberg called Angels games from 1969 through 1978 before leaving for greener pastures, becoming perhaps the busiest sportscaster in the land. He returned to the baseball scene with the Padres in 2010. (National Baseball Hall of Fame and Museum)

Enberg, with Autry in his corner, was promoted to the top on-air spot. This move stunned Wells, who believed he was in line for the promotion. Enberg had never before called a professional baseball game, and a resentful Wells only fitfully meshed with Enberg, going so far as to insult his partner on the air.

KTLA began airing more regular-season games and, as a result, showed fewer exhibitions from Palm Springs. During the 1960s, the Angels — like other teams showing 30 or fewer games — often put no September games on the tube, avoiding competition with football.

In 1970, Dick Enberg became quite busy, calling the Rams, Angels, and UCLA basketball in addition to his syndicated *Sports Challenge* television quiz show. Hugely influenced by Vin Scully, Enberg claimed, "You can be enthusiastic and still be impartial."

Enberg's M.O. was a professional demeanor at all times: even his trademark "Oh, my!" rarely conveyed much excitement. This quality made him a natural for a wide variety of sports on the national stage, but was perhaps not ideal for local baseball fans, who expected hometown rooters or, at least, excitement in the booth.

As part of the general industry trend toward more commercial spots from more companies, the Angels in 1971 began selling one-eighth advertising sponsorships. Jerry Coleman, let go by the Yankees and not yet anchored with the San Diego broadcast team, helmed the KTLA postgame show.

For its 26 road telecasts in 1972, KTLA was able to afford a half-hour pregame show. During TV games, Dave Niehaus, KMPC's Angels host and voice of the Rams, worked radio play-by-play.

In November 1972, the Angels made a big splash, inking Don Drysdale to their broadcast team. Drysdale, who replaced Wells, had called games for the Expos, Cardinals, and Rangers in the previous two seasons. Autry wanted the charismatic former pitcher so badly that he hired Drysdale even though Wells had time remaining on his contract.

After a two-decade run, Wells had broadcast his last big-league game, losing his battle with Enberg. Wells caught on with local radio powerhouse KFWB as a sportscaster, but never got over not being named the lead announcer.

The frosty relationship between Wells and Enberg was exemplified in 1972 by an incident on a team flight forced to make an emergency landing in Boston. Enberg shot from his seat next to Wells and claimed another, saying later that if he had to die, he didn't want to go while listening to Don Wells.

Like Blattner before him, Drysdale was an ex-player brought in to provide both color and play-by-play. The ex-Dodgers' hurler got a three-year deal with an option, reportedly making more money than any No. 2 in the game. Enberg professed to love working with the "Big D."

It's difficult to know just how much money the Angels could have earned for their broadcast rights in the 1960s and 1970s: For many years, the Angels broadcast on two of their owner's stations, reporting media revenue of exactly $1,000,000.

In late 1976, Niehaus landed a job as the expansion Seattle Mariners' first radio voice. KMPC hired 26-year-old Al Wisk to fill the gap and cover both the Angels and Rams. Wisk had experience broadcasting Dallas Cowboys football, but not much baseball. In the mid-to-late 1970s, the third man in the Angels' booth did a lot of weekend work subbing for the over-scheduled Enberg.

That year, the Angels telecast their normal 30 games, picking up 28 regular-season contests and two exhibitions. California also dipped its toe into the pay cable television pool in 1977 with National Subscription Television, run by entertainment mogul Jerry Perenchio, which aired via scrambled signal on UHF channel 52. Wired-up Angelenos could see NSTV for $54.95 (including installation and deposit on the de-scrambling device) plus a $17 monthly fee — a lot of money back then for something considered a novelty. NSTV showed a lot of old movies, a few entertainment specials, and some local sports, telecasting the Dodgers-Angels preseason Freeway Series in 1977 plus six regular-season home games from Anaheim and six from Chavez Ravine.

More than 20,000 area homes had subscribed to NSTV by January 1978, with Perenchio reporting nearly 50,000 customers by July. NSTV claimed to spend between $7,500 and $10,000 to televise a ballgame.

The Angels and KTLA went for a little glamour in the booth in 1978 with Christine Seubert, a young blonde being groomed as a star by the station, appearing on some telecasts. The club certainly needed someone to step in; by that time, Enberg was transitioning to bigger national assignments, while Drysdale was announcing ABC's *Monday Night Baseball*. This meant Al Wisk was very busy.

The Angels entire on-air crew turned over within a year. Enberg took his leave in fall 1978, going full-time to football, basketball, and tennis. After 1979, the Angels declined to renew Wisk's contract; he soon resigned his Rams commitment as well. Shortly thereafter, Drysdale and KMPC came to an impasse on his 1980 salary, and the station cut the future Hall of Famer loose.

Wisk, whose style was not universally appreciated in Anaheim, initially said he was going to attend law school, but instead hooked on with the Royals' and Chiefs' broadcast teams in Kansas City. He was replaced by Steve Shannon, coming off a two-year gig in the Royals' booth. Some Los Angeles columnists intimated that Wisk left with a knife in his back; he returned to Dallas to get his law degree from SMU.

KMPC and the Angels had gone hard after Harry Caray, who instead remained in Chicago and received a new contract. Bob Starr, previously Jack Buck's second in St. Louis and for eight seasons the voice of the NFL Cardinals, got the Angels gig, apparently on Enberg's recommendation. The Pirates had pursued Starr to succeed Milo Hamilton, but Starr headed west to team with Shannon on radio and Ron Fairly on television. He also assumed Rams play-by-play duties.

For many years, both KMPC and the Angels implicitly assumed that one announcer could be the voice of two sports and call both effectively. While that might have been convenient, it often seemed that the Angels' talent was more familiar with football (Starr, Wisk, Kelley, Niehaus) than baseball.

Like Drysdale, the recently retired Fairly was a Southern California prep star who was tremendously popular due to his career with the Dodgers. Fairly enjoyed 25 years as a baseball broadcaster with three clubs despite occasional verbal glitches.

In 1980, the Angels slated 30 games on television, eight of them at home from The Big A — a first. The club broadcast six more pay cable home games via NSTV. Interestingly, the Angels also discussed signing free-agent hurler Don Sutton — yet another former Dodgers star — for 1980 and even talked about using him in the booth between starts. This never came to pass, but Sutton would later enjoy a lengthy and successful broadcasting career following the end of his playing days.

Making the whole celebrity wheel spin even faster, Drysdale made personal overtures to Autry during 1980 to get his old job back. This tactic worked: in 1981, Drysdale returned to the California booth, doing play-by-play on both conventional and subscription television as well as on the radio.

The return of the Big D had an immediate domino effect. Shannon fell first, ending up in Milwaukee helming the Brewers' telecasts. Starr fell next, demoted to solely to second-chair duty. Fairly also suffered, losing most of his mike time.

Drysdale's ardor for the Angels lasted only one season, after which he jumped to the White Sox, leaving Starr to reassume his No. 1 role with California in 1982. KTLA brought on sportscaster Joe Buttitta to work on the club's 35 free telecasts — a franchise high.

In 1983, the Angels finally reported a realistic media rights figure, almost quadrupling from the reported $1.1 million in 1982 to $4 million. By now the club was earning money from both KTLA's and ON-TV's telecasts as well as its Spanish-language radio. The reason for the huge increase was that KTLA had been sold and, with the station no longer under Autry's control, the club demanded much higher rights fees when they inked a new deal in 1984.

A slate of high-profile sponsors that included Chevrolet, Chevron, and Anheuser-Busch and a radio network of almost 30 stations meant that California's broadcast income ranked near the top in the AL. Yet the 1980s were an uncertain period among the team's broadcasting personnel.

Al Conin, hired to back up Starr as a relief radio play-by-play man in 1984, assumed top duty in 1986 when Starr transferred exclusively to television. (Born Allen Elconin, he had changed his name to Allen L. Conin.) Enberg returned to call 50 home games on radio in 1985 before again flying the celestial coop, while Fairly stepped back onto the field as the Angels' batting coach in 1984.

Meanwhile, California's TV package suffered. From 1983 through 1992, a star-studded but uninspired crew of Angels announcers and commentators included Starr, Buttitta, Geoff Witcher, Harmon Killebrew, Joe Torre, Joel Meyers, Charlie Jones, Reggie Jackson,

Joe Garagiola, Ken Brett, Ken Wilson, and Paul Olden — many working but one year for the Halos.

Adding to the confusion, ON-TV capitulated in late 1984 and sold its subscriber information to SelectTV, another local pay operation that couldn't turn a profit. So in 1986 the Angels, unable to cut a deal with Prime cable, decided to test pay-per-view (PPV) by airing four games on AngelVision.

Produced by the same company that did DodgerVision, these PPV games cost $5.95 each or $17.95 for all four (the first of which aired in July). Fans could also opt for a $47.95 package of four Angels and eight Dodgers games. That season, California reached the ALCS for the second time, dropping a heartbreaking five-game series.

In 1987, assisted by independent cable packager Spectacor (owned by Philadelphia sports mogul Ed Snider), the club tried yet another cable option, Z Channel, which also aired movies and Dodgers games. Z Channel provided both English and Spanish-language audio for its baseball telecasts.

Z Channel — which had locked up PPV rights through 1994 — outsourced them to SportsChannel Los Angeles in 1990, with SCLA carrying 35 Angels home games annually for three seasons.

In the early 1990s, the Angels could boast $9 million in media revenue, yet the junior league club remained a frustrating second in the local market to SoCal's dominant Dodgers. In an apparent move of desperation, KMPC opted to can both Conin and his assistant, Bob Jamison, in October 1992, though the local media wondered just what Conin and Jamison had done wrong. Conin's replacement was none other than Bob Starr, returning from several years in Boston.

While observers mooted Geoff Witcher, radio reporter Larry Kahn, and former Angels players Jay Johnstone and Bobby Grich as potential second chairs, KMPC hired Billy Sample as Starr's numero duo. TV broadcaster Ken Wilson had campaigned for the lead job in both media, but the Angels and their broadcast partners now wanted distinct presences on television and radio.

Sample lasted just one campaign before Mario Impemba, who had previously called games at Double A and Triple A, took over the lead mike in 1998 when Starr retired. Within months, Starr passed away.

After 35 years, Gene Autry sold a controlling interest in the Angels to the Disney Company in 1996. This meant that longtime broadcast partners KMPC and KTLA were shown the door as the new era saw the Angels pair with KCAL (television) and KTZN (radio).

A third major change in 1996 came when KCAL hired Steve Physioc, another Rams announcer, as the Angels' play-by-play voice. Physioc's baseball experience was limited, consisting mostly of one year of Reds TV games plus being part of the star-crossed ABC-NBC-MLB "Baseball Network" venture. While he had his fans, others wondered how he had earned a big-league play-by-play job; he endured some brusque interactions with his color men.

Physioc's gig with the Angels lasted for 14 years, though; he teamed with Jerry Reuss, Jeff Torborg, Sparky Anderson, and, from 1999 on, Rex Hudler. Dubbed the "Wonder Dog" by admiring fans, Hudler was a hyperactive former Angels infielder whose lighthearted manner belied the intensity he brought to the booth. Hudler fell ill in 2001 then was temporarily suspended from the team's broadcasts in late 2003 when busted for possession of marijuana.

To the Angels' credit, they began beating the bushes for talented young radio broadcasters after their unsuccessful 1980s' raiding of the Old Broadcasters Home. In addition to Impemba, the team hired Brian Barnhart and Terry Smith. The former didn't work out so well, but the latter did. Smith, heretofore voice of the Triple-A Columbus Clippers, has been part of the Angels team since 2002, first teaming with Rory Markas, a former TV play-by-play voice of the Milwaukee Brewers.

Markas made his mark out west not only with the Angels but also as USC's basketball announcer. He made the radio call when the Angels captured the 2002 World Series, the single greatest moment in club history.

Jose Mota, a former big-league player, joined the team's broadcast crew in 2002 doing Spanish-language radio. Good and charismatic, Mota was soon being used on Spanish-language television, English-language radio, and English-language television. He also became a guest analyst on the Fox's Saturday network telecasts.

Advertising magnate Arte Moreno purchased the Angels in 2005, setting out immediately to improve the team's status in Southern California. Moreno fixed up the Angel Stadium, changed ticket plans, gave more muscle to the club's Spanish-language marketing and, unlike Autry and Disney, refused to concede that the Dodgers owned SoCal.

Engaging in Autry-like media synergy, Moreno bought KMXE radio in early 2006, which in 2006–2007 carried the team's Spanish-language broadcasts. The next season, KMXE changed its call letters to KLAA (as in the franchise's new name, the Los Angeles Angels of Anaheim), became an Anglo sports-talk station, and took over the team's English-language radio package.

Even with Moreno's careful planning, Angels broadcasts have bounced around various TV and radio outlets in recent years as baseball clubs and media outlets have spent the Internet age seeking the right balance between long-term stability, short-term profit, and scheduling flexibility.

Nothing could have prepared the club for the upheavals of 2009 and 2010. Before and after a season during which pitcher Nick Adenhart and organizational eminence Preston Gomez died, the Angels overhauled their broadcasts, not fully by choice.

The Angels had kept at least 40 games on free television even after Fox Sports West ramped up its cable coverage to more than 100 contests a year. But in 2009, KCOP showed just 24 games, while FSW presented 125. This was the lowest total of over-the-air games the Angels had aired since 1967.

In November 2009, the club and Fox Sports West jointly announced that Steve Physioc and Rex Hudler would not return for 2010. Markas would move to TV with Mark Gubicza,

One of the game's more prominent Latino voices, Jose Mota has worked for the Angels on Spanish-language TV and radio as well as English-language TV and radio. (Wikipedia Commons)

while Terry Smith earned a promotion to radio top voice, teaming with the versatile Mota. Physioc and Hudler had been well-compensated, leading to rumors that the decision was partially financial. But changing announcers also gave the club a more streamlined media presence: during the late 2000s, it had been unclear who would be calling the game on what outlet on a particular day.

On January 4, 2010, however, the popular Markas passed away. Two seasons earlier, he had been laid up with a blood clot in the brain, but had recovered fully. The shock of Markas' death forced the Angels to act quickly. Shortly before spring training, the Angels announced that Victor Rojas, formerly on Rangers radio and a 2009 MLB Network anchor, would become the club's new TV play-by-play announcer.

If the new-look Angels — looking to establish themselves as the region's No. 1 baseball franchise — can catch up to the foundering Dodgers, it may have to be through broadcasting. Rojas had received mixed reviews in the past, and Gubicza was in his first season as a full-time voice in the booth when hired. The two have meshed together well, but are in no way a top duo. Angel Stadium does not have the reputation and the romance of Dodger Stadium, and the AL franchise is still catching up to the NL Dodgers' global marketing approach.

Moreno and his organization shook some things up before the 2012 season, primarily in Spanish television coverage. The Angels cut a deal to air 50 home games in Spanish on local Time Warner cable, with legendary Amaury Pi-Gonzalez at the mike with Jose Mota.

The Angels' flagship, KLAA, also welcomed Mark Langston to the radio broadcast in 2012. He worked with Terry Smith when Mota, the regular color man, went to television. For 2013, Mota went full-time to Spanish-language radio and Langston took over as chief radio analyst. In addition, the club pioneered a new radio concept in 2012. Compass Media Networks signed to sell and beam a package of 25 games, one per week, to various terrestrial radio stations across the country.

Steve Quis, formerly a fill-in play-by-play man for the Padres, was lead announcer on most games, with Steve Carrino doing the remainder. Either Steve Phillips or Darryl Hamilton filled the analysts' chair for each contest. For 2013, Quis was retained to do all play-by-play with Rob Dibble, Jeff Nelson, and Phillips revolving as analysts.

Compass, a big player in syndicated radio (its owner and founder, Peter Cosann, was CEO of Westwood One), also acquired the rights to air some Tampa Bay Rays games in 2013, but was out of baseball the following year.

FISH ON THE RADIO

FLORIDA/MIAMI MARLINS BROADCASTING HISTORY

"AND HIS NAME IS DAN UGGLA!!"
— Yelled in unison by television broadcasters Rich Waltz and Tommy Hutton
after each Uggla round-tripper

THE EXPANSION FLORIDA MARLINS HAD HIGH EXPECTATIONS FOR their 1993 entry into the National League. Local observers considered the area's huge Latino community to be a tremendous potential audience for Major League Baseball. Moreover, who had any doubts about the ability of the fourth-most populous state — which also hosted a majority of MLB teams in spring training — to support the new franchise?

Unfortunately, despite two World Series championships in the franchise's first decade, things have not worked out as hoped. Playing in an enormous football stadium was a problem almost from the beginning, and the team's original owner almost destroyed his franchise in a fit of pique before selling it.

Through all the ups and downs, the Marlins' broadcasting philosophy, however, has competently served its English- and Spanish-speaking audiences well, even improving over time.

As is often the case with expansion clubs, Florida's original English-language voices were plain vanilla types who wouldn't engender any controversy or inundate the fans with unnecessary analysis.

Journeyman Joe Angel — already a veteran of San Francisco, Oakland, Minnesota, Baltimore, and New York — handled the new team's radio assignment on WQAM, making no waves and generating little excitement. He was assisted by Dave O'Brien, who had come off two years with the Braves' radio team. Angel lasted until the 2000 campaign.

WQAM, which remained Florida's flagship until 2008, made a four-year bet on the expansion ballclub, obtaining English-language radio rights for $2 million per year. It looked like a steal at the time.

The Marlins' first television broadcaster was Jay Randolph, previously the Cardinals' lead TV voice for 15 years. Sports director for the Redbirds' over-the-air TV station, Randolph had worked with Jack Buck late in his career in the Gateway City and had also helmed a season's worth of Reds games. Teamed with Gary Carter (who never held a full-time analyst job in the majors before or after), Randolph was competent but unexciting.

Over the franchise's first four seasons, the pair telecast 110 games per season on UHF channel WBFS and over the Sunshine cable network. The video package netted the team $9.5 million annually. Like other sports teams, the Marlins originally wanted to be on a VHF channel; over time, however, the greatly expanded penetration of cable made over-the-air channel frequencies irrelevant.

Soon WBFS was the town's sports leader, broadcasting games of the Marlins, the NBA's Miami Heat, and the NHL's Florida Panthers. The station, sold to the UPN Network in 1995, carried the Fish through 1998.

The Sunshine Network had debuted in Florida during 1988 as an all-purpose cable net, carrying sports, entertainment, and government/political programming. Like most MLB cable outlets, Sunshine carried a heavy slate of home games, leaving most road contests to the over-the-air station. The Marlins aired on Sunshine from 1993 through 1997.

Randolph semi-retired after the 1996 season. He had never called more than 46 games in a year before joining the Marlins, and the relatively heavy schedule may have worn him down. He continued as the pregame host through 2000. Carter was not retained, but later resurfaced on the occasional Expos' telecast on TSN.

For 1997, the Marlins went into broadcast economy mode, hiring Tommy Hutton, who teamed with O'Brien for TV games. (Strangely, the Marlins have never had a former player in their radio booth, even as a color man.) Hutton is a fine commentator, intelligent and willing to be funny when appropriate. In his first year, the Marlins split a 70-game cable schedule evenly between Sunshine and SportsChannel; for the next two years, SportsChannel covered all 70. Sunshine was later rebranded as Sun Sports, and has carried occasional Florida games since 2006 that Fox hasn't had room to broadcast.

The surprising Marlins won the 1997 World Series — the first Wild Card team to achieve that feat. Within hours of Game 7, however, angry owner Wayne Huizenga ordered the championship team completely dismantled, destroying the young franchise's momentum as well as the outpouring of goodwill from its suddenly much larger fan base.

Even before the order to strip Florida's roster, many baseball fans in Florida were unhappy with Huizenga, who as the expansion club's original owner won a stipulation that no radio station in the state could broadcast any major league games other than the Marlins. For baseball fans in the spring training homes of several MLB clubs who followed those teams on the radio during the regular season, this was infuriating — especially in Tampa Bay, where fans were used to hearing Yankees' and Braves' broadcasts.

The denuded club lost 108 games in 1998 and finished with by far the worst record in the majors. Yet SportsChannel Florida — whose majority owner was Huizenga — obtained all the Marlins' TV rights for six years at $10 million per season, then sold a six-year, 55-game, "free TV" package to WAMI for a total of $19.2 million. Huizenga's insistence on retaining the revenue from that relatively lucrative package even after selling the franchise was one of the sticking points that delayed the sale of the club for a year.

That arrangement only carried through the end of the 2001 campaign when Latino media powerhouse Univision bought WAMI. Spanish-language broadcasting has always been a critical component of the Marlins' media coverage; the Florida management embraced the concept from the very beginning, more quickly than any franchise previously.

The organization's original Spanish-language broadcast team teamed the beloved Cuban-born Felo Ramirez with fellow countryman Manolo Alvarez. Ramirez, born in 1921, has been in radio for nearly 70 years. During that time he has broadcast more than 40 Serie Caribe (Caribbean Series, the annual winter league championship) and worked with the legendary Buck Canel to bring more than 30 World Series to Latin America.

Ramirez emigrated from Cuba in 1961 and eventually settled in Puerto Rico. He endured his share of hard knocks along the way — during the 1997 World Series, he fell down some stairs and was hospitalized for several days — but continued to call every Marlins game even in his late 80s. He is a true superstar and one of the most well-known Spanish-language voices in the Western hemisphere.

Alvarez, while not as famous as Ramirez, was much appreciated in Florida and points south for his work as a journalist and announcer, and his 2009 passing was mourned all over Latin America.

Miami has a very strong Cuban connection and is also a Spanish-language media center. Thus the Marlins' radio stations have made their heritage clear. Between 1993 and 1997 the team was carried in Spanish on WCMQ, which was named in tribute to popular Havana station CMQ, where Ramirez had broadcast Cuban baseball from 1953 through 1961. In 1993, WCMQ began paying $1 million per season to carry Marlins games to the Latin community of South Florida.

For 11 seasons starting in 1998, the Marlins' Spanish-language home was WQBA, with its call letters phonetically referring to Cuba. For 2009, Los Marlins moved to WAQI, which, like WQBA, is owned by broadcasting giant Univision. WAQI phonetically emulates the Spanish word aqui, meaning here. The 50,000-watt AM station can clearly be heard in Cuba, at least when it is not jammed by the Cuban government.

In 2001, Felo Ramirez was named a Ford Frick Award winner, the third Spanish-language mikeman to be so honored. The late, legendary Buck Canel had been the first to receive the award in 1995, and Jamie Jarrin of the Dodgers gained the honor in 1998.

Ramirez' recent partners in the booth have carried a bit more of the load. Jesus Diaz joined Ramirez in 1999, then ex-Cuban Angel "Tito" Rodriguez worked with Ramirez for two years before contracting lung cancer and passing away at age 48 on April 10, 2002.

Since then, "Yiki" Quintana, another Cuban who left the island to pursue a media career in the US, has served as the club's second Spanish voice. The Marlins continue to carry all 162 games in Spanish on the radio each year, and the club also makes available a Spanish-language TV option. By using the SAP button on their remote controls, fans have been able to watch their team on television since 2003, listening to audio from Raul Striker Jr. A Puerto Rican whose father is also a famous broadcaster, Striker worked with former big-league infielder Cookie Rojas, a native of Cuba, through 2013.

Since 2001, Florida's English radio voice has been Dave Van Horne, who had previously spent 32 years calling games for the Montreal Expos.

Van Horne formed a solid team for four seasons with Jon "Boog" Sciambi, an enthusiastic rookie making his first appearance in the booth, while O'Brien and Hutton handled "free TV" and cable.

The hearty Sciambi, who resembles former Orioles first baseman Boog Powell, departed for Atlanta, making way for Roxy Bernstein in 2005. A California native who had made a name as the voice of University of California–Berkeley basketball, Bernstein had earned his first regular big-league job at age 32 after calling the action for four minor league teams, filling in on some Giants games, and also working some Expos games in San Francisco with Elliot Price in 2003 and 2004, when the team's penurious MLB caretaker management refused to pay for a second announcer to travel to Montreal's road games.

Despite Bernstein's experience and ability, the Marlins did not renew him after his three-year contract expired in October 2007; the team was annoyed that he had refused to give up his off-season residence in California. Glenn Geffner, former Padres and Red Sox radio man, has paired with Van Horne since then. Geffner has called baseball from college on up, and also spent time as the Padres' PR director. He lives in Florida year-round and does significant promotional work for the franchise, although the on-air reviews have not always been positive.

When the Marlins took on a new radio partner (local ESPN affiliate WAXY) in 2008, it was via a fundamentally different relationship. Rather than selling broadcast rights to the station, the club retained its rights, purchasing airtime directly from the station while selling ads and covering announcer and equipment costs.

The Marlins were pleased to move to WAXY, as their previous home station had dramatically cut back its baseball-related programming. Like WQAM, WAXY is a 5,000-watt station during the day but broadcasts at 25,000 watts at night.

After nine years on TV in South Florida, Dave O'Brien left for the Mets for 2002 and was replaced by Len Kasper, who had broken into the business by substituting on Brewers telecasts for two years. WPXM, the PAX Network's Miami-area station, made a four-year deal to show 45-55 Marlins games per season, replacing WAMI, which had converted entirely to Spanish-language programming.

A clever promotional campaign got the Marlins in trouble in May 2003, when the federal government objected to the defacing of 75,000 dimes with the Fox Sports Florida logo. The club put these altered coins into circulation as part of a "free ticket" promotion. After a visit from Treasury Department personnel, the club was allowed to continue the gimmick, which let fans redeem the dimes for seats at Pro Player Stadium.

Before the last season of the WPXM contract, Kasper jumped at the opportunity to take the plum No. 1 role in the Cubs' TV booth. Rich Waltz, who had worked in baseball for years as a host and fill-in with the Mariners while also calling college football and basketball, finally got a crack as a lead announcer. He and Hutton are quite comfortable in the booth, emblemized by their creation of a special home-run call for slugging former Marlins second baseman Dan Uggla.

When PAX rebranded itself as iNetwork and moved away from baseball, Sun Sports and Fox Sports Florida took over the full slate of the Marlins' 150-game television package in 2006. Since then, the Marlins have been seen almost exclusively on local cable TV and the web. The team has rarely been shown nationally in recent years, partly because its attendance is so embarrassingly low.

Renamed Miami as part of the deal to get their new retro ballpark built, the Marlins began a new era in 2012, although the team crashed and burned in its first (and last) year under manager Ozzie Guillen. Moving to their splashy new park and escaping the teal-and-orange football prison they had inhabited since 1993, the Marlins hoped to rekindle interest and win back the affection of a baseball-crazy population. It continues to be a hard

The legendary Felo Ramirez, Spanish-language voice of the Miami Marlins since the franchise's first game in 1993. (Courtesy Florida Marlins)

sell, however, to induce the South Florida fan base — burned too many times by ownership that reaped huge profits from non-competitive clubs — to return to the park or to their televisions to watch the new-look Marlins.

In November 2013, the Marlins announced that their English-language radio broadcasts would henceforth be on WINZ-AM, a Clear Channel station that also broadcasts the NFL Dolphins and Florida Gators college basketball and football.

If the Marlins ever get it right on the field for a sustained period of time, their bilingual broadcast emphasis will enhance the club's popularity. While the franchise was, as of 2013, in dire straits on the field, their broadcasting record is far from the worst thing to build on.

PLAYING THE UKE

SEATTLE PILOTS/MILWAUKEE BREWERS
BROADCASTING HISTORY

*"I remember working first with Milo Hamilton and Ernie Johnson. And I was all
fired up about that, too, until I found out that my portion of the broadcast was being
used to jam Radio Free Europe."*
— *Bob Uecker (from his 2003 Frick Award acceptance speech)*

THE AMERICAN LEAGUE AWARDED AN EXPANSION FRANCHISE TO
Seattle in October 1967. While the new Pilots didn't have a suitable ballpark or any players,
they did sign a radio announcer in February 1968. Management hired Jimmy Dudley, fired
the previous month after 20 years with the Cleveland Indians, to call the Pacific Northwest's
first big-league baseball club over powerhouse Seattle station KVI.

KVI's adult contemporary music format made it a good fit for sports coverage. Part of
Gene Autry's Golden West Radio Network, KVI paid big bucks — an estimated
$750,000 — for the Pilots' radio rights, beaming the expansion team across the state of
Washington, as far east as North Dakota, and as far north as Alaska on a 51-station network.

Tabbed to team with Dudley was Bill Schonely, KVI's 39-year-old sports director. Schonely
had called 11 years of Seattle Totems minor league hockey and a few seasons of the Seattle
Angels' Triple-A games (at home from Sick's Stadium and recreating road games via teletype).

Dudley and Schonely paired in fall 1968 on University of Washington football, learning
to work together and getting sports fans in the Emerald City acclimated to their broadcasts.
They also joined the Pilots' early 1969 promotional tour around the northwest.

Schonely sported a deep, rich, mellifluous voice, while Dudley had a different tone. He was out of the Red Barber school and had done national broadcasts. Some listeners in Cleveland had wished for a bit more passion and flash.

KVI wanted Dudley's well-known voice, feeling that it was the right fit for their middle-of-the-road listener base. The station lined up Lucky Lager, a Vancouver (Washington) beer, to be the Pilots' primary advertiser, taking a quarter of the broadcasts. Chevron gasoline and Kent cigarettes bought time as well, but KVI could sell only three-quarters of its available ad inventory.

The Pilots had no television deal. Local stations asserted that the team wanted too much money for its TV rights. Max Soriano, one of the club's three owners, said that it wasn't smart to show home games and that video transmission costs for away games were so high that there "wouldn't be any revenue for the ball club." The Pilots' owners didn't really know what they were doing, as it would seem a logical imperative to use television as a promotional tool for a small-market expansion team with a huge hinterland.

Entering 1969 with a barely upgraded minor league ballpark that was still having seats bolted down on Opening Day made it clear that the club was in trouble from the start. In order to provide major-league-caliber facilities for the visiting radio and television crews, the Pilots constructed a new press box atop the grandstand of decrepit Sick's Stadium. The views were not good, and announcers often struggled to follow fly balls into the outfield corners.

The Pilots played fairly well through August of their debut season before collapsing, losing 18 of 20. Eventually KING-TV, channel 5, produced one telecast on August 31 from Detroit as the Pilots lost to the Tigers, 7–2.

During the season, it became clear that the Pilots did not have the necessary capital to make needed improvements to Sick's, much less build a new ballpark. That fall, a new Seattle-based group bought the team, but couldn't make the promised payments.

In early spring 1970, Milwaukee auto dealer Allan H. "Bud" Selig, who for several years had led the charge to replace Wisconsin's departed Braves, entered the picture. Selig was asked by American League owners, in secret, to make an offer for the team.

On hearing of Selig's involvement, the city of Seattle sought a court order to ban the transfer of the franchise, but no local burghers stepped up with enough money. Throughout this traumatic time, Dudley and Schonely continued to broadcast Pilots spring training games from Mesa, Arizona.

On April 1, as the regular season inched closer, the bankrupt team was sold to Selig by order of a federal court. Equipment trucks on the way to Seattle were diverted east to Milwaukee. Two days later, the new Milwaukee Brewers named Merle Harmon their radio voice on WEMP, which quickly cobbled together a network of nearly 50 stations to carry the games. Hometown brewer Schlitz was the key advertiser.

Local fans remembered Harmon, who had called Braves games in 1964–1965. With the Twins' broadcasting team for several years, Harmon wanted to get back to being a lead announcer. Though he considered taking a job with the Kansas City Royals for 1970, he instead leapt at the chance to return to Milwaukee even though the uncertain situation kept him on pins and needles all spring. Harmon signed up as soon as the official word came.

Left behind, Schonely and Dudley called collegiate football for the University of Washington again in fall 1970 then split. Schonely, who had broadcast one year of the NBA's Seattle SuperSonics in 1967, landed a gig broadcasting the NBA Portland Trail Blazers in 1970 and never looked back, holding that position until 1998.

Dudley never landed another big-league job. He announced minor league games in the 1970s and was in the running for jobs with the White Sox, Blue Jays, and even the Mariners. In 1997, two years before his death, the Baseball Hall of Fame honored Dudley with the Ford C. Frick Award. He is the only Frick winner to finish his career in the minor leagues.

Harmon eased comfortably back into the County Stadium booth. Tom Collins, the NBA Milwaukee Bucks' telecaster and WEMP sports director, served as his sidekick. On April 23, 1970, the Brewers announced they'd televise 26 games on WTMJ, the first coming on May 22. Eddie Doucette, radio voice of the Bucks, assisted Harmon and Collins on radio during Brewers telecasts.

Just after Thanksgiving, WTMJ radio, which boasted the strongest signal in the city, announced that it had acquired the Brewers' radio rights for the 1971 season and for 14 spring games with Schlitz again sponsoring. Schlitz continued its involvement with Brewers broadcasts until 1975. Appropriately for beer 'n' brats Milwaukee, Oscar Mayer co-sponsored the radio broadcasts for several seasons.

Except for 1981–1982, when WISN was the club's radio carrier, the Brewers have been a mainstay of WTMJ's lineup ever since. The club added more local companies as sponsors in the mid-1970s and 1980s, including Mautz Paint, Allis-Chalmers, Hardware Hank stores, and Klement's sausages.

Another key decision the Brewers made in 1971 was to hire Bob Uecker, former light-hitting reserve receiver for the Braves and other clubs, as the director of the club's speaker's bureau after their first attempt to use Uecker as a scout didn't work out. Following his playing days, Uecker had built a new career doing standup comedy using material almost entirely based on his on-field misadventures.

Uecker's gift of the gab made him an excellent conduit to the community. One year later, the Brewers chose to add the funny and telegenic personality, who'd done color on Atlanta Braves telecasts in 1969 and had already appeared several times on the *Tonight Show*, to their TV broadcasts.

During one 1972 telecast, Collins and Harmon coordinated a mutual exit from the TV booth when the ad spots ended, forcing Uecker to do an inning of solo play-by-play. After completely blanking on the first batter, Uecker got his bearings. He improved with every game.

WTMJ chose to add Uecker to the radio team in 1973, making him an everyday member of the broadcasts. Collins moved exclusively to television, teaming with former Braves shortstop Johnny Logan — also known for his humor, albeit unintentional. (Once at a banquet he referred to "the immoral Babe Ruth.") Schlitz hired Collins as "assistant manager and director of radio operations" for the brewery's broadcast division.

Harmon and Uecker worked together, often hilariously, through 1979 on WTMJ and a large regional network. On Saturday, September 21, 1974, Uecker broadcast the day's pregame show from a hot-air balloon hovering over County Stadium, though it was too windy to risk doing the entire game from the lofty perch. "Uke" also called a game with Harmon from Bernie Brewer's chalet in the left-center field stands, even taking a trip down Bernie's home-run slide.

Later famous for his Miller Lite beer commercials, Uecker also worked on ABC's *Monday Night Baseball* and as a television sitcom star. It said something about the times — baseball was hardly *au courant* in the 1970s — that arguably baseball's biggest media star of the decade built his media persona by making jokes about the game. That said, old-time baseball comics like Al Schacht and Joe E. Brown weren't as serious as Uecker was about baseball when behind the mike.

Brewers broadcasts were on a different financial planet from New York or even Chicago. The club earned $600,000 in both 1972 and 1973 for its broadcast rights, less than any team in baseball — even San Diego, which didn't televise in those seasons! In 1973, WTMJ's radio network boasted 40 affiliates; their television coverage, 11. Big-market clubs made even more money by appearing frequently on national games, increasing the disparity in media monies.

Engaging in a common practice, WTMJ tried to hold down expenses by using sportscasters already on its staff. Jim Irwin called Brewers games in 1971 and 1975, working with another sportscaster, Gary Bender, in an odd two-man play-by-play setup for the latter season. Unfortunately, the Brewers were still earning just $600,000 for their broadcast rights in 1977, more than only the Royals.

Home run king Hank Aaron, his storied career nearing its end, returned to Milwaukee in 1975 for a victory lap as a DH. That year's radio pregame featured Aaron with Harmon and manager Del Crandall (who had also starred for the Milwaukee Braves). Selig's adulation for the idols of his youth did not always make for good casting decisions.

After parting company with CBS in 1973, former Green Bay Packers voice Ray Scott had stayed busy with NBA and NFL gigs: Phoenix Suns basketball and Kansas City Chiefs football. In 1976, Scott called 30 Brewers contests on television — flying solo, with Uecker and Harmon only on radio.

Once Uecker joined ABC's *Monday Night Baseball* in 1976, becoming the best element of that little-watched, unlamented show, a third voice was needed. Former Brewers first-sacker Mike Hegan joined the crew in 1978 after Scott had departed.

From 1977–1979, WTMJ lost a troubling 20 radio affiliates. Just as troubling was Milwaukee's instability in the booth. The ambitious Harmon was offered a deal by NBC that gave him, among other assignments, a chance to cover the 1980 Moscow Olympics. When the Brewers understandably balked at allowing Harmon to take a month-long leave during the middle of the season, he left. Regrettably for Harmon, America ended up boycotting that Olympiad, so the veteran voice instead called NBC's backup *Game of the Week* with former umpire Ron Luciano that summer.

WTMJ hired Lorn Brown, formerly of the White Sox, in 1980 to replace Harmon. Brown ignored a competing offer from Pittsburgh to make the move to Milwaukee, stating that the reason he took the job was to be a No. 1 announcer. Brown never caught on with Beer City fans and also clashed with Uecker; both broadcasters felt they were the top dog.

After 1980, the Brewers opened the bidding for their radio rights. WISN unexpectedly offered about $2 million for a two-year deal, which some in the baseball industry thought was over-market. The new flagship also brought in more than 50 affiliates, but WISN's signal was not nearly as strong as that of WTMJ, especially at night, and didn't even carry to some of Milwaukee's suburbs.

On the tube, NBC network affiliate WTMJ could not provide the bigger television package that Selig wanted. Joining a developing trend of independent UHF channels televising baseball, WVTV assumed the Brewers' rights for 1981–1983, airing an all-time high of 60 games per season along with six affiliates. This kind of shift was happening all over; independent stations were devoting more airtime to sports as network stations experienced increased pressure to air programming from New York.

In addition to their new over-the-air home, the Brewers in September 1981 announced the formation of the Wisconsin All-Sports Network (WASN) with the NBA Bucks. The new net, which featured the two professional teams' as well as Marquette University and University of Wisconsin sports, was scheduled to go live in 1983.

Manager Harvey Kuenn's free-swinging, homer-happy team won the 1982 AL pennant, so the club took advantage of the incredible popularity of "Harvey's Wallbangers" to make a new radio deal. The club went back to WTMJ, but this time retained its rights to sell ads, paying the station $300,000 for air time and reaping the profits.

Who called the Brew Crew's pennant-winning final out against the California Angels in the 1982 ALCS? Not Uecker, who was working the national telecast for ABC that day, but rather No. 2 Dwayne Mosley, whose two years (1982–1983) with the club ended mysteriously when the organization decided that Mosley was just not up to the assignment. Mosley went on to a year's worth of cable TV games in Kansas City and then became a sportscaster in northern Wisconsin.

The new radio deal with WTMJ worked well for the Brewers, whose 1983 broadcast revenue jumped to a tidy $2.7 million, 15th among 26 MLB teams and impressive for a very small metropolitan area. Television advertisers lined up for Brewers games on WVTV in 1983 as Toyota, True Value, and Miller each paid $1,200 per 20-second spot — at the time a good sum for the size of their market.

A 1984 *Milwaukee Journal* article noted that radio advertising on Brewers games cost $325 for a one-minute local spot and $500 to be heard on the entire network. Major 1984 sponsors on WTMJ radio included Pabst, Pepsi, Chevrolet, and the local Mr. B's pizza chain.

While Milwaukee made money on radio, it did not capitalize on its ambitious pay TV plans. Due to funding and infrastructure problems, WASN didn't get off the ground until April 1984. The Brewers' plan was to show 30 road games on free TV and home contests over WASN, which had joined with other young sports channels such as Detroit's PASS and the Seattle SuperSonics SuperChannel to form The Sports Network. The amalgamation would allow for regional programming to be exchanged, thus increasing the number of games that could be aired on each channel.

WASN renamed itself SportsVue prior to its debut, but only 4,000 subscribers had signed up for the pay channel at that time, largely because the city of Milwaukee itself was not yet wired for cable. SportsVue aired 67 Brewers games in 1984, charging $8–$9 per month and ending up with only 18,000 suburban subscribers.

At the end of the baseball season, the two founding franchises folded up the channel. Selig was clearly deeply disappointed by the experience, and the Brewers did not become involved with cable television again until 1996. Many other small- or mid-market Midwestern teams — the Reds, Indians, Twins, Royals, Pirates, and Cardinals — also failed with pay-TV ventures around this time.

MLB teams that prospered with cable and pay TV in the 1980s were mostly located in larger markets or medium-size markets that were growing: the Cubs, Braves, White Sox, Red Sox, Orioles, Tigers, Yankees, Mets, Padres, Giants, Phillies, Rangers, Blue Jays, Astros, and even Expos. These teams succeeded either by putting their terrestrial (i.e., free, over-the-air) broadcasts on satellite, so they could be picked up by local cable systems, or by letting another interested party — in the Yankees' case, for example, Cablevision — build their pay-cable infrastructure.

With the demise of SportsVue, most of the Brewers' public presence landed on the Bob Uecker–Pat Hughes radio team. This was a good thing, because the pair comprised one of the best announcing duos of the modern age. Uecker, now a national star, had honed his play-by-play skills to a keen edge as he developed his own smooth style, alternating between serious one moment and dryly witty the next. He became a local icon, hugely entertaining without ever dumbing the game down.

Pat Hughes, a 29-year-old added to the broadcasts in 1984, was a perfect second chair, ably contributing commentary and play-by-play. Raised in California, he had announced Triple-A games and a season of cable TV for the Twins. Hughes bested more than 100 applicants to win the Brewers' position, handling three (or four, if the game was televised) innings of play-by-play as well as the pregame and postgame shows over WTMJ's network of 60-plus stations.

Uke and Pat worked together from 1984–1995, when Hughes moved south to take the reins of the Cubs' broadcasts. The pair described lots of highlights, particularly in 1987 when the club won its first 13 games en route to a surprise third-place finish as Paul Molitor hit in 39 straight games.

Bob Uecker was a big league catcher before converting his unique, funny take on the game into a spot on the Brewers' broadcast team in 1972. He's been the team's "voice" since 1980. (National Association of Broadcasters)

By the late 1980s, media consolidation was in full swing, especially in smaller markets such as Milwaukee. Journal Communications, owner of the two Milwaukee dailies, the *Journal* and the *Sentinel*, merged them in 1995. Journal also owned WTMJ. Milwaukee's broadcasters were not employees of the club, but rather the rights holders, and so walked a tightrope between accurate, objective reporting and boosterism. Uecker and Hughes toed this line with credibility intact, which was not always true among mikemen in other cities.

WVTV, also television home of the Bucks, was the Brewers' sole TV outlet from 1985–1988. Journeyman Steve Shannon did play-by-play for two seasons with Hegan (soon bound for Cleveland) on color. It was Shannon's final big-league job.

Prior to 1987, WVTV chose to have one voice handle all its play-by-play. Jim Paschke, heretofore sports director at WGCV, another local UHF station, took over for Shannon on Brewers games and called the Bucks as well. Despite being far more experienced with roundball, Paschke handled baseball play-by-play from 1987–1991 and again in 1995–1996. His color man from for the 1987–1991 stint was Pete Vukovich, a former Brewers hurler who during his playing days was known for having little tolerance for the media.

While the parade of TV announcers passed by, Bob Uecker's stature grew with his role in the ABC-TV sitcom *Mr. Belvedere*. With Selig's approval, Uecker took off significant blocks of time in the 1980s to videotape episodes of the Hollywood sitcom, with a variety of replacements filling in. Few owners would have allowed anyone that much time off, and few announcers merited it. Uecker would also portray Cleveland Indians announcer Harry Doyle in the successful *Major League* film series.

Rory Markas, who had called NBA basketball and minor league baseball on the West Coast, teamed with Del Crandall from 1992–1994 on over-the-air telecasts. When Paschke returned in mid-decade, he paired with affable Bill Schroeder, another ex-Milwaukee catcher who is still on the telecasts.

The big news in 1996 was the Brewers' reappearance on cable, as the Wisconsin Sports Network produced a slate of games. Following the season, the Minnesota-based Midwest Sports Channel took over WSN, rebranding it MSC in 1998. Fox Sports Net eventually bought MSC and since 2001, Brewers games have aired on Fox Sports Wisconsin, which unlike WSN/MSC is a 24-hour operation.

The Brewers have always used the same telecasters for their over-the-air and cable telecasts. Matt Vasgersian joined the crew to do play-by-play in 1997, musing over games for five seasons before heading to San Diego. Sharp-tongued Daron Sutton, son of Hall of Famer and former Brewers hurler Don, called the games on TV with Schroeder from 2002–2006 before leaving to fill Arizona's play-by-play chair.

Brian Anderson, a former college baseball player and longtime announcer for The Golf Channel, succeeded Sutton and earned accolades for a lighthearted, professional style well suited for the Midwestern audience. He and Schroeder work well together.

After Hughes departed in 1995, the club selected Jim Powell, a Triple-A voice who had subbed on Twins games the previous two years, to team with Uecker. Powell made the transition seamlessly with his conversational manner.

When the club's radio deal with WTMJ ended in 2001, WTMJ had to ante up a little more to retain the rights. From 2000–2002, though, the Brewers ranked either 28th or 29th in the majors in broadcast revenue.

In 2004, when the radio contract came up again, WTMJ was the only serious contender. The nationwide consolidation of radio stations under a few huge banners reduced small-market clubs' flexibility and leverage, and as a result the Brewers received less favorable terms this time around. WTMJ now had enough clout that it could pay the club a fairly small $3 million rights fee, sell its own ads, and cut the Brewers out of the profits.

Like most clubs, the Brewers came late to broadcasting in Spanish; interestingly, the franchise produced Spanish-language video before radio. WYTU began televising the English-language television feed for selected Brewers home contests in 2003, overlaying commentary from Francisco Romero and longtime White Sox voice Hector Molina. The pair eventually began calling all Sunday home games in Spanish on the box.

Milwaukee added Spanish-language radio in 2008 when Oscar Lopez and Juan Carlos Lozano took the mike for a couple of dozen contests.

Jim Powell's departure for Atlanta at the end of that year meant that the Brewers needed a new play-by-play man to pair with Uecker. Cory Provus, the third chair on Cubs radio games for a couple of seasons, got the gig.

Uecker, who had suffered a mild heart attack in 1989, underwent surgery in January 2010 to remove part of his pancreas. He was sidelined for a significant portion of the same season after undergoing emergency surgery to repair a heart valve.

With Uke on the DL, Provus experienced a trial by fire, assuming the reins as the club's voice with Davey Nelson, the postgame TV co-host, slipping into the analyst's chair. Provus seized the opportunity and showed himself to be a solid everyday voice, and as a result landed the lead announcing role in Minnesota for 2012.

Joe Block, at 34 a baseball veteran who had done a lot of minor league ball and had substituted in several big-league booths, copped the role as Provus' replacement.

Brewers fans were overjoyed to hear Uecker return to WTMJ at full strength in 2011, but the broadcasting franchise of the Brewers' franchise is not immortal. Milwaukee has always been a terrific baseball town despite the widespread but uninformed opinion that Wisconsin deserved to lose the Braves in the 1960s.

As one of MLB's three smallest markets, Milwaukee has always faced serious challenges with its media presence and revenue that have sometimes hampered the franchise. The ubiquitous and friendly presence of Bob Uecker has transcended those limitations for four decades, helping the club retain a loyal fan base even when it struggled on the diamond.

Block and Anderson are young in age, while Uecker remains youthful in spirit. That's why the Brewers' media package still crackles with life. But there won't be another like Uecker, and the club needs a solid plan for the sad day that the Milwaukee legend retires.

Stay tuned for an important message from the club's sponsors.

THE HAPPY RECAP

NEW YORK METS BROADCASTING HISTORY

by Stuart Shea and Greg Spira

"And the world champion New York Mets take the field…that has a ring to it!"
— Lindsey Nelson on Opening Day 1970

WHEN THE EXPANSION NEW YORK FRANCHISE JOINED THE NATIONAL
League in 1962, the ballplayers who took the field for the Mets did not always perform
professionally. In the broadcast booth, however, things were very different. From the beginning, the Mets' management took their broadcast policies and talent seriously, establishing
a top-notch on-air team of Lindsey Nelson, Bob Murphy, and Ralph Kiner.

New York NL fans had been used to watching their home teams on television for more
than a decade. In 1957, the last year before their move west, the Dodgers had broadcast more
than 100 games and the Giants 77. Convinced that this extensive coverage had been bad for
business at the gate, both the Giants and Dodgers drastically cut back their telecasts when
they moved to California for the 1958 season.

Furthermore, in each of their four years as New York City's only big-league team, the
Yankees had aired more than 120 telecasts. No other team in the majors showed anywhere
close to that many but, up against the mighty Yankees, the Mets couldn't afford to be
conservative with their television strategy. So in their inaugural season, the Mets beamed
133 TV games, far more than any NL team ever had to that point.

In the early 1960s, clubs still sold their broadcasting rights to sponsors rather than to
stations or networks. When the Mets put their radio-TV rights up for bid, local breweries

were often the most interested parties, which held true for the Mets. Liebmann, the brewer of Rheingold beer, secured the club's broadcast rights for five years with a bid of $6 million.

During the company's heyday in the 1950s, Liebmann Breweries had been a Fortune 500 company (ranking as high as No. 297 in 1955), and Rheingold was the best-selling beer in Gotham with a 35% share of the market. The brand's popularity was partially attributable to the company's annual pageant, in which a pulchritudinous new Miss Rheingold was crowned every year from 1940–1965.

The Mets and Liebmann conducted an exhaustive search process in the autumn of 1961 to put together their announcing team. Norm Varney, Liebmann Breweries' account manager at the J. Walter Thompson Advertising Agency, listened to more than 250 audition tapes and read a thousand resumes.

Nowhere to be found in those applications, however, was anyone matching what Varney, the brewery, and the Mets all wanted in their lead announcer. Before the Mets had made the deal for the team's broadcast rights, club president George Weiss had talked extensively to former Senators announcer Bob Wolff, then doing Twins games, about the lead position, but Weiss wasn't willing to sign a key announcer without the involvement of his future sponsor. (Wolff did end up in New York with Madison Square Garden.) The search team also inquired about Chris Schenkel, football announcer for CBS and the NFL New York Giants, but he was not interested. So Varney set his sights on Lindsey Nelson, lead announcer for NBC's *Game of the Week*.

Known just as much for his football broadcasting and loud sports jackets as for his work with the Mets, Lindsay Nelson was a mainstay at the Polo Grounds and Shea Stadium from 1962 until 1978 when he took a job with the San Francisco Giants. (National Baseball Hall of Fame and Museum)

"Hello, everybody, I'm Lindsay Nelson" were the opening words of almost every Mets television broadcast during the team's first 17 years of play. But two obstacles almost kept the Mets from signing Nelson. First, the announcer didn't seem all that enthusiastic about the gig. Nelson had not applied, and reacted to Varney's entreaties politely but without overt enthusiasm. Second, while Mets officials and Liebmann execs were familiar with Nelson's work as a football announcer, some had no idea that he was also covering baseball — blackout rules of the day prevented NBC's *Game of the Week* from being broadcast into major league cities. While Nelson had also called college football for NBC, the Big Apple was never a big college football town.

Most Mets fans, therefore, got their first exposure to Nelson as he described their bumbling infant team. While Nelson came in cold, he quickly gained the fans' affection with his enthusiasm, good humor, and ability to make even a 15–2 drubbing sound exciting. The Mets audience came to love him, eccentrically viewing Nelson — and his garish sports coats — as a creation of New York itself, rather than as a top professional who had already spent decades at the mike.

Bob Murphy, who would ultimately spend over 40 years behind the mike for the Mets, was the second play-by-play announcer. Before joining the Mets' team, Murphy had spent several years with the Red Sox and Orioles. When the New York job opened, he sent a tape of his call of Roger Maris' 60th home run as part of his application. Of the hundreds of reel-to-reel tapes and resumes received, Murphy's was the only one that led to a job.

Bob Murphy called baseball in Boston and Baltimore before landing a job with the expansion Mets in 1962. A beloved presence, Murphy remained with the club until 2003, among the best radio announcers baseball has known. (National Baseball Hall of Fame and Museum)

In his second generation behind the mike in Flushing, Murphy truly blossomed into the voice most identified with the team. At the beginning, though, the Mets viewed Murphy not as a future lead announcer but as merely one part of their broadcast crew. Since Nelson was obviously the lead play-by-play man and Ralph Kiner was hired as lead analyst, Murphy was really No. 3.

Murphy's broadcasting partners and fans enjoyed his work more than some key figures in the Mets' front office. In 1961, Weiss had asked Nelson if he knew "a fellow from Baltimore named Bob Murphy?"

"I know a fellow from Baltimore, Boston, Oklahoma City, and Tulsa named Bob Murphy," Nelson replied, "and he's one of the best sportscasters in the business." M. Donald Grant, the chairman of the Mets, was never a fan, constantly criticizing Murphy during the early years. The announcer finally obtained some relief by going to Weiss and threatening to take an offer to return to Boston if Grant didn't back off. Grant backed off.

Kiner took well to the rapidly growing role of ex-player and analyst. Best known at the time as a prodigious home-run hitter who played for awful teams for most of his career (only twice did his team finish over .500), Kiner was later inducted into the Baseball Hall of Fame in 1975.

Retiring after the 1955 season, Kiner had worked as a minor league executive before being hired for his first announcing job with the 1961 White Sox. Kiner's year on WCFL did not go smoothly, as his partner, the legendary Bob Elson, couldn't stand what he called "jock announcers." Moreover, Kiner was no natural at the microphone.

Kiner's season in the Windy City involved a lot of hard work: every day when the Sox were playing at night, the novice analyst practiced by re-creating another game in the afternoon. His apprenticeship paid off and, when the Mets offered a chance to join them, Kiner — unappreciated in Chicago — didn't think twice. In New York, he called play-by-play as well as contributing analysis.

Though Kiner did not bring the common attributes of a professional announcer — a great voice and a smooth style — to the booth, he was immensely likeable and conveyed a great deal of baseball intelligence. While he always needed a good partner to help him, Kiner at his best had a lot to say and could captivate his audience with loads of entertaining stories.

Ralph's other claim to fame was "Kiner's Korner," the Mets' postgame wrap-up and interview show that aired following every televised road game. He interviewed virtually every Mets player, many of the biggest stars in the league, and even some show business stars. Kiner's first show ran on April 30, 1963; the Korner was a regular feature for three decades in Queens.

Nelson, Murphy, and Kiner helped usher baseball back into the living rooms of New Yorkers who had been starved for National League baseball since being abandoned by the Dodgers and Giants. The trio covered the Mets for their first 17 seasons, becoming as known as any announcing team in the game.

The Mets averaged 113 losses during their first four seasons — bad for sure, but were they appreciably worse than the Astros, Cubs, Senators, or Athletics of the time? Not really. Yet New York was New York, where everything was amplified. Before they had even played a game, the Mets had already made more money on broadcasting rights than any other NL club.

New York loved the Mets even if they were horrid, and some idiosyncratic fans loved them because they were downtrodden. Nelson, when asked by Curt Smith to describe what it was like to broadcast a bad team, simply said, "What can you say after you say you're sorry?" Listeners to those 1960s broadcasts, however, would never have known the Mets were cellar-dwellers if they didn't read the daily newspapers. Nelson, Murphy, and Kiner worked with verve, skill, and palpable enjoyment no matter what end of the score their team was on.

Over the years, Liebmann sold sub-sponsorships. Viceroy cigarettes placed ads on Mets games for many years, as did Allstate Insurance, Sun Oil, and Shell. The lilting tones of "My beer is Rheingold, the dry beer" became indelibly linked with the Mets; it also became as famous an ad jingle as any in the land.

Following two years on WABC, where Howard Cosell served as pregame host, working with former Brooklyn pitcher Ralph Branca, the Mets signed a three-year deal in 1964 with WHN radio. WHN put together a 13-station network. That season, the Mets became the first club to broadcast its entire 81-game home schedule in color via WOR. The 52 road telecasts, though, remained monochromatic.

During the 1960s, the Mets tended to put Friday night, Saturday, and Sunday road games on the box, along with a few selected others. Five television stations in the Northeast also picked up a portion of the Mets' TV slate.

One of the most memorable days in Mets history came May 31, 1964, with the Giants in town for a Sunday doubleheader. San Francisco won the first game 5–3 in two hours and 29 minutes. Game 2 was a different story, as New York rallied from a 6–1 deficit to tie it up. The game went into extra innings…and extras…and more extra frames. Nelson, Murphy, and Kiner reported, almost disbelieving, the seemingly endless contest in which the clubs used 41 players. Willie Mays had to play shortstop, and Gaylord Perry tossed 10 innings in relief. The Mets had two relievers combine to pitch 16 innings.

After being held scoreless for 19 innings, the Giants finally pushed across two runs in the top of the 23rd, and the game came to a close after seven hours and 23 minutes as the twin bill consumed ten-and-a-half hours of airtime.

Befitting a bad team, the Mets engaged in their share of gimmicks, with Nelson once calling a game from a gondola in the Houston Astrodome some 200 feet in the air. Another time, Nelson reported from a blimp above Shea Stadium.

Prior to 1967, WHN landed the Yankees' broadcasts, forcing the Mets to find a new radio home. A triumvirate of smaller stations — WJRZ in Newark, WGLI on Long Island, and WNAB in Bridgeport, Connecticut — signed on as the club's new flagships with a three-year deal. While not having a station in the city itself was unusual, the Mets' new sponsorship deal with Liebmann netted a small raise as the brewery began selling off more ads to companies such as Allstate Insurance to increase revenue.

Because the new flagship stations were low-profile with low wattage, the Mets built a network of more than 40 stations for 1968 to make sure that their games could be heard all over the Northeast. In 1969, the Mets also signed WABC-FM as an affiliate.

The Miracle Mets' shocking 1969 world championship produced a windfall for the team's TV and radio partners. Ratings skyrocketed and, with the Yankees in a down cycle, the city was talking Mets all the time. Even having low-power radio outlets didn't dampen the fans' enthusiasm, as the voices of Nelson, Murphy, and Kiner were everywhere during the summer of 1969. After the season, a commemorative Mets LP album, *Miracle Mets*, was released, featuring interviews, play-by-play, and other memories of the magical year.

WJRZ decided in 1971 to change formats and forsake renewal of its Mets contract, so the Mets returned to WHN, which had dropped and then re-added sports. The three-year deal started in 1972, with 30 stations as part of a new network. Strangely, however, WHN did not clear time for Mets afternoon broadcasts on weekdays, other than for the home and road openers, meaning that fans literally could not hear all the team's games in 1972–1973. This bizarre policy, unheard of in baseball since the 1930s, was remedied due to fan protest, but not until 1974 — after colorful relief pitcher Tug McGraw's "Ya gotta believe" teammates had won the 1973 NL pennant.

By the early 1970s the Mets had changed their television plan, slowly cutting back on home games while increasing road telecasts. The number of games WOR showed generally hovered around 120.

In 1975, Nelson, Murphy, and Kiner called the Mets on WNEW-AM, which signed on for three years to do most regular-season games and some spring contests. WRVR-FM agreed to air the 17 weekday afternoon games as the club's network reached 25 stations. Unfortunately the Mets were entering a dark period on the field while the Yankees were on the way up, and ratings sagged. WRVR refused to broadcast weekday games in 1976, so WNEW shunted those contests to tiny city-owned WNYC, whose signal didn't even cover all five boroughs. WOR also refused to televise the team's Monday–Friday day games in 1976 as well.

After the 1977 season, the world champion Yankees jumped from WMCA to a bigger, better radio deal with WINS. The Mets, pleased to have an option to broadcast their entire schedule, filled the gap with WMCA via a deal that lasted through 1982.

Many teams at this time still did not spend the money to send their own camera crews on the road, instead accepting the feed from the home team's telecast while announcing over it. The pitfalls of such a practice became apparent on April 21, 1978. On a frigid day at Wrigley Field, with the Mets taking WGN's video feed, former Mets slugger Dave Kingman homered off New York's Craig Swan —"King Kong's" first round-tripper of the season. WGN replayed the home run seven times, enraging the Mets' TV announcers as well as more than a Mets few fans.

On January 8, 1979, Lindsey Nelson announced he was leaving the Mets' broadcast team. Two weeks later, he accepted the job as the Giants' radio voice. Within three days of Nelson's announcement, the Mets had received 50 resumés. Nelson did not explain his decision, other than averring that, with a daughter attending USC, the time was right to head west.

With Nelson gone, Bob Murphy felt that he had a chance to be the Mets' lead play-by-play man. Inexplicably, though, the Mets hired Steve Albert, who had no baseball experience, and declined to appoint a lead. The younger brother of prominent New York sportscaster Marv Albert, Steve filled Nelson's chair, but not his shoes, from 1979–1981. Albert injected some youthful energy into the broadcasts, but his talents were not compatible with baseball's pace. While adept at play-by-play, he had neither the knowledge to do analysis nor the temperament to offer any insight during the many "in-between" moments that occur during a baseball broadcast.

The emergence of cable television in the early 1980s put the Mets in a different situation than most other MLB franchises. Unlike most of their counterparts, the Mets in the late 1970s were still telecasting the majority of their games. In 1979, the year before the Mets first moved games to cable, WOR aired 99 Mets contests, which was the lowest number the club had ever permitted. WOR would have televised more had the team been competitive.

Before the cable sports revolution, most baseball teams saw local television foremost as a promotional tool and secondarily as a revenue stream. Thus clubs rationed TV home games carefully in order to protect their attendance. Given the immense physical size of the New York metropolitan area and the enormous size of its television market, however, local TV had long been one a primary revenue stream for both the Mets and Yankees (not to mention the Dodgers in the 1950s). So the Mets didn't hesitate to sign a deal before the 1980 season authorizing SportsChannel New York to air any games that Channel 9 eschewed broadcasting.

Cable TV was far from ubiquitous in metropolitan New York in 1980 as a result of legal disputes that kept four of the five boroughs without service until 1985. So the first year of Mets cable games was largely an experiment, and their quality was decidedly inferior to WOR's broadcasts, from production to announcing. SportsChannel's announcing team paired former Mets player Art Shamsky with local sportscaster Bob Goldsholl.

While SportsChannel's production quality remained mediocre for two decades, at least the cable net started using Murphy, Kiner, and Steve Albert in 1981. SCNY retained Shamsky that year to differentiate its broadcasts from Channel 9's, but the onetime World Series hero was soon let go.

In 1982, with SportsChannel in only 215,000 area homes, the network had no distinct Mets voice. Former Mets shortstop Bud Harrelson was hired to fill the "local hero" role for 1983, but he also didn't last, eventually winding up back in uniform as a coach. In the cable booth with Kiner and Harrelson was a new partner, Tim McCarver. Aside from Nelson's departure, McCarver's arrival was the most significant change to the team's broadcasting lineup since it went on the air in 1962.

Albert and Shamsky had been let go on the same day that manager Joe Torre was fired at the end of the 1981 season. The most significant change was not the shifting of personnel in the booth, but rather the change in broadcast philosophy. No longer would the team's announcers switch between radio and television, providing a similar experience in both media and ensuring continuity for the team and its sponsors. Now the radio and television broadcasts would be free to establish individual identities. In the long run, this shift would benefit the Mets as well as both Murphy and Kiner.

Mets GM Frank Cashen moved Bob Murphy exclusively to radio. Everyone, especially Murphy, considered it a demotion. Kiner was shifted entirely to television, where he could tell more stories and not worry about precision on the play-by-play. Cashen explained to a crestfallen Murphy that his skills were better suited to radio, but that hardly soothed the disappointment. Later, Murphy would realize that the "demotion" was the best thing that could have happened to him.

While television offers the most exposure, radio is still the ideal medium through which to broadcast baseball. Fans have to rely on the radio announcer's ability to paint word pictures of the game, and as a result a good announcer forms a far more intimate bond with radio listeners than anyone can on TV. People also listen to games in places where there is no television, such as in the car, while walking around town, in remote locations, or at the beach. In that subtle way, dozens of people within earshot can be instantly teleported to

Shea Stadium by — as New York commentator Mike Francesa liked to call Murphy — "The Voice of Summertime."

Hearing Murphy every day on the radio made Mets fans appreciate him even more. He was no homer, but he kept the broadcasts relentlessly positive. His folksy, warm style and homespun wisdom ensured that his calls always rang true, even when Murphy seemed happier than the final score would allow.

In 1994, Murphy was awarded the Ford C. Frick Award, an honor he almost certainly would have not received if not for his 1982 "demotion." Nelson had received the same prestigious award in 1988, three years after retiring from the Giants' baseball booth.

Working exclusively on radio, Murphy worked with Steve Lamar starting in 1982. Though Lamar came equipped with a mellifluous voice and a gift for language, he was not especially knowledgeable about baseball and did not seem dedicated to becoming more so; his analysis often consisted solely of agreeing with whatever Murphy had just said. After three years, the Mets and WFAN (formerly WHN) replaced him with Gary Thorne.

Lorn Brown teamed with Kiner on WOR and SportsChannel in 1982. While Brown was pleasant, his style was understated and he often filled airtime with tedious statistics. Kiner, rendered ineffective without an engaging partner, was as a consequence often left flailing, and Brown lasted only one year in Flushing.

The Mets hired Tim McCarver for 1983 to liven things up — and did he ever. The ex-catcher was everything Brown was not. Folksy, energetic, and irreverent, McCarver immediately put a charge into Mets broadcasts. Talkative but not overly so during his early years with the Mets, McCarver pulled Kiner back into the swing of things and brought Kiner's baseball IQ to the fore.

Immediately, McCarver displayed an eagerness to bring viewers inside the game and to inform them of the finer points of on-field strategy and tactics. That eagerness would eventually try the patience of some viewers, but at first it was universally welcomed, as was McCarver's willingness to criticize the Mets when necessary.

Fran Healy arrived in the Mets' booth in 1984 as SportsChannel's "house broadcaster" after several years describing the Yankees on the RSN. In 1981, WPIX executive producer Art Adler had fired Healy from the station's Yankees games because of poor play-by-play skills and his refusal to take voice lessons. Given that, who would have guessed that Healy would remain in the Mets broadcast booth for 22 years? Few sports broadcasters have worked for two decades without being embraced by either fans or critics.

Curt Smith wrote in *Voices of the Game* that announcers such as Healy seem to "consider it…their martial call to reshape baseball in a cast of boredom." Handicapped with a poor voice, Healy rarely added any "inside the game" insights that viewers like to hear from ex-players, even though he was an ex-catcher like McCarver. Healy was liked by most of his partners and knew baseball and its history, but those qualities do not by themselves make a good broadcaster. His interviewing skills were good, which made him a competent host for the *Mets Weekly* highlight show and in other long-form interview programs.

Longtime fan favorite Rusty Staub, who had just retired, joined Healy in the booth in 1986. From 1986–1988 Healy was the fourth announcer on all telecasts, after which he went exclusively to cable to replace McCarver, who was cutting back on his commitment to the Mets.

Kiner, Healy, and Staub telecast nearly every Mets cable game through 1995, though the combination was not felicitous. Staub showed obvious personal appeal, yet never fully adjusted to broadcasting; he was unable to shake his ballplayer mentality and was loath to criticize. He tended, when teamed with Healy, to discuss everything but the game.

Meanwhile, McCarver's star was rising by the mid-1980s, as were the fortunes of the resurgent Mets. By 1986, McCarver was ABC's top national baseball analyst and appeared on the cover of GQ magazine, which praised McCarver's "wit, southern charm, [and] baseball savvy."

Local TV critics also sung McCarver's praises. Phil Mushnick of the *New York Post* allowed that "McCarver is hotter than a five-alarm bowl of chili." Neil Postman, professor of communications at New York University, called McCarver "uncanny." The academic further enthused, "His [McCarver's] command of language is surprisingly sophisticated. One wouldn't expect that sentence structure from someone who spent all those years behind the plate."

Overexposure, along with a penchant for awful puns and occasional preaching, led some viewers to protest that McCarver didn't know when to stop, but he was for many years America's preeminent television baseball analyst and has announced more World Series games on television than anyone else.

Two other Mets mikemen of the same era, Gary Thorne and Steve Zabriskie, are often remembered fondly, which has a lot to do with the Mets' success at the time they worked.

Thorne, an attorney, had caught the ear of several prominent baseball observers while broadcasting the Triple-A Maine Guides, a team in which he also had an ownership stake. Thorne proved to be an energetic and deferential partner to Murphy when brought on board in 1984. Perhaps due to his legal training, Thorne's approach to his job was very different from Lamar's; Thorne soaked up information and rarely was at a loss for words — as Murphy's second chair he was an asset.

Zabriskie came on board in 1983, the same year as McCarver. The Californian had come to attention doing play-by-play for USA Network's *Thursday Game of the Week* national package in 1982. While Zabriskie worked the team's entertaining and successful run through the 1980s, he came off a little like vanilla compared to partner Tim McCarver's chocolate sundae with extra toppings. Relegated to the shrinking schedule of over-the-air games, Zabriskie faded from the picture by the end of the decade, leaving just Kiner and McCarver on Channel 9.

In 1987, as cable found its way into an increasing percentage of the New York market, the Mets decided to split their TV schedule evenly between WWOR-TV (the station added an extra "W" to its call letters in 1987) and SportsChannel. While this increased the club's local profile on cable, it decreased the Mets' exposure across the country.

WOR/WWOR was retransmitted by the Comsat satellite and seen by fans all over the country in the mid-1980s. This meant Kiner became a national figure, perhaps as much for his frequent and funny malaprops as for his skills. When Gary Carter first joined the Mets, he sometimes was transformed into "Gary Cooper," and Kiner once referred to his partner as "Tim McArthur." Cubs star second baseman Ryne Sandberg caused Kiner the most trouble: he might be "Ryne Sandbag" one day and "Ryne Rhineberg" on another.

Other Kiner-style Yogi-isms included: "All of the Met road wins this year against the Dodgers are at Dodger Stadium"; "Today is Father's Day, so everybody out there, Happy Birthday"; "All of his saves have come during relief appearances"; "He's going to be out of action the rest of his career"; and "If Casey Stengel were alive today, he'd be spinning in his grave."

Verbal gaffes aside, Kiner communicated well. Not only was he a great storyteller, but he was also ahead of his time. His own style of hitting — power and walks — returned to vogue in the 1990s thanks in part to the rise in prominence of sabermetric research. Of course, Kiner didn't do statistical analysis; like Ted Williams, he smartly thought it made sense to combine patience and aggressiveness at the plate. As Kiner liked to say, "Home run hitters drive Cadillacs and singles hitters drive Fords."

As with most broadcasters who stay in place for decades, Kiner's career with the Mets endured ups and downs. Seriously unhappy about the sale of the club during the Linda de Roulet era, he applied for a job with the Dodgers in 1977. Los Angeles eventually went with Ross Porter and Kiner settled permanently in Flushing.

The widely praised Murphy-Thorne partnership on radio lasted only four years, ending after 1988 because Frank Cashen was upset at the number of games Thorne missed in order to broadcast the NHL's New Jersey Devils.

Queens native Gary Cohen replaced Thorne on radio in 1989. Though Cohen had never before broadcast for a major league team, six years of broadcasting minor-league ball made him ready for The Show. And growing up as a hardcore Mets fan in the 1960s and 1970s enabled Cohen to come up with historical comparisons and tidbits quickly and effectively.

Cohen immediately proved to be a technically proficient partner for Murphy; few announcers convey what happens on the field as well as Cohen. Unfortunately, he lacked the chemistry with Murphy that Thorne had shown. It seemed almost as if Cohen respected Murphy too much to banter with him. Cohen didn't really loosen up on the air until being paired with Howie Rose, who had also grown up a Mets fan. The two shared an easy chemistry in the booth.

Thorne returned to the Mets, primarily on over-the-air games, in 1994. His enthusiasm remained infectious, but his strengths on radio sometimes seemed like "too much information" coming from a lead TV announcer. The rapidly diminishing number of games on broadcast television also made it harder for Thorne and his partners to establish a good working rhythm. With multiple opportunities available to him, Thorne again left the Mets after the 2002 season.

McCarver's term with the Mets, meanwhile, ended after 1998 when the club decided it no longer would tolerate his on-air criticisms. After cutting ties with someone as high-profile as McCarver, New York management knew they had they couldn't hire just any announcer as a replacement. So the franchise went out and bagged "The Franchise": Tom Seaver.

The oddest aspect about Seaver's hiring was that it had taken so long for the club to retain the Hall of Famer in some capacity. Seaver had not been employed by the organization since the White Sox plucked him off the Mets' roster in the 1984 free-agent draft. (Seaver tried a brief comeback with the Mets before retiring for good in 1987, but signed no contract). By the time the Mets hired "Tom Terrific," he had already worked five years as an analyst on WPIX's Yankees telecasts. Seaver also had network postseason broadcasting experience dating back to the 1970s.

Mets fans were glad to have Seaver back in the fold, but the Hall of Famer's broadcasting skills were not as fluid as his pitching motion. Like McCarver, Seaver was a genuine student of the game, but his presentation was far drier: McCarver was often effusive, but Seaver could come off as reserved or even guarded.

Always alert and attentive to the action, Seaver never seemed to have his heart fully invested in broadcasting. Like most ex-pitchers behind the mike, his almost exclusive focus on pitching analysis was understandable, but not ideal. It seems as if the studiousness and professionalism that had made Seaver one of the game's greatest pitchers made it impossible for him to be a great announcer. After seven seasons, both Seaver and Mets fans were ready to move on.

By this time, the Mets were seen almost exclusively on cable. In 1997, SportsChannel for the first time had broadcast a clear majority of their games. In 1998, Fox Sports, rapidly expanding its family of regional cable sports networks, acquired most of the SportsChannel franchises. The technical quality of the broadcasts improved with Fox's increased spending, and Kiner, Healy, and Staub remained at the mikes.

In the final four years of the Mets' contract with Fox Sports Net, the network aired half its Mets games on the Madison Square Garden channel (which had earlier merged with FSN) because MSG had lost the Yankees to the team's own YES Network.

Kiner struggled with facial paralysis caused by Bell's palsy in 1998, but by the next year was able to fully enunciate again and returned to the booth for a full slate. He semi-retired after 2002 but returned for 10-15 broadcasts each year through 2013, his 52nd season broadcasting the Mets.

After he retired from game-calling, Kiner's bloopers grew even more legendary — whether it was referring to himself as "Ralph Korner" or announcing an upcoming commercial from "Manufacturers Hangover" bank. Like Jerry Coleman, Kiner came to be defined as much by his verbal missteps as by his accomplished playing and broadcasting. Which is a shame.

The Mets' television broadcasts improved when Gary Cohen transferred to the tube in 2005. A stellar game-caller on radio, he successfully shifted gears to become more of a conversationalist. Cohen's move to TV meant that Howie Rose ascended to the role of the club's top radio man. It would be hard to find a baseball announcer who identifies with his team more than Rose, who seems to have spent his entire life preparing to be a Mets announcer.

The Brooklyn-born Rose started his career doing updates for Sportsphone; in New York in 1975, calling 976-1313 was the fastest way to get the latest scores. Twelve years later, WHN radio hired Rose to host Mets Extra, a pregame and postgame show. When WHN morphed into WFAN, the nation's first all-sports radio station, Rose picked up the weekday evening slot when there wasn't a Mets game, soon proving that there was nothing about the club's history that he didn't know.

Rose broke into play-by-play in the early 1990s with the NHL's New York Rangers, calling the team's first Stanley Cup triumph in 54 years. Rose occasionally appeared on Mets cablecasts starting in 1996. Seven years later, with Bob Murphy's retirement approaching, Rose's cameos shifted to radio.

After Murphy retired on September 25, 2003, there were no more of Murphy's "happy recaps"; the iconic announcer died of lung cancer the next summer.

The Mets wore commemorative patches in his honor for the rest of the 2004 season, and the radio booth at Shea Stadium was renamed in his honor. Kiner said, "It's like losing a brother. We worked together for 40-plus years. We did everything together; we went to movies, ate together and traveled together. It's so hard to fathom he's gone. It's been a terrible year for me. First I lose my wife to cancer and now Bob. I just pray that he was at peace at the end."

Rose became Cohen's full-time No. 2 in 2004. When Cohen moved to television the next year, Rose assumed the captain's seat on radio, initially working with former Phillies mikeman Tom McCarthy. After three seasons in which he did not seem to create much of an impression, McCarthy returned to the Phillies as journeyman Wayne Hagin joined the radio team for 2008. Ed Coleman, who took over as Mets Extra host in 1996, occasionally filled in on play-by-play.

Successful because of his genuine enthusiasm and extensive knowledge, Rose's play-calling is accurate, but his voice and command of language are not especially memorable. He is fair and does not hesitate to criticize when it's called for. He occasionally gets too excited, but he never patronizes the fans, who accept him as one of them.

The Mets and WFAN declined to retain Hagin for 2012, replacing him with Josh Lewin, for several years the TV voice of the Rangers. This is Lewin's first shot at doing big-league ball on the radio. Lewin and Texas had parted ways after 2010 because the club (and many listeners) objected to the announcer's commitment to broadcast the NFL's San Diego Chargers, which took him out of town on August and September weekends. The Mets tolerate it, however.

Consistent with the franchise's overall thoughtful planning about broadcasting, the Mets produced Spanish-language broadcasts from Day One. The Brooklyn Dodgers had established Spanish-language broadcasts in their market before moving to Los Angeles, and the Mets enthusiastically embraced the concept. The original radio team of Miguel Angel Torres and Salomon Volpe were behind the microphones from the club's inception through 1973 on WHOM radio.

Former major league infielder Jose Valdivielso, Juan Vene, and legendary Latino voice Eloy "Buck" Canel took over the broadcasts in 1974 on a network organized by Vene to carry games throughout Latin America from 1969–1986.

Buck Canel was the first Spanish-language broadcaster to win the Frick Award (posthumously in 1985, five years after his death) and among the most influential voices in the history of the sport. He started calling major league action in the late 1930s, broadcasting the Dodgers' final three years in Flatbush and also handling some Yankees games. Canel was at the microphone for many big games — World Series, All-Star, and crucial regular-season contests — for decades, with his voice carrying throughout Latin America on various radio networks.

Many ballplayers from Latin America grew up listening to Canel describe big-league action. As a result the announcer developed an almost messianic following in Cuba, Mexico, Puerto Rico, the Dominican, and in Central America, making it easy for him to get interviews with players who had grown up under his spell.

In 1982 Juan Alicea, who had been working for the Mets in various capacities since 1969, teamed with Vene in the booth. Alicea was a Puertorriqueño raised in New York City. After joining the Mets, he worked as a scout and in the community relations and broadcasting departments before going on-air. With three consecutive decades in the broadcast booth, Alicea had more service time than any Mets broadcaster in history besides Kiner and Murphy.

The 1983 season was Vene's last year in the booth and Max Perez Jimenez's first. The next year, Oscar Polo joined the team. The Polo, Alicea, and Jimenez trio worked together through the Mets' championship season of 1986.

In 1987, Billy Berroa and Armando Talavera joined Alicea, serving until 1990 when Renato Morffi was added to make the Mets' Spanish broadcasting team a quartet. Those four announcers split the broadcasts through 1993, at which point Berroa and Talavera left.

Berroa, who had been broadcasting games long before the Mets were born, was the top baseball announcer in the Dominican Republic before moving part-time to the U.S. He was honored with induction into the Dominican Republic Sports Hall of Fame in 1998. He returned to the Mets' booth in 1997, replacing Morffi, and partnered with Alicea in one of the most highly-regarded broadcasting teams in the majors. Unfortunately, just as the Mets signed a deal to have their Spanish-language announcers do 25 simulcasts of cable games, Berroa fell ill and died in 2007. Jimenez, already back part-time, replaced him.

In 2006, following years of planning and negotiation, the Mets followed the Yankees' lead and launched their own regional sports network, SportsNet New York (SNY). Both

Time Warner Cable and Comcast invested in the venture, with the latter handling negotiations to put the channel on satellite and local cable systems.

The Mets' new RSN differed from YES in ways other than negotiating style. While YES is unabashedly Yankees-centric — often hagiographic — in historical broadcasts, SNY has established strong sports news programming across the board, with the requisite Mets' programming sprinkled in.

SNY sells about two dozen Mets games each year to WPIX, which after many years as the Yankees' over-the-air station, started airing Mets games in 1999. Longtime Mets rights holder WWOR-TV now handles over-the-air Yankees games.

Along with the network came a new announcing trio: Cohen, Ron Darling, and Keith Hernandez, all three familiar to Mets fans. Cohen had already called play-by-play on WFAN for 17 years as well as for one season on Fox. With either Darling or Hernandez (often both) in the booth with him, Cohen's role shifted to ringmaster rather than play-by-play announcer. He adapted well to television, and relaxing his on-air persona significantly since he first came on the air.

Hernandez and Darling were key components of the 1986 world champions; the former had been an occasional contributor to Mets telecasts since 1999, while Darling had a year of experience on Washington Nationals telecasts.

The disparate trio gelled quickly even though the three announcers do not have strongly defined roles. Cohen does play-by-play, but neither Hernandez nor Darling assumes the role of a typical ex-jock. Darling is unusually incisive and thoughtful, while Hernandez — willing to poke fun at himself via advertisements and in that famous episode of *Seinfeld* — skillfully plays the "loose cannon" role.

Little of the trio's repartee sounds scripted. Cohen, in fact, has described the broadcasts as similar to free-form jazz. While it's unusual to compare viewing a Mets game to listening to Ornette Coleman, there is some relevance to the analogy, as all three are capable of engaging in long digressions, especially during lulls in the game. Those digressions often provide far more interesting than the oft-clichéd analyses of other announcers. Cohen and his team are also not afraid to cover the game from different locations in the ballpark, like the upper deck on a May afternoon during Shea Stadium's final year in 2008, or the Pepsi Porch at Citi Field during a hot night in 2011.

Unfortunately, the three are only together in the booth approximately 60 times per year. For the remaining games, Cohen works with one or the other.

The Mets' new team is the most popular group of announcers to inhabit Flushing Meadows since Nelson, Murphy, and Kiner. Today's broadcasters carry over the original group's professionalism, minimizing "homerism" while commanding the respect and affection of the fans.

As the Mets continued a tough rebuild after moving to new Citi Field, change intruded on the radio broadcasts. The club's deal with WFAN expired following the 2013 season, and the Yankees signed a deal to be heard over the all-sports behemoth. That left the Mets, coming off a 74–88 campaign, without a radio home after being with the Fan for 27 seasons.

There would be no shortage of suitors for the team, but few could match WFAN's 50,000-watt signal, which allowed for huge coverage in the Northeast. (Ironically, both WFAN and the Yankees' former home, WCBS, are owned by CBS radio.)

Early in November 2013, the Mets officially moved to WOR-AM, a Clear Channel station and, like WFAN, a 50,000-watt blowtorch. The two parties signed up for five years, but the deal does not include simulcasts on WOR-FM. The futures of lead announcer Howie Rose and #2 Josh Lewin remained secure.

Sadly, Ralph Kiner passed away on February 6, 2014, bringing to an end the team's final link to its 1962 broadcasts. Kiner was 91.

On the field, the history of the New York Mets is one of several memorable championship crests interrupting long droughts of futility. In the executive suites, the Mets' ownership history has been erratic and sometimes contentious. In the broadcast booths, however, the club's half-century history has been generally well-planned, marked by forethought, consistency, and judicious risk-taking. Whether the team's starting nine were awful or exceptional, their broadcasting teams have typically bonded with their fans in a way all clubs strive for, but not all achieve.

STEPCHILDREN OF THE GOLDEN WEST

THE SAN DIEGO PADRES BROADCASTING HISTORY

"You can hang a star on that baby!"
— Jerry Coleman

FROM 1949-68, SOUTHERN CALIFORNIA BASEBALL FANS ENJOYED
veteran Al Schuss' radio broadcasts of the Pacific Coast League Padres, variously affiliated
with the White Sox, Reds, and Phillies in the 1960s.

When the National League granted San Diego an expansion franchise for 1969, however,
the major league Padres shunned local hero Schuss and instead searched outside the city
for well-known veteran broadcasters with big-league experience. The club announced the
hiring of its on-air trio — Frank Sims, Jerry Gross, and Duke Snider — in late August 1968.

Sims had been the third man in the Phillies' booth from 1960–62 before calling games
for the Dodgers' short-lived 1964 foray into pay TV. Gross, third behind Harry Caray and
Jack Buck in St. Louis from 1963–67, was hired to share time with Sims. The Padres selected
former Dodgers superstar Snider to be the color analyst. Sims and Snider certainly were
familiar to the new club's management, which was headed by former Dodgers GM Buzzie
Bavasi, the Padres' first president. Snider served as a scout and spring training instructor
for the club as well as a color man.

Gross had local connections as the broadcaster of the NBA's expansion San Diego Rockets
(soon to relocate to Houston), while Sims had put in several years with The Sports Network,
a company that rented video trucks and equipment in multiple cities for producing sports

broadcasts. He had also done Michigan and Michigan State sports as well as Detroit Pistons basketball.

Unfortunately for everyone concerned, nobody at flagship station KOGO or in the Padres' front office designated a No. 1 announcer. In fact, Bavasi made a point of refusing to make either Sims or Gross the top dog. Therefore, the two "co-lead" broadcasters developed an uncomfortable balance that soon became a bitter rivalry. Sims departed after 1970, with Gross and Snider following a year later.

In 1969, KOGO radio-TV paid the Padres $700,000 for exclusive broadcast rights only to eventually learn that they couldn't book enough advertising to pay for the six road telecasts originally scheduled. U.S. National Bank was one of the club's most reliable early guarantors, but both television and radio sponsorships seemed very hard to come by in the early going.

Part of the problem with televising the new club was the team's location. Line charges to transmit away games over AT&T could cost thousands of dollars per game in the late 1960s. A club official told Television Age in 1969 that it would cost $10,000 just to beam one Sunday telecast from St. Louis back to San Diego.

The expansion Padres were terrible on the field and not a lot better in the booth. Following a June 13 loss to Philadelphia at San Diego, Jerry Gross tried to interview Richie Allen for his postgame show. Allen — annoyed to learn that his fee for the show was a supply of trading stamps — said, on-air, that he refused to do an interview for something so relatively valueless. Allen later admitted that he didn't like Gross, so the temperamental slugger may have wanted to purposely embarrass the broadcaster on the air.

Taking the opposite approach, two of the other three 1969 expansion teams, Kansas City and Montreal, had their eyes on the future and hired young voice talent. Denny Matthews and Dave Van Horne, respectively, became cornerstones of their nascent franchises' identity, and both continue to broadcast today. By contrast, neither of the Padres' first play-by-play men enjoyed long or distinguished careers.

Sims, following his Padres experience, never broadcast baseball again, working instead in various front offices. Gross' only future baseball work was with the Padres for a small slate of 1978 TV games — which he called, ironically, with Al Schuss.

While the Padres foundered on the diamond in their first decade, management did make a couple of excellent off-field moves before the 1972 season, calling on Jerry Coleman and Bob Chandler to serve as their voices.

Coleman, a World War II and Korean War hero as a Marine Corps pilot, had starred at second base for the Yankees in the 1950s and had served on New York's broadcast crew from 1963 through 1969. A longtime favorite in San Diego for his affable manner and humorous malapropisms, Coleman in 2006 cut back his schedule to include only home games yet remained a great ambassador of San Diegos baseball.

Chandler, a respected local sportscaster, served as the Padres' television broadcaster for their tiny slate of games in 1969, then helped negotiate a deal to get the team on his home station, KCST, for 1970. For the next three seasons, Chandler described the Padres' road telecasts, all of which originated from Los Angeles and San Francisco due to their relatively limited production costs. Starting in 1972, he also spelled Coleman on the radio. Over the years, Chandler dealt capably with a myriad of different radio and TV partners, becoming a favorite for his class and adaptability as well as for his smooth, easygoing manner.

San Diego retained its own TV and radio rights in the early 1970s, assuming all costs for producing its broadcasts. Unfortunately, the team was bad enough on the field that few advertisers wanted to underwrite the games.

In addition to being bad, the Padres were — even worse — uninteresting, so much so that they could not obtain a local television deal for several years in the mid-1970s. It had been more than a decade since a big-league team went without a single local TV broadcast; the Milwaukee Braves in 1961 had been the last to be completely dark.

Like most teams in smaller markets, San Diego initially eschewed televising home games: the club didn't show a game from Jack Murphy Stadium until 1984, when they aired a slate on Cox Cable.

One area in which the Padres were very progressive was in Spanish-language radio. Starting in 1969, XEXX aired the new club's games with Arnaldo Sanchez Fontes as the lead and Mario Thomas as his second chair. Thomas took over the lead the next year and served until 1997. Both the legendary Thomas and current play-by-play man Eduardo Ortega hail from Mazatlán, Mexico.

The Padres are currently one of only a handful of teams broadcasting the entire schedule on Spanish-language radio. The club maintains its strong ties with the local Latino community through myriad marketing efforts, including showing TV games with Spanish audio, which they began in 1992.

Another former second baseman — Dave Campbell, who played with San Diego from 1970–72 — joined the radio team in 1978. Chandler moved to public relations, although he returned to the San Diego booth a couple of years later and spent many years as a sort of broadcast utility man through 2001. Having already sat in the radio booth for a dozen games while on the disabled list in 1972, the articulate Campbell had the voice, experience, and even the suntan to be a media star.

Once Campbell smoothed out his delivery, he became even more important to the radio package, especially in 1980, when Coleman stepped down into for a disastrous single season as the Padres' manager. When Coleman returned to the booth, Ted Leitner also joined the broadcast team.

Leitner, a successful, garrulous on-air presence who speaks of the team as "my Padres," has a most unusual announcing timbre. He is a novelty among broadcasters in the way he leaves empty space. Many in conservative San Diego who don't agree with his liberal politics still enjoy his work for the Pads as well as for San Diego State sports (and, formerly, for the NFL Chargers and NBA Clippers). Just as many who do agree with his point of view can become annoyed with his unusual turns of phrase and off-balance phrasing.

When the station where Leitner worked, KFMB, took over the Padres' telecasting rights in 1980, he was off and running. KFMB lost the club's telecasting rights after three seasons, but Leitner remained as a pay cable telecaster, also starting to work some of KFMB's radio broadcasts in the mid-1980s. When KOGO outbid competitors for the radio rights in 2000, Leitner moved to KOGO, assuming more of the workload as Coleman slowed down. XPRS obtained San Diego's radio rights in 2004, with Leitner remaining the lead voice.

After their youthful struggles, the Padres eventually matured as a team and a media property, with 1984 the watershed year. Not only did the team institute its first cable-casts — Cox Cable, a pay-per-view setup, produced 40 home games — but the Padres also won their first pennant after 15 years of never finishing higher than fourth in the NL West Division.

For the first time in club history, fans could watch their local heroes on the tube when they were playing at home, and they could also view an all-time high of 85 TV games between pay cable and over-the-air. Due to the fact that Cox was not universally available in the San Diego area, the club's 1984 media revenue of $2.4 million was, as usual for the Padres, near the bottom of the league. Cox's local market penetration remained limited for years, even after the local channel spun off and rebranded itself the San Diego Cable Sports Network.

The number of TV games broadcast grew in the coming years as San Diego went with a consistent four-man team: Coleman and Campbell on radio and free TV, with Leitner and Chandler serving as the relief team on radio while also calling the cable TV games. Campbell departed in 1989, replaced by Rick Monday, who stayed a few years before landing a job with the Dodgers.

Prior to 1986, the Padres signed new TV, English-language radio, Spanish-language radio, and cable contracts as they opted to return to producing their own radio broadcasts, selling ad time themselves and paying KFMB a fee to air the contests. Even with a very successful cable package, San Diego's rights revenue ranked lowest in the NL. While the Padres had a wealthy and dedicated fan base, the club's small market and proximity to Los Angeles limited its ability to broaden its coverage geographically — and, therefore, grow its media dollars.

In the early 1990s, San Diego Cable Sports Network went under, with various cable outlets including Fox, Prime, and Cox picking up the baton to carry Padres games. By that time, free TV broadcasts were on their way out in San Diego, as they were in many other cities.

In 1997, the club, in association with Cox, unveiled C4 Padres, a local cable outlet that showed 96 games, roughly evenly split between home and road. Veteran Mel Proctor took over as the team's TV announcer, both on C4 Padres and for a 23-game Sunday package on KUSI. Proctor was the team's first dedicated TV announcer since the cable revolution began; former pitchers Mark Grant and Rick Sutcliffe split analyst duties.

Following 2001, when the team's Sunday deal with KUSI ran out, games aired only on C4 Padres, with about 140 games per season being seen on the cable net. The enthusiastic

Matt Vasgersian took over as the play-by-play announcer, staying until the MLB Network hired him after 2008.

Hall of Fame right fielder Tony Gwynn joined the telecasts on a part-time basis in 2005, lending authentic first-person Padres playing history to the broadcasts. With Sutcliffe leaving after a short term, Grant remained the No. 1 television color man.

With Leitner firmly in control on radio, and Coleman working a smaller slate of games, the Padres needed a third radio voice in 2006. They hired Andy Masur, who had spent nearly a decade with the Cubs' radio team, as a host, third chair, and all-around fill-in. Good in his role, Masur also showed a wicked sense of humor on occasion.

Even when San Diego's nine sank into the lower levels of the NL West, their broadcasts remained professional. Vasgersian's departure led to the hiring in 2009 of Mark Neely, a proper professional voice who had put in his time in the minors, working all over the country for various teams at all levels.

The hiring of Masur and Neely, and Bob Scanlan's employment as a radio color man starting in 2011, gave a clear hint about the need to plan for the future; Leitner and Coleman have served long and well as spokesmen for the team, but new voices were needed to engage a new generation of San Diego fans. This obvious truth made the late 2009 announcement of Dick Enberg's hiring so shocking.

The 74-year-old Enberg was handed the no. 1 TV role, with Neely being bumped to a secondary spot after just one season. Enberg, a generalist who has done football, golf, and tennis as well as other sports, had not had worked a regular gig in baseball since a stint with the Angels in 1985. But Enberg, inducted into the Sports Broadcasting Hall of Fame in December 2009, wanted back into the game and found a willing partner.

The Padres have always been hampered by their small market and by the long shadow of the Dodgers and the Angels to the north. Yet after a difficult birth and infancy, San Diego managed to hire broadcasters that would develop the kind of deep, long-lived bonds with the community that are crucial to keeping fans as listeners and viewers — especially when they have so many alternative entertainment options. One of the few downsides of such longevity is difficulty in transitioning to a new era.

Perhaps mixing his baseball metaphors, Enberg averred at his welcoming press conference that he still had his fastball at his age, but couldn't locate it as well. The reverse is likely true: the well-traveled veteran can still spot his mediocre stuff, but there's not as much gas in the tank. Enberg's presence risks that this could become true of San Diego's broadcasts as well.

While Enberg's work in San Diego has shown his continuing competence behind the mike, and he works well with Grant, it is also clear that the team's broadcasts feel a little less than topical and a little less than relevant. Mark Neely did not stick around, as Enberg's fame and favored position seemed like a guarantee that he could work as long as he wanted.

Following several months of speculation, the Padres announced in August 2011 their intention to sever their association with Channel 4, the team's cable carrier since 1997. Shortly after, the club inked a 20-year broadcast deal with the new Fox Sports San Diego. The first year of the deal promised the Padres some $28 million, and by the end of the contract the annual fee could be nearly three times as high.

Unfortunately, moving to a new cable home proved difficult, and many local systems, balking at the price asked by Fox Sports, did not pick up the Padres' games in 2012. By the end of the season, most local carriers had signed on, but Time Warner, which is in one of five area households, had still not agreed to carry Fox Sports San Diego.

Early in 2012, Fox hired a new pregame and postgame host, Mike Pomeranz, who had been a news anchor in Minneapolis. Pomeranz, a former minor-league pitcher, is seen as a comer; he announced a slate of spring training contests in 2013.

In retrospect, Jerry Coleman—a former New York Yankee and a genuine war hero—was always a great fit for San Diego. He brought his deep knowledge, friendly voice, and occasional scrambled phrases to Padres broadcasts from 1972 until his death in early 2014. (SD Dirk)

The Padres also moved Bob Scanlan, previously a pregame/postgame analyst, into the regular radio rotation. In addition, beginning in 2013, Andy Masur shifted part-time to television, doing 25 games of play-by-play as Dick Enberg reduced his schedule to some 120 contests.

But even that wasn't the end of change. Early in 2014 the Padres announced that Andy Masur had been let go in favor of Jesse Agler, a Miami sports reporter with no baseball in his profile. To be fair, Agler was really hired to manage the Padres' social media function, with some broadcast duties thrown in. When working in Florida, Agler apparently caught the eye of Mike Dee, formerly the Miami Dolphins' CEO, who took the same job with the Padres in 2013.

Mark Sweeney, usually a field reporter for Fox, took on some color work in 2014, subbing on occasion for Mark Grant. Mike Pomeranz also increased his workload.

Sadly, the Padres took two big hits in 2014.

First, Jerry Coleman passed away at age 89 on January 5, 2014. While Coleman had been doing only 30 or so games, all from Petco Park, over the last few seasons, he was still an icon.

Then, Hall of Fame right fielder Tony Gwynn, an occasional Padres TV color man for a decade, died on June 16. Both men have statues outside of Petco Park; neither man is replaceable.

DAVE IN THE (NIE) HAUS

SEATTLE MARINERS BROADCASTING HISTORY

"It will fly away!"
— *Dave Niehaus' home run call*

SEATTLE'S FIRST EXPERIENCE WITH MAJOR LEAGUE BASEBALL WAS short and bitter, as the expansion American League Pilots debuted in April 1969 and departed a year later. Under political pressure, the AL awarded the city a second expansion team to begin play in 1977, and, while it took two decades for the club to become a contender, the Mariners captured the imagination and hearts of the Pacific Northwest much sooner.

One reason for the club's popularity was Dave Niehaus, the Mariners' longtime voice. In his nearly 35 years with the franchise, Niehaus became a household name in the Northwest, describing the exploits of local heroes like Glenn Abbott, Alvin Davis, Alex Rodriguez, and Felix Hernandez.

Born in 1935, Niehaus called games for both the Yankees and Dodgers for the Armed Forces Radio Network in the 1950s and 1960s. He started doing play-by-play for the NFL's Los Angeles Rams in 1966. In 1970, Niehaus joined the Angels broadcast team — beating several other candidates including football voice Keith Jackson — when Steve Bailey bowed out to head the Golden West Sports Network.

Niehaus, as No. 3 in Anaheim behind Dick Enberg and Don Wells (and later Don Drysdale), did pregame and postgame shows and called the plays during the middle innings. It was a good gig and, although he lost the Rams' assignment in 1973, he filled his winters with UCLA football and basketball. Already a big name in Southern California, Niehaus still threw his hat in the ring for a broadcasting job when the AL again expanded for 1977.

What led the Mariners to choose Niehaus? For starters, he knew AL teams and players well, especially the West Division; he had baseball experience; and he sported a rich, enthusiastic timbre. The M's signed Niehaus and 29-year-old Ken Wilson, his sidekick, to three-year deals in December 1976. Unlike Niehaus, Wilson had no previous big-league experience, though he had done Triple-A ball in Hawaii and was handsome, well-spoken, and ambitious. Wilson's lack of experience soon became apparent, however: probably the best trick in his bag was the exclamation, "Oh, Baby!"

Far removed from the whirl and twirl of Los Angeles and San Francisco, Seattle was somewhat parochial about its sports teams — quite natural given its experience with the Pilots and with Major League Baseball. Bill Schonely, the Pilots' No. 2 voice in 1969, was strongly considered for one of the jobs in the Seattle booth, but was passed over. The fact that neither Niehaus nor Wilson had any prior connection to the Pacific Northwest rankled some.

Nonetheless, Niehaus quickly quelled any resentment with his enthusiastic manner and distinctive phrasings. Few contemporary announcers bother to create a special home run call for a grand slam, or alter their voices to a near-growl when the home team does something particularly exciting, but Niehaus was both excitable — with his trademark "My, oh, my!" — and fun to listen to throughout his long career.

KVI, the Pilots' flagship in 1969, became the new team's first flagship station. It was a smart gambit: the Pacific Northwest was fertile territory, with an expanding, upscale market. Thus in 1977, despite a tiny television package, the Mariners made $800,000 in broadcast revenue — nearly as much as Baltimore, more than Texas or Milwaukee, and more than twice that of the Royals.

Seattle management chose to retain its radio rights in 1977, buying air time for the broadcasts on KVI and hiring a local agency to sell the commercial spots on behalf of the club. By 1979, KVI was itself selling the ad time, and the station purchased the Mariners' rights in the early 1980s.

While the Mariners proved popular in Seattle, their radio network — which began with 25 stations — fell to 15 in 1978 and just 10 by 1979. This type of decline is not unusual; the novelty wears off unless the new club wins immediately.

Seattle's 1977 TV package was the smallest in the American League. KING-TV, the club's first flagship, broadcast just 17 games with six other

Hired as the Seattle Mariners' first radio voice, Dave Niehaus brought his big voice and hearty appetite for language to the northwest and outlasted some initial fan and media skepticism to become a beloved regional figure. "It will fly away!" (National Baseball Hall of Fame and Museum)

stations in the network. Apparently viewing television as nothing more than an occasional promotional tool for ticket sales, Seattle did not permit a home telecast until 1982 and, until 1995, local fans could not even view half the team's games.

In the days before cable television brought near-ubiquitous coverage, radio was the quotidian baseball experience for most dedicated fans — radio broadcasters were the team's voice and, in many ways, its identity. So a crucial part of the announcers' job back then was off-season promotion. Some broadcasters worked in their team's publicity departments during the winter; others were tasked with building the franchise's radio network by grooming or stroking local broadcast executives in the hinterland. Winter caravans had been part of most clubs' marketing since the 1920s or 1930s, bringing players, broadcasters, and executives to various outposts in each team's territory. Niehaus and Wilson dutifully spent part of their off-seasons with the Seattle caravan, spreading the M's gospel. Both grew to love the area, and both settled there.

The two mikemen worked with a rotating cast of TV analysts beginning in 1978, when ex–second-sacker Bill Mazeroski — the club's minor league defensive instructor — carried most of the extra duty, with former infielder Rico Petrocelli filling in. From 1979 through 1987, ex-catcher Bill Freehan, former Mariners pitching coach Wes Stock, retired hurlers Ken Brett and Nelson Briles (fired for being too critical of Seattle's pitchers), and college sports announcer Don Poier all spent time in the booth.

Only when Joe Simpson, a onetime Mariners outfielder, successfully auditioned for the job before 1987 did Seattle get a truly acute analyst. Simpson quickly cultivated a relaxed, insightful manner and a pleasant, informative tone.

The M's original booth duo was broken up in the early 1980s when Niehaus signed a five-year contract in December 1981, while his co-pilot received just a one-year deal. Spurned, Wilson quit the team prior to Seattle's final series in 1982, skipping town to become the voice of the NHL Chicago Blackhawks. Wilson later would do play-by-play for the NHL St. Louis Blues as well as four other MLB clubs before purchasing a minor-league team and moving to the administrative side of the game.

Seattle and KVI re-upped for three more years in 1982, but the Mariners took a new direction for their television package. KING-TV had shown just 102 games total in its five-year deal, and the Mariners opted for a much larger package with KSTW for 1982. The station signed a two-year contract for 50 telecasts annually, paying to control the broadcast rights and, therefore, the lucre to be reaped from ad sales.

Wilson's replacement was Rick Rizzs, who signed a one-year deal. Rizzs, who grew up in Chicago, had worked his way up, doing five years in Double-A and two seasons with Triple-A Columbus. Professional, studious, and bellowing a decent home run call ("Goodbye, baseball!"), Rizzs was clearly intended to be Niehaus' caddy, and he was offered only one-year contracts for his first three seasons before gaining some traction. Meanwhile, the big dog in the booth inked another five-year pact after 1986.

With the Mariners continuing to stumble on the field, KVI decided it wanted out following 1984. KIRO — already airing the NBA's SuperSonics, the NFL's Seahawks, and University of Washington football — snared the radio contract, becoming the city's sports behemoth.

The new deal, which gave KIRO the ad rights, boosted the team's total broadcast revenue to $2.1 million by 1986, but it was the lowest figure in the majors except for Kansas City. Nevertheless, the club's new radio package included a larger network and a strong set of advertisers, including Budweiser, GTE, and Chevron.

Unfortunately, there were also negative aspects. Washington had always been a sports hotbed, and the city's major league status had grown quickly. The NBA SuperSonics began play in 1967, the NFL Seahawks in 1976, and the M's in 1977. Football's "seniority" meant that the Seahawks and UW Huskies commandeered KIRO on football weekends, bouncing the Mariners to a smaller station.

Before the 1986 season, the Mariners and KIRO-TV signed a $1 million deal. The next year, they signed a two-year contract for 70 games per season with an option for 1989. The station optioned 40 of those games to a smaller TV station, KTZZ, because CBS network affiliate KIRO didn't have the necessary airtime.

With the Mariners still far from contention, however, ratings weren't as good as hoped, and KIRO opted out for 1989 after paying more than $3 million over three years. By the late 1980s, though, the Mariners were at least garnering the kind of rights fees that the area's economic profile should project: Seattle's media revenue now ranked eighth among AL clubs and would continue to rise.

KSTW became the new TV rightsholder, inking a three-year contact with the team and Simpson who, unlike Niehaus and Rizzs, did not work directly for the Mariners. The series of short-term TV partners meant that, despite negotiations in 1983–1984 with various cable outlets including Group W, no M's games were seen on cable for more than another decade. The NBA SuperSonics' experiment with subscription television, a $120 full-season pay package in 1981 which didn't come close to getting into the black, provided a cautionary tale, but the M's were definitely late joiners to baseball's cable TV revolution. As a result, the Mariners showed just 12 home games — total — in their first 15 seasons.

An external event some 2,000 miles away radically changed the Mariners' broadcasts following the 1991 season. When Detroit's Ernie Harwell was forced out, Rizzs successfully sought the opportunity to succeed Harwell, putting his John Hancock on a three-year contract for the impossible task of replacing a legend.

So the Mariners needed to replace Rizzs. Should they make their second voice a seasoned baseball announcer? Or maybe change things up by bringing in a popular ex-athlete? How about a comedy writer and former DJ! In March 1992, the Mariners announced that Ken Levine would be their new color man.

Levine had begun his career in radio in the 1970s and later wrote for *M*A*S*H*, *Cheers*, and several other popular TV sitcoms. After calling games for three years in Triple A, he landed a job in the Orioles' booth in 1991. In Seattle, Levine lasted three years on the M's broadcast team, with the listeners split between those that loved him and those who couldn't stand him.

Also in 1992, Billy Sample replaced Joe Simpson — who departed to begin his long association with Atlanta — in the television booth. The problem? Neither Levine nor Sample were really suited for play-by-play, though Sample improved significantly and later landed at MLB.TV, where he broadcasted on MLB.COM. Sample lasted just one season, replaced by former Giants mikeman Ron Fairly in 1993.

Broadcasting legacy Chip Caray joined the broadcasting team at the same time as Fairly, handling most TV play-by-play for three years before heading off to bigger opportunities (*Fox Saturday Baseball*, then the Cubs).

The club's real seismic shift came in June 1992, when owner Jeff Smulyan sold the Mariners to a consortium headed by Hiroshi Yamauchi, CEO of Japanese gaming giant Nintendo Co. Ltd. The changeover led the club to adopt a global perspective in many areas, particularly regarding cable television. It was not coincidental that, once a more progressive and better financed ownership group was operating the club, Prime Cable and the Mariners started serious negotiations that would result in a partnership in 1995.

John Ellis, former CEO of Puget Sound Power and Light, became the club's public face as chair and CEO. "Locally" controlled by Nintendo of America, the team began to adopt some interesting Japanese principles, one of which was airing condensed games on TV. In 1994, KSTW ran an edited, one-hour version of Seattle games called *Fast Forward*. Rich Waltz, who years later graduated to the play-by-play chair in Miami, provided the narration for the condensed broadcasts.

Of course, the delayed and strike-shortened 1995 season was hardly the best time to begin any baseball venture but for Mariners fans, this was a huge year. Their club made the postseason for the first time while 104 regular-season games were telecast locally (40 on cable via Prime). Rizzs returned from Detroit just in time to join Niehaus in calling the exploits of Ken Griffey Jr., Edgar Martinez, and Randy Johnson for a suddenly fanatical local audience.

The comfortable Niehaus-Rizzs-Fairly team was retained for 1996 as the amount of games on "free TV" began declining in favor of cablecasts. Fox Northwest purchased Prime for 1997, ramping up its broadcasts to approximately 60 per year through 2000.

In his 23rd season calling Mariners' games, Niehaus was a no-brainer to throw out the ceremonial first pitch at Safeco Field's inaugural game in midseason 1999. Such honors aren't often bestowed on broadcasters, but Niehaus had become an institution in the Pacific Northwest long before then.

The Mariners opted to run even more of their games on Fox in the new century. For 2001 and 2002, KIRO showed a combined 77 games, with cablecasts of 106 and 107 per year. From 2003–2007, KSTW aired only 33 games annually as Fox eventually went to 117 cablecasts.

Niehaus, Fairly, and Rizzs described the television action during these years with ex-Mariners players Dave Valle, Dave Henderson, Jay Buhner, and occasionally Bill Krueger alternately in the analyst's chair. Another popular ex-Seattle player, Tom Paciorek, also filled in on radio in 2001.

Focused more and more on international marketing opportunities, Seattle eagerly collaborated with the transmission of telecasts in Japan when Nippon Pro Baseball superstar Ichiro Suzuki joined the club in 2001 — even though the Mariners didn't control those rights. (International broadcast rights for all teams were vested in MLB, with revenue distributed equally among the 30 clubs.)

The M's added a Spanish-language broadcast in 2003, hiring the acknowledged best in the business, Amaury Pi-Gonzalez (a veteran of Giants and A's games) to work with former second baseman Julio Cruz. The two teamed up for four years on home games.

When Pi-Gonzalez returned full-time to the Bay Area, Alex Rivera slipped into the play-by-play chair. KFTH was been Seattle's Spanish-language flagship from 2004-2010, and audio *en Español* is now also available as the SAP component of home TV games.

Fairly retired after 2006, and Rizzs transferred exclusively to radio, while Dave Henderson was exiled after a DUI incident. To fill the TV vacancy, the Mariners hired Dave Sims, just the second full-time African American to call play-by-play in MLB history.

Sims' journey to the Mariners was atypical. After college, he spent a few years as a sportswriter before being hired by ESPN, where called several different sports on the national stage. Though he did not work his way through the minors, Sims has the gift of gab and knows the game from being a catcher in college. Following Niehaus' manner, Sims is excitable and will yell — loudly — when called for.

Along with Sims, the Mariners welcomed former Seattle third baseman Mike Blowers, for several years prior a studio analyst. He and Sims work together effectively, and the young duo should serve the team well for years. Because the industry belief is that baseball radio listeners are older and more settled in their habits, it wasn't happenstance that Seattle's TV team was younger, while veterans Rizzs and Niehaus reigned on KIRO radio (which renewed its broadcast agreement again for 2009).

Along with the stability in the booth, the Mariners have been served by the same radio and TV producers for many years. Kevin Cremin has worked on radio more than 30 years, and Mark Engelbrekt on television production for more than two decades. They are among the more well-known producers in the game, along with famous figures like Kent Sommerfeld of Brewers radio, Glenn Diamond of Braves TV, and the late Arne Harris of Cubs telecasts.

Niehaus joined the pantheon of Frick Award winners in 2008. Yet the twilight of an aging broadcast legend (especially when on-air mistakes occur more often) always gives rise to questions about succession. That question was called on November 10, 2010, when the 75-year-old Niehaus died of a heart attack at his home in suburban Bellevue.

The nationwide outpouring of grief and support for Niehaus' family was genuine. Ken Griffey Jr. was moved to tears, while longtime Mariners outfielder Jay Buhner called it the worst day of his life. Niehaus had called all but 101 of Seattle's 5,385 games from 1977 through 2010, so no one could ever truly fill his trademark white shoes.

It is always interesting to watch how franchises handle the succession path for their veteran voices. Forward-thinking clubs are often proactive, grooming successors for that inevitable sad day mandated by retirement or death. San Diego brought in Andy Masur to ease Jerry Coleman's later years; the Phillies have always had a big broadcast crew to deal with emergencies and routine transitions. In contrast, the Braves, whose mainstays aged out at the same time, hit a rough patch.

Seattle had neither groomed anyone, nor had an obvious replacement ready when Niehaus passed. Rizzs is a perfectly capable lead radio announcer, as is Sims on TV. In the immediate aftermath, the Mariners made many choices rather than one. In lieu of hiring a full-time second chair to Rizzs, the club and KIRO recalled voices from the past such as Fairly, Valle, Levine, Wilson, and Henderson to make appearances with Rizzs.

The M's finally hired a full-time no. 2 radio announcer for the 2013 season to assist Rick Rizzs. Aaron Goldsmith, who had spent the previous year at Triple-A Providence — the latest breeding ground for big-league voices — became, at age 29 the youngest full-time radio man in the majors.

The process of selecting a new announcer is always complex — just sifting through the resumes can take months. Seattle received 160 applications for the job, and whittled the candidates down to four. Goldsmith, who worked his way up from indie ball and the Cape Cod League, impressed the Mariners' brass with his skill, attitude, and ambition.

Mike Curto, longtime voice of the Mariners' Triple-A franchise in Tacoma, was not among the finalists considered for the position. The well-traveled Ken Levine, who worked for the Mariners in the 1990s, also applied.

Early in 2013 the Mariners announced that they would be taking a controlling interest in Root Sports, their telecaster since 2011. Just a few months before, the team had denied that it would be making such a move. But it's clearly a smart investment on Seattle's part, as teams that own their own RSNs can evade much of the revenue-sharing component of broadcast income.

WAVES OF SOUND, RAYS OF LIGHT

TAMPA BAY DEVIL RAYS/RAYS BROADCASTING HISTORY

"This one's gonna go!"
— Dewayne Staats' home-run call

LIKE MANY EXPANSION TEAMS, THE DEVIL RAYS CONSTRUCTED
their early rosters around experienced players such as Wade Boggs, Roberto Hernandez, Fred McGriff, Jose Canseco, and Wilson Alvarez. They also used experienced broadcasters, hoping that familiar faces and voices in the booth would help the hometown fans bond with the new team.

On the field, the plan failed miserably. Tampa Bay finished last regularly while losing at least 90 games each year from its inaugural season in 1998 through 2007. In the broadcast booth, however, the expansion team was more competent.

The franchise's broadcasting department hired Paul Olden and Charlie Slowes as its original radio voices. Neither one was particularly well-known. The peripatetic Olden had previously handled TV broadcasts for the Indians, Angels, and Yankees (working in the Bronx for the three years preceding his hiring by Tampa Bay). Cleveland had made Olden the first dedicated African-American play-by-play man in baseball history when it tapped him for television games in 1988.

Even in recent years, few black broadcasters have worked in MLB broadcast booths, with most African Americans serving as analysts (also known as "color men"). In recent years, Ken Singleton has graduated from analyst status to become a good lead announcer when Michael Kay isn't in the Yankees' booth, and Dave Sims has made progress with Seattle.

Eric Collins began doing Dodgers games in 2009, and Robert Ford took over Astros radio duties in 2013.

Olden, a professional photographer and longtime radio veteran, had served as the PA announcer for the Super Bowl; in 2009, he became the PA announcer at Yankee Stadium, subbing for ailing Bob Sheppard. Despite his varied resume, Olden unfortunately never made much of a mark broadcasting baseball, and St. Petersburg was no exception to the pattern as he persevered through seven years of describing the fortunes of a very bad club.

Prior to being hired as the Devil Rays' No. 2 radio voice, Charlie Slowes had announced several seasons of Triple-A baseball at the Mets' affiliate in Tidewater. He also did fill-in work on Cardinals, Orioles, and Mets games from 1984–1991.

Between his tenure with the Rays (1998–2004) and his later work with the Nationals, Slowes called a lot of bad baseball — certainly more in percentage terms than any other active big-league announcer. Slowes provided an affable presence with a friendly, laid-back approach even though he had come out of Fordham's high-powered broadcasting school. While he was in St. Petersburg, though, there wasn't much to get excited about.

The Rays parted ways with WFLA — their flagship radio station since the club's inception — after 2004. The new carrier, WHNZ, and the Rays chose not to retain Slowes and Olden, instead committing to "youth" on their radio broadcasts. Dave Wills and Andy Freed, who had worked their way up through the bushes, became the team's co-voices.

Both WFLA and WHNZ were, at the time of the transfer, owned by Clear Channel radio, but the latter station's programming and identity was seen as a better fit for the upper-income, older fans believed to be more apt to listen to baseball on the radio.

Freed, a broadcaster since college, spent 10 years at the mike with the Red Sox' Double-and Triple-A affiliates. Wills worked in suburban Chicago before toiling for more than a decade for the White Sox, doing pregame and postgame work as well as weekend broadcasts.

During their long climb uphill, Wills and Freed supplemented their baseball jobs with basketball and football work. Wills also coached baseball at NCAA Division III Elmhurst College, where he had played as an undergraduate. Neither is an ex-big-league player, but both know the game and can handle analytical chores as well as taking the lead.

The most interesting broadcaster the Rays have ever had is Enrique Oliu. Despite being blind from birth, Oliu has served as a Spanish-language color commentator for the club since its inaugural season. The club does not send Oliu and popular play-by-play man Ricardo Taveras on the road, but the Dominican-born pair cover all home games at Tropicana and call road games from the club's television broadcasts.

Oliu can't see, but he can synthesize baseball information, recall player statistics and abilities, and analyze, making him a perfect complement to a quality play-by-play announcer. He is respected enough inside the game that nobody was surprised when, in 2009, filmmaker Ziam Hanseh released a well-received documentary about Oliu, ¡Henry O! Indicating baseball's unsteady position on Spanish-speaking radio, however, Oliu and Taveras have scrambled for a home on the airwaves, working for several different stations.

In contrast to the radio, the television side of Rays broadcasts has not changed much in the team's history. From 1998-2002, the Rays showed about 130 games per season on TV, split among two over-the-air channels and Fox Sports on cable. The local CBS affiliate aired 15 games per season for the duration of the deal.

From 2003–2007, Tampa Bay cut back to two outlets, licensing around 65 over-the-air games per season to the local PAX affiliate and increasing the team's Fox Sports broadcasts to a high of 80 in 2007. Beginning in 2009, the Rays eschewed free TV, negotiating a deal to show a franchise-high 150 regular-season contests exclusively on Fox Sports.

Sometimes, consistency in a broadcast operation is good. Sometimes, it just feels like ossification. Dewayne Staats has been Tampa Bay's play-by-play announcer on TV since the beginning, from the misery of the Bryan Rekar era to the glory of the Evan Longoria age, but his tenure sometimes has had the feel of playing out the string.

Staats, who began his big-league career in 1977 with the Astros, has worked almost everywhere — ESPN, the Baseball Network, New York, and Chicago — without carving out a niche as more than a "professional voice." He has a pleasing Southern tone and a his laconic, old-school style, but excitement doesn't seem to be his primary gear.

Fortunately, for the first 11 years of Staats' tenure with the Rays, he worked with Joe Magrane, a former Cardinals hurler who could effectively get into pitchers' heads while bringing his analysis to the broadcast. The MLB network hired Magrane in 2009; he was replaced by Kevin Kennedy, former Rangers manager and Fox game-of-the-week analyst. Kennedy joined Staats in the booth for most of the action on Sun Sports, which had picked up televising the club.

Brian Anderson, a former Rays pitcher who had done some broadcasting for the Indians and had filled in for Magrane when the latter covered the 2008 Olympics, was tabbed for a smaller slate of games in 2009. While Kennedy toted a sack full of good-old-boy bonhomie, it was felt that he lacked some of Magrane's charm and insight, and the reviews of Kennedy were not kind. Following the 2010 season, the Rays and Sun Sports hired Anderson as full-time analyst, where he provides depth and color to Staats' reliable if not blood-stirring play-by-play call.

Another interesting chapter in Tampa Bay's broadcast history is the presence of Todd Kalas, son of late Philadelphia mike legend Harry Kalas. The younger K, one of several active broadcasting legacies, has been with the Rays' on-air team since 1998. In a career spanning two decades, he has gone from Philadelphia to New York to Florida without snagging a lead broadcaster's job, working instead as a roving reporter and occasional fill-in. He's always employed, but has failed to find his métier or an adoring audience — which can also be said for the team's broadcasts in general.

Although the Rays have fielded an exciting team since 2008, the club has not yet hit its stride on the air. A challenge that the astute and forward-looking club management has not yet met is figuring out how to put together a broadcast team equal to its starting nine — a broadcast team that Tampa Bay fans will truly adopt as their own.

FINALLY AT HOME ON THE RANGE

WASHINGTON SENATORS II/TEXAS RANGERS BROADCASTING HISTORY

"I actually liked Jimmy Piersall and hated that he was fired…
what other team in baseball had a guy who viewed his full-time job
as going around telling lawyers and ad executives to fuck off?"
— Mike Shropshire, Seasons in Hell

CALVIN GRIFFITH MOVED THE WASHINGTON SENATORS — WHO WERE finally getting good after nearly three decades — to Minnesota in 1961. The idea of not having baseball in the District of Columbia was enough to send the powers that be into spasms, so baseball hastily prepared its first modern expansion.

Owned by non-baseball people and stocked with cronies and incompetents, the new Senators had a terrible expansion draft that hamstrung the club for most of its 11 years in the nation's capital. It was an unexciting squad to watch, and didn't have a particularly interesting broadcast crew.

WTOP, radio home of the original American League Senators, secured the radio rights to the new club. Dan Daniels, WTOP's sports director, had been on the Senators' announcing crew in 1960 and also served as Redskins' play-by-play man. With the Griffith-era Senators radio team of Bob Wolff and Chuck Thompson gone to Minnesota and Baltimore, respectively, Daniels decided to do it himself.

Daniels had first sat at the microphone in 1940 while at the University of Florida. Working his way up the radio ladder, he took jobs in Orlando and Birmingham before coming to Washington in 1956.

His new partner, Massachusetts-raised John MacLean, had started his career in 1941. He called minor-league Baltimore Orioles games in the early 1950s and had been a *Game of the Day* announcer from 1956 through 1960. MacLean had also manned the NFL Colts' radio chair in 1953–54.

For 1961, the club's only summer at ancient Griffith Stadium, Sears and Ballantine Beer were the club's top radio sponsors. R.J. Reynolds also bought time on WTOP-TV's 30-game package of Senators games, all but six of which were shown on weekends.

While reviewers of the team's broadcasts did not deem them exciting, at least Washington fans knew where to tune in. For the club's first eight years, WTOP was the Senators' home on both radio and television. The TV slate presented 30–35 games per season, 11 at home (13 in 1961) and the balance from the road. Many clubs of the day showed a smaller percentage of home contests on the tube than did Washington. One interesting aspect of the Senators' broadcast philosophy was to try to feature every AL opponent at least once per season. Of course, AL clubs could never go wrong by showing the dynastic Yankees: in 1963, the Bombers were on six of the 30 Senators' telecasts.

Daniels and MacLean remained mikeside for each Senators game from 1961 through 1968. Shiny new District of Columbia Stadium — which opened in 1962 as the first of a wave of superstadia that would change the way the game was played — was the one attractive thing about the sad-sack club.

In 1962, the club aired just four exhibition games on radio. Later that season, NBC chose John MacLean to help announce the All-Star Game held at D.C. Stadium, the last year that two Midsummer Classics were played. Daniels also manned a mike for NBC at the 1964 All-Star Game from Shea Stadium.

Even with an array of high-powered sponsors, in both 1962 and 1963 the Nats' TV-radio revenue totaled only $300,000, the lowest in the majors — even the Kansas City Athletics earned $400,000 in 1963. Sponsors of the Senators' broadcasts in 1963 were Ballantine Beer, Atlantic Refining, General Cigar, Guardian Maintenance, R.J. Reynolds, and General Mills.

A key reason for the club's poor rights fees was that the team had literally no radio or television network. Many radio stations on the Middle Atlantic and Southeastern seaboard had switched from the moribund old Senators over to the Orioles in the late 1950s. As a 50,000-watt clear-channel station, WTOP signal reached a wide region at night, making the club's lack of a radio network a little less important, but the club didn't even have a radio affiliate in their spring training home of Pompano Beach, Florida, in 1961.

The Brooklyn Dodgers' unusual secondary network of re-created games — called by Nat Allbright and Bob Best from a studio in Arlington, Virginia — served more than 100 smaller radio stations in the region during the 1950s. But by 1962, the Dodgers' re-creations had lost their audience because games from the West Coast ended too late for Eastern listeners. The Senators leapt into the breach.

Washington's new plan included hiring Best as their radio-TV director, the first such position created in the majors. They then signed Allbright and Best to re-create 158 Senators games, hoping to build a secondary network of their own that would allow them to offer re-created games to small, budget-minded radio outlets. Unfortunately, few wanted to listen to the Senators, live or re-created, and the venture failed. Allbright permanently left the baseball airwaves.

On September 6, 1963, before an Indians-Senators game, a team of Hollywood All-Stars that included Bing Crosby, Pat Boone, and Jerry Lewis played a three-inning charity game at D.C. Stadium against the local press corps. MacLean pitched, reportedly impressively, for the local press. Shortly afterward, Daniels won a golf tournament between the press and the Senators' coaching staff.

For 1964, WTOP and WTOP-TV inked new three-year deals with the team for $333,333 per season. That wasn't much of an increase, but the club had little leverage since it was both bad and boring. To make matters worse, WTOP-TV pushed hard for a revolutionary clause in its contract that decreased payment to the Senators if any national telecast was broadcast to the D.C. market during a WTOP Senators telecast.

WTOP began simulcasting its Senators games over WTOP-FM in 1964, adding six stations to a skeleton network. By 1966, there were nine stations on the lines, though the Senators still had no TV network.

Having a team located in the populous, growing, and relatively wealthy Washington metropolitan area might have seemed to be a potential bonanza, but Daniels understood that it was actually a challenge. Daniels told *The Sporting News* in 1966 that his job was different from most, since a lot of listeners to Washington broadcasts were government workers, from other places, rooting for the Senators' opposition.

"You must avoid the hometown approach," he noted. "You have to try not to be a rooter, yet you also must recognize that a lot of fans are pulling for Washington. You must sort of walk a tightrope."

Meanwhile, prior to the 1966 campaign, MacLean joined the Nats to do offseason promotional work, consisting mostly of speaking to various organizations that were potential buyers of season tickets or group outing packages.

For 1965 and 1966, National Brewing — previously associated with the Orioles — replaced Ballantine and joined R.J. Reynolds as the club's chief co-sponsor. A new high of 13 stations composed the team's radio network in 1966 as the Senators broadcast 10 spring exhibition games for the first time. Also that spring, former Senators' pitcher Chuck Stobbs signed on as an analyst on the club's TV crew, staying only one year. Once again, however, the Senators endured another disappointing season on the field, despite the managerial skills of Gil Hodges.

WTOP presented all of the team's 35 televised games in color for the first time in 1967. The club's new sponsors on radio were B.F. Goodrich, Atlantic Richfield, Dodge Motors, and Household Finance. On television, the sponsors were Carling, General Cigar, and Allstate Insurance.

Following another last-place Senators finish in 1968, WTOP radio chose to drop all sports, including the Senators, Colts, and University of Maryland, in favor of an all-news format. Daniels, deposed as the Nats' voice, went on to do sports news at WRC-TV. MacLean, in his next big-league announcing job, lasted only a month with the Red Sox in 1972 before collapsing in Minneapolis with a condition that required open-heart surgery the next year.

Many things changed in Washington baseball for 1969. Bob Short, a lawyer and trucking industry magnate who a decade before had bought the Minneapolis Lakers and then moved them to Los Angeles, purchased the Senators, outbidding Cleveland Indians part-owner Bob Hope in the process. Despite little baseball experience, Short immediately appointed himself general manager.

Perennially short of cash, the new owner had little time to negotiate a new radio deal, but did receive $165,000 — a franchise high — for the radio rights on WWDC and a 10-station network. WTOP-TV continued to telecast Washington games in the last season of its contract, paying $250,000.

The new announcers were Shelby Whitfield, a longtime Armed Forces Network broadcaster, and Ron Menchine, sports director of WWDC and also an AFN veteran who had worked his way up doing mostly college sports. For the first time, the lead announcer was on the team's payroll, rather than the station's. Whitfield then hired Menchine, who was paid by WWDC. Building up the club's radio network was also one of Whitfield's responsibilities, even though he and Menchine were offered only one-year contracts.

Whitfield, a 37-year-old Texan, was one of more than 50 applicants for the job, beating out experienced broadcasters such as Jimmy Dudley and Ned Martin as well as ex-athletes Rex Barney and Jim Piersall. While Whitfield had called just one year of minor-league baseball, he'd been on AFN for more than a decade and had anchored and presented sports broadcasts all over the world. His AFN baseball gig involved providing between-innings commentary for big-league games carried by the network to military personnel around the globe.

Warner Wolf, WTOP's top sportscaster, assisted Whitfield and Menchine. Popular for his distillation of the razzle-dazzle style of the late 1960s, Wolf would later work on ABC's *Monday Night Baseball*, though reviews of his performance with the network were poor. Wolf and Whitfield clashed almost from the get-go.

WTOP came up with some weird ideas about jazzing up the game, including bringing non-baseball types into the booth during its telecasts. For example, Wolf spent broadcasts pumping football players John Mackey and Sonny Jurgensen for wacky stories while Whitfield tried to describe the action on the field. A riotous appearance in the booth by Flip Wilson brought the experiment to an end, with the third chair filled for the rest of the season by former ballplayers like Bob Feller and Moose Skowron.

In July, the D.C. chapter of AFTRA (the American Federation of TV and Radio Artists) went on strike, forcing Menchine and Whitfield off the air for two games, with Rex Barney taking over. Barney had also stepped in during a strike in Baltimore in 1968.

Broadcasting weirdness aside, 1969 was a good year for the Senators. Playing in a renamed Robert F. Kennedy Memorial Stadium, the club benefited from new uniforms and a charismatic new manager, Ted Williams. To everyone's surprise, Washington finished a shocking 86–76, jumping from last place to fourth during the club's only winning season in D.C.

Rather than build on the fragile new interest in the team, Short immediately shot himself in the foot — perhaps on purpose. Completely opposed to broadcasting home games on TV, he said that he would rather go without a contract than show even one home contest in 1970, undercutting his negotiating position. Instead of leveraging the team's success into bigger dollars and more exposure, he chose to join three other AL clubs (Angels, Royals, and Athletics) that did not telecast home games. The result was that WTOP paid only $160,000 in 1970, the lowest TV rights fee in the majors, to cover 32 road contests.

On the plus side, the team's strong 1969 meant that 31 stations joined WWDC and WWDC-FM's network for 1970. Williams, however, couldn't repeat his success as the Senators dropped below .500.

The untold tale of the time was that Short was micromanaging both on-field and off-field matters, professing fealty to D.C. while all the time aiming to move the club to what he felt a more profitable clime.

During 1970, Short ordered Shelby Whitfield to lie about attendance and weather conditions — in the opposite fashion than one might expect. Instead of having Whitfield pushing tickets and ignoring bad weather forecasts, as he had done in 1969, Short now told his lead broadcaster to announce incoming storms in order to hold down attendance and to underreport crowds at the games. The self-sabotage was in service of promoting Short's view that the club wasn't drawing well enough to remain in Washington.

Despite the club's poor 1970 finish, Short signed a new, two-year radio package with WWDC for $200,000 per season. He fired Whitfield, who did not want to return anyway, on December 2, 1970.

Since Short had no control over who WWDC hired for its pregame and postgame programming, the station retained Whitfield on the Senators' pregame show. Whitfield later wrote the scabrous and fascinating book *Kiss it Goodbye*, detailing Short's machinations to deprive the nation's capital of its team. After later becoming sports director of ABC Radio, Whitfield reunited with Menchine in the early 1980s to do United States Football League games.

Tony Roberts — Short's handpicked replacement for Whitfield — called the 1971 games on WWDC, assisted by Menchine. On WTOP-TV, however, Short changed things as Wolf and Ray Scott called 40 road games in the first year of a proposed three-year deal that netted the club $240,000 per season. Scott, a longtime football mainstay on CBS, had broadcast several years of Twins games in the 1960s. His summer golf broadcasting commitments, however, meant that he wasn't available for the entire 40-game slate — not that it mattered much, anyway.

The Senators' lease at RFK was up at the end of 1971, and the team had collapsed. Short saw the opportunity solve his short-term financial problems and stopped making rent payments for the stadium. He was spending increasing time with Tom Vandergriff, the mayor of Arlington, Texas, laying the groundwork for relocating the franchise.

Short obtained permission from his fellow AL owners to move the club on September 21, 1971. Washington fans were furious at being abandoned for the second time in 11 years. The team's final home game, nine days later against the Yankees, featured anti-Short banners and chanting. The fans gave a tearful ovation for star slugger Frank Howard, who homered, and delayed the game after the seventh by running onto the field. The curtain dropped for good with the Senators up 7–5 with two out in the top of the ninth as the fans streamed back onto the field in a riot, causing the umpires to award New York a 9–0 win by forfeit. *Exeunt omnes.*

With the Senators gone, Tony Roberts moved to NBA Baltimore Bullets basketball and collegiate gridiron action for Navy and the University of Indiana. He then began a 26-year career calling Notre Dame football, a long way from the exploits of Paul Casanova and Denny Riddleberger.

As the carpetbagging Short — who owed D.C. banks $3.3 million — romanced Texas, astonishing figures like one million dollars in annual broadcast revenue were tossed around. Yet that kind of big money did not materialize in 1971, even with the help of Broadcast Partners Corp., an organization founded to assist in creating a radio network and selling commercial time for the new Texas Rangers.

In a highly unusual arrangement, Arlington Park, Inc. (owned by the city of Arlington) took a 10-year option on the team's broadcast rights. The city paid Short $7.5 million upfront in that deal, with revenue the company realized from selling radio ads going to pay down debts the city had assumed on behalf of Short.

The Rangers' 1972 radio network boasted 30 stations in its first year, but only 16 in its second. In 1972 and 1973, Short's $750,000 pro-rated annual share of the $7.5 million media rights payment ranked ahead of only Kansas City and Milwaukee among AL clubs, but far better than what he had been making in Washington.

KRLD, a 50,000-watt station, became the Rangers' first radio flagship. With baseball on the tube still a novel event in Texas — the Houston Astros rarely televised games, and then only on weekends — success on the radio was critical. Thus Rangers management made brave pronouncements about invading Houston's radio territory.

Local talent Bill Mercer was the Rangers' first radio voice; he had served as the NFL Dallas Cowboys' announcer from 1965 to 1971. Mercer predicted in August 1972 that, with football the big sport in Texas, the Rangers would have to be good to attract attention. He was right: the Rangers were bad, and few attended, watched, or listened. As a result, the club's sponsorship situation did not firm up until 1974.

Don Drysdale joined Mercer in the Rangers' original radio booth. The former Dodgers' great had broadcast the Expos in 1970–71 while also calling a few 1971 games on the Cardinals' television network. The Rangers and KRLD hired him late that year, giving the handsome ex-star his first full-time broadcasting job.

KDTV (soon to be called KDFW) and 12 network stations carried a 24-game TV package in 1972 that included five home contests, despite Short's antipathy to telecasting from his own park. Mercer and Drysdale teamed with Dick Risenhoover, who had played on the 1949 University of Texas' national championship baseball team.

A high school athletics coach, Risenhoover began broadcasting in Amarillo in the early 1960s before coming to Dallas in 1970 to join KDTV's sports department. Risenhoover was well-loved in the area and truly adored his Rangers.

Drysdale left Texas after one season for the Angels broadcast crew, and Risenhoover assumed an everyday role in 1973. During that season, Risenhoover quit his KDTV sports job to work for the Rangers.

Following two last-place, 100-loss seasons in Texas, Mercer departed for WMAQ in Chicago to be Harry Caray's sidekick, a difficult job but one that at least promised some winning baseball. At the same time, Short finally got out of baseball, selling the Rangers to a group led by Brad Corbett.

Local sportscaster Bill Merrill, who wasn't really suited for the analyst's role and who never called MLB games before or after his tenure with the Rangers, became Risenhoover's radio and TV partner. Jim Piersall, fresh from the Charles Finley zoo in Oakland, did the TV color.

Originally hired by the club's promotions department, Piersall didn't last long. Annoying local civic leaders with ill-timed comments about the Dallas area and publicly insulting Schlitz beer (the club's main radio and television sponsor), Piersall also picked a fight with sportswriter Mike Shropshire, who had noted in print that the club was partying a lot during spring training.

The early 1970s Rangers were not just bad, they were also out of control — a combustible mix of green kids and hardcore, cynical veterans. Manager Billy Martin, hired late in the 1973 season, wasn't much of a calming influence on this crew.

All this played out on new broadcast outlets. The city of Arlington had underwritten much of Short's debt as part of the deal to bring the team to Texas, and it was important for the city to earn more broadcast revenue after the broadcasting setup had lost money in 1972 and had broken even in 1973.

During 1972 and 1973, KRLD had bumped the Rangers to air the Cowboys, both for exhibitions and in the regular season. KDFW-TV also aired Cowboys games, which made it an easy call for the Rangers to look for greener media pastures.

Texas shifted to WBAP for both radio and TV coverage in 1974. WBAP-TV was an NBC affiliate so, in order to run both the network's *Game of the Week* and the Rangers' contests, WBAP scheduled many of its 22 road games in prime time. This was a boon to the club, but the station bailed after only one year.

WBAP radio and the Rangers, however, formed a team until 1994. The 50,000-watt station from Fort Worth easily reached into the Astros' territory in Louisiana and East Texas. Two stations joined the club's network in 1974, then 20 signed on in 1975, but the network was back to eight affiliates in 1976. From 1975 to 1984, KXAS was the team's TV flagship. In 1976 and 1977, Texas again earned $700,000 in media revenue, third-lowest in the AL in 1977, even below expansion Seattle.

Tom Vandergriff, mayor of Arlington from 1951 to 1977, was not only a big player in bringing the team to Texas, but also a superfan. He began doing commentary on Rangers TV games in 1974, taking no salary and even reportedly paying his own way on road trips for the three years he shared a mike with Risenhoover.

The popular Risenhoover, however, was diagnosed in January 1978 with cancer of the liver. With the prognosis dire, the Rangers needed a broadcaster. The club quickly settled on Jon Miller, who had spent 1974 with the Athletics but had been working college basketball and pro soccer since.

Risenhoover died on Opening Day in 1978 at age 51. His grief-stricken fans and friends in the local media took out some of their anguish, regrettably, on the new guy. Miller departed after two seasons, finding like so many others that it was nearly impossible to walk in the shoes of a dead man.

When Risenhoover took ill, Merrill moved exclusively to radio, working with Miller. Frank Glieber, the famous "round mound of sound" from CBS' NFL broadcasts, became the club's television voice for three seasons over KXAS and 17 network stations.

When Miller decamped for Boston in 1980, the Rangers pulled 33-year-old Mel Proctor out of Triple-A, where he had done for years of play-by-play for the Padres' affiliate in Hawaii. Proctor was also the voice of the NBA Washington Bullets. A proud collector of baseball-themed neckties, the enthusiastic Proctor brought vigor to the Rangers' broadcasts for the two years he worked for WBAP and KXAS.

Rangers pitcher Sparky Lyle had signed a contract with the Rangers in 1979 that promised him a 10-year, $50,000-per-year job as a broadcaster on the club's network after his playing career ended. Lyle was soon dealt to Philadelphia, however, and the contract was not brought up again. Lyle never did take the mike for a big-league game.

For the first time in 1981, the Rangers also attempted Spanish-language broadcasts, with legendary ex-Dodgers and Astros announcer Rene Cardenas manning a network that stretched from San Juan, Puerto Rico, to Tijuana in Baja California. Cardenas, though, departed after one year and the Rangers did not return to the airwaves in Spanish until 1992.

With Bill Merrill retiring following the 1981 season — he died in 2003 at age 79 — and Mel Proctor moving on, the Rangers adopted a whole new broadcasting philosophy for 1982. The agreement with the city of Arlington had expired, and the Rangers opted to retain broadcast rights on radio and television and sell their own ad time. This turned out to be extremely profitable, as longtime sponsors Chevrolet, State Farm, Dr. Pepper, and Coca-Cola remained connected with the club and other local and national businesses like 7-11 became sponsors.

The Rangers hired Eric Nadel and Mark Holtz as the club's new radio voices. Merle Harmon, who had been calling NBC's *Game of the Week*, joined former Royals pitcher Steve Busby on television. Nadel had begun working Rangers broadcasts in 1979, both on WBAP and doing some fill-in TV work. A sports nut with an eye for arcane knowledge, Nadel wrote a book of interesting baseball stories called *The Man Who Stole First Base*. Nadel's is the longest tenure of any AL broadcaster save Denny Matthews.

Holtz had aired Triple-A Denver Bears games from 1976 through 1980 and had worked Dallas Mavericks NBA games before becoming WBAP's sports director. He was loud, excitable, and in love with his job. "It's Baseball Time in Texas!" he'd almost sing before each home game. Every Rangers victory was greeted with a hearty, "Hello, win column!"

Holtz' first Rangers work had come in 1981 with the Vue-Pay cable television network, a venture of Gene Autry's Golden West Broadcasting. Golden West paid the Rangers $600,000 for the rights to approximately 20 games.

In 1982, Vue-Pay changed its name to Five Star Cable and broadcast 20 contests. For 1983, Home Sports Entertainment (HSE), owned by Warner-Amex, consummated a lucrative five-year deal to carry Texas games on cable, with the Rangers' broadcast income jumping to $5.5 million per year, second-highest among AL clubs.

Harmon, hired specifically for his national broadcast profile, manned KXAS and HSE telecasts. He also owned the Merle Harmon's Fan Fair sporting-goods chain. Curt Gowdy, who like Harmon had been let go by NBC, also joined the Rangers as director of TV planning and evaluation.

By July 1984 HSE had 52 affiliates and 40,000 subscribers at about $10 per month. Warner-Amex soon sold the network to a syndicate that included the Rangers and Astros along with the NBA Dallas Mavericks and Houston Rockets. HSE continued to broadcast games in several sports through 1994 when it became part of the Prime Sports Network, which later became part of the growing group of regional Fox Sports networks.

In 1982, all Rangers' exhibition games were carried on the radio for the first time as the team was making strides in a long climb toward respectability. Holtz and Nadel cemented themselves as local favorites on radio, while various TV voices came and went without making much of an impact.

Busby left HSE after 1985, going exclusively to over-the-air broadcasts with new TV rightsholder KTVT. Busby, in fact, became a play-by-play man and remained with the club through 1995, teaming with longtime Rangers fan favorite Jim Sundberg beginning in 1990.

Distributed via satellite since the late 1970s, KTVT became one of baseball's superstations, joining WTBS, WGN, WWOR, and WPIX. Even though KTVT was beaming Texas baseball to cable systems in the South and Southwest and as far away as Montana, the Rangers did not earn the enmity from other clubs that Turner (WTBS) and the Tribune

Company (WGN) did, because most of the cable systems KTVT serviced were inside the club's proscribed five-state territory. KTVT continued carrying Rangers over-the-air contests through the end of 1995.

The 1994 work stoppage coincided with the end of the team's final radio deal with WBAP. KRLD took over the following year, starting another long-term relationship that continued through 2010. Nadel began working directly for the Rangers, teaming with Brad Sham, heretofore a Cowboys voice. Holtz shifted to cable TV, pairing with Tom Grieve, a former Senators player and the Rangers' GM from 1984 to 1994.

Sham lasted three seasons, receiving mixed reviews, but Grieve showed a dry wit and the ability to dissect the game from both the playing and administrative viewpoints. Grieve and Holtz called the club's first division championship in 1996, though all the TV coverage was over-the-air that summer as the sale of Prime Networks to Fox was delayed.

Holtz became ill in 1997 and had to leave his post on May 22 in favor of Bill Jones. On September 7, Holtz died from leukemia after a career at the mike that spanned two perfect games and four no-hitters — including Nolan Ryan's seventh no-no in 1991, which thanks to Holtz and the manic Rangers fans was one of the most thrilling broadcasts in modern baseball history.

Holtz was, oddly enough, the third Rangers' announcer to pass away at age 51, following Risenhoover and Frank Glieber, who had collapsed in 1985 and died of a heart attack while working out. Despite his untimely death, Holtz's legacy is strong, as he was an eight-time Texas broadcaster of the year and his catchphrases remain part of the baseball lexicon in North Texas.

Jones, a sportscaster at KXAS from 1990 until he took over for Holtz, stepped into the breach until he began to suffer from health problems and had to step down during the 2001 season. He returned to local newscasts with a greatly reduced sports broadcasting schedule.

The Rangers were back on cable in 1997, though the club would be one of the last holdouts in keeping a significant number of games on free TV. Only in 2008 did Fox get to carry more than 80 Texas games, upping its schedule to 110, with KDFI and KDFW splitting 50 games that year and 25 in 2009.

Nadel teamed with Vince Cotroneo for six years beginning in 1998, then with Victor Rojas (later of the MLB Network and the Los Angeles Angels) for five more. In 2009, Dave Barnett, a generalist more known for his football and basketball work, became Nadel's sidekick at 100,000-watt KRLD-FM. By that time, Nadel had signed a lifetime contract with the Rangers.

Nadel was unusually durable through 2008; the last time he had missed a game was in 1989, when his father had passed away. In 2009, however, eye surgery knocked Nadel out for six games. Former TV voices Jim Sundberg and Steve Busby helped out, as did former Rangers PR director John Blake, then Vice President for Communications.

Although the English-language radio broadcast picture had been secure for quite some time, fans saw big changes in 2009. KRLD began moving all weekday games to the station's

FM frequency, with the weekend games broadcast on AM. Having an FM option games allowed the club to have more of its spring training games aired than previously.

The Rangers had brought back Spanish-language coverage in 1992. Luis Mayoral, a longtime baseball broadcaster, journalist, and scout in Puerto Rico, joined the organization at the behest of new Rangers owner Tom Hicks to promote the team in the Latino community. He also manned the mike for the club's new Spanish broadcasting slate. In 1993, the Rangers became the first MLB team to broadcast all their games, home and road, in Spanish. (In 2014, the White Sox, Red Sox, and Rangers were the only AL clubs covering each home and road contest in two tongues.)

Mayoral, also responsible for counseling and teaching the club's Spanish-speaking stars (a large contingent, which during his time included Ivan Rodriguez, Juan Gonzalez, and Ruben Sierra), remained the radio voice through 1999, at which time he was replaced by Eleno Ornelas, who today remains at the mike and also coordinates the club's Spanish broadcasts.

During home games, Ornelas is joined by former Rangers infielder Benji Gil. Like their English-language counterparts, Ornelas and Gil work directly for the club, also doing community relations work.

Josh Lewin came on as the Rangers' TV voice in 2002 after serving with the Orioles and the Cubs. One of *Fox Saturday Baseball's* announcers, Lewin was usually on network duty on the weekends, requiring a substitute — either Bill Land or Barnett. The excitable Lewin often sounded younger than his years. As a relative "young turk" familiar with contemporary baseball research and the Internet, he received some criticism, reinforcing the age-old truism that no announcer can please everyone.

Unfortunately, Lewin's ambition caused a problem. In 2005, he took the NFL San Diego Chargers' radio job. The Rangers had tolerated his other baseball work, but were unhappy playing second fiddle to an NFL commitment that took their lead announcer away for a quarter of their September games. Therefore, the Rangers mandated, when re-upping Lewin for 2010 with a mutual option for 2011, that he limit his absences to three games in the season's last month.

Lewin and Grieve had an on-again, off-again chemistry, reportedly with some friction off the air. On August 7, 2009, the analyst had an embarrassing moment during a broadcast. As the broadcast returned following a series of commercials, viewers heard Grieve — who didn't know he was on the air — let fly with an annoyed, "I don't give a shit!"

Once the 2010 season concluded, Lewin exited the Rangers booth, temporarily giving up full-time baseball work. Rather than hiring a well-known outside voice or picking an eligible announcer from the Triple-A tree for their lead television voice, the Rangers chose John Rhadigan.

Rhadigan came to the job with little baseball play-by-play experience, although he had been host of the Rangers' pregame and postgame shows for several years. Texas management made it clear that Rhadigan was not its first choice, but the club claimed to be content with someone would be a conversationalist and, just as importantly, work effectively with Grieve.

The "television isn't really a play-by-play medium" trope — which is sometimes used to rationalize hiring less expensive talents who lack experience as lead baseball announcers — proved unsound in this case. Rhadigan was an almost immediate failure, appearing uncomfortable and lacking baseball knowledge, before being relieved of in-game duty on May 27, 2011.

Fox and the club returned Rhadigan to his studio job and transferred Dave Barnett from radio to team with Grieve as the new TV play-by-play man. Busby, who had been filling in on TV and radio in recent years, assumed the full-time radio analyst chair, with occasional help from Bryan Dolgin, KRLD's pregame and postgame host.

The Rangers took a huge PR hit in the Rhadigan affair, both for asking the well-liked local personality to do a job he wasn't qualified for and for providing a poor broadcast experience. The damage was limited, however, at least for the moment.

The Rangers' broadcast teams shifted during 2012, though, due to an unusual situation.

On June 18 of that season, during a game in San Diego, TV announcer Dave Barnett suddenly began to speak what sounded like gibberish.

During the bottom of the eighth, Barnett was calling the play, noting, "…a single by Chase Headley. The tying run is on second and lead run is on…fifth…in what Adams is insisting on calling it (sic) a botched robbery. What happened was, his henchman literally took a piece…out…" before he fell silent for some 20 seconds.

Barnett, who for much of his life has suffered migraine headaches, finished the game with no further incident, but was taken off the job the next day and did not return. Happily, he had not suffered a stroke, but he still has no medical explanation for what happened. Following the season, the Rangers announced that they would not renew the 54-year-old Barnett's one-year contract.

On June 19, radio color man Steve Busby shifted over to call the action on TV with Tom Grieve, and after pregame and postgame host Bryan Dolgin filled in as the No. 2 radio guy for a few games, the Rangers and KESN-FM welcomed their new radio man, Matt Hicks, on June 30. Hicks had heretofore been the lead announcer for Texas' Double-A Frisco affiliate.

While Busby is an experienced broadcaster, he won't win any medals for his delivery, but then again the Rangers haven't had a riveting television broadcast for many years. Nadel and Hicks work just fine on the wireless.

Texas hired former infielder Mark McLemore to handle some 25 television games for 2014, giving Tom Grieve a few days off; some rumors had Grieve wanting to retire outright. This is McLemore's first in-the-booth job after several years as an in-studio host.

With consecutive World Series appearances in 2011 and 2012 and a new $80 million per year TV deal kicking in for 2014, the club has plenty to smile about when it looks at its broadcasting future.

CHEEKY CANADIANS

THE TORONTO BLUE JAYS BROADCASTING HISTORY

"Tony Kubek always brought along the juiciest rumors in town.
He would pass them along, glancing over his shoulder to make sure he wasn't
being overheard, and warn me not to tell where I had got the tip. Then he would
go on the air and spill the beans himself. Some tip!"
— *Alison Gordon,* Foul Ball! Five Years in the American League

TORONTO HAD FOR MANY YEARS BEEN A TRIPLE-A CITY, THOUGH
only in a baseball sense. With the Maple Leafs having last played in 1967, however, the civic
leaders in Canada's largest city were hungry for baseball and ready to commit when the
American League granted its first non–U.S. franchise. But once the Blue Jays were assembled
for the 1977 season, with the popular Labatt's Brewery as its majority owner, the organization
seemed to have a tough time turning Canadians into fans.

A major problem was that the new club's 20-station radio network covered only Ontario
and parts of New York State. Stations all over Canada might have been interested in carrying
the Blue Jays–brand of Major League Baseball, but a combination of factors led to the small
footprint. Lack of vision or unsuccessful marketing, plus the success of the Expos, meant
that neither the Hewpex nor Télémedia radio networks could spread the Jays' new gospel.

When the Toronto franchise was born, Montreal was already well established as "Canada's
team" and had a roster burgeoning with exciting young talent. Thus the Blue Jays were in
a bind from the start.

Toronto's broadcasting rights netted the expansion franchise $1.2 million in 1977, in the
middle of the pack among AL teams — not bad considering that the club's television package

was far less robust than most major-league teams'. National network CBC showed just 13 Jays games in 1977, all on Wednesday nights save for the club's first-ever contest on Opening Day, April 7.

The new club decided to eschew hiring experienced big-league broadcasters, figuring that the Canadian audience would not know most American baseball voices anyway. In making this choice, Toronto — like other visionary expansion teams — provided its fans with a voice that came to personify its franchise.

At the radio mike for the team's first season, and in fact covering every single Blue Jays game through June 2004, was Tom Cheek. After spending three years as a part-time broadcaster with the Expos — where he did radio play-by-play for about 20 games each season when Dave Van Horne shifted to TV — Cheek had both attended college and worked in the Northeastern U.S. He was married to a Quebeçois woman.

A quality baseball broadcaster with an affable air and an easy grace, Cheek was an understated presence, which went a long way for someone broadcasting baseball in Canada. While baseball is popular in Canada, it's still a distant second to hockey and vies for fans with other sports like Canadian football, American football, and even curling.

Hewpex made overtures to two American former players, Tim McCarver and Tommy Davis, about working with Cheek. Eventually the network settled on the much older Early Wynn as its radio color man on CKFH. Wynn was a cantankerous, idiosyncratic Hall of Fame pitcher who could break down the pitcher's strengths and weaknesses; he lasted five seasons with the Jays' network.

On the television side, veteran Don Chevrier — who also had some experience filling in on Expos broadcasts — took the lead chair. A legendary presence with a big voice and a huge resume that included Olympic hockey and curling, CFL football, boxing, and golf, Chevrier was aided from 1977 to 1980 by CBC veteran Tom McKee, who would later move into reporting and hosting roles. In 1977, the two also worked with Hall of Fame pitcher Whitey Ford on all 13 telecasts.

Tapes of the team's first-ever game on April 7, 1977 survive, detailing a 9–5 win over the White Sox that was played in bitterly cold wind and snow. The inaugural contest was played at Exhibition Stadium, a football facility hurriedly retrofitted for baseball. During this first telecast, Chevrier, McKee, and Ford constantly marveled at the hardy Canadian fans' enthusiasm for their brand-new franchise.

Even though the honeymoon wore off as the Jays lost more than 100 games in each of their first three seasons, Cheek developed a devoted following on the radio. Chevrier remained on Blue Jays telecasts through 1996; he was the club's main TV presence as Toronto clambered into contention, finishing above .500 every year from 1983 through 1993 in the very competitive AL East Division.

During the club's second season on CBC, another onetime Yankees' player entered the booth: Tony Kubek, a successful color man on NBC's *Game of the Week* telecasts. Working alongside Chevrier for 12 years, the intelligent but sometimes gruff Kubek explained the intricacies of the game during the club's growing years and ascent into contention.

In July 1978, the CBC's groundbreaking tactic of employing McKee as a dugout-level reporter raised hackles with the local Baseball Writers' Association of American chapter, which demanded equal access. The Jays responded that if the local papers wanted to pay the one million dollars that the CBC paid to air their games, then the club would also make field-level access available to the ink-stained wretches.

Despite its limited radio territory, Toronto made an effort to appeal to all of Canada by simultaneously telecasting games from 1977 to 1980 on CBC's French network, SRC (Société Radio-Canada). Jean-Pierre Roy and Gui Ferron, the network's announcers for Montreal games, also called the action on the Toronto broadcasts, coordinated not to conflict with Expos telecasts.

After 1980, however, Toronto left the CBC, which the club felt was too closely affiliated with the Expos. The Blue Jays decided to sell their video rights to Labatt's Brewery, which then sublicensed them to CTV, Canada's second television network and a powerhouse in its own right. The independent net forged a relationship with Blue Jays fans that lasted through 1992. Toronto games were not telecast in French again until 2011 and were never on the radio *en Français* until a pair of French-language games aired over Montreal's CKAC in May 2010.

The Labatt/CTV deal brought the Jays $4 million in rights fees per year in 1981 and 1982. The brewery undertook all production costs and sold most (if not all) of the advertising time. Toronto CTV affiliate station CFTO was the flagship.

Toronto wanted more money — Carling/O'Keefe was paying approximately $6 million for the Expos TV rights at that time — but Labatt was operating under two disadvantages. First, the brewer couldn't sell its product at dry Exhibition Stadium, and second, the Blue Jays did not control their scoreboard advertising, as the Expos did.

While the CBC and SRC had televised a high of 22 games in 1978, CTV ramped up to 30 games immediately, gradually increasing the number to 60 by 1991. In 1987 the network's sponsors were Chrysler, Honda, AMC, Mazda, Michelin, Goodyear, Standard Auto Glass, Imperial Oil, Labatts, and a local bank.

Chevrier, Kubek, and former minor-league pitcher Fergie Olver formed the CTV team through 1989, when Kubek retired. He was replaced by Tommy Hutton, one of few to play for both the Jays and Expos. The handsome and personable Hutton had covered the Expos on TV and radio from 1982 to 1986 then served a three-year hitch with the Yankees. By the time Hutton joined the Jays, CTV had company in the form of the cable Sports Network (TSN).

Owned by Labatt's, TSN began operations in November 1984. Like ESPN in the U.S., TSN began with a heavy diet of fringe sports, but the net started pouring serious money into the Expos' and Blue Jays' pockets in 1985. The cable cash infusion helped raise Toronto's media rights fees to $7 million that season, higher than any AL club aside from New York.

Labatt, as majority owner of the Jays, also telecast Expos games on TSN, even becoming Montreal's primary sponsor in 1986. Labatt continued this unusual arrangement until it sold the Blue Jays to Interbrew NA following the 1994 strike.

The Jays' first cable broadcasts came on a short-lived network called Superchannel, which carried 10 games across Canada with Cheek at the mike in 1984. The following season, TSN hit the ground running with Olver calling the action, paired with Kubek and recently retired outfielder Ken Singleton. Kubek and Singleton split color duties for the 40-game slate, with Singleton getting the full-time gig in 1985.

Smart and smooth, Singleton has never hurt for broadcast work; he moved over to the Expos' telecasts in 1987. Former Jays catcher Buck Martinez took over the Toronto mike after hanging up his spikes after the 1986 campaign. Martinez quickly became one of TSN's main on-air personalities, staying with the network through 2000 as he provided color first for Olver, then for Jim Hughson and, finally, for Dan Shulman.

While the television outlook for Toronto changed tremendously during the 1980s, the club's radio broadcasts were a sea of calm. With Cheek at the helm, Jerry Howarth provided color and shared some of the play-by-play work over the wireless.

The deeply religious Howarth provided a friendly, reserved presence with a certain charm. Like Cheek, he had never enjoyed a full-time job in the majors before joining the Jays. Howarth arrived in 1981 after five years doing broadcasts in Triple-A; the felicitous pairing continued, unaccompanied by others, through 1999.

As the Jays increased the TV schedule in the 1990s, the club remained popular on the radio. CJCL took over radio rights in 1982; later that year, Télémedia Broadcast Systems of Ontario bought the station and the Hewpex Sports Network.

In 1985, when the Jays won their first AL East title, Télémedia undertook its first national coverage with a network of 45 stations transmitting Cheek's and Howarth's voices across Canada's vast landscape. When the Expos began to falter and the Jays rose to contention, the audience in the Canadian hinterlands seemed to switch its allegiance almost overnight.

From the beginning, the Jays attracted many of Canada's biggest companies as sponsors: McDonald's, CIBC (Canadian Imperial Bank of Commerce), GM Canada, and others. For many years in the 1980s, their radio inventory was completely sold out. In 1986, Télémedia raised the 30-second spot rate on Jays radio from $40,000 to $60,000, but sponsors kept buying up time. Télémedia's President, Len Bramson, called Toronto games "the biggest show in Canada."

CJCL, rebranded as "The Fan" in 1992, carried Cheek and Howarth's cheery descriptions through 1997. CHUM took over from 1998 through 2002. CJCL, now a division of Rogers Communications, regained the rights in 2003.

TSN experienced competition following Toronto's world championship in 1992 when the CBC got back into baseball with veteran sportscaster Brian Williams in the play-by-play seat through 2003. The new ONT (Ontario Network Television) system, a subgroup of CTV, also telecast from 1993 to 1996 with Chevrier and crew in the booth.

TSN was set to carry an all-time high of 80 Blue Jays games in 1994 until labor problems destroyed the season. With three separate television outlets beaming the action, the 1995 season turned into a disaster; fan interest deteriorated as the Jays finished last in the East, 30 games out. Despite the troubles of the previous two years, in 1996 Jays fans could watch all-time high 141 contests on the box.

In 1997 and 1998, only the CBC and TSN televised Toronto games, with CTV returning in 1999–2001. In the first two years of its three-year deal, CTV's broadcast team featured Rod Black and Joe Carter, whose dramatic Game Six home run had won the 1993 World Series for the Jays.

CTV bought TSN in 2001, with Rob Faulds assuming play-by-play duties. By this time, a new crew of ex-players was working as analysts on Toronto's various radio and TV broadcasts, including hurlers Tom Candiotti and John Cerutti, outfielder Gary Matthews, and first baseman Pat Tabler.

The biggest new player in the Jays' broadcasts for 2002, however, had never seen action on a major-league diamond. Instead Ted Rogers had made his mark in the corporate boardroom. Long a superstar in the media and wireless communications fields, Rogers purchased 80 percent of the Blue Jays in 2000, acquiring the remaining shares from Labatt Communications four years later.

With the team's broadcast contracts expiring after 2001, Rogers folded the Blue Jays into his cross-Canada TV sports network, Rogers Sportsnet. CTV Sportsnet had first taken the air in 1998, gradually increasing its programming as it challenged heretofore superior TSN. CTV's 2001 purchase of TSN, and the subsequent sale of Sportsnet to Rogers, created a perfect synergy between ballclub and television.

During the 2002 season, Rob Faulds described nearly 120 games on Rogers, the largest TV package ever for any Canadian network airing the Blue Jays. Rogers showed the contests throughout Canada, producing extensive pregame and postgame content as well as weekly features.

Faulds, perhaps best as a studio host, did not have an ideal style for play-by-play and was not retained after 2004, a year when two tragedies shook the Blue Jays' organization. Tom Cheek missed his first radio broadcast in June when his father passed away. Cheek had been experiencing headaches and, shortly after returning to the booth, was diagnosed with a malignant brain tumor. The second shock came when John Cerutti died suddenly of a heart attack on October 3, 2004, before the season's last game in Toronto.

Although he returned to do some home games later in 2004, Cheek had to leave the booth after only a few innings on Opening Day, 2005, in Tampa Bay. The Toronto legend passed away on October 14, 2005, after calling occasional home games that season. Cheek had broadcast 4,303 consecutive Blue Jays games from 1977 through 2004, a streak that no future announcer is likely to match. With his death, the franchise officially shifted Howarth to the lead chair.

Local broadcaster Mike Wilner, engaged in 2002 to take some of the load off veterans Cheek and Howarth, assumed the no. 2 role permanently, with former replacement player Warren Sawkiw filling out the Jays' new radio team.

On television, young Jamie Campbell was tapped for full-time duties in 2005. Campbell had covered Triple-A ball in Edmonton, occasionally filling in on Sportsnet. While somewhat awkward at first, Campbell improved quickly with experience, interacting with an assortment of analysts that included Candiotti, Tabler, Rance Mullinks, and Darrin Fletcher. Even with this advancement, Campbell had a hard time winning over the fan base used to a more slick presentation.

Howarth and Wilner were joined in 2007 by newly hired Alan Ashby, a former Blue Jays receiver who arrived fresh from Houston's radio booth to replace Sawkiw.

Ted Rogers passed away in 2008, but Sportsnet remained the big player in Jays' telecasts as TSN's slate hovered around 20–30 per year. CBC, sponsored by Rogers, made another foray into Blue Jays baseball in 2007, with Hughson, the network's top hockey voice, calling the action. This time around, CBC bowed out after two seasons of telecasting a mediocre team to a mid-sized audience.

With so many games being carried by Rogers Sportsnet (RSN) — most Jays games are shown on all four of the RSN regional networks — more Canadian fans can watch the Blue Jays than ever before, and more often, too. Via a nationwide radio network, MLB.com's Webcasts, and satellite dishes, the whole of Canada finally has convenient and frequent access to what now is the only national team.

Campbell was shifted from play-by-play to studio work after 2009. Rogers and the Jays then made an ill-considered but defensible move; rather than bring in a qualified play-by-play announcer, the club chose to re-hire Buck Martinez who, like most athletes-turned-broadcasters, is better suited to handle color than play-by-play even when aided by the quality of the RSN production team.

Martinez's workload grew unexpectedly in May 2010, when TSN and the Blue Jays agreed to shift all 25 of the network's games to Sportsnet. The 2010 season was the last year of TSN's contract to carry the Blue Jays, and both parties chose to save some time by making the changeover. The decision also meant a sudden end for Rod Black's career as a baseball play-by-play voice, but few fans seemed to mourn that loss.

Thus, for the first time in a quarter-century, TSN was not telecasting the Blue Jays. TSN had counted on the prestige of Major League Baseball and the attraction of the Blue Jays and Expos as key factors in gaining respectability when the network debuted in 1984. But the American game is now viewed by many as a niche sport in Canada, and the Blue Jays are a perfect fit for Rogers, which as team owner can promote the club more effectively than anyone.

Free of carrying the product of its biggest competitor, TSN showed only one major league baseball game per week — the ESPN Sunday night show — as all 162 of the Jays' 2010 games were now on Sportsnet.

The late Tom Cheek described Toronto Blue Jays action from the franchise's start in 1977 through 2005. (Courtesy Toronto Blue Jays)

The Jays resumed French-language broadcasting in 2010 in a limited fashion when Montreal's CKAC aired Jeremy Filosa and Alex Agostino covering a pair of May home games. The experiment was repeated the following season, with Filosa and Agostino expanding their schedule to 15 contests from the Rogers Centre. Unfortunately, CKAC had changed format by 2012 and was no longer a sports station, so the French radiocasts ended.

But even more surprising was the 2011 development that saw the Blue Jays add a television package *en Français*. New French-language sports network TVA contracted to carry a handful of games, putting former Expos airmen Jacques Doucet and Rodger Brulotte back at the mike. The experiment was successful enough that for 2012, TVA scheduled 60 games, looking to fill the void for French-Canadian baseball fans created after Les Expos left for Washington, D.C., after the 2004 season.

Partnering with Rogers Sportsnet, TVA used the English-language video feed for most of the action, eliminating the costs of employing a dedicated television crew. The new arrangement felt even better for Quebec's baseball fans because Doucet and Brulotte were two of the stalwart banner-carriers for baseball in the province.

Alan Ashby departed for Houston's television booth in January 2013, meaning that Toronto needed a new color man for its radio broadcasts. (Mike Wilner, the club's #3 on radio, was apparently not strongly considered for a promotion).

Instead, the Jays hired Jack Morris, who had done several years of part-time work with the Twins, for his first-ever full-time radio job.

Popular opinion seemed almost evenly split concerning Morris, whose Hall of Fame candidacy has become a lightning rod for opposing views about player excellence. Some locals looked forward to hearing Morris talk about the "old days" and discuss pitching, while others felt his voice was grating and that his point of view about the game was outmoded.

Morris and Dirk Hayhurst, another former pitcher (and accomplished author) and occasional Jays radio fill-in, got into trouble almost immediately, accusing Boston's Clay Buchholz in May 2013 of throwing doctored baseballs. Morris ended up apologizing publicly to Buchholz, and neither he nor Hayhurst returned to the broadcasts in 2014.

Instead, the Jays hired Joe Siddall, a former big-league catcher, to work with Howarth, a move that so far looks to be a strong one.

The Jays continued to make games available on French cable TV in 2013 and 2014, with TVA network airing 60 contests a year with Doucet and Brulotte at the microphones. It's a welcome thing to see the Jays attempting to truly become Canada's team.

NOS AMOURS SONT PARTIS

MONTREAL EXPOS/WASHINGTON NATIONALS
BROADCASTING HISTORY

"Breaking in doing football and basketball, you needed to call those games at a rapid pace. Baseball opened the door to a world of creativity. A lot of what goes into calling a baseball game is about what you do between pitches, and I enjoyed that."
— *Dave Van Horne, Baseball Prospectus interview, 2003*

FEW OBSERVERS THOUGHT THAT MONTREAL WOULD BE SUCCESS-ful in its attempt to land a National League expansion franchise for 1969. While the city was certainly prestigious, having just hosted the Expo '67 World's Fair, Montreal had no suitable ballpark to house a big-league team and no plans to build one. Factoring in the cold weather, few viable television broadcast options, the absence of professional baseball in the city for nearly a decade, and no evidence of overwhelming fan support, it was a surprise that Les Expos were ever born.

But Charles Bronfman, owner of Seagram's and head of the investor group, would not rest until Montreal had a team. He put $5 million of his own money into a large ownership group to help guarantee the new club's solvency.

The biggest problems the new team faced were arguably not the serious ones of finding a suitable stadium, dealing with the weather, growing a fan base, or even the lack of on-field talent. Perhaps the biggest issue was sorting out the radio and television situations.

Montreal's potential baseball audience was split into two languages, and the numbers didn't favor the Expos; some believed that the roughly three-quarters of city residents who were Francophones (i.e., spoke French as their first or only language) were less inclined to watch baseball than the minority Anglophone community.

Neither French nor English radio stations lined up to carry the nascent team, which could not find a home on the radio until spring training.

On television, the Expos had only two options. The Canadian Broadcasting Corporation, a government-mandated monopoly, was the country's only television network until 1961, when the government deregulated television and began taking applications from potential operators in other cities who wanted to own TV stations.

In 1961, the new CTV took to the air in eight Canadian cities. Despite some early inroads into sports broadcasting, however, CTV was not a high-profile network until the 1970s, making CBC the Expos' preferred choice.

The CBC and SRC (Société Radio-Canada, CBC's French component) obviously felt some responsibility to the Expos, as not airing the Canada's first Major League Baseball club on the national TV network would have been a PR disaster.

The immediate issue, however, was serious: when could the networks show the games? The CBC and CTV both had contracts with the Canadian Football League in the summer and with the National Hockey League during the spring and fall. Haggling over money and scheduling kept a baseball deal from coalescing until mid-March.

Carling–O'Keefe, a 100-year-old concern owned in 1969 by Canadian Brewers but soon to be sold to international tobacco conglomerate Rothmans, stepped up and paid $300,000 for a half-sponsorship and editorial control of both the English and French telecasts. O'Keefe Ale would continue its association with the Expos for nearly two decades.

To its credit, O'Keefe didn't just sponsor the games; the company poured a million dollars into reviving youth baseball in Quebec, setting up winter clinics and camps all over the province. Montreal players and front-office staff traveled to these camps, creating grass-roots interest.

There was no time to work the Expos' games into a regular television slot for 1969, so the CBC chose to beam 15 games to the nation: four on Sundays and nine on Wednesday nights, plus the Expos' season opener and the club's home opener, both on weekdays. SRC chose to air all 15 of the CBC's games plus six additional contests. Both networks transmitted all games in color.

Amazingly enough, the CBC didn't even have to pay to show games in 1969 and 1970, as the Expos purchased telecast time from the network. This gamble paid off for the club; strong ratings in the initial years led to a new contract for 1971 in which the CBC and SRC remunerated the Expos.

SRC and CBC televised the Expos' first-ever game from New York on April 8 as well as the first home game, both of which Montreal won. The next four early-season games aired on Sundays, with the remainder of the 1969 schedule shown Wednesdays during the network's summer rerun period, going directly against CTV's football telecasts.

While the Expos' TV picture wasn't profitable at the beginning, at least it didn't cause embarrassment as did the English-language radio rights situation. In March 1969, the Expos named WEAV of Plattsburgh, New York — an hour away from Montreal and previously a Yankees radio affiliate — as their first English-language flagship. Eventually CFCF in Montreal, which decades before had been the first radio station to take the air in Canada, signed on in 1970 as the club's local English-language affiliate.

Choosing announcers turned out to be a sticky exercise. The Expos made it known that they wanted Bob Wolff, formerly voice of the Washington Senators, to be their English-language voice, but negotiations broke down and Wolff remained as a P.R. man and announcer at Madison Square Garden.

Shortly afterward, the club named Dave Van Horne as its English-language announcer. Though without previous big-league experience, the Virginia native had called three years of Triple-A ball for the Richmond Braves. In 1966 and 1967 he had been named Virginia Sportscaster of the Year.

Though not yet 30 but prematurely balding, Van Horne was the NL's youngest No. 1 announcer at the time, as well as one of the youngest ever. Among MLB's broadcasters in 1969, four, including Van Horne, remain active at least on a half-time basis in 2014 (the others are Dick Enberg, Denny Matthews, and Vin Scully).

Blessed with a pleasant baritone and displaying an easy feel for the game, Van Horne never attempted to make himself the star, doing his best to simultaneously stay out of the way of the action while reminding the listeners that he was there to guide them.

Van Horne's first sidekick was Russ Taylor, a Montreal broadcaster since 1948 and previously sports director of CFCF-TV. Taylor wasn't really a baseball guy, but he showed a lot of enthusiasm and is credited with helping the Expos obtain the rights to use Jarry Park.

The team signed a five-year lease to play at — and expand — Jarry, a small community stadium, in October 1968. Taylor added to the fun by hanging a fishing net out of the Jarry Park radio booth to snag foul balls.

Parc Jarry was among the smallest parks in recent major-league history and almost certainly the most Spartan. On Opening Day, fans were guided to seats barely bolted in, and a lack of adequate walkways delayed the large crowd from entering.

Somehow, this tiny ballpark held a press box big enough not only for newspaper writers supplying copy in two languages, but also for six radio-TV booths outfitted to serve French radio, French-language television, English-language radio, English-language television, visiting team radio, and visiting team television. The intimate ballpark's broadcast booths were, by necessity, small, and radio listeners could often hear whoever was announcing next door.

Jean-Pierre Roy and Jean-Paul Sarault narrated the original French-language broadcasts. CHRD, based in Drummondville, was mooted as the French flagship station until CKLM, in Montreal proper, signed on shortly before Opening Day. Unfortunately, the French network carried just 130 games in 1969, omitting 32 afternoon contests.

Sarault, a sportswriter with the *Montreal-Matin* and the first Montreal BBWAA chairman, called Expos games with Roy for three years before returning to his typewriter. In 1978, Sarault was named BBWAA president while with the *Matin*, but lost his job the next year when the afternoon newspaper closed down.

Roy enjoyed hero status in his native Canada, as he had starred with the Montreal Royals in the 1940s and had even pitched for the Brooklyn Dodgers in 1946. He was the first of many ex-Royals to find their way into the team's broadcast booth. Another was Jim Hearn, former Cardinals, Giants, and Phillies right-handed pitcher, hired by CBC as its color man. Hearn had previously done between-innings commentary on CBC's rebroadcast of NBC's *Game of the Week*.

Hal Kelly was the CBC's first Expos play-by-play announcer. For many years, Kelly had called the Triple-A Toronto Maple Leafs' games. The Canadian Baseball Hall of Fame honored him and Joe Crysdale, the color man on Leafs games, with its Jack Graney Award, given for meritorious media service, in 1991. Hal was the older brother of Dan Kelly, who in 1969 was rapidly becoming one of hockey's best-loved play-by-play men, covering the St. Louis Blues and helming CBS' national NHL telecasts.

Roy and Guy Ferron, a veteran sportscaster, teamed in the Société Radio-Canada booth. Ferron, little remembered today, served as a TV commentator on Expos games until his passing in 1981.

The Expos hired all four radio broadcasters, but the TV personnel were under the control of the networks. In 1969, the man in charge of all the radio broadcasters and various broadcast arrangements was Gene Kirby, doing double duty as Expos' traveling secretary and radio-TV director after years of experience on the administrative end of the network *Game of the Week* in the U.S.

The Expos' front office in 1969 also had a director & producer of broadcast operations, Ray Blomquist, so the overlapping job responsibilities must have been confusing. Kirby departed after just one year; Blomquist, after three.

In previous years, NBC had sold its *Game of the Week* to the CBC, and it continued this relationship in 1969, sending 12 Saturday afternoon games, the World Series, and the All-Star Game across Canada via the CBC. Kelly and Hearn were on hand for all of these games to provide Canadian-specific commentary between innings.

The Expos finished 52–110 in 1969, but were hugely popular anyway. SRC and CBC telecasts, not bound by American conventions, utilized some interesting techniques. One example was that players and coaches could be miked while in uniform. Another was that the networks stationed reporters adjacent to, and even in, the dugouts. The level of production was high, with multiple camera angles and frequent replays.

Late in August, injured Expos first baseman Ron Fairly sat in the radio booth with Van Horne and Taylor for several games. It was the beginning of a long second career for Fairly; years later in California, following his playing days, Fairly initiated a 27-year run as a broadcaster.

Even with interest in two languages and national exposure, Montreal didn't enjoy a big return financially on radio and TV in 1969: the team's total broadcast revenue of $450,000 ranked with Pittsburgh's as the smallest in the NL.

Television deals for 1970 were completed early enough that SRC and CBC instituted a pattern of showing most games on Wednesday nights. SRC beamed 22 contests, while the English net aired 16. Jim Hearn was out, with Don Drysdale — another ex-Royals player — coming aboard as TV color man as well as a roving pitching instructor in the Montreal system.

CBC and SRC could at least boast strong sponsorships, not because the Expos were a good team, but simply because the networks broadcast games all over Canada and reached a large number of viewers. Aside from O'Keefe, other big Canadian companies to buy on-air sponsorships included Bank of Montreal, Texaco Canada, and MacDonald Tobacco. The network's overall commitment to baseball took a dive, however, for 1970, as CBC stopped airing NBC's *Game of the Week*.

On the English radio side, CFCF assumed the role of Expos' chief English-language radio station in 1970, continuing through 1988. CKLM remained Les Expos' French flagship, with Roy and Sarault manning the mikes. Jacques Doucet, a beat writer from Montreal newspaper *La Presse* and an official scorer, filled in when Roy went over to television.

Building a fan base was made easier by the unlikely popularity of slugger Rusty Staub, one of the original Expos (via trade), who became the club's only All-Star in 1969. Staub became both a local and a national hero for his hitting, winning smile, and flaming copper hair (leading to his nickname "Le Grand Orange"). During the winter of 1970–71, the CBC aired a one-hour primetime special on Staub.

In early 1971, the CBC and SRC linked new a three-year deal with the Expos. CBC showed 18 games, again all on Wednesday nights, while SRC aired 21. Van Horne became the Expos' English-language TV voice, teaming with Drysdale.

The deposed Hal Kelly eventually became an itinerant television play-by-play man for various mediocre NHL teams (North Stars, Islanders, and Capitals) and never again called big-league baseball.

Starting in 1971, the Expos utilized Ron Reusch — known for his work on Montreal Canadiens radio broadcasts — in the CFCF booth when Van Horne assumed the CBC-TV mike. Reusch remained associated with the Expos in this secondary role for most seasons through 1990.

Also in 1971, the Expos hopped to their third French-language radio flagship in three years, but this was a lasting relationship as CKAC held the radio rights through 1999. On the English side, Toronto's CFKH signed on as a radio affiliate. The Expos by then were broadcast over radio stations in New York, Quebec, and Ontario, but nowhere west. One station in Windsor in Southwestern Ontario wanted to join the Expos' network; the Detroit Tigers controlled that territory, however, so the station's request was denied. Montreal's 1971 media rights added up to just $500,000, among the lowest in MLB.

Big changes came in 1972, when the Expos' media revenue rose to $600,000 as the club's 23-station French-language radio network was the largest yet. Jacques Doucet, the 1971 Montreal BBWAA chair, replaced Sarault as the lead voice on French broadcasts while also helping to administer the radio network. The reliable and personable Doucet remained the team's primary voice until its departure from Montreal.

Producing French-language broadcasts was not easy: even though the broadcasters were bilingual, reinterpreting press materials written in English took extra time and effort. Pregame shows in French were problematic because, aside from relief pitcher Claude "Frenchy" Raymond, no Expos players even spoke French, so nearly all interviews had to be translated.

Nevertheless, the Francophone communities in Montreal, Laval, Chicoutimi, Temiscaming, and Sherbrooke certainly appreciated the broadcasts, and a province already known for its love of youth baseball took to Les Expos in a major way.

The CBC, racked by strikes in 1972, had to call off an early April telecast. Van Horne went it alone that season on television, as Drysdale had moved on to a regular broadcasting job in Texas. Two decades later, Drysdale — who had credited Van Horne as a major factor in his on-air success — died in Montreal while on a road trip broadcasting his beloved Dodgers.

That winter, O'Keefe began awarding $10,000 to the team's Most Valuable Player, as selected by the local BBWAA chapter. The following year, the brewery instituted a $1,000 Player of the Month award, reducing the annual prize to $5,000. Reliever Mike Marshall captured the first two Montreal MVP honors.

In 1973, the brewer ("Have another O'Keefe ... a great moment at any time!") had begun airing historical "Great Moments in Baseball" highlights during Expos telecasts on SRC and CBC. Jean-Pierre Roy gave up the radio gig, instead helping O'Keefe expand its baseball commitment while continuing to call TV games with Ferron on SRC.

At Doucet's request, Raymond joined the radio broadcasts on a full-time basis in 1973. The charismatic pitcher from St. Jean, Quebec, who finished his 12-year big-league career with the Expos from late 1969 through 1971, had assisted on some broadcasts in 1972.

Only 150 of Montreal's 1973 games were carried on French radio, the last time that any games were pre-empted en Français until 2002. The colorful Raymond, like Russ Taylor, used a fishing net to grab foul balls from the radio booth.

The team's rights fees jumped to $800,000 in 1973, which at least ranked ahead of San Diego, if no one else in the NL. With few television channels available in Canada, and CBC and SRC's mandated responsibility to present a varied range of programming, the Expos were somewhat constrained in their ambitions. However, for the first time that season, CBC and SRC did extend their baseball coverage to hookups in the Yukon and the Northwest Territory.

The Expos added another ex-Montreal Royals player in February 1973 when Duke Snider joined the CBC telecasting team to pair with Van Horne. The following year, Snider was hired as the club's hitting coach. After two seasons in uniform, the future Hall of Famer assumed full-time duties as a third man in the radio booth, also serving as Van Horne's co-pilot on TV.

The Expos finished 79–83 in 1973, but the young team still contended through the final days of the season in a weak NL East Division. As a result, CBC added a couple of late September contests to its schedule to sate the appetite of ravenous Canadian baseball fans.

Once the season was done, trouble arose between the team and its chief sponsor; Mike Marshall refused to accept his 1973 O'Keefe award, averring that he didn't want to compete against his teammates. Marshall, who had set a new MLB record for games pitched and had finished second in NL Cy Young balloting in 1973, first asked that O'Keefe pay the income tax on the award, then requested that the brewery donate the prize to sickle-cell anemia research.

O'Keefe did not heed Marshall's request, which annoyed the famously cantankerous pitcher, who criticized one of his teammates shortly after in an interview and then became the subject of a $75,000 defamation of character suit from *La Presse* sportswriter J.P. Sarault, who Marshall had accused of being unscrupulous in his methods.

Marshall was soon dealt to the Dodgers. According to contemporaneous reports, annoyed O'Keefe representatives had pressured Expos GM Jim Fanning into making the trade — the reports were denied, of course.

From 1974 through 1976, Tom Cheek took over from Reusch as the relief man on English-language radio, using this experience to introduce himself to the Canadian baseball audience. The Toronto Blue Jays, granted an American League franchise for 1977, wisely named Cheek their lead radio voice.

In 1974, 56 CBC and SRC affiliates carried the 20-game Expos' television package across Canada, while on radio, 24 stations broadcast the team in French and 11 more in English. O'Keefe was now a major sponsor on radio as well as on television, joined by "outside" corporations Pepsi, Texaco, and AMC (American Motors), plus Canadian concerns Air Canada, Steinberg's supermarkets, and the Bank of Montreal. Overall, the varied set of broadcasters and sponsors paid the club $950,000 for its radio-TV rights.

The next year, due to an exclusive six-year CBC/SRC TV contract that had involved a bidding war with CTV, the Expos' media revenue rose to a nice, even million dollars — as much as Houston, Atlanta, and St. Louis, and more than San Diego. O'Keefe remained the major sponsor both on radio and television, along with the national lottery, Texaco, GM, and the like, but AMC dropped out of the radio package. Televised games aired on Wednesdays and Saturdays.

Some radio stations, mostly outside of Quebec, had dropped off the French network by this time. The English network, though, was now carried in New Brunswick and Prince Edward Island as well as on stations in Quebec, Ontario, Vermont, and New York.

The team did some market research at this time that indicated that 40 percent of the team's 1974 television audience had been female — an unusual breakdown for baseball or other team sports, given the proportion of ads for beer and autos on their broadcasts.

The Expos by this time aired pregame and postgame shows on both their radio networks although, unlike many teams, Montreal controlled the sales of commercials on those programs, rather than the stations.

When the Blue Jays began play in 1977, some of the Expos' English-language radio stations either defected to the AL team or were prohibited from carrying Montreal games because they were now in Toronto's territory. Thanks to the continuing partnership with Carling–O'Keefe, though, the value of the Expos' media rights rose to $1.2 million, among the highest in the NL.

Russ Taylor retired from the English-language radio team in spring 1977 to become the team's director of broadcasting. Sadly, he passed away of a heart attack on August 19, his 51st or his 55th birthday, depending on the source.

As Montreal developed a talented cohort of popular young players, the Expos' broadcast teams of Van Horne and Snider on the English side, and Roy and Ferron on the French, virtually became national institutions. During the late 1970s, Bob McDevitt was the third man in the booth as well as the field reporter on CBC Expos broadcasts. McDevitt had previously done hockey and tennis for the network. Don Wittman, later known for his work on *Hockey Night in Canada*, also filled this role on occasion.

With veteran manager Dick Williams at the helm, Montreal made its first serious runs at the postseason, finishing a strong second in 1979 and 1980 after never before having cleared .500. The number of radio stations in the Expos' network had dropped to around 30 by 1979, largely because of the Blue Jays, but Montreal's television ratings remained good.

The radio network swelled in September 1979 when four stations in the Maritimes and another in Manitoba signed up as the Expos fought for a division title. CBC even pre-empted a scheduled Blue Jays game that month to follow the Expos.

With the Expos viewed as an exciting and popular club with a bright future, Carling–O'Keefe saw baseball as a good investment and, as a result, the brewery laid down serious money. After the season, the Expos voided the final year of their six-year contract with CBC and SRC and put their entire broadcast package, not just the rights to carry the games, up for bids. Carling–O'Keefe, heretofore a sponsor, chose to purchase the team's television rights, offering twice as much as Labatt Brewing, the CBC, or CTV.

The unprecedented five-year, $32.5 million agreement raised Montreal's broadcast rights to a staggering $6.3 million per annum, by far the highest in the majors at a time when most teams had taken control of their broadcasts from sponsors and awarded them instead to stations or networks.

Carling–O'Keefe chose to lease Expos games back to the CBC. The brewery also returned to the practice of showing more games on SRC than on the English network. It all seemed like a great plan; Canada was gaga for its Expos, who were on the rise.

But the team's moment passed very quickly. In 1981, the year of the midseason player strike, Montreal won the second half NL East race and then defeated Philadelphia in commissioner Bowie Kuhn's *ad hoc* divisional playoffs. The Expos then lost to the Dodgers in the fifth and final game of the NLCS on a ninth-inning home run by Rick Monday. The painful 2–1 loss at home ended the club's first and only postseason appearance.

The Expos continued to produce good young players for years, but mismanagement and an oddly limited payroll kept the club from contending again until the NL expanded in 1993. After the 1981 strike, the Expos and O'Keefe had agreed to extend their deal through 1986. Instead of allying itself with a rising team, however, O'Keefe had bought in just as the party was ending.

The club's recently formed French-language network, Télémedia, inked a five-year deal in 1981 as Les Expos' success and the poor play of the expansion Blue Jays increased demand for Expos games. Montreal's English-language radio network included 24 stations in 1982. Two years later, the club boasted 35 English-language affiliates, only one of which — flagship station CFCF — was located in Quebec.

The Blue Jays chose to play hardball, invoking early in 1981 a clause in their charter that gave them exclusive television rights within 50 miles of their stadium in order to prevent the Expos from infringing on the huge Toronto market. The Expos had been shown in Ontario since 1969 on the CBC. The matter went all the way to the commissioner's office before it was eventually settled with a compromise that pleased no one, allowing the Expos to show 15 games each season in Toronto and the Jays to air the same number in Montreal. On some nights, the CBC was forced to broadcast both teams, with the Jays airing across most of Canada and the Expos seen only in Quebec.

In 1982, Ferron left the SRC telecasts, making way for Raymond Lebrun, a legendary figure in Canadian sports media who had most notably called football and amateur sports. He provided Expos play-by-play through 1993. In 1984, Lebrun got a new partner, Claude Raymond, who abdicated his radio duty for a lighter TV schedule. Joining Doucet on the radio was Rodger Brulotte, a team employee since 1969 and a tireless advocate of baseball in Canada. His signature home-run call was "Bonsoir! Elle est partie!"

CBC was now showing the Expos in many different slots, on Saturdays and Sundays as well as on Wednesday and Thursday nights, beaming 24 games in 1984. The following season, the new TSN (The Sports Network) began a more than a decade-long run of carrying Expos games. TSN, a cable net owned by Labatt Brewing, was Canada's first 24-hour sports TV network; as such, it needed to fill a lot of airtime, making baseball a summertime natural.

At the request of both Canadian franchises, the commissioner's office suspended the 1981 blackout rules during the 1985 season so that baseball fans across Canada could see every one of the 40 Jays games, 40 Expos games, and the 50 other MLB games that TSN cablecast in its inaugural year.

Labatt, which owned nearly half of the Blue Jays at the time, had its sights set on cornering the Canadian baseball market, and it got close to doing so in 1986 when Carling–O'Keefe relinquished the last year of its Expos deal to Labatt. This was a huge turning point in

Expos history; O'Keefe was the only lead sponsor the franchise had ever known, and had in fact run the show for much of the club's history.

CFCF and CKAC signed new contracts for 1986, continuing as solid radio partners with large networks. The 40-station French and 20-station English nets broadcast throughout Canada and parts of the United States.

TSN, with 800,000 subscribers, also inked a new two-year pact to transmit 40 Montreal road games. Former Expos players Ken Singleton and Tommy Hutton, who had started new careers as mikemen the previous year, called the action. While both have forged long careers in the booth, Singleton, in particular, distinguished himself for his easy manner and clear diction.

Duke Snider retired from Expos broadcasts in early 1987, with former Montreal GM and manager Jim Fanning stepping in to team with Van Horne on radio. Although the overall media rights amount had shrunk to $7 million (down from $8 million the previous year), the Expos' media revenue still ranked sixth-best in the majors. Labatt and the team established a new five-year sponsorship agreement which brought the team $30 million over five seasons.

For 1987, the Expos and Labatt sold a number of over-the-air broadcasts to CTV, with some games airing on nationally and some only over CFCF-TV in Montreal, the network's local affiliate. CBC and SRC continued to telecast Les Expos as well. While fans could see more games than before, the diffuse television arrangements and announcers were confusing and, with all the new stations, it was hard to keep track of the team's announcers. From 1987 through 1991, 17 men called games for the Expos: Dave Van Horne, Rob Faulds, Richard Griffin, Jerry Trupiano, Jim Fanning, Ken Singleton, Tommy Hutton, Jim Hughson, Ron Reusch, Bobby Winkles, Elliot Price, Jacques Doucet, Rodger Brulotte, Raymond Lebrun, Claude Raymond, P.J. Arsenault, and Denis Casavant.

In 1989, CJAD assumed English-language radio rights, signing a three-year deal. Jerry Trupiano replaced Fanning as Van Horne's second; Trupiano had called baseball, football, and basketball in Houston and later would work with Joe Castiglione on Red Sox games.

TSN went from a subscriber-based channel to a basic cable channel in 1990, broadening the network's audience to more than five million pairs of Canadian eyes. Unfortunately, the resulting drop in revenue led TSN to pare its commitment from 40 Expos games to 25.

In 1993, Montreal's media rights were still worth only $8 million. It was a sign of trouble to come for the Expos, who in the 1980s had competitive revenues but now watched as the rights fees other MLB franchises could command went through the roof. The stake through the franchise's heart came in 1994, when the owner-forced strike killed the last third of the regular season and the postseason. When the strike occurred, what was probably the best-ever Expos squad was playing .649 ball and leading the NL East, on target for Montreal's first postseason appearance since 1981.

In the wake of the work stoppage, Montreal ownership began an ongoing purge of higher-salaried veteran players, a move which undermined fan loyalty. It was difficult for the Expos to interest any network in a television deal given the bitterness engendered by the strike, with Canadian baseball fans less forgiving than U.S. fans. The Canadian networks that did carry baseball eventually showed fewer and fewer games. Sadly, many Montreal fans, burned before a long-awaited potential moment of triumph, soon learned to live without baseball.

By 1996, the club was earning just $3.5 million in broadcast rights, the lowest in MLB by a wide, wide margin — and that was with 45 games telecast in English, 80 over three French-Canadian networks, and all contests aired on radio over both English and French stations.

After the Expos' CTV contract expired in 1996, no over-the-air English-language TV station ever showed the Expos again. The Blue Jays, winner of back-to-back World Series in 1992–93, assumed the mantle of Canada's team, with the Expos' market limited mostly to Quebec.

Even as late as 1998, half of Montreal games were televised in French. In 1989, RDS (TSN's new French-language arm) had first carried Montreal games. SRC trooped along, with Camille Dubé and then René Pothier manning the play-by-play chair. A Quebec network, Television Quatre-Saisons (TQS), broadcast Expos games for four years, but its on-air team of Michel Villenueve and former minor-league player Marc Griffin failed to engage the fans.

TQS dropped out after 1998 and SRC let the Expos go forever following the 1999 season. In 2000, new owner Jeffrey Loria — either in a misguided attempt to get fans into the ballpark or an ill-advised attempt to negotiate higher rights fees — refused to sign any media deals until late in spring training, when CKAC agreed to carry the games in French on the radio for a year. It was an embarrassingly clear sign of how far things had deteriorated that no television network — SRC, CBC, CTV, RDS, TSN, or TQS — carried a single Expos game in 2000.

The lack of an English-language radio contract forced the Expos into new territory, as they became the first club to broadcast the entire schedule over the Internet. The only place to hear Dave Van Horne's call was at MontrealExpos.com. His sidekick was Joe Cannon, a talk-show host and squash-playing buddy of former owner Claude Brochu who was well out of his comfort zone.

After that nightmare of a season, Van Horne decamped for the Florida Marlins, snapping one of the last and most important links to the Expos' past. Elliot Price helped negotiate a new radio deal for CKGM, which took to the air on May 7, 2001. His second was Terry Haig, an actor and sometime talk-show host.

For 2001, RDS televised 48 games in French, with TSN carrying 12 in English. Two years later, however, the Expos were reduced to Price doing radio broadcasts at home with Mitch Melnick (another talk-radio host). On the road, Melnick worked with a revolving set of color men, usually a radio veteran from the city being visited. Les Grobstein sat in at Wrigley Field; Russ Langer joined Price in Los Angeles; Roxy Bernstein did the honors in San Francisco. It was a stunning comedown for the Expos who, less than two decades earlier, had been Canada's team.

On the French side, Doucet continued to call the games with dignity, assisted by Griffin, who fit better on radio than on television. The team's standing had declined enough that in 2002, CKAC pre-empted 10 games. The next season, the channel aired only 102.

Doucet, along with Rodger Brulotte and Denis Casavant on RDS, did their best as things went from bad to worse. When Loria badly bungled negotiations for a new, downtown retro ballpark — the only thing that could save baseball in Montreal — the team entered its death throes.

Major League Baseball considered contracting the franchise after the 2001 season, but instead purchased the club from Loria in 2002 in a complex deal that allowed Loria to buy the Marlins. Under MLB's management, the Expos operated on a shoestring for the next three seasons, allowing Expos fans and players to twist in the wind as various relocation scenarios were openly explored.

In 2004, the Expos signed a deal with the fledgling Score TV network to air 25 games in English. This was an interesting deal, as Score TV kept its expenses low by airing all the games off of the opposing team's TV feed, adding its own live audio from the network's Toronto studio.

Sam Cosentino, Score's resident baseball expert, called the action with former Expos Warren Cromartie and Darrin Fletcher and former Blue Jay Rance Mulliniks taking turns in the color role. (Cosentino moved on to become the third man on the Jays' TV team in 2008–10.)

Of course a small, low-profile TV plan couldn't stave off the inevitable, but at least Score TV broadcast the Expos' final game in Montreal on September 29, 2004. During the 9–1 loss to the Marlins, visiting play-by-play man Dave Van Horne must have been riding a wave of emotions.

That winter, the Expos became the first major-league club to pull up stakes in 33 years, shifting to Washington, D.C., to become the Nationals. For the club's French-language broadcasters — Doucet, Griffin, Brulotte, and Casavant — it was a sad farewell after a long decline. The four dispersed, with Casavant taking a reporting job with RDS and Doucet eventually announcing independent minor-league baseball in Quebec City.

Elliot Price had been promised one of the Nationals' English-language radio posts, working alongside ex-Tampa Bay broadcaster Charlie Slowes, but had difficulty securing a U.S. visa. When Price still hadn't obtained safe passage by spring training, the team hired Dave Shea, a former voice of the Boston Bruins sidelined by the NHL owners' lockout. With no baseball experience, Shea struggled to master such intricacies as the double switch.

Slowes' hiring was as much about name recognition — he had called games for the NBA Washington Bullets for a decade — as about his baseball work. After announcing for the Devil Rays, though, he knew how to prepare fans for the worst. With non-local ownership of a bad team that had just relocated, the new Nationals radio situation was problematic. The Nats quickly linked up with WFED, a small radio station owned by Bonneville International.

It took much longer to iron out the multiple layers of complex issues related to the Nationals' potentially lucrative television rights. In order to avoid threatened litigation by Baltimore Orioles owner Peter Angelos over the relocation of the Expos to Washington, the MLB-owned Nationals agreed to broadcast their games on a new RSN, the Mid-Atlantic Sports Network. MASN was created by Angelos and MLB to carry both the Nationals and the Orioles, though the O's would not be free of their existing deal with Comcast Sports Net Mid-Atlantic until after the 2006 season.

The solution greatly benefitted the Orioles' owner, with MLB paying Angelos $75 million to purchase a minority stake in MASN for the Nationals. The Nationals' ownership share in the RSN began at 10 percent and will ultimately rise to a maximum of 33 percent at a rate of one percentage point per year; the Orioles own the rest of MASN. A key part of the deal was that the Orioles agreed to share their exclusive broadcast territory with the Nationals, which ran from Harrisburg, Pennsylvania, all the way to Charlotte, North Carolina, and included the states of Delaware, Maryland, and Virginia; the District of Columbia; and parts of the states of Pennsylvania, West Virginia, and North Carolina.

The highly unusual situation compromised the Nationals' ability to fully exploit the huge and rich Washington TV market. That issue resurfaced in 2011 when the Nationals asked for a huge increase in the annual rights fee they received from MASN under a five-year reset provision in the original agreement. The dispute continues to drag on without resolution; Bud Selig's inability to solve the crisis means that the Nats-Orioles fight seems headed for the courts.

Mel Proctor, known locally for his Orioles and Bullets work, had long been anticipated as the television voice of the relocated club. He and color man Ron Darling formally signed agreements with the Nationals just before the regular season.

Fewer than half of the Nats' 2005 games were shown over MASN. The other games were optioned to over-the-air TV stations WDCA and WTTG. Unfortunately, few viewers in the Washington metropolitan area even had the option of receiving MASN on their cable systems for the team's first year and a half in D.C., as a result of a bitter carriage dispute with Comcast, the dominant cable provider in the area.

After the District of Columbia council had agreed to pay for a new ballpark for the Nationals, MLB sold the club to billionaire real estate developer Ted Lerner in 2006. The Nationals didn't wait for the new ownership to be approved to change their broadcasting plans for 2006, dumping Dave Shea in January. His replacement, Dave Jageler, was some 25 years younger. Jageler had spent a term with the Pawtucket PawSox, a Triple-A club that in recent years has produced several big-league announcers. With new announcers came a new radio station, as the Nats and Bonneville struck a three-year deal to put the team on WTWP, a higher-profile station.

On the TV side, Ron Darling flew the coop to join the Mets' broadcast team, and Mel Proctor was not asked to return. Therefore, all but one of the club's 2006 broadcast team was new for the Nationals' sophomore season.

Bob Carpenter, the club's newly hired television voice, had been involved in big-league broadcasting since the early 1980s, first with the Rangers, then the Cardinals, and also on a national basis. Tom Paciorek, his seasoned partner, had spent 12 seasons with the White Sox and then had worked in the Braves' booth.

MASN created a second channel for 2007 so that the net could carry nearly all the Nats' games. Just 30 of the team's contests were shown over-the-air in 2007 and 2008, and only 20 in each of the following two years.

Paciorek lasted just one year in Washington; the club reportedly only wanted a commentator who had been either a pitcher or a catcher. He was succeeded by Don Sutton, veteran of nearly two decades in the Braves' booth, joined Carpenter in 2007–08. Sutton's relationship with Stan Kasten, the new Washington club president and his former boss in Atlanta, was a key.

Sutton's first love was always the Braves, so when an opportunity to return presented itself in January 2009, he moved back to Atlanta's radio crew. Rob Dibble, onetime Reds "Nasty Boys" closer and former ESPN analyst, moved into the vacant color role. Carpenter and Dibble showed a good rapport, with the former always professional and with the latter promising to tone down his hyperbolic antics.

The Nats started Spanish-language broadcasts in June 2008, working with Bill Kulik's Spanish Baseball Network.

The Nationals began to generate a lot of excitement in 2010. Third baseman Ryan Zimmerman had become a fine player, and young pitcher Stephen Strasburg, the first pick in the 2009 June draft, drew huge crowds when the team promoted him to "The Show" in June.

Strasburg soon began experiencing serious elbow pain, and had to come out of his August 21 start after $4\frac{1}{3}$ innings. Two days later, during his regular turn on XM Radio, Dibble chose to rail against what he saw as the stereotype of the modern crybaby player, as personified by his employer's well-paid young phenom.

"OK, you throw a pitch, it bothers your arm, and you immediately call out the manager and the trainer? Suck it up, kid. This is your profession," he said. "You chose to be a baseball player. You can't have the cavalry come in and save your butt every time you feel a little stiff shoulder, sore elbow…Stop crying, go out there and pitch. Period."

As it turned out, it was Washington management, not Strasburg, that had put the brakes on their hot-shot prospect — and for good reason, as the club soon disclosed that the 22-year-old right-hander had suffered a torn elbow ligament and needed transplant surgery.

Dibble couldn't have pulled the foot out of his mouth with a tractor. The Nationals first handed him a suspension, then fired him on September 2, proving that they have final say on broadcasters even though MASN pays the salaries.

If Dibble's rant wasn't the biggest screw-up in sports broadcasting history, it certainly was in the running. Dibble still had a year and change left on his contract, but it's tough to see him ever getting another job in a team's broadcast booth, especially after he burned his bridges by accusing Strasburg's father of getting him fired.

Maybe only in the aftermath of this particular situation could Washington bring in a new broadcaster implicated in the Mitchell Report and not cause controversy. The decision to hire former Expos utility player F.P. Santangelo as Carpenter's color man for 2011 made surprisingly few waves. At least, the thinking seemed to go, he's not Rob Dibble.

Not amazingly, Dibble reverted to form after his firing. On his Sirius/XM radio show in August 2011, he complained that the Nats were rushing Strasburg back too quickly from his "Tommy John" surgery.

While all that was going on, Carpenter and Santangelo were working to improve what began as a somewhat shaky teaming. By season's end, however, the two voices were working well enough to merit even more interest in their future — like the promising young Washington club itself.

Shown here with analyst Rob Dibble (left), smooth-voiced Bob Carpenter called games for the Texas Rangers and St. Louis Cardinals prior to his hiring as the Nationals' television announcer in 2006. (Wikipedia Commons)

MAJOR LEAGUE BASEBALL ON TELEVISION: THE TOP 10 EVENTS

by Jim Walker & Rob Bellamy

THE HISTORY OF BASEBALL ON TELEVISION HAS ITS OWN trajectory, its own pioneers and Luddites, and its own watershed events. Here are 10 key turning points we have selected as experts in the field and authors of the exhaustive *Center Field Shot: A History of Baseball on Television.*

FIRST TELEVISED MLB GAME,
BROOKLYN DODGERS VS. CINCINNATI REDS, AUGUST 26, 1939

Although experimental telecasts of baseball date back to 1931, the first televised game in the U.S. was a college game between Princeton and Columbia at New York's Baker Field on May 17, 1939. With a perplexed Bill Stern handling announcer duties, this first NBC attempt, using a single camera, received pans in the local press.

Three months later, NBC mounted a much more successful two-camera effort with Red Barber calling the action from the third base upper-deck in Ebbets Field. The telecast, the first game of a doubleheader, included commercials for Wheaties, the Socony Vacuum Oil Co., and Ivory Soap. Barber used a monitor to follow the camera coverage and received occasional instructions from director Burke Crotty in the NBC control truck. The visiting Reds won, 5–2.

This telecast was well-received. NBC later marked Barber's contribution to television history with an engraved silver cigarette case — accompanied by a $35 bill to cover the souvenir's cost! In 1951, CBS tapped Barber to call the action in their experimental color telecasts of major-league games.

FIRST TELEVISED WORLD SERIES, OCTOBER 1947

The first World Series coverage was limited to a few East Coast stations; in fact, it nearly didn't happen. Commissioner "Happy" Chandler completed negotiations with Gillette and Ford to sponsor the Series less than a month before the contests began, rejecting a higher offer from a Brooklyn brewer because, "It would not be good public relations for baseball to have the Series sponsored by the producer of an alcoholic beverage."

Fall Classic coverage expanded to the country's interior in 1948 when an experimental "Stratovision" airplane-based relay system linked East Coast and Midwest game coverage. In 1949, with televisions still in limited supply, Chandler allowed movie theaters to charge patrons to see the televised Series via "theater television," a method used to project the TV images onto movie screens. By 1950, the World Series, telecast on multiple networks, would be dubbed "the greatest advertising force on earth" by A. Craig Smith, Gillette's head of advertising.

Chandler incurred the wrath of the owners when he agreed to give most of the proceeds of the sale of World Series and All-Star Game rights to the players' pension fund. After the owners failed to reappoint him, Chandler undersold the rights to the World Series for the next six years to Gillette.

GAME OF THE WEEK BEGINS, MAY 1953

Taking an idea from the DuMont Network, ABC signed contracts with the White Sox, Indians, and Athletics in early 1953 to produce national weekly telecasts in TV markets without MLB teams. (At this time, the market for each major-league team was blacked out.) Audiences in these small and medium markets made ABC's lead announcer, Hall of Famer Dizzy Dean — a dictionally-challenged Arkansan — the darling of rural America.

In 1955, the much stronger CBS network snatched away Dean and the *Game of the Week*, making it Saturday afternoon tradition in the summer.

NBC added its own weekly version of the national pastime in 1957 with Lindsey Nelson and Leo Durocher at the mikes, while CBS expanded to Sunday coverage in 1958. ABC challenged its stronger competitors with another network weekly game in 1960, hiring Jack Buck to handle the play-by-play.

Each of these network contracts, made with individual teams, spread the influence of the major leagues into minor-league markets, making "Major League Baseball" and "baseball" synonymous to most Americans.

CONGRESSIONAL HEARINGS ON TELEVISING BASEBALL, 1953 AND 1958

The impact of televised baseball on the rapidly shrinking minor leagues was the main theme of Congressional hearings of 1953 chaired, respectively, by Senator "Big Ed" Johnson (D-Colorado), himself president of the Western League, and Representative Emmanuel "Manny" Celler (D-New York). Along with the relocation of franchises and Organized Baseball's antitrust exemption and its effect on players, this issue was also a theme of the 1958 Celler Committee hearings.

Despite Commissioner Ford Frick's less-than-stellar leadership, baseball was the big victor in these hearings, demonstrating its power as well as its hold on Congress. The game continued to expand its television and radio presence, relocated franchises with alacrity, and maintained its traditional reserve clause. With a couple of exceptions, Organized Baseball's operations were not altered. The committee members exhibited near-worship of baseball icons Casey Stengel and Mickey Mantle when they took the witness stand.

The hearings were a key demonstration of Congressional infatuation with a valence issue that was popular with the public — at least those living in areas that had lost major- or minor-league teams — but was unlikely to produce legislative action. The hearings cleared the path for MLB's national TV contract negotiations in the 1960s after the Sports Broadcasting Act was passed.

THE SPORTS BROADCASTING ACT OF 1961

In a reversal of Congressional posturing during the 1950s, the passage of the SBA was a major turning point for MLB and all professional sports. The SBA gave all professional leagues a limited antitrust exemption to sell broadcast rights as a joint league package.

No league benefited more from the act than the National Football League, whose young and media-savvy Commissioner Pete Rozelle was the major lobbyist for its passage. The power of individual pro teams to protect their own exclusive interests was seriously thwarted by the act. As a result, NFL owners began to see themselves as both TV partners and on-field rivals. The same applied to their counterparts in the competing American Football League.

Major League Baseball also benefited from the SBA, as did the National Basketball Association and, later, the National Hockey League. Professional football, however, most effectively leveraged the new exemption, becoming the most popular sport by the end of the decade. MLB lost its supremacy as the only pro sport with an antitrust exemption, albeit one more broad than that provided by the SBA.

In contrast to the progressive attitudes of the two rival pro football leagues, baseball appeared increasingly feudal, with the American and National Leagues often warring and with its traditional strong individual ownership structure. Decades would pass before MLB centralized its administration effectively and took full advantage of the collective value of its product.

FIRST COMPREHENSIVE MLB TV CONTRACTS: ABC 1965, NBC 1966

In the *Game of the Week's* first decade, participation in network TV contracts was a team-by-team decision, but the Sports Broadcasting Act of 1961 changed everything. Almost immediately, sports became a critical component of network programming, especially for primetime-challenged ABC.

In 1965, ABC tried to work its sports magic on the national pastime. In ABC's comprehensive MLB contract — the first allowing national games to be broadcast into major-league markets — teams shared *Game of the Week* revenues equally. The contract produced disappointing results for ABC, however, due to continuing competition from CBS's *Yankee Baseball Game of the Week* as well as from local telecasts, especially in New York and Chicago.

ABC made only a half-hearted effort to keep baseball in 1966, losing the national contract to NBC, the longtime holder of World Series and All-Star Game rights. NBC was, in the public's eye, Major League Baseball's network for the next quarter century. For 1966, NBC ignored pressures to hire Dizzy Dean, rural America's favorite announcer, and instead gave its national baseball spotlight to Curt Gowdy, a professional, but ultimately replaceable, performer. At NBC, the lead announcer would no longer be the biggest star of its weekly baseball broadcast.

ABC AND NBC SHARE THE MLB CONTRACT AS MONDAY NIGHT BASEBALL BEGINS ON ABC, 1976

Finally taking a cue from the NFL, where competitive network bidding and primetime placement had dramatically increased the league's rights fees, MLB granted both NBC and ABC the keys to the national pastime. NBC would offer the traditional Saturday game, while ABC attempted to extend its successful *Monday Night Football* brand to baseball. The two big prizes of the package alternated each year between the networks, with one network carrying both League Championship Series and All-Star Game, and the other broadcasting the World Series.

Early in the history of the ALCS & NLCS when the games were all scheduled during the day, the network would start the first game at about 1 p.m. Eastern Time and the second about 4 p.m., an especially effective gambit if games were being played on the West Coast. In 1969, when all four division winners were from the East and Midwest, the games started at 1 and 2:30 ET and there was some overlap. As more postseason night games were scheduled, the network would schedule a day game and then a prime time night game. If the games overlapped, they would intercut the coverage to capture the key action from each game.

The record $92.8 million contract helped owners pay the market-level salaries players now demanded after having escaped the reserve clause's perpetual servitude. Network television became MLB's sugar daddy, providing ready cash to solve its problems. After a failed three-announcer experiment in 1976, ABC brought in its biggest star: Howard Cosell, a noted critic of the game's slow pace. Cosell dominated ABC's crowded booth and served as a lightning rod for baseball writers' criticism. At NBC, Curt Gowdy gave way to the more flashy, folksy, and humorous Joe Garagiola.

Despite much criticism, night World Series, All-Star, and League Championship Series games became fixtures, producing record ratings in prime time. Although its ratings were never that strong, *Monday Night Baseball* offered a huge primetime promotional stage for MLB in the pre-cable era when the three commercial broadcast TV networks dominated the airwaves.

MLB GOES CABLE, 1990

MLB jumped a major hurdle in 1990, entering a four-year contract with ESPN for about $400 million. The owners now saw cable and satellite delivery as a viable source of national revenue, not just as a competitor for their gate receipts and the game's broadcast coverage. As of 2013, ESPN became the national network with the longest consecutive relationship with Major League Baseball.

Cable's influence inside MLB, which began tentatively in local markets during the 1970s, went national in 1981. Taking advantage of the judicial overthrow of the FCC's onerous sports pay-television rules, MLB offered a weekly national game on Thursday evening via the USA Network from 1981–83, although four of the then 26 teams (the Astros, Braves, Cardinals, and Mets) refused to participate. The 1990 ESPN deal was, therefore, the first truly national cable contract.

Although ESPN has complained about the amount of money it claims to have lost on its baseball deals, the network used baseball programming to reduce its schedule of low-brow and low-viewership events like tractor pulls and funny-car rallies and to brand itself as the national home of professional sports. As for MLB, its extensive schedule of contests was for the first time a plus, as its huge inventory became a new source of media revenue. This advantage increased with the advent of more baseball-related television program offerings, such as the "Extra Innings" cable and satellite package, and the dawn of the World Wide Web.

MLBAM AND THE INTERNET AGE, 2000

The large inventory of MLB product became an even greater benefit with the creation of a subsidiary called Major League Baseball Advanced Media (MLBAM or BAM). In the digital age, even the most obscure getaway-day game between two last-place teams matters to transplanted fans and fantasy players. MLBAM provided audio, and eventually video, of every game for a relatively small fee. BAM made additional money for MLB owners by controlling all 30 team websites, ticket-buying, and online shopping, as well as by offering products and services to other media companies, sports organizations, and leagues, including handling digital streaming for ESPN and various RSNs. In 2005, BAM began providing the website and official statistics for Minor League Baseball (MiLB.com) and all of its affiliated teams and leagues.

MLBAM's overreaching editorial arm also controlled each team's storyline, presenting a unified presence for the game in the fragmented Internet age. After an initial investment of $30 million (one million per team), BAM was writing annual checks to each team within a few years. MLBAM is now believed to be worth $3 billion or more if it were to go public.

As commissioner, Bud Selig spearheaded MLBAM's formation, which may turn out to be his most lucrative business decision. MLBAM is widely regarded as having the best online presence of any sport.

Revenue from the site is shared equally by the 30 teams, narrowing somewhat the "rich team/ poor team" divide created by local TV rights differentials. Although BAM stumbled in its misguided attempt to control the rights to fantasy baseball, it continues to grow and has introduced new video and audio packages, archival broadcasts of classic games, and fantasy games enhanced with proprietary material.

THE MLB NETWORK, APRIL 2009

With a tagline of "The National Pastime All the Time," the MLB Network began telecasting on January 1, 2009 to about 50 million households, making it the largest launch of any cable network to date. Although MLB lagged the NFL and NBA in starting its own TV network, the MLB Network quickly gained cable and satellite carriage by offering equity positions to major television carriers Comcast, Time Warner Cable, Cox, and DirecTV.

This very successful debut contrasted markedly with the mid-1990s creation of MLB's failed "Baseball Network." That early attempt at in-house production by MLB failed to generate sufficient ratings for its network partners (ABC and NBC), largely because of the 1994–95 strike that killed the 1994 World Series. The Baseball Network never had a chance.

Like MLB.com, the MLB Network lets baseball control its message while staying in constant contact with its most avid fans. It offered over 50 live games in 2009 via its Thursday Night Baseball program and an additional Saturday night game simulcast via a local/regional telecaster. Afternoon games were added in 2010. The World Baseball Classic, winter league, and spring training games provide even more telecasts. In 2012, MLB network added the postseason to its slate, with exclusive coverage of two Division Series games.

MLB Network hired experienced commentators like Bob Costas and many former players to host its original programming, including *MLB Tonight*, *Quick Pitch*, *Diamond Demos*, and *Hot Stove*. Previously unseen vintage telecasts, such as Game 7 of the 1960 World Series, have also become an attraction. Because MLB now owns an alternative distribution system, it has substantial leverage in future negotiations with both its broadcast (Fox) and cable (ESPN and Turner) networks.

BASEBALL'S NATIONAL BROADCASTING PICTURE

by Gary Gillette and Stuart Shea

MANY OF THE MOST IMPORTANT BROADCASTERS OF BASEBALL DO not appear in the team chapters of this book because they did not cover a specific team. These were national, rather than local, voices.

Ted Husing, Graham McNamee, Bob Costas, Joe Morgan, Gordon McLendon, Dizzy Dean, Tony Kubek, and Tim McCarver are far better known for covering baseball on a national stage than for their local work. Some of these men, in fact, never announced for a team. All of them are profiled in Curt Smith's *Voices of the Game* and Ted Patterson's *Golden Voices of Baseball*.

The game's portrayal on national radio and television also differs in significant ways from local presentations, with much larger-scale economics, broader coverage, and a complex web of complications that have impacted the way the game is both presented and played. It is because of national TV coverage and the millions of dollars in rights fees paid, for example, that postseason ballgames are played at night and that two extra layers of postseason play have been added in the last two decades.

Here is a brief portrait of the national broadcasting scene in radio and television from the early 1920s through today, the scene in which these men made their mark and the media-driven landscape that baseball executives and TV networks have created.

RADIO DAYS

In the first decades of the twentieth century, little difference existed between a local and a national radio broadcast. Unlike today, few stations were operating in any one city, so it was possible to tune into Pittsburgh's KDKA if you lived in Australia, or pick up a London station from your home in the Hollywood hills.

Many operators set up radio frequencies in the 1910s, but entrepreneurs began to exploit the commercial applications for radio following World War I. The first licensed radio station in the U.S. was Pittsburgh's KDKA. Owned by Westinghouse, KDKA went on the air November 2, 1920. Less than a year later, the station broadcast a big-league ball game from Forbes Field with Harold Arlin at the microphone.

In October 1921, three Westinghouse stations — KDKA, WJZ of New York, and WBZ of suburban Boston — hooked up a line to the Polo Grounds, where the Yankees and Giants were playing the World Series, and broadcast the games to anyone who would listen. Sportswriter Grantland Rice supplied the play-by-play for that Fall Classic as well as in 1922.

In fall 1923, Bill McGeehan, a *New York Herald-Tribune* sportswriter who had assisted Rice in 1922, got the job calling the games. Astonishingly, a frustrated McGeehan quit in the middle of Game 3, reportedly bored by the scoreless pitching duel! His young assistant, Graham McNamee, took the microphone and never looked back.

McNamee, heard over the Westinghouse network from 1923 through 1927 and on NBC until 1932, called World Series games with a perhaps overenthusiastic style that became his trademark. In the early days of radio, there was no conventional wisdom, no playbook, and no consultants to advise a budding radio performer or station manager about what made "good radio."

What should radio personalities sound like? Should they have the booming, lush tones of an opera singer? The clipped, strict cadence of a reporter with a snap-brim fedora? The comic timing of a Vaudeville star? It has been said that each baseball game is a debate about how baseball should be played. In the same way, the early days of radio were a debate about how the revolutionary new form of communication should develop.

In 1929, the new CBS network hired Ted Husing, another early radio legend, to compete with NBC's World Series broadcasts. After several years of popularity, McNamee — truly a pioneer in the business — faded from the baseball airwaves and re-

Ted Husing's authoritarian tones described many of the country's major sporting events during the 1930s. He called World Series from 1929-1934 before earning a ban from Commissioner Landis for his on-air candor. Husing influenced broadcasters such as Mel Allen, Bob Elson, Jack Brickhouse, Harry Caray, and Bob Prince. (National Baseball Hall of Fame and Museum)

In the early days of radio, men with big voices did it all—sports, world affairs, human interest stories. Graham McNamee, blessed with a great instrument and a facility for describing things in detail, brought to a national audience political conventions, the Lindbergh flight, world championship boxing matches, and, from 1923 through 1935, every World Series broadcast. (National Baseball Hall of Fame and Museum)

turned to his first love, music. Husing, another "big voice," influenced many future baseball announcers.

Through the 1930s, the World Series was broadcast simultaneously by several radio networks, including CBS, Mutual, and both NBC's Red and Blue networks. Many local baseball voices, such as Cleveland's Tom Manning, Chicago's Bob Elson and Hal Totten, Boston's Fred Hoey, and Cincinnati's Red Barber, polished their resumés by describing October Classic action — but always at the pleasure of Judge Landis, who as baseball's commissioner ruled the game with an iron fist.

Even a famous announcer like Husing wasn't immune to Landis's power. While he was the biggest name in sports radio in 1934, Husing apparently was too critical of the umpiring in that fall's World Series, and Landis banished him from further October assignments.

Baseball on the radio was an almost immediate hit. Forward-thinking teams in the Midwest like Chicago, Cincinnati, and St. Louis aired many of their home games — and soon, all their home games. In some years, the Cubs and White Sox were on five different stations concurrently, employing as many different broadcast teams.

With local broadcasting opening up unheard-of streams of advertising revenue, the idea of tying stations into national networks became attractive to those interested in maximizing income. In order to restrict the broadcasters covering the World Series, Landis's office awarded only one or two networks the honor of covering the games, and the Judge continued to personally control the selection of announcers for baseball's annual autumn showcase.

FIRST SPORT IN THE GILLETTE CAVALCADE

In 1939, Gillette Razors paid $100,000 for exclusive rights to broadcast the World Series and partnered with the Mutual Broadcasting System, which remained the sole radio provider for October baseball through 1956. These exclusive rights meant that no team could air its own local World Series radio broadcast.

Having paid such a grand sum, Gillette demanded input on content, scheduling, and announcers. Red Barber called the Fall Classic through 1943, assisted by Elson and Mel

Allen. Bill Slater did the 1944 and 1945 Series. Landis died in 1944; though no subsequent commissioner wielded the nearly absolute power of Landis, the ascension of Happy Chandler did not seem to change the October routine. Mutual hired Mel Allen as its lead announcer for five years, Al Helfer for four, and Bob Wolff for one, utilizing various local voices as the No. 2 men.

It would not be an exaggeration to say that advertising legend Craig Smith, who coordinated efforts between baseball and Gillette for many years, was one of the most powerful men in the game.

Of course, national baseball broadcasts were not only heard in October. Mutual began airing the All-Star Game exclusively in 1943, when the contest was only a decade old and remained tremendously popular.

GOING REGIONAL, NATIONALLY

Outside looking in at this early ferment was a big thinker named Gordon McLendon, who called himself "The Old Scotchman." Seeing that many major markets in the West, North, and South lacked their own major-league teams, and therefore their own major-league broadcasts, McLendon came up with a hot idea in the late 1940s: Why not bring broadcasts of AL and NL games to radio stations in those far-flung markets?

Prior to the relocations of the 1950s and the expansions of the 1960s, the entire country west of St. Louis and south of Cincinnati and Washington was not served by the major leagues, meaning that McLendon had plenty of virgin territory as his market.

McLendon founded the Liberty Broadcasting System, paid the commissioner's office the $1,000 fee for play-by-play rights, and re-created games from a Western Union ticker-tape feed, using canned sound effects to spice up the proceedings. (McLendon was accused, a year or so later, of also pirating accounts from other radio broadcasts.)

This was the first time that a national audience could hear regular-season games on a routine basis. McLendon's foresight demonstrated that a national market existed not just for postseason baseball, but also throughout the daily grind of the game's long season. Fans across the country could now hear a game happening in St. Louis, Philadelphia, New York, or Washington, D.C. Previously regular-season baseball had been a local or regional phenomenon.

Starting in 1949, Liberty presented a daily *Game of the Day* during the season, unexpectedly pulling in huge ratings throughout the country. McLendon was the network's sole announcer that year. In 1950, however, up-and-coming young professionals like Buddy Blattner, Wes Wise, Don Wells, Jerry Doggett, and Lindsey Nelson — all of whom had experience calling minor-league contests — joined the Liberty broadcast crew as the network often presented two games per day.

Blackout rules kept fans in major-league cities from hearing McLendon's networks, but the *Game of the Day* afforded fans in smaller cities in the East and North and both major and smaller locales in the South and West the special privilege of hearing these games.

In 1950 and 1951, the network's heyday, Liberty announcers would call a week's worth of games live from various ballparks, spending the rest of the month re-creating contests at the Liberty studios at Dallas station KLIF to hold down costs.

Liberty's success did not go unnoticed by the club owners, who did not enjoy watching McLendon making literally thousands of dollars each day outsourcing their games–raw material for which he was paying virtually nothing.

Before the 1952 season, the commissioner's office decided to simply take the business out of McLendon's hands. The leagues returned some control of broadcasts to the clubs, and the Yankees immediately served notice that they would no longer allow Liberty announcers in their parks. Most other clubs followed suit. In addition, baseball raised McLendon's rights payment from $1,000 to $250,000.

Intending to crush the business, furthermore, baseball instituted a blackout on broadcasts of the program in minor-league cities, removing a huge number of Liberty's markets. Altogether, 13 of the 16 major-league clubs served notice that they would ban Liberty broadcasters. Those not going along were the Dodgers, Reds, and White Sox, the last of which entered into a separate contract with Liberty to produce the club's radio broadcasts for 1952, 1953, and 1954.

With only three teams to air as a result, the Old Scotchman had to fold the *Game of the Day* operation on May 15, 1952 after filing a $12 million lawsuit against the major leagues and 13 of its clubs. Liberty filed for bankruptcy two weeks later. The White Sox' carrier, former Liberty station WCFL, took over their three-year deal. This left the field open for the Mutual radio network, already baseball's favored postseason carrier, to appropriate McLendon's business model.

After careful study, Mutual adopted a somewhat altered Liberty model for its new *Game of the Day*. At the behest of Organized Baseball, Mutual refused to air games at night or on Sundays to protect the minor leagues. It also broadcast all of its games live, from the ballparks.

In undercutting Liberty, Mutual had three advantages: an already huge network of stations, a large budget, and a longstanding relationship with baseball.

From 1950 through 1960, past, current, and future big-league voices such as Al Helfer, Bob Wolff, Gene Elston, Dizzy Dean, Art Gleeson, John MacLean, Van Patrick, and even Hal Totten worked Mutual's slate of contests. Some of these men used the *Game of the Day* as a springboard to land permanent jobs in a big-league market.

While this in some ways represented baseball's zenith on radio, it didn't last. The incredibly quick rise of television, and the amount of baseball broadcast on both the local and national levels, dimmed the luster of what had formerly been a shining example of radio's ability to tell stories. In addition, the grueling travel to different locations burned out some of Mutual's prime voices. Shorn of its novelty, the radio *Game of the Day* was cancelled prior to the 1961 season.

Gillette, still sponsoring the World Series on radio and television, transferred its loyalty and its business to NBC radio beginning in 1957, continuing the policy of using a rotating crew of announcers, some local to one of the teams in the Series, some not.

Eventually, as also happened in local markets, sponsors began to cede control of the broadcasts to the radio and TV networks and the rightsholder stations. Sponsors stopped allocating so much money to the big events and began spreading their cash around. Networks, meanwhile, were happy to be able to work with more advertisers and retain control of their own product.

AS THE NATIONAL PASTIME STRUGGLES, PRO FOOTBALL GROWS

During the 1960s, football began to overtake the national pastime in terms of fan base, media attention, and glamour. While NBC was baseball's network, it was also deeply committed to football. In 1967 the Peacock Network increased its commitment to pro football on radio, taking on Super Bowl broadcasts to go along with its already large schedule of pigskin on television.

All three major networks — CBS, NBC, and ABC — had by this time begun to use multisport announcers, both for continuity and to save money. This meant that on NBC radio, Jim Simpson became the dedicated World Series play-by-play man from 1969 through 1974, working with the lead announcer from the home team for each Series game — despite having no previous experience calling major-league baseball and admittedly not even liking the game!

This was just part of the decline in NBC's radio presentation in the 1960s and 1970s. The network did a poor job promoting baseball on radio, even outsourcing the scheduling and administration of postseason play to its affiliate stations. During the 1970s, with many fans and pundits believing baseball was in decline, some NBC radio affiliates declined to even carry MLB postseason games.

With the support of Commissioner Bowie Kuhn, CBS won baseball's national radio rights in 1976, signing a four-year deal at $75,000 per season. As part of the deal, longtime CBS radio sports director Win Elliot took the No. 2 seat on the network's World Series broadcasts for three seasons. Like Simpson, Elliot had no previous experience behind the mike doing baseball.

In 1981, baseball finally allowed local radio rightsholders to produce and air their own World Series broadcasts; up until then, the only choice the local fan had was to listen to the national network. CBS continued its exclusive national radio coverage of the postseason through 1997, paying $2 million per year starting in 1983, with Vin Scully and Jack Buck splitting most of the lead announcing duties.

For the 1985 campaign, CBS also signed on to become baseball's first national radio carrier during the regular season in three decades, paying more than $32 million for five years.

During the 1980s and 1990s, the network did great work with baseball. Most games featured a "hometown inning" in which the lead announcers for whatever clubs were playing would do a half-inning each of play-by-play on the national broadcast. It was a nice touch in the pre-Internet days, when a fan in New England would never otherwise hear an announcer working for Seattle or Oakland.

The Big Eye network broadcast two games each Saturday, one in the afternoon and one in the evening, with most of the net's affiliates taking one or the other. Play-by-play announcers included on-the-rise talent like John Rooney and Gary Cohen as well as veterans such as Ernie Harwell, Lindsey Nelson, and Curt Gowdy. When CBS aired the World Series, Vin Scully sat in the No. 1 chair from 1979 through 1982 and again from 1990 through 1997. Jack Buck was the lead voice from 1983–89.

CBS radio bowed out after 1997 and remains involved in baseball only by local affiliation. Currently seven major-league clubs' flagship stations are owned by or are affiliates of CBS.

TODAY

ESPN won exclusive national rights for World Series and All-Star Game radio broadcasts in 1998; it eventually hired Jon Miller and Joe Morgan as its top postseason radio team in 2001. Miller and Morgan also teamed up to call ESPN's televised *Sunday Night Baseball* over the same span. After the 2010 campaign, ESPN, reported to want to go "younger," cut loose Miller and Morgan from both their radio and TV gigs, bringing in Dan Shulman as its new lead baseball voice.

During the postseason, ESPN Radio has four crews of announcers, one for each Division Series. The network then pares down to two crews for the League Championships and one for the World Series. Shulman, Orel Hershiser, and Bobby Valentine, the network's primary radio team, worked ESPN's biggest games in 2011 (with Terry Francona replacing Valentine in 2012 when Bobby V. supplanted Francona as manager of the Boston Red Sox). This threesome also called ESPN's televised *Sunday Night Baseball* action.

Between 1998 and 2009, ESPN Radio employed three different play-by-play men for Sunday Night Baseball: Charley Steiner, Shulman, and Gary Thorne. Jon "Boog" Sciambi, formerly with the Marlins and Braves, has held the job since 2010. Chris Singleton is the current analyst, replacing Dave Campbell, who memorably manned the position from 1999 through 2010. One of the more eloquent ex-players in the booth, Campbell was comfortable both on radio and TV.

ESPN Radio also carries Opening Day, holiday, and key pennant race games, though these broadcasts are carried on fewer stations than are the marquee Sunday Night and postseason contests.

ON THE SMALL SCREEN

When television seized the American imagination in the late 1940s, the networks — first NBC and CBS, soon joined by ABC — formed after the U.S. government forced NBC to rid itself of one of its two networks — realized that sports on the tube meant big money.

NBC televised the 1948 World Series, with Bob Stanton at the mike, and the network also handled the 1949 and 1950 Fall Classics. The first truly national baseball telecast, however, was the final game of the 1951 National League playoff series. Broadcast coast-to-coast from New York, the epic battle between the Dodgers and the Giants ended with Bobby Thomson's home run off Ralph Branca. While the "shot heard 'round the world" would have lived forever in baseball legend even without TV, there is no doubt that its fame was enhanced by the live telecast.

It was only a matter of time before the small screen adopted the Old Scotchman's idea of bringing regular-season action to markets starved for major-league play.

Baseball at this time had a blackout rule intended to protect every major-league team from what most owners felt to be the "evils" of television. As was true on radio, regular-season national TV games could not be shown in cities with AL or NL teams. In the 1950s, only the Northeast and Midwest had big-league ball, so that left most of the rest of the country open for business.

In 1953, fledgling ABC decided to air Saturday baseball over its small but growing network of stations, even though it could only purchase rights to Browns, White Sox, and Indians home games. Sponsored by Falstaff, this was the first-ever network television *Game of the Week*.

Dizzy Dean, for a long time the voice of Falstaff Beer, was heavily promoted as the play-by-play man, a canny move which brought the broadcasts high ratings in the West and South. The program was successful, and CBS took notice. The bigger net soon outbid ABC for the rights to show a *Game of the Week*. In 1955 and 1956, CBS aired games on Saturdays; from 1957 on, they showed a Sunday contest as well. Dean continued to hold court and fracture the English language, with Buddy Blattner at his side.

Working with the phenomenally successful but egocentric Dean was no picnic. In 1959, after a disagreement over covering that year's Dodgers-Braves NL playoff series, Blattner resigned rather than continue to work with Ol' Diz.

Pee Wee Reese joined Dean on CBS from 1960 through 1964. Dean's likeable, though somewhat calculated, country-bumpkin routines, fed by the genial Reese, personified baseball for a huge portion of the nation.

NBC, which was already televising the World Series, joined the fray in 1957 with games on Saturday and Sunday, buying up rights to beam teams that CBS hadn't tied up, such as the Braves, Red Sox, Tigers, Pirates, and Cubs. Despite the clever work of Lindsey Nelson and Joe Garagiola on the NBC broadcasts, however, Dean and CBS garnered far superior ratings.

In 1960, ABC got back into the game as the three networks divvied up the teams, a confusing situation for viewers. After 1964, however, CBS had to bow out of the national contract because the company had purchased the New York Yankees and chose to show their games exclusively on weekends.

ABC had one crack at exclusivity in 1965, paying $5.7 million to become the sole national baseball TV provider. All teams but the Yankees and Phillies opted into the package. Unfortunately, the network made key mistakes. Dividing the country into three coverage areas was a good idea, but hiring Chris Schenkel and Keith Jackson — both known almost entirely for their work in other sports — to handle play-by-play was a big mistake. Merle Harmon, the third lead announcer, was decent.

NBC TAKES OVER

Following ABC's disastrous year as exclusive broadcaster of the TV Game of the Week, NBC became baseball's network in 1966, paying $18 million over a three-year period for exclusivity. The network held that position for most of the next 25 years, garnering decent ratings and occasional plaudits.

NBC decided not to hire Dizzy Dean, ending an era. The network desired a presence familiar to fans nationally and not so strongly identified regionally. Curt Gowdy, ascending to national stardom for his football and *American Sportsman* work, became NBC's No. 1 man both for *Game of the Week* and postseason play.

Gowdy's enthusiastic delivery masked a lack of in-depth knowledge about baseball's finer points, but his personality was popular in much of the country. While Gowdy lobbied NBC to hire Ted Williams to assist him, the network went with Pee Wee Reese, Dean's former second chair.

Absolute exclusivity on national telecasts worked fine for NBC and brought in a large amount of money to Major League Baseball. It also made the administration of the telecasts easier. Many believe, though, that Gowdy was the wrong choice for baseball's top nationwide voice because he was ubiquitous and so strongly identified with other sports and games.

The network executives then, and to some extent now, didn't understand that baseball fans love the game because it is in so many ways *unlike* other team sports. In fact, many people like baseball because of its singular charm, and because it provides a respite from the pace of contemporary society. Trying to fit baseball into a homogenous format that works for football, basketball, golf, and other sports only cheapens the unique appeal of the national game.

Gowdy and Reese didn't mesh, with the latter drawing a pink slip after the 1968 season. NBC's backup game broadcast team, Jim Simpson and Sandy Koufax, fared even less well.

Simpson was far too dry and Koufax, like so many other star athletes before him, was unable to transition to analysis.

Tony Kubek ascended to color duties in the late 1960s on some national broadcasts, working hard to overcome his early-career clipped delivery and awkward pauses. During the 1970s, the former Yankees' shortstop was the best thing about NBC's TV games, analyzing exactly what was happening and seeming to have no filter. Aside from Kubek, though, it was a rough patch as Gowdy, Garagiola, Simpson, Maury Wills, Monte Moore, and others employed at the time as lead announcers and analysts, failed to overcome the prevailing belief that NBC, and by extension Major League Baseball, were yesterday's news.

Beginning in 1966, NBC also showed a few games in prime time on Monday nights. By 1971, NBC had convinced Major League Baseball to play all World Series games at night, with LCS games also aired in the evenings by 1975. The network ramped up the number of evening telecasts to 15 during the regular season that year. It was the end of a four-year deal with MLB that worth $18 million per annum, and the concept of regular-season night games on a major network was not yet ready for prime time.

BARBARIANS AT THE GATE

In 1976, Major League Baseball decided to maximize national broadcast revenue and divide the regular and postseason schedules between NBC and ABC. This was the first time in more than 25 years that more than one network participated. The 1976–79 contract netted baseball nearly $93 million.

NBC produced the Saturday *Game of the Week* all four years, aired the World Series in even-numbered seasons, and showed the LCS in odd years. ABC carried the postseason the other years and instituted a new *Monday Night Baseball* telecast.

ABC Sports had made its fortune on the gridiron, first by airing the new American Football League in 1960 and then, beginning in 1970, by producing the tremendously popular *Monday Night Football*. When the network decided to get involved again with the national pastime, it tried to use the same formula — flash, trash, and superstars — for baseball. Why baseball owners and executives thought this was a good idea can be put down to desperation — and $93 million.

ABC's initial play-by-play men included former Giants and Reds voice Al Michaels and Pirates legend Bob Prince, but the network was always perceived as football-first. The result was some of the worst allocation of on-air talent on baseball broadcasts ever. Michaels, soon shunted to backup games, was wasted for several years as Keith Jackson, a football announcer with little regard for baseball, manned the mike for most key games. To make matters worse, Howard Cosell couldn't stop talking about baseball's many problems, contributing to the debacle by pouring scorn on the game he was covering.

Filling the other "designated quote-machine" role on *Monday Night Baseball* was former Senators play-by-play man Warner Wolf. The concomitant hiring of Bob Uecker was a fine idea, but he was initially featured more for his comedy than for actual analysis. Former players Norm Cash and Bob Gibson were not successful at doing color.

One thing ABC Sports did right was regionalizing its coverage, at times making three games available to different parts of the country. But ratings for ABC's *Monday Night Baseball* were weak and the reviews were worse. The network never seemed to understand or like baseball and promoted its own brand far more than it promoted the game.

Regardless, ABC was making money from baseball, and both networks re-upped during the 1979 campaign, signing new deals that brought MLB what then seemed like a staggering $185 million through 1983 (NBC for $90 million and ABC for $95 million). For 1980, ABC decided to carry some games on Sunday afternoons as well as Monday nights.

Over at NBC, the on-air situation improved greatly. When Curt Gowdy was retired, Vin Scully got a shot at the *Game of the Week* and the postseason in 1983, immediately becoming the best baseball voice on national TV. Garagiola, finally teamed with someone who could bring out his best as well as rein in his ego, made an excellent partner for Scully during these years.

Another upgrade was NBC's new backup game crew that featured Kubek and a relatively unknown young man with a Prince Valiant haircut. Bob Costas' first significant sports assignment involved covering the ill-fated American Basketball Association's St. Louis Steamers. Costas never covered baseball regularly on his way up, but NBC management loved his voice, versatility, and enthusiasm. By the mid-1980s Costas was a rising star in baseball, both for his detailed understanding of the game and especially because of his obvious love for it. He and Kubek made an excellent duo — both had strong opinions and the fortitude to elucidate them.

NBC's excellent *Game of the Week* presentation during these years overshadowed ABC's ham-handed attempts to remake baseball in pro football's sexy image. While Michaels became the Monday Night top dog in 1983, critics still panned the ABC broadcasts. A stream of big-name analytical talent, including Jim Palmer, Tim McCarver, Joe Morgan, Reggie Jackson, and Don Drysdale, failed to fully fix baseball's image problem.

Both networks re-upped for new pacts in 1984, with national rights fees reaching new highs. Most media observers were amazed to learn that NBC committed $575 million to baseball through 1989 and that ABC committed another $625 million. These seemingly stratospheric figures were possible because national advertisers wanted to be associated with baseball, even after the 1981 work stoppage.

The big money, though, came at a hefty price: the need to accommodate the networks by putting more postseason games in prime time. This proved a vexing problem when the Chicago Cubs won the 1984 NL East Division title, causing apoplexy among network execs. New Commissioner Peter Ueberroth immediately threatened that, if the Cubs did not add lights to their park, future Cubs home postseason games would be removed to other venues.

Another negative for baseball was that the national contracts prohibited MLB from signing national cable TV contracts throughout the five-year term. By this point, that was a significant strategic liability.

CABLE RUMBLINGS

USA Network had been the first national cable channel to present a slate of big-league contests, showing Major League Baseball on Thursday evenings from 1979 through 1983. Few remember those broadcasts today because the USA games were only shown outside of major markets. The deal was reported to be worth some $500,000 a year at the beginning and maybe three times that by the end.

Although MLB's new 1984 agreements attempted to lock out the burgeoning cable industry, the increase in viewing options could not be controlled by the commissioner's office, ABC, or NBC. The proven success of some of the so-called "superstations" — over-the-air TV stations holding rights to the Chicago Cubs (WGN), New York Yankees (WPIX), New York Mets (WWOR), Texas Rangers (KTVT), Boston Red Sox (WSBK), and, most notably, Atlanta Braves (WTBS) — beamed their signals via satellite, where they were licensed by regional cable operators across the U.S as well as into Central America and even South America.

Baseball may not have been the only reason that so many cable systems added WTBS, WGN, and other superstations. There is no doubt, though, that the large number of baseball games carried on the superstations was a major attraction and meant that the Braves and Cubs could each legitimately call themselves "America's Team," although only Atlanta actually had the hubris to do so.

The networks and MLB management vociferously opposed what they saw as unregulated games diluting their rightful hold on the market. Ueberroth, backed by the other club owners, pressured the superstations into making payments to MLB's Central Fund, with the monies distributed to the other teams as de facto damages for invading their exclusive markets. But the superstations were so popular that they couldn't be stopped: the market had spoken, and MLB spent the next few years behind the curve. Commissioner Fay Vincent was reduced to claiming in a 1992 interview with the trade magazine *Broadcasting* that the superstations were showing so many games that big-league clubs were in danger of going out of business.

ABC found it impossible to earn back its hefty investment, suffering from both a weak advertising climate and its own inability to showcase the game properly. Eventually the network scrapped its Monday night schedule, instead moving games to Sunday afternoons and Thursday nights. Perhaps the weak ratings were due not to the time slots but to how people watched baseball differently from football.

In spring 1986, ABC Sports president Dennis Swanson summed up his network's attitude: "Boy, I can't wait until 1989 gets here." His network's confidence when signing the 1984 deal bordered on arrogance, as ABC seemed to have an unshakeable conviction that it could produce a product that baseball fans liked despite the network having no real love for, or affinity with, the sport. By 1987, ABC scheduled only nine regular-season games plus the World Series, which meant it had given up on its attempt to build a brand.

ABC was unhappy about its financial losses and asked for givebacks; even though MLB denied that request, ABC still made a failed bid for the new contract. The big surprise, though, was that NBC — the only network to that time ever to produce consistently good national baseball telecasts — would be shut out as well after 42 years. The Peacock Network also claimed to have lost money on its MLB broadcasts in 1988, but the reported revenue figures didn't quite bear this out. While national productions were not inexpensive and it's possible that creative accounting could have made a modest profit or breakeven situation look like a loss, NBC was shocked when it was outbid by the Big Eye. CBS, the "Tiffany Network," was looking to benefit from a synergy with its excellent MLB radio productions and eager to pluck a valuable sports property from its competitors. So it stepped into the breach with what turned out to be unfounded enthusiasm.

EPIC FAIL BY CBS

Long dormant in presenting baseball, but angling to get back into the game since 1984, CBS signed a four-year contract (1990–93) and agreed to pay MLB $1.06 billion to become the game's sole over-the-air television carrier. That covered Saturday *Game of the Week* broadcasts, the All-Star Game, and all postseason action. By the end of the first year, however, it was clear that CBS had paid far too much without understanding how to market or produce baseball properly — the same mistake made by ABC in 1984.

Because CBS had spent such a huge sum of money, there was tremendous pressure for early success, yet the network was allowed by the contract to schedule only 12 regular-season telecasts. Though CBS didn't seem to care about continuing the *Game of the Week* tradition, this restriction immediately limited its ad revenue and delayed building a relationship with fans unfamiliar with CBS's new presentation of the game.

The reason that MLB strictly limited CBS's regular-season telecasts was the desire of the large-market and the more popular clubs to maximize income from local broadcast rights. Baseball executives reportedly did not feel that they were profiting enough from the negotiated superstation payments, so MLB decided to meet cable head-on. By the late 1980s, the big three broadcast networks were becoming less dominant on the sports television scene as ESPN and other cable networks presented a smorgasbord of sports never before available. Cable television, with its multiplicity of channels, expanded viewer options and offered opportunities for specialized programming. This made cable a perfect match for the national pastime: what better fit for 24/7 sports programming than MLB and its 2,106 scheduled regular-season games?

ESPN HITS A HOME RUN

Not having been able to squelch the demand for more games, baseball eventually decided to look for its own lucrative cable deal, and after several years of searching they found a partner. In 1979, a fledgling channel named ESPN (for Entertainment and Sports Programming Network), went on the air, initially showing college sports and quasi-sporting events like monster truck rallies while gaining influence and prestige for its news coverage and all-out, round-the-clock commitment to sports.

In 1989, ESPN had gained enough cachet and enough cash to offer MLB $400 million for a precedent-setting new package, which included the rights to air six games each week for four years, starting in 1990. The biggest sports cable network in the country was now a partner with Major League Baseball, immediately gaining a regular-season following that CBS had forsworn.

ESPN telecast baseball as an ongoing narrative, its 24/7 focus giving the channel an opportunity to track a daily story that no broadcast network could. The self-anointed (but accurately so) "Worldwide Leader in Sports" created a signature telecast, *Sunday Night Baseball*, which debuted in 1990 with Jon Miller in the lead announcer's seat. It was a brilliant idea to show a Sunday night game in prime time, since almost no other games were being played to detract attention from it. (In the 1990s, only the Rangers regularly scheduled games on Sunday nights because of the extreme heat, and then only in the summer.) Before *Sunday Night Baseball* aired each week at 8 p.m. Eastern, an hour-long pregame edition of *Baseball Tonight* touted the upcoming game and summed up the past week in the world of baseball.

This was a doubleheader presentation made for real baseball fans — why hadn't anyone thought of it before? Obviously the ratings and the revenue that ESPN needed to make its baseball program work were lower than what the broadcast networks needed, but ESPN seemed to have no trouble lining up advertisers.

The Sunday night baseball programming immediately proved a winner for ESPN, and the network filled its spring and summer schedule with baseball, showing regional double-headers on some nights and, on holidays like July 4 and Labor Day, showing as many as four games in succession. (The last game of these marathons was a 10 p.m. ET game from the West Coast.) For baseball fans, this was more than a little like Nirvana, although ESPN's demand for Wednesday evening exclusivity through 1998 annoyed many viewers put off by the national blackout on their local teams' broadcasts.

While ESPN's game coverage has expanded and contracted over the years as it has signed new contracts with MLB and as ESPN has changed its schedule to accommodate other sports (primarily football), the cable network has remained an incredibly important partner of MLB for almost a quarter century.

In addition to broadcasting ballgames, ESPN's daily (during baseball season) *Baseball Tonight* news program became an institution both inside and outside the game. Some of the battalions of sportscasters, writers, and ex-players used by *Baseball Tonight* as hosts and analysts over the years have been top-notch, and some have been forgettable, but there is constant and significant value in the program's daily recap of the action, chronicling the unfolding story of baseball's long season in a way that only newspapers had been able to previously.

Baseball Tonight has helped define the way the game is seen in the twenty-first century via its barrage of video recaps, highlights, and look-ins as well as its daily home-run count and unique features like "Web Gems."

Both ESPN and CBS lost money in their landscape-altering 1990–93 deals, although almost certainly not as much as claimed; TV networks can spin their financial numbers as creatively as can baseball teams. CBS dropped baseball with many regrets and hard feelings, whereas ESPN learned from its initial overbid and negotiated a series of new contracts with MLB in the intervening years.

With the large number of national telecasts on ESPN — plus the superstation schedules and the growing number of games carried on cable by regional sports networks — MLB was now perceived as having glutted the market with its product. MLB didn't want to admit that CBS had wildly overvalued baseball, and it needed to keep the other (i.e., aside from CBS) three broadcast networks interested.

The solution was to increase the number of postseason games. So in 1994, MLB realigned both the AL and NL into three divisions, added a wild card team in each league to the postseason, and added a third round of postseason action — the Division Series. But who would televise it?

Needing both MLB's inventory as well as its associated prestige, ESPN wanted baseball back and kept it, agreeing to pay $255 million through 1999. The six-year package included exclusive Sunday and Wednesday night games and other non-exclusive games on weeknights and holidays. In November 1995, ESPN and MLB restructured the contract at a reported $455 from 1996–2002, adding for the first time ever on cable, some daytime postseason contests that neither Fox nor NBC wanted. While the average annual value of the contract was substantially less than the $100 million per season paid by ESPN from 1990–93, the total was still impressive and the ongoing coverage by the increasingly important ESPN remained invaluable to MLB.

NETWORK FAILURE

On the traditional broadcast network side, CBS was out and the young-but-growing Fox TV Network was not quite ready to bid for baseball. Unable to sell a standard rights package at anything like the megamillions CBS had previously paid, MLB was forced to innovate. NBC and ABC returned to the national pastime after a four-year hiatus as part of "The Baseball Network (TBN)," a unique arrangement crafted by the commissioner's office that eliminated virtually all risk to the networks because they had to pay no rights fees. While MLB would retain the vast majority of any profits that the network generated, the only investment NBC and ABC had to commit to was their broadcast time — which in the summer, when most network shows were reruns with low ratings, was no big deal at all.

Unfortunately, the blandly branded Baseball Network seemed less a strategy for bringing baseball to the country on "free TV" than an attempt to kill the sport outright. Certainly TBN was unique in that it will be a long time before anyone tries such a bad idea again. With no risk to the networks, ABC and NBC had little incentive not to publicly trash the game when things began to go badly. With little reward but advertising dollars, MLB simply chased the highest bidder and found itself in a partnership with companies who cared little about the game.

Ken Schanzer, formerly a broadcast industry lobbyist and powerbroker at NBC Sports, ran the new tripartite venture between MLB-NBC-ABC, which produced the games itself and then brokered them to the two networks. This potentially interesting concept was undermined by several catastrophic strategic errors.

First, the network's signature product, its once-per-week slate of *Baseball Night in America* games, were shown in a confusing schedule over various evenings and carried on two different networks. This left many fans unsure of where to go and certainly didn't contribute to the kind of "appointment television" viewing that broadcast network series needed to draw the large audiences national advertisers demanded. Would this week's games be on a Friday? Saturday? Monday? What channel?

Second, the overly showbizzy tenor of the broadcasts sometimes detracted from the game itself. Repeating earlier mistakes, the fear that baseball was not exciting enough to attract and hold viewers' interest led to unnecessary razzle-dazzle that alienated devoted fans and didn't draw many casual fans.

Third, many of the new network's announcers and analysts were clearly not of major-league caliber. Some announcers were best known for their work in other sports, and some rookie ex-player analysts were clearly not ready for their roles.

Fourth, another killer was that, in two-team markets, one team simply wouldn't be shown on a given night, leading to large numbers of aggrieved Yankees, Mets, Cubs, White Sox, Dodgers, Angels, Giants, and Athletics fans.

Fifth and perhaps worst of all, the networks demanded that all Division Series and LCS games be scheduled simultaneously in the evenings, meaning that it was impossible for hardcore fans to watch all October games. Bob Costas later noted in his memoir, *Fair Ball*, that TBN's postseason approach was "stupid and an abomination," a huge and disastrous surrender by MLB to the networks.

Having games on various weeknights and weekends in prime time, and enforcing blackouts of local broadcasts the same evening, was bound to confuse and annoy most fans. In addition, the huge schedule of games — on most Baseball Network nights, all MLB games were covered — led to very high production costs. MLB's network partners themselves seemed to have little faith in the new model.

In retrospect, it seems appropriate in a tragic way that The Baseball Network was in place during the national pastime's darkest hour since World War II. The owner-forced strike of 1994, the cancellation of the World Series, the folly and farce of replacement baseball, and the game's tentative return with a shortened 1995 season resulted in a steep plunge in baseball's popularity. Even devoted fans had trouble forcing themselves to watch Baseball Network presentations during these angry times, and legions of casual fans couldn't have cared less.

By mid-1995, both NBC and ABC were fed up, especially after The Baseball Network was dissolved at the end of the season by MLB. Both NBC and ABC publicly expressed their lack of interest in working with Major League Baseball again, though NBC did a 180 within a few months and bid successfully on the next contract. It was clear that fans would not miss the ill-fated experiment, which never really had a chance given the climate when it was launched. The financial loss to MLB was reported to at nearly $600 million for the two-year debacle (when comparing what TBN earned to the previous network payments).

FOXIFICATION AND ESPINNING

NBC and the newest major network, Fox Broadcasting, split up MLB's national broadcast TV rights for 1996 through 2000. The new contracts were a welcome relief even though annual payments were about one-quarter less than from 1990–93, as many clubs were still suffering from the effects of the strike and its associated Baseball Network disaster.

Fox secured the rights to three World Series, two All-Star Games, and a new quasi–*Game of the Week* that would be broadcast on most, but not all, Saturdays. NBC paid for two World Series and three All-Star Games. The two networks also divided up the Division Series and LCS, with daytime Division Series games that neither network wanted laid off to ESPN. Fox paid $575 million over five years for its share of the package, with NBC paying $425 million.

From the start, Fox wanted to change things and put its own unique stamp on the game's broadcast conventions. The network's goal was to bring its young demographic to baseball, an aim that MLB was happy to collaborate with. The use of up-tempo, rock-based theme music was new to baseball broadcasts, and the increased reliance on information graphics, quick cuts, and reaction shots made for a very different experience — one that many fans embraced but some fans hated.

In 1997, a joint venture between Fox Sports and Liberty Media paid $172 million for a four-year cable deal. Airing games on Fox's FX channel on Saturday nights and on Fox Sports Net on Thursday evenings through the 2000 season, the package never gained traction due to competition from local broadcasts and the fact that FX — unlike dominant cable sports giant ESPN — was not known for its sports coverage.

Not that ESPN always did right by the national pastime. In 1998 ESPN, feeling its oats partially because of the prestige carrying baseball had lent it before other major sports leagues signed on, began shifting MLB games to ESPN2. MLB understandably objected because ESPN was bumping September games that impacted pennant races to ESPN2 in order to carry early-season NFL games on its lead channel. ESPN, having recently paid a huge sum for Sunday night football games, refused to reconsider. So MLB canceled the final three years of the deal, and ESPN then sued MLB.

Literally hours before the trial in federal court was to start in December 1999, MLB and ESPN announced that they had agreed on a new, eye-popping $815 million pact that added three additional years (2003–05) to their current contract. Essentially ESPN, afraid it was going to lose both the trial and its rights to MLB games, agreed to pay very handsomely to retain its 2000–02 rights and to extend the contract at about five times its previous rights fees for the three added years. ESPN immediately remitted to MLB $125 million — described as a "signing bonus," but better understood as a kind of damages payment. ESPN also took over as baseball's national radio outlet under the contract, for an additional $36 million from 2000–05.

"Oddly, the settlement vastly increases ESPN2's baseball coverage," wrote Richard Sandomir in the *New York Times*. As part of the agreement, not only did MLB consent to allow ESPN to put September games on ESPN2 so that NFL games could be featured on ESPN, but MLB agreed to allow many other ballgames to be broadcast on ESPN2.

Sandomir's piece also included quotes from Commissioner Bud Selig, who did his best to spin the deal as a positive thing despite the assertions made by MLB in response to the shift of games to ESPN2. "'You want to be practical, and when I looked at this entire deal, it's a different picture,' said Selig, who denounced ESPN's plan to move the late-season games to ESPN2 last year, but is happy now. 'Under these conditions, I find it quite acceptable and it wasn't difficult to accept in the end.'"

Fox also re-signed, becoming the exclusive over-the-air provider of baseball from Opening Day 2001 through the last game of the 2006 World Series. The six-year, $2.5 billion deal turned more than a few heads given that, five years earlier, baseball had seemed to be on its deathbed. Since 2001, Fox has been the sole over-the-air TV network to carry baseball.

By continuing to carry Major League Baseball, Fox has achieved status as a major sports "supernetwork," something that NBC and ABC had hoped to become in the 1960s and

1970s. In fact, Fox has surpassed the earlier dreams of network sports dominance, as Fox currently features NFL games and NASCAR as well.

As its older network siblings NBC, CBS, and ABC have eschewed Major League Baseball, Fox's postseason, All-Star Game, and weekly Saturday games have kept MLB on national broadcast television even as the broadcast-versus-cable distinction has become increasingly irrelevant. Apart from its technical achievements, however, Fox's presentation has not been 100% positive for baseball.

Like every other network, Fox likes to brand its "own" talent and use it as much as possible. This means that multisport generalists like Dick Stockton, Kenny Albert, Thom Brennaman, Josh Lewin, and Joe Buck have received Fox's high-profile assignments, blurring the lines that distinguish baseball from its competitors for sports fans' attention.

ESPN America, which beams American sports events overseas, broadcasts MLB games every week during the regular season as well as much of the postseason. European, North African, and Middle Eastern fans, unfortunately, do not get the A team, as the lead World Series announcing duo of Gary Thorne and Rick Sutcliffe is far from ESPN's or baseball's best.

SATELLITE RADIO IS LAUNCHED

Satellite radio became prominent during the mid-2000s, enabling listeners around the world to listen to programming via a special proprietary device in automobiles, which could also be installed at home. Baseball fans benefitted significantly from this new medium, as subscribers to the XM satellite service could now listen to any major-league baseball game without dealing with radio interference.

This meant that fans in New York could hear the home team calls of games from the West Coast for the first time, and displaced Orioles rooters in Phoenix could now pick up local broadcasts from Crabtown. While old-time radio bugs missed late-night dial-fiddling, no one could deny the convenience, the choices, or the superb fidelity of satellite radio. In addition, a wealth of additional baseball-oriented programming — some of it produced by MLB itself — was available on the satellite channels.

THE GAME GOES ONLINE

MLB teams began developing their own websites, slowly, in the early 1990s. The Cleveland Indians had the first successful site of any major-league team, actually generating revenue from their proprietary content. The Indians, Yankees — who in the late 1990s were the first baseball team to sell their own web rights for millions of dollars — and a few other clubs thus were unhappy when MLB centralized the rights to all team websites in 2000 with the creation of MLB Advanced Media. Abbreviated MLBAM (or simply BAM), the separate

New York–based corporation was controlled by the commissioner's office but owned equally by all 30 clubs. It produced all team websites and managed all online ticket sales, with each MLB club agreeing to commit up to $5 million as initial financing. In a long overdue move, MLB also purchased the MLB.com domain name from the prominent Philadelphia law firm of Morgan Lewis Bockius. Previously MLB's domain name had been the unwieldy MajorLeagueBaseball.com, even though MLB retained Morgan Lewis Bockius to handle much of baseball's legal work.

MLB.com's new website was launched in early 2001. It experienced its share of startup hiccups, but BAM quickly won plaudits for its aggressive deal-making and cutting-edge technology. Dissenting teams were mollified when analysts predicted a high value were MLBAM to go public, and a positive cash flow meant that their initial investment was capped at less than $3 million per club. Profit-sharing checks soon began to stream in.

The first real-time baseball radio Webcasts came during the 1998 season, with audio streamed through individual team websites. Eventually all MLB games were made available via live audio streaming in 2001, and some games were available via nascent live video streaming technology.

Beginning in 2003, with video streaming technology having improved, MLB.com elected to offer fans the ability to watch all "out-of-market" games on their computers. The subscription fee included the ability to listen to and watch all such games at a price that is extremely affordable.

MLB.com has generated its own video-based analytical content, contests, and features, forging a separate, high-tech, cutting-edge identity that has helped turn around MLB's previous stodgy image as a follower rather than a trendsetter. MLBAM now employs scores of writers and has become a major news source in its own right, though one clearly conscious of the positions staked out by the commissioner's office. As major newspapers and magazines have dramatically cut back on their news coverage, their ranks of reporters, and their editorial staffs in the past decade, MLB.com has filled the gaps.

The burgeoning market based on smart phone technology has led baseball to increase its tiny-screen presence. MLB.com and MLB.TV have produced very popular apps for cell phones that allow fans to watch or listen to games, view highlights, and check scores and statistics.

Commissioner Bud Selig and president and CEO Bob Bowman have been given most of the credit for BAM's success. Selig is credited for insisting that the clubs centralize Internet rights and share equally in the equity and revenue generated, as with baseball's national TV contracts. Bowman, the only chief executive BAM has ever known, is given credit for building an advanced and innovative technological infrastructure so good that it counted other minor sports leagues and media networks as its clients.

Major League Baseball's success on the World Wide Web has in many ways been similar to ESPN's success with baseball in the 1990s: a visionary belief that the unique aspects of the game could best be served by customized formats and dedicated features. While BAM experienced some blowback from MLB's TV rightsholders wary of diminished ratings due to Internet streaming, it has consistently and aggressively promoted baseball's enormous inventory of current audio and video content. Interestingly enough, however, many historical radio broadcasts and telecasts had to be purchased from private collectors, who retained films, kinescopes, and tapes that the networks and baseball itself once believed had no value.

HAPPY DAYS

In the middle of the first decade of the new millennium, MLB was enjoying record attendance and overall revenue. A major reason for the latter was the huge amount of money that baseball's national TV partners were willing to pay for rights despite the game's across-the-board weak Nielsen numbers.

ESPN and MLB agreed in September 2005 to continue their winning partnership for eight more years (2006–13) in a megadeal that netted baseball $2.4 billion. In return, ESPN continued its exclusive *Sunday Night Baseball* centerpiece, plus its nonexclusive rights to another two games per week. The cable net also nabbed many of the valuable new-media rights it had sought.

Fox Broadcasting agreed to a new seven-year contract with MLB in July 2006 that covered the 2007–13 seasons and continued Fox's exclusive broadcasts of the All-Star Game and World Series. Fox committed to broadcast one League Championship Series each year, alternating leagues annually, with the other LCS awarded to Turner Broadcasting and its prime cable outlet, TBS. Both parties agreed to move the start of the World Series from Saturday night to Wednesday evening in an attempt to bolster the Fall Classic's ailing ratings.

The $257 million per year that Fox paid during the term of that contract was almost 40% less than the previous arrangement. For that money, Fox also received the rights to a full-season slate of Saturday games that were initially televised in an exclusive 3:30-7 p.m. ET window that began with Fox's studio pregame show. The increased Saturday schedule gave MLB its first April-to-October *Game of the Week* broadcast since 1989, and the return of that tradition seemed like good news for baseball fans — except for fans who wanted to watch their local games during that window but were effectively blacked out when Fox opted not to show those particular contests. Fox's exclusive window pushed many teams to schedule their former Saturday afternoon games in the evenings.

Fox's commitment to its Saturday Baseball *Game of the Week* quickly deteriorated, however, due to the games' low ratings despite regionalized broadcasts. First, Fox cancelled its pregame show after 2008. Worse, Fox in 2010 started changing the Saturday start times around to accommodate other sports, with some MLB starts pushed up to 3 p.m. to accommodate NASCAR broadcasts and others pushed back to 7 p.m. to accommodate European Cup soccer. In 2012, most games began at 3:30 ET, but some began at 12:30 ET and others at 7 p.m. Fox even skipped two weeks of Saturday games in August 2012 due to the summer

Olympics — on NBC. By 2014, most Saturday games had been shunted to the Fox Sports 1 startup, which many cable viewers don't even have.

The decrease in Fox's rights fees was made up by Turner Broadcasting, which stepped up to the plate and agreed to pay $149 million per year to become the exclusive home of all four of MLB's low-rated Division Series — which both Fox and ESPN seemed quite glad to shed.

Turner also received the rights to broadcast a Sunday afternoon game each week during the regular season as well as any tiebreaker games before the postseason began. The Turner Sunday schedule began in 2008 on TBS, thus ending the Atlanta Braves' three-decade run on the superstation and its basic cable network successor. (Some Braves games continued to be carried on WTBS in the Atlanta area.)

Since becoming a national partner for MLB, TBS has carried some postseason games as well as Sunday games during the season, but its choice of announcers has sometimes been uninspired. Turner Broadcasting, once a pioneer in the field, has a solid video component but has a long way to go to become a high-quality national baseball presenter. It has become just one of the many places fans can watch games, with nothing innovative to distinguish it from the plethora of other channels carrying the sport.

Overall, the new Fox, and Turner contracts totaled more than $3 billion dollars from 2007–13. When combined with the 2006–13 ESPN deal, they represented a modest increase in MLB's average annual rights payments.

MLB DOES NETWORK BASEBALL RIGHT

After watching the other three major professional team sports do it first, Major League Baseball formed its own cable TV network in 2009 to show live games, highlights, historical broadcasts, and the like. The net's first-ever host was Matt Vasgersian, onetime television voice of the Brewers and Padres.

The MLB Network has a major presence in the market, being the exclusive national television provider for a large number of games. Because of its unique and unwavering focus, it is perfectly positioned to take advantage of unexpected finds like airing a previously unknown kinescope of Game 7 of the 1960 World Series (in 2010). With Bob Costas at the helm, MLB Network turned the program into an event, booking a theater in Pittsburgh, flying in several surviving members of the 1960 Pirates and Yankees, and conducting discussions and interviews between innings of the broadcast.

The channel also produces and shows its own documentaries, instructional programs, game shows, as well as the interview show *Studio 42* with Bob Costas, which often presents more candid talk than one might expect on a house network. Costas and Vasgersian serve as the network's play-by-play announcers, with several well-known veteran analysts rotating as color men.

Since CBS bought the Yankees in 1964, several other MLB clubs have been owned by media companies. The owners of some other clubs have created their own regional sports networks, and other clubs have become equity holders in regional sports networks. This synergy helped put the MLB Network in a record number of homes for a basic cable network when it launched. It continues to reach more households than the NFL Network or the NBA and NHL channels in the United States.

In 2012, Major League Baseball showed its serious plans for its proprietary cable channel by making two Division Series games available exclusively on MLB Network — making it tough on those fans whose cable operators don't provide MLB Network as a basic service.

DISAPPOINTING RATINGS AND EXPLODING RIGHTS FEES

The twenty-first century brought both good and bad news for baseball on national TV. Ratings for MLB's so-called "jewel events" — the All-Star Game, League Championship Series, and World Series — declined steadily, repeatedly setting record lows. Yet the Balkanization of television audiences in the era of digital cable, DVRs, online viewing, and an almost unlimited number of viewing choices paradoxically resulted in ever-higher rights fees being paid for live sports properties.

In August 2012, ESPN and MLB announced an eight-year extension of their TV deal for the years 2014–21 at a reported price of $700 million per year. ESPN will continue to broadcast regular-season tilts on Sunday, Monday, and Wednesday night. It will also carry any potential tiebreaker games at the end of the regular season plus one of the sport's two Wild Card games. The Disney subsidiary received many other ancillary broadcast, digital, and highlights rights in the package, and ESPN will no longer have to black out its broadcasts on Monday and Wednesday nights in the local markets of the teams shown. *Sunday Night Baseball* will continue as an ESPN exclusive.

Two months later, Fox and Turner agreed to new contracts to continue their MLB coverage. Both of these deals also ran for an initial term of eight years (2014–21). Fox retained the World Series, All-Star Game, and one LCS, and added coverage of two Division Series annually. Turner retained the other LCS and two Division Series. From 2007–13, Turner had covered all four Division Series, showing marquee games on TBS and overlapping coverage on TNT.

ESPN, Fox, and Turner all obtained the increasingly important "TV Everywhere" rights that the networks covet. Turner also received additional online and interactive rights. Fox obtained the right to transfer some LCS games to Fox Sports 1, though the Fall Classic is guaranteed to remain on over-the-air TV.

During the regular season, Fox will now carry 52 Saturday games (one at 4 p.m. ET, the other at 7 ET). One of those games is carried by Fox Sports 1 cable channel, the network's new competition for ESPN. Turner will also broadcast 13 Sunday afternoon games in the second half of the season, half of TBS' previous annual Sunday schedule.

MLB Network retained its two Division Series games, which will come from the series broadcast by Fox, and added one Wild Card game. In the first two years of the Wild Card playoff, TBS had carried both games.

Fox paid a reported $525 million per year for the rights, with Turner paying an average of $325 million annually. MLB Network was reported to be paying $30 million each year to Fox for the two DS games.

MLB's total rights fees for the eight years amounted to $12.4 billion ($1.55 billion annually), more than double the amount of the annual combined value of the contracts that expired in 2013.

THE NATIONAL GAME ON NATIONAL TV: AN UNEASY MARRIAGE

One of baseball's greatest strengths is its seeming constancy in a changing world — as dependable a part of one's spring, summer, and fall as the rhythms of the seasons. But the advent of the 24-hour news cycle, and its concomitant noise factor, leaves little romance in the way the game is presented. Very little is left to the imagination by the drumbeat of business and scandal. The simple presentation of baseball on radio or TV has morphed in the last half century into glitzy telecasts or jarring radio broadcasts increasingly crowded with commercials, sponsorship labels, and promotional announcements.

Many baseball fans feel, in some ways, trapped. Serious fans don't want to sever the reassuring bonds with their team, but the level of crass marketing, of subtle condescension, and of borderline contempt for fans emanating from the media on both local and national levels is astounding. Many casual fans appeared to have been turned off enough by the ads, the scandals, and the substandard presentation of the game that they won't ever become serious about baseball.

For decades, baseball owners and commissioners claimed that the game was spiraling out of control, that they were losing money, and that teams would go bankrupt or even have to be contracted.

Virtually none of that was true, of course, and the few clubs that went bankrupt did so because of bad management. Yet the fact that few reporters and media pundits bothered to challenge those overblown assertions led to a great loss of credibility that removed baseball from its pedestal and made it just another game — or worse, just another business.

In a more innocent era, national broadcasts were a novelty, a way to bring the national game to those who without local access to it. Now that everyone has 24/7 access to the game, its machinations, and its dirty laundry, fewer and fewer people are watching. Baseball deserves better than that; the national pastime is more important than that. Baseball deserves better than interchangeable "professional voices" hired by corporate suits, just as it deserved better than Curt Gowdy or Monte Moore or The Baseball Network. It deserves voices with character and personality, hired by executives who care about the game and the fans — and who understand the intimate and complicated relationship between the two.

The past 25 years of MLB's national television broadcasts have been characterized by a constant tension between the game's declining ratings and the hefty rights fees demanded by baseball. While that trend began earlier, the watershed moment was the signing of the two national TV contracts that began in 1990.

Bickering over the magnitude of the losses incurred under the new national contracts in 1990 and 1991 resulted in sharp public comments from both sides. Fed up with complaining by CBS and ESPN, as well as with the black eye baseball was receiving, Commissioner Fay Vincent was in no mood to discount the agreed-upon rights fees or soften the networks' losses in any other way.

Vincent sarcastically told off both ESPN and CBS in his December 1991 state-of-the-game remarks. "I think there is more to the story. I believe ESPN has wisely used baseball to dominate cable programming throughout the summer. Where would ESPN be without baseball? There are only so many tractor pulls and billiard matches you can televise."

A December 10 piece in the *Los Angeles Times* ran with the headline "TV Gravy Will Run Out Soon"; the *Boston Globe*'s piece carried the headline, "A brushback from Vincent / He defends deals, though networks are taking a hit."

The result of this war of words was that CBS further deemphasized its already weak baseball coverage during the last two years of its contract. The CBS disaster was only the first of three major events that combined to give baseball a reputation for incompetence and fratricidal warfare that greatly diminished its stature vis-à-vis football and basketball.

The second event was the owners' 1992 coup d'etat that deposed Vincent and installed Milwaukee owner Bud Selig as acting commissioner. Though Selig has been lauded as his tenure rolled toward its end, his stewardship of the national pastime was widely derided in his first decade on the job.

The third game-changing event was the course of virtual self-immolation that MLB owners pursued in the early 1990s, resulting in the bloody 1994–95 strike that wiped out the World Series for the first time in 90 years. The creation of The Baseball Network was part of the owners' strategy for crushing the players' union, since TBN didn't pay any rights fees and the ultimate return to the clubs would be hard to project and would remain unreported. (Prior to that time, the game's national TV revenue had been an important factor in labor negotiations in one way or another, so eliminating an substantial source of guaranteed revenue bolstered the owners' claims of impending economic doom.)

Bob Costas noted in his book, "The Baseball Network was idiotic, but it was a television idiocy. It didn't fundamentally corrupt the game (except, of course, in the sense that for their steadfast, spaniel-like loyalty, the most impassioned fans in baseball were now prevented from watching many of the playoff games they wanted to see)." True, TBN didn't corrupt the game; it was a manifestation of the corruption and greed inherent in the game due to the huge influence that television was exerting on baseball's management and direction.

The perfect demonstration of that kind of endemic corruption was how MLB, even though it emphatically trounced ESPN in its 1999 legal skirmish, also agreed to let ESPN carry many more games on ESPN2 than before. The convincing victory MLB scored over ESPN in the settlement made two things crystal clear.

First, that baseball was a valuable property for ESPN, and it was prepared to pay accordingly. Second, that despite this, the NFL was far more valuable to ESPN, and even early-season NFL games — no matter which teams were playing — were far more important to ESPN than late-season MLB games that involved teams fighting for the pennant.

The difference between MLB's attitude about ESPN2 broadcasts before and after the 1999 settlement was simply a matter of money — how much could MLB extract from ESPN in order for MLB to acknowledge its secondary status. In a way, MLB was lucky that ESPN violated its contact and had to pay dearly to bump baseball to ESPN2 because, if ESPN had simply waited till the contract expired, it could have done the same without paying any "damages." In that event, MLB might have huffed and puffed about taking its games elsewhere, but it really had no options.

By the dawn of the twenty-first century, MLB's national TV ratings were in such decline that its value to the networks seems to have been centered more on its value as a promotional platform than its value in selling ad time based on the size and demographics of its audience. One only has to look at the musical-chairs history of the Division Series broadcasts to see that even postseason baseball can't draw enough eyeballs to the tube to compel the broadcast networks to carry all October games.

In the first decade of the new millennium, MLB suffered plenty of indignities on TV. Division Series games originally broadcast mostly on network TV from 1996–2000 ended up on such low-rent cable networks as FX, Fox Family, and ABC Family in the early 2000s, sometimes drawing ratings of 1 or even less than 1 — not single digits, but literally one percent of the potential television audience.

MLB's League Championship Series weren't spared, either. Despite the three-decade history of the LCS and the many classic moments of October baseball that the American League Championship Series and the National League Championship Series had generated, LCS games were sometimes scheduled simultaneously, preventing fans from seeing all the games that decided the AL & NL pennants. In 2001, this unhappy scheduling conflict was blamed on the 9/11 schedule disruption that pushed the postseason a week later into football season.

The next five years, however, also saw ALCS and NLCS games pitted against each other, with Fox deciding (based on the market) which game to show on its local broadcast affiliate and which game to bump to cable on FX. While FX was widely distributed on cable systems, not every viewer was a cable subscriber, and most bars and hotels didn't carry FX.

By 2007, Fox — baseball's broadcast network champion since 1996 — was faced with a dilemma: how to keep MLB rights without having to carry any of the low-rated Division Series games. The solution was for MLB to sell all DS games from 2007–13 to Turner, a legitimate player in cable TV sports but hardly as prestigious as Fox or ESPN. TBS also picked up one League Championship Series each year, moving half of the potential LCS games exclusively to cable as another demonstration of the national lack of interest in October baseball.

BACK TO THE FUTURE

In the twenty-first century, the Internet and World Wide Web give displaced fans the ability to see and listen to live games with their favorite team's local broadcasters from almost anyplace on the planet. That ubiquity can only be good for a sport with so many more games and so much more history than other team sports. It also directly raises the question of the future of national baseball broadcasts in general.

ESPN will continue into the 2020's as baseball's primary cable partner, with Fox chipping in with some regular-season games on broadcast TV. Will the Fox game be on Saturday nights? Afternoons? Is it on Fox, or Fox Sports 1? Does anyone really care? (And what IS Fox Sports 1, anyway?)

Whether it's good or bad, the world in which the *Game of the Day* narrative flowed from living-room radios in the 1940s, or the world in which the NBC *Game of the Week* poured from televisions on Saturday afternoons in the 1960s, is as long gone as a Tigers home run called by the late, great Ernie Harwell.

The cable age, the satellite age, and the Internet age have increased the choices available to fans, regardless of whether Major League Baseball or its broadcasters *want* fans to have more choices. Most baseball fans have demonstrated over decades of devotion to the national pastime that they like their announcers and their broadcasts best when served with a strong local flavor. Each baseball season is a marathon, a summer-long soap opera that rewards sustained attention and in-depth knowledge of history — key elements that national TV broadcasts cannot provide.

Increased network coverage in recent decades has brought more news about baseball that has little or nothing to do with the game on the field. As pundits have pointed out many times, baseball has, through incompetence and greed, stripped the veneer from its inner workings. As a result, fans now pay attention to things like rights deals, arbitrations, contracts, and legal battles that they either used to ignore or did not care a lot about. In many cases, the fans truly don't concern themselves about the nuts and bolts of how the game's business gets done, but it is in their face, nevertheless. In many places, it once was true that you could watch or listen to your team's games in the same place — physically or on the dial — for decades. Not so much now.

Baseball's overall popularity has plunged from its "glory days" of the 1950s and 1960s, when the NFL hadn't yet gained its dominant hold on the American sports fan's imagination. As pro football earned its enviable position as the undisputed king of network sports, baseball has undergone a long, slow decline in popularity. The arrogance of baseball's owners and their intractability in addressing their declining market position — along with a love of short-term dollars brought in from disadvantageous network deals — has seemingly doomed the national game to also-ran status among the big three team sports.

It is unclear whether the major networks can do anything to keep the national game from further becoming a niche sport. That the nets have made baseball more like their other sports programming is great for network continuity, but does that help baseball teams, fans, or the game itself? Making baseball just another part of the endless year-long parade of sporting events punctuated by beer advertisements doesn't bring anything new to the game. In fact, making baseball more like sports such as college football, auto racing, or golf robs the national pastime of much of its strength and unique charm.

A large portion of baseball's fan base loves the game precisely because it is so different from other sports. Unfortunately, that difference makes many network executives, sports editors, and pundits dislike baseball because its quotidian rhythm isn't as predictable and because it doesn't easily fit into schedules or time slots. Think of the difference between the NFL playoffs — with dates etched in stone well in advance — and baseball's championship series, where the date of the decisive game cannot be predicted (except for the newly instituted Wild Card play-in game). Nor can the time of the final out be accurately estimated because of the lack of a clock and the real possibility of extra innings.

One compensating factor in the MLB/television network dynamic of declining popularity and ratings is that, as more and more people watch the games or highlight packages on devices other traditional television sets, the importance of BAM and its centralized web and Internet rights will grow. That won't compensate for a lack of eyeballs, but it might play a lot better to the game's strengths, resulting in new media rights becoming as important as TV rights.

So far, the history of MLBAM is encouraging, as baseball has often been ahead of the technological curve compared to rival sports since 2001. That stands in distinct contrast to the way the men that ran baseball approached the onrushing popularity of television during the critical decades of the 1950s and 1960s, when TV went from a promising new medium to dominating the media landscape. The game's leadership also failed to deal collectively or effectively with the cable television boom of the 1980s, leaving the individual clubs to sort things out for themselves.

Unlike in pro football, where the American Football League was literally founded to provide television programming, and where the National Football League quickly embraced the new technology wholeheartedly and took a long-term view of its potential, the national pastime was reactionary and reactive rather than progressive and proactive. The failure to centralize local television rights and revenue led to destabilizing inequities between large-market and small-market clubs in MLB that drove much of the owners' zeal to crush the players' union — and that directly led to the Great War of 1994–95.

Also unlike the NFL and the NBA, Major League Baseball never seemed to develop a long-range strategy for managing its increasingly valuable national TV rights. From the 1970s through the present, MLB has lurched from one short-term plan to another, with the only constant being the willingness to sell the game's video presentation to the highest bidders. To be sure, maximizing profit is what business is all about, but maximizing revenue today can be counterproductive to maximizing revenue in the future. Baseball is complex and intensely local: it developed that way in a different century and in a pre-electronic era. The game rewards sustained attention and undying devotion over a long season in which a club might play 100 or more games after being effectively eliminated from postseason play. It also rewards the studious and those with a passion for history. Football is simpler, episodic, and far more flashy: gridiron combat seems built for TV and football broadcasts have become national in scope because the game is relatively easy to follow.

There is no doubt that the networks' technical innovations have substantially helped baseball productions, with innovations like the "Fox Box" and its relatives, the "K Zone" and its cousins, and super slo-mo making for compelling as well as informed viewing. More aggressive exploration of technical advances might have mitigated MLB's anemic national TV ratings somewhat in the past decade.

In addition, broadcasting more than one audio track, as the White Sox attempted for a while in the 2000s, could have helped. Baseball broadcasts might have featured, along with Spanish-language audio, a stats-heavy audio, a traditional audio, a comedy audio, or even commentary aimed specifically at women or young people — two huge audiences that the game now has trouble reaching.

Looking at the past three decades of baseball on TV, the conclusion that cable television actually saved baseball, rather than harmed it, is very appealing. The early 1980s were a low time for the game, and the 1981 strike left long-term scars. At the same time, though, fans were for the first time getting the chance to watch out-of-market games regularly. Many displaced fans could now follow the arc of their "hometown" team live on the tube for the first time ever, thanks to superstation broadcasts on TBS, WGN, etc.

The explosion of national broadcasts on ESPN and other cable outlets in the 1990s, plus other national factors like fantasy baseball, brought new interest to baseball and paved the way for a huge increase in revenue for both players and owners. The web and Internet, it can be argued, sealed the deal against national broadcasting, giving all fans almost unlimited choice.

Viewed in this light, it's not clear that any broadcast network could have arrested the slide toward irrelevance of weekly national broadcasts on "free TV." Once fans — especially casual fans — acquired the taste for following their own teams throughout the year, why would they watch a national game unless they were fantasy players?

The best scenario for baseball in the next decade would be for web and Internet access across many platforms to become the norm for baseball fans, even when following local teams. If so, traditional television might become merely part of the rights package that MLB offers to potential media partners when its current deals expire after 2021. That kind of evolution would materially strengthen the game as the tech-savvy youngest demographics become a larger part of MLB's fan base.

The alternative is a scenario where the current explosion in rights fees paid to local clubs by RSNs, or the formation of RSNs by individual clubs, continues, with large-market clubs like the Yankees and Dodgers reaching new levels of revenue and spending. That would exacerbate the already large and growing revenue disparities between clubs and could destroy the game's competitive balance. Should that scenario develop, MLB may find that the day of reckoning arrives seven years hence, when baseball's lackluster — to be very kind — TV ratings could result in a decrease in national rights fees like that seen in the 1990s after the implosion of the CBS deal and The Baseball Network. One wonders whether the Nationals vs. Orioles rights war, or the trouble Time Warner is having getting other SoCal cable carriers to offer SportsNet LA, could rip open the industry and change the nature of how, and how much, money baseball teams make from rights fees.

Whether the future is "TV Everywhere" with its centralized digital rights, or whether MLB's national broadcast picture fades into the background as the clubs' local broadcasting rights become the game's key economic engine, the game's come a long way. What we don't know is where the fork in the road will lead, or which route baseball will take.

AFTERWORD

BASEBALL NORTH OF THE BORDER

by Jacques Doucet, La voix des Expos de Montreal, 1972–2004

THE EARLY DAYS

By 1968, Montreal had been without professional baseball for nearly a decade since the Montreal Royals of the International League moved to Syracuse at the end of the 1960 season.

But interest still lingered among baseball fans, since both English and French newspapers in Canada's largest city carried daily stories about the major leagues.

When the Expos were born in 1969, the fans could not wait to see in person the stars they had heretofore only read about or watched from time to time on television.

Dave Van Horne, who'd cut his teeth in the Atlanta Braves farm system, and Russ Taylor, a well known Montreal broadcaster, were the first on-air talent the club hired. Jean-Pierre Roy, a former star pitcher with the Royals, and Jean-Paul Sarault, a writer with the *Montreal-Matin* newspaper, were soon brought on as the Expos' first French-language broadcasting team.

I was at that time a sportswriter for *La Presse*, following the daily activities of the Expos. In addition, I was one of four official scorers hired by the National League, although my only experience in the game had been as a writer covering junior baseball in the Montreal area.

About half way through the 1969 season, the Expos realized they needed a "pinch-broadcaster" to replace J.P. Roy when he left the radio booth to act as analyst on the SRC (French CBC) telecasts. The people who initially tried their hand at filling Roy's spot on radio did not seem to satisfy the Expos, and Sarault suggested that I should be given an opportunity to do so.

I was fortunate enough that my editor at *La Presse*, Gerry Champagne, was a diehard baseball fan; in addition, since I was writing for an afternoon newspaper, I did not have an early deadline for my game stories. So my editor gave me permission to pinch-hit on radio once a week. Three years later, the Expos offered me the full-time broadcasting job.

WORKING THE GAME

In my first year, 1972, I worked with Jean-Pierre Roy. At the end of the season, he moved to the O'Keefe Brewery (the Expos' main sponsor) and kept his job as a TV analyst. I strongly recommended that Claude Raymond, a former major league pitcher with the White Sox, Braves, Astros, and finally the Expos, be hired for radio duties, and we worked together for 12 seasons. I also worked with Rodger Brulotte for 17 seasons and Marc Griffin for the last three campaigns.

Working with Claude, who was just out of uniform, was a great help for me, since he knew almost every player in the National League. So we split our pregame activities, with Claude handling the players while I mostly talked with managers, coaches, and general managers.

Every bit of information was shared before each broadcast and, since we were both new to the broadcasting business, we met after each road game to discuss how we handled the flow of the game, discarding what we felt was not right and insisting on what we thought was more interesting for the listener. And we eventually used more and more French expressions during our broadcasts.

In order to improve my broadcasting techniques, I used to carry a small transistor radio on the road in order to listen to some of my favorite baseball announcers. I handled the play-by-play portion of our broadcasts for the first and last three innings and Claude pitched in for the middle three innings. So it allowed me to listen to Hall of Famers like Vin Scully of the Dodgers and Harry Kalas of the Astros and Phillies. Listening to those broadcasting greats, who later became good friends, was a big help.

Mentioning Vin Scully leads me to recall that once in Vero Beach, during spring training, I was talking with Vin when a fan asked him to pose for a picture. As I started to move away so the fan could have a picture of him, Vin said to the fan, "Take the picture of the two of us. This is Jacques Doucet, young French broadcaster of the Expos, a good friend of mine." I never forgot that moment.

Vin also invited me on the Dodger telecast once to broadcast a couple of innings in French, which was a great honor.

CALLING PERFECTION

In working with Claude Raymond, I had one thing to settle at the very start of our relationship.

Knowing how superstitious professional athletes are, I had to convince him that if a pitcher was working on a no-hitter or a perfect game after four or five innings, that this fact had to be mentioned during our broadcast — which was, after all, a radio broadcast — in order to keep the listener aware of what was happening on the field.

In 1972, my first season with Jean-Pierre Roy, Bill Stoneman pitched his second no-hitter, against the New York Mets, and Jean-Pierre adamantly refused to talk about it until the last out was recorded. He had noted during the game only that "something special" was happening on the field! Being a rookie broadcaster, I did not want to create animosity with my partner.

Once the game was over, I told Jean-Pierre that never again would I refrain from mentioning that a pitcher had a no-hitter or a perfect game going during our broadcast.

And I had, over the 33 years that I spent in the radio booth, the privilege of broadcasting five no-hitters and two perfect games (Dennis Martinez against the Dodgers, in Los Angeles on July 28, 1991, and David Cone against the Expos at Yankee Stadium on July 18, 1999).

June 3, 1995, Pedro Martínez also pitched nine perfect innings at San Diego before allowing a hit in the bottom of the tenth. He was immediately removed from the game, and was the winning pitcher in Montreal's 1–0 victory. As far as I am concerned, this was also a perfect game, since a "regular" baseball game is made of 27 outs.

TOUCH 'EM ALL

I was also privileged to broadcast All-Star, playoff, and World Series games from 1982 through 1995. I'll never forget Kirk Gibson's home run against Dennis Eckersley — I can still see him limping around the bases — in the 1988 World Series, or the earthquake that hit San Francisco at 5:04 pm before game three of the 1989 Series, or Joe Carter's title-clinching homer in 1993.

In Game 6 of that series, with the Blue Jays up three games to two, Carter came to bat with one out in the bottom of the ninth with Toronto trailing 6–5. Rickey Henderson and Paul Molitor were on base. On a 2–2 count, Carter hit a three-run walk-off homer off Phillies pitcher Mitch Williams.

This is still the only time that a home run has been hit by a player whose team was trailing in the bottom of the ninth in a potential championship clincher. As Carter went hysterical, jumping up and down while rounding the bases, my good friend Tom Cheek, the late radio broadcaster for the Blue Jays, shouted, "Touch 'em all, Joe! You'll never hit a bigger home run in your life!"

Those moments, like many others, are ones that I'll never forget.

My only regret is that I never had the opportunity to broadcast a World Series game involving the Expos.

APPENDIX: BROADCASTER STATS

AL Teams' Longest-Serving #1 Radio Voices

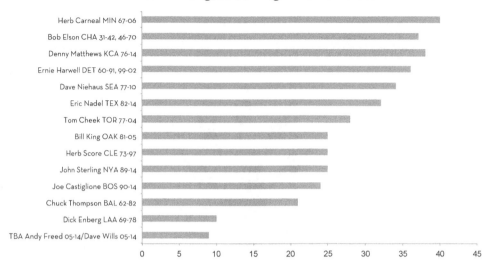

Herb Carneal MIN 67-06	
Bob Elson CHA 31-42, 46-70	
Denny Matthews KCA 76-14	
Ernie Harwell DET 60-91, 99-02	
Dave Niehaus SEA 77-10	
Eric Nadel TEX 82-14	
Tom Cheek TOR 77-04	
Bill King OAK 81-05	
Herb Score CLE 73-97	
John Sterling NYA 89-14	
Joe Castiglione BOS 90-14	
Chuck Thompson BAL 62-82	
Dick Enberg LAA 69-78	
TBA Andy Freed 05-14/Dave Wills 05-14	

NL Teams' Longest-Serving #1 Radio Voices

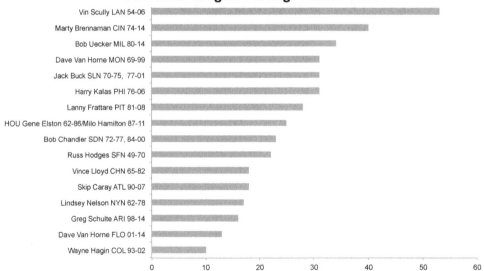

Vin Scully LAN 54-06	
Marty Brennaman CIN 74-14	
Bob Uecker MIL 80-14	
Dave Van Horne MON 69-99	
Jack Buck SLN 70-75, 77-01	
Harry Kalas PHI 76-06	
Lanny Frattare PIT 81-08	
HOU Gene Elston 62-86/Milo Hamilton 87-11	
Bob Chandler SDN 72-77, 84-00	
Russ Hodges SFN 49-70	
Vince Lloyd CHN 65-82	
Skip Caray ATL 90-07	
Lindsey Nelson NYN 62-78	
Greg Schulte ARI 98-14	
Dave Van Horne FLO 01-14	
Wayne Hagin COL 93-02	

AL Teams' Longest-Serving #2 Announcers

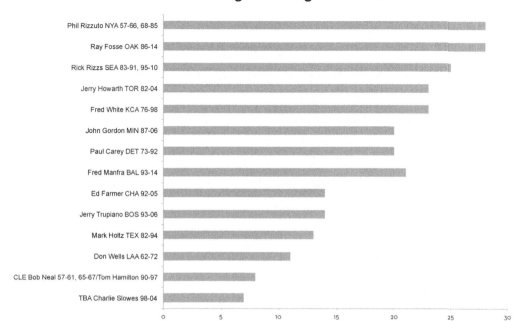

Phil Rizzuto NYA 57-66, 68-85
Ray Fosse OAK 86-14
Rick Rizzs SEA 83-91, 95-10
Jerry Howarth TOR 82-04
Fred White KCA 76-98
John Gordon MIN 87-06
Paul Carey DET 73-92
Fred Manfra BAL 93-14
Ed Farmer CHA 92-05
Jerry Trupiano BOS 93-06
Mark Holtz TEX 82-94
Don Wells LAA 62-72
CLE Bob Neal 57-61, 65-67/Tom Hamilton 90-97
TBA Charlie Slowes 98-04

NL Teams' Longest-Serving #2 Announcers

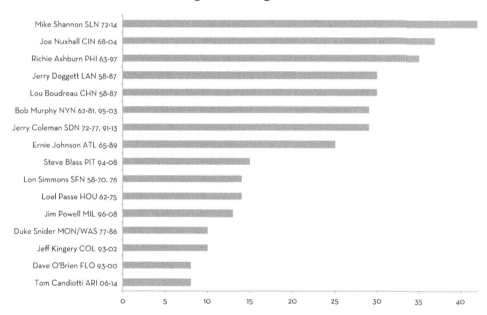

Mike Shannon SLN 72-14
Joe Nuxhall CIN 68-04
Richie Ashburn PHI 63-97
Jerry Doggett LAN 58-87
Lou Boudreau CHN 58-87
Bob Murphy NYN 62-81, 95-03
Jerry Coleman SDN 72-77, 91-13
Ernie Johnson ATL 65-89
Steve Blass PIT 94-08
Lon Simmons SFN 58-70, 76
Loel Passe HOU 62-75
Jim Powell MIL 96-08
Duke Snider MON/WAS 77-86
Jeff Kingery COL 93-02
Dave O'Brien FLO 93-00
Tom Candiotti ARI 06-14

AL Teams' Announcers with Longest Radio Careers

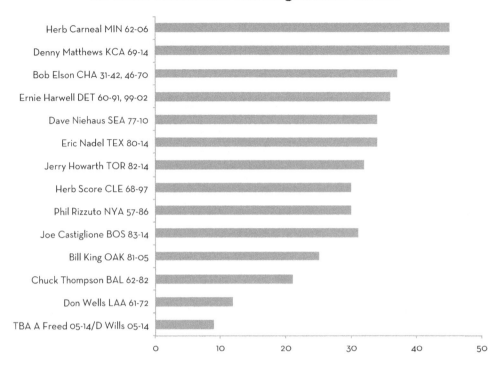

Herb Carneal MIN 62-06	
Denny Matthews KCA 69-14	
Bob Elson CHA 31-42, 46-70	
Ernie Harwell DET 60-91, 99-02	
Dave Niehaus SEA 77-10	
Eric Nadel TEX 80-14	
Jerry Howarth TOR 82-14	
Herb Score CLE 68-97	
Phil Rizzuto NYA 57-86	
Joe Castiglione BOS 83-14	
Bill King OAK 81-05	
Chuck Thompson BAL 62-82	
Don Wells LAA 61-72	
TBA A Freed 05-14/D Wills 05-14	

NL Teams' Announcers With Longest Radio Careers

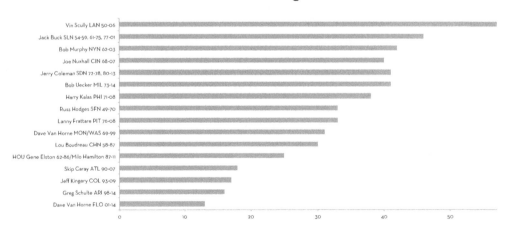

Vin Scully LAN 50-06	
Jack Buck SLN 54-59, 61-75, 77-01	
Bob Murphy NYN 62-03	
Joe Nuxhall CIN 68-07	
Jerry Coleman SDN 72-78, 80-13	
Bob Uecker MIL 73-14	
Harry Kalas PHI 71-08	
Russ Hodges SFN 49-70	
Lanny Frattare PIT 76-08	
Dave Van Horne MON/WAS 69-99	
Lou Boudreau CHN 58-87	
HOU Gene Elston 62-86/Milo Hamilton 87-11	
Skip Caray ATL 90-07	
Jeff Kingery COL 93-09	
Greg Schulte ARI 98-14	
Dave Van Horne FLO 01-14	

AL's Longest-Serving Radio Duos

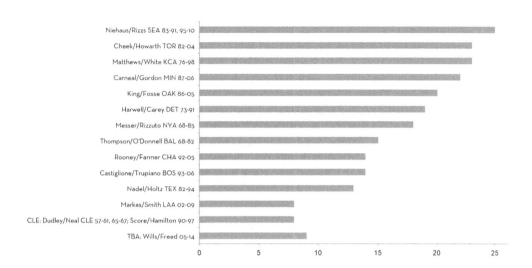

NL's Longest-Serving Radio Duos

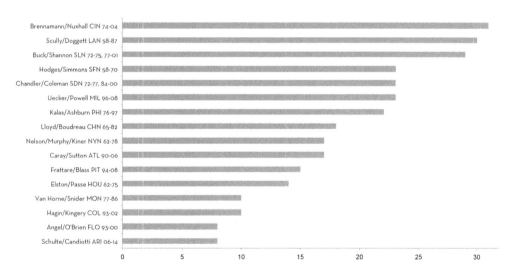

MLB Announcers With the Longest On-Air Tenure

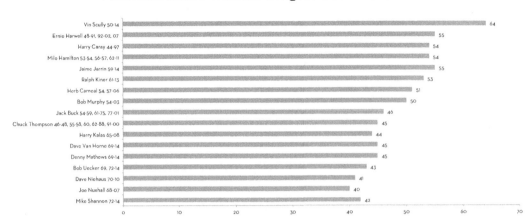

Announcer	Years
Vin Scully 50-14	64
Ernie Harwell 48-91, 92-02, 07	55
Harry Caray 44-97	54
Milo Hamilton 53-54, 56-57, 62-11	54
Jaime Jarrin 59-14	55
Ralph Kiner 61-13	53
Herb Carneal 54, 57-06	51
Bob Murphy 54-03	50
Jack Buck 54-59, 61-75, 77-01	46
Chuck Thompson 46-48, 55-58, 60, 62-88, 91-00	45
Harry Kalas 65-08	44
Dave Van Horne 69-14	45
Denny Mathews 69-14	45
Bob Uecker 69, 72-14	43
Dave Niehaus 70-10	41
Joe Nuxhall 68-07	40
Mike Shannon 72-14	42

ABOUT THE AUTHOR

STUART SHEA is the author of *Wrigley Field: The Long Life and Contentious Times of the Friendly Confines*, published in 2014. Having first joined SABR in the 1980s, he has edited SABR's *Baseball Research Journal* and *National Pastime*. He is a contributing editor to *The Emerald Guide to Baseball* and *Who's Who in Baseball*. Shea collects baseball audio and also writes about popular music, having co-created the FAQ series for Backbeat Books; he is the author of *Pink Floyd FAQ* and co-author of *Fab Four FAQ*.

SABR BioProject Books

In 2002, the Society for American Baseball Research launched an effort to write and publish biographies of every player, manager, and individual who has made a contribution to baseball. Over the past decade, the BioProject Committee has produced over 2,200 biographical articles. Many have been part of efforts to create theme- or team-oriented books, spearheaded by chapters or other committees of SABR.

THE YEAR OF THE BLUE SNOW:
The 1964 Philadelphia Phillies
Catcher Gus Triandos dubbed the Philadelphia Phillies' 1964 season "the year of the blue snow," a rare thing that happens once in a great while. This book sheds light on lingering questions about the 1964 season—but any book about a team is really about the players. This work offers life stories of all the players and others (managers, coaches, owners, and broadcasters) associated with this star-crossed team, as well as essays of analysis and history.
Edited by Mel Marmer and Bill Nowlin
$19.95 paperback (ISBN 978-1-933599-51-9)
$9.99 ebook (ISBN 978-1-933599-52-6)
8.5"x11", 356 pages, over 70 photos

DETROIT TIGERS 1984:
What a Start! What a Finish!
The 1984 Detroit tigers roared out of the gate, winning their first nine games of the season and compiling an eye-popping 35-5 record after the campaign's first 40 games—still the best start ever for any team in major league history. This book brings together biographical profiles of every Tiger from that magical season, plus those of field management, top executives, the broadcasters—even venerable Tiger Stadium and the city itself.
Edited by Mark Pattison and David Raglin
$19.95 paperback (ISBN 978-1-933599-44-1)
$9.99 ebook (ISBN 978-1-933599-45-8)
8.5"x11", 250 pages (Over 230,000 words!)

SWEET '60: The 1960 Pittsburgh Pirates
A portrait of the 1960 team which pulled off one of the biggest upsets of the last 60 years. When Bill Mazeroski's home run left the park to win in Game Seven of the World Series, beating the New York Yankees, David had toppled Goliath. It was a blow that awakened a generation, one that millions of people saw on television, one of TV's first iconic World Series moments.
Edited by Clifton Blue Parker and Bill Nowlin
$19.95 paperback (ISBN 978-1-933599-48-9)
$9.99 ebook (ISBN 978-1-933599-49-6)
8.5"x11", 340 pages, 75 photos

RED SOX BASEBALL IN THE DAYS OF IKE AND ELVIS: The Red Sox of the 1950s
Although the Red Sox spent most of the 1950s far out of contention, the team was filled with fascinating players who captured the heart of their fans. In Red Sox Baseball, members of SABR present 46 biographies on players such as Ted Williams and Pumpsie Green as well as season-by-season recaps.
Edited by Mark Armour and Bill Nowlin
$19.95 paperback (ISBN 978-1-933599-24-3)
$9.99 ebook (ISBN 978-1-933599-34-2)
8.5"x11", 372 pages, over 100 photos

THE MIRACLE BRAVES OF 1914
Boston's Original Worst-to-First Champions
Long before the Red Sox "Impossible Dream" season, Boston's now nearly forgotten "other" team, the 1914 Boston Braves, performed a baseball "miracle" that resounds to this very day. The "Miracle Braves" were Boston's first "worst-to-first" winners of the World Series. Refusing to throw in the towel at the midseason mark, George Stallings engineered a remarkable second-half climb in the standings all the way to first place.
Edited by Bill Nowlin
$19.95 paperback (ISBN 978-1-933599-69-4)
$9.99 ebook (ISBN 978-1-933599-70-0)
8.5"x11", 392 pages, over 100 photos

THAR'S JOY IN BRAVELAND!
The 1957 Milwaukee Braves
Few teams in baseball history have captured the hearts of their fans like the Milwaukee Braves of the 1950s. During the Braves' 13-year tenure in Milwaukee (1953-1965), they had a winning record every season, won two consecutive NL pennants (1957 and 1958), lost two more in the final week of the season (1956 and 1959), and set big-league attendance records along the way.
Edited by Gregory H. Wolf
$19.95 paperback (ISBN 978-1-933599-71-7)
$9.99 ebook (ISBN 978-1-933599-72-4)
8.5"x11", 330 pages, over 60 photos

NEW CENTURY, NEW TEAM:
The 1901 Boston Americans
The team now known as the Boston Red Sox played its first season in 1901. Boston had a well-established National League team, but the American League went head-to-head with the N.L. in Chicago, Philadelphia, and Boston. Chicago won the American League pennant and Boston finished second, only four games behind.
Edited by Bill Nowlin
$19.95 paperback (ISBN 978-1-933599-58-8)
$9.99 ebook (ISBN 978-1-933599-59-5)
8.5"x11", 268 pages, over 125 photos

CAN HE PLAY?
A Look At Baseball Scouts and their Profession
They dig through tons of coal to find a single diamond. Here in the world of scouts, we meet the "King of Weeds," a Ph.D. we call "Baseball's Renaissance Man," a husband-and-wife team, pioneering Latin scouts, and a Japanese-American interned during World War II who became a successful scout—and many, many more.
Edited by Jim Sandoval and Bill Nowlin
$19.95 paperback (ISBN 978-1-933599-23-6)
$9.99 ebook (ISBN 978-1-933599-25-0)
8.5"x11", 200 pages, over 100 photos

SABR Members can purchase each book at a significant discount (often 50% off) and receive the ebook editions free as a member benefit. Each book is available in a trade paperback edition as well as ebooks suitable for reading on a home computer or Nook, Kindle, or iPad/tablet.

To learn more about becoming a member of SABR, visit the website: sabr.org/join

The SABR Digital Library

The Society for American Baseball Research, the top baseball research organization in the world, disseminates some of the best in baseball history, analysis, and biography through our publishing programs. The SABR Digital Library contains a mix of books old and new, and focuses on a tandem program of paperback and ebook publication, making these materials widely available for both on digital devices and as traditional printed books.

CLASSIC REPRINTS

BASE-BALL: How to Become a Player
by John Montgomery Ward
John Montgomery Ward (1860-1925) tossed the second perfect game in major league history and later became the game's best shortstop and a great, inventive manager. His classic handbook on baseball skills and strategy was published in 1888. Illustrated with woodcuts, the book is divided into chapters for each position on the field as well as chapters on the origin of the game, theory and strategy, training, base-running, and batting.
$4.99 ebook (ISBN 978-1-933599-47-2)
$9.95 paperback (ISBN 978-0910137539)
156 pages, 4.5"x7" replica edition

BATTING
by F. C. Lane
First published in 1925, Batting collects the wisdom and insights of over 250 hitters and baseball figures. Lane interviewed extensively and compiled tips and advice on everything from batting stances to beanballs. Legendary baseball figures such as Ty Cobb, Casey Stengel, Cy Young, Walter Johnson, Rogers Hornsby, and Babe Ruth reveal the secrets of such integral and interesting parts of the game as how to choose a bat, the ways to beat a slump, and how to outguess the pitcher.
$14.95 paperback (ISBN 978-0-910137-86-7)
$7.99 ebook (ISBN 978-1-933599-46-5)
240 pages, 5"x7"

RUN, RABBIT, RUN
by Walter "Rabbit" Maranville
"Rabbit" Maranville was the Joe Garagiola of Grandpa's day, the baseball comedian of the times. In a twenty-four-year career that began in 1912, Rabbit found a lot of funny situations to laugh at, and no wonder: he caused most of them! The book also includes an introduction by the late Harold Seymour and a historical account of Maranville's life and Hall-of-Fame career by Bob Carroll.
$9.95 paperback (ISBN 978-1-933599-26-7)
$5.99 ebook (ISBN 978-1-933599-27-4)
100 pages, 5.5"x8.5", 15 rare photos

MEMORIES OF A BALLPLAYER
by Bill Werber and C. Paul Rogers III
Bill Werber's claim to fame is unique: he was the last living person to have a direct connection to the 1927 Yankees, "Murderers' Row," a team hailed by many as the best of all time. Rich in anecdotes and humor, Memories of a Ballplayer is a clear-eyed memoir of the world of big-league baseball in the 1930s. Werber played with or against some of the most productive hitters of all time, including Babe Ruth, Ted Williams, Lou Gehrig, and Joe DiMaggio.
$14.95 paperback (ISNB 978-0-910137-84-3)
$6.99 ebook (ISBN 978-1-933599-47-2)
250 pages, 6"x9"

ORIGINAL SABR RESEARCH

INVENTING BASEBALL: The 100 Greatest Games of the Nineteenth Century
SABR's Nineteenth Century Committee brings to life the greatest games from the game's early years. From the "prisoner of war" game that took place among captive Union soldiers during the Civil War (immortalized in a famous lithograph), to the first intercollegiate game (Amherst versus Williams), to the first professional no-hitter, the games in this volume span 1833–1900 and detail the athletic exploits of such players as Cap Anson, Moses "Fleetwood" Walker, Charlie Comiskey, and Mike "King" Kelly.
Edited by Bill Felber
$19.95 paperback (ISBN 978-1-933599-42-7)
$9.99 ebook (ISBN 978-1-933599-43-4)
302 pages, 8"x10", 200 photos

NINETEENTH CENTURY STARS: 2012 EDITION
First published in 1989, Nineteenth Century Stars was SABR's initial attempt to capture the stories of baseball players from before 1900. With a collection of 136 fascinating biographies, SABR has re-released Nineteenth Century Stars for 2012 with revised statistics and new form. The 2012 version also includes a preface by John Thorn.
Edited by Robert L. Tiemann and Mark Rucker
$19.95 paperback (ISBN 978-1-933599-28-1)
$9.99 ebook (ISBN 978-1-933599-29-8)
300 pages, 6"x9"

GREAT HITTING PITCHERS
Published in 1979, Great Hitting Pitchers was one of SABR's early publications. Edited by SABR founder Bob Davids, the book compiles stories and records about pitchers excelling in the batter's box. Newly updated in 2012 by Mike Cook, Great Hitting Pitchers contain tables including data from 1979-2011, corrections to reflect recent records, and a new chapter on recent new members in the club of "great hitting pitchers" like Tom Glavine and Mike Hampton.
Edited by L. Robert Davids
$9.95 paperback (ISBN 978-1-933599-30-4)
$5.99 ebook (ISBN 978-1-933599-31-1)
102 pages, 5.5"x8.5"

THE FENWAY PROJECT
Sixty-four SABR members—avid fans, historians, statisticians, and game enthusiasts—recorded their experiences of a single game. Some wrote from inside the Green Monster's manual scoreboard, the Braves clubhouse, or the broadcast booth, while others took in the essence of Fenway from the grandstand or bleachers. The result is a fascinating look at the charms and challenges of Fenway Park, and the allure of being a baseball fan.
Edited by Bill Nowlin and Cecilia Tan
$9.99 ebook (ISBN 978-1-933599-50-2)
175 pages, 100 photos

SABR Members can purchase each book at a significant discount (often 50% off) and receive the ebook editions free as a member benefit. Each book is available in a trade paperback edition as well as ebooks suitable for reading on a home computer or Nook, Kindle, or iPad/tablet.

To learn more about becoming a member of SABR, visit the website: sabr.org/join

Join SABR today!

If you're interested in baseball — writing about it, reading about it, talking about it — there's a place for you in the Society for American Baseball Research.

SABR was formed in 1971 in Cooperstown, New York, with the mission of fostering the research and dissemination of the history and record of the game. Our members include everyone from academics to professional sportswriters to amateur historians and statisticians to students and casual fans who merely enjoy reading about baseball history and occasionally gathering with other members to talk baseball.

SABR members have a variety of interests, and this is reflected in the diversity of its research committees. There are more than two dozen groups devoted to the study of a specific area related to the game — from Baseball and the Arts to Statistical Analysis to the Deadball Era to Women in Baseball. In addition, many SABR members meet formally and informally in regional chapters throughout the year and hundreds come together for the annual national convention, the organization's premier event. These meetings often include panel discussions with former major league players and research presentations by members. Most of all, SABR members love talking baseball with like-minded friends. What unites them all is an interest in the game and joy in learning more about it.

Why join SABR? Here are some benefits of membership:

- Two issues (spring and fall) of the *Baseball Research Journal*, which includes articles on history, biography, statistics, personalities, book reviews, and other aspects of the game.
- One expanded e-book edition of *The National Pastime*, which focuses on baseball in the region where that year's SABR national convention is held (in 2015, it's Chicago)
- 8-10 new and classic e-books published each year by the SABR Digital Library, which are all free for members to download
- *This Week in SABR* newsletter in your e-mail every Friday, which highlights SABR members' research and latest news
- Regional chapter meetings, which can include guest speakers, presentations and trips to ballgames
- Online access to back issues of *The Sporting News* and other periodicals through Paper of Record
- Access to SABR's lending library and other research resources
- Online member directory to connect you with an international network of SABR baseball experts and fans
- Discounts on registration for our annual events, including SABR Analytics Conference & Jerry Malloy Negro League Conference
- Access to SABR-L, an e-mail discussion list of baseball questions & answers that many feel is worth the cost of membership itself
- The opportunity to be part of a passionate international community of baseball fans

SABR membership is on a "rolling" calendar system; that means your membership lasts 365 days no matter when you sign up! Enjoy all the benefits of SABR membership by signing up today at SABR.org/join or by clipping out the form below and mailing it to SABR, Cronkite School at ASU, 555 N. Central Ave. #416, Phoenix, AZ 85004.

SABR MEMBERSHIP FORM

	Annual	3-year	Senior	3-yr Sr.	Under 30
U.S.:	❏ $65	❏ $175	❏ $45	❏ $129	❏ $45
Canada/Mexico:	❏ $75	❏ $205	❏ $55	❏ $159	❏ $55
Overseas:	❏ $84	❏ $232	❏ $64	❏ $186	❏ $55

Add a Family Member: $15 for each family member at same address (list on back)
Senior: 65 or older before 12/31/2015
All dues amounts in U.S. dollars or equivalent

Participate in Our Donor Program!
I'd like to desginate my gift to be used toward:
❏General Fund ❏Endowment Fund ❏Research Resources ❏_____
❏ I want to maximize the impact of my gift; do not send any donor premiums
❏ I would like this gift to remain anonymous.

Note: Any donation not designated will be placed in the General Fund.
SABR is a 501 (c) (3) not-for-profit organization & donations are tax-deductible to the extent allowed by law.

Name _____

Address _____

City _____ ST_____ ZIP_____

Phone _____ Birthday _____

E-mail: _____
(Your e-mail address on file ensures you will receive the most recent SABR news.)

Dues $_____

Donation $_____

Amount Enclosed $_____

Do you work for a matching grant corporation? Call (602) 496-1460 for details.

If you wish to pay by credit card, please contact the SABR office at (602) 496-1460 or visit the SABR Store online at SABR.org/join. We accept Visa, Mastercard & Discover.

Do you wish to receive the *Baseball Research Journal* electronically?: ❏ Yes   ❏ No
Our e-books are available in PDF, Kindle, or EPUB (iBooks, iPad, Nook) formats.

Mail to: SABR, Cronkite School at ASU, 555 N. Central Ave. #416, Phoenix, AZ 85004

04/15

Made in the USA
Coppell, TX
04 June 2021

56894208R10227